READINGS IN SEMANTICS

READINGS IN SEMANTICS

Edited by
FARHANG ZABEEH, E. D. KLEMKE,
and ARTHUR JACOBSON

UNIVERSITY OF ILLINOIS PRESS
Urbana   Chicago   London

Library of Congress Cataloging in Publication Data

Zabeeh, Farhang, comp.
  Readings in semantics.

  Includes bibliographies.
  1. Semantics (Philosophy) — Addresses, essays,
lectures. 2. Modality (Logic) — Addresses, essays,
lectures. I. Klemke, E. D., 1926-   joint comp.
II. Jacobson, Arthur, 1929-   joint comp.
III. Title.
B840.Z32   149'.94   74-639
ISBN 0-252-00196-6
ISBN 0-252-00421-3 (pbk.)

PREFACE

As anyone who is familiar with the development of contemporary philosophy knows, the field of semantics and the philosophy of language has become increasingly significant. A vast body of literature on various aspects of this area of recent philosophy has appeared in journals and books from Frege to the present. We have assembled here, under seven main topics, selections which we believe are among the most important contributions to the field. In addition, we have written expressly for the volume a general introduction plus introductions to each part. With the help of these introductions, we believe that the book will be suitable for undergraduate and graduate courses in philosophy, and perhaps for the general reader as well.

Though all three of us collaborated in various ways with regard to the researching and writing of the introductions, the chief responsibility was divided as follows: Farhang Zabeeh, for the general introduction and the introductions to Parts I, V, and VII; Arthur Jacobson, for the introductions to Parts II and IV; E. D. Klemke, for the introductions to Parts III and VI (the latter in collaboration with Marshall Green).

We express our gratitude to all of the authors, editors, and publishers who have kindly granted permission to reprint previously published articles and selections from books. We also acknowledge our warm appreciation to all those who assisted with various aspects of the preparation of the volume. Among these, we are especially grateful to: Mary L. Facko, who undertook the arduous task of typing and preparing the manuscript; Marshall Green, who coauthored the introduction to Part VI; and James M. Warzecha, Martin F. Farrell, Steven R. Bayne, and G. Moor, who helped with bibliographical research and other tasks. In addition, we express our thanks to the staff of the University of Illinois Press, who were most helpful and patient. Finally, we express our deep gratitude to President Rolf Weil, Dean Ralph Carnes, and former Dean Paul Olscamp of Roosevelt University, who helped make this project possible under the university's selective load reduction program.

CONTENTS

GENERAL INTRODUCTION   1

I. ASPECTS OF THE STUDY OF SIGNS   17

  A. *Semantics, Syntax, and Pragmatics*

  1. Some Pragmatic Aspects of Meaning   33
     C. L. STEVENSON

  2. Semantical Concepts   79
     ARTHUR PAP

  B. *Use and Mention*

  1. Use Versus Mention   89
     W. V. QUINE

  2. Varieties of Use and Mention   95
     NEWTON GARVER

  3. On Using Inverted Commas   105
     LEONARD LINSKY

II. MEANING AND REFERENCE   111

  1. On Sense and Reference   117
     GOTTLOB FREGE

  2. On Denoting   141
     BERTRAND RUSSELL

  3. On Referring   159
     P. F. STRAWSON

  4. Identifying Reference and Truth-values   193
     P. F. STRAWSON

  5. The Theory of Meaning   217
     GILBERT RYLE

III. CRITERIA OF MEANINGFULNESS   245

  1. The Elimination of Metaphysics   255
     A. J. AYER

2. Verifiability and Meaningfulness 271
A. J. AYER

3. The Criterion of Significance 285
PAUL MARHENKE

4. Empiricist Criteria of Cognitive Significance:
Problems and Changes 309
CARL G. HEMPEL

5. The Methodological Character of Theoretical Concepts 331
RUDOLF CARNAP

IV. MEANING AND USE 371

1. Wittgenstein's *Philosophical Investigations* 381
PAUL FEYERABEND

2. The Meaning of a Word 419
J. L. AUSTIN

3. Knowledge of Other Minds 443
NORMAN MALCOLM

4. Ordinary Language 455
GILBERT RYLE

5. Use, Usage and Meaning 477
GILBERT RYLE AND J. N. FINDLAY

6. Meaning 499
H. P. GRICE

7. The Assertion Fallacy 513
JOHN R. SEARLE

V. KINDS OF STATEMENTS:
THE ANALYTIC-SYNTHETIC DISTINCTION 525

1. The A Priori 545
A. J. AYER

2. Analytic — Synthetic 565
FRIEDRICH WAISMANN

3. Two Dogmas of Empiricism 583
W. V. QUINE

4. Two Cornerstones of Empiricism 611
GUSTAV BERGMANN

5. In Defense of a Dogma 641
H. P. GRICE AND P. F. STRAWSON

VI. TRUTH 661

1. The Semantic Conception of Truth 675
ALFRED TARSKI

2. Truth 713
P. F. STRAWSON

3. Truth and Correspondence 731
G. J. WARNOCK

4. True to the Facts 743
DONALD DAVIDSON

VII. MODALITIES 761

1. Modalities 769
RUDOLF CARNAP

2. Reference and Modality 777
W. V. QUINE

3. Semantical Considerations on Modal Logic 801
SAUL A. KRIPKE

4. Quine on Modality 815
DAGFINN FØLLESDOL

5. The Problem of Interpreting Modal Logic 829
W. V. QUINE

6. Modalities and Intensional Languages 837
RUTH BARCAN MARCUS

GENERAL INTRODUCTION

A Historical Perspective

The word 'semantics' comes from the Greek adjective *semantikos* ('significant'). It was used by Aristotle in *On Interpretation* in connection with grammar, and by others as a term to denote various subject matters falling under the headings of logic, grammar, and rhetoric. 'Semantics,' in a modern and technical sense, is used to signify the study of the relation between the items of language, such as words, names (proper and common), predicate expressions, and sentences; and the items of the world, such as objects, events, states of affairs, truth values, and situations. This discipline in ancient Greece and medieval Europe was intermixed with grammar, subservient to metaphysics, and in the seventeenth and eighteenth centuries was infected with epistemology. But the logic of the *Old Stoa,* the theories of Occam and Hobbes on designation of names, Locke's semiotic or 'the doctrine of signs,' and Mill's theory of denotation-connotation, set the stage for the emergence of semantics as an independent discipline.

It has been said that "preoccupation with the theory of meaning could be described as the occupational disease of twentieth-century Anglo-Saxon and Austrian philosophy."[1] But the history of semantics is in effect as old as the history of philosophy. Viewed retrospectively, from the vantage point of the twentieth century, it was Socrates' mission to make his interlocutor see that first-order questions, e.g., questions as to whether an act is virtuous, or a law is just, or an entity is knowable, could not be answered without answering second-order questions about the meanings of such predicate expressions as '. . . is virtuous,' '. . . is just,' and '. . . is knowable.' Indeed, what is called elenchus, namely, examination of the interlocutor's statements by asking him questions calling for further statements of his first statement (which is the most striking aspect of the Socratic dialogues), is similar to what is now called "semantic analysis." However, this purely therapeutic

[1] Gilbert Ryle, "The Theory of Meaning," in *British Philosophy in the Mid-Century,* ed. C. A. Mace (London: Allen and Unwin, 1957), 239.

1

aspect of inquiry led to dialectic, which, according to Plato, aims at the discovery of the one underlying the many, i.e., the forms, which are not merely semantic properties but also ontological models for imperfect particulars. Plato's theory of forms begins with semantics, but ends up in metaphysics, epistemology, and cosmology.

The Stoic logicians made a significant contribution to semantics by making a threefold distinction between the linguistic expressions, the significate or *lekton* ("that which is meant" or "that which the barbarians do not understand when they hear Greek words spoken"), and the denotation of a sign. This distinction corresponds closely to Frege's categories of *Zeichen* (sign), *Sinn* (sense), and *Bedeutung* (reference).[2]

In the Middle Ages philosophers again turned their attention to semantics, primarily as a means of finding a solution to the controversial problem of universals. Ockham's elaborate semantico-grammatic theory of signs, their various *intentions,* and their corresponding *nomina* was devised to prove that universals are neither in the world nor in the mind; rather, their being is their being understood.[3]

Classical Empiricists

In *An Essay Concerning Human Understanding,* essentially an epistemological work, John Locke devotes a whole book (Book III, "Of Words") to semantics. According to Locke, significant words denote not things, but Ideas, which are mental entities. He realized that there are significant words which do not stand for Ideas, but he tried to show that even words such as *nihil* in Latin, and 'ignorance' and 'barrenness,' 'Spirit' and 'Angel' in English, may refer to ideas obliquely. He argues that "negative or privative words cannot be said properly to belong to or signify no ideas, for then they would be perfectly insignificant sounds; they relate to positive ideas and signify their absence."[4] With regard to words like 'Spirit' and 'Angel' Locke argues that, if we trace their etymology, we shall find that they "have had their rise from sensible ideas . . . thus *Spirit,* in its primary significance, is breath; *Angel,* a messenger. . . ."[5] Locke, in the concluding

---

[2] Benson Mates, *Stoic Logic* (Berkeley: University of California Press, 1953). Note that Zeno, the founder of the Stoic school, apparently lived 350-260 B.C., and Frege from 1848 to 1925.

[3] E. Moody, *The Logic of William Ockham* (New York: Sheed and Ward, 1935).

[4] Book III, Chs. 1 and 4.

[5] Book III, Ch. 1, Pt. 5.

chapter of the *Essay,* "Of the Division of the Sciences," divides knowledge into natural philosophy, moral philosophy, and the doctrine of signs, σημειωτική.

Let us turn our attention to another classical empiricist, David Hume, a precursor of modern empiricism. Hume writes:

> When we entertain, therefore, any suspicion that a philosophical term is employed without any meaning or idea (as is but too frequent), we need but enquire, *from what impression is that supposed idea derived?* And if it be impossible to assign any, this will serve to confirm our suspicion. By bringing ideas into so clear a light we may reasonably hope to remove all dispute, which may arise, concerning their nature and reality.[6]

According to Hume, some expressions denote simple ideas and others denote complex ideas. But since complex ideas are ultimately analyzable into simple ones, every significant expression can be linked to a simple idea. An idea which is not caused by an impression is a dubious entity, and a word which purports to be linked to such a dubious entity is a word without meaning.

This theory, despite its simplicity and its reference to entities such as impressions or ideas, is very similar to some theories of meaning which have been expounded by Russell and Schlick in more recent times. In early stages of their work, both Russell and Schlick followed Hume, seeking to explain the relation between language and experience in terms of a one-to-one correspondence between words and the data of experience. Russell once suggested, "Every proposition which we can understand must be composed wholly of constituents with which we are acquainted."[7] Likewise Schlick, in an early attempt to construct a theory of meaning, wrote, "In order to find the meaning of a sentence we have to transform it by the introduction of successive definitions until finally it contains only words that are not further defined, but whose meanings can be given by direct ostension."[8] However, both Russell and Schlick, upon realizing the inadequacy of their theories, modified their criteria. Russell observed that the elements of a sentence

[6] David Hume, *Enquiries,* Book I, sec. II, par. 17, ed. L. A. Selby-Bigge (Oxford: Clarendon Press, 1951).

[7] Bertrand Russell, *Mysticism and Logic* (New York: Longmans, Green, 1921), 219.

[8] Quoted in Paul Marhenke, "The Criterion of Cognitive Significance," *Proceedings and Addresses of the American Philosophical Association,* XXIII (1950), 1-21.

like "Quadruplicity drinks procrastination" are ostensibly definable, yet the whole sentence lacks significance. The attempt to present a more adequate theory of meaning, without diverging from the Humean conviction that meaning and experience are closely connected, led Schlick and others to formulate various criteria of verifiability.

Nonetheless, the Humean approach to the problem of meaning has not been forsaken. Of late, various theories about the mechanism of language learning have been developed by psychologists, linguists, and philosophers.

In the introductory chapters of *Word and Object,* the American logician Quine developed, in Chomsky's words, "what appears to be a narrowly Humean theory of language acquisition in recent philosophy."[9] However, Quine takes (with Bentham and Tooke) sentences as the unit of language, and not terms, and refers to "the impossible term-by-term empiricism of Locke or Hume."

On Quine's view there are three possible mechanisms by which sentences can be learned: direct conditioning to appropriate stimulations, associations of sentences with sentences, and "analogical synthesis" — that is, producing a new sentence by analogy with the old sentences. The theory of language learning is only a part of the more comprehensive theory of meaning. As Quine recently hinted, "The way to a full and satisfactory theory of meaning is, I begin to suspect, a phenomenology of act and intention, but one in which all concepts are defined finally in behavioral terms."[10]

The main difficulty with the views of the classical empiricists was not merely that their semantic analyses were infected with psychologism, nor was it that their ontologies were populated with entities which could in no way constitute objective referents for various expressions. Rather, their most serious shortcoming was their failure to provide an explanation of the meaningfulness of mathematical statements, for mathematical truths are not statements of fact, and numbers are neither mental nor physical entities. Hume, following Leibniz, argued that mathematical truths are significant, even though they do not express matters of fact. He endeavored to make a place in his system for the significance of mathematical statements by a distinction between two kinds of relations: those which are dependent upon their relata

[9] Noam Chomsky, "Quine's Empirical Assumptions," *Synthese,* XIX (1968), 53.

[10] W. V. Quine, "Replies," *Synthese,* XIX (1968), 313.

and those which are not (*Treatise*), or between relations of ideas and matters of fact (*Enquiries*). On Hume's account a mathematical proposition is to be regarded as *a priori*, in the sense of requiring no empirical verification in order to be assertable as true or false, even though all the concepts that constitute such a proposition are derived from experience. But Hume neither explained the supposed impressions corresponding to arithmetic ideas, nor could he in his framework of "internal and perishing impressions," conjoined by links of association, account for the apodictic nature of mathematical truths.

Kant correctly noted that the empirical position of Hume is incompatible with the necessity and universality of mathematical judgments: "This empirical deduction, which was adapted by both philosophers (Locke and Hume), cannot be reconciled with the reality of our scientific knowledge *a priori*, namely pure *mathematics*."[11]

While Hume tried to give an account of the significance of mathematical statements by placing them in the class of analytic truths, his successor, J. S. Mill, stated: "The science of number is thus no exception to the conclusion we previously arrived at, that the processes even of the deductive sciences are altogether inductive, and that their first principles are generalizations from experience."[12]

Logical Empiricists

The investigations of Frege and Russell on the foundations of mathematics, and their rejection of psychologism of the Hume-Mill type, paved the way for construction of semantic theories which could both account for the meaningfulness of mathematical truths and factual statements, and at the same time exclude metaphysical assertions from the class of cognitive discourse.

However, Frege's and Russell's attempts at the reduction of mathematics to logic, i.e., logicism, encountered serious difficulties. Commenting on logicism, a mathematical logician states:

> This seemed to be an excellent program, but when it was put into effect, it turned out that there is simply no logic strong enough to encompass the whole of mathematics. Thus what remained from this program is a reduction of mathematics to set theory. This can hardly be said to be a satisfactory solution of the problem of founda-

[11] Immanuel Kant, *Critique of Pure Reason,* trans. Max Miller (London: Macmillan, 1949), 742.

[12] John Stuart Mill, *A System of Logic*, 8th ed. (1872), I, 298.

tions of mathematics since among all mathematical theories it is just the theory of sets that requires clarification more than any other.[13]

Russell nonetheless thought that by means of this program an old philosophical puzzle was solved: "We get rid of numbers as metaphysical entities. They become, in fact, merely linguistic conveniences with no more substantiality than belong to 'etc.' or 'i.e.'," and "Numbers are classes of classes, and classes are symbolic conveniences."[14]

Logical empiricists were influenced by the earlier Wittgenstein. Wittgenstein in the *Tractatus* develops a theory about the nature of logic, the relation of logic to language, and the relation which holds between a proposition and a fact by virtue of which a proposition states a fact. His so-called picture theory of language is designed to explain the nature of fact-stating propositions, and thereby to characterize metaphysical assertions as senseless inasmuch as they do not picture atomic facts. At that stage Wittgenstein did not consider the role or function of other linguistic expressions. Following his lead, logical empiricists concentrated their attention mainly upon the language of science.

Logical empiricists used the apparatus of formal logic to construct criteria of meaningfulness which would exclude metaphysical assertions without assimilating mathematical truths into the realm of empirical truths, and to construct idealized languages. Logical empiricists such as Schlick, Carnap, and Ayer formulated criteria of significance which could be used to determine whether any given statement is cognitively significant or cognitively meaningless, and a criterion for distinguishing between analytic and synthetic statements.

In an early stage of his work, Carnap attempted to construct various artificial languages in which no metaphysical statements could be formulated. He states:

> The fact that natural languages allow the formation of meaningless sequences of words without violating the rules of grammar, indicates that grammatical syntax is, from the logical point of view, inadequate. If grammatical syntax corresponds exactly to logical syntax, pseudo-statements . . . could not arise. . . . It follows that if our thesis

[13] A. Mostowski, *Thirty Years of Foundational Studies* (New York: Barnes & Noble, 1966), 7.

[14] Bertrand Russell, *My Philosophical Development* (New York: Simon and Schuster, 1948), 7, 234.

that the statements of metaphysics are pseudostatements is justifiable, then metaphysics could not be expressed in a logically constructed language. This is the great philosophical importance of the task, which at present occupies the logicians, of building a logical syntax.[15]

Carnap distinguished various levels of language, differentiating object language from metalanguage, material from formal modes of speech, and assertions about a linguistic framework from assertions in the framework. Carnap also utilized the three aspects of semiotics: pragmatics, semantics, and syntactics. His later works fall primarily under the heading of semantics. However, the logical empiricists' criteria of significance and of analyticity were the objects of severe scrutiny. In this country W. V. Quine, in his famous "Two Dogmas of Empiricism," leveled some fundamental objections, on both technical and philosophical grounds, against the adequacy of both criteria.

Wittgenstein and his followers at Oxford seriously questioned both the method and the value of constructing such criteria. Despite the fact that logical empiricists were inspired by the early work of Wittgenstein (*Tractatus*), Wittgenstein himself denied that he ever advocated a criterion of verifiability. It is reported that he said:

> I used at one time to say that, in order to get clear how a certain sentence is used, it was a good idea to ask oneself the question, 'How could one verify such an assertion?' But this is just one way among others of getting clear about the use of a word or a sentence. For example, another question which is often very useful to ask oneself is, 'How is this word learned?' 'How would people set about teaching a child this word?'
>
> But some people have turned this suggestion about asking for the verification into a dogma — as if I'd been advancing a *theory* about meaning.[16]

Several philosophers have argued that the stipulations offered by constructive semanticists are too arbitrary to serve as a basis for solving or dissolving philosophical controversies on the meaning of 'meaning' or 'truth.' Among these stipulations are Schlick's criterion of verifi-

[15] Rudolf Carnap, "The Elimination of Metaphysics through the Logical Analysis of Language," in *Logical Positivism*, ed. A. J. Ayer (New York: Macmillan, 1959).
[16] From "Ludwig Wittgenstein," by D. A., J. G. and A. C., *Australasian Journal of Philosophy*, XXIX, 2: 79.

ability, Carnap's postulates and semantical rules, and Tarski's formal treatment of truth (which provides a formal condition that any definition of truth for any object language must meet). However, the critics who made this objection admitted that in some cases (e.g., that of Tarski's formal treatment of truth) a semantic paradox was dissolved. Such philosophers have also argued that the relation between an ideal or artificial language and natural language is not like the relation between the language of science (i.e., one employing idealizations and models) and a body of empirical data. This is because the formalized languages of semanticists, unlike the language of science, are not under strict empirical controls. The descriptive semanticists thus believed that the best way to solve philosophical problems is via the study of the uses of expressions in natural language. Metalinguistic rules can be provided for idealized languages; these would include rules about the correct formation and valid derivation of formulae. But in natural language there are no analogous rules by which we can determine the use and hence the meaning of a word or sentence in any given context.

Wittgenstein's view that philosophical problems arise when language is misused[17] led to the belief that, in order to solve such problems, we should discover the ordinary use (or normal use) of expressions in various language games. Despite his insistence upon looking at the facts of language and not constructing dogmas about it, and his appeal to avoid hasty generalizations, Wittgenstein does say something very general about the meaning of a word: "For a *large* class of cases — though not for all in which we employ the word 'meaning' it can be defined thus: the meaning of a word is its use in the language."[18]

Wittgenstein is not defining the meaning of an expression in terms of its use; he is recommending to philosophers that, if they were to look at an expression from the aspect of its use in the language, they would get a clearer picture of it than by looking at it from the aspect of meaning. In this sense, use and meaning, like Jastrow's duck-rabbit picture (I, 144) are two aspects of the same thing, i.e., words.

This interpretation is based on numerous passages in the *Philosophical Investigations*. For example: "Let the use of words teach you their meaning. Similarly one can often say in mathematics: let the proof teach you *what* was being proved" (II, 220).

---

[17] Ludwig Wittgenstein ("Philosophical problems arise when language *goes on holiday*"), *Philosophical Investigations* (Oxford: Basil Blackwell, 1953), 19e.

[18] Wittgenstein, *Philosophical Investigations,* 43e.

Following Wittgenstein's lead, many linguistic philosophers examined the uses of expressions conducive to the generation of philosophical puzzles. For almost twenty years the philosophical periodicals contained close examinations of expressions like 'freedom of the will,' 'cause,' 'motive,' 'obligation,' the misuse of which was taken to be a prominent feature of philosophical problems.

However, soon the complaints were heard: that at best such discussions clarify the subtleties of the English language, but they do not clarify philosophical concepts which are independent of the contingencies of any specific language; and that the mere pursuit of facts without the employment of theory is useless. Ayer wrote, "The current philosophical emphasis on fact, as opposed to theory, has been overdone."[19] Though some philosophers moved toward an empirical theory of semantics (J. L. Austin's "performative utterances," Strawson's "referring expressions," Hart's "defeasible concepts," R. M. Hare's "phrastic-neustic" expressions, etc.), linguists such as Chomsky and Katz objected that, without making use of data already obtainable in the field of structural linguistics, the findings of Oxford philosophers in descriptive semantics lack scientific significance.

In referring to ordinary language philosophy in his recent book, *The Philosophy of Language,* J. J. Katz writes: "It is indeed somewhat strange that a movement that achieved such a quantity of competent description should have done almost nothing in the way of theorizing about linguistic structure. The comparison with Babylonian astronomy or Greek geometry before Euclid comes most readily to mind."[20]

A shift from linguistic philosophy (i.e., the attempt to solve problems of philosophy by analysis of the meanings of words and their logical structure in sentences) to philosophy of language (a general theory of meaning) came with the later work of J. L. Austin. Austin's emphasis on speech acts, rather than on meanings of words, may be noticed by the problem which he sets for himself to solve in his last work, *How to Do Things with Words.* Namely, "What are the different kinds of speech acts speakers perform when they utter expressions?" The problem thus formulated falls within the domain of descriptive pragmatics.

[19] A. J. Ayer, *Philosophy and Language* (Oxford: Oxford University Press, 1960).
[20] Jerrold J. Katz, *The Philosophy of Language* (New York: Harper and Row, 1966), 88.

Logic and Semantics

Viewing deductive logic as the study of formal structure and semantics as the study of meaning and reference of linguistic expressions, we may clearly see their interdependency. We cannot do logic without knowing the meanings or references of words which appear in a sentence and without knowing the meaning and the truth value of the whole sentence, and we know very little about the meaning of a sentence if we do not know its role in the logical scene, e.g., what follows from it.

From the dawn of logic, it was recognized that if we want to apply the laws of logic to a natural language, we should make some adjustments in their application. It is said, for example:

> Even Aristotle had to introduce a certain stylization of language in order to carry out his investigations. . . . For instance, although the sentence
> > All men are mortal or not all men are mortal
> is an exact substitution-instance of the matrix
> > S or not S,
> i.e., can be obtained from it by putting 'all men are mortal' for the letter 'S' (though even here we must make a slight adjustment by capitalizing the initial 'a' in one of its occurrences and not in the other), the sentence
> > Socrates is mortal or Socrates is not mortal
> is not strictly such an instance. In connection with this particular matrix the difficulty stems from the fact that, although the denial of an English sentence is usually formed by adding the word 'not,' there is no simple rule for determining *where* the addition is to be made. We form the denial of 'Socrates is mortal' by inserting the word 'not' right after the verb, but if we try to deny the sentence 'all men are mortal' in the same way, the result is
> > All men are not mortal,
> whereas what is wanted is the much weaker sentence
> > Not all men are mortal.[21]

In their quest for precision, many logicians sought, therefore, to employ various devices for the regimentation of natural language so that it would be amenable to logical manipulations obviating fallacies and paradoxes which we encounter throughout the use of a natural lan-

[21] Benson Mates, *Elementary Logic* (New York: Oxford University Press, 1965), 14-15.

guage. The idea of creating an artificial language which is grammatically simpler than the natural language and in which there exists an algorithm or a method of computation for determining whether a formula is well formed or not is put into practice by most modern logicians, though it goes back to Leibniz.

Leibniz projected a scheme for the reform of all knowledge by the use of a universal language (*characteristica universalis*) and a calculus of reasoning (*calculus ratiocinator*) for the manipulation of that language. He stated, "Telescopes and microscopes have not been so useful to the eye as this instrument would be in adding to the capacity of thought. . . ." And, "If we had it, we should be able to reason in metaphysics and morals in much the same way as in geometry and analysis." And, "If controversies were to arise, there would be no more need of disputation between two philosophers than between two accountants. For it would suffice to take their pencils in their hands, to sit down to their slates, and say to each other (with a friend as witness if they liked) : Let us calculate."[22]

The idea of an artificial language may give the false impression that the logical inquiries carried on in such a language have no bearing upon the semantic of natural languages. However, the utility of an artificial language lies in its approximations to natural language.

The charge of artificiality which is often brought against formal semantics is unfounded. Tarski, the founder of formal semantics, explicitly stated a criterion for the formal as well as the material adequacy of the definition of truth. "The definition must not lead to contradiction and besides it should do justice to the intuitions which adhere to the classical Aristotelian conceptions of truth."[23]

As another logician points out, "The logical complexities and logical systems are not dreamed up artificially; they are simply there, embodied in natural languages, as it were, waiting to be brought to light and suitably characterized."[24]

Frege was the first logician who tried to construct an artificial language (*Begriffsschrift*, 1879). In his quantification theory, by the use of predicate letters, variables, and quantifiers, he showed the possibility

[22] Gottfried Wilhelm von Leibniz (G. VII. 14), (G. VII. 21), (G. VII. 200), quoted in Bertrand Russell, *A Critical Exposition of the Philosophy of Leibniz*, 2nd ed. (London: Allen and Unwin, 1937), 169-70.

[23] A. Tarski, "The Semantic Conception of Truth," in this volume.

[24] R. M. Martin, *Intension and Decision* (Englewood Cliffs, N.J.: Prentice-Hall, 1963), 152.

of capturing some of the usage of words such as 'all,' 'every,' 'some,' 'each,' 'none,' and others in natural language. He emphasized that his logic is not like Boole's, only a *calculus ratiocinator*, but *lingua characterica*, that is, a logic in which semantical components of propositions as well as their formal structures were analyzed.

We may comprehend the relation between natural language and an artificial language by using an analogy of Ryle's. "The cartographer," Ryle writes, "finds no Euclidean straight hedgerows in Euclidean plane meadows. Yet he could not map the sinuous hedgerows that he finds or the undulating meadows save against the ideally regular boundaries and levels. . . . The cartographer is one of the clients of geometry. The possibility of his map being approximately correct or precise is the gift of Euclid."[25]

We should note also that though the Euclidean geometry in an abstract way depicts some properties of objects, it is less abstract and less artificial in comparison to Hilbert's formal language constructed for the Euclidean geometry.

The regimentation of language into the logic of truth functions, quantification, and identity was the first step in modern logic. There are, however, a host of expressions whose occurrences in declarative sentences alter the truth values of such sentences.

Insert words such as 'possible,' 'necessary,' 'probable,' 'believes that,' 'said that,' in a certain place in a simple declarative sentence; then create a name of that sentence by quotation device, and you will see that you have changed the logical structure of your sentence. (See the introduction to Part One.) There are, moreover, various classes of sentences such as optatives, imperatives, and interrogatives which do not have truth value and hence could not be dealt with by truth functional and quantificational logic (though it is possible to state compliance conditions for the imperative and fulfillment conditions for the optative, i.e., something akin to truth conditions).

Lately an attempt has been made to develop neoclassical logic. Various systems of logic such as modal logic, deontic logic, event logic, and intentional logic have already been constructed, though the logic of counterfactual, causal, and future contingency statements has not yet been developed. (See introductions to Part One and Part Seven.)

[25] G. Ryle, *Dilemmas* (Cambridge: Cambridge University Press, 1960), 123.

Formal Semantics and Speech Acts

Finally, we have to adumbrate two different trends in the philosophy of language, i.e., the discipline of formal semantics and the theories of speech acts.

In formal semantics, the attempt has been made by Frege, Church, Tarski, and others to lay bare the skeleton of two cardinal concepts of meaning and truth. Quine succinctly describes the ongoing of formal semantics as such.

> What goes by the name of semantics falls into two domains, the theory of reference and the theory of meaning. Truth is on one side of the boundary, meaning on the other. The two domains are conspicuously distinct, but still there is this fundamental connection between them: You have given all the meanings when you have given the truth conditions of all sentences.[26]

A formal semanticist, Donald Davidson, argues negatively against certain informal theories of meaning (see introduction to Part One) and proposes a way to construct a systematic account of meanings for a language by building Tarski's recursive definition of truth for that language. Rejected is the familiar idea that knowledge of the meaning of each word in a sentence — which is obtainable by observing the use or by consulting a dictionary — plus knowledge of grammar and syntax would necessarily provide the meaning of the whole sentence. For example, though we may know the meaning of each word in belief sentences, and though the syntax is relatively unproblematic, "we cannot account for even as much as the truth conditions of such sentences on the basis of what we know of the meanings of the words in them."

In Davidson's essays we can see clearly the blueprint of the Leibnizean project. He writes: "What we need as part of a theory of language is a mechanical procedure for pairing a sentence with a representation of its logical form; with a formula which formally determines the entailments of the sentence."[27] The relation between knowing the logical form of a sentence, its truth value, and its meaning is thus revealed: "To know the semantic concept of truth for a language is to know what it is for a sentence — any sentence — to be true, and this amounts, in one good sense we can give to the phrase, to under-

[26] Quine, "Replies," *Synthese,* XIX (1968), 303.
[27] Donald Davidson, "Truth and Meaning," *Synthese,* XVII (1967), 3.

standing the language."[28] And: "The obvious connection between a definition of truth of the kind Tarski has shown how to construct, and the concept of meaning ... [is]: the definition works by giving necessary and sufficient conditions for the truth of every sentence, and to give truth conditions is a way of giving the meaning of a sentence."[29]

Davidson recognizes Tarski's awareness of the problem of defining truth in natural languages. Tarski states:

> *The problem of the definition of truth obtains a precise meaning and can be solved in a rigorous way only for those languages whose structure has been exactly specified.* For other languages — thus, for any natural, "spoken" languages — the meaning of the problem is more or less vague, and its solution can have only an approximate character.[30]

Nonetheless, Davidson seeks a way to determine the meaning of a sentence by giving its truth condition.

> I am aware that many people, including Tarski ... have felt that it is hopeless to expect to give a truth definition for even the indicative sentences of a natural language, much less imperatives, interrogatives and so on. Then we must find alternative ways of showing how the meanings of sentences depend on their structure, or give up the attempt at theory.[31]

Davidson's project is applauded by Quine, yet Quine's comment on the project indicates that such a project could not be carried on into natural language.

> A defense of plain talkers against regimentalists ... has been to equate clarity with familiarity and so to declare ordinary language clear ex-officio. What better can we equate clarity to? A central importance of Davidson's idea is that it offers an answer, thus telling us what is wrong with ordinary language. You cannot launch it into a truth definition.[32]

There are philosophers of language, the later Wittgenstein and the speech acts theorists (Austin, Grice, Searle), who argue that appeal to

[28] *Ibid.,* 310.
[29] *Ibid.*
[30] Tarski, "The Semantic Conception of Truth," in this volume.
[31] Donald Davidson, "Theories of Meaning and Learnable Languages," in Y. Bar-Hillel, *Logic, Methodology and Philosophy of Science* (Amsterdam: North Holland, 1965), 387.
[32] Quine, "Replies," 304.

formal structure of a language alone, without reference to the intention of the user or speaker of that language and without knowledge of a particular situation in which the utterance is made, is insufficient for understanding that language. In the words of Strawson: "The particular meanings of words and sentences are, no doubt, largely a matter of rule and convention; but the general nature of such rules and conventions can be ultimately understood only by reference to the concept of communication-intention."[33]

According to the view of the formalists, the syntactic and semantic rules together determine the meanings of all sentences of a language via determination of their truth conditions. Strawson objects that, even if we limit our language to sentences having truth conditions, truth conditions themselves cannot be explained without reference to the function of communication, since "the idea of truth leads straight to the idea of *what* is *said,* the content of what is said, when utterances are made, and that in turn to the question of what is *done* when utterances are made."[34] He concludes, "We connect meaning with truth and truth, too simply, with sentences, and sentences belong to language. But, as theorists, we know nothing of human *language* unless we understand human *speech.*"[35]

It seems to us that there is no real conflict between the theories of formal semantics and those of speech acts, but only division of labor. The inquiries into the dynamics of speech fall within the domain of descriptive pragmatics, whereas the inquiries about the statics of language form the subject matter of formal semantics. As there is no theoretical conflict in classical mechanics between statics (the branch which treats bodies at rest or forces in equilibrium) and dynamics (the branch which considers the motion and equilibrium of systems under the action of forces outside the system), there is no and need not be any conflict between theories of language and theories of speech. Indeed, the welcome growth of semantics into a science may very well hinge upon the cooperation between these seemingly diverse trends on the present scene of philosophy of language.

We do not desire to speculate about the future of semantics. Whatever direction it will take in the future, it cannot avoid following the

[33] P. F. Strawson, *Meaning and Truth* (Oxford: Clarendon Press, 1970), 4.
[34] *Ibid.,* 18.
[35] *Ibid.,* 25.

path of other sciences in utilizing both fact and theory. Though semantics is still in its infancy, an inquiry into the more recent history (roughly sixty years) of this discipline is indispensable for the adequate understanding of this branch of philosophy. To assist in providing this understanding, we have collected, organized, and edited materials which cover more than half a century of work in semantics. We have reproduced here works by famous logicians and semanticists before the rise of logical empiricism, and various important essays written by logical empiricists on such issues as criteria of meaningfulness and analyticity. In order to give a balanced view, we have also included some criticisms of the semantic theories of logical empiricism which were made by competent philosophers outside this school. Thus we have not limited our scope to the work of logicians and semanticists who either came before the logical empiricists or who were logical empiricists. We have also included significant works by the followers of Wittgenstein, Oxford philosophers, and American logicians and semanticists. We have excluded theories of meaning and analyticity in the works of some classical empiricists or continental rationalists, and the more recent works of some structural linguists.

We have divided the book into seven parts. For each part we have provided an introduction which sets the background for the various issues to be discussed; it briefly deals with the articles included and shows the changes and developments of a specific aspect or problem of semantics. We have also included a selected bibliography for each part.

We hope this book, which is a compendium of the most important works in semantics in the past several decades, will be an asset for the study of what has gradually become a significant and well-defined discipline.

PART

I

ASPECTS OF THE STUDY OF SIGNS

INTRODUCTION

A. Semantics, Syntax, and Pragmatics

The American philosopher Charles Sanders Peirce (1839-1914) made use of Locke's conception of semiotic, or the general theory of signs, and divided it into pure grammar (the inquiry into the necessary conditions of meaningfulness of propositions), logic proper (the study of the necessary conditions of truth), and pure rhetoric ("the study of laws by which in every scientific intelligence one sign gives birth to another, and especially one thought brings forth another").

Peirce's classification of semiotic was borrowed by C. W. Morris and used by Rudolf Carnap under the designation pragmatics, semantics and syntactics or syntax.

Carnap suggested construction of a metatheory of semiotics, i.e., the theory about pragmatics, semantics, and logical syntax of the object language, which is formulated in a metalanguage.[1] Three aspects of the object language may be considered. We may view linguistic expressions in relation to the speaker's intention, linguistic ability, belief, audience, and contexts of use. This is called pragmatics. Eliminating the speaker and the hearer from the scene, what remains is language and the relation of each of its parts to objects, events, or in general their designata. This is called semantics. Abstracting once more the designata from this picture, we are left with linguistic expressions themselves, and with their relations. This is called syntactics, which may include grammar. Exclude grammar, and we have logical syntax. Each dimension may be subdivided into pure or formal, empirical or descriptive.

---

[1] Rudolf Carnap, "Foundations of Logic and Mathematics," *International Encyclopedia of Unified Science* (Chicago: University of Chicago Press, 1949).

The central problem of formal semantics is the problem of definition of truth or the criteria for truth conditions for the sentences of certain specified languages. Tarski's massive contributions to the formulation of the concept of truth, and his notion of truth in a model for formalized languages of specified structure, are considered to be classics in formal semantics. In the early 1950's Tarski introduced to semantics the notion of truth in a model; since then, formal semantics has turned into the theory of models. Starting from a given language L and a class C of objects called models of sentences of L, truth is then defined in terms of satisfaction in a model. Some Polish logicians such as Lesniewski and Ajdukiewicz had already dealt with formal semantics. Tarski, however, made the first comprehensive and systematic study of this dimension.

The basic idea of semantics — i.e., relations between objects; for example, mathematical objects and expressions naming them, whether expressions in natural or formalized languages — is for the first time applied by Tarski to the study of formalized languages, and later is carried over to the study of relations between mathematical objects and formal expressions naming them which is called "logical semantics."[2]

In descriptive semantics there have been various inquiries into the nature of referring expressions, proper names, sense, and reference by logicians such as Frege, Russell, Quine, and Strawson — though such work should not be described as purely empirical. The pioneer study of formal syntax has been achieved by Carnap.[3]

The descriptive study of syntactics is under investigation by linguists. The descriptive work in pragmatics was pioneered by the later Wittgenstein and has been carried more systematically by Austin, Grice, Searle, and others. However, some work of American philosophers, though programmatic and speculative, falls within this domain. Almost half a century before the rise of what is called "speech acts theory," John Dewey viewed language as essentially a social phenomenon and only accidentally a private matter: "Language is specifically a mode of interaction of at least two beings, a speaker and a hearer; it presupposes an organized group to which these creatures belong, and from whom they have acquired their habits of speech. It is there-

    [2] See A. Mostowski, *Thirty Years of Foundational Semantics* (New York: Barnes and Noble, 1966), 27.
    [3] Rudolf Carnap, *Logical Syntax of Language* (London: Kegan Paul, 1937).

fore a relationship."[4] We should note also that some of Charles Stevenson's observations (with regard to the similarity of moral pronouncements and persuasive definition and his emphasis upon the emotive rather than the descriptive role of ethical expressions) belong to pragmatics of language rather than to semantics.[5]

We may view descriptive pragmatics as the study of speech or speech acts: the linguistic acts performed by the speaker in making assertions, claims, promises, inferences, requests, insults, and so on. We may then study various aspects of a speech act by formulating necessary and sufficient conditions for a successful or normal performance of the act (consider Austin's notion of an infelicity); by stating the intention, beliefs, and expectations of the speaker; and by specifying the context of the utterance, such as time, place, and audience.

Of late, various steps have been taken toward construction of formal pragmatics. As early as the 1940's Carnap encouraged such a program.

> There is an urgent need for a system of theoretical pragmatics, not only for psychology and linguistics, but also for analytic philosophy. Since pure semantics is sufficiently developed, the time seems ripe for attempts at constructing tentative outlines of pragmatical systems. Such an outline may first be restricted to small groups of concepts (e.g., those of belief, assertion, and utterance); it may then be developed to include all those concepts needed for discussions in the theory of knowledge and the methodology of science.[6]

Following Carnap's suggestion, R. M. Martin in *Intension and Decision*[7] developed a language for talking about pragmatic concepts such as preference, acceptance, reasonableness, and evidence, together with an elaborate theory of intensions. One of Carnap's disciples, Bar-Hillel, suggested that pragmatics may concern itself with what C. S. Peirce called 'indexical expressions' (called by Russell 'egocentric particulars' and by Reichenbach 'token-reflexive expressions').[8]

[4] John Dewey, *Experience and Nature* (La Salle, Ill.: Open Court, 1925).

[5] See Charles Stevenson, *Ethics and Language* (New Haven: Yale University Press, 1944), Ch. 4, "Persuasive Definition," and Ch. 2, "Some Pragmatic Aspects of Meaning."

[6] Rudolf Carnap, *Meaning and Necessity* (Chicago: University of Chicago Press, 1946), 250.

[7] R. M. Martin, *Intension and Decision* (Englewood Cliffs, N.J.: Prentice-Hall, 1963).

[8] Y. Bar-Hillel, "Indexical Expressions," *Mind,* LXIII (1954), 359-76.

Since in formal pragmatics, as in formal semantics and formal syntax, we are interested in determining truth conditions of a sentence, and since the referent of indexical expressions cannot be determined without considering the context of use, we should study the context of use in order to determine the truth of the assertion. Such inquiries could be carried on in formal pragmatics. Consider the sentence:

I will do the job.

The truth value of this sentence cannot be determined without knowledge of the context of use: the bearer of the indexical expression, i.e., the pronoun 'I'; the description of "the job"; the time of the utterance; and the time in which "the job" will be done.

Finally, Richard Montague in various papers tried to construct pragmatic systems. He suggested that pragmatics should at least initially follow the lead of semantics or its modern version, model theory — which is concerned with the notion of truth and satisfaction (satisfaction in a model, or under an interpretation). He considered a pragmatic language L, the utterer or the speaker and the moment of utterance, and suggested that "if the only indexical features of L were the presence of tense operators and the first person pronoun 'I,' then a point of reference might be an ordered pair consisting of a person and a real number, understood respectively as the utterer and the moment of utterance."[9] Thus viewed, pragmatics becomes an extension of formal semantics containing indexical expressions.

B. Use and Mention

Speaking about persons, places, institutions, material objects, events, experiences, concepts, etc., we make use of linguistic expressions which are available and appropriate for each occasion. We use proper names, pronouns, definite descriptions for the purpose of referring to persons, places, institutions, and the like — spatio-temporal predicates for talking about material objects and events, emotive expressions to convey our experiences and certain technical expressions such as class names or numerals, operational signs in speaking about concepts, numbers, and mathematical operations. (On occasion we communicate without using linguistic expression, such as by pointing to an object or to ourselves, miming, or gesturing. We are not concerned here with non-linguistic communication.)

[9] Richard Montague, "Pragmatics and Intensional Logic," *Synthese,* XXII (1970).

We seldom confuse a linguistic expression with what that expression names or describes, e.g., the place name Chicago with the city which goes by that name, the clan name Montague or Capulet with the members of the clan. We see through Shakespeare's eyes the essential irrelevancy of names (in particular, proper names).

> O, be some other name:
> What's in a name? that which we call a rose
> By any other name would smell as sweet;

Though it is said that blasphemy is a sin, and though obscene words are regarded as taboo, we do ordinarily distinguish the name of a person from the bearer of that name, or the name of an act from the act. However, when the bearer or the description of an expression is either an abstract entity or another expression, we may confuse the expression used to say something about an abstract entity with that entity itself, or the expression used to refer to another expression with that expression. The confusion between numerals (names of numbers) and numbers (e.g., between the Arabic numeral '3,' the Roman numeral 'III,' the Greek numeral 'γ,' and the number 3), between variables and their substituends, between names or descriptions of signs and signs, or between symbols and their meaning is not uncommon.

Such confusions are removable by paying due attention to the contexts or frames of reference in which the expressions occur. Thus the context:

(1) Chicago is an Indian name,

or

(2) The Latin title *Tractatus Logico-Philosophicus* was proposed by G. E. Moore for *Logisch-Philosophische Abhandlung*,

or

(3) Dreary rhymes with weary,

or

(4) Ghost Town has more letters than people,

indicates that in (1) we are talking about a place name and not about the city by that name, that in (2) we are saying something about a title of a book and not about the book, that in (3) we are speaking about rhyming of two words and not about their meaning, and that in (4) we are saying that a certain place name has more letters than that place has people.

However, it is of fundamental importance to note that in fields such as logic, semantics, and grammar, where the language itself is the subject of investigation and is talked about as frequently as it is used, we should sharply distinguish the linguistic expression in general, or the language which is the object of the inquiry, from the linguistic expressions or the language in which the inquiry is made. Indeed, unless some distinction is made, no progress could be made in such fields. For example, understanding semantical paradoxes, the Russell theory of types, Gödel's incompleteness proof, and the theory of syntax requires awareness of cases in which a given linguistic expression is spoken about and used. For this purpose logicians beginning with Frege have used various techniques. The technique of making a distinction between the use and the mention of linguistic expressions, and the use of categorical distinction between the object language and the metalanguage in formal systems, is now a common practice among logicians.

Since we are not here concerned with formal systems, we shall not delve into the issue of levels of languages. It will suffice to mention that in formal systems of logic and semantics a distinction is made between the language about which we talk and which is the object of our inquiry (the object language) and the language in which we talk and in which the inquiry is carried out (the metalanguage).

The practice of talking about one language by using another is not uncommon. There are books about the grammar of some foreign languages written in English. In such cases the English language is the metalanguage and the foreign language is the object language. The practice of using the same language in order to talk about it is very common. Most English grammars are written in English, and there are many books about the English language in English.

Where the object language and the metalanguage are the same, the need for some device to keep them distinct is obvious. This need is most crucial when we wish to investigate the semantics or the logic of natural or artificial languages. Corresponding to the object language/metalanguage distinction, a distinction is made between the use and the mention of linguistic expressions. (A linguistic expression may be a proper name, a predicate, a phrase, a sentence.)

In the vernacular of logicians, when I say:

(5) Chicago is large,

I am said to be using the word 'Chicago' and not Chicago itself.

Obviously Chicago, being a city and not a word, cannot be used in (5). Whereas if I say:

(1) Chicago is an Indian name,

then I am said to be mentioning a place name and saying something about its origin.

Logicians say that (1) does not have the proper form. According to a convention, the way to mention an expression is to create a name for it; this could be done by surrounding that expression in single quotes. Thus (1) should be rendered:

(6) 'Chicago' is an Indian name.

Accordingly, in (6) I am not mentioning Chicago, but its name. (6) is about 'Chicago,' not Chicago. It does not use 'Chicago' but ' 'Chicago.' ' (Note the double quotes around the last word of the last sentence. It shows how we can create a name for a name and so on by using an additional quote.) (5) is about Chicago and contains 'Chicago.' Following the mentioned convention, (2) should be written as:

(7) The Latin title *'Tractatus Logico-Philosophicus'* was proposed by G. E. Moore for *Logish-Philosophische Abhandlung*.

(Note that in [7] the whole expression in quotes is the name of the title of a book. Since the title is a linguistic expression, if we wish to speak of it, we should use its name and not the title itself, whereas the three German capitalized words constitute a German title.)

We can represent this idea by using the arrow mark as a sign for 'denotes':

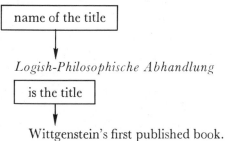

'Tractatus Logico-Philosophicus'

name of the title

Logish-Philosophische Abhandlung

is the title

Wittgenstein's first published book.

Likewise (3) should be written as:

(8) 'Dreary' rhymes with 'weary.'

Finally, (4) goes into:

(9) 'Ghost Town' has more letters than Ghost Town has people.

Carrying over the idea of mentioning a linguistic expression by creating its name through the quotation device, we are able to state unambiguously various properties of a word or a sentence without confusion. Such a perspicuous mode of talking and writing is essential for appreciating many important philosophical issues, from Plato's Third Man argument, to the puzzle about the amendability of the clause about the amendability of the American constitution, to Tarski's semantic conception of truth, and so on.

You may omit the suggested method of name-making by using quotation marks around an expression in cases where your interest does not hinge upon logical or semantical properties of that expression — perhaps without much loss. It is possible that the context of the following sentence,

Chicago is a noun, is trisyllabic, has seven letters, appears in one of Mayakoysky's poems,

reveals that we are talking about certain grammatic, phonetic, morphological, and literary properties of a place name and not the big town. But note that without knowledge of the name-making device you cannot get the meaning, much less the significance, of

(10) 'Chicago is large' is true, if and only if, Chicago is large.

which satisfies Tarski's schema (T), through which the condition of material adequacy for a correct definition of truth is expressed.

The use of the word 'mention' in the context of 'use versus mention' is liable to confusion. Students often ask why it is said that in (5) we are "using" the word 'Chicago,' whereas in (6) it is said that we are "mentioning" it. Granted the distinction, is it not the case that strictly speaking in each we are using the said expression?

It is also stated that the case of pure mentioning of an expression is an exception rather than a rule.[10] The answer is that in (5) the word 'Chicago' is used in order to say something about the city, whereas in (6) ' 'Chicago' ' is used plus quotation marks for saying something about the word 'Chicago.' Hence the expression 'mention' is used in semantics to take care of cases like (6) in which an expression is used *as a topic of discussion.*

---

[10] Newton Garver, "Varieties of Use and Mention," *Philosophy and Phenomenological Research* (1965), 230-36.

An informal rule about mentioning an expression is the following: "To mention an object one shall use a name or description of that object, and not just the object itself. The word 'just' is inserted here in order to take account of those few cases in which a name or description of the object contains the object as a part, as for example in the expression 'Bertrand Russell's name.' "[11]

One way of creating a name for an object which is a linguistic expression is to enclose it within quotation marks, though the use of quotation marks is not the only device available for mentioning an expression. The other device is the use of the colon as equivalent to quotation marks when followed by displayed text, i.e., text centered in a new line. (Some instances of the use of this device have already appeared in this essay.) Yet another technique is to form a name by spelling. We may mention (5) as "the sentence constituted by three words, the first of which consists of the capitalized third letter, followed by the eighth, followed by the ninth, followed by the third, followed by the first, followed by the ninth, followed by the fifteenth letters . . . of the English alphabet, etc. etc."

Tarski in the *Wahrheitsbegrif*[12] suggests that the structural-descriptive names are obtained either by spelling or by using names of letters together with hyphen by way of concatenation sign. Using this device, we may mention (5) as:

$$\text{'C'} \frown \text{'h'} \frown \text{'i'} \frown \text{'c'} \frown \text{'a'} \frown \text{'g'} \frown \text{'o'} \frown \text{'i'} \frown \text{'s'} \frown \text{'l'} \frown \text{'a'} \frown \text{'r'} \frown \text{'g'} \frown \text{'e'}$$

The most common technique for creating a name for an expression is the use of quotation marks.

As Quine has observed,[13] Frege seems to have been the first logician to recognize the importance of scrupulous use of quotation marks for avoidance of confusion between use and mention. In *Grundgesetze* Frege points out:

> The frequent use made of quotation marks may cause surprise. I use them to distinguish the cases where I speak about the sign itself from those where I speak about what it stands for. Pedantic as this may appear, I think it necessary. It is remarkable how an inexact

---

[11] Benson Mates, *Elementary Logic* (New York: Oxford University Press, 1965), 20.

[12] A. Tarski, translated as "The Concept of Truth in Formalized Languages," in his *Logic, Semantics, Meta-mathematics* (Oxford: Oxford University Press, 1956), 152-278.

[13] W. V. Quine, *Mathematical Logic* (Cambridge: Harvard University Press, 1951).

mode of speaking or writing, which perhaps was originally employed only for greater convenience or brevity and with full consciousness of its inaccuracy, may end in a confusion of thought when once that consciousness disappeared. People have managed to mistake numerals for numbers, names of the things named, the mere devices of arithmetic for its proper subject matter. Such experiences teach us how necessary it is to demand the highest exactness in manner of speech and writing.[14]

However, not all logicians took Frege's advice seriously. Quine said that carelessness over the distinction of use and mention in *Principia Mathematica* allowed a confusion of material conditional with the relation of implication. "Properly, whereas '⊃' or 'if-then' connects statements, 'implies' is a verb which connects names of statements and thus expresses a relation of the named statements."[15]

As early as 1933 Tarski made some insightful suggestions about the way we may refer to a linguistic expression by creating a name for that expression, a device for creating a name for an expression by using quotation and other techniques, and how the inside of the quoted expression may be treated. He writes:

The fundamental conventions regarding the use of any language require that in any utterance we make about an object it is the name of the object which must be employed, and not the object itself. In consequence, if we wish to say something about a sentence, for example, that it is true, we must use the name of this sentence, and not the sentence itself.[16]

In another place he writes:

Quotation-mark names may be treated like single words of a language and thus like syntactically simple expressions. The single constituents of these names — the quotation marks and the expressions standing between them — fulfill the same function as the letters and complexes of successive letters in single words. Hence they can possess no independent meaning. Every quotation-mark name is then a constant individual name of a definite expression — and in fact a name of the same nature as the proper name of a man.[17]

[14] Gottlob Frege, translated in *From the Philosophical Writings of Gottlob Frege,* ed. P. Geach and Max Black (Oxford: Blackwell, 1966).
[15] W. V. Quine, *The Ways of Paradox* (New York: Random House, 1966).
[16] A. Tarski, "The Semantic Concept of Truth," in *Readings in Philosophical Analysis* (New York: Appleton-Century-Crofts, 1949).
[17] *Ibid.,* 159.

Quine also makes the same suggestion:

> From the standpoint of logical analysis each whole quotation must
> be regarded as a single word or sign, whose parts count for no more
> than serifs or syllables. A quotation is not a *description,* but a *hiero-*
> *glyph,* it designates its object not by describing it in terms of other
> objects, but by picturing it. The meaning of the whole does not de-
> pend upon the meanings of the constituent words. The personal name
> buried within the first word of the statement:
>
> 'Cicero' has six letters,
>
> e.g., is logically no more germane to the statement than is the verb
> 'let' which is buried within the last word.[18]

He compares the occurrence of an expression inside quotation marks
with the occurrence of letters in words: 'cat' in 'cattle,' 'can' in
'canary,' 'let' in 'letters.' According to Quine, an expression in quotation marks occurs merely "as a fragment of a longer name which contains besides this fragment, the two quotation marks."[19]

  The point of these suggestions seems to be this: beginning with the
idea that to mention an expression we have to create a name for it,
and a name for an expression could be constructed by surrounding it
in a pair of quotation marks, we may come to see that these marks
function as referring signs which refer to the expression inside. But
then we should take the referent of the whole interior of quotes as a
particular object. The rule about the referent of quotation marks is
formulated as: "The denotation of the result of enclosing any expression in quotes is the expression itself."[20] According to both Tarski's and
Quine's suggestions, we should take the quotation contents as a single
entity, as "a proper name" or "an orthographic accident." There
are, however, two main objections with regard to the above suggestions.
The first is brought forward by some philosophers who are concerned
mostly with pragmatics of language, and particularly with what is
called speech acts, and has to do with Tarski's first two suggestions,
above. The second objection is stated by some formal semanticists and
is concerned with some technical implications with regard to his third
suggestion. Let us take John Searle as a representative of the former
and Donald Davidson as a representative of the latter group.

---

[18] Quine, *Mathematical Logic,* 26.
[19] W. V. Quine, *From a Logical Point of View* (Cambridge: Harvard University Press, 1953).
[20] R. M. Smullyan, "Languages in Which Self Reference Is Possible," *Journal*
of Symbolic Logic, **XXII** (1957), 55-67.

Searle objects to the view that what occurs within the quotation is not the expression itself but a new expression, the proper name of the first expression. He considers:

(1) Socrates was a philosopher, and
(2) 'Socrates' has eight letters.

He remarks, first, that "the obvious truth that the same word begins both sentences" is denied by logicians, and, second, that it is claimed that in cases like (2) "the word 'Socrates' does not occur at all"; rather, a completely new word occurs, the proper name of the word, which is formed by putting quotation marks around the expression, or around what would be the expression if it were a use of the expression and not just a part of a new proper name. On this account, the word which begins (2) is not, as you might think, 'Socrates'; it is ' 'Socrates.' ' And the word I just wrote, elusively enough, is not ' 'Socrates,' ' but ' ' 'Socrates,' ' '[21] and, third, contra Tarski, there is no fundamental convention regarding the use of any language that "in any utterance we make about an object it is the name of the object which must be employed, and not the object itself."

Searle's main effort is to draw our attention to the disanalogy which he sees between the proper name and the quotation marks. He writes:

> If we ask ourselves why we have the institution of proper names at all, part of the answer is that we need a convenient device for making identifying references to commonly referred to objects when the objects are not always themselves present. But the device has no point when the object we wish to talk about is itself a stretch of discourse, and hence is easily produceable and does not require a separate linguistic device to refer to it. With very few exceptions, such as sacred words or obscenities, if we wish to speak of a word we don't need to name it or otherwise refer to it, we can simply produce (a token of) it.
>
> The odd cases where we do need names of words are those cases where it is improper, taboo or inconvenient to produce the word itself. We have conventions in written discourse, e.g., quotation marks, to mark the fact that the word is not being used normally but is being used as a topic of discussion.[22]

Searle concludes:

> Bits of discourse or other oral or visually presentable items can

[21] J. R. Searle, *Speech Acts* (Cambridge: Cambridge University Press, 1969).
[22] *Ibid.*, 74-75.

quite easily occur in discourse as the topic of the discourse. For example, an ornithologist might say "The sound made by the California Jay is . . ." and what completes the sentence is a sound, not a proper name of a sound.[23]

Searle's objection seems innocuous insofar as it points to some dissimilarities between the concept of proper name and the idea of making a name for an expression by the quotation marks device. But it overlooks the fact that Tarski's fundamental principle is meant to be employed in formal systems of logic and semantics, where we do need to refer to expressions in order to state their formal and semantical structures. One way to refer to an expression is to create a name for it. Note that Gödel's method of arithmetization of metamathematics, Tarski's general theory of semantic relations, and the discovery of paradoxes in semantically closed systems are based on cognition of some method of classifying the object language and the metalanguage which is the extension of use-mention distinction.

The deeper and technical objections against some aspects of the use of quotation marks as a name-making device are brought forward by some formal semanticists. It has been mentioned that, if we accept the suggestion that we can create a name for an expression by surrounding it with quotation marks, we have to treat the quotation contents as single words. Accordingly, what appears within the quotation marks should be taken as a proper name, as suggested by Tarski, or as an orthographic accident, as suggested by Quine. But now consider:

  (1) Nine is greater than five,
  (2) Canines are larger than felines,
  (3) 'Nine is greater than five' is a truth of Arithmetic.[24]

The appearance of 'nine' in (1) is, according to Quine, "referential." That is: in (1) we can substitute 'the number of planets' for 'nine' without changing its truth value; (1) is also open to existential generalization, i.e., the result of replacing the occurrence of 'nine' by the variable 'x' and prefixing '($\exists$x)' would not lead from truth to falsehood. If 'Nine is greater than five' is true, then it is also true that

  ($\exists$x) (x is greater than five).

The appearance of 'nine' in (1) also contributes to the meaning of the

---

[23] *Ibid.*, 76.

[24] These examples and the points about their contrast are taken from David Kaplan's "Quantifying In," *Synthese,* XIX (1968), 178-214.

sentence which contains it. We cannot replace it by other expressions having different meanings without changing the meaning of the whole sentence.

The appearance of 'nine' in (2), however, is purely accidental. 'Nine' is a part of a longer word 'canines' and so does not refer to anything, and it fails the other criteria mentioned for being counted as a referential occurrence. If we accept the suggestion that quotation marks denote its interior and the interior should be taken as an orthographic accident, we have to treat the occurrence of 'nine' in (3) just like the occurrence of 'nine' in (2). Quine calls the occurrence of an expression 'opaque' if it makes the context in which it appears nonreferential; one mark of a referentially opaque context is "that it cannot properly be *quantified into* (without quantifier outside the context and variable inside)."[25]

It follows that "Quotation, again, is the referential opaque context par excellence." Thus to render (3) into

$(\exists x)$ ('x is greater than five' is a truth of Arithmetic)

is misguided. (Since the 'x' replacing 'nine' in [1] cannot be reached by a quantifier, the quantifier is followed by no germane occurrence of its variable.) Note that (3) also fails the other tests. Substituting 'the number of planets' for 'nine,' we will get nonsense or falsehood:

'The number of planets is greater than five' is a truth of Arithmetic.

The view about referential opacity of quotation marks is at least counterintuitive. Many object that to assimilate the occurrence of 'nine' in 'canine' in (2) to the occurrence of 'nine' in quotation marks in (3) is to overlook certain dissimilarities. We may legislate that 'nine' in (3) has no separate meaning, but we cannot close our eyes to the fact that every word in (3) is translatable (including 'nine') and has meaning, whereas 'nine' in 'canine' is not translatable.

Taking into account Quine's remarks that quotations have a "certain anomalous feature" and Tarski's comments showing that paradoxes result in favorable cases, and that the expression within has no meaning in unfavorable cases, Davidson remarks: "We must therefore give up the idea that quotations are 'syntactically composite expressions, of which both quotation marks and the expressions within them

[25] Quine, *The Ways of Paradox*, 172.

are parts.' "[26] According to Davidson, there is no serious problem either about identifying quotations on the basis of form, or in giving informal rules for producing a wanted quotation ("enclose the expression you want to mention in quotation marks"). However, "the puzzle comes," he says, "when we try to express those rules as a fragment of a theory of meaning." For Davidson, a theory of meaning "must give a constructive account of the meaning of the sentences in the language. . . . We must be able to specify, in a way that depends effectively and solely on formal considerations, what every sentence means."[27] He concludes that informal suggestions about quotations "do not provide even the kernel of a theory in the required sense, as both authors (Tarski and Quine) are at pains to point out."[28]

Students who are interested in formal semantics and problems concerning name-making devices may refer to the following technical essays. In some of them attempts have been made to overcome Quine's puzzle of referential opacity of quotation contexts.

SELECTED READINGS

Bar-Hillel, Y. "Indexical Expressions." *Mind,* LXIII (1954), 359-76.
Carnap, Rudolf. *Logical Syntax of Language.* London: Kegan Paul, 1937.
———. "Foundations of Logic and Mathematics." *International Encylopedia of Unified Science.* Chicago: University of Chicago Press, 1949.
Davidson, Donald. "On Saying That." *Synthese,* XIX (1968).
Kaplan, David. "Quantifying In." *Synthese,* XIX (1968).
Montague, Richard. "Pragmatics and Intensional Logic." *Synthese,* XXII (1970).
Wallace, John. "On the Frame of Reference." *Synthese,* XXII (1970), 117-50.

[26] Donald Davidson, "Theories of Meaning and Learnable Languages," in *Logic, Methodology and Philosophy of Science,* ed. Y. Bar-Hillel (Amsterdam: North Holland, 1965).
[27] *Ibid.,* 383.
[28] *Ibid.,* 388.

1

Some Pragmatic Aspects of Meaning

C. L. STEVENSON

III

Some Pragmatic Aspects of Meaning

1

IF we are to reach a more detailed understanding of ethics, guarding its issues from confusion, and opening them to economical types of inquiry, we must pay constant attention to ethical language, and the logical and psychological factors which permit it to have its characteristic functions. The need of this approach, and the central topics it introduces, will be evident from the preceding chapter.

Certain parts of the study could be developed immediately, with reference to ethical examples alone; but there are other parts of it which require more comprehensive treatment. A background must be sought in a general theory of signs, yielding conclusions that can subsequently be extended to the more specific problems that concern us. This is especially necessary in connection with the emotive uses of language, which in spite of many recent studies are still in need of careful examination. And care is needed, no less urgently, in showing how emotive and descriptive meanings are related, each modifying the other. These topics, lying somewhat beyond the narrower province of ethical analysis, will form the subject matter of the present chapter. There can be no hope or pretense, of course, of exhausting so large a subject, but perhaps enough can be said to serve present purposes.

2

THE emotive meaning of words can best be understood by comparing and contrasting it with the expressiveness of laughs, sighs, groans, and all similar manifestations of the emotions, whether by voice or gesture. It is obvious that these "natural" expressions are direct behavioristic symptoms of the emotions or feelings to which they testify. A laugh gives direct "vent" to the amusement which it accompanies, and does so in such an intimate, inevitable way that if the laugh is checked, some degree of amusement is likely to be checked as well. In much the same way a sigh gives immediate release to sorrow; and a shrug of the shoulders integrally expresses its nonchalant carelessness. One must not, merely on this account, insist that laughs, sighs, and so on, are literally a part of language, or that they have an emotive meaning; but there remains an important point of analogy: Interjections, which *are* a part of language, and which do have an emotive meaning, are *like* sighs, shrieks, groans, and the rest in that they can be used to "give vent" to the emotions or attitudes in much the same way. The word "hurrah," for instance, serves much the same purpose as any simple cry of enthusiasm, and releases the emotions with equal directness.

There is clearly a difference between interjections, which directly vent emotions, and words like "emotion" itself which *denote* them. The exact difference, with all its ramifications, will require patient analysis, but this much is obvious at the outset: words which denote emotions are usually poor vehicles for giving them active expression. One has only to pronounce "enthusiasm" like an interjection, trying to accompany it with the gestures and intonation characteristic of a shriek or of "hurrah," to see what a relatively impotent instrument it is for use in giving the emotions any direct outlet.

Emotive words, then, whatever else must be said of them, are suitable for "venting" the emotions, and to that extent are akin not to words which denote emotions, but rather to the laughs, groans, and sighs that "naturally" manifest them. But here the analogy ends. From the point of view of linguistic theory, interjections and "natural" manifestations of the emotions must be contrasted. The former make up a recognized grammatical part of speech, whereas the latter do not; the former are of interest to the etymologist and phonetician, whereas the latter are of scientific interest only to the psychologist or physiologist. And one speaks of the "meaning" of an interjection in a narrow sense, whereas one would hesitate to speak so narrowly of the "meaning" of a groan or laugh. There is a sense, to be sure, in which a groan "means" something, just as a reduced temperature may at times "mean" convalescence, or a tariff may "mean" restricted trade; but this sense of "meaning" is wider than any that are common in linguistic theory. Why is it that "natural" manifestations of emotions are ascribed meaning only in this broader sense, whereas interjections, so like them in function, may be ascribed meaning in a narrower sense?

An essential part of the answer is simply this: The expressiveness of interjections, unlike that of groans or laughs, depends on conventions that have grown up in the history of their usage. Had interjections been used in different living contexts, they would have been suited to the venting of somewhat different feelings. People groan in all languages, so to speak, but say "ouch" only in English. In learning French, one must learn to substitute "helas" for "alas," but one may sigh just as usual. Linguists are largely concerned with the study of verbal conventions; hence they are more interested in interjections than in expressions which are not conventionalized. And philosophers will do well to share this interest, though for a different reason. Conventionalized emotive meaning, far more than natural expressiveness, is likely to be confused with the descriptive aspects of language, and so fill the world with fictitious philosophical "entities."

In Edgar Rice Burroughs' extravaganzas, it is narrated that the Green Men of Mars always express their amusement (even a relaxed, kindly sort of amusement) by piercing shrieks, and express their anger by hearty laughter. Such practices, it is explained, are all accidental matters of convention, and seem surprising to us earth-dwellers only because we are not habituated to them. If this were so, if we laughed and groaned only because we happened to be trained to do so, rather than because of almost inevitable predispositions, then laughs and groans would be interesting subject matter for linguistic theory. They would, in all essentials, *be* interjections. But until Mr. Burroughs' psychology finds stronger confirmation, such sounds need give earthborn philologists and philosophers no concern.

To a certain extent some interjections retain, in addition to their conventionalized powers, a "phonetic suitability" that parallels the naturalness of laughs or sighs. The pure sound of a word may have a physiological fitness for venting certain emotions, which coöperates with the habits formed by past usage. (This is similar to onomatopoeia, but not wholly so. An onomatopoetic word mimics the sound of what it *designates;* hence its fitness for expressing feelings is secondary to its fitness for naming an object.) But on the whole, phonetic suitability is a minor factor. A man may learn to pronounce a foreign oath before he knows its use, and will not yet feel that it is an easy vehicle for expressing his temper. Even when he learns that it is an oath, he will find it less forceful than some corresponding word in his own language, which has behind it the accumulated energy of his linguistic habits.

Once a word has become ingrained into our habits of emotional expression, it retains its place with no little persistence. This is easily observed in daily life. In fact it is often discovered by children. When boys simulate a sweet, kindly tone of voice, and then proceed to swear at their dog—trying to see if the dog "really understands" their words—they find the experiment difficult. The habits that attend the abusive words are too strong, and stultify the agreeable intonation.

Emotive terms remain fully subject, of course, to the general forces of philological change. Slang words come and go; the profanities of yesterday may become the parlor terms of tomorrow.[1] And yet emotive change has sluggish rules of its own. One cannot easily introduce emotive terms by fiat, as one can introduce technical scientific terms. They must run their course, not easily interrupted, and some have an emotive life that outlasts their descriptive one.

So far we have seen only how emotive terms are dependent on the habits of the *speaker*. There is an equally important aspect of their use which concerns the habits of the *hearer*. This can most readily be seen where one interjection replaces another, all else remaining roughly the same. When an actress properly utters the word "alas" she heightens the sympathies of her audience. In good measure the audience is swayed by her gestures and intonation, and by the general situation presented in the play. But the audience's habitual reaction to "alas" must not be neglected. For suppose that the actress should train herself, with all the care that such a feat would require, to preserve the same tragic gestures and intonation, but to replace the word "alas" by the word "hurrah." The scene would then become crude burlesque, so forcibly and incongruously would the habitual responses to "hurrah" clash with the manner of its utterance. To evoke sympathy the actress must use a word-vehicle whose emotive meaning is appropriately ingrained into the hearers' habits, else her gestures and intonation will be unavailing.

1. See H. L. Mencken *The American Language* (Alfred A. Knopf, New York, 1919). In 4th ed. chap. vi, Secs. 5–8.

It is clear, then, so far as one may generalize from these extremely simple examples, that emotive words are fitted both to express the feelings of the speaker and to evoke the feelings of the hearer, and that they derive this fitness from the habits that have been formed throughout the course of their use in emotional situations.

A very close parallel to emotive meaning, in some ways more instructive than that of laughs and groans, can be found in the customs of etiquette. The parallel is so close that one might almost call etiquette a form of emotive sign language. There are certain aspects of "good manners," of course, which are aesthetic in nature, and others which are practical; but a great many others are conventions as arbitrary as linguistic ones, and as unintelligible to foreign eyes as words are to foreign ears. That a man should tip his hat, or walk on the curb side, that the hostess at dinner should be served first, that the fork should be conducted to the mouth with the right hand, and so on, are conventional "symbols" for expressing social deference, and some are parts of the American "dialect," unfamiliar in England. To trace the origin of these customs is to trace their "etymology," and leads one to similarly heterogeneous sources. Like interjections (and unlike laughs and sighs) good manners owe their expressiveness to force of habit, and with changing habits may become "archaic" or "obsolete." And just as interjections must be attended, to reach their full emotional effect, by a relevant situation and suitable intonation, so the conventional gestures of etiquette must be executed in their appropriate place and with suitable graciousness, if they are actually to manifest the deference which they, much more than less habitual gestures, are particularly suited to express.

3

THE above account has explained how certain emotive terms are put to use, but it has presented no clear *definition* of "emotive meaning." Although no rigorous definition of the term can here be attempted, let us work toward an approximate one, freely digressing to examine any points of interest that arise in the course of doing so.

It will be misleading to use the term at all unless "meaning" can be ascribed some conventional sense that marks off a genus, of which emotive meaning will be a species, and descriptive meaning another. Emotive meaning must be a kind of meaning, or else it had better be rebaptized. So our first task will be to single out the generic sense of "meaning" that is required.

There is one sense (among many others) which, though conventional enough, will be unsuitable for our purpose. In this sense the "meaning" of a sign is that *to which* people *refer* when they use the sign. (E.g.: "The meaning of 'cake' is edible"; "The meaning of 'hardness' is a characteristic of flint.") It will be convenient to replace "meaning," so used, by the term "referent," following Ogden and Richards.[2] The sense cannot be the generic one required, for we shall want to say that some words (such as "alas") have no referent, but do have a kind of meaning—namely, emotive meaning.

Another sense of "meaning" promises to be more serviceable. In this sense, the "meaning" of a sign must be defined in terms of the psychological reactions of those who use the sign. It may be called "meaning in the psychological sense," or in Morris'[3] terminology, "meaning in the pragmatic sense." (E.g.: "The meaning of 'cake' cannot conceivably be eaten, even though cake is edible." "The meaning of 'hardness' is not a characteristic of flint, even though hardness itself is.") If this sense of "meaning" were sufficiently clear, it could readily be taken as designating the required genus, of which emotive and descriptive meanings would be species; for the species could be distinguished by the kind of psychological processes that were involved.

But this generic, psychological sense of "meaning" is unfortunately not clear. Indeed, a proper definition of it has long been one of the most troublesome aspects of linguistic theory. The reason for this can readily be seen:

2. *Meaning of Meaning,* pp. 10 ff. Perhaps Ogden and Richards would prefer to recognize only *objects* as referents, and not *qualities* such as hardness. But note that if "hardness" is replaced in any sentence by "softness," empirical verification will be wholly changed. Hence "hardness" has an analogue of a naming function, and since this cannot be easily absorbed into the pure sign or the refere*nce* (concept), the other corners of the well-known meaning triangle, it is suggested that the term "referent" (or Morris' term, "designatum") be extended to include it. There is unquestionably something perplexing in the language that we use in talking about qualities—as any philosophical discussion of universals will testify—but until someone carefully untangles the perplexity, it will not do to dismiss qualities with a nonchalant nominalism or conceptualism. Such a procedure only goes on with the old controversies, adding nothing, and is equally non-commonsensical.

3. Charles W. Morris, "Foundations of the Theory of Signs," *International Encyclopedia of Unified Science,* Vol. I, No. 2 (University of Chicago Press, 1938).

PRAGMATIC ASPECTS OF MEANING   43

One of the requirements for any definition of "meaning," so long as that term is to remain suitable for talking about language, is that meaning *must not vary* in a bewildering way. Some variation must of course be allowed, else we shall end with a fictitious entity, serene and thoroughly useless amid the complexities of actual practice; but "meaning" is a term wanted for marking off something relatively constant amid these complexities, not merely for paying them deference. A sense is needed where a sign may "mean" less than it "suggests"—a sense in which meanings are helpful to the understanding of *many* contexts, not some vagrant sense in which a word has a wholly different "meaning" every time it is used.

If the meaning of a sign must be relatively constant, how can "meaning" possibly be defined in terms of the psychological reactions that attend the sign? These reactions are by no means constant, but vary markedly from situation to situation. At a football game "hurrah" may express vigorous emotion, but elsewhere it may be attended by only the faintest echo of emotion. For one who assorts mail, "Connecticut" may cause only a toss of the hand, but for an old resident it may bring a train of reminiscences. How can a constant "meaning" be found amid this psychological flux?

As the latter example shows, the problem of defining a psychological sense of "meaning" is by no means confined to emotive situations; it is equally perplexing for situations which involve a referent. Between sign and referent (e.g., between the word "Connecticut" and the state of Connecticut) a rather constant relation must hold. This relation is preserved by *meaning* in the psychological sense in question; for if "Connecticut" is divorced from the psychological habits of those who use the word, it becomes devoid of any referent, no more interesting than any other complex noise. And yet the psychological responses that attend the word are observed to vary. How can a constant relation be maintained by such inconstant means? How is it possible (so one may confusedly picture the situation) to suspend a weight at a fixed distance from a frame, when the only string that can suspend it is continually varying in length?

Let us illustrate the perplexity a little further, still emphasizing the generic sense of "meaning," but taking examples from situations that we shall later want to designate more specifically as "emotive."

Just as one may not identify the meaning of "Connecticut"

with its immediate psychological repercussions, even for the psychological sense in question, so one may not identify the meaning of an interjection with the full-bodied emotion that at any time accompanies its use in a living context. The accompanying emotions vary with so many inconstant factors (such as voice, gesture, situation, mood, etc.) that the actual degree and kind of emotion which attend a word at one time are rarely the same as those which attend it at another. If we called each of these emotions a different "meaning," we should divert "meaning" to the vagrant sense that we have decided to avoid.

For the same reason we may not define the "meaning" of an interjection as the "emotional association" of a word, or as "the aura of feeling that hovers about a word." *Which* associations? *Which* aura? Do not these shadowy associations vary, just as the full-bodied emotions do? And if it is suggested that the associations must be those which accompany the word out of any living context (as when "alas" is pronounced experimentally in the comfort of one's study) then the way is opened to serious confusions: In the first place, since the immediate associations of a word out of its living context are very slight, one would naturally conclude that "emotive meaning," defined in terms of them, is very slight, and so think of it as having little importance. This would be unfortunate, for "emotive meaning" is often used, however vaguely and confusedly, in a sense that merits the attention it is beginning to receive. In the second place, the identification of emotive meaning with associations may foster a crude distortion of introspection. It may suggest that the associations continue to accompany the word in concrete, living situations, contributing to the general emotional tone of the situations in a purely additive way. As if the word "alas," in the above example of the actress, were suitable because it introduces its "associations" as "extra units" of emotion—units that are introspectively distinguishable, all at one glance, from those due to the general situation presented in the play. No one would believe this if he stopped to think about it; but misleading terminology has perpetuated fictions that are still more absurd, and it must not be allowed to confuse the present issue.

Emotive meaning, then, is not a full-bodied emotion, and not a shadowy association; nor is descriptive meaning an image or a toss of the hand. To say this is to rule out an inconvenient way of speaking, not to state a fact. We must, to reiterate, retain for the term "meaning" a sense which, although psychological, permits us to say that meaning is relatively unchanging. How shall such a sense be found?

The question is perplexing only when we look for the answer in a naïve way. It is as if we were trying to define the "purchasing power" of a dollar,[4] and, properly requiring that this be something relatively constant, were puzzled to find that dollars were always being used to buy different things. "Is the purchasing power the book I bought yesterday, or is it really the dinner I bought last night?" Or let us take a further example. Let us compare the meaning of a word with the stimulating power of coffee, and consider how we might proceed to define "stimulating power."

Is this power of the coffee simply the stimulated feeling that attends drinking it? This will clearly not do. The stimulating power must be relatively constant, varying only with different brands used, or with different ways of preparing it, and so on; but the feelings that attend drinking it are subject to a much greater variation. When a man is thoroughly exhausted, coffee may be insufficient to stimulate him at all; but when he is nervously wrought up, the same amount of coffee may stimulate him to the highest degree. How can the constant power to stimulate be identified with these inconstant states of mind?

Perhaps the stimulating power may be identified with the stimulation that coffee produces under some specified, artificially simple set of circumstances. But this too is inadvisable. It is not easy to specify simple circumstances under which the stimulation will be sufficiently constant. Even if this could be done, misconceptions might arise. In the first place, if the stimulation produced under these circumstances were unusually slight, one might think that the stimulating power of coffee was slight, and so negligible. In the second place, one might think that this same degree of stimulation attends coffee under all other circumstances, augmenting one's energy in a purely additive way . . .

And so on. It will now be clear how closely these suggestions parallel our repudiated definitions of "meaning," particularly in connection with the emotive situations. The attendant problem is precisely the same. We have a term—whether "meaning" or "stimulating power"—that must be defined with reference to

4. The example is borrowed from Max Black, who may, however, wish to reject much of the analysis of meaning that is to follow.

psychological reactions. These reactions fluctuate; but the term must designate something relatively stable. So an analysis of the one term is likely to throw light on the other.

A clue is readily given by the word "power." This term, so familiar in Locke, and a descendant of Aristotle's "potentiality," is in many cases very misleading, since it tempts one to hypostatization and anthropomorphism; but in several modern studies[5] the important aspects of its use have been subject to a very promising analysis. In these studies the term "power" usually gives place to the term "dispositional property," and from now on the latter term will be used here. Before employing the term for present purposes, however, let us become clearer about its usage. Space will permit only a cursory study, in which accuracy will often have to be sacrificed to simplicity; but such a treatment will even so be helpful. It will lead us to a better understanding of "meaning," and so in the direction of a definition of "emotive meaning."

4

THE word "disposition" (or "power," or "potentiality," or latent ability," or "causal characteristic," or "tendency," etc.) is useful in dealing with complicated *causal* situations, where some specified sort of event is a function of many variables. To illustrate, let us continue the above example. Although coffee often "causes" stimulation, it is never the *only* cause. The degree of stimulation will depend as well on many other factors—the initial state of a man's fatigue, the absorptive state of his stomach, the constitution of his nervous system, and so on. The situation may accordingly be schematized in this way:

Variations in $\left\{\begin{array}{l} \text{C (amount of} \\ \quad\text{coffee drunk)} \\ \text{A} \\ \text{B} \end{array}\right\}$ $\left\{\begin{array}{l}\text{determine} \\ \text{variations} \\ \text{in}\end{array}\right\}$ $\left\{\begin{array}{l}\text{(actual} \\ \text{stimulation).}\end{array}\right\}$

Here A stands for a *set* of conditions which are subject to change

5. C. D. Broad, *Mind and Its Place in Nature* (Harcourt, Brace, 1925), pp. 430–436; *Examination of McTaggart's Philosophy* (Cambridge, 1933), I, 266–272; *The Philosophy of Francis Bacon* (Cambridge, 1926), pp. 30–39. And Rudolph Carnap, "Testability and Meaning," *Philosophy of Science*, Vol. III, No. 4, and Vol. IV, No. 1.

The present account will be closer to Broad than to Carnap, since Broad's analysis lends itself more readily to a simplified presentation.

from time to time—the "attendant circumstances" under which the coffee is drunk. B stands for other conditions, less markedly subject to change, such as the chemical components of the coffee. The B factors have an important place in any discussion of dispositional properties; but for the next few pages let us be content to ignore them, to simplify exposition.

There will, of course, be no constant correlation between C and S taken alone; for the correlation will vary with variations in A. And yet the relation of C to S may be very important. With *each* constant condition of A, S may vary with C in *some* way; and with certain conditions of A, variations in C may cause S to vary greatly. To designate this relation, it is convenient to say that coffee (to which C makes conspicuous reference) has a "disposition" to produce S—which is of course only another way of saying that coffee "is a stimulant."

Let us take a further example. The "solubility" of sugar is its disposition to dissolve. And for this disposition, as for all others, we may distinguish factors corresponding to those above. Putting the sugar into water is a factor comparable to C; the temperature of the water and the degree to which it is stirred are factors comparable to A; the chemical composition of the sugar is comparable to B; and the actual dissolving of the sugar is comparable to S. The statement, "Sugar is soluble," refers to such a causal milieu, though it does not stipulate precisely what the A and B factors are.

These examples are by no means equivalent to a formal definition of "disposition," but they will permit us to proceed with freedom from the more serious confusions.

We must now consider in what sense an object may have an "unchanging" disposition to produce some effect, even though no fixed degree of that effect constantly attends it. This, of course, is simply our problem of explaining how the stimulating power of coffee may remain unchanged, even though the degree of stimulation that attends drinking it does not; and we shall soon see that much the same explanation must be given for *meaning*. With reference to the symbols previously used, the explanation is briefly this:

If for each constant state of A, there is some or another *fixed* way in which C is correlated with S, then the disposition of coffee to stimulate (and so, *mutatis mutandis,* for parallel examples) is said to remain unchanged.

48   *ETHICS AND LANGUAGE*

More specifically: Let A retain some constant state, say A_1, and suppose that on each day of a given week it is found that the number of units of C is always double the number of units of S. Again, let A retain some other constant state, say A_2, and suppose that on each day of the same week it is found that the number of units of C is always triple the number of units of S. By a continuation of such experiments it would be possible to conclude, inductively, that for *each* constant condition of A, there is *some* correlation between C and S that remains fixed over the week; or in other words, that the disposition of coffee to stimulate has remained unchanged during that interval. (Note that this correlation need not be the same for all states of A; all that is required is that for each state of A there should be one or another fixed correlation.)

On the other hand, let A retain some constant state, say A_1; and suppose that on *one day* the number of units of C is double the number of units of S, but that on a *later day* it is triple. Here the correlation between C and S has not remained fixed, *even though A has*. The disposition of coffee to stimulate has *changed* during the interval.

Thus the disposition *need* not be said to change just because the effects do; though a change in the effects may *sometimes* indicate a change in the disposition. The unchanging disposition does not require an unchanging S, but rather a correlation between C and S that changes *only* if A changes.

It will be obvious that our imagined experimental tests have been artificially simple. The references to the "number of units" of stimulation, for instance, are more definite than practice may permit, and "more-or-less" comparisons must often take the place of numerical ones. Again, it may be practically impossible to hold the A factors constant; hence their variation must be "allowed for," or be made to cancel out, roughly, by statistical methods. But these and other points, however important they would be to a full study, are more detailed than our simplified treatment can include, and will be granted no further attention.

Let us now give somewhat closer attention to the several factors that any dispositional property involves, and provide a terminology for discussing them:

(a) There will be some relatively simple factor, like C above, which conspicuously affects the object that *has* the disposition. Let us call this a "stimulus." For dispositions assigned to living

PRAGMATIC ASPECTS OF MEANING   49

organisms, this term will have the sense that is current in psychology. For other dispositions it must be taken in an extended sense. Thus the stimulus for the disposition of water to freeze is a temperature of 32° F. or less.

In a similarly extended sense we may use "response" to designate whatever it is that an object has a disposition to·do.

A disposition is said to exist at a given time even though the stimulus and response are not occurring at that time. And we may conveniently say, introducing an ambiguity that is too obvious to be misleading, that a disposition *has* a stimulus even when no concrete stimulus is occurring, and that it *has* a response even when no concrete response is occurring—meaning thereby that there is a *kind* of factor lawfully correlated with another, given the general situation, in stimulus-response fashion. A disposition will be "realized" whenever its response concretely occurs, along with a concrete stimulus, and "unrealized" when the response does not occur.

(b) There will be a more complicated set of factors, like A above, which are the "attendant circumstances" under which the disposition may be realized. A variation in these factors may alter the precise form that the response assumes, but as we have seen the disposition is not said to alter *merely* because these factors do. It is sometimes convenient to say that the disposition continues to exist when certain of these factors are totally absent, even though the response may then fail to occur with the stimulus; but unless they are usually present in some form, the disposition will be realized so infrequently that it probably will not be worth mentioning.

(c) There will be other factors, like B of page 47, that have hitherto been relatively neglected, and must now receive more attention. They are likely to be more permanent than the attendant circumstances, and differ conspicuously in that a variation in them *does* lead us to say that the disposition has varied. Whether or not a given factor is to be classified as belonging to this group, rather than to the attendant circumstances, will largely be determined by the usage of the specific names for dispositions, such as "solubility," "resiliency," "stimulating power," and so on. When a person decides that a variation in a certain factor is to be a criterion for saying that a dispositional property, so named, has itself varied (as distinct from saying that the manner of its realization has varied), he thereby decides that this factor is a B factor, relative to the specific name in question. (Many of the specific names for dispositions are vague, of course, permitting certain factors to be classified either as attendant circumstances or as B factors, at will; hence the criterion for change in a disposition is often rough.) Some of the B factors will be remote and others immediate. Thus in the example of the "stimulating powers" of coffee, a remote factor would be the way the coffee was grown, and an immediate one would be the amount of caffeine present. The most immediate set of factors, varying when and only when the disposition is said to vary, will be called the "basis" of the disposition.

The bases of a great many dispositions are unknown; and indeed, much of the usefulness of the term "disposition," and of the many common terms that designate specific dispositional properties, lies in permitting one to talk about correlations between stimulus and response, under attendant circumstances, before knowing what the basis of a disposition is. As Broad has remarked,[6] not a little was known about heat, taken as a disposition of certain objects to affect the human organism, long before the basis of the disposition was explained by the atomic theory. And there are many other dispositional properties—almost all of those mentioned in psychology, and a great many even in physics and chemistry—where the nature of the basis is still highly problematical. This is by no means a fatal difficulty; for some or another basis can often be inferred to be present, and can be presumed, even though little else is known about it, to retain rather permanently such qualities as it has. That is to say, realizing that the stimulus and attendant circumstances are not sufficient to produce the response, and finding that they in fact produce it, an experimenter can infer that some basis is present as an additional factor. And finding that the correlation between stimulus and response varies in a predictable manner with variations in the attendant circumstances, he can infer that the basis is not changing. To be sure, if he knows the precise basis, he will be in a more secure position, having richer inductive evidence from which to judge whether the correlations between stimulus and response will continue in the future; but his ignorance of the basis is simply a difficulty, not a fatal one. Nor is "basis" a name that *disguises* his ignorance; for the term marks off causal factors which he knows about indirectly, through their effect, and

6. *The Philosophy of Francis Bacon*, p. 32.

it may guide him progressively to a more adequate knowledge of them.

If the basis were always known, changes in it could be taken as definitive tests for changes in the disposition. But since it is usually unknown, there is a practical advantage in explaining changes in the disposition with reference to correlations between stimulus, response, and attendant circumstances, as was done in the preceding pages.[7]

It will be observed that neither the term "disposition" nor the terms designating the several factors in a dispositional property have been formally defined. For the most part they have been clarified by examples. Since the issue is highly controversial on points of detail, the writer will not presume to attempt any more rigorous analysis, hoping that a simplified approximation will not be without practical use.[8] There are, however, two sources of confusion that must receive passing attention:

It is tempting to hypostatize a disposition, taking it as a special "object" that exists over and above its more "tangible" components. In point of fact, one who gives the stimulus, response, attendant circumstances, and basis of a disposition, and who states in detail their correlation, has said all about the disposition that there is to say. The correlation between the several factors is of primary importance, but a correlation is not, to be sure, an extra object. In the same quest for "tangibility," it is tempting to identify a disposition with its basis; but this again will not do. One may know a great deal about certain factors that

---

7. There is a further reason for this procedure. It may be that certain fundamental dispositions have no basis, as Broad has in effect maintained in *Mind and Its Place in Nature*, pp. 435 f. This is a matter which the present account cannot take time to discuss, but it is well not to explain "change" in a disposition in a way that presupposes a contrary view.

8. A full analysis would introduce certain broader topics, such as (a) the meaning of "cause" and "law," and (b) the meaning of "perception" and "matter." As to (b), it will be noted that by Locke's views, the secondary qualities of an object, as predicates of that object, would be dispositional, whereas the primary ones would not. But by subsequent and more plausible theories, the primaries and secondaries are given much the same status. Are there *any* qualities of an object, then, which are *not* dispositional? If so, are they wholly unknowable qualities of a Kantian thing-in-itself? It is the writer's assumption that an adequate development of the problem would serve both to preserve certain properties of objects as nondispositional and also to avoid any wholly unknowable "substances"; but this cannot be developed here, and is mentioned only as an indication of the elementary level on which the present account is regrettably but inevitably compelled to proceed.

in fact constitute the basis of a disposition, but unless he knows how these factors are correlated with the stimulus, response, and attendant circumstances, he cannot be said to know a great deal about the disposition.[9]

A further source of confusion lies in a vacuous way of taking a disposition as the cause of its own response. Consider, for instance, the statement, "This ball bounces because it has a disposition to do so." This does not explain why the ball bounces; for although the term "disposition" implies that the response of bouncing comes with *some* stimulus, under *some* attendant circumstances, coöperating with *some* basis, its complete indeterminateness about what these factors are renders it trivial. The statement, "Man's rational faculty causes him to reason" is trivial in the same way.

It must not be thought, however, that all such idioms are equally open to criticism. The statement, "This ball bounced higher than that because of its greater resiliency" is by no means trivial, even though "resiliency" may partially be defined as a disposition to bounce. Here an empirical advance is indicated by the fact that certain other possible explanations are excluded: the ball might have bounced higher because it was dropped farther, or because it was dropped on a more resilient surface. Again, "Bees build hives because they have an instinct to do so" need not be trivial. An instinct, though a complicated disposition, is not *any* disposition, but one which, unlike a habit, is relatively free from changes with changing environments; and to know this about hive-building is not unimportant. (The "faculty psychology" was vacuous not because it used the dispositional terms, but because it misused them.) In general, any statement of the form "D caused R," where D is a disposition and R its response, will be of empirical interest to whatever extent it specifies definite tests for D that extend beyond the tests for R, and so relates R to a larger inductive setting. Our last cases, unlike the first ones, succeeded in meeting this requirement. The word "cause" may seem objectionable in such contexts, but common usage

9. If "disposition" were adequately defined, the definition would presumably have to be given "in use." Any terms so defined tempts one to hypostatize. For an account of "definitions in use" see A. N. Whitehead and Bertrand Russell, *Principia Mathematica*, Introduction to the 1st ed., chap. iii. A very lucid account is given by A. J. Ayer, in *Language, Truth and Logic* (Gollancz, 1936), chap. iii.

sanctions the idiom, and for many purposes it is quite useful, so long as the underlying considerations are understood.

When a disposition, D, is said to be the cause of E, and when E is *not* any part of the response of D, there is no special difficulty. If there is a lawful connection between the appearance of D and that of E, the connection may be called "causal" in a rough but familiar sense. Thus the *poisonous* nature of certain drugs may cause the government to restrict their sale. The causes *of* a disposition are usually the same as the *remote* B factors; and these too bring no difficulty so long as the disposition itself is not defined in terms of them. Thus the process of heating, hammering, and cooling steel in a certain way causes it to become more *elastic*. There is no objection, of course, to defining a specific name for a dispositional property with reference to some of its causes; but it must then be realized that any assertion which ascribes these causes to the disposition, so named, will not give additional information about it.

Broad has called attention to "orders" of dispositions,[10] in a way that is best clarified by example. If magnetism is taken as a disposition of the first order, then the disposition of a metal to *acquire* magnetism (which iron has, but copper has not) will be a disposition of the second order. In general, a first-order disposition may be the response of a second-order disposition, which may conceivably be the response, in turn, of a third-order one, and so on. Once we have seen, as above, that a *disposition* may be the *effect*, in an intelligible sense, of something else, we can readily see that it may itself be a response—i.e., that kind of effect whose causes are constituted by some stimulus, basis, and attendant circumstances. The possibility of orders of dispositions is thus manifest.

5

HAVING now explained (very roughly, but perhaps serviceably) the nature of dispositional properties, and the sense in which a disposition may be "unchanging," we may return to our problem about meaning. Let us at first consider meaning-situations entirely from the point of view of a hearer, neglecting any reader,

10. See his *Examination of McTaggart's Philosophy*, I, 48, where the distinction has an interesting application to the old controversies about "Innate Ideas."

speaker, or writer. So simplified, the view to be defended is essentially this:

The meaning of a sign, in the psychological sense required, is not some specific psychological process that attends the sign at any one time. It is rather a dispositional property of the sign, where the response, varying with varying attendant circumstances, consists of psychological processes in a hearer, and where the stimulus is his hearing the sign.

This implies that the relation between the hearing of a sign and the reaction to the sign is an elaborate causal one; for dispositional properties always involve a causal milieu. Although causal theories of meaning are often criticized, it is difficult to see how, for the sense of "meaning" in question, any other view can be plausible. The sign produces certain effects in the ear or eye, and in the nerves; and any further processes must be effects of a more remote sort.[11] Moreover, the hearing of the sign (stimulus) is not the only cause of the psychological processes that ensue (response); and for the remaining causal factors, it is possible to indicate attendant circumstances, and infer to the presence of a basis, in the way that any dispositional property requires.

Such a view all but eliminates the difficulty that was mentioned in Section 3—the need, and seeming impossibility of obtaining, a sense in which the "meaning" of a sign can remain constant even though its psychological effects vary. We shall find that the difficulty reappears for certain of the more controversial aspects of the analysis; but on the whole it vanishes when the problem is freed from artificial simplification and hypostatization. Variations in the response do not imply, necessarily, variations in the disposition. We have seen, for the analogous case of coffee, that whenever a variation in the response can be accounted for by a variation in the attendant circumstances, the disposition can be said to remain unchanged.[12] This holds no less obviously for the particular sort of disposition which is called the meaning of a sign. The psychological processes that attend the sign may vary, but the meaning of the sign need not be said to vary to the same extent; for the meaning is a disposition, whereas the psychological processes are simply the response. Thus a sign's meaning, for the dispositional sense of "meaning" in question, will be

11. Or "epiphenomena"; but see Chap. XIV, p. 301, n. 7.
12. Cf. pp. 48 ff.

more constant than the sign's psychological effects—and that is precisely what the considerations of Section 3 demanded.

It cannot be pretended, of course, that these remarks stipulate any precise test for determining when the meaning of a given sign has changed. Any such precision would require a sharp demarcation between the factors that are to be considered among the attendant circumstances of a meaning and those that are not, whereas the present account will provide the demarcation only by means of occasional examples. Hence the phrase "change in meaning" will itself be vague; there will be border-line cases in which it becomes arbitrary whether one says, "The meaning of this sign has changed," or, "Although the meaning of this sign has not changed, the attendant circumstances have come to be such that people's usual reaction to it has changed." The vagueness can *partially* be eliminated for the phrase "change in descriptive meaning," as we shall later see; but it cannot, within the compass of the present work, be eliminated for the phrase "change in emotive meaning"—nor is it likely that any more exhaustive account would be able, in practice, to attain full precision. It can reasonably be hoped, however, that the vagueness will not be fatal to our present purposes.[13] The phrase "change in meaning" is roughly serviceable in common usage, and becomes confusing only when, amid the artificialities of insensitive theory, it is pressed into some hypostatic sense, where unique "entities" take the place of analysis. For our subsequent problems in ethics, little more will be needed than to dispel these artificialities. Though a great deal will remain for an adequate linguistic theory, we must here be content with the initial, modest steps of pointing to its complexities, as yet little explored.

Passing attention must now be given to a point that might otherwise be misunderstood. Meaning has been taken as a dispositional property of a *sign*, not of the *persons* who *use* the sign. The latter alternative, however, would not have been impossible. In general, whenever a dispositional property has factors that involve several objects (as distinct from events) it makes little difference which object is said to *have* the disposition. Thus one may say either that sugar has a disposition to dissolve in water

13. In dealing with the ethical terms the present work does not seek permanently to remove vagueness, for its object there is to call attention to the flexibilities of ordinary language. In dealing with "change in meaning," however, where it would be convenient to have a term for technical use, vagueness would be removed if that were possible.

or that water has a disposition to dissolve sugar, and one may say either that coffee has a disposition to stimulate people or that people have a disposition to be stimulated by coffee. In the same way, one may say either that a sign has a disposition to produce responses in people or that people have a disposition to respond to the sign. The former way of speaking, though not mandatory, will here be adopted. We usually ascribe meaning to a sign, not a person; so if "meaning" is to designate a disposition, the disposition too had better be ascribed to the sign.

This way of speaking may at first seem odd, simply because we usually expect the basis of a disposition to be *in* the object said to have the disposition. In the case of meaning this will obviously not be so. The basis, whatever its ultimate psychological nature may be, will be in the people who use the sign, not in the sign itself. But this seems only of idiomatic interest; it can make no great difference where the basis is located, so long as its presence can be inferred. In fact we implicitly recognize this in parallel cases. If people permanently ceased to be stimulated by coffee under all the usual circumstances, we should doubtless say that coffee had *ceased* to be "a stimulant," and we should say this even if we knew that the change was not in the coffee but in the permanent constitution of human beings. In effect, we recognize aspects of human nature as parts of the basis of the "stimulant," rather than as attendant circumstances; for a change in attendant circumstances *without* a change in the basis would not bring a change in the disposition.[14] The basis, even in this example, need not be confined to the object that has the disposition; and the same holds for the basis of a sign's meaning.

In adopting the idiom, "This sign has a meaning," we must remember that the phrase is elliptical, and must often be expanded to the form "This sign has a meaning for people of sort K." This is parallel to saying that "X is a stimulant" is elliptical, and must often be expanded to the form "X is a stimulant for people of sort K." Just as an X may be a stimulant for certain people and not for others, so a sign may have a meaning for certain people and not for others.

Let us now proceed, still seeking no more than a rough analysis, to limit the *kind* of disposition that is to be called a "meaning." To all words, even nonsense syllables, may be ascribed

14. Cf. p. 49 (b) and (c).

some disposition to affect a hearer; and we shall not want to say that all of them are meaningful. The restriction can partially be obtained by specifying the causes of the disposition, as follows:

A sign's disposition to affect a hearer is to be called a "meaning" (for the not unconventional sense in question) only if it has been caused by, and would not have developed without, an elaborate process of conditioning which has attended the sign's use in communication.[15]

This proviso, though it will be subject to implicit qualification as we proceed, does much to limit "meaning" to a sense that is suitable for linguistic theory. It excludes nonsense syllables, and the ordinary "nonlinguistic" signs. A cough may, in a sense, "mean" that a person has a cold, but will not have a meaning in the present sense; for the elaborate conditioning, developed for purposes of communication, will be lacking.

Let us next drop the artificial restriction of considering only the hearer, and include the reader, speaker, and writer as well. The reader is easily included. We need only recognize that meaning is a disposition whose stimulus must be specified disjunctively, as *either* reading *or* hearing the sign. This is often done in the case of other dispositional properties. E.g., the stimulus for the disposition of powder to explode may be *either* a shock *or* a spark.

The speaker and writer introduce greater complexity into the analysis. They call attention to the need of recognizing a "passive" disposition of a sign—that is to say, a disposition *to be* used. If there is a correlation between some range of a person's psychological processes and his use of a sign, we may say, granted that the other factors can be classified as attendant circumstances and basis, that the sign has a disposition *to be* used. This disposition will be a part of the "meaning" of the sign, granted the proviso introduced just above. The psychological processes, which from the hearer's point of view were the response, become from the speaker's point of view the stimulus.

Meaning thereby becomes a conjunction of dispositions, one passive and one not. But it will be convenient to speak of it as "one" disposition, in spite of this. The criterion of unity for a disposition is rarely precise in ordinary parlance, and often need not be. Thus we may say that magnetism is "one" disposition; or we may say that it is "two," namely, a disposition of an ob-

15. Cf. pp. 39, 52 f.

ject to draw certain others to it *and* a disposition to induce electric currents in a coil of wire. The criterion of unity is often conveniently allowed to vary with one's purposes.

Having seen that the psychological correlates of a sign may be both a stimulus and a response, we must note that their relationship with signs is often reciprocal. When a man is trying to "clear up his ideas," for instance, he may "talk things over with himself," or "write them down" with many revisions. Certain crude psychological processes lead to certain words, which in turn lead to less crude processes, which in turn lead to other words, which in turn lead to still less crude processes, and so on. As Sapir has remarked, "The product grows with the instrument, and thought may be no more conceivable, in its genesis and daily practice, without speech than is mathematical reasoning practicable without the lever of an appropriate symbolism." [16] In addition to clarifying one's ideas in this way, one may give form to one's moods by use of poetic language. The causal relation between the physical and psychological aspects of language is thus not confined to one simple interplay. It is as if, to press an analogy now grown painfully forced, a man who was stimulated by coffee used his increased energy to make and drink more coffee.

It is this complicated interplay between signs and their psychological correlates which may have led certain theorists to view causal theories of meaning with suspicion. Language has so elaborate a function that any causal explanation seems too clumsy. But one need only imagine the causal situation more sensitively, with a full appreciation of its complexities. The present emphasis on dispositions, with parallels to nonpsychological examples, only hints at the complexity; it is half analysis, half analogy. But so far as it is analogy, it must be taken not as a permanent substitute for a more involved scheme, but only as a device for pointing to it, and for suggesting the further work that must be done. Advances in biology have come not from postulating vital forces, but from a sensitivity to multiple causes; and those who have come to realize, with Wittgenstein, that "colloquial language is a part of the human organism and is not less complicated than it," [17] will expect linguistic theory to take the same course.

A practical mastery of a language like our own, though it makes

16. Edward Sapir, *Language* (Harcourt, Brace, 1921), pp. 14 f.
17. *Tractatus Logico-Philosophicus* (Harcourt, Brace, 1922), 4.002.

great strides in early childhood, reaches its maturity only with the full maturity of an individual's intellect; and this development is itself possible only in a linguistic environment that has been developing over a vast period of history. It is scarcely to be expected that meaning, with so complicated a growth, should prove simple in its nature. We become insensitive to this complexity, among other reasons, because we consciously deal with only a part of it. We feel that the meaning of a term is as simple as the process of explaining its use to one who understands many other terms. But in such a process the meaning is by no means built up from the beginning. The old machinery, so to speak, need only be connected up to a new switch. The definition of a term makes use of the complicated dispositions that have already been developed for the definiens; nor would the definition be recognized for what it is, had we not some such word as "definition" with which to christen it.

6

WE must now leave meaning in the generic sense and return to emotive meaning. The latter may be taken as a more specific disposition, in the following way:

Emotive meaning is a meaning in which the response (from the hearer's point of view) or the stimulus (from the speaker's point of view) is a range of emotions.

Thus emotive meaning will be a kind of meaning, as the considerations of Section 3 demanded. And it will be so in the way that any disposition may be a kind of another. In general, when the stimulus, or response, or both, of one disposition have ranges that fall within those of another disposition, the first is commonly called a specific kind of the second. Thus a medicine's disposition to cure some limited class of illnesses is more specific than its disposition to cure a broader class of them. The dispositions may be realizable under different attendant circumstances, and a part, only, of the basis for the general one may be relevant to the more specific one; but for many purposes it is sufficient to mention only the stimulus and response. Emotive meaning can be considered a "kind" of meaning in this familiar way; for emotions fall within the broader range of psychological responses that were specified for meaning in general. In a similar way, we may classify kinds of emotive meaning with reference to kinds of emotion.

The term "emotion" is introduced temporarily, since the term "emotive" suggests it; but hereafter it will be convenient to replace "emotion" by "feeling or attitude"—both to preserve terminological uniformity throughout the book and to emphasize an important distinction. The term "feeling" is to be taken as designating an affective state that reveals its full nature to immediate introspection, without use of induction. An attitude, however, is much more complicated than that, as our previous examples will have suggested. It is, in fact, itself a complicated conjunction of dispositional properties (for dispositions are ubiquitous throughout all psychology), marked by stimuli and responses which relate to hindering or assisting whatever it is that is called the "object" of the attitude. A precise definition of "attitude" is too difficult a matter to be attempted here; hence the term, central though it is to the present work, must for the most part be understood from its current usage, and from the usage of the many terms ("desire," "wish," "disapproval," etc.) which name specific attitudes. Meanwhile it is important to see that immediate feelings are far more simple than attitudes, and that attitudes must not, amid temptations to hypostatize, be confused with them.

To whatever extent the emotive meaning of a sign is a disposition to evoke attitudes, it will be a disposition of the second order.[18] But it remains possible to include dispositions to produce feelings as well; and to that extent emotive meaning will be a first-order disposition.

We may now see, more clearly than before, that emotive meaning may remain roughly constant even though the immediately introspectable states of mind that attend it may vary. In the first place, the meaning will be less subject to variation than its responses (or stimuli); for different concrete responses, given a constant disposition, are only to be expected with different attendant circumstances. In the second place, if the responses are themselves dispositions (i.e., if the meaning is in part a second-order disposition to evoke attitudes) there will be still greater latitude for change in the immediately introspectable states of mind; for the same attitude may have a variety of introspective manifestations.

It may be presumed, in spite of this, that a meaning will remain only *roughly* constant. The continual variation of our psychological make-up leaves nothing unaltered, including the basis

18. Cf. p. 53.

of meaning. But only marked changes are of practical importance. With slight changes people say "there is no change"; and
for most purposes this way of speaking is not only permissible
but of great convenience.

These remarks help us to see that an attention to emotive
meanings, and a careful selection of certain emotive terms rather
than others, may enable a speaker to evoke attitudes that are of
great strength. For example:

> A (in debate) : I favor this bill because it restricts the degree
> of *license* allowed to business.
> B: License? It is really a way of suppressing *liberty*—that
> freedom of enterprise which is the cornerstone of our de-
> mocracy.

Although B's rejection of "license" in favor of "liberty" need
not, of course, be a purely emotive change—for the terms lend
themselves to definitions that sharply differentiate their descriptive meaning—it will be obvious that if B does not trouble to
define either of them, or to clarify their usage by his subsequent
examples, the change will be primarily emotive. And the effect
on the audience may be no less strong on that account. Now if we
thought of emotive meaning as the pale associations of a word
out of context, and confusedly assumed that these associations
must augment attitudes in a purely additive way, we might ask
how the "mere" emotive meaning of the words could make so
much difference. But the perplexity vanishes when we envisage
the manifold conditions under which language operates. An emotive word makes use of an elaborate process of conditioning, of
long duration, which has given it its emotive disposition. This
disposition, granted suitable attendant circumstances, enables
the word to act not additively but much more strongly, like a
spark that ignites prepared tinder. To be sure, the suitable attendant circumstances cannot be taken for granted, but an effective orator will be careful to control them. He will first try to
hold his audience's attention, win their respect, enliven them by
his gestures, and so on. But when the attendant circumstances
are thus prepared, he must take care to select, at strategic moments, a word which has a strong and fixed emotive disposition.
Without the appropriate circumstances, the word will be unavailing; but without the appropriate word, the circumstances may
amount to nothing. It is upon this latter fact that the importance

62   *ETHICS AND LANGUAGE*

of a study of emotive meaning depends. Whether we wish to employ emotive terms or to avoid them, it is imperative to understand the strong effect that they can often produce.

7

OUR study of emotive meaning must now be interrupted by a discussion of descriptive meaning. This will be of interest on its own account, and doubly so in permitting emotive and descriptive meaning to be compared and related, as will be undertaken in the next section. Two questions about descriptive meaning will require particular attention:

(a) What *kind* of psychological processes is a sign, in virtue of its descriptive meaning, disposed to produce?

(b) How do descriptive meanings attain the precision that is needed for practicable communication?

To the first of these questions it is natural enough to answer that a sign's descriptive meaning is its disposition to produce *cognitive* mental processes, where "cognitive" is to be taken as a general term designating such specific kinds of mental activity as believing, thinking, supposing, presuming, and so on. But this answer is far from a full solution; it is merely a step toward envisaging the broader problem with which meaning-theory must inevitably deal—the nature of cognition. This is an involved matter that has long been a stumbling block in psychology and epistemology, nor can the present work pretend to throw fresh light upon it. Some passing remarks, however, may not be amiss.

A "cognitive" reaction cannot plausibly be identified, if we are to preserve the intended sense of the term, with a "flat piece of experience" that reveals its full nature to introspection at the time that the reaction occurs. Those who have sought to identify it with imagery, as Hume did, have been criticized too often to require further attention here. And those who take it as a unique experience, with an indefinable "self-transcendence," are working on a hypothesis which, since indefinables put an end to further analysis, should be accepted only as a last resort. There are, perhaps, certain feelings that are peculiar to cognition, like the feeling of tension that comes from "expecting something to happen"; but these do not readily allow one to understand what "self-transcendence" could be.[19] There remains, then, the alternative

19. For a discussion of such views, see E. B. Titchener, *Lectures on the Experimental Psychology of the Thought Processes* (Macmillan, 1909),

of supplementing a purely introspective definition—though there is no occasion for abandoning introspection altogether—by making reference to dispositions to action. (Note that the term "disposition" is again making its appearance.) That there is *some* connection between cognition and action will not be denied; and perhaps it is impossible even to give an adequate definition of "cognition" when actions are left out of account.[20]

Analyses which take cognition as (in part) a disposition to actions have several points in their favor. They are much better than others in providing for the variety of introspective manifestations that attend "the same thought" or "the same belief." Thus when a man believes something for several days, we commonly take this as exemplifying cognition. But clearly, during the several days there will be no constant introspective manifestation of his belief. At most times it will be totally outside his conscious attention. And even when he is "consciously aware" of his belief, there will be no single, fixed experience by which his awareness is always marked. This latter point is perplexing to a purely introspective psychology; but to a psychology which takes the affective aspects of a belief as varying manifestations of a constant disposition to action, there is relatively little difficulty. Moreover, the dispositional view readily explains how one can "have a belief without acting on it"; for in such a case the disposition is simply unrealized.[21] And the view can give an intelligible analysis of such a phrase as, "Although his belief was false, it *referred to* something." What the belief is said to "refer to" must be related, though in a very complicated manner, to the stimulus or response factor of the belief. A false belief will then *have* a reference to something else in much the same sense that a disposition *has* a stimulus or response, even though no concrete stimulus or response exists.[22] These are respects in which a dispositional view of cognition promises to have no little fidelity to the distinctions of common sense—nor is common sense an unworthy ally.

In developing the view, however, one immediately encounters

Lecture II; and Ledger Wood, *The Analysis of Knowledge* (Princeton, 1941), chap. i.

20. See William James, "The Function of Cognition," *The Meaning of Truth.* Written in 1884, this article does not represent James's final views, nor is it wholly tenable; but it remains of great interest as an attempt to supplement an "image theory" of cognition with a more behavioristic one.

21. Cf. p. 49.

22. Cf. p. 49.

an overwhelming complexity. *What kind* of disposition to actions is to be called "cognitive"? Unless this is answered, the definition will have only its genus, without the required differentiae; yet in providing the differentiae it is impossible, in practice, to hope for more than the vaguest approximation. When a man "puts his knowledge into action" he may do any one of a great number of things. Now if his actions are the *response* of a disposition, they may vary even when the disposition does not; but we must at least limit the *range* over which they may vary, else the disposition will not be marked off as "cognitive." That is the difficulty; and it is equally difficult to specify the range for the *stimulus*.

How, for instance, will a man "act on" the belief that it is raining? Perhaps he will put on his raincoat, or reach for his umbrella; perhaps he will simply pick up a book, instead of going out; perhaps he will close the windows, and fold up the chairs on the porch; perhaps he will phone a friend to cancel a tennis game for the afternoon, and so on. Any of these actions, and the list might have been extended indefinitely, will be among the possible responses for this cognitive disposition. The stimuli will be no less complicated. It is not enough to mention the sight and sound of the rain, for these are more likely to be the causes of the belief itself than stimuli which prompt a specific action upon it; so among the stimuli must be included, say, the man's sight of his raincoat, or someone's reminding him of the open windows, or his remembering his tennis engagement, and so on. It is easy to draw up such partial lists, but quite another thing to specify the general classes into which the members of the lists must fall. If it is difficult to specify them for a particular belief, it is no less difficult to make clear what distinguishes beliefs in general, and cognitive dispositions in general, from all other dispositions to action.

If the problem lay wholly in this complexity, perhaps it would not be of great importance. We should need only to acknowledge, with Frank Ramsey, that philosophy is often less a "system of definitions" than a "system of descriptions of how definitions might be given,"[23] not forgetting that such a "system of descriptions," even when it is imperfect, may be sufficient to clear away the more troublesome confusions. But in fact the complexity seems indicative of a further problem, to which we must now attend. Suppose that a man, believing that it is raining, should in

23. *Foundations of Mathematics*, p. 263.

fact put on his raincoat. Is he acting *solely* on the belief that it is raining? Clearly not. He would not have put it on unless he *also believed* that it would serve to keep him dry when he went out, and unless he *wanted* both to go out and to keep dry. This example illustrates a principle whose application is quite general, namely: No concrete action can be related exclusively to one, simple belief; it must also be related to many *other* beliefs —usually a complicated system of them—and must be related to attitudes as well. Thus there are many dispositions involved, all of them relevant to any given action. Change *any* of these dispositions, and, with all else constant, the action will change as well.

How shall we account for this? Shall we say that the man's putting on his raincoat was in fact the response of his belief that it was raining, and classify his other beliefs and his attitudes among the *attendant circumstances* which, with a certain stimulus, made the response take just this form? Perhaps; but we must remember that the term "attendant circumstances" has been introduced largely by examples, and that the previous examples have none of them prepared us for attendant circumstances like these, which are themselves dispositions.

For a study of the present sort, where no empirical contribution to the problem is sought, but only a schema that will guard against the more gross oversimplifications, it will be sufficient to suggest an analogy—some example which is more easily understood, and which will illustrate how dispositional properties may mutually influence each other. Perhaps the following will serve, though very humbly: A small ball of iron is surrounded by electromagnets; the current is switched on, and the ball moves in a certain way. Now each of the magnets has a disposition to affect the motion of the ball, but the actual motion of it cannot be related to one of these dispositions alone; it must be related to all. Change any of the magnets, and, all else remaining constant, the motion of the ball will change as well. In spite of many differences, this case parallels the one in question. Several dispositional properties are present together, each making a difference to the way any other is realized.

There is clearly nothing mysterious about such a situation. The term "disposition" is used, as always, to refer to a complicated milieu in which a given sort of event has many causes. Here the situation is complicated enough to require the mention of several dispositions. It is convenient to distinguish them, and give separate attention to each, so long as a knowledge of how each would be realized in the absence of the others permits one to infer, with only a little more inductive evidence, how they will be realized when present conjointly. Even if the dispositions cannot be studied in isolation—as is the case for cognition but not the case for the magnets—one can observe what difference is made by a *change* in one of them, all else remaining roughly constant; and if this change is evidenced by other tests than that involving the given response to be predicted, a knowledge of it may be of practical use.

It is after this fashion, perhaps, that cognition must be conceived—as a disposition whose response is modified by that of many other dispositions. But two points must be clearly understood: In stressing dispositions to *action*, the present account is not presenting an uncompromising defense of behavioristic psychology. As has previously been remarked, there are certain immediate experiences which are involved, in various ways, in the processes to which the term "cognitive" is usually applied. An adequate study would undoubtedly have to take account of them —though it would seem that they too are only dispositionally present in cognition. The present emphasis on overt action is intended to supplement an introspective analysis, not to discredit it. And further: any mechanical analogy such as that of the magnets must serve, here as elsewhere, not to disguise the full complexity of the problem but rather to reveal it. A belief is much more complicated than any phenomenon studied in physics, and may involve, so far as anyone can now know, causal explanations that are irreducibly peculiar to biology or psychology. But if the mechanical examples serve as a starting point for the imagination, foreshadowing much more complicated conceptions, they may help to dispel those too simple "simple entities" which so often enter philosophy and psychology as fictitious substitutes for logical constructions.

These remarks do no more than suggest why it is difficult to give the differentiae for "cognition"; they do not surmount the difficulty. Nor will there be any attempt here to present an adequate definition of the term. Since a parallel difficulty arises for defining "attitude," one that again has not been surmounted, it will be observed that the key terms that are used in the present work—in the analysis both of meaning in general and of ethical meanings—have only such clarity as is afforded by instances of their usage, together with admonitions not to hypostatize and oversimplify. This is not an agreeable admission; but it is difficult to see how, at the present stage of linguistic and psychological theory, any more persistent quest for a definition would be rewarding. An inquiry cannot rest until its key terms are perfectly clear; for it is only by pressing on the inquiry, in any such way as is possible, that greater clarity can ultimately be obtained.

We must be content, then, to say that descriptive meaning is the disposition of a sign to affect cognition, though we must remember that this remark only approximates to a proper definition. To whatever extent cognition is itself dispositional in nature, descriptive meaning will be a second-order disposition. Thus the distinction between descriptive and emotive meaning depends largely on the kind of psychological disposition that a sign, in its turn, is disposed to evoke.

No attempt has been made here to deal with one of the most difficult problems that meaning-theory includes—that of explaining how separate words, each one with its own meaning, can combine to yield sentence-meanings. It is feasible, perhaps, to take each word as having a disposition to affect cognition, just as the full sentence does. The problem reduces, then, to one of explaining the interplay of the dispositions of the several words, when realized conjointly. The analogy of the magnets will still serve, used now to illustrate the relationship of *meanings* rather than of *beliefs*. We may compare the meaning of each word with the disposition of some one of the magnets, and compare the meaning of the sentence with the disposition that may be assigned to the group of magnets. Each word has an independent meaning in the sense that if it is replaced by certain others in any context, there will be a typical sort of difference in the meaning of the context; but the precise way in which the word's meaning is realized will depend on the meaning of the other words that accompany it.

Of the two questions mentioned at the beginning of this section, we may now proceed to the second, namely: How do descriptive meanings attain the precision that is needed for practicable communication? This question is best developed by example:

Compare "It is 99 miles from X to Y" with "It is 100 miles from X to Y." With suitable substitutions for "X" and "Y," each of these phrases becomes a sentence that has a descriptive meaning. We have no difficulty in distinguishing the meaning of the one from that of the other. But if descriptive meanings are dispositions of signs to produce further dispositions, how, amid this causal complexity, can such nice distinctions be preserved? By what device do we keep our reactions to the one sentence permanently different from those to the other?

To understand this, we must consider the function of *linguistic rules,* which relate symbols *to each other.* (To speak in Morris' terminology: an understanding of this part of "pragmatics" requires that we look to certain related aspects of "syntax.") Let us see this by example:

Consider how a child uses large numbers before he has learned arithmetic. "100" means *many,* "1,000" means *very, very many,* and "1,000,000" means *an enormously great many.* How do these symbols attain a more precise meaning as the child grows older? In great measure, precision is due to arithmetical *rules.* A child learns to say "100 comes next after 99," "10 times 10 is 100," "1,000 divided by 10 is 100," and so. By acquiring a *mechanical* ability to speak in this way, the child is conditioned to go from one numerical expression to another, and thereby comes to react more constantly to any one of them than he would to a sign for which no rules were provided. The meaning of each symbol is modified by that of every other symbol to which the rules of arithmetic relate it. (Note that the modification of the meaning (disposition) itself is in question, not merely the circumstances under which the disposition is realized.) A child does not first acquire a full understanding of a mathematical symbol, and then learn rules for manipulating it; rather, these rules are a part of the very conditioning process upon which a full understanding of the symbol depends. It is thus (to repeat Sapir's phrase) that "the product grows with the instrument."

In the context that was previously mentioned—"It is 100 miles from X to Y"—such rules are readily seen at work. Any variation in its descriptive meaning is counteracted by an activity with symbols ("100, that's twice fifty," or "100 miles, that's two hours at fifty miles per hour," etc.) to which recourse is made when occasion requires it. The rules which this symbolic activity follows are simply fixed procedures, established by rote memory or written tables of reference, of going from one symbol to another in a mechanical way. They are by no means sufficient to establish a meaning from the beginning, but they render more fixed any rough meanings that may have developed in other ways.[24] The precise way in which rules do this—the way in which, by mechanically relating signs, they alter the meanings of the signs —is a problem in the psychology of language that has never been investigated; but it is obvious, whatever the detailed explanation may be, that rules do have some such effect, and that they are necessary for any precise communication.

Linguistic rules are not confined to mathematics; they have a function that pervades the whole of descriptive language. Suppose, for instance, that a man is deciding whether he has any living great aunt. In a rough way he understands the term "great aunt" to begin with; but so long as the term is isolated from others his reaction will be too inconstant for practical use. He may accordingly say, "Great aunt—that would be a sister of one of my grandparents; or in other words, a sister of one of the parents of my parents." To talk in this way requires only rote memory of definitions, though this may be supplemented by other devices, such as written definitions, or a diagram of a family tree. It is by such a procedure—that of referring back to other signs— that we preserve a fixed descriptive meaning. The process of referring back is more a preliminary to knowledge than its attainment; but it is often indispensable for clearing up a sign's meaning, making it suitable for some empirical context in which it is later used.

Again, consider the sentence, "John is a remarkable athlete." This might have a disposition to make people think that John is tall, simply because so many athletes are. But we should not ordinarily say that it "meant" anything about tallness, even though it "suggested" it. The reason for this is simply that linguistic rules do not connect "athlete" with "tall." Rather, we say, "An athlete may or may not be tall"; and this very remark emphasizes a rule. It *isolates* the disposition of the word "athlete" from that of "tall," and so isolates what "athlete" *means* from what it *suggests*.

24. It is sometimes maintained that the logical constants, like "or" and "not," acquire their meaning solely from the linguistic rules that govern them. But obviously, the actual learning process is much more complicated than that. A child who is told to bring either this *or* that is frowned upon when he brings neither and praised when he brings one. The frowns and praises are parts of the nonlinguistic circumstances that help to give "or" its meaning; and it is not easy to see, for the psychological sense of "meaning" that is here in question, how they or their equivalent could be dispensed with.

70   *ETHICS AND LANGUAGE*

Under linguistic rules we must include all manner of "a priori" statements, definitions,[25] and the stipulations that exclude certain combinations of words. (An instance of the last is, "A preposition must not be used without its object.") Whether such statements have any *other* function than that of rendering descriptive meanings permanent is a question that cannot here be discussed; but they obviously have at least this function.

The relation of rules to descriptive meanings is so close that it must be mentioned, qualifying the remarks that have preceded, in course of defining "descriptive meaning." Thus the full definition (rough to whatever extent "cognition" is improperly analyzed) can be given in this way:

The "descriptive meaning" of a sign is its disposition to affect cognition, provided that the disposition is caused by an elaborate process of conditioning that has attended the sign's use in communication, and provided that the disposition is rendered fixed, at least to a considerable degree, by linguistic rules. (Exception: a term without previous use in communication may be assigned a descriptive meaning if linguistic rules relate it to words that have had such a use.)

The proviso about linguistic rules is essential if we are to distinguish between what a sign means and what it suggests—as in the example of "athlete" above. When a sign persistently suggests something, this may be taken as a disposition of the sign; but being unchecked by linguistic rules, it will not be a "descriptive meaning" in the sense (not at all unconventional) which is here defined. Moreover, this proviso gives a little more precise test for determining when a sign's meaning has *changed*,[26] for among the many criteria for change in meaning we may now include a change in the linguistic rules with which the sign is made to comply.

---

25. But definitions need not always be so classified. When they describe how people actually use language, or predict how the speaker will subsequently use it, they become ordinary contingent statements about language. Only when they are used as symbolic exercises for clearing one's head, or establish a routine procedure of referring back from the definiendum to the definiens, do they serve to preserve linguistic rules. Note that it is one thing to give a psychological *description of* clarifying one's meanings, and another thing to clarify them. The latter, though it is the subject matter of an empirical (psychological) inquiry, is not itself an empirical inquiry—just as taking physical exercise, though it may be empirically studied, is not empirical study.

26. Cf. p. 55.

Note that a sign may be said to have a descriptive meaning even though its disposition to affect cognition is not *wholly* fixed by linguistic rules. It need only be fixed "to a considerable degree." This more lenient requirement permits one to say that a word may have a descriptive meaning which is *vague*. Whenever a descriptive meaning is vague, it is subject to constant changes of a slight nature, the linguistic rules being insufficient or too poorly specified to prevent this.[27] Vagueness is often removed by *stipulating* additional rules for a sign's use; but before these are stipulated, we shall want to say (so long as there were a number of rules to begin with, applied in people's habits) that the sign, for all its vagueness, was not void of all descriptive meaning. This useful way of speaking is readily preserved by the lenient requirement that has been introduced—that descriptive meaning must be fixed "to a considerable degree" by linguistic rules. When a sign becomes subject to fewer and fewer rules, and so more and more vague, there comes a point where we may say that it loses descriptive meaning altogether (even though it may still, on occasion, affect cognition); but the exact point at which this occurs can itself conveniently remain vague, since any sharp distinction is unnecessary for our purposes.

8

HAVING distinguished between emotive and descriptive meaning, we are now in a position to ask how the two are related.

It is evident that a sign may have both kinds of meaning. That is to say, it may at once have a disposition to affect feelings or attitudes and a disposition to affect cognition. Since most common words do in fact have a meaning of both sorts, let us begin by giving this aspect of the relationship closer attention.

The growth of emotive and descriptive dispositions in language does not represent two isolated processes. There is a continual interplay. It may happen—to take only a simple and not wholly typical instance—that a word acquires a laudatory emotive meaning partly because it refers, *via* its descriptive meaning, to some-

27. Cf. pp. 34 ff. "Vagueness" was there explained in terms of the relation between a sign and its designatum—i.e., semantically. It will be obvious, however (since a sign and its designatum are always related *via* descriptive meaning, in the present, psychological sense) that there will be a "pragmatic" counterpart to vagueness; and since descriptive meaning depends on linguistic rules, in part, there will also be a "syntactical" counterpart of vagueness.

thing which people favor. "Democracy" has a pleasing emotive meaning to most Americans because its referent pleases them. But if the two sorts of meaning often grow up together, it does not follow that they must always change together. Either may come to vary while the other remains roughly constant; and it is largely on this account that the distinction between them is important.

Suppose, for example, that a group of people should come to disapprove of certain aspects of democracy, but continue to approve of other aspects of it. They might leave the descriptive meaning of "democracy" unchanged, and gradually let it acquire, for their usage, a much less laudatory emotive meaning. On the other hand, they might keep the strong laudatory meaning unchanged, and let "democracy" acquire a descriptive sense which made reference only to those aspects of democracy (in the older sense) which they favored. It is often essential, if failures in communication are to be avoided, to determine which of these changes is taking place; and the distinction between emotive and descriptive meaning is of great use in studying the matter.

A particularly interesting phenomenon depends upon the "inertia," so to speak, of meaning. Suppose, though quite artificially, that a term's laudatory emotive meaning has arisen *solely* because its descriptive meaning refers to something which people favor. And suppose that a given speaker succeeds in changing the descriptive meaning of the term, in a way which his audience temporarily sanctions. One might expect that the emotive meaning will undergo a parallel change, automatically. But in fact it often will not. Through inertia, it will survive a change in the descriptive meaning on which it originally depended. And if we remember, dropping the artificial assumption above, that emotive meaning seldom depends on descriptive reference alone, but likewise on the gestures, intonations, and emotionally vigorous contexts with which the term has previously been associated, it is easy to see why emotive meaning can often survive quite sharp changes in descriptive meaning.

We shall find that the inertia of emotive meaning is of great interest to our subsequent study of ethics. Let us accordingly introduce the following terminology: To whatever extent emotive meaning is *not* a function of descriptive meaning, but either persists without the latter or survives changes in it, let us say that it is "independent." Thus nonmetaphorical interjections will have a wholly independent emotive meaning, but most words, including "democracy," "liberty," "magnanimity," and so on, will have an emotive meaning which is independent only in part. On the other hand, to whatever extent emotive meaning is a function of descriptive meaning, changing with it after only a brief "lag," let us say that it is "dependent."

The independence of emotive meaning can be roughly tested by comparing descriptive synonyms which are not emotive synonyms. Thus to whatever extent the laudatory strength of "democracy" exceeds that of "government where rule is by popular vote," the emotive meaning of the former will be independent. But such a test is far from exact, since it makes no allowance for the independent emotive meaning that may be common to *both* terms. Nor is it always easy to find descriptive synonyms; for whenever such synonyms differ emotively, people usually proceed (for reasons that will be given in Chapter IX) to redefine one of them in a way that brings a descriptive difference as well.

To see some further relations between emotive and descriptive meaning, let us turn briefly to the subject of metaphor. Though metaphors are not of primary concern to the present work, they will be useful in illustrating important distinctions.

People often say that although a metaphorical statement "has" a literal meaning, it is not to be "taken" literally. Let us see what that implies. A statement such as "All the world's a stage" has a verbal similarity to "All the third floor is a laboratory," "All the eastern district is an army camp," etc., and so suggests that application of the linguistic rules by which the cognitive dispositions of language are usually preserved. To say that the metaphorical statement "has a literal meaning" is a way of saying that, in accordance with these rules, including the rules that govern the individual words in other contexts, it has an ordinary descriptive meaning. To say that this meaning is "not taken literally" is to say that the attendant circumstances—the living context in which the sentence is uttered, and particularly the hearer's expectations of what the speaker would be likely to intend—are such that the descriptive disposition is not in fact realized in any usual way. This is by no means an exact analysis of the situation, but it points to a truth which is obvious once it is stated: The very distinction between a sentence's metaphorical and literal import cannot adequately be made without reference to the linguistic rules (syntax) that govern its component words throughout a linguistic system, and thereby preserve descriptive dispositions that are *usually* realized in a nonmetaphorical way.

The literal meaning of a metaphorical sentence must be sharply distinguished from what may be called its "interpretation." For example: If a person were instructed to express "All the world's a stage" in plain prose, he might give such "interpretations" as, "Real life is often like a play," or "There is a routine in real life, each man going through a prearranged course," or even "There is a great deal of trivial make-believe in each man's conduct." Now clearly, none of these interpretations has a descriptive meaning which is identical with the literal meaning (in the sense above explained) of the metaphorical sentence; for the latter is "not taken" in its literal meaning, whereas any of the interpretations is. Rather, the "interpretation" may be defined as a sentence which is to be taken literally, and which *descriptively means* what the metaphorical sentence *suggests*. We have seen elsewhere that a sentence may suggest, with regard to cognition, much more than it descriptively means.[28] Metaphorical sentences are replete with such suggestions. The function of an interpretation is to reduplicate the suggestive force of the metaphor in other terms—terms which have the same effect not as a part of their suggestiveness, but as a part of their descriptive meaning, realized in the ordinary way.

It must be remembered, however, that no sentence can ever descriptively mean *exactly* what another suggests. This is so, if for no other reason, because the descriptive meaning of a sentence is made definite by the operation of linguistic rules, which cause it systematically to be modified by the descriptive dispositions of many other terms in the language; whereas the suggestiveness of a sentence, going beyond any fixed rules, will be far more vague. There is no such thing as giving an exact translation of a metaphor into nonmetaphorical terms. One can only give interpretations, and these are always approximate. It is usually necessary to give not one interpretation but many, each of which will give, with too great a precision, a small part of what the metaphor suggests by its richly vague figure. What sometimes passes as "the" interpretation of a metaphor is in fact only a foveal one, which may too easily cause one to forget the many that are peripheral. Thus the second of the three interpretations above for "All the world's a stage" might seem "the" interpre-

28. Cf. pp. 69, 70.

PRAGMATIC ASPECTS OF MEANING   75

tation, since it is most developed in Shakespeare's context; but the third one, even though it is not developed, could plausibly be taken as pointing out a partial but relevant aspect of the metaphor's full reverberations.[29]

Let us now see how these cognitive aspects of metaphor have a bearing on its emotive aspects. It will be clear that the strongly moving effect of certain metaphors has relatively little to do with "independent" emotive meaning; it is closely related to the metaphor's descriptive meaning (even though this is not taken literally) and to its possible interpretations. Just *how* this relationship takes place is an endlessly complicated matter, on which any attempt at an adequate analysis would be only rash. But perhaps the following observations will have a modest use.

For certain simple metaphors, such as the colloquialism, "He is a pig," the emotional effect seems in part due to the full realization of dependent emotive meaning even though the descriptive meaning is not, in the context, fully realized. Thus "he" is given the derogation that the word "pig," simply because it literally refers to pigs, has come to acquire. To that extent a metaphor serves merely to separate off the emotive effect of a word from its usual descriptive effects, and so to increase the number of emotive tools that language offers.

But metaphor is obviously much more than this. It often happens that a word which has relatively little emotive effect when used literally has a much greater one when used metaphorically. "All the world's a stage" is much more moving than any set of literal contexts that use the same words. No doubt this is in part due to the dependent emotive meaning of the possible interpretations, and to the music of the line; but it is difficult to believe that these factors are sufficient to complete, or even to suggest, a full explanation. It would seem that the attendant circumstances, preventing the metaphor's literal meaning from being realized in any ordinary way, serve thereby to intensify the form in which each term's emotive disposition is realized. The general problem lies in explaining how the unusual realization of the one disposition affects the realization of the other. Now it is easy to suggest rough physical analogues. A match, having dispositions to produce both flame and smoke, will produce more than the usual

29. See William Empson's *Seven Types of Ambiguity* (Harcourt, Brace, 1931) for a wealth of illustrative material on this and other aspects of poetic language.

amount of smoke whenever certain attendant circumstances make it produce less than the usual amount of flame. But such parallels, as we have seen, can do no more than point to a greater complexity; and they are so inadequate for suggesting the rich complexity of poetic metaphors that their usefulness is meager. It can only be remarked, then, that an adequate explanation of the emotional effects of metaphor lies in a little-charted region of psychology—where a psychophysical explanation is barely to be hoped for, and where any purely introspective analysis is less likely to indicate the *modus operandi* than to provide a series of interesting but disorganized examples.

This much, however, may profitably be concluded: Emotive and descriptive meaning, both in their origin and practical operation, stand in extremely close relationship. They are distinguishable *aspects* of a total situation, not "parts" of it that can be studied in isolation. For varying purposes, the one or the other may require a preponderance of theoretical *attention*. And in practice it is often necessary, lest general intelligibility be sacrificed to an overwhelming body of details, to pretend that they are more neatly separable than they are. Such a compromise must often be made in the analysis of ethics that is to follow, and as a compromise it will serve its purpose. But should the procedure seem anything more than a compromise, the subject of metaphor must stand as a reminder of all that is left unmentioned.[30]

9

BEFORE concluding these remarks about meaning, it may be well to guard against the tendency, too common among popular writers, to separate meanings into the sheep and the goats—a procedure which militates against detachment, and hides the need of a more detailed classification.

In particular, the term "emotive" is sometimes used in an extremely rough way, until it labels a wastebasket for the many aspects of linguistic usage that are detrimental or irrelevant to the purposes of science. Under "emotive" utterances come to be included not only those which are disposed to alter feelings or

30. For some remarks dealing specifically with "sleeping metaphors" see p. 143. An instructive study of metaphor has been made by I. A. Richards, *The Philosophy of Rhetoric* (Oxford, 1936), chaps. v and vi, and *Interpretation in Teaching* (Harcourt, Brace, 1938), *passim*. Since the present account sometimes diverges from Richards, he must not be credited with its inadequacies; but the writer must express an indebtedness to him, both on this topic and on many others.

attitudes, but also those which are hypostatic, anthropomorphic, ambiguous, vague, misleading, incoherent, or in any way confused. Now this use of the term is natural enough, and not always inconvenient, for linguistic confusions are often attended by strong emotive effects; but the usage is not at all fortunate when it leads one to suppose, as it too readily does, that any expression classifiable as "emotive" is thereby perfectly put in its place, requiring no further attention.

It would be well to supplement the terms "emotive" and "descriptive" by subdividing meaning in a number of other ways. If meaning is taken as a disposition of a sign to produce psychological reactions, one may subdivide it by classifying the psychological reactions in any way that occasion requires. Thus for certain terms that have a marked, persistent disposition to produce images, it may be convenient to speak of "pictorial meaning."[31] If some form of pictorial meaning proved always to attend emotive or descriptive meaning, that would be a contingent matter that would in no way jeopardize the distinction. At certain times, even for purposes of science, pictorial meaning may be definitely sought, in the hope of making graphic certain complicated conceptions. James' expression, "the stream of consciousness," is useful in this respect. At other times, when the images may intervene to obscure or give a fictionalizing simplicity to complicated descriptive phrases, it may be helpful to find descriptive equivalents which are relatively free from pictorial meaning.

To take another instance: There are certain expressions which on account of inadvertent hypostatization, grammatical incoherency, and the like, are persistently disposed to evoke the state of mind that John Wisdom calls "philosophical perplexity."[32] In the broad, psychological sense here employed these expressions may be said to have a "meaning." One may deny, however, that they have a descriptive meaning, on the ground that their linguistic rules are too rough, or that the perplexed state which they are disposed to evoke is not cognitive; and one may deny that their meaning is *wholly* emotive, on the ground that the perplexed state which they evoke is so different from what is

31. See Virgil C. Aldrich, "Pictorial Meaning and Picture Thinking," *The Kenyon Review* (summer issue, 1943).
32. See the article bearing that title in *Proceedings of the Aristotelian Society* for 1936–37.

usually called a "feeling or attitude" that it is best classified in some other way. It may consequently be useful to recognize a separate kind of meaning for these cases—one that could be designated, for instance, as "confused meaning."

There will be inevitable controversies about just where to draw the line between descriptive and confused meanings, for the distinction is itself no clearer than the meaning of the term "cognitive." But such controversies exist in any case, and until they are settled, the term "confused" seems more fortunate than "emotive" as a temporary counter with which the matter can be discussed. Emotive meaning, so long as it is not attended by any confusion, has such a variety of uses in literature and daily life that no judicious person could consider it a "linguistic ill"; and if on occasion it becomes troublesome, there are recognized ways of nullifying or diminishing its effect, as by the use of a compensating tone of voice, or by the alternation of laudatory and derogatory terms. Confused meaning, however (if we judge by those instances that would certainly be so rated, and not those whose status is still a matter of controversy), is always a "linguistic ill"; and the means of correcting and controlling it are very complicated. Some confusions are eradicable only after the most careful analysis, and perhaps only after a careful diagnosis of how the confusion has originated.

In certain cases a statement which has a confused meaning (again neglecting the controversial cases) will *also* have an emotive meaning; and it may be that the latter is largely a consequence of the former. Once the confusion is dispelled, the emotive meaning greatly decreases. The emotive meaning is then related to the confused meaning just as "dependent" emotive meaning[33] is related to descriptive meaning. Let us accordingly generalize the usage of the terms "dependent" and "independent," previously introduced, giving the former a reference to any kind of meaning whose existence is conditional to that of any other kind of meaning. Thus there will be emotive meaning dependent on descriptive meaning, as before; but there will also be emotive meaning dependent on confused meaning. One may go on, of course, recognizing emotive meaning dependent on pictorial meaning; and there will be use for such a term as "quasi-dependent emotive meaning," designating that which is conditional to the cognitive *suggestiveness* of a sign—i.e., conditional

33. See pp. 72 f.

to a descriptive disposition which, though too inconstant and too little modified by linguistic rules to be called a "descriptive meaning," may yet make a great difference to the way in which any emotive disposition is usually realized. It must be remembered, of course, that any sort of dependent emotive meaning will not be identical with the sort of meaning *on which* it depends, for there will be a difference in the kind of response in question—a difference which it may be important to emphasize even though both kinds of response repeatedly occur together. It must be remembered further that the distinction between *dependent* and *independent* emotive meaning does not rest (thus differing from the distinction between laudatory and derogatory emotive meaning) on the kind of feelings or attitudes that constitute the response, but rather upon the conditions under which the disposition itself has originated and will continue to exist. If these points are kept clear, the term "dependent" is of no little service in discussing many aspects of a sign's range of effects.

Any more detailed classification of meanings, and of dependent emotive meanings, must be expected to vary with varying purposes. There is nothing mandatory about the present classification; but it is certainly mandatory that the term "emotive," whether by these distinctions or others, be kept as a tool for use in careful study, not as a device for relegating the nondescriptive aspects of language to limbo.

10

THE object of this chapter has been to outline a psychological (or "pragmatic") sense of meaning, of which emotive meaning may be considered a specific kind. By taking meaning as a dispositional property of a sign, it has defended an essentially causal view of meaning. More specifically, it has sought to explain how a sign's meaning can be constant even though its psychological effects vary, and how the effect of a sign on feelings and attitudes, in virtue of emotive meaning, can be much more powerful than any "additive" effect of its passing associations. It has sought further to show that the several aspects of language are closely interrelated.

At no time has the account sought to develop an empirical study of meaning. That would require a vast and detailed inquiry into the conditions under which meaning-dispositions originate, into the way in which their realization varies with various attendant circumstances, and into the basis of the dispositions. Such matters lie far beyond the present work, which hopes only to free the rough empirical knowledge of language that we acquire in common life from naïve confusions and oversimplifications. Indeed, the chapter sometimes does little more than show that language about language must share some of the complexities of all language. But even this has its modest use in cutting through the vacuities of much traditional theory, and will be of assistance in forwarding a workable understanding of ethics.

2

Semantical Concepts

ARTHUR PAP

CHAPTER I

Semantical Concepts

A. SEMANTIC MEANING
AND VERIFIABILITY

To begin with, the verifiability principle as stated is ambiguous, and so it is apt to give rise to purely verbal disputes, i.e., disputes that arise only because the same word is interpreted in different ways. For what is the meaning of "meaning"? In their famous pioneer work *The Meaning of Meaning*, Ogden and Richards distinguished something like seventeen meanings of the word "meaning." For our purposes discrimination of three senses will suffice; we shall label them *semantic, syntactic,* and *pragmatic* meaning. Semantic meaning, as we propose to use the term, is exclusively a property of statements: the semantic meaning of a statement is that state of affairs whose existence would make the statement true. The word "fact" is more current in ordinary language than the clumsy "state of affairs," but we avoid it here for a good reason: if a statement is false, then it has just as definite a semantic meaning as it would have if it were true—indeed, it has the same semantic meaning whether it be true or false. But to a false statement no fact corresponds at all; to speak here of a fact that does not exist though it might have existed would be far more clumsy than to speak of a state of affairs in the sense of a *possibility* that may or may not be actualized. To illustrate: What is the semantic meaning of the statement, "The train really (not just apparently) moves now"? This is to ask which state of affairs must exist at the time denoted by "now" if the statement is to be true. As an alternative terminology, which has the advantage of reminding us of the close connection between the concept of semantic meaning and the concept of truth, let us call this state of affairs the *truth-condition* of the

[6]

Semantical Concepts   [7]

statement. Now, our principle is best interpreted as a guide to the discovery of the truth-condition (not to be confused with the truth!) of a statement. How, indeed, do we go about verifying whether the train really moves? If we notice that it changes its position relative to a train on the parallel track, we are still in doubt, for it may be the latter train that really moves. But if we observe a change of position relative to the station platform, or relative to any object that is fixed on the earth, then we are convinced. Conclusion: The statement means semantically that the train changes its position relative to the earth.

Let us keep in mind that the verifiability principle addresses itself only to semantic meaning, not to meaning in any other sense of this highly ambiguous word. It is a proposed analysis of the concept of semantic meaning, or "truth-condition," in terms of the concept of *verification*. As we shall see in due course, even after this initial clarification it still faces great difficulties, but first let us appreciate its usefulness a little. Suppose somebody were to jump to conclusions and say, "I guess 'X really moves' generally means 'X changes its position relative to the earth, or relative to an object fixed on the earth,' since this is the way we verify the occurrence of a real motion." He could easily be refuted if we pointed out that a man might walk in a moving train in the direction opposite to its motion and with exactly the train's speed, so that relative to the earth he would remain stationary. Suppose he then modified his analysis as follows: " 'X *really moves*' means 'X changes position relative to *some* visible body in the environment of X.' " But this analysis is even more absurd, since it would then be just as true to say that the station platform really moves as that the train really moves— whereas the station platform just does *not* move in the sense in which the word is ordinarily used. Let us take one more step: how would one verify that, contrary to appearances, the earth really moves, as asserted by scientists and educated laymen since Copernicus? Surely not by observing that the earth changes position relative to itself! But then "real motion" does not mean in this context what it means in the context "the train really moves." If the evidence that, practically unattainable though it may be, would establish it as certain that the earth really moves is that an observer stationed on a fixed star and equipped with a powerful telescope would observe the earth to change position, then "the earth really moves" means that the earth changes position relative to the fixed stars.[1] One result, therefore, of the application of the verifiability prin-

---

1. ". . . The question whether the earth moves or not amounts in reality to no more than this, to wit, whether we have reason to conclude, from what has been observed by astronomers, that if we were placed in such and such circumstances, and such or such a position and distance both from the earth and sun, we should perceive the former to move among the choir of the planets, and appearing in all respects like one of them." (Berkeley, *The Principles of Human Knowledge*, sec. 58.)

ciple to this case is that the expression "real motion" does not stand for one concept, but for a family of similar concepts. A more interesting consequence, however, is the following: Suppose we asked a classical physicist whose semantic self-consciousness was not above average whether the earth would still move if all other bodies in the universe were destroyed. He would probably reply, "Yes, according to the law of inertia it would move on forever along that straight line which was the direction of the tangential velocity component at the moment when its gravitational attraction by the sun discontinued." But how could one even in principle verify that it moved if there was no other body relative to which it changed position? If one could not, then the verifiability principle seems to force the conclusion that the statement, "The earth would still move," has no semantic meaning at all. As we shall see later, an implicit adherence to this principle has indeed led physicists to abandon the Newtonian concepts of absolute space, time, and motion, though we shall also see that the story is far more complicated than this over-simplified preliminary version.

One more illustration may be useful to convey a preliminary under-standing of the verifiability principle, though it may at the same time foreshadow a serious criticism of it. Suppose that in your rare moments of speculation you entertained the possibility that absolutely every body in the universe is constantly expanding, though it is impossible to detect this because all bodies expand at the same rate. What, now, is the semantic meaning of this hypothesis? The positivist, who may be said to be a refiner of the pragmatist principle, "A difference that makes no difference is no difference," will argue that it has no semantic meaning at all: for the only way of verifying that a body expands is by comparison with other bodies (e.g., yardsticks) that themselves do not expand or at least do not expand the same rate; and if all bodies expand at the same rate, then one cannot verify whether any of them expands. If the statement *seems* to be true or false, seems to describe a genuine possibility, the positivist will say the reason is its grammatical similarity to statements which are verifiable, e.g., "All heated pieces of iron expand at the same rate." A critic of the positivist principle might reply: "How could you find out that the statement was in principle unverifiable unless you understood it? Unless you understood it, you would not be able to conclude that the very supposition of its being either confirmed or dis-confirmed by observations contradicts what it asserts. And since, as the positivists themselves have emphasized, understanding a statement and knowing its truth-condition are one and the same thing, you should admit that a statement may be unverifiable and still have a semantic meaning."

We shall see later that this criticism cannot be lightly dismissed. Un-doubtedly there is in science a usage of the word "meaningless" accord-

Semantical Concepts   [9]

ing to which a statement like the above hypothesis would be condemned as meaningless just because it is in principle unverifiable, i.e., just because it cannot be specified in what way observations made in a world in which it was true would differ from observations made in a world in which it was false. More accurately, what the word "meaningless" *means* in this usage is just "in principle unverifiable"—though we have not yet made the meaning of the latter expression precise. But though nobody could hope to know whether a statement that was meaningless in this sense was true or false, and though it would make no practical difference whatever whether it was true or false, it does not follow that it could not *be* true or false, i.e., describe a conceivable state of affairs.

B. SEMANTIC AND PRAGMATIC MEANING

Semantic meaning, we have said, is a property of statements. Imperatives, for example, have no semantic meaning; we do not call them true or false, but obeyed or disobeyed. Now, in a derived sense we can also speak of the semantic meaning of a *predicate*, because it is of the nature of predicates to be used in statements characterizing a certain subject-matter. The semantic meaning of a predicate is that aspect of it which determines whether an ascription of it to something or other is true or false. For example, whether or not a statement of the form "X is a father" is true depends upon the semantic meaning of the predicate "father." If "X is a father" is true if and only if X is a male parent, then the property of *being a male parent* is the semantic meaning of "father."[2] Following John Stuart Mill, many logicians call this the *connotation* of the predicate: the criterion by which it is determined whether the predicate is applicable to this or that object. But the word "connotation" itself has certain connotations in its everyday use that make it desirable to avoid it in an exact discussion. For example, we might say that for so-and-so the word "father" connotes financial worries, and for so-and-so self-confidence, and for so-and-so an age of at least thirty. But the properties that we psychologically associate with a predicate are no part of its semantic meaning unless the truth or falsehood of an ascription of the predicate depends on their presence. To be sure, statements are true or false not just by virtue of the "facts" but also by virtue of the conventional meanings of the words. If everybody in a given society observed the rule to apply the word "father" to X if and only if X was a

2. The distinction between properties and classes is a controversial subject that may be ignored in this context.

male parent older than thirty, then the property of being older than thirty would be part of the semantic meaning of "father" *in that society*, and statements of the form "X is a father" as interpreted in that society would be true only if X was older than thirty.

Nevertheless, even with regard to predicates for which no explicit definitions are codified we can distinguish properties that, within a given language community, are *criteria of true applications* from properties that are not so regarded though most or all of the objects of which the predicate is true may have them and though some people may mentally associate them with the predicate. Suppose, for example, that all Republican congressmen were corruptible and that this was so widely known that every voter immediately thought of corruptibility when he heard the expression "Republican congressman." (That on the supposition made there soon would be no Republican congressmen is probable, but irrelevant in this context.) Still, corruptibility would not be *semantically* meant by "Republican congressman" as long as the voters granted the logical possibility of there being incorruptible Republican congressmen, for if it were so meant then "incorruptible Republican congressman" would be as self-contradictory an expression as "square with unequal sides."

Now, thoughts and other kinds of mental states that are causally connected with a linguistic expression without being directly relevant to the question of truth constitute the *pragmatic* meaning of the expression. Normally, a man who utters the sentence, "It will rain," with a tone of conviction believes that it will rain. But whether or not he believes what he said is irrelevant to the question of whether what he said is true. Therefore the belief is no part of the truth-condition of the sentence. Banker X who hates all communists without exception may feel a surge of hatred whenever he hears someone referred to as a communist; nevertheless this hatred has nothing to do with the semantic meaning of "communist" in X's usage as long as X admits that a person could *be* a communist even if he did not hate him. Or imagine a man in whose experience there never have been any blonde girls except slim and blue-eyed ones, and who therefore inevitably imagines a slim and blue-eyed girl whenever he hears the expression "a blonde girl." Such images constitute part of the pragmatic meaning of the expression for that man, but as long as he answers the question, "Could you conceive of a blonde who is fat, or who is not blue-eyed?" affirmatively, slimness and blue-eyedness are not *semantically* meant by "blonde girl" even for him.

What is frequently called "emotive" meaning is a species of pragmatic meaning as here conceived. Some philosophers, notably logical positivists, have maintained that value statements, such as "It is wrong to steal from the poor," "Beethoven was a great composer," "It is your duty to fight for your fatherland," have *only* emotive meaning. But whether or not

Semantical Concepts [11]

they have semantic meaning also, we can see that their semantic meaning, whatever it may be, must be distinct from their emotive meaning relative to the speaker. For otherwise they would be descriptions of the speaker's emotions, hence true or false according to whether or not the described emotions were present, and hence not *value* statements at all. If in an autobiographical mood I reported, "I dislike seeing the poor robbed, I greatly admire Beethoven as a composer," and so on, I would be engaged in introspective description, not in evaluation. But here we touch upon a subtle problem of the analysis of evaluation discourse only in passing,[3] our sole purpose being to clarify the concept of semantic meaning by differentiation from other senses of "meaning." It should be noted that in spite of the differences between the various kinds of meaning, they all have in common their involving, in addition to the sign that is said to have meaning and that which is said to be the meaning of the sign, people who produce or interpret the sign. If people in linguistic communication are not mentioned, the reason is simply that a more or less constant class of sign interpreters and sign users is presupposed. Thus the statement, " 'Father' semantically means a male parent," is really short for " 'Father' semantically means a male parent for English-speaking people using the word in a biological sense." Even where the sign is a *natural* sign as in "Black clouds signify rain," there is a tacit reference to people whose perception of black clouds causes them to expect rain.

C. SYNTACTIC MEANING

Semantic meaning and pragmatic meaning moreover share the following feature: that which is meant by the linguistic expression is usually not itself a linguistic expression; it is a state of affairs, or a property, or a mental state, or the like. In this respect *syntactic* meaning is a peculiar sort of meaning. One expression syntactically means other expressions. Thus the word "uncle" means the word "man" as well as the word "brother," in the sense that if "X is an uncle" is true, it follows that "X is a man" and "X is a brother" are also true. In natural language syntactic meaning derives from semantic meaning: if "X is a man" is deducible from "X is an uncle," the reason lies not in any intrinsic properties of the words "man" and "uncle," but in the fact that "man" semantically means a property that is part of the semantic meaning of the word "uncle."

One might allege as an exception to this principle of the priority of semantic meaning to syntactic meaning the case in which one sentence is derivable from (as a consequence of) other sentences not by virtue of

3. A more detailed analysis may be found in Chapter 21.

any reference of descriptive terms to something outside of language, but by sole virtue of the rules for manipulating so-called *logical* words, i.e., words such as "or," "and," "not," and "all" that are determinants of the total meaning of a statement but do not mean anything by themselves. Thus "Either X is not introverted or X is not a mathematician" follows from "X is not an introverted mathematician," and this logical relation is independent of the meanings of the descriptive words "introverted" and "mathematician." The second sentence is *formally* derivable from the first; i.e., one needs no understanding of the descriptive words to see that this logical relation holds. But even here the semantic dimension of meaning is prior to the syntactic dimension. No statement can be true *solely* by virtue of its form: even the tautology "He is a scientist or he is not a scientist" is a tautology only if the word "scientist" has the same meaning in both occurrences. Note that we sometimes say, without being guilty of contradiction, "X is, and is not, an A," intending of course, the word represented by A in different senses. Again, if relations of logical consequence depended only on syntactic form, then "All good musicians are good people" should follow from "All musicians are people" just as "All brown horses are brown animals" follow from "All horses are animals."

For the above reasons, it is really confusing to speak of meaning in the syntactic sense at all, and of a kind of truth, "formal truth," that allegedly derives exclusively from syntactical rules, i.e., rules governing manipulation of symbols without regard to any semantic meanings.[4] In any ordinary use of the word "meaning," to say that one word means other words is to say that it is used in order to refer to other words, as when the grammarian uses the word "adjective" in order to refer to such words as "red" and "hard." And again this is meaning in the semantic sense (note that semantic meaning is sometimes called "reference"). But since some prominent writers do speak of a syntactical dimension of meaning, we do well to distinguish this sense of "meaning" from the others.

D. A PRIORI AND EMPIRICAL
STATEMENTS

We turn now to a preliminary differentiation of kinds of *statements* in order to single out the kind of statement to which alone the verifiability principle addresses itself. We have seen that the latter is intended as a

4. For a detailed discussion of formal or logical truth, see Chapter 6.

Semantical Concepts   [13]

guide to the discovery of the truth-condition of a statement. As synonym for "truth-condition," we have also used the expression "state of affairs described," where a state of affairs was informally defined as a possibility which may or may not be actual. (If it is actual, then the statement describes a fact, or is true.) But in this sense no state of affairs is described by such statements as "All bachelors are unmarried," "Anything that is red is colored," "If *A* is father of *B* and *B* is father of *C*, then *A* is grandfather of *C*," "If this is a metal and all metals expand when heated, then this will expand when heated." Whether or not it makes sense to speak of empirical verification of such statements, it will be agreed that they do not *require* empirical verification. We can see that they are true by just thinking about the meanings of the terms, without recourse to experience. In this sense they are *a priori* statements, not empirical statements. Now, most advocates of the verifiability principle in one form or another would restrict it to statements that are claimed to be empirical. For if one were to hold that with regard to any statement whatever, to understand its semantical meaning is to be able to specify the kind of experience or observations that would lead one to assert it as true, then it is doubtful whether a priori statements could be said to be semantically meaningful; and then the very concept of "a priori truth" would be thrown out, whereas logical positivists would in general accept the distinction between a priori and empirical truth, though they reject traditional interpretations of the concept "a priori truth" (cf. Chapters 5 and 6).

The logical positivist, then, says: If you claim to be making an empirical statement, you must substantiate this claim by describing the kind of experience that would establish your statement as true—in other words, you must specify what difference the truth of the statement would make to human experience. If no such difference can be specified, then either your statement is a priori and so says nothing specifically about the actual world (a priori statements following a phrase of Leibnitz, are often said to be true in all possible worlds), or it lacks semantical meaning altogether, however rich it may be in pragmatic meaning.

E. MEANING AND MEANINGFULNESS

But it is time to become somewhat more precise. In the first place, the logical positivist as portrayed so far seems to do two jobs at once: to offer a guide to the discovery of the semantical meaning of an empirical statement, and also to set up a criterion for deciding whether a statement claimed to be empirical has a semantical meaning at all, or more simply, *is* empirical. But these are different jobs. If to specify the meaning of an empirical statement is to describe the method of its verification, then of course it follows that the statement is meaningless if it is not verifiable. But one could consistently agree that a statement that is not a priori must be empirically verifiable if it is semantically meaningful at all, and reject the claim that describing the method of verification of a statement, or the sort of *evidence* that would lead one to accept it, is *the same as* saying what it means. For example, if I asked a physicist how he would verify that there was an electrical field in a certain spatial region, he would describe experiments such as placing an electroscope at the appropriate place and seeing whether its leaves diverged. But he might well deny that what he meant by his theoretical statement was just that such and such experiments would, were they performed, have such and such outcomes. Let us, therefore, split the positivist principle into the verifiability principle of *meaning* and the verifiability principle of *meaningfulness*. The former says that the meaning of a statement is identical with the empirical evidence that would establish its truth; the latter that a statement is meaningful if and only if it is empirically verifiable. The former entails the latter, but it is not obvious that the latter entails the former.

Secondly, the term "verifiable" has so far been used rather loosely. For example, is the empirical statement "All bodies near the surface of the earth fall with approximately constant acceleration" verifiable in the sense that one can describe the sort of experience that would establish it as true? Certainly not; experience can only render it more and more probable; to suppose it false would be logically consistent with any conceivable, and any conceivable amount of, experience of which the human race is capable. The example calls attention to the distinction between verification and confirmation, to be explored in the next chapter.

1

Use versus Mention

W. V. QUINE

§ 4. *Use versus Mention*

IN THE literature on the logic of statements, and in other foundational studies of mathematics as well, confusion and controversy have resulted from failure to distinguish clearly between an object and its name. Ordinarily the failure to maintain this distinction is not to be attributed to any close resemblance between the object and the name, even if the object happens to be a name in turn; for even the discrimination between one name and another is a visual operation of an elementary kind. The trouble comes rather in forgetting that a statement about an object must contain a name of the object rather than the object itself. If the object is a man or a city, physical circumstances prevent the error of using it instead of its name; when the object is a name or other expression in turn, however, the error is easily committed.

As an illustration of the essential distinction, consider these three statements:

(1)   Boston is populous,
(2)   Boston is disyllabic,
(3)   'Boston' is disyllabic.

The first two are incompatible, and indeed (1) is true and (2) false. Boston is a city rather than a word, and whereas a city may be populous, only a word is disyllabic. To say that the place-name in question is disyllabic we must use, not that name itself, but a name of it. The name of a name or other expression is commonly formed by putting the named expression in single quotation marks; the whole, called a *quotation*, denotes its interior. This device is used in (3), which, like (1), is true. (3) contains a name of the disyllabic word in question, just as (1) contains a name of the populous city in question. (3) is *about* a word which (1) *contains;* and (1) is about no word at all, but a city. In (1) the place-name is *used*, and in this way the city is *mentioned;* in (3) a quotation is used, and the place-name is mentioned. We mention x by using a name of x; and a statement about x contains a name of x.[1]

[1] By these considerations, the first sentence of the present paragraph might be

The foregoing treatment of (1)–(3) is itself replete with mention of expressions, yet free from quotations. These were avoided by circumlocution. As an exercise in quotation marks, however, it may be useful now to add a few comments involving them. 'Boston is populous' is about Boston and contains 'Boston'; ''Boston' is disyllabic' is about 'Boston' and contains ''Boston''. ''Boston'' designates 'Boston', which in turn designates Boston. To mention Boston we use 'Boston' or a synonym, and to mention 'Boston' we use ''Boston'' or a synonym. ''Boston'' contains six letters and just one pair of quotation marks; 'Boston' contains six letters and no quotation marks; and Boston contains some 800,000 people.

Such examples as (3), or:

(4)   'Boston' has six letters,
(5)   'Boston' is a noun,
(6)   'Boston' occurs in Walt Whitman's *Chants Democratic*,

must not be thought of as exhausting the kinds of things that can be said about an expression. These four statements ascribe properties to 'Boston' which might be classed respectively as phonetic, morphological, grammatical, and literary; roughly speaking, they have nothing to do with meaning. But an expression which has use in language will also have *semantic* properties, or properties which arise from the meaning of the expression. Such properties are ascribed to 'Boston' by these statements:

(7)   'Boston' designates Boston,
(8)   'Boston' designates a populous city,
(9)   'Boston' designates the capital of Massachusetts,
(10)   'Boston' is synonymous with 'the capital of Massachusetts'.

(7)–(10) are just as genuinely statements about 'Boston' as are (3)–(6), and omission of the quotation marks from (7)–(10) would give results no less objectionable than (2); for it is only

criticized for failure to enclose the whole statements (1)–(3) in quotation marks. But it is clearer to avoid quotation, in such cases, by agreeing to regard the colon as equivalent to quotation when followed by displayed text (text centered in a new line).

§ 4   USE VERSUS MENTION   25

expressions, not places, that can designate or be synonymous. A statement about an expression may depend for its verification upon considerations of sound or shape or literary locale, or even upon considerations of population or other extra-linguistic matters of fact with which the expression is indirectly connected by its use; but so long as the statement is about the expression it must contain a name of the expression.

Lack of care in thus distinguishing the name from the named is common in mathematical writings. The following passage, from a widely used textbook on the differential calculus, is fairly typical:

> The expression $D_x y \Delta x$ is called the *differential* of the function and is denoted by dy:
>
> $$dy = D_x y \Delta x.$$

The third line of this passage, an equation, is apparently supposed to reproduce the sense of the first two lines. But actually, whereas the equation says that the entities dy and $D_x y \Delta x$ (whatever these may be) are the same, the preceding two lines say rather that the one is a name of the other. And the first line of the passage involves further difficulties; taken literally it implies that the exhibited expression '$D_x y \Delta x$' constitutes a name of some other, unexhibited *expression* which is known as a differential. But all these difficulties can be removed by a slight rephrasing of the passage: drop the first two words and change 'and is denoted by' to 'or briefly'.

Expository confusions of this sort have persisted because, in most directions of mathematical inquiry, they have not made themselves felt as a practical obstacle. They do give rise to minor perplexities, indeed, even at the level of elementary arithmetic. A student of arithmetic may wonder, e.g., how 6 can be the denominator of $\frac{4}{6}$ and not of $\frac{2}{3}$ when $\frac{4}{6}$ is $\frac{2}{3}$; this puzzle arises from failure to observe that it is the *fractions* '$\frac{4}{6}$' and '$\frac{2}{3}$' that have denominators, whereas it is the designated *ratios* $\frac{4}{6}$ and $\frac{2}{3}$ that are identical. But it is primarily in mathematical logic that carelessness over these distinctions is found to have its more serious effects. At the level of the logic of statements, one effect is obliteration of the distinction between predicates of statements and

composition of statements — a distinction which will be considered in the next section.

Scrupulous use of quotation marks is the main practical measure
against confusing objects with their names.   But it has already
been suggested that this particular method of naming expressions
is not theoretically essential.   E.g., using elaborately descriptive
names of 'Boston', we might paraphrase (3) in either of the following ways:

> The word composed successively of the second, fifteenth,
> nineteenth, twentieth, fifteenth, and fourteenth letters of the
> alphabet is disyllabic.

> The 4354th word of *Chants Democratic* is disyllabic.

Quotation is the more graphic and convenient method, but it has
a certain anomalous feature which calls for special caution: from
the standpoint of logical analysis each whole quotation must be
regarded as a single word or sign, whose parts count for no more
than serifs or syllables.   A quotation is not a *description*, but a
hieroglyph; it designates its object not by describing it in terms of
other objects, but by picturing it.   The meaning of the whole does
not depend upon the meanings of the constituent words.   The
personal name buried within the first word of the statement.

> (11)   'Cicero' has six letters,

e.g., is logically no more germane to the statement than is the verb
'let' which is buried within the last word.   Otherwise, indeed, the
identity of Tully with Cicero would allow us to interchange these
personal names, in the context of quotation marks as in any other
context; we could thus argue from the truth (11) to the falsehood:

> 'Tully' has six letters.

Frege seems to have been the first logician to recognize the importance of scrupulous use of quotation marks for avoidance of confusion between use and mention
of expressions (cf. *Grundgesetze*, vol. 1, p. 4); but unfortunately his counsel and good
example in this regard went unheeded by other logicians for some thirty years.
For further discussion of this topic see Carnap, *Syntax*, pp. 153-160.   Concerning
the necessity of treating a whole quotation as a single sign, see also § 1 of Tarski's
"Wahrheitsbegriff".

2

Varieties of Use and Mention

NEWTON GARVER

Reprinted with the kind permission of the author and editor from *Philosophy and Phenomenological Research*, XXVI (1965).

VARIETIES OF USE AND MENTION

When a word is used in a straightforward way in a context where its employment is "ordinary," there is no problem about what it means or what it refers to; nor is there any question of the word itself being referred to. But on many occasions a word is not used in such a straightforward way, but to refer to itself. One common way of speaking of this distinction is as that between "use" and "mention." [1] This way of putting the matter has an intuitive appeal, and is undoubtedly useful in certain cases; but it can do more harm than good if taken as a panacaea for dealing with questions of use and mention.

One source of trouble is that the very statement of the distinction suggests that there are instances of "pure mention," where the ordinary use of the symbol mentioned is wholly irrelevant. This suggestion, which we might call the Postulate of Pure Mention, attractive because of the sharpness and simplicity is gives to the original distinction, challenges us to find instances of "pure" mention. The most plausible place to look is among the paradigms for the distinction between use and mention. Hence it seems reasonable to suppose that in the sentence " 'Cat' is a noun" the word 'cat' is *just* mentioned. If so, then it must be arbitrary, and dictated by convenience rather than necessity, that the word 'cat' appears as a part of the symbol

(1) 'cat'.

If a person is mentioned, for example, it is obvious that he need not be a part of the device used to mention him (though he may be, in conjunction with a gesture); nor need he even be a living human being. Similarly in the case of words, it cannot be necessary for the word itself to be part of the symbol used to mention it, if the instance is one of pure mention. Thus the inscription

(2) cat

cannot really be the word 'cat' when it occurs as a part of the symbol (1), if (1) is an instance of pure mention; it must rather be an arbitrary

---

[1] See for example W. V. O. Quine: *Mathematical Logic* (New York, 1940) #4, 6, or *Methods of Logic* (New York, 1959), pp. 37-38; L. Linsky: "On Using Inverted Commas," *Methodos* II (1950), pp. 232-236; A. Church: *Introduction to Mathematical Logic* (Princeton, 1956) #.08.

index, and the fact that it has the same shape as inscriptions of the *word* 'cat' cannot be essential to the way in which (2) serves as an index to show which word is mentioned when we use (1). The point is often put by saying that (1) is a "(proper) name" of the word 'cat'.

Followed out in this manner the Postulate of Pure Mention loses its plausibility. I cannot recognize (1) as denoting the word 'cat' unless I recognize (2) to be a word, and more particularly, to be that very word which is being mentioned; and then the ordinary use of (2) is not wholly irrelevant, for to recognize something as a word is to recognize that it has a regular use in a language. Therefore (1) must be some rather interesting *function* of (2) rather than a *name* of (2), if, as accords with usage, we mean by a "name" a symbol that can be recognized and understood without understanding or recognizing its parts. So (1) is not an instance of pure mention, and it begins to appear very doubtful indeed whether there are any such instances. Thus we must acknowledge that in the paradigms of mentioning the word mentioned is also in some way used — and that this fact in no way impugns the practical effectiveness of the use-mention distinction.

This intellectual snare was noticed some time ago by Wittgenstein:

> The arguments of functions are readily confused with the indices of names. For both arguments and indices enable me to recognize the meaning *Bedeutung* of the signs containing them. For example, when Russell writes '$+_c$', the '$_c$' is an index which indicates that the sign as a whole is the addition-sign for cardinal numbers. But the use of this sign is the result of arbitrary convention and it would be quite possible to choose a simple sign instead of '$+_c$'; in '$\sim p$', however, 'p' is not an index, but an argument: the sense of '$\sim p$' *cannot* be understood unless the sense of 'p' has been understood already.[2]

Wittgenstein points out that this consideration leads to a decisive criticism against Frege's theory of the *Bedeutung* of propositions and functions. Frege assimilates complex designations, such as definite descriptions, to simple ones, and thus he regards a proposition or a function-cum-argument as a name *(Eigenname)* and its distinctive constituent part as mere index. In the case of functions it is easy to see that such a view turns directly upon neglecting the distinction on which Wittgenstein insists. In the case of propositions Frege holds that the *Bedeutung* or reference of any proposition is either the True or the False, and that the propositional sign must therefore be a name *(Eigenname)* of either the True or the False, and as such a logically simple sign; whereas, as

---

[2] L. Wittgenstein: *Tractatus Logico-Philosophicus* (London, 1962), 5.02. Readers who want to look behind this cryptic statement may find it useful to consult M. Black: "Frege on Functions" in *Problems of Analysis* (Ithaca, 1954), pp. 229-254.

232   PHILOSOPHY AND PHENOMENOLOGICAL RESEARCH

Wittgenstein cryptically reminds us, I cannot understand a proposition or know its "*Bedeutung*" unless I first understand its parts.[3]

The Postulate of Pure Mention is in the same pickle as Frege's theory of the *Bedeutung* of propositions — as might be expected, since both conceptions grew historically from Frege's theory of sense and reference. The trouble, in Wittgenstein's terms, is that although what lies between the single quotes in the symbol we use when we mention a word is what enables us to recognize which word is being mentioned, nevertheless this identification is not accomplished in the manner in which an arbitrary index shows which individual is meant, but in the manner in which the argument of a function shows what the value of the function is in the instance at hand.[4]

A second source of trouble is that the use-mention distinction, once stated, comes to be regarded as exhaustive as well as exclusive. This view, which I shall call the Postulate of Comprehensiveness, receives its most serious challenge from a typical simple explanation of what a word means, such as might be conveyed by the meaning-statement

> (3) The meaning of 'courage' is — steadfastness in the face of danger.

For the phrase 'steadfastness in the face of danger' cannot be straightforwardly regarded as either used or mentioned in (3), and in certain respects it must be regarded as both.

Examination of an argument recently used by Professor William Alston will illustrate the difficulty.[5] Alston points out that a meaning-statement like (3) appears on the surface to express an identity, as do

> (4) The need of the moment is steadfastness in the face of danger.

and

> (5) The engineer of the Express is Svendsen.

He argues, however, that the similarity is only apparent, and that (3) does not express an identity. The decisive reason is that whereas whatever is true of one member of an identity must be true of the other,

---

[3] The view I have ascribed to Frege may not in fact have been held by Frege, although the elements of it certainly were held by him. For a critically sympathetic account of Frege's view, see Geach's essay on Frege in G. E. M. Anscombe and P. T. Geach: *Three Philosophers* (Oxford, 1961), esp. pp. 136-147. But in any event Wittgenstein must have read Frege as holding that view, or he would have lacked grounds for the criticism presented in *Tractatus* 5.02.

[4] G. E. M. Anscombe presents a powerful criticism of what I have called the Postulate of Pure Mention, also based on Wittgenstein's *Tractatus* and drawing in addition on some work of K. Reach (*Journal of Symbolic Logic*, vol. III, 1938), in *An Introduction to Wittgenstein's Tractatus* (London, 1959), pp. 82-85.

[5] W. P. Alston: "The Quest for Meanings," *Mind*, LXXII (1963), pp. 79-87.

this inference-possibility does not hold in the case of (3). For example, if (5) is true and Svendsen has a pretty wife, then the engineer of the Express must have a pretty wife. Similarly (4) and

(6) Steadfastness in the face of danger is a rare virtue.

entail

(7) The need of the moment is a rare virtue.

But to argue, from the grounds presented in (3) and (6), that

(8) The meaning of 'courage' is a rare virtue.

would be absurd. So the thesis that (3) is an identity statement is refuted by *reductio ad absurdum*.

This is an interesting argument, about which four things deserve to be said. The first is that when Alston uses the word 'meaning' he is referring to sense rather than to denotation or reference; for (8) would be true rather than absurd if we put 'denotation' for 'meaning'. I shall follow him in this use of the word 'meaning'.

The second point is that the argument has a compelling quality. Even if it proves wrong in some respect, it does at least demonstrate that the "deep grammar" or the "logic" of (3) is different from that of (4). This is a main point of Alston's paper, and in it he is surely correct.

The third point is that the argument is clearly fallacious. It presupposes that the phrase 'steadfastness in the face of danger' has the same mode of occurrence, or signifies in the same way, in both (3) and (4). If the mode of occurrence is not the same, then (since intuitively we can see that the phrase signifies in the same way in (4) and (6)) the inference to (8) is based on an equivocation between two senses presented by the same phrase, and the *reductio* fails. And in this crucial presupposition Alston is wrong, for the mode of occurrence of an expression in the predicate of a standard-form meaning-statement is radically different from the mode of its occurrence in other statements. The principal clue to this difference is the shift from the normal intonation pattern following the copula in (3), a shift which Alston and I have transcribed with a dash. The significance of the intonation shift can perhaps be seen more clearly in the case of a phrase which has a different grammatical function in its two occurrences, such as 'on time' in

(9) The express is on time.

and

(10) The meaning of 'punctual' is — on time.

The meaning of 'punctual' is certainly not being said to be among the things which are prompt or on schedule rather than dilatory or tardy. Indeed, the meaning of 'punctual' is not being qualified or described at all, for the intonation shift has transformed what is normally an adjectival or adverbial phrase into an expression that functions as a noun.

Thus there is a radical differences in the mode of occurrence of 'on time' in (9) and (10), and the change is one that is effected by the special intonation pattern characteristic of meaning-statements. Because of his equivocation between these two modes of occurence of a phrase, Alston's *reductio* fails.

The fourth point to be made is that the most plausible explanation for the fallacy is an acceptance, conscious or unconscious, of the Postulate of Comprehensiveness. The fallacy is an obvious one, and it was stumbled into by a man who is neither dull nor incompetent. Why? Well, if Alston assumed the Postulate of Comprehensiveness and asked whether the phrase 'on time' might be mentioned rather than used in (10), the answer, clear and quick, would be negative. If the phrase 'on time' were simply mentioned in (10), then the perspicuous way to transcribe the meaning-statement would be

(11) The meaning of 'punctual' is 'on time'.

and the meaning of the word 'punctual' would be a certain linguistic expression. This is absurd. Meanings are expressed by linguistic expressions; but whatever they are, they are not identical with linguistic expressions. Therefore (still assuming the Postulate of Comprehensiveness) the predicate phrases in (3) and (10) and other such meaning-statements must be used rather than mentioned.[6] And so the predicate phrases of (3) and (10) must be comparable in status with the predicate phrases of (4) and (9). In this manner adherence to the distinction between use and mention as simple and comprehensive nudges us into equivocating.[7]

A comparison of (9) and (10) shows that 'on time' is not simply used in the meaning-statement, and a comparison of (10) and (11) shows that

---

[6] They are of course "used" in some sense, though not in the sense intended in the "use-mention" distinction. Black presents similar considerations, and then concludes: "Since "mention" is opposed to "use," we must say that the accusative is used in a meaning formula, though in a peculiar way. . . ." (*Models and Metaphors*, Ithaca, 1962, p. 19). The point is sound enough. But we could equally start by contrasting such an accusative with a case where the same phrase is used in a straightforward manner, and conclude that we must say that the accusative is *mentioned* in a meaning formula, "though in a peculiar way."

[7] Although this is a most plausible explanation for such a fallacy, it may not be the correct one in Alston's case. The contrary evidence is that in another recent article ("Meaning and Use", *Philosophical Quarterly*, Vol. XIII, 1963, pp. 107-124) Alston explicitly rejects the Postulate of Comprehensiveness and points out that the phrase in the accusative of a meaning-statement is neither used nor mentioned "in the ordinary way" (p. 111n). But if Alston had these distinctions in mind when he wrote "The Quest for Meanings" he would have known his *reductio* was fallacious, and it is beyond belief that he would knowingly rely on a fallacious argument.

VARIETIES OF USE AND MENTION   235

it is not simply mentioned either. Existing notations are too poor to allow us to represent its mode of occurrence perspicuously. In (10) what we hold up to view in the predicate of the statement is not the string of words 'on time' but the meaning of that string of words — or a meaning of them, which they have in many common contexts. The trouble with single quotes is that they enable us to refer to words, whereas we wish to refer to meanings of words.[8] Let us therefore invent a notation, using double slanting lines, which will enable us to refer to meanings:

> Whenever X is a linguistic expression of a sort that can be said to have a meaning, the statement expressed by the formula 'The meaning of X is //X//' is trivially true.
>
> Whenever X and Y are linguistic expressions of a sort that can be said to have a meaning, the statement expressed by the formula 'The meaning of X is //Y//' is true if X and Y have the same meaning.

Then the meaning-statement we intended to transcribe by (3) will be written either as

> (3a) The meaning of 'courage' is //'steadfastness in the face of danger'//.

or as

> (3b) The meaning of 'courage' is //steadfastness in the face of danger//.

Of these alternatives, it will immediately be seen that (3b) will not do, since steadfastness in the face of danger is a virtue rather than a linguistic expression. Thus we have a convention which allows us to transcribe the mode of occurrence of the predicate phrase of a meaning-statement, and which suggests, appropriately, that such a use is built upon, or is a function of, the case where words refer to themselves and are transcribed in single quotes.

Using this new notation, we can say that the trouble with Alston's *reductio ad absurdum* is that it depends upon taking the phrase 'steadfastness in the face of danger' to be unambiguous, whereas in the course of the argument this phrase is used at one time to refer to //'steadfastness in the face of danger'// and at another time to refer to a certain virtue.

Alston is by no means alone in falling prey to this fallacy. I have heard Wittgenstein rebutted as follows:

---

[8] Russell apparently wishes to use single quotes when he is referring to the meanings of the quoted words; but this is both unconventional and inconvenient. See below; see also Searle's comments, cited in note 9.

> A moment's reflection shows that the meaning of an expression is not the same as its use. (See Wittgenstein: *Philosophical Investigations*, I. 43) The meaning of 'obfuscate' is to confuse, but we cannot say truly the use of 'obfuscate' is to confuse.

A second moment's reflection uncovers the fallacy in this "refutation." The propositions we must consider are:

    (12) The meaning of 'obfuscate' is to confuse.

    (12a) The meaning of 'obfuscate' is //'to confuse'//.

    (13) The use of 'obfuscate' is to confuse.

    (13a) The use of 'obfuscate' is //'to confuse'//.

(12) is nonsense, assuming that the infinitive is supposed to have some straightforward use. The meaning-statement which is presumably intended by (12) is correctly transcribed by (12a). What we cannot say in general is (13); although it may be true on some occasions, as a generalization it is patently false. (13a), on the other hand, has a good deal of plausibility as a general statement; if it is wrong, it is at any rate not *obviously* wrong. If its premises are to be clearly true, the argument against Wittgenstein must therefore use first (12a) and then (13), and consequently it is equivocal.

Alston has also the distinguished company of Bertrand Russell, whose argument against the adequacy of Frege's conception of meaning *(Sinn)* and denotation *(Bedeutung)* contains a similar equivocation.[9] The root of the problem is again a paucity of distinctions. Russell begins by introducing an unusual quoting convention: "When we wish to speak about the *meaning* of a denoting phrase, as opposed to its *denotation*, the natural mode of doing so is by inverted commas" (p. 48). Russell gives two examples of this convention — unfortunately ambiguous ones — and then states his problem:

> Thus taking any denoting phrase, say C, we wish to consider the relation between C and 'C', where the difference of the two is of the kind exemplified in the above two instances (p. 49).

At this point there are two difficulties: (1) so far as the examples go, the difference in question could, in our notation, be that between C and

---

[9] B. Russell: "On Denoting," in *Logic and Knowledge* (ed. R. C. Marsh, London, 1956), pp. 41-56, esp. pp. 48-51. There have been several able comments on the argument recently, and all agree that the position which Russell attacks was not really Frege's. See R. J. Butler: "The Scaffolding of Russell's Theory of Descriptions," *Philosophical Review*, LXIII (1954), pp. 350-364; J. R. Searle: "Russell's Objections to Frege's Theory of Sense and Reference," *Analysis*, XVIII (1958), pp. 137-143; P. T. Geach: "Russell on Meaning and Denoting," *Analysis*, XIX (1959), pp. 69-72; and R. Jager: "Russell's Denoting Complex," *Analysis*, XX (1960), pp. 53-62.

'C', that between C and //C//, or that between C and //'C'//; and (2) it is not clear whether the symbol 'C' is meant to be a name, an abbreviation, or the meaning of the denoting phrase in question. To provide the necessary distinctions, let us introduce the following abbreviations to replace the two symbols in terms of which Russell states his problem:

    'A' for 'the first line of Grey's *Elegy*'
    'B' for ' 'the first line of Grey's Elegy' '
    'D' for '//the first line of Grey's *Elegy*//'
    'E' for '//'the first line of Grey's *Elegy*'//'

A is thus a line of poetry, B is a denoting phrase whose denotation is A, and both are linguistic expressions whose meanings are respectively D and E.

If Russell is using his symbol 'C' consistently, he must mean to discuss either the relation between A and D or the relation between B and E, but for lack of the necessary distinctions he is forced to stir the matters together in the same pot. The crux of his argument runs:

> The one phrase C was to have both meaning and denotation. But if we speak of 'the meaning of C', that gives us the meaning (if any) of the denotation. 'The meaning of the first line of Grey's *Elegy*' is the same as 'The meaning of "The curfew tolls the knell of parting day" ', and is not the same as 'The meaning of "the first line of Grey's *Elegy*" '. Thus in order to get the meaning we want, we must not speak of 'the meaning of C', but of 'the meaning of "C" ', which is the same as 'C' by itself. Similarly, 'the denotation of C' does not mean the denotation we want, but means something which, if it denotes at all, denotes what is denoted by the denotation we want (p. 49).

He elaborates on these difficulties, and then concludes:

> This is an inextricable tangle, and seems to prove that the whole distinction between meaning and denotation has been wrongly conceived (p. 50).

There can be no doubt about the tangle, but Russell is wrong about what it proves. The tangle is of his making rather than Frege's, for his argument cannot be plausibly restated. If we take C = A, the first sentence of Russell's argument makes little sense, and the whole argument has no bearing on the issue at hand, namely whether the distinction between meaning and denotation can be applied to denoting phrases. Since B is a denoting phrase and A is not, Russell must have intended C = B. But if we take C = B, the second sentence and the fifth are both patently false. On either interpretation the fourth sentence is a howler, since Russell uses inverted commas in two ways, first to refer to the symbol itself and then to refer to the meaning of the symbol. In any case the tangle is easily avoided, so long as we are provided with a means for mentioning separately both a phrase and its meaning.

The Postulate of Pure Mention, the Postulate of Comprehensiveness,

238   PHILOSOPHY AND PHENOMENOLOGICAL RESEARCH

and Russell's unusual quoting convention all treat the use-mention distinction as sharp and simple, and they all founder. The moral to be drawn is that the distinction, considered generally, is neither exclusive nor exhaustive, and that there are varieties of mention just as there are varieties of use. These considerations do not, of course, call for abandoning the use-mention distinction, but rather for paying more attention to varieties of use and mention, so that use of the distinction can be more effective and its misuse eschewed.[10]

NEWTON GARVER.

STATE UNIVERSITY OF NEW YORK AT BUFFALO.

---

[10] The notation using double slanting lines is adapted from one discussed in a seminar of Max Black's in 1956-57 at Cornell University and recorded in the mimeographed reports of that seminar; its employment in analyzing Russell's argument stems from the same source. I have beneifted from comments made on this paper by W. T. Parry and William Baumer.

3

On Using Inverted Commas

LEONARD LINSKY

Reprinted with the kind permission of the author and editor from *Methodos,* II (1950), 232-36.

232   [II, 6-7

ON USING INVERTED COMMAS (*)

LEONARD LINSKY

Department of Philosophy
University of Wisconsin
Madison 6, Wisconsin (U.S.A.)

[Received on May 22nd, 1950

I

The purposes of this note are to point out some apparent confusions in the use of inverted commas in referring to linguistic expressions, and to suggest a convention restricting the use of this device. Adherence to the proposed convention would result in considerably greater clarity of expression although the restriction which it imposes is, we believe, not an onerous one.

In the following it will be necessary to distinguish between sign-events and sign-designs ([1]). The only sign-events which will be relevant will be printed (or written) expressions, and a sign-design is a maximal class of similar sign-events. We shall not be concerned with the analysis of the relation of similarity just referred to, since the points to be discussed do not depend on this. For convenience the reader may think of printed expressions as sign-events and, for the relation of similiarity, have in mind some close approximation to geometrical congruence.

In writing about a sign-event one ordinarily uses a second sign-event either as a name or as a description of the first. In order to form a name, *in situ*, of a sign-event Reichenbach ([2]) has introduced

---

*) I would like to express my thanks to Professor H. E. Vaughan of the Department of Mathematics, University of Illinois, for the help which he gave me in the writing of this paper. He is not, however, to be held responsible for anything which is said here.

This paper was read at the annual meetings of the Western Division of the American Philosophical Association, May 4, 5, 6, 1950, Minneapolis, Minnesota.

[1]) We here use Carnap's terminology; see: *Introduction to Semantics*, p. 5.
[2]) *Elements of Symbolic Logic*, p. 284.

token-quotes. For example,

(1): ⌐ of ⌐ is a word-event

expresses a fact concerning the sign-event enclosed by the little arrows. (Consequently the corresponding sentence-events in two copies of this note express different facts). Token-quotes cannot be used in expressing the fact which is expressed by

(2): The sign-event composed of the twelfth and thirteenth letter-events occurring in this note is a word-event.

Now consider

(3): ' of ' is a word-event.

We propose to interpret (3) as a universal sentence-event of which (1) and (2) are instances. Thus the initial word-event of (3) is to be construed as what is sometimes called an ambiguous name, and (3) as equivalent in meaning with:

Every ' of ' is a word-event.

(That (3), when so interpreted, turns out to be false is, of course, irrelevant.) This interpretation of quoted sign-events also allows us to paraphrase (2) by:

The first ' of ' which occurs in this note is a word-event.

The proposed convention is then:

(A) *An expression obtained by enclosing a sign-event in inverted commas is a word-event which refers ambiguously to the membership of the sign design to which the sign-event belongs* ([3]).

We shall later need a third device for constructing names of signs-designs. For this purpose dots will be used to enclose an event of the design which we desire to name. We shall, for example, use sign-events similar to ⌐ • of • ⌐ as names for the sign-design of which any ' of ' is a member.

---

[3] If the language in which inverted commas are to be used also uses variables (A) might be replaced by the more precise statement: *An expression obtained by enclosing a sign-event in inverted commas is a variable-event whose range is the sign-design to which the sign-event belongs.* In such a case (3) might be translated (using the universal quantifier): (' of ') (' of ' is a word-event). Thus our proposal seems to be in accordance with Reichenbach's proposal. He says, "...ordinary quotes should be interpreted as variable-quotes of a restricted range of substitution ". (See his discussion, *op. cit.*, p. 14).

II

In order to justify our adherence to convention A) we will now attempt to show that while in *discussing* the use of inverted commas some logicians appear to adhere to other conventions; nevertheless the meanings which they seem to wish to express in contexts in which thay *use* them usually requires adherence to convention (*A*).

First let us turn to Carnap's discussion of this matter ([4]). His argument may be paraphrased as follows. Referring to a sign-event of the same sign-design as ⅄ signs ⅄ , Carnap says

(4): There are two letters ' s ' in the eighth word of this paragraph.

(5): The letter ' s ' occurs twice in the word ' signs '.

Now, Carnap argues, sentence (4) implies that there are at least two letters ' s ', while sentence (5) implies that there is at least and at most only one letter ' s '. Thus if we hold both of these sentences to be true, we must maintain that the phrase " letter ' s ' " has a different meaning in each of them.

Carnap gives the following explication of the two meanings involved: " In (4), a letter is a single thing or event, e.g. a body consisting of printer's ink or a sound event; therefore, it is at a certain time-moment or during a certain time-interval, and at each time-moment within its duration it occupies a certain place. In (5), on the other hand, a letter is not a single thing but a class of things to which many things may belong, e.g. the letter ' s ' is that class of written or printed marks to which all lower case S's belong " ([5]). By way of further explication of this ambiguity in the meaning of expressions enclosed in inverted commas, Carnap writes, "In an expression-event all elements are different... there is no repetition of sign-events, because an event... can only be at one place at a time. On the other hand, in an expression-design a certain sign-design may occupy several positions; in this case we speak of the several *occurrence* of the sign-(design) within the expression (-design) " ([6]).

Now, a sign-design is a class. What, therefore, can it mean to say that a given sign-design may occupy a position (or several positions) in another sign-design? What is a position in a class? It

[4]) *op. cit.*, pp. 5-8.
[5]) *op. cit.*, p. 6.
[6]) *op. cit.*, p. 7.

seems to us that a clear formulation of what Carnap desires to say can be made in accordance with our convention (*A*). In accordance with convention (*A*), expressions enclosed in inverted commas are not ambiguous in meaning in the way that Carnap says they are in his discussion of " letter ' s ' ". Thus on our view Carnap's sentence (4) says of a particular sign-event similar to ⌐ signs ⌐ , that it contains two events which are members of the same design as ⌐ s ⌐ .   Sentence (5), on the other hand, is a universal sentence which says that every event similar to the event which appears between inverted commas at its very end, contains two events which are similar to the event which occurs between inverted commas near its beginning.   On our view, therefore, the only ambiguity associated with expressions in inverted commas is that of a variable which ambiguously denotes over a certain class (range of significance).

At this point the objection might be raised that our convention does not enable us to use expressions in inverted commas to name sign-designs as, for example, Carnap seems to desire to do.   It is true that our convention excludes this use of inverted commas. We do not, however, feel that this restriction is a serious objection to our convention, since we rarely desire to talk about sign-designs anyway.   Examples of sentences in which sign-designs are mentioned are:

(6): • of • is a sign-design,

and

(7): • of • is different from • sit •.

Notice, however, that

(8): • of • consists of two letters,

is nonsense.   Our contention is that though Carnap seems to treat expressions such as (8) as significant (as, for example, in his discussion of (5) above), the meaning which is actually intended requires no use of names for sign-designs and can be rendered by the use of inverted commas in their unambiguous meaning as proposed in (*A*).

Quine offers us another example of a logician who sometimes speaks as though he adhered to some other convention than our (*A*). In his discussion of the use of inverted commas he says, " The name of a name or other expression is commonly formed by putting the named expression in single quotation marks; the whole, called a *quotation*, denotes its interior '' ([7]).   But the interior of such a whole as Quine is speaking of is a sign-event. Thus the convention expressed by Quine for the use of inverted commas seems to be in accordance with Reichenbach's convention for token-quotes rather than our convention (*A*).   That Quine's *use* of inverted commas is in accordance with our proposal rather than the one quoted above is seen by an examination of Quine's examples:

' Boston is populous ' is about Boston and contains ' Boston '
" Boston " designates ' Boston '
' Boston ' occurs in Walt Whitman's *Chants Democratic.*

The above sentences are taken by Quine as true ([8]).   But if a quotation denotes its interior, then each of them is false.   (For example, the event which is the interior of the quotation in the third sentence above, does not occur in Whitman's *Chants Democratic.*)   By our proposal (*A*), on the contrary, each of the above three sentences is true as Quine wants them to be.

Consider the first of these.   On our view it is a sentence which asserts that every sign-event of the same design as the one which appears between the first pair of inverted commas is about the city of Boston, and contains as a part, a sign-event of the same design as the event which appears between the last pair of inverted commas.   Using bound variables whose ranges of significance are the last mentioned sign-designs (see footnote ([3])), we may represent the meaning of this sentence as follows:

(' Boston is populous ') (∃ ' Boston ') (' Boston is populous ' is about Boston and contains ' Boston ').

The second of Quine's sentences may be translated as a doubly universally quantified sentence:

(" Boston ") (' Boston ') (" Boston " designates ' Boston ').

In order to translate the third of Quine's sentences we shall introduce ' *X* ' as a variable whose range of significance is the class of all copies of Whitman's *Chants Democratic.*   The sentence then becomes:

(*X*) (∃ ' Boston ') (' Boston ' occurs in *X*).

---

[7]) *Mathematical Logic*, p. 23.
[8]) *op. cit.*, p 24.

II

MEANING AND REFERENCE

INTRODUCTION

The selections in this part are arranged in order of publication. The advanced student, already to some degree acquainted with the philosophical issues connected with the discussions of meaning and reference, will profit from reading the selections in the order in which they are presented. The editors are not suggesting that later stages in this unfolding debate are more nearly correct than earlier ones. The last word is not necessarily the best word; an argument's soundness is not determined by its historical location in a continuing philosophical discussion. But by the same token our understanding of the issues, and an appreciation of the philosophical problems and perplexities connected with meaning and reference, can be materially assisted by an understanding of the historical development of the discussion about them. This is particularly true in the case at hand, where explicit reference is made in later papers to positions defended in the earlier ones. One final comment of a historical nature may be called for. It is interesting to note that this tightly focused discussion of meaning and reference covers the broadest span of time of any topic in this volume. Frege's paper, "On Sense and Reference," was first published in 1892, and Russell published a reply to Strawson in 1959.

The student coming to this material for the first time is strongly urged, however, to begin his reading with Gilbert Ryle's paper, "The Theory of Meaning." Ryle presents an admirably clear summary and overview of the problems which gave rise to the discussions of the first four papers. His article serves not only as an introduction to the topic of this chapter, but as a bridge to Chapter 4, "Meaning and Use," as well.

There is certainly not much that the editors need add to Ryle's article by way of introduction to this chapter. He points out that most of the problems connected with the theory of meaning arise from holding a quite natural and cosily naive view about words and their meanings. Put most crudely, it is the view that nearly all words are names and that all names are proper names, or mean the way proper names mean. Thus the meaning of a word is the object, event, or state of affairs it names, denotes, or refers to. The problem that forces itself upon us now is that there are many words or expressions which have meaning, which add to or alter the meanings of sentences in which they occur, but which have no attached objects. 'Other' is a significant word in English, yet there is not, obviously at least, any object denoted by it which could be its meaning. Our puzzlement may grow greater still when we consider such expressions as 'the round square' or 'the present king of France' functioning as the grammatical subjects of sentences. 'The round square does not exist' is a true sentence. But if true, then there is no round square to be denoted, and if there is nothing denoted by the expression, then the sentence is meaningless. Or we must assert that round squares, while not real, still somehow subsist.

In response to difficulties of this nature, Russell, as Ryle says,

> ... found himself forced to say of some expressions which had previously been supposed to name or denote that they had to be given exceptional treatment. They were not names but what he called 'incomplete symbols,' expressions, that is, which have no meaning in the sense of denotation by themselves; their business was to be auxiliary to expressions which do, as a whole, denote.[1]

Before Russell both Meinong and Frege had recognized the problems presented by such denoting phrases as 'the present king of France' or 'the round square.' Meinong's view was that such phrases have meanings, that the meanings are objects denoted by the phrases, but that the objects do not exist in the ordinary way that tables and chairs do. This view Russell found intolerable on the grounds that such strange objects do not seem to obey the law of contradiction. When I say, 'The round square does not exist,' I seem to be saying both that it does and that it doesn't. Frege's distinction between sense and reference (which in his own article Russell translates as meaning and denotation, respectively) is extremely important in that it recognizes

---

[1] Gilbert Ryle, "The Theory of Meaning," in *British Philosophy in the Mid-Century,* ed. C. A. Mace (London: Allen and Unwin, 1957), 253.

a greater range of meaning for 'meaning' than simply denotation. A denoting phrase will be said to express a meaning, while both phrase and meaning will be said to denote a denotation. The advantage here is that this enables us to make sense of the fact that expressions like 'the evening star' and 'the morning star' have different meanings, even though they denote the same object — in this case, the planet Venus. Further, sentences like 'The present King of France is bald' are not made meaningless by virtue of the fact that there is no present king of France to be denoted. Where denoting phrases lack a denotation, as in the case of 'the round square,' one is provided for them by definition in the form of the null class. Russell's objection to this is that although it avoids violation of the law of contradiction, as he believed Meinong's account did not, it is at best artificial. At worst, it does not really provide a proper analysis of the meaning of denoting phrases and the sentences in which they occur.

Russell's advance on the views of Meinong and Frege is contained in the extremely important essay, "On Denoting." Russell has called this his finest philosophical essay. Five years after the publication of "On Denoting," the theory put forward in it, the full statement of which is the well-known theory of descriptions, was published in *Principia Mathematica*.

This essay, and the following one by P. F. Strawson, may well be the pivotal papers around which the entire discussion of meaning and reference revolves. It would be out of place for the editors to offer a detailed summary of these two papers here, because they speak for themselves. At the same time, it will perhaps be a help to the student approaching this material for the first time if something is said about the strategy of Russell's argument, and about the main thrust of Strawson's critique.

To begin with, Russell defines the expression 'denoting phrase.' Phrases like 'the fiftieth president of the United States,' 'the round square,' 'a man,' 'some man,' etc., are all denoting phrases. Phrases of this sort are titled 'denoting phrases' not by virtue of any denotation they have or might have, but solely by virtue of their form. Such phrases may not, indeed, have any denotation at all, as the phrase 'the round square' does not. Next, such phrases do not in and of themselves have any meaning. They are not the names of anything; they do not denote. As Ryle says in the passage quoted earlier, "Their business was to be auxiliary to expressions which do, as a whole, denote." Essentially, if crudely, such phrases have work to do in sentences expressing propositions. But although they are the grammatical subjects of certain sentences, they are not, as it were, the logical subjects of the propositions the sentences express; they are not constituents of any sort of the propositions. The strategy behind the denial that they are constituents can be shown fairly easily. Consider the phrase 'the round square' as it occurs in the sentence, 'The round square does not exist.' Now suppose that the phrase 'the round square' is a constituent of the proposition *The round square does not exist.* We are now faced with a dilemma; we can say neither that it denotes nor that it doesn't. If we say that it does *not* denote, then the proposition seems to become meaningless because we have deprived one of its constituents of meaning. But, on the other hand, if we assert that the phrase 'the round square' *has* meaning, then we seem to be guilty of a violation of the principle of contradiction when we assert that the round square does not exist. There must be something which is round and square to be denoted by the phrase if it is to have meaning. One alternative is not open to Russell. He could not hold that the phrase has meaning and at the same time assert that there is no equivalent to it in the proposition expressed by the sentence containing the phrase. In that case there would be some additional meaning in the sentence which was not in the proposition it expressed. Hence Russell claims that denoting phrases have a grammatical function in sentences, but that they have no meaning in themselves and are not constituents of the propositions that such sentences express. In order to make good on this view, Russell must now show that he can offer "a reduction of all propositions in which denoting phrases occur to forms in which no such phrases occur."[2] "On Denoting" is concerned with the pattern of this reduction and the illustration of its ability to deal with certain key logical puzzles.

P. F. Strawson's analysis and criticism of Russell, and the development of the consequences of his own view, form a long and intricately detailed piece of philosophical writing. It has been the occasion of considerable discussion and debate and deserves the reader's most careful attention. Whether Strawson's criticisms are well founded and, indeed, whether he has understood the main thrust of Russell's theory

---

[2] Bertrand Russell, "On Denoting," in *Logic and Knowledge,* ed. R. C. Marsh (New York: Macmillan, 1956), 45.

are issues upon which the editors reserve judgment for others. The core of Strawson's argument is an attack on the very heart of a theory of meaning which he takes to underlie Russell's views. Strawson's understanding of the matter seems to be roughly as follows.

Russell noted that certain sentences occur which have denoting phrases like 'the present king of France' as their grammatical subjects. But the logical subjects of propositions expressed by those sentences cannot (for whatever reasons) be taken to be the grammatical subjects of the sentences. "To exhibit the logical form of the proposition, we should re-write the sentence in a logically appropriate grammatical form."[3] This program seems to imply that sentences containing denoting phrases like 'the present king of France,' which are grammatically of the subject-predicate form and where the subject fails of denotation, must be either meaningless or not logically of the subject-predicate form at all. This in turn would seem to suggest that there are at least some sentences which *are* both grammatically and logically of the subject-predicate form. The subjects of such sentences are what Russell calls logically proper names, and the meaning of such a name is the thing it designates, or denotes, or refers to. Strawson is at pains to deny this thesis. This denial amounts to a rejection of the denotationist or reference theory of meaning; it is at the heart of the attempt to treat meaning as a function of the way words and sentences are used to refer, rather than as a function of the things they are used to refer to.

The relation of meaning and use is the topic of Part IV of this collection of readings.

SELECTED READINGS

ON STRAWSON

Sellars, Wilfrid. "Presupposing." *Philosophical Review,* LXIII, 2 (Whole no. 366), 197-215.
Strawson, P. F. "A Reply to Mr. Sellars." *Philosophical Review,* LXIII, 2 (Whole no. 366), 216-31.

ON RUSSELL

Cartwright, R. L. "Negative Existentials." *Journal of Philosophy,* LVII (1960), 629-39. Reprinted in *Philosophy and Ordinary Language,* ed. Charles E. Caton. Urbana: University of Illinois Press, 1963, 55-66.

[3] P. F. Strawson, "On Referring," in *Essays in Conceptual Analysis,* ed. A. Flew (New York: Macmillan, 1956), 24.

IN GENERAL

Caton, Charles E. "Strawson on Referring." *Mind*, LXVIII (1959), 539-44.
Fitch, Frederick B. "Some Logical Aspects of Reference and Existence." *Journal of Philosophy*, LVII (1960), 640-47.
Linsky; Leonard. "Reference and Referents." In *Philosophy and Ordinary Language*, ed. Charles E. Caton. Urbana: University of Illinois Press, 1963, 74-89.
Russell, Bertrand. "Mr. Strawson on Referring." *Mind,* LXVI (1957), 385-89.

ON FREGE AND RUSSELL

Mace, Cecil Alec, ed. *British Philosophy in the Mid-Century.* London: Allen and Unwin, 1957.
Searle, J. R. "Russell's Objections to Frege's Theory of Sense and Reference." *Analysis,* XVIII (1957-58), 137-43.

1

On Sense and Reference

GOTTLOB FREGE

Reprinted with the kind permission of the publisher from Geach and Black, eds., *Philosophical Writings of Gottlob Frege* (Oxford: Basil Blackwell, 1960), 56-78.

ON SENSE AND REFERENCE

First published in *Zeitschrift für Philosophie und philosophische Kritik*, vol. 100 (1892), pp. 25–50

25] EQUALITY* gives rise to challenging questions which are not altogether easy to answer. Is it a relation? A relation between objects, or between names or signs of objects? In my *Begriffsschrift*ᴬ I assumed the latter. The reasons which seem to favour this are the following: $a=a$ and $a=b$ are obviously statements of differing cognitive value; $a=a$ holds *a priori* and, according to Kant, is to be labelled analytic, while statements of the form $a=b$ often contain very valuable extensions of our knowledge and cannot always be established *a priori*. The discovery that the rising sun is not new every morning, but always the same, was one of the most fertile astronomical discoveries. Even to-day the identification of a small planet or a comet is not always a 26] matter of course. Now if we were to regard equality as a relation between that which the names 'a' and 'b' designate, it would seem that $a=b$ could not differ from $a=a$ (i.e. provided $a=b$ is true). A relation would thereby be expressed of a thing to itself, and indeed one in which each thing stands to itself but to no other thing. What is intended to be said by $a=b$ seems to be that the signs or names 'a' and 'b' designate the same thing, so that those signs themselves would be under discussion; a relation between them would be asserted. But this relation would hold between the names or signs only in so far as they named or designated something. It would be mediated by the connexion of each of the two signs with

---

* I use this word in the sense of identity and understand '$a = b$' to have the sense of 'a is the same as b' or 'a and b coincide.'

ᴬ The reference is to Frege's *Begriffsschrift, eine der arithmetischen nachgebildete Formelsprache des reinen Denkens* (Halle, 1879).

ON SENSE AND REFERENCE 57

the same designated thing. But this is arbitrary. Nobody can be forbidden to use any arbitrarily producible event or object as a sign for something. In that case the sentence $a=b$ would no longer refer to the subject matter, but only to its mode of designation; we would express no proper knowledge by its means. But in many cases this is just what we want to do. If the sign 'a' is distinguished from the sign 'b' only as object (here, by means of its shape), not as sign (i.e. not by the manner in which it designates something), the cognitive value of $a=a$ becomes essentially equal to that of $a=b$, provided $a=b$ is true. A difference can arise only if the difference between the signs corresponds to a difference in the mode of presentation of that which is designated. Let a, b, c be the lines connecting the vertices of a triangle with the midpoints of the opposite sides. The point of intersection of a and b is then the same as the point of intersection of b and c. So we have different designations for the same point, and these names ('point of intersection of a and b,' 'point of intersection of b and c') likewise indicate the mode of presentation; and hence the statement contains actual knowledge.

It is natural, now, to think of there being connected with a sign (name, combination of words, letter), besides that to which the sign refers, which may be called the reference of the sign, also what I should like to call the *sense* of the sign, wherein the mode of presentation is contained. In our example, accordingly, the 27] reference of the expressions 'the point of intersection of a and b' and 'the point of intersection of b and c' would be the same, but not their senses. The reference of 'evening star' would be the same as that of 'morning star,' but not the sense.

It is clear from the context that by 'sign' and 'name' I have here understood any designation representing a proper name, which thus has as its reference a definite object (this word taken in the widest range), but not a concept or a relation, which shall be discussed further in another article.[B] The designation of a single object can also consist of several words or other signs. For brevity, let every such designation be called a proper name.

The sense of a proper name is grasped by everybody who is sufficiently familiar with the language or totality of designations

---

[B] See his 'Ueber Begriff und Gegenstand' (*Vierteljahrsschrift für wissenschaftliche Philosophie* XVI [1892], 192–205).

to which it belongs;* but this serves to illuminate only a single aspect of the reference, supposing it to have one. Comprehensive knowledge of the reference would require us to be able to say immediately whether any given sense belongs to it. To such knowledge we never attain.

The regular connexion between a sign, its sense, and its reference is of such a kind that to the sign there corresponds a definite sense and to that in turn a definite reference, while to a given reference (an object) there does not belong only a single sign. The same sense has different expressions in different languages or even in the same language. To be sure, exceptions to this regular behaviour occur. To every expression belonging to a complete totality of signs, there should certainly correspond 28] a definite sense; but natural languages often do not satisfy this condition, and one must be content if the same word has the same sense in the same context. It may perhaps be granted that every grammatically well-formed expression representing a proper name always has a sense. But this is not to say that to the sense there also corresponds a reference. The words 'the celestial body most distant from the Earth' have a sense, but it is very doubtful if they also have a reference. The expression 'the least rapidly convergent series' has a sense but demonstrably has no reference, since for every given convergent series, another convergent, but less rapidly convergent, series can be found. In grasping a sense, one is not certainly assured of a reference.

If words are used in the ordinary way, what one intends to speak of is their reference. It can also happen, however, that one wishes to talk about the words themselves or their sense. This happens, for instance, when the words of another are quoted. One's own words then first designate words of the other speaker, and only the latter have their usual reference. We then have signs of signs. In writing, the words are in this case enclosed in quotation marks. Accordingly, a word standing between

* In the case of an actual proper name such as 'Aristotle' opinions as to the sense may differ. It might, for instance, be taken to be the following: the pupil of Plato and teacher of Alexander the Great. Anybody who does this will attach another sense to the sentence 'Aristotle was born in Stagira' than will a man who takes as the sense of the name: the teacher of Alexander the Great who was born in Stagira. So long as the reference remains the same, such variations of sense may be tolerated, although they are to be avoided in the theoretical structure of a demonstrative science and ought not to occur in a perfect language.

ON SENSE AND REFERENCE   59

quotation marks must not be taken as having its ordinary reference.

In order to speak of the sense of an expression 'A' one may simply use the phrase 'the sense of the expression "A"'. In reported speech one talks about the sense, e.g., of another person's remarks. It is quite clear that in this way of speaking words do not have their customary reference but designate what is usually their sense. In order to have a short expression, we will say: In reported speech, words are used *indirectly* or have their *indirect* reference. We distinguish accordingly the *customary* from the *indirect* reference of a word; and its *customary* sense from its *indirect* sense. The indirect reference of a word is accordingly its customary sense. Such exceptions must always be borne in mind if the mode of connexion between sign, sense, and reference in particular cases is to be correctly understood.

29] The reference and sense of a sign are to be distinguished from the associated idea. If the reference of a sign is an object perceivable by the senses, my idea of it is an internal image,* arising from memories of sense impressions which I have had and acts, both internal and external, which I have performed. Such an idea is often saturated with feeling; the clarity of its separate parts varies and oscillates. The same sense is not always connected, even in the same man, with the same idea. The idea is subjective: one man's idea is not that of another. There result, as a matter of course, a variety of differences in the ideas associated with the same sense. A painter, a horseman, and a zoologist will probably connect different ideas with the name 'Bucephalus.' This constitutes an essential distinction between the idea and the sign's sense, which may be the common property of many and therefore is not a part or a mode of the individual mind. For one can hardly deny that mankind has a common store of thoughts which is transmitted from one generation to another.†

---

* We can include with ideas the direct experiences in which sense-impressions and acts themselves take the place of the traces which they have left in the mind. The distinction is unimportant for our purpose, especially since memories of sense-impressions and acts always go along with such impressions and acts themselves to complete the perceptual image. One may on the other hand understand direct experience as including any object, in so far as it is sensibly perceptible or spatial.

† Hence it is inadvisable to use the word 'idea' to designate something so basically different.

In the light of this, one need have no scruples in speaking simply of *the* sense, whereas in the case of an idea one must, strictly speaking, add to whom it belongs and at what time. It might perhaps be said: Just as one man connects this idea, and another that idea, with the same word, so also one man can associate this sense and another that sense. But there still remains a difference in the mode of connexion. They are not prevented from grasping the same sense; but they cannot have the same 30] idea. *Si duo idem faciunt, non est idem.* If two persons picture the same thing, each still has his own idea. It is indeed sometimes possible to establish differences in the ideas, or even in the sensations, of different men; but an exact comparison is not possible, because we cannot have both ideas together in the same consciousness.

The reference of a proper name is the object itself which we designate by its means; the idea, which we have in that case, is wholly subjective; in between lies the sense, which is indeed no longer subjective like the idea, but is yet not the object itself. The following analogy will perhaps clarify these relationships. Somebody observes the Moon through a telescope. I compare the Moon itself to the reference; it is the object of the observation, mediated by the real image projected by the object glass in the interior of the telescope, and by the retinal image of the observer. The former I compare to the sense, the latter is like the idea or experience. The optical image in the telescope is indeed one-sided and dependent upon the standpoint of observation; but it is still objective, inasmuch as it can be used by several observers. At any rate it could be arranged for several to use it simultaneously. But each one would have his own retinal image. On account of the diverse shapes of the observers' eyes, even a geometrical congruence could hardly be achieved, and an actual coincidence would be out of the question. This analogy might be developed still further, by assuming A's retinal image made visible to B; or A might also see his own retinal image in a mirror. In this way we might perhaps show how an idea can itself be taken as an object, but as such is not for the observer what it directly is for the person having the idea. But to pursue this would take us too far afield.

We can now recognize three levels of difference between words,

ON SENSE AND REFERENCE   61

expressions, or whole sentences. The difference may concern at most the ideas, or the sense but not the reference, or, finally, the reference as well. With respect to the first level, it is to be 31] noted that, on account of the uncertain connexion of ideas with words, a difference may hold for one person, which another does not find. The difference between a translation and the original text should properly not overstep the first level. To the possible differences here belong also the colouring and shading which poetic eloquence seeks to give to the sense. Such colouring and shading are not objective, and must be evoked by each hearer or reader according to the hints of the poet or the speaker. Without some affinity in human ideas art would certainly be impossible; but it can never be exactly determined how far the intentions of the poet are realized.

In what follows there will be no further discussion of ideas and experiences; they have been mentioned here only to ensure that the idea aroused in the hearer by a word shall not be confused with its sense or its reference.

To make short and exact expressions possible, let the following phraseology be established:

A proper name (word, sign, sign combination, expression) *expresses* its sense, *stands for* or *designates* its reference. By means of a sign we express its sense and designate its reference.

Idealists or sceptics will perhaps long since have objected: 'You talk, without further ado, of the Moon as an object; but how do you know that the name 'the Moon' has any reference? How do you know that anything whatsoever has a reference?' I reply that when we say 'the Moon,' we do not intend to speak of our idea of the Moon, nor are we satisfied with the sense alone, but we presuppose a reference. To assume that in the sentence 'The Moon is smaller than the Earth' the idea of the Moon is in question, would be flatly to misunderstand the sense. If this is what the speaker wanted, he would use the phrase 'my idea of the Moon.' Now we can of course be mistaken in the presupposition, and such mistakes have indeed occurred. But the question whether the presupposition is perhaps always mistaken 32] need not be answered here; in order to justify mention of the reference of a sign it is enough, at first, to point out our intention in speaking or thinking. (We must then add the reservation: provided such reference exists.)

So far we have considered the sense and reference only of such expressions, words, or signs as we have called proper names. We now inquire concerning the sense and reference for an entire declarative sentence. Such a sentence contains a thought.* Is this thought, now, to be regarded as its sense or its reference? Let us assume for the time being that the sentence has reference. If we now replace one word of the sentence by another having the same reference, but a different sense, this can have no bearing upon the reference of the sentence. Yet we can see that in such a case the thought changes; since, e.g., the thought in the sentence 'The morning star is a body illuminated by the Sun' differs from that in the sentence 'The evening star is a body illuminated by the Sun.' Anybody who did not know that the evening star is the morning star might hold the one thought to be true, the other false. The thought, accordingly, cannot be the reference of the sentence, but must rather be considered as the sense. What is the position now with regard to the reference? Have we a right even to inquire about it? Is it possible that a sentence as a whole has only a sense, but no reference? At any rate, one might expect that such sentences occur, just as there are parts of sentences having sense but no reference. And sentences which contain proper names without reference will be of this kind. The sentence 'Odysseus was set ashore at Ithaca while sound asleep' obviously has a sense. But since it is doubtful whether the name 'Odysseus,' occurring therein, has reference, it is also doubtful whether the whole sentence has one. Yet it is certain, nevertheless, that anyone who seriously took the sentence to be true or false would ascribe to the name 'Odysseus' a reference, not merely 33] a sense; for it is of the reference of the name that the predicate is affirmed or denied. Whoever does not admit the name has reference can neither apply nor withhold the predicate. But in that case it would be superfluous to advance to the reference of the name; one could be satisfied with the sense, if one wanted to go no further than the thought. If it were a question only of the sense of the sentence, the thought, it would be

---

* By a thought I understand not the subjective performance of thinking but its objective content, which is capable of being the common property of several thinkers.

ON SENSE AND REFERENCE   63

unnecessary to bother with the reference of a part of the sentence; only the sense, not the reference, of the part is relevant to the sense of the whole sentence. The thought remains the same whether 'Odysseus' has reference or not. The fact that we concern ourselves at all about the reference of a part of the sentence indicates that we generally recognize and expect a reference for the sentence itself. The thought loses value for us as soon as we recognize that the reference of one of its parts is missing. We are therefore justified in not being satisfied with the sense of a sentence, and in inquiring also as to its reference. But now why do we want every proper name to have not only a sense, but also a reference? Why is the thought not enough for us? Because, and to the extent that, we are concerned with its truth value. This is not always the case. In hearing an epic poem, for instance, apart from the euphony of the language we are interested only in the sense of the sentences and the images and feelings thereby aroused. The question of truth would cause us to abandon aesthetic delight for an attitude of scientific investigation. Hence it is a matter of no concern to us whether the name 'Odysseus,' for instance, has reference, so long as we accept the poem as a work of art.* It is the striving for truth that drives us always to advance from the sense to the reference.

We have seen that the reference of a sentence may always be sought, whenever the reference of its components is involved; and that this is the case when and only when we are inquiring after the truth value.

34] We are therefore driven into accepting the *truth value* of a sentence as constituting its reference. By the truth value of a sentence I understand the circumstance that it is true or false. There are no further truth values. For brevity I call the one the True, the other the False. Every declarative sentence concerned with the reference of its words is therefore to be regarded as a proper name, and its reference, if it has one, is either the True or the False. These two objects are recognized, if only implicitly, by everybody who judges something to be true—and so even by a sceptic. The designation of the truth values as objects may

* It would be desirable to have a special term for signs having only sense. If we name them, say, representations, the words of the actors on the stage would be representations; indeed the actor himself would be a representation.

appear to be an arbitrary fancy or perhaps a mere play upon words, from which no profound consequences could be drawn. What I mean by an object can be more exactly discussed only in connexion with concept and relation. I will reserve this for another article.[c] But so much should already be clear, that in every judgment,[*] no matter how trivial, the step from the level of thoughts to the level of reference (the objective) has already been taken.

One might be tempted to regard the relation of the thought to the True not as that of sense to reference, but rather as that of subject to predicate. One can, indeed, say: 'The thought, that 5 is a prime number, is true.' But closer examination shows that nothing more has been said than in the simple sentence '5 is a prime number.' The truth claim arises in each case from the form of the declarative sentence, and when the latter lacks its usual force, e.g., in the mouth of an actor upon the stage, even the sentence 'The thought that 5 is a prime number is true' contains only a thought, and indeed the same thought as the simple '5 is a prime number.' It follows that the relation of the thought to the True may not be compared with that of subject to predicate. 35] Subject and predicate (understood in the logical sense) are indeed elements of thought; they stand on the same level for knowledge. By combining subject and predicate, one reaches only a thought, never passes from sense to reference, never from a thought to its truth value. One moves at the same level but never advances from one level to the next. A truth value cannot be a part of a thought, any more than, say, the Sun can, for it is not a sense but an object.

If our supposition that the reference of a sentence is its truth value is correct, the latter must remain unchanged when a part of the sentence is replaced by an expression having the same reference. And this is in fact the case. Leibniz gives the definition: 'Eadem sunt, quae sibi mutuo substitui possunt, salva veritate.' What else but the truth value could be found, that belongs quite generally to every sentence if the reference of its components is relevant, and remains unchanged by substitutions of the kind in question?

---

c See his 'Ueber Begriff und Gegenstand' (*Vierteljahrsschrift für wissenschaftliche Philosophie* XVI [1892], 192–205).

* A judgment, for me is not the mere comprehension of a thought, but the admission of its truth.

ON SENSE AND REFERENCE   65

If now the truth value of a sentence is its reference, then on the one hand all true sentences have the same reference and so, on the other hand, do all false sentences. From this we see that in the reference of the sentence all that is specific is obliterated. We can never be concerned only with the reference of a sentence; but again the mere thought alone yields no knowledge, but only the thought together with its reference, i.e. its truth value. Judgments can be regarded as advances from a thought to a truth value. Naturally this cannot be a definition. Judgment is something quite peculiar and incomparable. One might also say that judgments are distinctions of parts within truth values. Such distinction occurs by a return to the thought. To every sense belonging to a truth value there would correspond its own manner of analysis. However, I have here used the word 'part' in a special sense. I have in fact transferred the relation between the parts and the whole of the sentence to its reference, by calling the reference of a word part of the reference of the sentence, if the 36] word itself is a part of the sentence. This way of speaking can certainly be attacked, because the whole reference and one part of it do not suffice to determine the remainder, and because the word 'part' is already used in another sense of bodies. A special term would need to be invented.

The supposition that the truth value of a sentence is its reference shall now be put to further test. We have found that the truth value of a sentence remains unchanged when an expression is replaced by another having the same reference: but we have not yet considered the case in which the expression to be replaced is itself a sentence. Now if our view is correct, the truth value of a sentence containing another as part must remain unchanged when the part is replaced by another sentence having the same truth value. Exceptions are to be expected when the whole sentence or its part is direct or indirect quotation; for in such cases, as we have seen, the words do not have their customary reference. In direct quotation, a sentence designates another sentence, and in indirect quotation a thought.

We are thus led to consider subordinate sentences or clauses. These occur as parts of a sentence complex, which is, from the logical standpoint, likewise a sentence—a main sentence. But here we meet the question whether it is also true of the

66 TRANSLATIONS FROM THE WRITINGS OF GOTTLOB FREGE

subordinate sentence that its reference is a truth value. Of indirect quotation we already know the opposite. Grammarians view subordinate clauses as representatives of parts of sentences and divide them accordingly into noun clauses, adjective clauses, adverbial clauses. This might generate the supposition that the reference of a subordinate clause was not a truth value but rather of the same kind as the reference of a noun or adjective or adverb—in short, of a part of a sentence, whose sense was not a thought but only a part of a thought. Only a more thorough investigation can clarify the issue. In so doing, we shall not follow the grammatical categories strictly, but rather group together what is logically of the same kind. Let us first search for cases in which the sense of the subordinate clause, as we have just supposed, is not an independent thought.

37] The case of an abstract[D] noun clause, introduced by 'that,' includes the case of indirect quotation, in which we have seen the words to have their indirect reference coinciding with what is customarily their sense. In this case, then, the subordinate clause has for its reference a thought, not a truth value; as sense not a thought, but the sense of the words 'the thought, that . . .,' which is only a part of the thought in the entire complex sentence. This happens after 'say,' 'hear,' 'be of the opinion,' 'be convinced,' 'conclude,' and similar words.* There is a different, and indeed somewhat complicated, situation after words like 'perceive,' 'know,' 'fancy,' which are to be considered later.

That in the cases of the first kind the reference of the subordinate clause is in fact the thought can also be recognized by seeing that it is indifferent to the truth of the whole whether the subordinate clause is true or false. Let us compare, for instance, the two sentences 'Copernicus believed that the planetary orbits are circles' and 'Copernicus believed that the apparent motion of the sun is produced by the real motion of the Earth.' One subordinate clause can be substituted for the other without harm to the truth. The main clause and the subordinate clause together have as their sense only a single thought, and the truth of the whole includes neither the truth nor the untruth of the subordinate clause.

D A literal translation of Frege's 'abstracten Nennsätzen' whose meaning eludes me.

* In 'A lied in saying he had seen B,' the subordinate clause designates a thought which is said (1) to have been asserted by A (2) while A was convinced of its falsity.

ON SENSE AND REFERENCE   67

In such cases it is not permissible to replace one expression in the subordinate clause by another having the same customary reference, but only by one having the same indirect reference, i.e. the same customary sense. If somebody were to conclude: The reference of a sentence is not its truth value, for in that case it could always be replaced by another sentence of the same truth value; he would prove too much; one might just as well claim that the reference of 'morning star' is not Venus, since one may not always say 'Venus' in place of 'morning star.' One has the right to conclude only that the reference of a sentence is not *always* its truth value, and that 'morning star' does not always 38] stand for the planet Venus, viz. when the word has its indirect reference. An exception of such a kind occurs in the subordinate clause just considered which has a thought as its reference.

If one says 'It seems that . . .' one means 'It seems to me that . . .' or 'I think that . . .' We therefore have the same case again. The situation is similar in the case of expressions such as 'to be pleased,' 'to regret,' 'to approve,' 'to blame,' 'to hope,' 'to fear.' If, toward the end of the battle of Waterloo,[E] Wellington was glad that the Prussians were coming, the basis for his joy was a conviction. Had he been deceived, he would have been no less pleased so long as his illusion lasted; and before he became so convinced he could not have been pleased that the Prussians were coming—even though in fact they might have been already approaching.

Just as a conviction or a belief is the ground of a feeling, it can, as in inference, also be the ground of a conviction. In the sentence: 'Columbus inferred from the roundness of the Earth that he could reach India by travelling towards the west,' we have as the reference of the parts two thoughts, that the Earth is round, and that Columbus by travelling to the west could reach India. All that is relevant here is that Columbus was convinced of both, and that the one conviction was a ground for the other. Whether the Earth is really round and Columbus could really reach India by travelling west, as he thought, is immaterial to the truth of our sentence; but it is not immaterial whether we replace 'the Earth' by 'the planet which is accompanied by a

---

[E] Frege uses the Prussian name for the battle—'Belle Alliance.'

moon whose diameter is greater than the fourth part of its own.'
Here also we have the indirect reference of the words.

Adverbial final clauses beginning 'in order that' also belong
here; for obviously the purpose is a thought; therefore: indirect
reference for the words, subjunctive mood.

A subordinate clause with 'that' after 'command,' 'ask,' 'for-
bid,' would appear in direct speech as an imperative. Such a
clause has no reference but only a sense. A command, a request,
are indeed not thoughts, yet they stand on the same level as
thoughts. Hence in subordinate clauses depending upon
39] 'command,' 'ask,' etc., words have their indirect reference.
The reference of such a clause is therefore not a truth value but a
command, a request, and so forth.

The case is similar for the dependent question in phrases such
as 'doubt whether,' 'not to know what.' It is easy to see that here
also the words are to be taken to have their indirect reference.
Dependent clauses expressing questions and beginning with
'who,' 'what,' 'where,' 'when,' 'how,' 'by what means,' etc.,
seem at times to approximate very closely to adverbial clauses in
which words have their customary references. These cases are
distinguished linguistically [in German] by the mood of the verb.
With the subjunctive, we have a dependent question and indirect
reference of the words, so that a proper name cannot in general
be replaced by another name of the same object.

In the cases so far considered the words of the subordinate
clauses had their indirect reference, and this made it clear that the
reference of the subordinate clause itself was indirect, i.e. not a
truth value but a thought, a command, a request, a question.
The subordinate clause could be regarded as a noun, indeed one
could say: as a proper name of that thought, that command, etc.,
which it represented in the context of the sentence structure.

We now come to other subordinate clauses, in which the words
do have their customary reference without however a thought
occurring as sense and a truth value as reference. How this is
possible is best made clear by examples.

Whoever discovered the elliptic form of the planetary orbits died in misery.

If the sense of the subordinate clause were here a thought, it
would have to be possible to express it also in a separate sentence.

ON SENSE AND REFERENCE   69

But this does not work, because the grammatical subject 'whoever' has no independent sense and only mediates the relation
with the consequent clause 'died in misery.' For this reason the
sense of the subordinate clause is not a complete thought, and its
reference is Kepler, not a truth value. One might object that the
sense of the whole does contain a thought as part, viz. that there
was somebody who first discovered the elliptic form of the
planetary orbits; for whoever takes the whole to be true cannot
40] deny this part. This is undoubtedly so; but only because
otherwise the dependent clause 'whoever discovered the elliptic
form of the planetary orbits' would have no reference. If anything is asserted there is always an obvious presupposition that
the simple or compound proper names used have reference. If
one therefore asserts 'Kepler died in misery,' there is a presupposition that the name 'Kepler' designates something; but it does not
follow that the sense of the sentence 'Kepler died in misery'
contains the thought that the name 'Kepler' designates something.
If this were the case the negation would have to run not

> Kepler did not die in misery

but

> Kepler did not die in misery, or the name 'Kepler' has no reference.

That the name 'Kepler' designates something is just as much a presupposition for the assertion

> Kepler died in misery

as for the contrary assertion. Now languages have the fault of
containing expressions which fail to designate an object (although
their grammatical form seems to qualify them for that purpose)
because the truth of some sentence is a prerequisite. Thus it
depends on the truth of the sentence:

> There was someone who discovered the elliptic form of the planetary orbits

whether the subordinate clause

> Whoever discovered the elliptic form of the planetary orbits

really designates an object or only seems to do so while having in
fact no reference. And thus it may appear as if our subordinate
clause contained as a part of its sense the thought that there was

somebody who discovered the elliptic form of the planetary orbits. If this were right the negation would run:

Either whoever discovered the elliptic form of the planetary orbits did not die in misery or there was nobody who discovered the elliptic form of the planetary orbits.

41] This arises from an imperfection of language, from which even the symbolic language of mathematical analysis is not altogether free; even there combinations of symbols can occur that seem to stand for something but have (at least so far) no reference, e.g. divergent infinite series. This can be avoided, e.g., by means of the special stipulation that divergent infinite series shall stand for the number 0. A logically perfect language (*Begriffsschrift*) should satisfy the conditions, that every expression grammatically well constructed as a proper name out of signs already introduced shall in fact designate an object, and that no new sign shall be introduced as a proper name without being secured a reference. The logic books contain warnings against logical mistakes arising from the ambiguity of expressions. I regard as no less pertinent a warning against apparent proper names having no reference. The history of mathematics supplies errors which have arisen in this way. This lends itself to demagogic abuse as easily as ambiguity—perhaps more easily. 'The will of the people' can serve as an example; for it is easy to establish that there is at any rate no generally accepted reference for this expression. It is therefore by no means unimportant to eliminate the source of these mistakes, at least in science, once and for all. Then such objections as the one discussed above would become impossible, because it could never depend upon the truth of a thought whether a proper name had a reference.

With the consideration of these noun clauses may be coupled that of types of adjective and adverbial clauses which are logically in close relation to them.

Adjective clauses also serve to construct compound proper names, though, unlike noun clauses, they are not sufficient by themselves for this purpose. These adjective clauses are to be regarded as equivalent to adjectives. Instead of 'the square root of 4 which is smaller than 0,' one can also say 'the negative square root of 4.' We have here the case of a compound proper name constructed from the expression for a concept with the help of the

ON SENSE AND REFERENCE 71

singular definite article. This is at any rate permissible if the 42] concept applies to one and only one single object.*

Expressions for concepts can be so constructed that marks of a concept are given by adjective clauses as, in our example, by the clause 'which is smaller than 0.' It is evident that such an adjective clause cannot have a thought as sense or a truth value as reference, any more than the noun clause could. Its sense, which can also be expressed in many cases by a single adjective, is only a part of a thought. Here, as in the case of the noun clause, there is no independent subject and therefore no possibility of reproducing the sense of the subordinate clause in an independent sentence.

Places, instants, stretches of time, are, logically considered, objects; hence the linguistic designation of a definite place, a definite instant, or a stretch of time is to be regarded as a proper name. Now adverbial clauses of place and time can be used for the construction of such a proper name in a manner similar to that which we have seen in the case of noun and adjective clauses. In the same way, expressions for concepts bringing in places, etc., can be constructed. It is to be noted here also that the sense of these subordinate clauses cannot be reproduced in an independent sentence, since an essential component, viz. the determination of place or time, is missing and is only indicated by a relative pronoun or a conjunction.†

In conditional clauses, also, there may usually be recognized to

---

* In accordance with what was said above, an expression of the kind in question must actually always be assured of reference, by means of a special stipulation, e.g. by the convention that 0 shall count as its reference, when the concept applies to no object or to more than one.

† In the case of these sentences, various interpretations are easily possible. The sense of the sentence, 'After Schleswig-Holstein was separated from Denmark, Prussia and Austria quarrelled' can also be rendered in the form 'After the separation of Schleswig-Holstein from Denmark, Prussia and Austria quarrelled.' In this version, it is surely sufficiently clear that the sense is not to be taken as having as a part the thought that Schleswig-Holstein was once separated from Denmark, but that this is the necessary presupposition in order for the expression 'after the separation of Schleswig-Holstein from Denmark' to have any reference at all. To be sure, our sentence can also be interpreted as saying that Schleswig-Holstein was once separated from Denmark. We then have a case which is to be considered later. In order to understand the difference more clearly, let us project ourselves into the mind of a Chinese who, having little knowledge of European history, believes it to be false that Schleswig-Holstein was ever separated from Denmark. He will take our sentence, in the first version, to be neither true nor false but will deny it to have any reference, on the ground of absence of reference for its subordinate clause. This clause would only apparently determine a time. If he interpreted our sentence in the second way, however, he would find a thought expressed in it which he would take to be false, beside a part which would be without reference for him.

43] occur an indefinite indicator, having a similar correlate in the dependent clause. (We have already seen this occur in noun, adjective, and adverbial clauses.) In so far as each indicator refers to the other, both clauses together form a connected whole, which as a rule expresses only a single thought. In the sentence

If a number is less than 1 and greater than 0, its square is less than 1 and greater than 0

the component in question is 'a number' in the conditional clause and 'its' in the dependent clause. It is by means of this very indefiniteness that the sense acquires the generality expected of a law. It is this which is responsible for the fact that the antecedent clause alone has no complete thought as its sense and in combination with the consequent clause expresses one and only one thought, whose parts are no longer thoughts. It is, in general, incorrect to say that in the hypothetical judgment two judgments are put in reciprocal relationship. If this or something similar is said, the word 'judgment' is used in the same sense as I have connected with the word 'thought,' so that I would use the formulation: 'A hypothetical thought establishes a reciprocal relationship between two thoughts.' This could be true only if an indefinite indicator is absent;* but in such a case there would also be no generality.

If an instant of time is to be indefinitely indicated in both conditional and dependent clauses, this is often achieved merely by using the present tense of the verb, which in such a case however does not indicate the temporal present. This grammatical form is then the indefinite indicator in the main and 44] subordinate clauses. An example of this is: 'When the Sun is in the tropic of Cancer, the longest day in the northern hemisphere occurs.' Here, also, it is impossible to express the sense of the subordinate clause in a full sentence, because this sense is not a complete thought. If we say: 'The Sun is in the tropic of Cancer,' this would refer to our present time and thereby change the sense. Just as little is the sense of the main clause a thought; only the whole, composed of main and subordinate clauses, has such a sense. It may be added that several common components in the antecedent and consequent clauses may be indefinitely indicated.

* At times an explicit linguistic indication is missing and must be read off from the entire context.

ON SENSE AND REFERENCE   73

It is clear that noun clauses with 'who' or 'what' and adverbial clauses with 'where,' 'when,' 'wherever,' 'whenever' are often to be interpreted as having the sense of conditional clauses, e.g. 'who touches pitch, defiles himself.'

Adjective clauses can also take the place of conditional clauses. Thus the sense of the sentence previously used can be given in the form 'The square of a number which is less than 1 and greater than 0 is less than 1 and greater than 0.'

The situation is quite different if the common component of the two clauses is designated by a proper name. In the sentence:

Napoleon, who recognized the danger to his right flank, himself led his guards against the enemy position

two thoughts are expressed:

1. Napoleon recognized the danger to his right flank
2. Napoleon himself led his guards against the enemy position.

When and where this happened is to be fixed only by the context, but is nevertheless to be taken as definitely determined thereby. If the entire sentence is uttered as an assertion, we thereby simultaneously assert both component sentences. If one of the parts is false, the whole is false. Here we have the case that the subordinate clause by itself has a complete thought as sense (if we complete it by indication of place and time). The reference of the subordinate clause is accordingly a truth value. We can therefore expect that it may be replaced, without harm to the truth value of the whole, by a sentence having the same truth 45] value. This is indeed the case; but it is to be noticed that for purely grammatical reasons, its subject must be 'Napoleon,' for only then can it be brought into the form of an adjective clause belonging to 'Napoleon.' But if the demand that it be expressed in this form be waived, and the connexion be shown by 'and,' this restriction disappears.

Subsidiary clauses beginning with 'although' also express complete thoughts. This conjunction actually has no sense and does not change the sense of the clause but only illuminates it in a peculiar fashion.* We could indeed replace the concessive clause without harm to the truth of the whole by another of the same truth value; but the light in which the clause is placed by the

* Similarly in the case of 'but,' 'yet.'

conjunction might then easily appear unsuitable, as if a song with a sad subject were to be sung in a lively fashion.

In the last cases the truth of the whole included the truth of the component clauses. The case is different if a conditional clause expresses a complete thought by containing, in place of an indefinite indicator, a proper name or something which is to be regarded as equivalent. In the sentence

If the Sun has already risen, the sky is very cloudy

the time is the present, that is to say, definite. And the place is also to be thought of as definite. Here it can be said that a relation between the truth values of conditional and dependent clauses has been asserted, viz. such that the case does not occur in which the antecedent stands for the True and the consequent for the False. Accordingly, our sentence is true if the Sun has not yet risen, whether the sky is very cloudy or not, and also if the Sun has risen and the sky is very cloudy. Since only truth values are here in question, each component clause can be replaced by another of the same truth value without changing the truth value of the whole. To be sure, the light in which the subject then appears would usually be unsuitable; the thought 46] might easily seem distorted; but this has nothing to do with its truth value. One must always take care not to clash with the subsidiary thoughts, which are however not explicitly expressed and therefore should not be reckoned in the sense. Hence, also, no account need be taken of their truth values.*

The simple cases have now been discussed. Let us review what we have learned.

The subordinate clause usually has for its sense not a thought, but only a part of one, and consequently no truth value as reference. The reason for this is either that the words in the subordinate clause have indirect reference, so that the reference, not the sense, of the subordinate clause is a thought; or else that, on account of the presence of an indefinite indicator, the subordinate clause is incomplete and expresses a thought only when combined with the main clause. It may happen, however, that the sense of the subsidiary clause is a complete thought, in

---

* The thought of our sentence might also be expressed thus: 'Either the Sun has not risen yet or the sky is very cloudy'—which shows how this kind of sentence connexion is to be understood.

which case it can be replaced by another of the same truth value without harm to the truth of the whole—provided there are no grammatical obstacles.

An examination of all the subordinate clauses which one may encounter will soon provide some which do not fit well into these categories. The reason, so far as I can see, is that these subordinate clauses have no such simple sense. Almost always, it seems, we connect with the main thoughts expressed by us subsidiary thoughts which, although not expressed, are associated with our words, in accordance with psychological laws, by the hearer. And since the subsidiary thought appears to be connected with our words of its own accord, almost like the main thought itself, we want it also to be expressed. The sense of the sentence is thereby enriched, and it may well happen that we have more simple thoughts than clauses. In many cases the sentence must be understood in this way, in others it may be doubtful whether the subsidiary thought belongs to the sense of the sentence or only 47] accompanies it.* One might perhaps find that the sentence

Napoleon, who recognized the danger to his right flank, himself led his guards against the enemy position

expresses not only the two thoughts shown above, but also the thought that the knowledge of the danger was the reason why he led the guards against the enemy position. One may in fact doubt whether this thought is merely slightly suggested or really expressed. Let the question be considered whether our sentence be false if Napoleon's decision had already been made before he recognized the danger. If our sentence could be true in spite of this, the subsidiary thought should not be understood as part of the sense. One would probably decide in favour of this. The alternative would make for a quite complicated situation: We would have more simple thoughts than clauses. If the sentence

Napoleon recognized the danger to his right flank

were now to be replaced by another having the same truth value, e.g.

Napoleon was already more than 45 years old

not only would our first thought be changed, but also our third

* This may be important for the question whether an assertion is a lie, or an oath a perjury.

one. Hence the truth value of the latter might change—viz. if his age was not the reason for the decision to lead the guards against the enemy. This shows why clauses of equal truth value cannot always be substituted for one another in such cases. The clause expresses more through its connexion with another than it does in isolation.

Let us now consider cases where this regularly happens. In the sentence:

Bebel fancies that the return of Alsace-Lorraine would appease France's desire for revenge

two thoughts are expressed, which are not however shown by means of antecedent and consequent clauses, viz.:

(1) Bebel believes that the return of Alsace-Lorraine would appease France's desire for revenge
48] (2) the return of Alsace-Lorraine would not appease France's desire for revenge.

In the expression of the first thought, the words of the subordinate clause have their indirect reference, while the same words have their customary reference in the expression of the second thought. This shows that the subordinate clause in our original complex sentence is to be taken twice over, with different reference, standing once for a thought, once for a truth value. Since the truth value is not the whole reference of the subordinate clause, we cannot simply replace the latter by another of equal truth value. Similar considerations apply to expressions such as 'know,' 'discover,' 'it is known that.'

By means of a subordinate causal clause and the associated main clause we express several thoughts, which however do not correspond separately to the original clauses. In the sentence: 'Because ice is less dense than water, it floats on water' we have

(1) Ice is less dense than water;
(2) If anything is less dense than water, it floats on water;
(3) Ice floats on water.

The third thought, however, need not be explicitly introduced, since it is contained in the remaining two. On the other hand, neither the first and third nor the second and third combined

ON SENSE AND REFERENCE   77

would furnish the sense of our sentence. It can now be seen that our subordinate clause

> because ice is less dense than water

expresses our first thought, as well as a part of our second. This is how it comes to pass that our subsidiary clause cannot be simply replaced by another of equal truth value; for this would alter our second thought and thereby might well alter its truth value.

The situation is similar in the sentence

> If iron were less dense than water, it would float on water.

49] Here we have the two thoughts that iron is not less dense than water, and that something floats on water if it is less dense than water. The subsidiary clause again expresses one thought and a part of the other.

If we interpret the sentence already considered

> After Schleswig-Holstein was separated from Denmark, Prussia and Austria quarrelled

in such a way that it expresses the thought that Schleswig-Holstein was once separated from Denmark, we have first this thought, and secondly the thought that at a time, more closely determined by the subordinate clause, Prussia and Austria quarrelled. Here also the subordinate clause expresses not only one thought but also a part of another. Therefore it may not in general be replaced by another of the same truth value.

It is hard to exhaust all the possibilities given by language; but I hope to have brought to light at least the essential reasons why a subordinate clause may not always be replaced by another of equal truth value without harm to the truth of the whole sentence structure. These reasons arise:

> (1) when the subordinate clause does not stand for a truth value, inasmuch as it expresses only a part of a thought;
> (2) when the subordinate clause does stand for a truth value but is not restricted to so doing, inasmuch as its sense includes one thought and part of another.

The first case arises:

> (a) in indirect reference of words
> (b) if a part of the sentence is only an indefinite indicator instead of a proper name.

78   TRANSLATIONS FROM THE WRITINGS OF GOTTLOB FREGE

In the second case, the subsidiary clause may have to be taken twice over, viz. once in its customary reference, and the other time in indirect reference; or the sense of a part of the subordinate clause may likewise be a component of another thought, which, taken together with the thought directly expressed by the subordinate clause, makes up the sense of the whole sentence.

It follows with sufficient probability from the foregoing that the cases where a subordinate clause is not replaceable by another of the same value cannot be brought in disproof of our view 50] that a truth value is the reference of a sentence having a thought as its sense.

Let us return to our starting point.

When we found '$a=a$' and '$a=b$' to have different cognitive values, the explanation is that for the purpose of knowledge, the sense of the sentence, viz., the thought expressed by it, is no less relevant than its reference, i.e. its truth value. If now $a=b$, then indeed the reference of 'b' is the same as that of 'a,' and hence the truth value of '$a=b$' is the same as that of '$a=a$.' In spite of this, the sense of 'b' may differ from that of 'a', and thereby the thought expressed in '$a=b$' differs from that of '$a=a$.' In that case the two sentences do not have the same cognitive value. If we understand by 'judgment' the advance from the thought to its truth value, as in the above paper, we can also say that the judgments are different.

2

On Denoting

BERTRAND RUSSELL

Reprinted with the kind permission of the publisher from Bertrand Russell, *Logic and Knowledge,* ed. R. C. Marsh (London: George Allen and Unwin, Ltd.), 39-56.

1905

ON DENOTING

BY a 'denoting phrase' I mean a phrase such as any one of the following: a man, some man, any man, every man, all men, the present King of England, the present King of France, the centre of mass of the solar system at the first instant of the twentieth century, the revolution of the earth round the sun, the revolution of the sun round the earth. Thus a phrase is denoting solely in virtue of its *form*. We may distinguish three cases: (1) A phrase may be denoting, and yet not denote anything; e.g., 'the present King of France'. (2) A phrase may denote one definite object; e.g., 'the present King of England' denotes a certain man. (3) A phrase may denote ambiguously; e.g., 'a man' denotes not many men, but an ambiguous man. The interpretation of such phrases is a matter of considerable difficulty; indeed, it is very hard to frame any theory not susceptible of formal refutation. All the difficulties with which I am acquainted are met, so far as I can discover, by the theory which I am about to explain.

The subject of denoting is of very great importance, not only in logic and mathematics, but also in theory of knowledge. For example, we know that the centre of mass of the solar system at a definite instant is some definite point, and we can affirm a number of propositions about it; but we have no immediate *acquaintance* with this point, which is only known to us by description. The distinction between *acquaintance* and *knowledge about* is the distinction between the things we have presentations of, and the things we only reach by means of denoting phrases. It often happens that we know that a certain phrase denotes unambiguously, although we have no acquaintance with what it denotes; this occurs in the above case of the centre of mass. In perception we have acquaintance with the objects of perception, and in thought we have acquaintance with objects of a more abstract logical character;

but we do not necessarily have acquaintance with the objects denoted by phrases composed of words with whose meanings we are acquainted. To take a very important instance: there seems no reason to believe that we are ever acquainted with other people's minds, seeing that these are not directly perceived; hence what we know about them is obtained through denoting. All thinking has to start from acquaintance; but it succeeds in thinking *about* many things with which we have no acquaintance.

The course of my argument will be as follows. I shall begin by stating the theory I intend to advocate;* I shall then discuss the theories of Frege and Meinong, showing why neither of them satisfies me; then I shall give the grounds in favour of my theory; and finally I shall briefly indicate the philosophical consequences of my theory.

My theory, briefly, is as follows. I take the notion of the *variable* as fundamental; I use '$C(x)$' to mean a proposition† in which x is a constituent, where x, the variable, is essentially and wholly undetermined. Then we can consider the two notions '$C(x)$ is always true' and '$C(x)$ is sometimes true'‡. Then *everything* and *nothing* and *something* (which are the most primitive of denoting phrases) are to be interpreted as follows:

C (everything) means '$C(x)$ is always true';
C (nothing) means ' "$C(x)$ is false" is always true';
C (something) means 'It is false that "$C(x)$ is false" is always
            true'.§

Here the notion '$C(x)$ is always true' is taken as ultimate and indefinable, and the others are defined by means of it. *Everything*, *nothing*, and *something* are not assumed to have any meaning in isolation, but a meaning is assigned to *every* proposition in which they occur. This is the principle of the theory of denoting I wish

* I have discussed this subject in *Principles of Mathematics*, Chap. V, and § 476. The theory there advocated is very nearly the same as Frege's, and is quite different from the theory to be advocated in what follows.

† More exactly, a propositional function.

‡ The second of these can be defined by means of the first, if we take it to mean, 'It is not true that "$C(x)$ is false" is always true'.

§ I shall sometimes use, instead of this complicated phrase, the phrase '$C(x)$ is not always false', or '$C(x)$ is sometimes true', supposed *defined* to mean the same as the complicated phrase.

ON DENOTING   43

to advocate: that denoting phrases never have any meaning in themselves, but that every proposition in whose verbal expression they occur has a meaning. The difficulties concerning denoting are, I believe, all the result of a wrong analysis of propositions whose verbal expressions contain denoting phrases. The proper analysis, if I am not mistaken, may be further set forth as follows.

Suppose now we wish to interpret the proposition, ' I met a man'. It this is true, I met some definite man; but that is not what I affirm. What I affirm is, according to the theory I advocate:

' "I met x, and x is human" is not always false'.

Generally, defining the class of men as the class of objects having the predicate *human*, we say that:

'C (a man)' means ' "$C(x)$ and x is human" is not always false'. This leaves 'a man', by itself, wholly destitute of meaning, but gives a meaning to every proposition in whose verbal expression 'a man' occurs.

Consider next the proposition 'all men are mortal'. This proposition* is really hypothetical and states that *if* anything is a man, it is mortal. That is, it states that if x is a man, x is mortal, whatever x may be. Hence, substituting 'x is human' for 'x is a man', we find:

'All men are mortal' means ' "If x is human, x is mortal" is always true'.

This is what is expressed in symbolic logic by saying that 'all men are mortal' means ' "x is human" implies "x is mortal" for all values of x'. More generally, we say:

'C (all men)' means ' "If x is human, then $C(x)$ is true" is always true'.
Similarly
'C (no men)' means ' "If x is human, then $C(x)$ is false" is always true'.
'C (some men)' will mean the same as 'C (a man)',† and

* As has been ably argued in Mr. Bradley's *Logic*, Book I, Chap. II.

† Psychologically 'C (a man)' has a suggestion of *only one*, and 'C (some men)' has a suggestion of *more than one*; but we may neglect these suggestions in a preliminary sketch.

44   LOGIC AND KNOWLEDGE

'C (a man)' means 'It is false that "$C(x)$ and x is human" is always false'.

'C (every man)' will mean the same as 'C (all men)'.

It remains to interpret phrases containing *the*. These are by far the most interesting and difficult of denoting phrases. Take as an instance 'the father of Charles II was executed'. This asserts that there was an x who was the father of Charles II and was executed. Now *the*, when it is strictly used, involves uniqueness; we do, it is true, speak of '*the* son of So-and-so' even when So-and-so has several sons, but it would be more correct to say '*a* son of So-and-so'. Thus for our purposes we take *the* as involving uniqueness. Thus when we say 'x was *the* father of Charles II' we not only assert that x had a certain relation to Charles II, but also that nothing else had this relation. The relation in question, without the assumption of uniqueness, and without any denoting phrases, is expressed by 'x begat Charles II'. To get an equivalent of 'x was the father of Charles II', we must add, 'If y is other than x, y did not beget Charles II', or, what is equivalent, 'If y begat Charles II, y is identical with x'. Hence 'x is the father of Charles II' becomes: 'x begat Charles II; and "if y begat Charles II, y is identical with x" is always true of y'.

> Thus 'the father of Charles II was executed' becomes: 'It is not always false of x that x begat Charles II and that x was executed and that "if y begat Charles II, y is identical with x" is always true of y'.

This may seem a somewhat incredible interpretation; but I am not at present giving reasons, I am merely *stating* the theory.

To interpret 'C (the father of Charles II)', where C stands for any statement about him, we have only to substitute $C(x)$ for 'x was executed' in the above. Observe that, according to the above interpretation, whatever statement C may be, 'C (the father of Charles II)' implies:

> 'It is not always false of x that "if y begat Charles II, y is identical with x" is always true of y',

ON DENOTING   45

which is what is expressed in common language by 'Charles II had one father and no more'. Consequently if this condition fails, *every* proposition of the form '*C* (the father of Charles II)' is false. Thus e.g. every proposition of the form '*C* (the present King of France)' is false. This is a great advantage in the present theory. I shall show later that it is not contrary to the law of contradiction, as might be at first supposed.

The above gives a reduction of all propositions in which denoting phrases occur to forms in which no such phrases occur. Why it is imperative to effect such a reduction, the subsequent discussion will endeavour to show.

The evidence for the above theory is derived from the difficulties which seem unavoidable if we regard denoting phrases as standing for genuine constituents of the propositions in whose verbal expressions they occur. Of the possible theories which admit such constituents the simplest is that of Meinong.* This theory regards any grammatically correct denoting phrase as standing for an *object*. Thus 'the present King of France', 'the round square', etc., are supposed to be genuine objects. It is admitted that such objects do not *subsist*, but nevertheless they are supposed to be objects. This is in itself a difficult view; but the chief objection is that such objects, admittedly, are apt to infringe the law of contradiction. It is contended, for example, that the existent present King of France exists, and also does not exist; that the round square is round, and also not round, etc. But this is intolerable; and if any theory can be found to avoid this result, it is surely to be preferred.

The above breach of the law of contradiction is avoided by Frege's theory. He distinguishes, in a denoting phrase, two elements, which we may call the *meaning* and the *denotation*.† Thus 'the centre of mass of the solar system at the beginning of the twentieth century' is highly complex in *meaning*, but its *denotation* is a certain point, which is simple. The solar system, the twentieth century, etc., are constituents of the *meaning*; but the *denotation*

* See *Untersuchungen zur Gegenstandstheorie und Psychologie* (Leipzig, 1904) the first three articles (by Meinong, Ameseder and Mally respectively).

† See his 'Ueber Sinn und Bedeutung', *Zeitschrift für Phil. und Phil. Kritik*, Vol. 100.

46   LOGIC AND KNOWLEDGE

has no constituents at all.* One advantage of this distinction is that it shows why it is often worth while to assert identity. If we say 'Scott is the author of *Waverley*', we assert an identity of denotation with a difference of meaning. I shall, however, not repeat the grounds in favour of this theory, as I have urged its claims elsewhere (loc. cit.), and am now concerned to dispute those claims.

One of the first difficulties that confront us, when we adopt the view that denoting phrases *express* a meaning and *denote* a denotation,† concerns the cases in which the denotation appears to be absent. If we say 'the King of England is bald', that is, it would seem, not a statement about the complex *meaning* 'the King of England', but about the actual man denoted by the meaning. But now consider 'the King of France is bald'. By parity of form, this also ought to be about the denotation of the phrase ' the King of France'. But this phrase, though it has a *meaning* provided 'the King of England' has a meaning, has certainly no denotation, at least in any obvious sense. Hence one would suppose that 'the King of France is bald' ought to be nonsense; but it is not nonsense, since it is plainly false. Or again consider such a proposition as the following: 'If u is a class which has only one member, then that one member is a member of u', or, as we may state it, 'If u is a unit class, *the u* is a u'. This proposition ought to be *always* true, since the conclusion is true whenever the hypothesis is true. But 'the u' is a denoting phrase, and it is the denotation, not the meaning, that is said to be a u. Now if u is *not* a unit class, 'the u' seems to denote nothing; hence our proposition would seem to become nonsense as soon as u is not a unit class.

Now it is plain that such propositions do *not* become non-

* Frege distinguishes the two elements of meaning and denotation everywhere, and not only in complex denoting phrases. Thus it is the *meanings* of the constituents of a denoting complex that enter into its *meaning*, not their *denotation*. In the proposition 'Mont Blanc is over 1,000 metres high', it is, according to him, the *meaning* of 'Mont Blanc', not the actual mountain, that is a constituent of the *meaning* of the proposition.

† In this theory, we shall say that the denoting phrase *expresses* a meaning; and we shall say both of the phrase and of the meaning that they *denote* a denotation. In the other theory, which I advocate, there is no *meaning*, and only sometimes a *denotation*.

sense merely because their hypotheses are false. The King in *The Tempest* might say, 'If Ferdinand is not drowned, Ferdinand is my only son'. Now 'my only son' is a denoting phrase, which, on the face of it, has a denotation when, and only when, I have exactly one son. But the above statement would nevertheless have remained true if Ferdinand had been in fact drowned. Thus we must either provide a denotation in cases in which it is at first sight absent, or we must abandon the view that the denotation is what is concerned in propositions which contain denoting phrases. The latter is the course that I advocate. The former course may be taken, as by Meinong, by admitting objects which do not subsist, and denying that they obey the law of contradiction; this, however, is to be avoided if possible. Another way of taking the same course (so far as our present alternative is concerned) is adopted by Frege, who provides by definition some purely conventional denotation for the cases in which otherwise there would be none. Thus 'the King of France', is to denote the null-class; 'the only son of Mr. So-and-so' (who has a fine family of ten), is to denote the class of all his sons; and so on. But this procedure, though it may not lead to actual logical error, is plainly artificial, and does not give an exact analysis of the matter. Thus if we allow that denoting phrases, in general, have the two sides of meaning and denotation, the cases where there seems to be no denotation cause difficulties both on the assumption that there really is a denotation and on the assumption that there really is none.

A logical theory may be tested by its capacity for dealing with puzzles, and it is a wholesome plan, in thinking about logic, to stock the mind with as many puzzles as possible, since these serve much the same purpose as is served by experiments in physical science. I shall therefore state three puzzles which a theory as to denoting ought to be able to solve; and I shall show later that my theory solves them.

(1) If *a* is identical with *b*, whatever is true of the one is true of the other, and either may be substituted for the other in any proposition without altering the truth or falsehood of that proposition. Now George IV wished to know whether Scott was the author of *Waverley*; and in fact Scott *was* the author of *Waverley*. Hence we may substitute *Scott* for *the author of 'Waverley'*, and thereby prove that George IV wished to know whether Scott was Scott.

48   LOGIC AND KNOWLEDGE

Yet an interest in the law of identity can hardly be attributed to the first gentleman of Europe.

(2) By the law of excluded middle, either '*A* is *B*' or '*A* is not *B*' must be true. Hence either 'the present King of France is bald' or 'the present King of France is not bald' must be true. Yet if we enumerated the things that are bald, and then the things that are not bald, we should not find the present King of France in either list. Hegelians, who love a synthesis, will probably conclude that he wears a wig.

(3) Consider the proposition '*A* differs from *B*'. If this is true, there is a difference between *A* and *B*, which fact may be expressed in the form 'the difference between *A* and *B* subsists'. But if it is false that *A* differs from *B*, then there is no difference between *A* and *B*, which fact may be expressed in the form 'the difference between *A* and *B* does not subsist'. But how can a non-entity be the subject of a proposition? 'I think, therefore I am' is no more evident than 'I am the subject of a proposition, therefore I am', provided 'I am' is taken to assert subsistence or being,* not existence. Hence, it would appear, it must always be self-contradictory to deny the being of anything; but we have seen, in connexion with Meinong, that to admit being also sometimes leads to contradictions. Thus if *A* and *B* do not differ, to suppose either that there is, or that there is not, such an object as 'the difference between *A* and *B*' seems equally impossible.

The relation of the meaning to the denotation involves certain rather curious difficulties, which seem in themselves sufficient to prove that the theory which leads to such difficulties must be wrong.

When we wish to speak about the *meaning* of a denoting phrase, as opposed to its *denotation*, the natural mode of doing so is by inverted commas. Thus we say:

The centre of mass of the solar system is a point, not a denoting complex;
'The centre of mass of the solar system' is a denoting complex, not a point.
Or again,
The first line of Gray's Elegy states a proposition.

* I use these as synonyms.

'The first line of Gray's Elegy' does not state a proposition. Thus taking any denoting phrase, say C, we wish to consider the relation between C and 'C', where the difference of the two is of the kind exemplified in the above two instances.

We say, to begin with, that when C occurs it is the *denotation* that we are speaking about; but when 'C' occurs, it is the *meaning*. Now the relation of meaning and denotation is not merely linguistic through the phrase: there must be a logical relation involved, which we express by saying that the meaning denotes the denotation. But the difficulty which confronts us is that we cannot succeed in *both* preserving the connexion of meaning and denotation *and* preventing them from being one and the same; also that the meaning cannot be got at except by means of denoting phrases. This happens as follows.

The one phrase C was to have both meaning and denotation. But if we speak of 'the meaning of C', that gives us the meaning (if any) of the denotation. 'The meaning of the first line of Gray's Elegy' is the same as 'The meaning of "The curfew tolls the knell of parting day",' and is not the same as 'The meaning of "the first line of Gray's Elegy".' Thus in order to get the meaning we want, we must speak not of 'the meaning of C', but of 'the meaning of "C",' which is the same as 'C' by itself. Similarly 'the denotation of C' does not mean the denotation we want, but means something which, if it denotes at all, denotes what is denoted by the denotation we want. For example, let 'C' be 'the denoting complex occurring in the second of the above instances'. Then

$$C = \text{'the first line of Gray's Elegy', and}$$

the denotation of C = The curfew tolls the knell of parting day. But what we *meant* to have as the denotation was 'the first line of Gray's Elegy'. Thus we have failed to get what we wanted.

The difficulty in speaking of the meaning of a denoting complex may be stated thus: The moment we put the complex in a proposition, the proposition is about the denotation; and if we make a proposition in which the subject is 'the meaning of C', then the subject is the meaning (if any) of the denotation, which was not intended. This leads us to say that, when we distinguish meaning and denotation, we must be dealing with the meaning: the meaning has denotation and is a complex, and there is not something other than the meaning, which can be called the complex, and be said to *have* both meaning and denotation. The right phrase, on the view in question, is that some meanings have denotations.

But this only makes our difficulty in speaking of meanings more evident. For suppose C is our complex; then we are to say that C *is* the meaning of the complex. Nevertheless, whenever C occurs without inverted commas, what is said is not true of the meaning, but only of the denotation, as when we say: The centre of mass of the solar system is a point. Thus to speak of C itself, i.e., to make a proposition about the meaning, our subject must not be C, but something which denotes C. Thus 'C', which is what we use when we want to speak of the meaning, must be not the meaning, but something which denotes the meaning. And C must not be a constituent of this complex (as it is of 'the meaning of C'); for if C occurs in the complex, it will be its denotation, not its meaning, that will occur, and there is no backward road from denotations to meanings, because every object can be denoted by an infinite number of different denoting phrases.

Thus it would seem that 'C' and C are different entities, such that 'C' denotes C; but this cannot be an explanation, because the relation of 'C' to C remains wholly mysterious; and where are we to find the denoting complex 'C' which is to denote C? Moreover, when C occurs in a proposition, it is not *only* the denotation that occurs (as we shall see in the next paragraph); yet, on the view in question, C is only the denotation, the meaning being wholly relegated to 'C'. This is an inextricable tangle, and seems to prove that the whole distinction of meaning and denotation has been wrongly conceived.

That the meaning is relevant when a denoting phrase occurs in a proposition is formally proved by the puzzle about the author of *Waverley*. The proposition 'Scott was the author of *Waverley*' has a property not possessed by 'Scott was Scott', namely the property that George IV wished to know whether it was true. Thus the two are not identical propositions; hence the meaning of 'the author of *Waverley*' must be relevant as well as the denotation, if we adhere to the point of view to which this distinction belongs. Yet, as we have just seen, so long as we adhere to this point of view, we are compelled to hold that only the denotation can be relevant. Thus the point of view in question must be abandoned.

It remains to show how all the puzzles we have been considering are solved by the theory explained at the beginning of this article.

According to the view which I advocate, a denoting phrase is essentially *part* of a sentence, and does not, like most single words, have any significance on its own account. If I say 'Scott was a man', that is a statement of the form 'x was a man', and it has 'Scott' for its subject. But if I say 'the author of *Waverley* was a man', that is not a statement of the form 'x was a man', and does not have 'the author of *Waverley*' for its subject. Abbreviating the statement made at the beginning of this article, we may put, in place of 'the author of *Waverley* was a man', the following: 'One and only one entity wrote *Waverley*, and that one was a man'. (This is not so strictly what is meant as what was said earlier; but it is easier to follow.) And speaking generally, suppose we wish to say that the author of *Waverley* had the property ϕ, what we wish to say is equivalent to 'One and only one entity wrote *Waverley*, and that one had the property ϕ'.

The explanation of *denotation* is now as follows. Every proposition in which 'the author of *Waverley*' occurs being explained as above, the proposition 'Scott was the author of *Waverley*' (i.e. 'Scott was identical with the author of *Waverley*') becomes 'One and only one entity wrote *Waverley*, and Scott was identical with that one'; or, reverting to the wholly explicit form: 'It is not always false of x that x wrote *Waverley*, that it is always true of y that if y wrote *Waverley* y is identical with x, and that Scott is identical with x'. Thus if 'C' is a denoting phrase, it may happen that there is one entity x (there cannot be more than one) for which the proposition 'x is identical with C' is true, this proposition being interpreted as above. We may then say that the entity x is the denotation of the phrase 'C'. Thus Scott is the denotation of 'the author of *Waverley*'. The 'C' in inverted commas will be merely the *phrase*, not anything that can be called the *meaning*. The phrase *per se* has no meaning, because in any proposition in which it occurs the proposition, fully expressed, does not contain the phrase, which has been broken up.

The puzzle about George IV's curiosity is now seen to have a very simple solution. The proposition 'Scott was the author of

Waverley', which was written out in its unabbreviated form in the preceding paragraph, does not contain any constituent 'the author of *Waverley*' for which we could substitute 'Scott'. This does not interfere with the truth of inferences resulting from making what is *verbally* the substitution of 'Scott' for 'the author of *Waverley*', so long as 'the author of *Waverley*' has what I call a *primary* occurrence in the proposition considered. The difference of primary and secondary occurrences of denoting phrases is as follows:

When we say: 'George IV wished to know whether so-and-so', or when we say 'So-and-so is surprising' or 'So-and-so is true', etc., the 'so-and-so' must be a proposition. Suppose now that 'so-and-so' contains a denoting phrase. We may either eliminate this denoting phrase from the subordinate proposition 'so-and-so', or from the whole proposition in which 'so-and-so' is a mere constituent. Different propositions result according to which we do. I have heard of a touchy owner of a yacht to whom a guest, on first seeing it, remarked, 'I thought your yacht was larger than it is'; and the owner replied, 'No, my yacht is not larger than it is'. What the guest meant was, 'The size that I thought your yacht was is greater than the size your yacht is'; the meaning attributed to him is, 'I thought the size of your yacht was greater than the size of your yacht'. To return to George IV and *Waverley*, when we say, 'George IV wished to know whether Scott was the author of *Waverley*', we normally mean 'George IV wished to know whether one and only one man wrote *Waverley* and Scott was that man'; but we *may* also mean: 'One and only one man wrote *Waverley*, and George IV wished to know whether Scott was that man'. In the latter, 'the author of *Waverley*' has a *primary* occurrence; in the former, a *secondary*. The latter might be expressed by 'George IV wished to know, concerning the man who in fact wrote *Waverley*, whether he was Scott'. This would be true, for example, if George IV had seen Scott at a distance, and had asked 'Is that Scott?'. A *secondary* occurrence of a denoting phrase may be defined as one in which the phrase occurs in a proposition *p* which is a mere constituent of the proposition we are considering, and the substitution for the denoting phrase is to be effected in *p*, not in the whole proposition concerned. The ambiguity as between primary and secondary occurrences is hard to avoid in language;

but it does no harm if we are on our guard against it. In symbolic logic it is of course easily avoided.

The distinction of primary and secondary occurrences also enables us to deal with the question whether the present King of France is bald or not bald, and generally with the logical status of denoting phrases that denote nothing. If 'C' is a denoting phrase, say 'the term having the property F', then

'C has the property ϕ' means 'one and only one term has the

property F, and that one has the property ϕ'.*

If now the property F belongs to no terms, or to several, it follows that 'C has the property ϕ' is false for *all* values of ϕ. Thus 'the present King of France is bald' is certainly false; and 'the present King of France is not bald' is false if it means

'There is an entity which is now King of France and is not bald', but is true if it means

'It is false that there is an entity which is now King of France and is bald'.

That is, 'the King of France is not bald' is false if the occurrence of 'the King of France' is *primary*, and true if it is *secondary*. Thus all propositions in which 'the King of France' has a primary occurrence are false; the denials of such propositions are true, but in them 'the King of France' has a secondary occurrence. Thus we escape the conclusion that the King of France has a wig.

We can now see also how to deny that there is such an object as the difference between A and B in the case when A and B do not differ. If A and B do differ, there is one and only one entity x such that 'x is the difference between A and B' is a true proposition; if A and B do not differ, there is no such entity x. Thus according to the meaning of denotation lately explained, 'the difference between A and B' has a denotation when A and B differ, but not otherwise. This difference applies to true and false propositions generally. If '$a\,R\,b$' stands for 'a has the relation R to b', then when $a\,R\,b$ is true, there is such an entity as the relation R between a and b; when $a\,R\,b$ is false, there is no such entity. Thus out of any proposition we can make a denoting phrase, which denotes an entity if the proposition is true, but does not denote an entity

* This is the abbreviated, not the stricter, interpretation.

E

if the proposition is false. E.g., it is true (at least we will suppose so) that the earth revolves round the sun, and false that the sun revolves round the earth; hence 'the revolution of the earth round the sun' denotes an entity, while 'the revolution of the sun round the earth' does not denote an entity.*

The whole realm of non-entities, such as 'the round square', 'the even prime other than 2', 'Apollo', 'Hamlet', etc., can now be satisfactorily dealt with. All these are denoting phrases which do not denote anything. A proposition about Apollo means what we get by substituting what the classical dictionary tells us is meant by Apollo, say 'the sun-god'. All propositions in which Apollo occurs are to be interpreted by the above rules for denoting phrases. If 'Apollo' has a primary occurrence, the proposition containing the occurrence is false; if the occurrence is secondary, the proposition may be true. So again 'the round square is round' means 'there is one and only one entity x which is round and square, and that entity is round', which is a false proposition, not, as Meinong maintains, a true one. 'The most perfect Being has all perfections; existence is a perfection; therefore the most perfect Being exists' becomes:

'There is one and only one entity x which is most perfect; that one has all perfections; existence is a perfection; therefore that one exists'. As a proof, this fails for want of a proof of the premiss 'there is one and only one entity x which is most perfect'.†

Mr. MacColl (*Mind*, N.S., No. 54, and again No. 55, page 401) regards individuals as of two sorts, real and unreal; hence he defines the null-class as the class consisting of all unreal individuals. This assumes that such phrases as 'the present King of France', which do not denote a real individual, do, nevertheless, denote an individual, but an unreal one. This is essentially Meinong's theory, which we have seen reason to reject because it conflicts with the law of contradiction. With our theory of denoting, we are able to

* The propositions from which such entities are derived are not identical either with these entities or with the propositions that these entities have being.

† The argument can be made to prove validly that all members of the class of most perfect Beings exist; it can also be proved formally that this class cannot have *more* than one member; but, taking the definition of perfection as possession of all positive predicates, it can be proved almost equally formally that the class does not have even one member.

hold that there are no unreal individuals; so that the null-class is the class containing no members, not the class containing as members all unreal individuals.

It is important to observe the effect of our theory on the interpretation of definitions which proceed by means of denoting phrases. Most mathematical definitions are of this sort; for example '$m-n$ means the number which, added to n, gives m'. Thus $m-n$ is defined as meaning the same as a certain denoting phrase; but we agreed that denoting phrases have no meaning in isolation. Thus what the definition really ought to be is: 'Any proposition containing $m-n$ is to mean the proposition which results from substituting for "$m-n$" "the number which, added to n, gives m".' The resulting proposition is interpreted according to the rules already given for interpreting propositions whose verbal expression contains a denoting phrase. In the case where m and n are such that there is one and only one number x which, added to n, gives m, there is a number x which can be substituted for $m-n$ in any proposition containing $m-n$ without altering the truth or falsehood of the proposition. But in other cases, all propositions in which '$m-n$' has a primary occurrence are false.

The usefulness of *identity* is explained by the above theory. No one outside a logic-book ever wishes to say 'x is x', and yet assertions of identity are often made in such forms as 'Scott was the author of *Waverley*' or 'thou art the man'. The meaning of such propositions cannot be stated without the notion of identity, although they are not simply statements that Scott is identical with another term, the author of *Waverley*, or that thou art identical with another term, the man. The shortest statement of 'Scott is the author of *Waverley*' seems to be 'Scott wrote *Waverley*; and it is always true of y that if y wrote *Waverley*, y is identical with Scott'. It is in this way that identity enters into 'Scott is the author of *Waverley*'; and it is owing to such uses that identity is worth affirming.

One interesting result of the above theory of denoting is this: when there is anything with which we do not have immediate acquaintance, but only definition by denoting phrases, then the propositions in which this thing is introduced by means of a denoting phrase do not really contain this thing as a constituent, but contain instead the constituents expressed by the several words of the denoting phrase. Thus in every proposition that we can apprehend (i.e. not only in those whose truth or falsehood we can judge of, but in all that we can think about), all the constituents are really entities with which we have immediate acquaintance. Now such things as matter (in the sense in which matter occurs in physics) and the minds of other people are known to us only by denoting phrases, i.e. we are not *acquainted* with them, but we know them as what has such and such properties. Hence, although we can form propositional functions $C(x)$ which must hold of such and such a material particle, or of So-and-so's mind, yet we are not acquainted with the propositions which affirm these things that we know must be true, because we cannot apprehend the actual entities concerned. What we know is 'So-and-so has a mind which has such and such properties' but we do not know 'A has such and such properties', where A *is* the mind in question. In such a case, we know the properties of a thing without having acquaintance with the thing itself, and without, consequently, knowing any single proposition of which the thing itself is a constituent.

Of the many other consequences of the view I have been advocating, I will say nothing. I will only beg the reader not to make up his mind against the view—as he might be tempted to do, on account of its apparently excessive complication—until he has attempted to construct a theory of his own on the subject of denotation. This attempt, I believe, will convince him that, whatever the true theory may be, it cannot have such a simplicity as one might have expected beforehand.

3

On Referring

P. F. STRAWSON

Reprinted with the kind permission of the author and the publisher from A. Flew, ed., *Essays in Conceptual Analysis* (Houndmills Basingstoke Hampshire: Macmillan, 1956; New York: St. Martin's Press, Inc., 1956), 21-52.

Chapter II

ON REFERRING

BY P. F. STRAWSON

I

W E very commonly use expressions of certain kinds to
mention or refer to some individual person or single object
or particular event or place or process, in the course of
doing what we should normally describe as making a statement about that person, object, place, event, or process. I
shall call this way of using expressions the 'uniquely referring use'. The classes of expressions which are most
commonly used in this way are : singular demonstrative
pronouns ('this' and 'that') ; proper names (*e.g.* 'Venice',
'Napoleon', 'John') ; singular personal and impersonal pronouns ('he', 'she', 'I', 'you', 'it') ; and phrases beginning
with the definite article followed by a noun, qualified or
unqualified, in the singular (*e.g.* 'the table', 'the old man',
'the king of France'). Any expression of any of these classes
can occur as the subject of what would traditionally be
regarded as a singular subject-predicate sentence ; and
would, so occurring, exemplify the use I wish to discuss.

I do not want to say that expressions belonging to these
classes never have any other use than the one I want to
discuss. On the contrary, it is obvious that they do. It is
obvious that anyone who uttered the sentence, 'The whale
is a mammal', would be using the expression 'the whale'
in a way quite different from the way it would be used by
anyone who had occasion seriously to utter the sentence,
'The whale struck the ship'. In the first sentence one is
obviously *not* mentioning, and in the second sentence one
obviously *is* mentioning, a particular whale. Again if I

21

said, 'Napoleon was the greatest French soldier', I should be using the word 'Napoleon' to mention a certain individual, but I should not be using the phrase, 'the greatest French soldier', to mention an individual, but to say something about an individual I had already mentioned. It would be natural to say that in using this sentence I was talking *about* Napoleon and that what I was *saying* about him was that he was the greatest French soldier. But of course I *could* use the expression, 'the greatest French soldier', to mention an individual; for example, by saying: 'The greatest French soldier died in exile'. So it is obvious that at least some expressions belonging to the classes I mentioned *can* have uses other than the use I am anxious to discuss. Another thing I do not want to say is that in any given sentence there is never more than one expression used in the way I propose to discuss. On the contrary, it is obvious that there may be more than one. For example, it would be natural to say that, in seriously using the sentence, 'The whale struck the ship', I was saying something about both a certain whale and a certain ship, that I was using each of the expressions 'the whale' and 'the ship' to mention a particular object; or, in other words, that I was using each of these expressions in the uniquely referring way. In general, however, I shall confine my attention to cases where an expression used in this way occurs as the grammatical subject of a sentence.

I think it is true to say that Russell's Theory of Descriptions, which is concerned with the last of the four classes of expressions I mentioned above (*i.e.* with expressions of the form 'the so-and-so'), is still widely accepted among logicians as giving a correct account of the use of such expressions in ordinary language. I want to show in the first place, that this theory, so regarded, embodies some fundamental mistakes.

What question or questions about phrases of the form 'the so-and-so' was the Theory of Descriptions designed to answer? I think that at least one of the questions may be

ON REFERRING   23

illustrated as follows. Suppose someone were now to utter the sentence, 'The king of France is wise'. No one would say that the sentence which had been uttered was meaningless. Everyone would agree that it was significant. But everyone knows that there is not at present a king of France. One of the questions the Theory of Descriptions was designed to answer was the question: How can such a sentence as 'The king of France is wise' be significant even when there is nothing which answers to the description it contains, *i.e.*, in this case, nothing which answers to the description 'The king of France'? And one of the reasons why Russell thought it important to give a correct answer to this question was that he thought it important to show that another answer which might be given was wrong. The answer that he thought was wrong, and to which he was anxious to supply an alternative, might be exhibited as the conclusion of either of the following two fallacious arguments. Let us call the sentence 'The king of France is wise' the sentence S. Then the first argument is as follows:

(1) The phrase, 'the king of France', is the subject of the sentence S.

Therefore (2) if S is a significant sentence, S is a sentence *about* the king of France.

But (3) if there in no sense exists a king of France, the sentence is not about anything, and hence not about the king of France.

Therefore (4) since S is significant, there must in some sense (in some world) exist (or subsist) the king of France.

And the second argument is as follows:

(1) If S is significant, it is either true or false.

(2) S is true if the king of France is wise and false if the king of France is not wise.

(3) But the statement that the king of France is wise and the statement that the king of France is not wise are alike true only if there is (in some sense, in some world) something which is the king of France.

Hence (4) since S is significant, there follows the same conclusion as before.

These are fairly obviously bad arguments, and, as we should expect, Russell rejects them. The postulation of a world of strange entities, to which the king of France belongs, offends, he says, against 'that feeling for reality which ought to be preserved even in the most abstract studies'. The fact that Russell rejects these arguments is, however, less interesting than the extent to which, in rejecting their conclusion, he concedes the more important of their principles. Let me refer to the phrase, 'the king of France', as the phrase D. Then I think Russell's reasons for rejecting these two arguments can be summarized as follows. The mistake arises, he says, from thinking that D, which is certainly the *grammatical* subject of S, is also the *logical* subject of S. But D is not the logical subject of S. In fact S, although grammatically it has a singular subject and a predicate, is not logically a subject-predicate sentence at all. The proposition it expresses is a complex kind of *existential* proposition, part of which might be described as a 'uniquely existential' proposition. To exhibit the logical form of the proposition, we should re-write the sentence in a logically appropriate grammatical form; in such a way that the deceptive similarity of S to a sentence expressing a subject-predicate proposition would disappear, and we should be safeguarded against arguments such as the bad ones I outlined above. Before recalling the details of Russell's analysis of S, let us notice what his answer, as I have so far given it, seems to imply. His answer seems to imply that in the case of a sentence which is similar to S in that (1) it is grammatically of the subject-predicate form and (2) its grammatical subject does not refer to anything, then the only alternative to its being meaningless is that it should not really (*i.e.* logically) be of the subject-predicate form at all, but of some quite different form. And this in its turn seems to imply that if there are any sentences which are genuinely of the subject-predicate form, then the very fact of their being significant, having a

ON REFERRING   25

meaning, guarantees that there *is* something referred to by the logical (and grammatical) subject. Moreover, Russell's answer seems to imply that there are such sentences. For if it is true that one may be misled by the grammatical similarity of S to other sentences into thinking that it is logically of the subject-predicate form, then surely there must be other sentences grammatically similar to S, which *are* of the subject-predicate form. To show not only that Russell's answer seems to imply these conclusions, but that he accepted at least the first two of them, it is enough to consider what he says about a class of expressions which he calls 'logically proper names' and contrasts with expressions, like D, which he calls 'definite descriptions'. Of logically proper names Russell says or implies the following things:

(1) That they and they alone can occur as subjects of sentences which are genuinely of the subject-predicate form.

(2) That an expression intended to be a logically proper name is *meaningless* unless there is some single object for which it stands: for the *meaning* of such an expression just is the individual object which the expression designates. To be a name at all, therefore, it *must* designate something.

It is easy to see that if anyone believes these two propositions, then the only way for him to save the significance of the sentence S is to deny that it is a logically subject-predicate sentence. Generally, we may say that Russell recognizes only two ways in which sentences which seem, from their grammatical structure, to be about some particular person or individual object or event, can be significant:

(1) The first is that their grammatical form should be misleading as to their logical form, and that they should be analysable, like S, as a special kind of existential sentence.

(2) The second is that their grammatical subject should be a logically proper name, of which the meaning is the individual thing it designates.

I think that Russell is unquestionably wrong in this, and that sentences which are significant, and which begin with an expression used in the uniquely referring way, fall into neither of these two classes. Expressions used in the uniquely referring way are never either logically proper names or descriptions, if what is meant by calling them 'descriptions' is that they are to be analysed in accordance with the model provided by Russell's Theory of Descriptions.

There are no logically proper names and there are no descriptions (in this sense).

Let us now consider the details of Russell's analysis. According to Russell, anyone who asserted S would be asserting that :

(1) There is a king of France.
(2) There is not more than one king of France.
(3) There is nothing which is king of France and is not wise.

It is easy to see both how Russell arrived at this analysis, and how it enables him to answer the question with which we began, viz. the question : How can the sentence S be significant when there is no king of France ? The way in which he arrived at the analysis was clearly by asking himself what would be the circumstances in which we would say that anyone who uttered the sentence S had made a true assertion. And it does seem pretty clear, and I have no wish to dispute, that the sentences (1)-(3) above do describe circumstances which are at least *necessary* conditions of anyone making a true assertion by uttering the sentence S. But, as I hope to show, to say this is not at all the same thing as to say that Russell has given a correct account of the use of the sentence S or even that he has given an account which, though incomplete, is correct as far as it goes ; and is certainly not at all the same thing as to say that the model translation provided is a correct model for all (or for any) singular sentences beginning with a phrase of the form 'the so-and-so'.

It is also easy to see how this analysis enables Russell to answer the question of how the sentence S can be significant, even when there is no king of France. For, if this analysis is correct, anyone who utters the sentence S to-day would be jointly asserting three propositions, one of which (viz. that there is a king of France) would be false ; and since the conjunction of three propositions, of which one is false, is itself false, the assertion as a whole would be significant, but false. So neither of the bad arguments for subsistent entities would apply to such an assertion.

II

As a step towards showing that Russell's solution of his problem is mistaken, and towards providing the correct solution, I want now to draw certain distinctions. For this purpose I shall, for the remainder of this section, refer to an expression which has a uniquely referring use as 'an expression' for short ; and to a sentence beginning with such an expression as 'a sentence' for short. The distinctions I shall draw are rather rough and ready, and, no doubt, difficult cases could be produced which would call for their refinement. But I think they will serve my purpose. The distinctions are between :

> (A1) a sentence,
> (A2) a use of a sentence,
> (A3) an utterance of a sentence,

and, correspondingly, between :

> (B1) an expression,
> (B2) a use of an expression,
> (B3) an utterance of an expression.

Consider again the sentence, 'The king of France is wise' It is easy to imagine that this sentence was uttered at various times from, say, the beginning of the seventeenth century onwards, during the reigns of each successive French monarch ; and easy to imagine that it was also uttered during the subsequent periods in which France was not a monarchy. Notice that it was natural for me to speak of 'the sentence' or 'this sentence' being uttered at various times during this period ; or, in other words, that it would be natural and correct to speak of *one and the same* sentence being uttered on all these various occasions. It is in the sense in which it would be correct to speak of one and the same sentence being uttered on all these various occasions that I want to use the expression (A1) 'a sentence'. There are, however, obvious differences between different *occasions of the use* of this sentence. For instance, if one man uttered it in the reign of Louis XIV and another man uttered it in the reign of Louis XV, it would be natural to say (to assume) that they were respectively talking about different people ; and it might be held that the first man, in using the sentence, made a true assertion, while the second man, in using the same sentence, made a false assertion. If on the other hand two different men simultaneously uttered the sentence (*e.g.* if one wrote it and the other spoke it) during the reign of Louis XIV, it would be natural to say (assume) that they were both talking about the same person, and, in that case, in using the sentence, they *must* either both have made a true assertion or both have made a false assertion. And this illustrates what I mean by *a use* of a sentence. The two men who uttered the sentence, one in the reign of Louis XV and one in the reign of Louis XIV, each made a different use of the same sentence ; whereas the two men who uttered the sentence simultaneously in the reign of Louis XIV, made the same use [1] of the same sentence. Obviously in the case of this sentence, and equally obviously in the case of many others, we cannot talk of *the sentence* being true or false, but only of its being used to make a true or false assertion, or (if this is preferred) to express a true or a false proposition. And equally obviously we cannot talk of *the sentence* being *about* a particular person, for the same sentence may be used at different times to talk about

---

[1] This usage of 'use' is, of course, different from (*a*) the current usage in which 'use' (of a particular word, phrase, sentence) = (roughly) 'rules for using' = (roughly) 'meaning'; and from (*b*) my own usage in the phrase 'uniquely referring use of expressions' in which 'use' = (roughly) 'way of using'.

ON REFERRING   29

quite different particular persons, but only of *a use* of the
sentence to talk about a particular person. Finally it will
make sufficiently clear what I mean by an utterance of a
sentence if I say that the two men who simultaneously uttered
the sentence in the reign of Louis XIV made two different
utterances of the same sentence, though they made the same
use of the sentence.

If we now consider not the whole sentence, 'The king
of France is wise', but that part of it which is the expression,
'the king of France', it is obvious that we can make analogous, though not identical distinctions between (1) the
expression, (2) a use of the expression, and (3) an utterance
of the expression. The distinctions will not be identical;
we obviously cannot correctly talk of the expression 'the
king of France' being used to express a true or false proposition, since in general only sentences can be used truly
or falsely; and similarly it is only by using a sentence and
not by using an expression alone, that you can talk about a
particular person. Instead, we shall say in this case that
you *use* the expression to *mention* or *refer to* a particular
person in the course of using the sentence to talk about him.
But obviously in this case, and a great many others, the
expression (B1) cannot be said to mention, or refer to, anything, any more than the *sentence* can be said to be true or
false. The same expression can have different mentioning-
uses, as the same sentence can be used to make statements
with different truth-values. 'Mentioning', or 'referring', is
not something an expression does; it is something that
someone can use an expression to do. Mentioning, or
referring to, something is a characteristic of *a use* of an
expression, just as 'being about' something, and truth-or-
falsity, are characteristics of *a use* of a sentence.

A very different example may help to make these distinctions clearer. Consider another case of an expression
which has a uniquely referring use, viz. the expression 'I';
and consider the sentence, 'I am hot'. Countless people
may use this same sentence; but it is logically impossible

D

for two different people to make *the same use* of this sentence : or, if this is preferred, to use it to express the same proposition. The expression 'I' may correctly be used by (and only by) any one of innumerable people to refer to himself. To say this is to say something about the expression 'I' : it is, in a sense, to give its meaning. This is the sort of thing that can be said about *expressions*. But it makes no sense to say of the *expression* 'I' that it refers to a particular person. This is the sort of thing that can be said only of a particular use of the expression.

Let me use 'type' as an abbreviation for 'sentence or expression'. Then I am not saying that there are sentences and expressions (types), *and* uses of them, *and* utterances of them, as there are ships *and* shoes *and* sealing-wax. I am saying that we cannot say *the same things* about types, uses of types, and utterances of types. And the fact is that we do talk about types ; and that confusion is apt to result from the failure to notice the differences between what we can say about these and what we can say only about the *uses* of types. We are apt to fancy we are talking about sentences and expressions when we are talking about the uses of sentences and expressions.

This is what Russell does. Generally, as against Russell, I shall say this. Meaning (in at least one important sense) is a function of the sentence or expression ; mentioning and referring and truth or falsity, are functions of the use of the sentence or expression. To give the meaning of an expression (in the sense in which I am using the word) is to give *general directions* for its use to refer to or mention particular objects or persons ; to give the meaning of a sentence is to give *general directions* for its use in making true or false assertions. It is not to talk about any particular occasion of the use of the sentence or expression. The meaning of an expression cannot be identified with the object it is used, on a particular occasion, to refer to. The meaning of a sentence cannot be identified with the assertion it is used, on a particular occasion, to make. For to talk

ON REFERRING

about the meaning of an expression or sentence is not to talk about its use on a particular occasion, but about the rules, habits, conventions governing its correct use, on all occasions, to refer or to assert. So the question of whether a sentence or expression *is significant or not* has nothing whatever to do with the question of whether the sentence, *uttered on a particular occasion*, is, on that occasion, being used to make a true-or-false assertion or not, or of whether the expression is, on that occasion, being used to refer to, or mention, anything at all.

The source of Russell's mistake was that he thought that referring or mentioning, if it occurred at all, must be meaning. He did not distinguish B1 from B2; he confused expressions with their use in a particular context; and so confused meaning with mentioning, with referring. If I talk about my handkerchief, I can, perhaps, produce the object I am referring to out of my pocket. I cannot produce the meaning of the expression, 'my handkerchief', out of my pocket. Because Russell confused meaning with mentioning, he thought that if there were any expressions having a uniquely referring use, which were what they seemed (*i.e.* logical subjects) and not something else in disguise, their meaning must *be* the particular object which they were used to refer to. Hence the troublesome mythology of the logically proper name. But if someone asks me the meaning of the expression 'this' — once Russell's favourite candidate for this status — I do not hand him the object I have just used the expression to refer to, adding at the same time that the meaning of the word changes every time it is used. Nor do I hand him all the objects it ever has been, or might be, used to refer to. I explain and illustrate the conventions governing the use of the expression. This *is* giving the meaning of the expression. It is quite different from giving (in any sense of giving) the object to which it refers; for the expression itself does not refer to anything; though it can be used, on different occasion, to refer to innumerable things. Now as a matter of fact there is, in

English, a sense of the word 'mean' in which this word does approximate to 'indicate, mention or refer to'; *e.g.* when somebody (unpleasantly) says, 'I mean you'; or when I point and say, 'That's the one I mean'. But *the one I meant* is quite different from *the meaning of the expression* I used to talk of it. In this special sense of 'mean', it is people who mean, not expressions. People use expressions to refer to particular things. But the meaning of an expression is not the set of things or the single thing it may correctly be used to refer to : the meaning is the set of rules, habits, conventions for its use in referring.

It is the same with sentences : even more obviously so. Everyone knows that the sentence, 'The table is covered with books', is significant, and everyone knows what it means. But if I ask, 'What object is that sentence about ?' I am asking an absurd question — a question which cannot be asked about the sentence, but only about some use of the sentence : and in this case the sentence has not been used to talk about something, it has only been taken as an example. In knowing what it means, you are knowing how it could correctly be used to talk about things : so knowing the meaning has nothing to do with knowing about any particular use of the sentence to talk about anything. Similarly, if I ask : 'Is the sentence true or false ?' I am asking an absurd question, which becomes no less absurd if I add, 'It must be one or the other since it is significant'. The question is absurd, because the *sentence* is neither true nor false any more than it is *about* some object. Of course the fact that it is significant is the same as the fact that it *can* correctly be used to talk about something and that, in so using it, someone will be making a true or false assertion. And I will add that it will be used to make a true or false assertion *only* if the person using it *is* talking about something. If, when he utters it, he is not talking about anything, then his use is not a genuine one, but a spurious or pseudo-use : he is not making either a true or a false assertion, though he may think he is. And this points the way to the correct answer to the puzzle to which the Theory of Descriptions gives a fatally incorrect answer. The important point is that the question of whether the sentence is significant or not is quite independent of the question that can be raised about a particular use of it, viz. the question whether it is a genuine or a spurious use, whether it is being used to talk about something, or in make-believe, or as an example in philosophy. The question whether the sentence is significant or not is the question whether there exist such language habits, conventions or rules that the sentence logically could be used to talk about something; and is hence quite independent of the question whether it is being so used on a particular occasion.

III

Consider again the sentence, 'The king of France is wise', and the true and false things Russell says about it.

There are at least two true things which Russell would say about the sentence :

(1) The first is that it is significant; that if anyone were now to utter it, he would be uttering a significant sentence.

(2) The second is that anyone now uttering the sentence would be making a true assertion only if there in fact at present existed one and only one king of France, and if he were wise.

What are the false things which Russell would say about the sentence ? They are :

(1) That anyone now uttering it would be making a true assertion or a false assertion ;

(2) That part of what he would be asserting would be that there at present existed one and only one king of France.

I have already given some reasons for thinking that these two statements are incorrect. Now suppose someone were in fact to say to you with a perfectly serious air : 'The king of France is wise'. Would you say, 'That's untrue'? I think it is quite certain that you would not. But suppose he went on to *ask* you whether you thought that what he had just said was true, or was false; whether you agreed or disagreed with what he had just said. I think you would be inclined, with some hesitation, to say that you did not do either; that the question of whether his statement was true or false simply *did not arise*, because there was no such person as the king of France. You might, if he were obviously serious (had a dazed astray-in-the-centuries look), say something like: 'I'm afraid you must be under a misapprehension. France is not a monarchy. There is no king of France.' And this brings out the point that if a man seriously uttered the sentence, his uttering it would in some sense be *evidence* that he *believed* that there was a king of France. It would not be evidence for his believing this simply in the way in which a man's reaching for his raincoat is evidence for his believing that it is raining. But nor would it be evidence for his believing this in the way in which a man's saying, 'It's raining', is evidence for his believing that it is raining. We might put it as follows. To say 'The king of France is wise' is, in some sense of 'imply', to *imply* that there is a king of France. But this is a very special and odd sense of 'imply'. 'Implies' in this sense is certainly not equivalent to 'entails' (or 'logically implies'). And this comes out from the fact that when, in response to his statement, we say (as we should) 'There is no king of France', we should certainly *not* say we were *contradicting* the statement that the king of France is wise. We are certainly not saying that it is false. We are, rather, giving a reason for saying that the question of whether it is true or false simply does not arise.

And this is where the distinction I drew earlier can help us. The sentence, 'The king of France is wise', is certainly significant; but this does not mean that any particular use of it is true or false. We use it truly or falsely when we use it to talk about someone; when, in using the expression, 'The king of France', we are in fact mentioning someone.

ON REFERRING   35

The fact that the sentence and the expression, respectively, are significant just is the fact that the sentence *could* be used, in certain circumstances, to say something true or false, that the expression *could* be used, in certain circumstances, to mention a particular person; and to know their meaning is to know what sort of circumstances these are. So when we utter the sentence without in fact mentioning anybody by the use of the phrase, 'The king of France', the sentence does not cease to be significant: we simply *fail* to say anything true or false because we simply fail to mention anybody by this particular use of that perfectly significant phrase. It is, if you like, a spurious use of the sentence, and a spurious use of the expression; though we may (or may not) mistakenly think it a genuine use.

And such spurious uses [1] are very familiar. Sophisticated romancing, sophisticated fiction,[2] depend upon them. If I began, 'The king of France is wise', and went on, 'and he lives in a golden castle and has a hundred wives', and so on, a hearer would understand me perfectly well, without supposing *either* that I was talking about a particular person, *or* that I was making a false statement to the effect that there existed such a person as my words described. (It is worth adding that where the use of sentences and expressions is overtly fictional, the sense of the word 'about' may change. As Moore said, it is perfectly natural and correct to say that some of the statements in *Pickwick Papers* are *about* Mr. Pickwick. But where the use of sentences and expressions is not overtly fictional, this use of 'about' seems less correct; *i.e.* it would not *in general* be correct to say that a statement was about Mr. X or the so-and-so, unless there were such a person or thing. So it is where the romancing is in danger of being taken seriously that we might answer the question, 'Who is he talking about?' with 'He's not talking about anybody'; but, in saying this, we are not

---

[1] The choice of the word 'spurious' now seems to me unfortunate, at least for some non-standard uses. I should now prefer to call some of these 'secondary' uses.

[2] The unsophisticated kind begins: 'Once upon time there was . . .'

saying that what he is saying is either false or nonsense.)

Overtly fictional uses apart, however, I said just now that to use such an expression as 'The king of France' at the beginning of a sentence was, in some sense of 'imply', to imply that there was a king of France. When a man uses such an expression, he does not *assert*, nor does what he says *entail*, a uniquely existential proposition. But one of the conventional functions of the definite article is to act as a *signal* that a unique reference is being made — a signal, not a disguised assertion. When we begin a sentence with 'the such-and-such' the use of 'the' shows, but does not state, that we are, or intend to be, referring to one particular individual of the species 'such-and-such'. *Which* particular individual is a matter to be determined from context, time, place, and any other features of the situation of utterance. Now, whenever a man uses any expression, the presumption is that he thinks he is using it correctly : so when he uses the expression, 'the such-and-such', in a uniquely referring way, the presumption is that he thinks both that there is *some* individual of that species, and that the context of use will sufficiently determine which one he has in mind. To use the word 'the' in this way is then to imply (in the relevant sense of 'imply') that the existential conditions described by Russell are fulfilled. But to use 'the' in this way is not to *state* that those conditions are fulfilled. If I begin a sentence with an expression of the form, 'the so-and-so', and then am prevented from saying more, I have made no statement of any kind ; but I may have succeeded in mentioning someone or something.

The uniquely existential assertion supposed by Russell to be part of any assertion in which a uniquely referring use is made of an expression of the form 'the so-and-so' is, he observes, a compound of two assertions. To say that there is a ϕ is to say something compatible with there being several ϕs ; to say there is not more than one ϕ is to say something compatible with there being none. To say there is one ϕ and one only is to compound these two assertions. I have

ON REFERRING   37

so far been concerned mostly with the alleged assertion of existence and less with the alleged assertion of uniqueness. An example which throws the emphasis on to the latter will serve to bring out more clearly the sense of 'implied' in which a uniquely existential assertion is implied, but not entailed, by the use of expressions in the uniquely referring way.   Consider the sentence, 'The table is covered with books'.   It is quite certain that in any normal use of this sentence, the expression 'the table' would be used to make a unique reference, *i.e.* to refer to some one table.   It is a quite strict use of the definite article, in the sense in which Russell talks on p. 30 of *Principia Mathematica*, of using the article '*strictly*, so as to imply uniqueness'.   On the same page Russell says that a phrase of the form 'the so-and-so', used strictly, 'will only have an application in the event of there being one so-and-so and no more'.   Now it is obviously quite false that the phrase 'the table' in the sentence 'the table is covered with books', used normally, will 'only have an application in the event of there being one table and no more'.   It is indeed tautologically true that, in such a use, the phrase will have an application only in the event of there being one table and no more *which is being referred to*, and that it will be understood to have an application only in the event of there being one table and no more which it is understood as being used to refer to.   To use the sentence is not to assert, but it is (in the special sense discussed) to imply, that there is only one thing which is *both* of the kind specified (*i.e.* a table) *and is being referred to* by the speaker.   It is obviously not to assert this.   To refer is not to say you are referring.   To say there is *some table or other* to which you are referring is not the same as referring to a particular table.   We should have no use for such phrases as 'the individual I referred to' unless there were something which counted as referring.   (It would make no sense to say you had pointed if there were nothing which counted as pointing.)   So once more I draw the conclusion that referring to or mentioning a particular thing cannot be dissolved into any kind of assertion. To refer is not to assert, though you refer in order to go on to assert.

Let me now take an example of the uniquely referring use of an expression not of the form, 'the so-and-so'. Suppose I advance my hands, cautiously cupped, towards someone, saying, as I do so, 'This is a fine red one'. He, looking into my hands and seeing nothing there, may say: 'What is? What are you talking about?' Or perhaps, 'But there's nothing in your hands'. Of course it would be absurd to say that, in saying 'But you've got nothing in your hands', he was *denying* or *contradicting* what I said. So 'this' is not a disguised description in Russell's sense. Nor is it a logically proper name. For one must know what the sentence means in order to react in that way to the utterance of it. It is precisely because the significance of the word 'this' is independent of any particular reference it may be used to make, though not independent of the way it may be used to refer, that I can, as in this example, use it to *pretend* to be referring to something.

The general moral of all this is that communication is much less a matter of explicit or disguised assertion than logicians used to suppose. The particular application of this general moral in which I am interested is its application to the case of making a unique reference. It is a part of the significance of expressions of the kind I am discussing that they can be used, in an immense variety of contexts, to make unique references. It is no part of their significance to assert that they are being so used or that the conditions of their being so used are fulfilled. So the wholly important distinction we are required to draw is between

(1) using an expression to make a unique reference; and
(2) asserting that there is one and only one individual which has certain characteristics (*e.g.* is of a certain kind, or stands in a certain relation to the speaker, or both).

This is, in other words, the distinction between

(1) sentences containing an expression used to indicate

ON REFERRING   39

or mention or refer to a particular person or thing ; and
    (2) uniquely existential sentences.

What Russell does is progressively to assimilate more and
more sentences of class (1) to sentences of class (2), and consequently to involve himself in insuperable difficulties about
logical subjects, and about values for individual variables
generally : difficulties which have led him finally to the
logically disastrous theory of names developed in the *Enquiry
into Meaning and Truth* and in *Human Knowledge*. That
view of the meaning of logical-subject-expressions which
provides the whole incentive to the Theory of Descriptions
at the same time precludes the possibility of Russell's ever
finding any satisfactory substitutes for those expressions
which, beginning with substantival phrases, he progressively
degrades from the status of logical subjects.[1] It is not
simply, as is sometimes said, the fascination of the relation
between a name and its bearer, that is the root of the trouble.
Not even names come up to the impossible standard set.
It is rather the combination of two more radical misconceptions : first, the failure to grasp the importance of the
distinction (section II above) between what may be said of
an expression and what may be said of a particular use of
it ; second, a failure to recognize the uniquely referring use
of expressions for the harmless, necessary thing it is, distinct from, but complementary to, the predicative or ascriptive
use of expressions. The expressions which can in fact occur
as singular logical subjects are expressions of the class I
listed at the outset (demonstratives, substantival phrases,
proper names, pronouns) : to say this is to say that these
expressions, together with context (in the widest sense), are
what one uses to make unique references. The point of the
conventions governing the uses of such expressions is, along
with the situation of utterance, to secure uniqueness of
reference. But to do this, enough is enough. We do not,
and we cannot, while referring, attain the point of complete

[1] And this in spite of the danger-signal of that phrase, '*misleading* grammatical form'.

explicitness at which the referring function is no longer per-formed. The actual unique reference made, if any, is a matter of the particular use in the particular context; the significance of the expression used is the set of rules or con-ventions which permit such references to be made. Hence we can, using significant expressions, pretend to refer, in make-believe or in fiction, or mistakenly think we are refer-ring when we are not referring to anything.[1]

This shows the need for distinguishing two kinds (among many others) of linguistic conventions or rules: rules for referring, and rules for attributing and ascribing; and for an investigation of the former. If we recognize this dis-tinction of use for what it is, we are on the way to solving a number of ancient logical and metaphysical puzzles.

My last two sections are concerned, but only in the barest outline, with these questions.

IV

One of the main purposes for which we use language is the purpose of stating facts about things and persons and events. If we want to fulfil this purpose, we must have some way of forestalling the question, 'What (who, which one) are you talking about?' as well as the question, 'What are you saying about it (him, her)?' The task of forestalling the first question is the referring (or identifying) task. The task of forestalling the second is the attributive (or descriptive or classificatory or ascriptive) task. In the conventional English sentence which is used to state, or to claim to state, a fact about an individual thing or person or event, the performance of these two tasks can be roughly and approxi-mately assigned to separable expressions.[2] And in such a

[1 This sentence now seems to me objectionable in a number of ways, notably because of an unexplicitly restrictive use of the word 'refer'. It could be more exactly phrased as follows: 'Hence we can, using significant expressions, refer in secondary ways, as in make-believe or in fiction, or mistakenly think we are referring to something in the primary way when we are not, in that way, referring to anything'.]

2 I neglect relational sentences; for these require, not a modification in the principle of what I say, but a complication of the detail.

ON REFERRING   41

sentence, this assigning of expressions to their separate rôles corresponds to the conventional grammatical classification of subject and predicate. There is nothing sacrosanct about the employment of separable expressions for these two tasks. Other methods could be, and are, employed. There is, for instance, the method of uttering a single word or attributive phrase in the conspicuous presence of the object referred to ; or that analogous method exemplified by, *e.g.*, the painting of the words 'unsafe for lorries' on a bridge, or the tying of a label reading 'first prize' on a vegetable marrow. Or one can imagine an elaborate game in which one never used an expression in the uniquely referring way at all, but uttered only uniquely existential sentences, trying to enable the hearer to identify what was being talked of by means of an accumulation of relative clauses. (This description of the purposes of the game shows in what sense it would be a game : this is not the normal use we make of existential sentences.) Two points require emphasis. The first is that the necessity of performing these two tasks in order to state particular facts requires no transcendental explanation : to call attention to it is partly to elucidate the meaning of the phrase, 'stating a fact'. The second is that even this elucidation is made in terms derivative from the grammar of the conventional singular sentence ; that even the overtly functional, linguistic distinction between the identifying and attributive rôles that words may play in language is prompted by the fact that ordinary speech offers us separable expressions to which the different functions may be plausibly and approximately assigned. And this functional distinction has cast long philosophical shadows. The distinctions between particular and universal, between substance and quality, are such pseudo-material shadows, cast by the grammar of the conventional sentence, in which separable expressions play distinguishable rôles.[1]

To use a separate expression to perform the first of these

[1 What is said or implied in the last two sentences of this paragraph no longer seems to me true, unless considerably qualified.]

tasks is to use an expression in the uniquely referring way. I want now to say something in general about the conventions of use for expressions used in this way, and to contrast them with conventions of ascriptive use. I then proceed to the brief illustration of these general remarks and to some further applications of them.

What in general is required for making a unique reference is, obviously, some device, or devices, for showing both *that* a unique reference is intended and *what* unique reference it is; some device requiring and enabling the hearer or reader to identify what is being talked about. In securing this result, the context of utterance is of an importance which it is almost impossible to exaggerate; and by 'context' I mean, at least, the time, the place, the situation, the identity of the speaker, the subjects which form the immediate focus of interest, and the personal histories of both the speaker and those he is addressing. Besides context, there is, of course, convention; — linguistic convention. But, except in the case of genuine proper names, of which I shall have more to say later, the fulfilment of more or less precisely stateable contextual conditions is *conventionally* (or, in a wide sense of the word, *logically*) required for the correct referring use of expressions in a sense in which this is not true of correct ascriptive uses. The requirement for the correct application of an expression in its ascriptive use to a certain thing is simply that the thing should be of a certain kind, have certain characteristics. The requirement for the correct application of an expression in its referring use to a certain thing is something over and above any requirement derived from such ascriptive meaning as the expression may have; it is, namely, the requirement that the thing should be in a certain relation to the speaker and to the context of utterance. Let me call this the contextual requirement. Thus, for example, in the limiting case of the word 'I' the contextual requirement is that the thing should be identical with the speaker; but in the case of most expressions which have a referring use this requirement cannot be so precisely specified. A further, and perfectly

ON REFERRING 43

general, difference between conventions for referring and conventions for describing is one we have already encountered, viz. that the fulfilment of the conditions for a correct ascriptive use of an expression is a part of what is stated by such a use ; but the fulfilment of the conditions for a correct referring use of an expression is never part of what is stated, though it is (in the relevant sense of 'implied') implied by such a use.

Conventions for referring have been neglected or misinterpreted by logicians. The reasons for this neglect are not hard to see, though they are hard to state briefly. Two of them are, roughly : (1) the preoccupation of most logicians with definitions ; (2) the preoccupation of some logicians with formal systems. (1) A definition, in the most familiar sense, is a specification of the conditions of the correct ascriptive or classificatory use of an expression. Definitions take no account of contextual requirements. So that in so far as the search for the meaning or the search for the analysis of an expression is conceived as the search for a definition, the neglect or misinterpretation of conventions other than ascriptive is inevitable. Perhaps it would be better to say (for I do not wish to legislate about 'meaning' or 'analysis') that logicians have failed to notice that problems of use are wider than problems of analysis and meaning. (2) The influence of the preoccupation with mathematics and formal logic is most clearly seen (to take no more recent examples) in the cases of Leibniz and Russell. The constructor of calculuses, not concerned or required to make factual statements, approaches applied logic with a prejudice. It is natural that he should assume that the types of convention with whose adequacy in one field he is familiar should be really adequate, if only one could see how, in a quite different field — that of statements of fact. Thus we have Leibniz striving desperately to make the uniqueness of unique references a matter of logic in the narrow sense, and Russell striving desperately to do the same thing, in a different way, both for the implication of uniqueness and for that of existence.

It should be clear that the distinction I am trying to draw is primarily one between different rôles or parts that expressions may play in language, and not primarily one between different groups of expressions; for some expressions may appear in either rôle. Some of the kinds of words I shall speak of have predominantly, if not exclusively, a referring rôle. This is most obviously true of pronouns and ordinary proper names. Some can occur as wholes or parts of expressions which have a predominantly referring use, and as wholes or parts of expressions which have a predominantly ascriptive or classificatory use. The obvious cases are common nouns; or common nouns preceded by adjectives, including participial adjectives; or, less obviously, adjectives or participial adjectives alone. Expressions capable of having a referring use also differ from one another in at least the three following, not mutually independent, ways:

(1) They differ in the extent to which the reference they are used to make is dependent on the context of their utterance. Words like 'I' and 'it' stand at one end of this scale — the end of maximum dependence — and phrases like 'the author of *Waverley*' and 'the eighteenth king of France' at the other.

(2) They differ in the degree of 'descriptive meaning' they possess: by 'descriptive meaning' I intend 'conventional limitation, in application, to things of a certain general kind, or possessing certain general characteristics'. At one end of this scale stand the proper names we most commonly use in ordinary discourse; men, dogs, and motor-bicycles may be called 'Horace'. The pure name has no descriptive meaning (except such as it may acquire *as a result of* some one of its uses as a name). A word like 'he' has minimal descriptive meaning, but has some. Substantival phrases like 'the round table' have the maximum descriptive meaning. An interesting intermediate position is occupied by 'impure' proper

ON REFERRING   45

names like 'The Round Table' — substantival phrases which have grown capital letters.

(3) Finally, they may be divided into the following two classes : (i) those of which the correct referring use is regulated by some *general* referring-cum-ascriptive conventions ; (ii) those of which the correct referring use is regulated by no general conventions, either of the contextual or the ascriptive kind, but by conventions which are *ad hoc* for each particular use (though not for each particular utterance). To the first class belong both pronouns (which have the least descriptive meaning) and substantival phrases (which have the most). To the second class belong, roughly speaking, the most familiar kind of proper names. Ignorance of a man's name is not ignorance of the language. This is why we do not speak of the meaning of proper names. (But it won't do to say they are meaningless.) Again an intermediate position is occupied by such phrases as 'The Old Pretender'. Only an old pretender may be so referred to ; but to know which old pretender is not to know a general, but an *ad hoc*, convention.

In the case of phrases of the form 'the so-and-so' used referringly, the use of 'the' together with the position of the phrase in the sentence (*i.e.* at the beginning, or following a transitive verb or preposition) acts as a signal *that* a unique reference is being made ; and the following noun, or noun and adjective, together with the context of utterance, shows *what* unique reference is being made. In general the functional difference between common nouns and adjectives is that the former are naturally and commonly used referringly, while the latter are not commonly, or so naturally, used in this way, except as qualifying nouns ; though they can be, and are, so used alone. And of course this functional difference is not independent of the descriptive force peculiar to each word. In general we should expect the descriptive force of nouns to be such that they are more efficient tools

E

for the job of showing what unique reference is intended when such a reference is signalized; and we should also expect the descriptive force of the words we naturally and commonly use to make unique references to mirror our interest in the salient, relatively permanent and behavioural characteristics of things. These two expectations are not independent of one another; and, if we look at the differences between the commoner sort of common nouns and the commoner sort of adjectives, we find them both fulfilled. These are differences of the kind that Locke quaintly reports, when he speaks of our ideas of substances being *collections* of simple ideas; when he says that 'powers make up a great part of our ideas of substances'; and when he goes on to contrast the identity of real and nominal essence in the case of simple ideas with their lack of identity and the shiftingness of the nominal essence in the case of substances. 'Substance' itself is the troublesome tribute Locke pays to his dim awareness of the difference in predominant linguistic function that lingered even when the noun had been expanded into a more or less indefinite string of adjectives. Russell repeats Locke's mistake with a difference when, admitting the inference from syntax to reality to the extent of feeling that he can get rid of this metaphysical unknown only if he can purify language of the referring function altogether, he draws up his programme for 'abolishing particulars'; a programme, in fact, for abolishing the distinction of logical use which I am here at pains to emphasize.

The contextual requirement for the referring use of pronouns may be stated with the greatest precision in some cases (*e.g.* 'I' and 'you') and only with the greatest vagueness in others ('it' and 'this'). I propose to say nothing further about pronouns, except to point to an additional symptom of the failure to recognize the uniquely referring use for what it is; the fact, namely, that certain logicians have actually sought to elucidate the nature of a variable by offering such *sentences* as 'he is sick', 'it is green', as examples of something in ordinary speech like a *sentential function.* Now of course it is true that the word 'he' may be used on different occasions to refer to different people or different animals : so may the word 'John' and the phrase 'the cat'. What deters such logicians from treating these two expressions as quasi-variables is, in the first case, the lingering superstition that a name is logically tied to a single individual, and, in the second case, the descriptive meaning of the word 'cat'. But 'he', which has a wide range of applications and minimal descriptive force, only acquires a use as a referring word. It is this fact, together with the failure to accord to expressions, used referringly, the place in logic which belongs to them (the place held open for the mythical logically proper name), that accounts for the misleading attempt to elucidate the nature of the variable by reference to such words as 'he', 'she', 'it'.

Of ordinary proper names it is sometimes said that they are essentially words each of which is used to refer to just one individual. This is obviously false. Many ordinary personal names — names *par excellence* — are correctly used to refer to numbers of people. An ordinary personal name is, roughly, a word, used referringly, of which the use is *not* dictated by any descriptive meaning the word may have, and is *not* prescribed by any such general rule for use as a referring expression (or a part of a referring expression) as we find in the case of such words as 'I', 'this' and 'the', but is governed by *ad hoc* conventions for each particular set of applications of the word to a given person. The important point is that the correctness of such applications does not follow from any *general* rule or convention for the use of the word as such. (The limit of absurdity and obvious circularity is reached in the attempt to treat names as disguised description in Russell's sense ; for what is in the special sense implied, but not entailed, by my now referring to someone by name is simply the existence of someone, *now being referred to,* who is *conventionally referred to* by that name) Even this feature of names, however, is only a symptom of the purpose for which they are employed. At present our choice of names

48   ESSAYS IN CONCEPTUAL ANALYSIS

is partly arbitrary, partly dependent on legal and social observances. It would be perfectly possible to have a thorough-going *system* of names, based *e.g.* on dates of birth, or on a minute classification of physiological and anatomical differences. But the success of any such system would depend entirely on the convenience of the resulting name-allotments for the purpose of making unique references; and this would depend on the multiplicity of the classifications used and the degree to which they cut haphazard across normal social groupings. Given a sufficient degree of both, the selectivity supplied by context would do the rest; just as is the case with our present naming habits. Had we such a system, we could use name-words descriptively (as we do at present, to a limited extent and in a different way, with some famous names) as well as referringly. But it is by criteria derived from consideration of the requirements of the referring task that we should assess the adequacy of any system of naming. From the naming point of view, no kind of classification would be better or worse than any other simply because of the kind of classification — natal or anatomical — that it was.

I have already mentioned the class of quasi-names, of substantival phrases which grow capital letters, and of which such phrases as 'the Glorious Revolution', 'the Great War', 'the Annunciation', 'the Round Table' are examples. While the descriptive meaning of the words which follow the definite article is still relevant to their referring rôle, the capital letters are a sign of that extra-logical selectivity in their referring use, which is characteristic of pure names. Such phrases are found in print or in writing when one member of some class of events or things is of quite outstanding interest in a certain society. These phrases are embryonic names. A phrase may, for obvious reasons, pass into, and out of, this class (*e.g.* 'the Great War').

ON REFERRING   49

V

I want to conclude by considering, all too briefly, three further problems about referring uses.

(*a*) *Indefinite references.* Not all referring uses of singular expressions forestall the question 'What (who, which one) are you talking about?' There are some which either invite this question, or disclaim the intention or ability to answer it. Examples are such sentence-beginnings as 'A man told me that . . .', 'Someone told me that . . .' The orthodox (Russellian) doctrine is that such sentences are existential, but not uniquely existential. This seems wrong in several ways. It is ludicrous to suggest that part of what is asserted is that the class of men or persons is not empty. Certainly this is *implied* in the by now familiar sense of implication; but the implication is also as much an implication of the *uniqueness* of the particular object of reference as when I begin a sentence with such a phrase as 'the table'. The difference between the use of the definite and indefinite articles is, very roughly, as follows. We use 'the' either when a previous reference has been made, and when 'the' signalizes that the same reference is being made; or when, in the absence of a previous indefinite reference, the context (including the hearer's assumed knowledge) is expected to enable the hearer to tell *what* reference is being made. We use 'a' either when these conditions are not fulfilled, or when, although a definite reference *could* be made, we wish to keep dark the identity of the individual to whom, or to which, we are referring. This is the *arch* use of such a phrase as 'a certain person' or 'someone'; where it could be expanded, not into 'someone, but you wouldn't (or I don't) know who' but into 'someone, but I'm not telling you who'.

(*b*) *Identification statements.* By this label I intend statements like the following:

(i*a*) That is the man who swam the channel twice on one day.

(ii*a*) Napoleon was the man who ordered the execution of the Duc d'Enghien.

The puzzle about these statements is that their grammatical predicates do not seem to be used in a straightforwardly ascriptive way as are the grammatical predicates of the statements :

(i*b*) That man swam the channel twice in one day.

(ii*b*) Napoleon ordered the execution of the Duc d'Enghien.

But if, in order to avoid blurring the difference between (i*a*) and (i*b*) and (ii*a*) and (ii*b*), one says that the phrases which form the grammatical complements of (i*a*) and (ii*a*) are being used referringly, one becomes puzzled about what is being said in these sentences. We seem then to be referring to the same person twice over and either saying nothing about him and thus making no statement, or identifying him with himself and thus producing a trivial identity.

The bogy of triviality can be dismissed. This only arises for those who think of the object referred to by the use of an expression as its meaning, and thus think of the subject and complement of these sentences as meaning the same because they could be used to refer to the same person.

I think the differences between sentences in the (*a*) group and sentences in the (*b*) group can best be understood by considering the differences between the circumstances in which you would say (i*a*) and the circumstances in which you would say (i*b*). You would say (i*a*) instead of (i*b*) if you knew or believed that your hearer knew or believed that *someone* had swum the channel twice in one day. You say (i*a*) when you take your hearer to be in the position of one who can ask : 'Who swam the channel twice in one day ?' (And in asking this, he is not saying that anyone did, though his asking it implies — in the relevant sense — that someone did.) Such sentences are like answers to such questions. They are better called 'identification-statements' than 'identities'. Sentence (i*a*) does not assert more or less than sentence (i*b*). It is just that you say (i*a*) to a man whom you take to know certain things that you take to be unknown to the man to whom you say (i*b*).

This is, in the barest essentials, the solution to Russell's puzzle about 'denoting phrases' joined by 'is'; one of the puzzles which he claims for the Theory of Descriptions the merit of solving.

(*c*) *The logic of subjects and predicates.* Much of what I have said of the uniquely referring use of expressions can be extended, with suitable modifications, to the non-uniquely referring use of expressions; *i.e.* to some uses of expressions consisting of 'the', 'all the', 'all', 'some', 'some of the', etc. followed by a noun, qualified or unqualified, in the *plural*; to some uses of 'they', 'them', 'those', 'these'; and to conjunctions of names. Expressions of the first kind have a special interest. Roughly speaking, orthodox modern criticism, inspired by mathematical logic, of such traditional doctrines as that of the Square of Opposition and of some of the forms of the syllogism traditionally recognized as valid, rests on the familiar failure to recognize the special sense in which existential assertions may be implied by the referring use of expressions. The universal propositions of the fourfold schedule, it is said, must *either* be given a negatively existential interpretation (*e.g.* for A, 'there are no Xs which are not Ys') *or* they must be interpreted as conjunctions of negatively and positively existential statements of, *e.g.*, the form (for A) 'there are no Xs which are not Ys, and there are Xs'. The I and O forms are normally given a positively existential interpretation. It is then seen that, whichever of the above alternatives is selected, some of the traditional laws have to be abandoned. The dilemma, however, is a bogus one. If we interpret the propositions of the schedule as neither positively, nor negatively, nor positively *and* negatively, existential, but as sentences such that *the question of whether they are being used to make true or false assertions does not arise except when the existential condition is fulfilled for the subject term*, then all the traditional laws hold good together. And this interpretation is far closer to the most common uses of expressions beginning with 'all' and 'some' than is any Russellian alternative. For these expressions are most commonly used in the referring way. A literal-minded and childless man asked whether all his children are asleep will certainly not answer 'Yes' on the ground that he has none; but nor will he answer 'No' on this ground. Since he has no children, the question does not arise. To say this is not to say that I may not use the sentence, 'All my children are asleep', with the intention of letting someone know that I have children, or of deceiving him into thinking that I have. Nor is it any weakening of my thesis to concede that singular phrases of the form 'the so-and-so' may sometimes be used with a similar purpose. Neither Aristotelian nor Russellian rules give the exact logic of any expression of ordinary language; for ordinary language has no exact logic.

UNIVERSITY COLLEGE, OXFORD

4

Identifying Reference and Truth-values

P. F. STRAWSON

Reprinted with the kind permission of the author and editor from *Theoria*, XXX (1964), 96-118.

Identifying reference and truth-values

by

P. F. STRAWSON
(Oxford, England)

The materials for this paper are: one familiar and fundamental speech-function; one controversy in philosophical logic; and two or three platitudes.

We are to be concerned with statements in which, at least ostensibly, some particular historical fact or event or state of affairs, past or present, notable or trivial, is reported: as that the emperor has lost a battle or the baby has lost its rattle or the emperor is dying or the baby is crying. More exactly, we are to be concerned with an important subclass of such statements, viz. those in which the task of specifying just the historical state of affairs which is being reported includes, as an essential part, the sub-task of designating some particular historical item or items which the state of affairs involves. Not all performances of the reporting task include the performance of this sub-task—the task, I shall call it, of identifying reference to a particular item. Thus, the report that it is raining now, or the report that it was raining here an hour ago, do not. But the statement that Cæsar is dying, besides specifying the historical fact or situation which it is the function of the statement as a whole to report, has, as a part of this function, the sub-function of designating a particular historical item, viz. Caesar, which that situation essentially involves. And this part of the function of the whole statement is the whole of the function of part of the statement, viz. of the name 'Caesar'.

The speech-function we are to be concerned with, then, is the function of *identifying reference* to a particular historical item, when such reference occurs as a sub-function of statement. We are to be concerned with it in relation to a particular point of philosophical controversy, viz. the question whether a radical failure in the performance of this function results in a special case of falsity in statement or, rather, in what Quine calls a truth-value gap. The hope is not to show that one party to this dispute is quite right and the other quite wrong. The hope is to exhibit speech-function, controversy and one or two platitudes in a mutually illuminating way.

I introduce now my first pair, a complementary pair, of platitudes. One, perhaps the primary, but not of course the only, purpose of assertive discourse is to give information to an audience of some kind, viz. one's listener or listeners or reader or readers. Since there is no point in, or perhaps one should say, no possibility of, informing somebody of something of which he is already apprised, the making of an assertive utterance or statement—where such an utterance has in view this primary purpose of assertion—implies a presumption (on the part of the speaker) of ignorance (on the part of the audience) of some point to be imparted in the utterance. This platitude might be called the Principle of the Presumption of Ignorance. It is honoured to excess in some philosophical proposals for analysis or reconstruction of ordinary language, proposals which might appear to be based on the different and mistaken Principle of the Presumption of Total Ignorance. To guard against such excess, we need to emphasise a platitude complementary to the first. It might be called the Principle of the Presumption of Knowledge. The substance of this complementary platitude, loosely expressed, is that when an empirically assertive utterance is made with an informative intention, there is usually or at least often a presumption (on the part of the speaker) of knowledge (in the possession of the audience) of empirical facts relevant to the particular point to be imparted in the utterance. This is *too* loosely expressed. The connexion between the presumption of knowledge and the intention to impart just such-and-such a particular point of information may be closer than that of customary association; the connexion between the *identity* of the particular point it is intended to impart and the kind of knowledge presumed may be closer

98   P. F. STRAWSON

than that of relevance. Just as we might say that it could not be
true of a speaker that he intended to *inform* an audience of some
particular point unless he presumed their ignorance of that point,
so we might often say that it could not be true of a speaker that
he intended to inform the audience of just *that* particular point
unless he presumed in his audience certain empirical knowledge.
So the second principle, in which I am mainly interested, is truly
complementary to the first.

Now this may sound a little mysterious. But at least there will
be no difficulty felt in conceding the general and vague point that
we do constantly presume knowledge as well as ignorance on the
part of those who are the audiences of our assertive utterances,
and that the first kind of presumption, as well as the second,
bears importantly on our choice of what we say. The particular
application that I want to make of this general point is to the case
of identifying reference. To make it, I must introduce the not
very abstruse notion of identifying knowledge of particulars.

Everyone has knowledge of the existence of various particular
things each of which he is able, in one sense or another, though
not necessarily in every sense, to distinguish from all other things.
Thus a person may be able to pick a thing out in his current
field of perception. Or he may know there is a thing (not in his
current field of perception) to which a certain description applies
which applies to no other thing: such a description I shall call
an *identifying description*. Or he may know the name of a thing
and be able to recognise it when he encounters it, even if he can
normally give no identifying description of it other than one
which incorporates its own name. If a man satisfies any one of
these conditions in respect of a certain particular, I shall say he
has identifying knowledge of that particular. One is bound to
define such a notion in terms of its outlying cases, cases, here,
of minimal and relatively isolated identifying knowledge. So it is
worth emphasising that, in contrast with cases of minimal and
relatively isolated identifying knowledge, thre are hosts of cases
of very rich and full identifying knowledge, and that, in general,
our identifying knowledge of particulars forms an immensely
complex web of connexions and relations—the web, one might

say, of our historical and geographical knowledge in general, granted that these adjectives are not to be construed as qualifying academic subjects alone, but also knowledge of the most unpretentious kind about the particular things and people which enter into our minute-to-minute or day-to-day transactions with the world.

The notion of identifying reference is to be understood in close relation to the notion of identifying knowledge. When people talk to each other they commonly and rightly assume a large community of identifying knowledge of particular items. Very often a speaker knows or assumes that a thing of which he has such knowledge is also a thing of which his audience has such knowledge. Knowing or assuming this, he may wish to state some particular fact regarding such a thing, e.g. that it is thus-and-so; and he will then normally include in this utterance an expression which he regards as adequate, in the circumstances of utterance, to indicate to the audience *which* thing it is, of all the things in the scope of the audience's identifying knowledge, that he is declaring to be thus-and-so. The language contains expressions of several celebrated kinds which are peculiarly well adapted, in different ways, for use with this purpose. These kinds include proper names, definite and possessive and demonstrative descriptions, demonstrative and personal pronouns. I do not say that *all* expressions of these kinds are well adapted for use with this purpose; nor do I say, of those that are, that they are not regularly used in other ways, with other purposes.

When an expression of one of these classes *is* used in this way, I shall say that it is used to *invoke* identifying knowledge known or presumed to be in possession of an audience. It would now be easy to define identifying reference so that only when an expression is used to invoke identifying knowledge is it used to perform the function of identifying reference. But though it would simplify exposition thus to restrict attention to what we shall in any case count as the central cases of identifying reference, it would not be wholly desirable. For there are cases which cannot exactly be described as cases of invoking identifying knowledge, but which are nevertheless sufficiently like cases which *can* be so

100   P. F. STRAWSON

described to be worth classifying with them as cases of identifying reference. For instance, there may be within a man's current field of possible perception something which he has not noticed and cannot be said actually to have discriminated there, but to which his attention may be intentionally drawn simply by the use, on the part of a speaker, of an expression of one of the kinds I mentioned, as part of a statement of some fact regarding the particular item in question. In so far as the speaker's intention, in using the expression in question, is not so much to *inform* the audience of the existence of some particular item unique in a certain respect as to bring it about that the audience *sees for itself* that there is such an item, we may think this case worth classifying with the central cases of identifying reference. Again, there are cases in which an audience cannot exactly be credited with *knowledge* of the existence of a certain item unique in a certain respect, but can be credited with a strong *presumption* to this effect, can be credited, we might say, with *identifying presumption* rather than identifying knowledge. Such presumed presumption can be invoked in the same style as such knowledge can be invoked.

So we may allow the notion of identifying reference to a particular item to extend beyond the cases of invoking identifying knowledge. We must then face the unsurpising consequence that if, as we do, we wish to contrast cases in which a speaker uses an expression to perform the function of identifying reference with cases in which the intention and effect of a speaker's use of an expression is to inform the audience of the existence of a particular item unique in a certain respect, then we shall encounter some cases which do not *clearly* belong to either of these contrasting classes, which seem more or less dubious candidates for both. But this is not a situation which should cause us embarrassment, in philosophy; and, having made the point, I shall for simplicity's sake speak in what follows as if all cases of identifying reference were, at least in intention, cases of invoking identifying knowledge.

What I have said so far, in describing the function of identifying reference, is I think, uncontroversial in the sense that the description has proceeded without my having to take up a position on any well-worn point of controversy. It has a consequence, just alluded to, which should be equally uncontroversial, and which I shall labour a little now, partly in order to distinguish it from any *prise de position* on a matter which is undoubtedly one of controversy.

I have explained identifying reference—or the central case of identifying reference—as essentially involving a presumption, on the speaker's part, of the possession by the audience of identifying knowledge of a particular item. Identifying knowledge is knowledge of the existence of a particular item distinguished, in one or another sense, by the audience from any other. The appropriate stretch of identifying knowledge is to be invoked by the use of an expression deemed adequate by the speaker, in the total circumstances of utterance, to indicate to the audience which, of all the items within the scope of the audience's identifying knowledge, is being declared, in the utterance as a whole, to be thus-and-so. Depending upon the nature of the item and the situation of utterance, the expression used may be a name or a pronoun or a definite or demonstrative description; and it is of course not necessary that either name or description should in general be *uniquely* applicable to the item in question, so long as its choice, in the total circumstances of utterance, is deemed adequate to indicate to the audience which, of all the particular items within the scope of his identifying knowledge, is being declared, in the utterance as a whole, to be thus-and-so.

Now one thing that is absolutely clear is that it can be no part of the speaker's intention in the case of such utterances to *inform* the audience of the *existence* of a particular item bearing the name or answering to the description and distinguished by that fact, or by that fact plus something else known to the audience, from any other. On the contrary, the very task of identifying reference, as described, can be undertaken only by a speaker who knows or presumes his audience to be already in posession of such knowledge of existence and uniqueness as this. The task of identifying reference is *defined* in terms of a type of speaker-intention which *rules out* ascription to the speaker of the intention to impart the existence-and-uniqueness information in question. All this can be put, perfectly naturally, in other ways. Thus, that there exists a particular item to which the name or description is applicable and which, if not unique in this respect, satisfies some uniqueness-condition known to the hearer (*and* satisfies some uniqueness-condition known to the speaker) is no part of what the speaker *asserts* in an utterance in which the name or description is used to perform the function of identifying reference; it is, rather, a *presupposition* of his asserting what he asserts.

This way of putting it is still uncontroversial. For it is a natural way of putting what is itself uncontroversial. But it introduces a contrast, between the *asserted* and the *presupposed,* in words which are associated with an issue of controversy.

We can come at this issue by considering some of the ways in which an attempt to perform the function of identifying reference can either fail altogether or at least fall short of complete success and satisfactoriness. There are several ways in which such an attempt can fail or be flawed. For instance, it may be that, though the speaker possesses, the audience does not possess, identifying knowledge of the particular historical item to which the speaker intends to make an identifying reference; that the speaker credits the audience with identifying knowledge the audience does not possess. It may be that though the audience possesses identifying knowledge of the particular item in question, the expression chosen by the speaker fails to invoke the appropriate stretch of identifying knowledge and leaves the audience uncertain, or even misleads the audience, as to who or what is meant. Failures of this kind may be, though they need not be, due to flaws of another kind. For it may be that the speaker's choice of expression reflects mistakes of fact or language on his part; and such mistake-reflecting choices are still flaws, even where they do not mislead, as, for example, references to Great Britain as 'England' or to President Kennedy as 'the U. S. Premier' are not likely to mislead.

Though these are all cases of flawed or failed reference, they are not cases of the most radical possible kind of failure. For my descriptions of these cases imply that at least one fundamental condition of success is fulfilled, even if others are not fulfilled. They imply at least that there *is* a particular historical item within the scope of the speaker's identifying knowledge—even if not all his beliefs about it are true—such that he intends, by suitable choice of expression, to invoke identifying knowledge, presumed by him to be in possession of the audience, of that item. But this condition might fail too; and that in various ways. It might be that there just is no such particular item at all as the speaker takes himself to be referring to, that what he, and perhaps the audience too, take to be identifying knowledge of a particular item is not knowledge at all, but completely false belief. This is but one case of what might uncontroversially be called radical failure of the existence presupposition of identifying reference. It involves no moral turpitude on the part of the speaker. Different would be the case in which the speaker uses an expression, by way of apparently intended identifying reference, to invoke what he knows or thinks the audience thinks to be identifying knowledge, though he, the speaker, knows it to be false belief. The speaker in this case can have no intention actually to refer to a particular historical item, and so cannot strictly fail to carry out *that* intention. He can have the intention to be *taken* to have the former intention; and in *this* intention he may succeed. A full treatment of the subject would call for careful consideration of such differences. For simplicity's sake, I shall ignore the case of pretence, and concentrate on that case of radical reference-failure in which the failure is not a moral one.

Our point of controversy concerns the following question: given an utterance which suffers from radical reference-failure, are we to say that what we have here is just one special case of false statement or are we to say that our statement suffers from a deficiency so radical as to deprive it of the chance of being either true or false? Of philosophers who have discussed this question in recent years some have plumped uncompromisingly for the first answer, some uncompromisingly for the second; some have been eclectic about it, choosing the first answer for some cases and the second for others; and some have simply con-

104   P. F. STRAWSON

tented themselves with sniping at any doctrine that offered, while
wisely refraining from exposing any target themselves. In virtue of
his Theory of Descriptions and his views on ordinary proper names
as being condensed descriptions, Russell might be said to be the
patron of the first party—the "special case of false statement"
party. One recent explicit adherent of that party is Mr. Dummett
in his interesting article on *Truth* (P.A.S. 58–59). The second
party—the "neither true nor false" party—might be said, with
some reservations, to have included Quine, Austin and myself.
Quine invented the excellent phrase 'truth-value gap' to characterise what we have in these cases (See *Word and Object*).
Austin (see *Performative Utterances* and *How to Do Things
with Words*) contrasts this sort of defiviency or, as he calls it,
'infelicity' in statement with straightforward falsity and prefers
to say that a statement suffering from this sort of deficiency is
void—'void for lack of reference'.

Let us ignore the eclectics and the snipers and confine our
attention, at least for the moment, to the two uncompromising
parties. I do not think there is any question of demonstrating that
one party is quite right and the other quite wrong. What we have
here is the familiar philosophical situation of one party being
attracted by one simplified, theoretical—or 'straightened out'—
concept of truth and falsity, and the other by another. It might
be asked: How does ordinary usage speak on the point? And
this, as always, is a question which it is instructive to ask. But
ordinary usage does not deliver a clear verdict for one party or
the other. Why should it? The interests which ordinary usage
reflects are too complicated and various for it to provide overwhelming support for either way of *simplifying* the picture. The
fact that ordinary usage does not deliver a clear verdict does not
mean, of course, that there can be no other way of demonstrating,
at least, that one view is quite wrong. It might be shown, for
example, to be inconsistent, or incoherent in some other way.
But this is not the case with either of these views. Each would
have a certain amount of explaining and adjusting to do, but each
could perfectly consistently be carried through. More important,
each is *reasonable*. Instead of trying to demonstrate that one is

quite right and the other quite wrong, it is more instructive to see how both are reasonable, how both represent different ways of being impressed by the facts.

As a point of departure here, it is reasonable to take related cases of what are indisputably false statements and then set beside them the disputed case, so that we can see how one party is more impressed by the resemblances, the other by the differences, between the disputed case and the undisputed cases. The relevant undisputed cases are obviously of two kinds. One is that of an utterance in which an identifying reference is successfully made, and all the conditions of a satisfactory or allround successful act of empirical assertion are fulfilled except that the particular item identifyingly referred to and declared to be thus-and-so is, as a matter of fact, *not* thus-and-so. It is said of Mr. Smith, the new tenant of the Grange, that he is single, when he is in fact married: a statement satisfactory in all respects except that it is, indisputably, false. The other relevant case is that in which an explicit assertion of existence and uniqueness is made. It is said, say, that there is one and not more than one island in Beatitude Bay. And this is false because there is none at all or because there are several.

Now, it might be said on the one side, how vastly different from the ways in which things go wrong in either of these undisputed cases of falsity is the way in which things go wrong in the case of radical reference-failure. A judgment as to truth or falsity is a judgment on what the speaker asserts. But we have already noted the uncontroversial point that the existence-condition which fails in the case of radical reference-failure is not something asserted, but something presupposed, by the speaker's utterance. So his statement cannot be judged as a false existential assertion. Nor, evidently, can it be judged as an assertion false in the same way as the first undisputed example, i.e. false as being a *mis*-characterisation of the particular item referred to. For there is no such item for it to be a mischaracterisation of. In general, where there *is* such an item as the speaker refers to, and the speaker asserts, with regard to that item, that it is thus-and-so, his assertion is rightly assessed as true if the item is thus-and-so,

106   P. F. STRAWSON

as false if it is not. In the case of radical reference failure, the speaker, speaking in good faith, *means* his statement to be up for assessment in this way; he takes himself similarly to be asserting with regard to a particular item, that it is thus-and-so. But in fact the conditions of his making an assertion such as he takes himself to be making are not fulfilled. We can acknowledge the character of his intentions and the nature of his speech-performance by saying that he makes a statement; but we must acknowledge, too, the radical character of the way in which his intentions are frustrated by saying that his statement does not qualify as such an assertion as he takes it to be, and hence does not qualify for assessment as such an assertion. But then it does not qualify for truth-or-falsity assessment at all. The whole assertive enterprise is wrecked by the failure of its presupposition.

But now, on the other side, it could be said that what the disputed case has in common with the undisputed cases of falsity is far more important than the differences between them. In all the cases alike, we may take it a genuine empirical statement is made; a form of words is used such that if there were as a matter of fact in the world (in Space and Time) a certain item, or certain items, with certain characteristics—if, to put it differently, certain complex circumstances did as a matter of fact obtain in the world (in Space and Time)—then the statement would be true. The important distinction is between the case in which those complex circumstances do obtain and the case in which they don't. This distinction is the distinction we *should* use the words 'true' and 'false' (of statements) to mark, even if we do not consistently do so. And this distinction can be drawn equally in the disputed and the undisputed cases. A false empirical statement is simply any empirical statement whatever which fails for *factual* reasons, i.e. on account of circumstances in the world being as they are and not otherwise, to be a true one. Cases of radical reference-failure are simply one class of false statements.

It no longer seems to me important to come down on one side or the other in this dispute. Both conceptions are tailored, in the ways I have just indicated, to emphasise different kinds of interest in statement; and each has its own merits. My motives in bringing up the issue are three, two of which have already partially shown themselves. First, I want to disentangle this issue of controversy from other questions with which it is sometimes confused. Second, I want to dispel the illusion that the issue of controversy can be speedily settled, one way or the other, by a brisk little formal argument. Third, I want to indicate one way—no doubt there are more—in which, without positive commitment to either rival theory, we may find the issues they raise worth pursuing and refining. I shall say something on all three points, though most on the third.

First, then, the issue between the truth-value gap theory and the falsity theory, which has loomed so large in this whole area of discussion, has done so in a way which might be misleading, which might give a false impression. The impression might be given that the issue between these two theoretical accounts was the *crucial* issue in the whole area—the key, as it were, to all positions. Thus it might be supposed that anyone who rejected the view that the Theory of Descriptions gives an adequate general analysis, or account of the functioning, of definite descriptions was committed, by that rejection, to uncompromising adherence to the truth-value gap theory and uncompromising rejection of the falsity theory for the case of radical reference failure. But this is not so at all. The distinction between identifying reference and uniquely existential assertion is something quite undeniable. The sense in which the existence of something answering to a definite description used for the purpose of identifying reference, and its distinguishability by an audience from anything else, is presupposed and not asserted in an utterance containing such an expression, so used, stands absolutely firm, whether or not one opts for the view that radical failure of the presupposition would deprive the statement of a truth-value. It remains a decisive objection to the Theory of Descriptions, regarded as embodying a generally correct analysis of statements containing definite descriptions, that, so regarded, it amounts to a denial of these undeniable distinctions. I feel bound to labour the point a little, since I may be partly responsible for the confusion of these two issues by making the word 'presupposition' carry simultaneously

108   P. F. STRAWSON

the burden both of the functional distinction and of the truth-value gap theory. Only, at most, partly responsible; for the line-up is natural enough, though not inevitable; and though there is no logical compulsion one way, there is logical compulsion the other. One who accepts the Theory of Descriptions as a correct analysis is bound to accept the falsity theory for certain cases and reject the truth-value gap theory. One who accepts the truth-value gap theory is bound to reject the Theory of Descriptions as a generally correct analysis. But it is perfectly consistent to reject the view that the Theory of Descriptions is a generally correct analysis, on the grounds I have indicated, and also to withhold assent to the truth-value gap theory.

Now for my second point. I have denied that either of the two theories can be decisively refuted by short arguments, and I shall support this by citing and commenting on some specimen arguments which are sometimes thought to have this power. First, some arguments for the truth-value gap theory and against the falsity theory:

A (1) Let *Fa* represent a statement of the kind in question. If the falsity theory is correct, then the contradictory of *Fa* is not -*Fa,* but the disjunction of -*Fa* with a negative existential statement. But the contradictory of *Fa* is -*Fa.* Therefore the falsity theory is false.

(2) If 'false' is used normally, then from *It is false that S is P* it is correct to infer *S is not P.* But it is agreed on both theories that *S is not P* is true only if there is such a thing as *S.* Hence, if 'false' is used normally, *It is false that S is P* is true only if there is such a thing as *S.* Hence, if 'false' is used normally in the statement of the falsity theory, that theory is false.

(3) The question *Is S P?* and the command *Bring it about that S is P* may suffer from exactly the same radical reference failure as the statement *S is P.* But if an utterance which suffers from this radical reference failure is thereby rendered false, the question and command must be said to be false. But this is absurd. So the falsity theory is false.

Now arguments on the other side:

B (1) Let *Fa* represent a statement of the kind in question (e.g.*The king of France is bald*). Then there may be an equivalent statement, *Gb,* (e.g. *France has a bald king*) which is obviously false if there is no such thing as *a*. But the two statements are equivalent. So *Fa* is false if there is no such thing as *a*. So the truth-value gap theory is false.

(2) Let *P* be a statement which, on the truth-value gap theory, is neither true nor false. Then the statement that *P* is true is itself false. But if it is false that *P* is true, then *P* is false. In the same way we can derive from the hypothesis the conclusion that *P* is true, hence the conclusion that *P* is both true and false. This is self-contradictory, hence the original hypothesis is so too.

The defender of either view will have little difficulty in countering these arguments against it. Thus to B2 the reply is that if a statement lacks a truth-value, any statement assessing it as true *simpliciter* or as false *simpliciter* similarly lacks a truth-value. So no contradiction is derivable. To B1 the reply is that the argument is either inconclusive or question-begging. If 'equivalent' means simply 'such that if either is true, then necessarily the other is true', it is inconclusive If it also means 'such that if either is false, then necessarily the other is false', it is question-begging. To A3 the reply is that there is no reason why what holds for statements should hold also for questions and commands. To A2 the reply is that the inference is not strictly correct, though it is perfectly natural that we should normally make it. To A1 the reply is that it is question-begging, though again it is perfectly intelligible that we should be prone to think of contradictories in this way.

It is just an illusion to think that either side's position can be carried by such swift little sallies as these. What we have, in the enthusiastic defence of one theory or the other, is a symptom of difference of direction of interest. One who has an interest in actual speech-situations, in the part that stating plays in communication between human beings, will tend to find the simpler falsity theory inadequate and feel sympathy with—though, as I say, he is under no compulsion, exclusively or at all, to embrace— its rival. One who takes a more impersonal view of statement, who has a picture in which the actual needs, purposes and presumptions of speakers and hearers are of slight significance—in which, as it were, there are just statements on the one side and, on the other, the world they should reflect—he will naturally tend to brush aside the truth-value gap theory and embrace *its* simpler rival. For him, one might say, the subject of every statement is just the world in general. For his opponent, it is now this item, now that; and perhaps sometimes—rarely and disconcertingly enough—nothing at all.

And now for the third matter, which we shall find not unconnected with this last thought. It seems to be a fact which advocates of either, or of neither, theory can equally safely acknowledge, that the intuitive appeal, or prima facie plausibility, of the truth-value gap theory is not constant for all example-cases of radical reference-failure which can be produced or imagined. We can, without commitment to either theory, set ourselves to explain this variation in the intuitive appeal of one of them—which is also an inverse variation in the intuitive appeal of the other. The attempt to explain this fact may bring into prominence other facts which bear in interesting ways upon speech-situations in general, and those involving identifying reference in particular. I shall draw attention to but one factor—no doubt there are more—which may contribute to the explanation of this fact in some cases. In doing so, I shall invoke another platitude to set beside, and connect with, the platitudes we already have.

First, we may note that the truth-value gap theory can be expressed, in terms of the familiar idea of predication, in such a way as to secure for it a certain flexibility in application. Let us call an expression *as and when used in a statement with the role of identifying reference*—whether or not it suffers in that use from radical reference failure—a *referring expression*. Then any statement containing a referring expression, E, can be regarded as consisting of two expression-parts, one the expression E itself, to be called the subject-expression or subject-term, and the other the remainder of the statement, to be called the predicate-expression or predicate-term. In the case of a statement containing more than one, say two, referring expressions, it is to be open to us to cast one of these for the role of subject-expression, while the

IDENTIFYING REFERENCE AND TRUTH—VALUES   111

other is regarded as absorbed into the predicate-term which is attached to the subject-term to yield the statement as a whole. The adherent of the truth-value gap view can then state his view as follows.[1] The statement or predication as a whole is true just in the case in which the predicate-term does in fact apply to (is in fact 'true of') the object which the subject-term (identifyingly) refers to. The statement or predication as a whole is false just in the case where the negation of the predicate-term applies to that object, i.e. the case where the predicate-term can be truthfully denied of that object. The case of radical reference failure on the part of the subject-term is of neither of these two kinds. It is the case of the truth-value gap.

Now consider a statement consisting of two referring expressions one of which is guilty of reference failure while the other is not. Then it is open to us to carve up the statement in two different ways; and different decisions as to carving-up procedure may be allowed to result in different assessments of the statement for truth-value. Thus (1) we can see the guilty referring expression as absorbed into a predicate-term which is attached to the innocent referring expression to make up the statement as a whole; or (2) we can see the innocent referring expression as absorbed into a predicate-expression which is attached to the guilty referring expression to make up the statement as a whole. Now if we carve up the statement in the second way, we must say—according to our current statement of the truth-value gap theory—that the statement lacks a truth-value. But if we carve it up in the first way, we *may* say that it is false; (or, sometimes —when negative in form—that it is true). For to carve it up in the first way is to think of the statement as made up of the satisfactory or innocent referring expression together with one general term or predicate into which the guilty referring expression has been absorbed. The question whether that predicate does or does not apply to the object referred to by the satisfactory referring expression remains a perfectly answerable question; and the fact that the predicate has absorbed a guilty referring expression

[1] This way of stating it is in fact implicit in the fundamental definition of predication which Quine gives on p. 96 of *Word and Object*.

will, for most predicates affirmative in form, merely have the consequence that the right answer is 'No'. Thus, if we look at such a statement in this way, we can naturally enough declare it false or untrue, and naturally enough affirm its *negation* as true, on the strength of the reference failure of the guilty referring expression.

In this way, it might seem, the truth-value gap theory can readily modify itself to take account of certain examples which may seem intuitively unfavourable to it. For example, there is no king of France; and there is, let us say, no swimming-pool locally. But there is, let us say, an Exhibition in town; and there is, let us say, no doubt of Jone's existence. If we consider the statements

(1) that Jones spent the morning at the local swimming-pool

and (2) that the Exhibition was visited yesterday by the king of France

it may seem natural enough to say (1) that it is quite untrue, or is false, that Jones spent the morning at the local swimming-pool, since there isn't one; that, however Jones spent the morning, he did *not* spend it at the local swimming-pool, since there's no such place; and similarly (2) that it is quite untrue, or is false, that the Exhibition was visited yesterday by the king of France; that, whoever the Exhibition was visited by yesterday, it was *not* visited by the king of France, since there is no such person. And the modified truth-value gap theory accommodates these intuitions by allowing the guilty referring expressions, 'the local swimming-pool', 'the king of France', to be absorbed into the predicate in each case.

This modification to the truth-value gap theory, though easy and graceful, will scarcely seem adequate. For one thing, it will not be available for all intuitively unfavourable examples, but only for those which contain more than one referring expression. For another, it will remain incomplete inside its own domain unless some *principle of choice* between alternative ways of carving up a statement is supplied. The theory might resolve the latter question self-sacrificially, by declaring that the carving-up operation was always to be so conducted as to permit the assignment of a truth-value whenever possible. But this more might be too self-sacrificial, turning friends into enemies, turning intuitively favourable cases into unfavourable ones.

So let us consider further. Confronted with the classical example, "The king of France is bald", we may well feel it natural to say, straight off, that the question whether the statement is true or false doesn't arise because there is no king of France. But suppose the statement occurring in the context of a set of answers to the question: "What examples, if any, are there of famous contemporary figures who are *bald?*" Or think of someone compiling a list in answer to the question, "Who has died recently?" and including in it the term "the king of France". Or think of someone including the statement "The king of France married again" in a set of statements compiled in reply to the question: "What outstanding events, if any, have occurred recently in the social and political fields?" In the first two cases the king of France appears to be cited as an *instance* or example of an *antecedently introduced class.* In the last case the statement as a whole claims to report an event as an instance of an *antecedently introduced class.* The question in each case represents the antecedent centre of interest as a certain class—the class of bald notables, the class of recently deceased notables, the class of notable recent events in a certain field—and the question is as to what items, if any, the classes include. Since it is certainly false that the classes, in each case, include any such items as our answers claim they do, those answers can, without too much squeamishness, be simply marked as wrong answers. So to mark them is not to reject them as answers to questions which don't arise, but to reject them as wrong answers to questions which do arise. Yet the answers need include only *one* referring expression for a particular item, viz. the one guilty of reference failure; and the questions need not contain any at all.

This suggests a direction in which we might look for the missing principle of choice in the case of our previous examples, those about the swimming pool and the Exhibition, which contained two referring expressions. The point was not, or was not solely, that each contained an extra and satisfactory referring expression.

It was rather that we could easily see the centre of interest in each case as being the question, e.g. *how Jones spent the morning* or *what notable visitors the Exhibition has had,* or *how the Exhibition is getting on.* And the naturalness of taking them in this way was increased by the device of putting the satisfactory referring expression *first,* as grammatical subject of the sentence, and the unsatisfactory one last. We might, for example, have felt a shade more squeamish if we had written "The king of France visited the Exhibition yesterday" instead of "The Exhibition was visited yesterday by the king of France". We feel very squeamish indeed about "The king of France is bald" presented abruptly, out of context, just because we don't naturally and immediately think of a context in which interest is centred, say, on the question *What bald notables are there?* rather than on the question *What is the king of France like?* or *Is the king of France bald?* Of course, to either of *these* two questions the statement would not be just an incorrect answer. *These* questions have no correct answer and hence, in a sense, no incorrect answer either. They *are* questions which do not arise. This does not mean there is no correct *reply* to them. The correct reply is: "There is no king of France". But this reply is not an answer to, but a rejection of, the question. The question about bald notables, on the other hand, *can* be answered, rightly or wrongly. Any answer which purports to mention someone included in the class, and fails to do so, is wrong; and it is still wrong even if there is no such person at all as it purports to mention.

I should like to state the considerations I have been hinting at a little more generally, and with less dependence upon the notion of a question. Summarily my suggestions are as follows.

(1) First comes the additional platitude I promised. Statements,or the pieces of discourse to which they belong, have subjects, not only in the relatively precise senses of logic and grammar, but in a vaguer sense with which I shall associate the words 'topic' and 'about'. Just now I used the hypothesis of a *question* to bring out, with somewhat unnatural sharpness, the idea of the topic or centre of interest of a statement, the idea of what a statement could be said, in this sense, to be about. But

even where there is no actual first-order question to pin-point for us with this degree of sharpness the answer to the higher-order question, 'What is the statement, in this sense, about'?, it may nevertheless often be possible to give a fairly definite answer to this question. For stating is not a gratuitous and random human activity. We do not, except in social desperation, direct isolated and unconnected pieces of information at each other, but on the contrary intend in general to give or add information about what is a matter of standing or current interest or concern. There is a great variety of possible types of answer to the question what the topic of a statement is, what a statement is 'about',—about baldness, about what great men are bald, about which countries have bald rulers, about France, about the king, etc.—and not every such answer excludes every other in a given case.—This platitude we might dignify with the title, the Principle of Relevance.

(2) It comes to stand beside that other general platitude which I announced earlier under the title, the Principle of the Presumption of Knowledge. This principle, it will be remembered, is that statements, in respect of their informativeness, are not generally self-sufficient units, free of any reliance upon what the audience is assumed to know or to assume already, but commonly depend for their effect upon knowledge assumed to be already in the audience's possession. The particular application I made of this principle was to the case of identifying reference, in so far as the performance of this function rests on the presumption of identifying knowledge in the possession of the audience. When I say that the new platitude comes to stand beside the old one, I mean that the spheres of (a) what a statement addressed to an audience is *about* and (b) what, in the making of that statement, the audience is assumed to have some knowledge of already, are spheres that will often, and naturally, overlap.

But (3) they need not be co-extensive. Thus, given a statement which contains a referring expression, the specification of that statement's topic, what it is about, would very often involve mentioning, or seeming to mention, the object which that expression was intended to refer to; but sometimes the topic of a state-

116   P. F. STRAWSON

ment containing such an expression could be specified without
mentioning such an object. Let us call the first type of case Type 1
and the second type of case Type 2. (Evidently a statement could
be of Type 1 relative to one referring expression it contained and
of Type 2 relative to another).

Now (4) assessments of statements as true or untrue are commonly, though not only, topic-centred in the same way as the
statements assessed; and when, as commonly, this is so, we may
say that the statement is assessed *as* putative information *about
its topic*.

Hence (5), given a case of radical reference-failure on the part
of a referring expression, the truth-value gap account of the consequences of this failure will seem more naturally applicable if
the statement in question is of Type 1 (relative to that referring
expression) than if it is of Type 2. For if it is of Type 2, the
failure of reference does not affect the topic of the statement, it
merely affects what purports to be information *about its topic*. We
may still judge the statement as putative information *about its
topic* and say, perhaps, that the failure of reference has the consequence that it is *mis*informative *about its topic*. But we cannot
say this if it is a case of Type 1. If it is a case of Type 1, the
failure of reference affects the topic itself and not merely the
putative information about the topic. If we know of the reference-
failure, we know that the statement cannot really have the topic
it is intended to have and hence cannot be assessed as putative
information about that topic. It can be seen neither as correct,
nor as incorrect, information *about its topic*.

But, it might be said, this account is self-contradictory. For it
implies that in a Type 1 case of radical reference-failure the statement does not really *have* the topic which by hypothesis it does
have; it implies that a statement which, by hypothesis, is *about*
something is really about nothing. To this objection we must reply
with a distinction. If I believe that the legend of King Arthur is
historical truth, when there was in fact no such person, I may
in one sense make statements *about* King Arthur, *describe* King
Arthur and make king Arthur my *topic*. But there is another
sense in which I cannot make statements about King Arthur,

IDENTIFYING REFERENCE AND TRUTH—VALUES   117

describe him or make him my topic. This second sense is stronger than the first. I may suppose myself to be making statements about him in the second, stronger sense; but I am really only making statements about him in the first and weaker sense. If, however, my belief in King Arthur were true and I really was making statements about him in the second sense, it would still be true that I was making statements about him in the first sense. This is why the first is a weaker (i.e. more comprehensive) sense than the second and not merely different from it.

Bearing this distinction of sense in mind, we can now frame a recipe for distinguishing those cases of reference-failure which are relatively favourable to the truth-value gap theory from those cases which are relatively unfavourable to it. The recipe is as follows. Consider in its context the statement suffering from reference-failure and frame a certain kind of description of the speech-episode of making it. The description is to begin with some phrase like 'He (i.e. the speaker) was saying (describing) . . . . . .' and is to continue with an interrogative pronoun, adjective or adverb, introducing a dependent clause. The clause, with its introductory conjunction, specifies the topic of the statement, what it can be said (at least in the weaker, and, if there is no reference failure, also in the stronger, sense) to be *about;* while *what is said about its topic* is eliminated from the description in favour of the interrogative expression. Examples of such descriptions based on cases already mentioned would be:

He was describing *how Jones spent the morning*
He was saying *which notable contemporaries are bald*
He was saying *what the king of France is like.*

If the peccant referring expression survives in the clause introduced by the interrogative, the clause which specifies what the original statement was about, then we have a case relatively favourable to the truth-value gap theory. If the peccant referring expression is eliminated, and thus belongs to what purports to be information about the topic of the original statement, then we have a case relatively unfavourable to the truth-value gap theory. There can be no true or false, right or wrong, descriptions-of-what-the-king-of-France-is-like, because there is no king of

118   P. F. STRAWSON

France. But there can be right or wrong descriptions-of-how-Jones-spent-the-morning, and the description of him as having spent it at the local swimming-pool is wrong because there is no such place.

It is easy to see why the relevance of these factors should have been overlooked by those philosophers, including myself, who, considering a few example sentences in isolation from possible contexts of their use, have been tempted to embrace, and to generalise, the truth-value gap theory. For, first, it often is the case that the topic of a statement is, or includes, something referred to by a referring expression; for such an expression invokes the knowledge or current perceptions of an audience, and what is of concern to an audience is often what it already knows something about or is currently perceiving. And, second, it often is the case that the placing of an expression at the beginning of a sentence, in the position of grammatical subject, serves, as it were, to announce the statement's topic. The philosopher, thinking about reference failure in terms of one or two short and isolated example sentences beginning with referring expressions, will tend to be influenced by these facts without noticing *all* of what is influencing him. So he will tend to attribute his sense of something more radically wrong than falsity to the presence alone of what is alone obvious, viz. a referring expression which fails of reference; and thus will overlook altogether these considerations about aboutness or topic which I have been discussing.

Let me remark that I do not claim to have done more than mention one factor which may sometimes bear on the fact that a truth-value gap theory for the case of radical reference failure is apt to seem more intuitively attractive in some instances than it does in others.

5

The Theory of Meaning

GILBERT RYLE

Reprinted with the kind permission of the publisher from C. A. Mace, ed., *British Philosophy in the Mid-Century* (London: George Allen and Unwin, Ltd., 1957), 239-64.

GILBERT RYLE

THE THEORY OF MEANING

WE can all use the notion of *meaning*. From the moment we begin to learn to translate English into French and French into English, we realize that one expression does or does not mean the same as another. But we use the notion of meaning even earlier than that. When we read or hear something in our own language which we do not understand, we wonder what it means and ask to have its meaning explained to us. The ideas of understanding, misunderstanding and failing to understand what is said already contain the notion of expressions having and lacking specifiable meanings.

It is, however, one thing to ask, as a child might ask, What, if anything, is meant by 'vitamin', or 'abracadabra' or '$(a+b)^2 = a^2 + b^2 + 2ab$'? It is quite another sort of thing to ask What are meanings? It is, in the same way, one thing to ask, as a child might ask, What can I buy for this shilling?, and quite another sort of thing to ask What is purchasing-power? or What are exchange-values?

Now answers to this highly abstract question, What are meanings? have, in recent decades, bulked large in philosophical and logical discussions. Preoccupation with the theory of meaning could be described as the occupational disease of twentieth-century Anglo-Saxon and Austrian philosophy. We need not worry whether or not it is a disease. But it might be useful to survey the motives and the major results of this preoccupation.

Incidentally it is worth noticing that many of these issues were explicitly canvassed — and some of them conclusively settled — in certain of Plato's later Dialogues, and in the logical and other works of Aristotle. Some of them, again, were dominant issues in the late Middle Ages and later still with Hobbes; and some of them, thickly or thinly veiled in the psychological terminology of 'ideas', stirred uneasily inside British epistemology between Locke and John Stuart Mill. But I shall not, save for one or two back-references, discuss the early history of these issues.

The shopkeeper, the customer, the banker and the merchant are ordinarily under no intellectual pressure to answer or even ask the abstract questions What is purchasing-power? and What are exchange-values? They are interested in the prices of things, but not yet in the abstract question What is the real nature of that which is common to two articles of the same price? Similarly, the child who tries to follow a conversation on an unfamiliar topic, and the translator who tries to render Thucydides into English are interested in what certain expressions mean. But they are not necessarily interested in the abstract questions What is it for an expression to have a meaning? or What is the nature and status of that which an expression and its translation or paraphrase are both the vehicles? From what sort of interests, then, do we come to ask this sort of question? Doubtless there are many answers. I shall concentrate on two of them which I shall call 'the Theory of Logic' and 'the Theory of Philosophy'. I shall spend a good long time on the first; not so long on the second.

(1) *The Theory of Logic.* The logician, in studying the rules of inference has to talk of the components of arguments, namely their premisses and conclusions and to talk of them in perfectly general terms. Even when he adduces concrete premisses and conclusions, he does so only to illustrate the generalities which are his proper concern. In the same way, he has to discuss the types of separable components or the types of distinguishable features of these premiss-types and conclusion-types, since it is sometimes on such components or features of premisses and conclusions that the inferences from and to them pivot.

Now the same argument may be expressed in English or in French or in any other language; and if it is expressed in English, there may still be hosts of different ways of wording it. What the logician is exploring is intended to be indifferent to these differences of wording. He is concerned with what is said by a premiss-sentence or a conclusion-sentence, not with how it is worded.

So, if not in the prosecution of his inquiry, at least in his ex-

THE THEORY OF MEANING   241

planations of what he is doing, he has to declare that his subject-matter consist not of the sentences and their ingredient words in which arguments are expressed, but of the propositions or judgments and their constituent terms, ideas or concepts of which the sentences and words are the vehicles. Sometimes he may say that his subject matter consists of sentence-meanings and their constituent word-meanings or phrase-meanings, though this idiom is interestingly repellent. Why it is repellent we shall, I hope, see later on. So in giving this sort of explanation of his business, he is talking *about* meanings, where in the prosecution of that business he is just operating *upon* them.

For our purposes it is near enough true to say that the first influential discussion of the notion of meaning given by a modern logician was that with which John Stuart Mill opens his *System of Logic* (1843). He acknowledges debts both to Hobbes and to the Schoolmen, but we need not trace these borrowings in detail.

Mill's contributions to Formal or Symbolic Logic were negligible. It was not he but his exact contemporaries, Boole and de Morgan, and his immediate successors, Jevons, Venn, Carroll, McColl and Peirce who, in the English-speaking world, paved the way for Russell. On the other hand, it is difficult to exaggerate the influence which he exercised, for good and for ill, upon British and Continental philosophers; and we must include among these philosophers the Symbolic Logicians as well, in so far as they have philosophized about their technical business. In particular, Mill's theory of meaning set the questions, and in large measure, determined their answers for thinkers as different as Brentano, in Austria; Meinong and Husserl, who were pupils of Brentano; Bradley, Jevons, Venn, Frege, James, Peirce, Moore and Russell. This extraordinary achievement was due chiefly to the fact that Mill was original in producing a doctrine of meaning at all. The doctrine that he produced was immediately influential, partly because a doctrine was needed and partly because its inconsistencies were transparent. Nearly all of the thinkers whom I have listed were in vehement opposition to certain parts of Mill's doctrine, and it was the other parts of it from which they often drew their most effective weapons.

Q

Mill, following Hobbes's lead, starts off his account of the notion of meaning by considering single words. As we have to learn the alphabet before we can begin to spell, so it seemed natural to suppose that the meanings of sentences are compounds of the components, which are the meanings of their ingredient words. Word-meanings are atoms, sentence-meanings are molecules. I say that it seemed natural, but I hope soon to satisfy you that it was a tragically false start. Next Mill, again following Hobbes's lead, takes it for granted that all words, or nearly all words, are names, and this, at first, sounds very tempting. We know what it is for 'Fido' to be the name of a particular dog, and for 'London' to be the name of a particular town. There, in front of us, is the dog or the town which has the name, so here, one feels, there is no mystery. We have just the familiar relation between a thing and its name. The assimilation of all or most other single words to names gives us, accordingly, a cosy feeling. We fancy that we know where we are. The dog in front of us is what the word 'Fido' stands for, the town we visited yesterday is what the word 'London' stands for. So the classification of all or most single words as names makes us feel that what a word means is in all cases some manageable thing that that word is the name of. Meanings, at least word-meanings, are nothing abstruse or remote, they are, *prima facie*, ordinary things and happenings like dogs and towns and battles.

Mill goes further. Sometimes the grammatical subject of a sentence is not a single word but a many-worded phrase, like 'the present Prime Minister' or 'the first man to stand on the summit of Mt. Everest'. Mill has no qualms in classifying complex expressions like these also as names, what he calls 'many-worded names'. There do not exist proper names for everything we want to talk about; and sometimes we want to talk about something or somebody whose proper name, though it exists, is unknown to us. So descriptive phrases are coined by us to do duty for proper names. But they are still, according to Mill, names, though the tempting and in fact prevailing interpretation of this assertion differs importantly from what Mill usually wanted to convey. For, when Mill calls a word or phrase a 'name', he is using 'name' not, or not always, quite in the ordinary way. Sometimes he says that for an expression to be a name it must be able to be used as the subject or the predicate of a subject-predicate sentence — which lets in, e.g. adjectives as names. Sometimes his requirements are more stringent. A name is an expression which can be the subject of a subject-predicate sentence — which leaves only nouns, pronouns and substantival phrases. 'Name', for him, does not mean merely 'proper name'. He often resisted temptations to which he subjected his successors.

Before going any further, I want to make you at least suspect that this initially congenial equation of words and descriptive phrases with names is from the outset a monstrous howler — if, like some of Mill's successors, though unlike Mill himself, we do systematically construe 'name' on the model of 'proper name'. The assumption of the truth of this equation has been responsible for a large number of radical absurdities in philosophy in general and the philosophy of logic in particular. It was a fetter round the ankles of Meinong, from which he never freed himself. It was a fetter round the ankles of Frege, Moore and Russell, who all, sooner or later, saw that without some big emendations, the assumption led inevitably to fatal impasses. It was, as he himself says in his new book, a fetter round the ankles of Wittgenstein in the *Tractatus*, though in that same book he had found not only the need but the way to cut himself partially loose from it.

I am still not quite sure why it seems so natural to assume that all words are names, and even that every possible grammatical subject of a sentence, one-worded or many-worded, stands to something as the proper name 'Fido' stands to the dog Fido, and, what is a further point, that the thing it stands for is what the expression means. Even Plato had had to fight his way out of the same assumption. But he at least had a special excuse. The Greek language had only the one word ὄνομα where we have the three words 'word', 'name' and 'noun'. It was hard in Greek even to say that the Greek counterpart to our verb 'is' was a word but not a noun. Greek provided Plato with no label for verbs, or for adverbs, conjunctions etc. That 'is' is a word, but is not a name or even a noun was a tricky thing to say in Greek where ὄνομα did duty both for our word 'word', for our word 'name' and, eventually, for our word 'noun'. But even without this excuse people still find it natural to assimilate all words to names, and the meanings of words to the bearers of those alleged names. Yet the assumption is easy to demolish.

First, if every single word were a name, then a sentence composed of five words, say 'three is a prime number' would be a list of the five objects named by those five words. But a list, like 'Plato, Aristotle, Aquinas, Locke, Berkeley' is not a sentence. It says nothing, true or false. A sentence, on the contrary, may say something — some one thing — which is true or false. So the words combined into a sentence at least do something jointly which is different from their severally naming the several things that they name if they do name any things. What a sentence means is not decomposable into the set of things which the words in it stand for, if they do stand for things. So the notion of *having meaning* is at least partly different from the notion of *standing for*.

More than this. I can use the two descriptive phrases 'the Morning Star' and 'the Evening Star', as different ways of referring to Venus. But it is quite clear that the two phrases are different in meaning. It would be incorrect to translate into French the phrase 'the Morning Star' by 'l'Étoile du Soir'. But if the two phrases have different meanings, then Venus, the planet which we describe by these two different descriptions, cannot be what these descriptive phrases mean. For she, Venus, is one and the same, but what the two phrases signify are different. As we shall see in a moment Mill candidly acknowledges this point and makes an important allowance for it.

Moreover it is easy to coin descriptive phrases to which nothing at all answers. The phrase 'the third man to stand on the top of Mt. Everest' cannot, at present, be used to refer to anybody. There exists as yet no one whom it fits and perhaps there never will. Yet it is certainly a significant phrase, and could be translated into French or German. We know, we have to know, what it means when we say that it fits no living mountaineer. It means *something*, but it does not designate *somebody*. What it means cannot, therefore, be equated with a particular mountaineer. Nor can the meaning conveyed by the phrase 'the first person to stand on the top of

Mt. Everest' be equated with Hillary, though, we gather, it fits him and does not fit anyone else. We can understand the question, and even entertain Nepalese doubts about the answer to the question 'Is Hillary the first person to conquer Mt. Everest?' where we could not understand the question 'Is Hillary Hillary?'

We could reach the same conclusion even more directly. If Hillary was, *per impossibile*, identified with what is meant by the phrase 'the first man to stand on the top of Mt. Everest', it would follow that the meaning of at least one phrase was born in New Zealand, has breathed through an oxygen-mask and has been decorated by Her Majesty. But this is patent nonsense. Meanings of phrases are not New Zealand citizens; what is expressed by a particular English phrase, as well as by any paraphrase or translation of it, is not something with lungs, a surname, long legs and a sunburnt face. People are born and die and sometimes wear boots; meanings are not born and do not die and they never wear boots — or go barefoot either. The Queen does not decorate meanings. The phrase 'the first man to stand on the top of Mt. Everest' will not lose its meaning when Hillary dies. Nor was it meaningless before he reached the summit.

Finally, we should notice that most words are not nouns; they are, e.g. adverbs, or verbs, or adjectives or prepositions or conjunctions or pronouns. But to classify as a name a word which is not even a noun strikes one as intolerable the moment one considers the point. How could 'ran' or 'often' or 'and' or 'pretty' be the name of anything? It could not even be the grammatical subject of a sentence. I may ask what a certain economic condition, moral quality or day of the week is called and get the answer 'inflation', 'punctiliousness' or 'Saturday'. We do use the word 'name' for what something is called, whether it be what a person or river is called, or what a species, a quality, an action or a condition is called. But the answer to the question 'What is it called?' must be a noun or have the grammar of a noun. No such question could be answered by giving the tense of a verb, an adverb, a conjunction or an adjective.

Mill himself allowed that some words like 'is', 'often', 'not', 'of', and 'the' are not names, even in his hospitable use of 'name'. They

cannot by themselves function as the grammatical subjects of sentences. Their function, as he erroneously described it, is to sub-
serve, in one way or another, the construction of many-worded
names. They do not name extra things but are ancillaries to the
multi-verbal naming of things. Yet they certainly have meanings.
'And' and 'or' have different meanings, and 'or' and the Latin 'aut'
have the same meaning. Mill realized that it is not always the case
that for a word to mean something, it must denote somebody or
some thing. But most of his successors did not notice how important this point was.

Even more to Mill's credit was the fact that he noticed and did
partial justice to the point, which I made a little while back, that two
different descriptive phrases may both fit the same thing or person,
so that the thing or person which they both fit or which, in his un-
happy parlance, they both name is not to be equated with either
(or of course both) of the significations of the two descriptions.
The two phrases 'the previous Prime Minister' and 'the father of
Randolph Churchill' both fit Sir Winston Churchill, and fit only
him; but they do not have the same meaning. A French translation
of the one would not be a translation of the other. One might
know or believe that the one description fitted Sir Winston
Churchill while still questioning whether the other did so too.
From just knowing that Sir Winston was Prime Minister one
could not infer that Randolph Churchill is his son, or *vice versa*.
Either might have been true without the other being true. The
two phrases cannot, therefore, carry the same information.

Mill, in effect, met this point with his famous theory of denotation and connotation. Most words and descriptive phrases, according to him, do two things at once. They *denote* the things or persons that they are, as he unhappily puts it, all the names of. But
they also *connote* or signify the simple or complex attributes by
possessing which the thing or person denoted is fitted by the description. Mill's word 'connote' was a very unhappily chosen word
and has misled not only Mill's successors but Mill himself. His
word 'denote' was used by him in a far from uniform way, which
left him uncommitted to consequences from which some of his
successors, who used it less equivocally, could not extricate them-

selves. For Mill, proper names denote their bearers, but predicate-expressions also denote what they are truly predicable of. Fido is denoted by 'Fido' and by 'dog' and by 'four-legged'.

So to ask for the function of an expression is, on Mill's showing, to ask a double question. It is to ask Which person or persons, thing or things the expression denotes? in one or other of Mill's uses of this verb — Sir Winston Churchill, perhaps — ; but it is also to ask What are the properties or characteristics by which the thing or person is described? — say that of having begotten Randolph Churchill. As a thing or person can be described in various ways, the various descriptions given will differ in connotation, while still being identical in denotation. They characterize in different ways, even though their denotation is identical. They carry different bits of information or misinformation about the same thing, person or event.

Mill himself virtually says that according to our ordinary natural notion of meaning, it would not be proper to say that, e.g. Sir Winston Churchill is the meaning of a word or phrase. We ordinarily understand by 'meaning' not the thing denoted but only what is connoted. That is, Mill virtually reaches the correct conclusions that the meaning of an expression is never the thing or person referred to by means of it; and that descriptive phrases and, with one exception, single words are never names, in the sense of 'proper names'. The exception is just those relatively few words which really are proper names, i.e. words like 'Fido', and 'London', the words which do not appear in dictionaries.

Mill got a further important point right about these genuine proper names. He said that while most words and descriptive phrases both denote or name and connote, proper names only denote and do not connote. A dog may be called 'Fido', but the word 'Fido' conveys no information or misinformation about the dog's qualities, career or whereabouts, etc. There is, to enlarge this point, no question of the word 'Fido' being paraphrased, or correctly or incorrectly translated into French. Dictionaries do not tell us what proper names mean — for the simple reason that they do not mean anything. The word 'Fido' names or denotes a particular dog, since it is what he is called. But there is no room for anyone who hears the word 'Fido' to understand it or misunderstand it or fail to understand it. There is nothing for which he can require an elucidation or a definition. From the information that Sir Winston Churchill was Prime Minister, a number of consequences follow, such as that he was the leader of the majority party in Parliament. But from the fact that yonder dog is Fido, no other truth about him follows at all. No information is provided for anything to follow from. Using a proper name is not committing oneself to any further assertions whatsoever. Proper names are appellations and not descriptions; and descriptions are descriptions and not appellations. Sir Winston Churchill *is* the father of Randolph Churchill. He is not *called* and was not christened 'the father of Randolph Churchill'. He is called 'Winston Churchill'. The Lady Mayoress of Liverpool can give the name *Mauretania* to a ship which thenceforward has that name. But if she called Sir Winston Churchill 'the father of Sir Herbert Morrison' this would be a funny sort of christening, but it would not make it true that Morrison is the son of Sir Winston Churchill. Descriptions carry truths or falsehoods and are not just arbitrary bestowals. Proper names are arbitrary bestowals, and convey nothing true and nothing false, for they convey nothing at all.

Chinese astronomers give the planets, stars and constellations names quite different from those we give. But it does not follow that a single proposition of Western astronomy is rejected by them, or that a single astronomical proposition rejected by us is accepted by them. Stellar nomenclature carries with it no astronomical truths or falsehoods. Calling a star by a certain name is not saying anything about it, and saying something true or false about a star is not naming it. Saying is not naming and naming is not saying.

This brings out a most important fact. Considering the meaning (or Mill's 'connotation') of an expression is considering what can be said with it, i.e. said truly or said falsely, as well as asked, commanded, advised or any other sort of saying. In this, which is the normal sense of 'meaning', the meaning of a sub-expression like a word or phrase, is a functional factor of a range of possible assertions, questions, commands and the rest. It is tributary to sayings. It is a distinguishable common locus of a range of possible tellings, askings, advisings, etc. This precisely inverts the natural assumption with which, as I said earlier, Mill and most of us start, the assumption namely that the meanings of words and phrases can be learned, discussed and classified before consideration begins of entire sayings, such as sentences. Word-meanings do not stand to sentence-meanings as atoms to molecules or as letters of the alphabet to the spellings of words, but more nearly as the tennis-racket stands to the strokes which are or may be made with it. This point, which Mill's successors and predecessors half-recognized to hold for such little words as 'if', 'or', 'all', 'the' and 'not', holds good for all significant words alike. Their significances are their rôles inside actual and possible sayings. Mill's two-way doctrine, that nearly all words and phrases both denote, or are names, and connote, i.e. have significance, was therefore, in effect, though unwittingly, a coalition between an atomistic and a functionalist view of words. By the irony of fate, it was his atomistic view which was, in most quarters, accepted as gospel truth for the next fifty or seventy years. Indeed, it was more than accepted, it was accepted without the important safeguard which Mill himself provided when he said that the thing or person denoted by a name was not to be identified with what that name meant. Mill said that to mean is to connote. His successors said that to mean is to denote, or, more rarely, both to denote and to connote. Frege was for a long time alone in seeing the crucial importance of Mill's argument that two or more descriptive phrases with different senses may apply to the same planet or person. This person or planet is not, therefore, what those phrases mean. Their different senses are not their common denotation. Russell early realized the point which Mill did not very explicitly make, though Plato had made it, that a sentence is not a list. It says one thing; it is not just an inventory of a lot of things. But only much later, if at all, did Russell see the full implications of this.

I surmise that the reason why Mill's doctrine of denotation, without its safeguards, caught on, while his truths about connotation failed to do so, were two. First, the word 'connote' naturally suggests what we express by 'imply', which is not what is wanted.

What the phrase 'the previous Prime Minister of the United Kingdom' signifies is not to be equated with any or all of the consequences which can be inferred from the statement that Churchill is the previous Prime Minister. Deducing is not translating. But more important was the fact that Mill himself rapidly diluted his doctrine of connotation with such a mass of irrelevant and false sensationalist and associationist psychology, that his successors felt forced to ignore the doctrine in order to keep clear of its accretions.

Let me briefly mention some of the consequences which successors of Mill actually drew from the view, which was not Mill's, that to mean is to denote, in the toughest sense, namely that all significant expressions are proper names, and what they are the names of are what the expressions signify.

First, it is obvious that the vast majority of words are unlike the words 'Fido' and 'London' in this respect, namely, that they are general. 'Fido' stands for a particular dog, but the noun 'dog' covers this dog Fido, and all other dogs past, present and future, dogs in novels, dogs in dog breeders' plans for the future, and so on indefinitely. So the word 'dog', if assumed to denote in the way in which 'Fido' denotes Fido, must denote something which we do not hear barking, namely either the set or class of all actual and imaginable dogs, or the set of canine properties which they all share. Either would be a very out-of-the-way sort of entity. Next, most words are not even nouns, but adjectives, verbs, prepositions, conjunctions and so on. If these are assumed to denote in the way in which 'Fido' denotes Fido, we shall have a still larger and queerer set of nominees or *denotata* on our hands, namely nominees whose names could not even function as the grammatical subjects of sentences. (Incidentally it is not true even that all ordinary general nouns can function by themselves as subjects of sentences. I can talk about *this* dog, or *a* dog, or *the* dog which . . .; or about *dogs*, *all* dogs, or *most* dogs, and so on. But I cannot make the singular noun 'dog' by itself the grammatical subject of a sentence, save inside quotes, though I can do this with nouns like 'grass', 'hydrogen' and 'Man'.) Finally, since complexes of words, like descriptive and other phrases, and entire clauses and sentences have unitary meanings, then these too will have to be construed as denoting complex entities of very surprising sorts. Now Meinong in Austria and Frege in Germany, as well as Moore and Russell in this country, in their early days, accepted some or most of these consequences. Consistently with the assumed equation of signifying with naming, they maintained the objective existence or being of all sorts of abstract and fictional *entia rationis*.

Whenever we construct a sentence, in which we can distinguish a grammatical subject and a verb, the grammatical subject, be it a single word or a more or less complex phrase, must be significant if the sentence is to say something true or false. But if this nominative word or phrase is significant, it must, according to the assumption, denote something which is there to be named. So not only Fido and London, but also centaurs, round squares, the present King of France, the class of albino Cypriots, the first moment of time, and the non-existence of a first moment of time must all be credited with some sort of reality. They must *be*, else we could not say true or false things of them. We could not truly say that round squares do not exist, unless in some sense of 'exist' there exist round squares for us, in another sense, to deny existence of. Sentences can begin with abstract nouns like 'equality' or 'justice' or 'murder' so all Plato's Forms or Universals must be accepted as entities. Sentences can contain mentions of creatures of fiction, like centaurs and Mr. Pickwick, so all conceivable creatures of fiction must be genuine entities too. Next, we can say that propositions are true or false, or that they entail or are incompatible with other propositions, so any significant 'that'-clause, like 'that three is a prime number' or 'that four is a prime number', must also denote existent or subsistent objects. It was accordingly, for a time, supposed that if I know or believe that three is a prime number, my knowing or believing this is a special relation holding between me on the one hand and the truth or fact, on the other, denoted by the sentence 'three is a prime number'. If I weave or follow a romance, my imagining centaurs or Mr. Pickwick is a special relation holding between me and these centaurs or that portly old gentleman. I could not imagine him unless he had enough being to stand as the correlate-term in this postulated relation of being imagined by me.

Lastly, to consider briefly what turned out, unexpectedly, to be a crucial case, there must exist or subsist classes, namely appropriate *denotata* for such collectively employed plural descriptive phrases as 'the elephants in Burma' or 'the men in the moon'. It is just of such classes or sets that we say that they number 3000, say, in the one case, and 0 in the other. For the results of counting to be true or false, there must be entities submitting to numerical predicates; and for the propositions of arithmetic to be true or false there must exist or subsist an infinite range of such classes.

At the very beginning of this century Russell was detecting some local unplausibilities in the full-fledged doctrine that to every significant grammatical subject there must correspond an appropriate *denotatum* in the way in which Fido answers to the name 'Fido'. The true proposition 'round squares do not exist' surely cannot require us to assert that there really do subsist round squares. The proposition that it is false that four is a prime number is a true one, but its truth surely cannot force us to fill the Universe up with an endless population of objectively existing falsehoods.

But it was classes that first engendered not mere unplausibilities but seemingly disastrous logical contradictions — not merely peripheral logical contradictions but contradictions at the heart of the very principles on which Russell and Frege had taken mathematics to depend. We can collect into classes not only ordinary objects like playing-cards and bachelors, but also such things as classes themselves. I can ask how many shoes there are in a room and also how many pairs of shoes, and a pair of shoes is already a class. So now suppose I construct a class of all the classes that are not, as anyhow most classes are not, members of themselves. Will this class be one of its own members or not? If it embraces itself, this disqualifies it from being one of the things it is characterized as embracing; if it is not one of the things it embraces, this is just what qualifies it to be one among its own members.

So simple logic itself forbids certain ostensibly denoting expressions to denote. It is at least unplausible to say that there exist

objects denoted by the phrase 'round squares'; there is self-contradiction in saying that there exists a class which is a member of
itself on condition that it is not, and *vice versa*.

Russell had already found himself forced to say of some expressions which had previously been supposed to name or denote, that
they had to be given exceptional treatment. They were not names
but what he called 'incomplete symbols', expressions, that is,
which have no meaning, in the sense of denotation, by themselves;
their business was to be auxiliary to expressions which do, as a
whole, denote. (This was what Mill had said of the syncategorematic
words.) The very treatment which had since the Middle Ages
been given to such little words as 'and', 'not', 'the', 'some' and 'is'
was now given to some other kinds of expressions as well. In effect,
though not explicitly, Russell was saying that, e.g. descriptive
phrases were as syncategorematic as 'not', 'and' and 'is' had always
been allowed to be. Here Russell was on the brink of allowing that
the meanings or significations of many kinds of expressions are
matters not of *naming* things, but of *saying* things. But he was, I
think, still held up by the idea that saying is itself just another
variety of naming, i.e. naming a complex or an 'objective' or a
proposition or a fact — some sort of postulated *Fido rationis*.

He took a new and most important further step to cope with the
paradoxes, like that of the class of classes that are not members of
themselves. For he now wielded a distinction, which Mill had seen
but left inert, the distinction between sentences which are either
true or false on the one hand, and on the other hand sentences
which, though proper in vocabulary and syntax, are none the less
nonsensical, meaningless or absurd; and therefore neither true nor
false. To assert them and to deny them are to assert and deny
nothing. For reasons of a sort which are the proper concern of
logic, certain sorts of concatenations of words and phrases into
sentences produce things which cannot be significantly said. For
example, the very question Is the class of all classes which are not
members of themselves a member of itself or not? has no answer.
Russell's famous 'Theory of Types' was an attempt to formulate
the reasons of logic which make it an improper question. We need
not consider whether he was successful. What matters for us, and

what made the big difference to subsequent philosophy, is the fact that at long last the notion of meaning was realized to be, at least in certain crucial contexts, the obverse of the notion of the nonsensical — what can be said, truly or falsely, is at last contrasted with what cannot be significantly said. The notion of meaning had been, at long last, partly detached from the notion of naming and re-attached to the notion of saying. It was recognized to belong to, or even to constitute the domain which had always been the province of logic; and as it is at least part of the official business of logic to establish and codify rules, the notion of meaning came now to be seen as somehow compact of rules. To know what an expression means involves knowing what can (logically) be said with it and what cannot (logically) be said with it. It involves knowing a set of bans, fiats and obligations, or, in a word, it is to know the rules of the employment of that expression.

It was, however, not Russell but Wittgenstein who first generalized or half-generalized this crucial point. In the *Tractatus Logico-Philosophicus*, which could be described as the first book to be written on the philosophy of logic, Wittgenstein still had one foot in the denotationist camp, but his other foot was already free. He saw and said, not only what had been said before, that the little words, the so-called logical constants, 'not', 'is', 'and' and the rest do not stand for objects, but also, what Plato had also said before, that sentences are not names. Saying is not naming. He realized, as Frege had done, that logicians' questions are not questions about the properties or relations of the *denotata*, if any, of the expressions which enter into the sentences whose logic is under examination. He saw, too, that all the words and phrases that can enter into sentences are governed by the rules of what he called, slightly metaphorically, 'logical syntax' or 'logical grammar'. These rules are what are broken by such concatenations of words and phrases as result in nonsense. Logic is or includes the study of these rules. Husserl had at the beginning of the century employed much the same notion of 'logical grammar.'

It was only later still that Wittgenstein consciously and deliberately withdrew his remaining foot from the denotationist camp. When he said 'Don't ask for the meaning, ask for the use', he was imparting a lesson which he had had to teach to himself after he had finished with the *Tractatus*. The use of an expression, or the concept it expresses, is the rôle it is employed to perform, not any thing or person or event for which it might be supposed to stand. Nor is the purchasing power of a coin to be equated with this book or that car-ride which might be bought with it. The purchasing power of a coin has not got pages or a terminus. Even more instructive is the analogy which Wittgenstein now came to draw between significant expressions and the pieces with which are played games like chess. The significance of an expression and the powers or functions in chess of a pawn, a knight or the queen have much in common. To know what the knight can and cannot do, one must know the rules of chess, as well as be familiar with various kinds of chess-situations which may arise. What the knight may do cannot be read out of the material or shape of the piece of ivory or boxwood or tin of which this knight may be made. Similarly to know what an expression means is to know how it may and may not be employed, and the rules governing its employment can be the same for expressions of very different physical compositions. The word 'horse' is not a bit like the word 'cheval'; but the way of wielding them is the same. They have the same rôle, the same sense. Each is a translation of the other. Certainly the rules of the uses of expressions are unlike the rules of games in some important respects. We can be taught the rules of chess up to a point before we begin to play. There are manuals of chess, where there are not manuals of significance. The rules of chess, again, are completely definite and inelastic. Questions of whether a rule has been broken or not are decidable without debate. Moreover we opt to play chess and can stop when we like, where we do not opt to talk and think and cannot opt to break off. Chess is a diversion. Speech and thought are not only diversions. But still the partial assimilation of the meanings of expressions to the powers or the values of the pieces with which a game is played is enormously revealing. There is no temptation to suppose that a knight is proxy for anything, or that learning what a knight may or may not do is learning that it is a deputy for some ulterior entity. We could not learn to play the knight correctly without having learned to play the other pieces, nor can we learn to play a word by itself, but only in combination with other words and phrases.

Besides this, there is a further point which the assimilation brings out. There are six different kinds of chess-pieces, with their six different kinds of rôles in the game. We can imagine more complex games involving twenty or two hundred kinds of pieces. So it is with languages. In contrast with the denotationist assumption that almost all words, all phrases and even all sentences are alike in having the one rôle of naming, the assimilation of language to chess reminds us of what we knew *ambulando* all along, the fact that there are indefinitely many kinds of words, kinds of phrases, and kinds of sentences — that there is an indefinitely large variety of kinds of rôles performed by the expressions we use in saying things. Adjectives do not do what adverbs do, nor do all adjectives do the same sort of thing as one another. Some nouns are proper names, but most are not. The sorts of things that we do with sentences are different from the sorts of things that we do with most single words — and some sorts of things that we can significantly do with some sorts of sentences, we cannot significantly do with others. And so on.

There is not one basic mould, such as the 'Fido'-Fido mould, into which all significant expressions are to be forced. On the contrary, there is an endless variety of categories of sense or meaning. Even the *prima facie* simple notion of naming or denoting itself turns out on examination to be full of internal variegations. Pronouns are used to denote people and things, but not in the way in which proper names do so. No one is *called* 'he' or 'she'. 'Saturday' is a proper name, but not in the same way as 'Fido' is a proper name — and neither is used in the way in which the fictional proper name 'Mr. Pickwick' is used. The notion of denotation, so far from providing the final explanation of the notion of meaning, turns out itself to be just one special branch or twig on the tree of signification. Expressions do not mean because they denote things; some expressions denote things, in one or another of several different manners, because they are significant. Meanings are not things, not even very queer things. Learning the meaning of an expression is more like learning a piece of drill than like coming across

THE THEORY OF MEANING   257

a previously unencountered object. It is learning to operate correctly with an expression and with any other expression equivalent to it.

(2) *The Theory of Philosophy.* I now want to trace, rather more cursorily, the other main motive from which thinkers have posed the abstract question What are meanings? or What is it for an expression to have a certain sense?

Until fairly recently philosophers have not often stepped back from their easels to consider what philosophy is, or how doing philosophy differs from doing science, or doing theology, or doing mathematics. Kant was the first modern thinker to see or try to answer this question — and a very good beginning of an answer he gave; but I shall not expound his answer here.

This question did not begin seriously to worry the general run of philosophers until maybe sixty years ago. It began to become obsessive only after the publication of the *Tractatus.* Why did the philosophy of philosophy start so late, and how did it come to start when and as it did?

It is often not realized that the words 'philosophy' and 'philosopher' and their equivalents in French and German had for a long time much less specific meanings than they now possess. During the seventeenth, the eighteenth and most of the nineteenth centuries a 'philosopher' was almost any sort of a *savant.* Astronomers, chemists and botanists were called 'philosophers' just as much as were Locke, Berkeley or Hume. Descartes's philosophy covered his contributions to optics just as much as his contributions to epistemology. In English there existed for a long time no special word for the people we now call 'scientists'. This noun was deliberately coined only in 1840, and even then it took some time to catch on. His contemporaries could not call Newton a 'scientist', since there was no such word. When a distinction had to be made, it was made by distinguishing 'natural philosophy' from 'moral' and 'metaphysical philosophy'. As late as 1887, Conan Doyle, within two or three pages of one story, describes Sherlock Holmes as being totally ignorant of philosophy, as we use the word now, and yet as having his room full of philosophical, i.e. scientific, instruments, like test-tubes, retorts and balances. A not very

R

ancient Oxford Chair of Physics still retains its old label, the Chair of Experimental Philosophy.

Different from this quite important piece of etymological history is the fact that both in Scotland and in England there existed from perhaps the time of Hartley to that of Sidgwick and Bradley a strong tendency to suppose that the distinction between natural philosophy, i.e. physical and biological science on the one hand and metaphysical and moral philosophy, perhaps including logic, on the other, was that the latter were concerned with internal, mental phenomena, where the former were concerned with external, physical phenomena. Much of what we now label 'philosophy', *sans phrase*, was for a long time and by many thinkers confidently, but quite wrongly equated with what we now call 'psychology'. John Stuart Mill sometimes, but not always, uses even the grand word 'metaphysics' for the empirical study of the workings of men's minds. Protests were made against this equation particularly on behalf of philosophical theology, but for a long time the anti-theologians had it their own way. A philosopher, *sans phrase*, was a Mental and Moral Scientist — a scientist who was exempted from working in the laboratory or the observatory only because his specimens were collected at home by introspection. Even Mansel, himself a philosophical theologian with a good Kantian equipment, maintained that the science of mental phenomena, what we call 'psychology', was the real basis of even ontological or theological speculations.

So not only did the wide coverage of the word 'philosophy' encourage people not to look for any important differences between what scientists, as we now call them, do and what philosophers, as we now call them, do; but even when such differences were looked for, they were apt to be found in the differences between the investigation of physical phenomena by the laboratory scientist and the investigation of psychological phenomena by the introspecting psychologist.

As I see it, three influences were chiefly responsible for the collapse of the assumption that doing philosophy, in our sense, is of a piece with doing natural science or at least of a piece with doing mental science or psychology.

First, champions of mathematics like Frege, Husserl and Russell had to save mathematics from the combined empiricism and psychologism of the school of John Stuart Mill. Mathematical truths are not mere psychological generalizations; equations are not mere records of deeply rutted associations of ideas; the objects of geometry are not of the stuff of which mental images are made. Pure mathematics is a non-inductive and a non-introspective science. Its proofs are rigorous, its terms are exact, and its theorems are universal and not merely highly general truths. The proofs and the theorems of Formal or Symbolic Logic share these dignities with the proofs and theorems of mathematics. So, as logic was certainly a part of philosophy, not all of philosophy could be ranked as 'mental science'. There must, then, be a field or realm besides those of the material and the mental; and at least part of philosophy is concerned with this third realm, the realm of non-material and also non-mental 'logical objects' — such objects as concepts, truths, falsehoods, classes, numbers and implications.

Next, armchair mental science or introspective psychology itself began to yield ground to experimental, laboratory psychology. Psychologists like James began to put themselves to school under the physiologists and the statisticians. Scientific psychology began first to rival and then to oust both *à priori* and introspective psychology, and the tacit claim of epistemologists, moral philosophers and logicians to be mental scientists had to be surrendered to those who used the methods and the tools of the reputable sciences. So the question raised its head What then were the objects of the inquiries of epistemologists, moral philosophers and logicians, if they were not, as had been supposed, psychological states and processes? It is only in our own days that, anyhow in most British Universities, psychologists have established a Faculty of their own separate from the Faculty of Philosophy.

Thirdly, Brentano, reinforcing from medieval sources a point made and swiftly forgotten by Mill, maintained as an *a priori* principle of psychology itself, that it is of the essence of mental states and processes that they are *of* objects or contents. Somewhat as in grammar a transitive verb requires an accusative, so in the field of ideas, thoughts and feelings, acts of consciousness are directed upon their own metaphorical accusatives. To see is to see something, to regret is to regret something, to conclude or suppose is to conclude or suppose that something is the case. Imagining is one thing, the thing imagined, a centaur, say, is another. The centaur has the body of a horse and does not exist. An act of imagining a centaur does exist and does not have the body of a horse. Your act of supposing that Napoleon defeated Wellington is different from my act of supposing it; but what we suppose is the same and is what is expressed by our common expression 'that Napoleon defeated Wellington'. What is true of mental acts is, in general, false of their accusatives or 'intentional objects', and *vice versa.*

Brentano's two pupils, Meinong and Husserl, happened, for different reasons, to be especially, though not exclusively, interested in applying this principle of intentionality or transitivity to the intellectual, as distinct from the sensitive, volitional or affective acts of consciousness. They set out, that is, to rectify the Locke-Hume-Mill accounts of abstraction, conception, memory, judgment, supposal, inference and the rest, by distinguishing in each case, the various private, momentary and repeatable acts of conceiving, remembering, judging, supposing and inferring from their public, non-momentary accusatives, namely, the concepts, the propositions and the implications which constituted their objective correlates. Where Frege attacked psychologistic accounts of thinking from the outside, they attacked them from the inside. Where Frege argued, for instance, that numbers have nothing psychological or, of course, physical about them, Husserl and Meinong argued that for the mental processes of counting and calculating to be what they are, they must have accusatives or objects numerically and qualitatively other than those processes themselves. Frege said that Mill's account of mathematical entities was false because psychological; Husserl and Meinong, in effect, said that the psychology itself was false because non-'intentional' psychology. The upshot, however, was much the same. With different axes to grind, all three came to what I may crudely dub 'Platonistic' conclusions. All three maintained the doctrine of a third realm of non-physical, non-psychological entities, in which realm

THE THEORY OF MEANING   261

dwelled such things as concepts, numbers, classes and propositions.

Husserl and Meinong were both ready to lump together all
these accusatives of thinking alike under the comprehensive title
of Meanings (*Bedeutungen*), since what I think is what is conveyed by the words, phrases or sentences in which I express what
I think. The 'accusatives' of my ideas and my judgings are the
meanings of my words and my sentences. It easily followed from
this that both Husserl and Meinong, proud of their newly segre-
gated third realm, found that it was this realm which provided a
desiderated subject-matter peculiar to logic and philosophy and
necessarily ignored by the natural sciences, physical and psychological. Mental acts and states are the subject-matter of psychology.
Physical objects and events are the subject-matter of the physical
and biological sciences. It is left to philosophy to be the science of
this third domain which consists largely, though not entirely, of
thought-objects or Meanings — the novel and impressive entities
which had been newly isolated for separate investigation by the
application of Brentano's principle of intentionality to the specifically intellectual or cognitive acts of consciousness.

Thus, by the first decade of this century it was dawning upon
philosophers and logicians that their business was not that of one
science among others, e.g. that of psychology; and even that it was
not an inductive, experimental or observational business of any
sort. It was intimately concerned with, among other things, the
fundamental concepts and principles of mathematics; and it
seemed to have to do with a special domain which was not be-
spoken by any other discipline, namely the so-called third realm of
logical objects or Meanings. At the same time, and in some degree
affected by these influences, Moore consistently and Russell spas-
modically were prosecuting their obviously philosophical and
logical inquiries with a special *modus operandi*. They, and not they
alone, were deliberately and explicitly trying to give analyses of
concepts and propositions — asking What does it really mean to
say, for example, that this is good? or that that is true? or that centaurs do not exist? or that I see an inkpot? or What are the differences between the distinguishable senses of the verb 'to know' and

the verb 'to be'? Moore's regular practice and Russell's frequent practice seemed to exemplify beautifully what, for example, Husserl and Meinong had declared in general terms to be the peculiar business of philosophy and logic, namely to explore the third realm of Meanings. Thus philosophy had acquired a right to live its own life, neither as a discredited pretender to the status of the science of mind, nor yet as a superannuated handmaiden of *démodé* theology. It was responsible for a special field of facts, facts of impressively Platonized kinds.

Before the first world war discussions of the status and rôle of philosophy *vis-à-vis* the mathematical and empirical sciences were generally cursory and incidental to discussions of other matters. Wittgenstein's *Tractatus* was a complete treatise dedicated to fixing the position mainly of Formal Logic but also, as a necessary corollary, the position of general philosophy. It was this book which made dominant issues of the theory of logic and the theory of philosophy. In Vienna some of its teachings were applied polemically, namely to demolishing the pretensions of philosophy to be the science of transcendent realities. In England, on the whole, others of its teachings were applied more constructively, namely to stating the positive functions which philosophical propositions perform, and scientific propositions do not perform. In England, on the whole, interest was concentrated on Wittgenstein's description of philosophy as an activity of clarifying or elucidating the meanings of the expressions used, e.g. by scientists; that is, on the medicinal virtues of his account of the nonsensical. In Vienna, on the whole, interest was concentrated on the lethal potentialities of Wittgenstein's account of nonsense. In both places, it was realized that the criteria between the significant and the nonsensical needed to be systematically surveyed, and that it was for the philosopher and not the scientist to survey them.

At this point, the collapse of the denotationist theory of meaning began to influence the theory of philosophy as the science of Platonized Meanings. If the meaning of an expression is not an entity denoted by it, but a style of operation performed with it, not a nominee but a rôle, then it is not only repellent but positively misleading to speak as if there existed a Third Realm whose deni-

THE THEORY OF MEANING   263

zens are Meanings. We can distinguish this knight, as a piece of
ivory, from the part it or any proxy for it may play in a game of
chess; but the part it may play is not an extra entity, made of some
mysterious non-ivory. There is not one box housing the ivory
chessmen and another queerer box housing their functions in
chess games. Similarly we can distinguish an expression as a set of
syllables from its employment. A quite different set of syllables
may have the same employment. But its use or sense is not an additional substance or subject of predication. It is not a non-physical,
non-mental object — but not because it is either a physical or a
mental object, but because it is not an object. As it is not an object,
it is not a denizen of a Platonic realm of objects. To say, therefore,
that philosophy is the science of Meanings, though not altogether
wrong, is liable to mislead in the same way as it might mislead to
say that economics is the science of exchange-values. This, too, is
true enough, but to word this truth in this way is liable to make
people suppose that the Universe houses, under different roofs,
commodities and coins here and exchange-values over there.

Hence, following Wittgenstein's lead, it has become customary
to say, instead, that philosophical problems are linguistic problems
— only linguistic problems quite unlike any of the problems of
philology, grammar, phonetics, rhetoric, prosody, etc., since they
are problems about the logic of the functionings of expressions.
Such problems are so widely different from, e.g. philological problems, that speaking of them as linguistic problems is, at the
moment, as Wittgenstein foresaw, misleading people as far in
one direction, as speaking of them as problems about Meanings or
Concepts or Propositions had been misleading in the other direction. The difficulty is to steer between the Scylla of a Platonistic
and the Charybdis of a lexicographical account of the business of
philosophy and logic.

There has been and perhaps still is something of a vogue for saying that doing philosophy consists in analysing meanings, or
analysing the employments of expressions. Indeed, from Trans-
atlantic journals I gather that at this very moment British philosophy is dominated by some people called 'linguistic analysts'.
The word 'analysis' has, indeed, a good laboratory or Scotland

Yard ring about it; it contrasts well with such expressions as 'speculation', 'hypothesis', 'system-building' and ⌣ ⸳ ⸳n 'preaching' and 'writing poetry'. On the other hand it is a hopelessly misleading word in some important respects. It falsely suggests, for one thing, that any sort of careful elucidation of any sorts of complex or subtle ideas will be a piece of philosophizing; as if the judge, in explaining to the members of the jury the differences between manslaughter and murder, was helping them out of a philosophical quandary. But, even worse, it suggests that philosophical problems are like the chemist's or the detective's problems in this respect, namely that they can and should be tackled piecemeal. Finish problem A this morning, file the answer, and go on to problem B this afternoon. This suggestion does violence to the vital fact that philosophical problems inevitably interlock in all sorts of ways. It would be patently absurd to tell someone to finish the problem of the nature of truth this morning, file the answer and go on this afternoon to solve the problem of the relations between naming and saying, holding over until tomorrow problems about the concepts of existence and non-existence. This is, I think, why at the present moment philosophers are far more inclined to liken their task to that of the cartographer than to that of the chemist or the detective. It is the foreign relations, not the domestic constitutions of sayables that engender logical troubles and demand logical arbitration.

CRITERIA OF MEANINGFULNESS

INTRODUCTION

We began our study of meaning in Part II with a consideration of meaning in relation to reference. We examined, in particular, one theory according to which the relationship is very close, indeed, that of identity — the reference theory of meaning. We turn now to a related topic, an examination of various theories of meaningfulness. The notion of meaningfulness was already implicit in Part II, but we single out the topic here because of the special consideration given to it by a number of philosophers who were more concerned with the question "What are the conditions under which we may judge an expression (sentence or term) to be meaningful?" than with the question "What is the meaning of an expression?" Thus a theory of meaningfulness is actually a criterion, or at least a proposal for one. The criterion, when explicitly stated, is of the form:

(Expression) E is meaningful if and only if. . . .

or

E is meaningful ≡ . . . .

One major way of classifying such criteria of meaningfulness is on the basis of whether 'E' is a term or a sentence. (We shall refer to these as term theories and sentence theories, respectively.) Among the sentence theories, many were put forth in the 1930's and 1940's by various philosophers in the tradition of logical positivism (or logical empiricism). Many of these involved the notion of verifiability as an essential part of the criterion. Let us examine several of these criteria. Some of them are not explicitly formulated by their authors in the form 'E is meaningful ≡ . . . .' But it is clear that our schematic formulation corresponds to the authors' discussions.

We may begin with an early formulation by M. Schlick.[1] He begins his essay in a manner which was followed by many later positivists, describing the "anarchy of philosophical opinions" of the day and claiming that we are now at a turning point in philosophy, at which we may end all of these conflicts of systems. All of the traditional problems in theory of knowledge may be disposed of. All genuine investigations into human capacity for knowledge are either a part of psychology or are replaced by talk about every possible language. We need not ask questions about the validity and limits of knowledge, for everything that can be expressed is knowable, and we can ask significant questions only about what can be expressed. Thus there are no questions which are in principle insoluble. What have been taken to be insoluble problems are not genuine questions, but meaningless sequences of words. They may satisfy the rules of grammar, but they transgress the rules of logical syntax. Furthermore, such sequences of symbols fail the test of verifiability. All meaningful questions and statements are such that, for each, one can theoretically indicate the path that ends in an act of verification, that is, the occurrence of a definite fact that is confirmed by observation or direct experience. Let us use 'S' to designate any sentence and 'M' to mean 'meaningful'; then we may formulate Schlick's criterion as follows:

S is M $\equiv$ (a) S is (logically) syntactically correct; *and*
(b) S is verifiable through some direct observational experience.

In a paper written shortly after the one referred to above, Schlick formulates another version of a criterion of meaningfulness which is similar to the one just stated.[2] He here holds (p. 88) that a proposition (by which he means, a sentence) is meaningful if and only if it makes a verifiable difference whether it is true or false, i.e., a difference which is capable of being "exhibited in the given." Schlick points out that it need not be verifiable in practice, but only in principle. That is, it need not be either practically or technically possible for anyone to verify it, but it must be logically possible. 'There are mountains on the other side of the moon' was, at the time Schlick wrote, a sentence for which the verification was not possible in practice; but its verification was logically possible. 'There is a nucleus in every electron which has

[1] M. Schlick, "The Turning Point in Philosophy," in *Logical Positivism*, ed. A. J. Ayer (New York: Macmillan, 1959), 53-59.
[2] M. Schlick, "Positivism and Realism," in Ayer, ed., *Logical Positivism*, 82-107.

no external effects' is a sentence for which verification is not merely factually, but also logically, impossible. We may formulate Schlick's criterion in this way:

S is M ≡ S is verifiable, in principle.
　　　 ≡ It is logically possible for S to be shown to be true or false in experience.

At approximately the same time, Carnap put forth a more complex theory which involves both a term criterion and a sentence criterion.[3] Like Schlick and other logical positivists, Carnap holds that the statements of traditional philosophy, and especially of metaphysics, are, in the strict sense, meaningless. They are all pseudo-statements, either because they contain words which have no meaning, or because the constituent words may be meaningful, but the sentence as a whole violates the rules of syntax. Thus we must consider two kinds of meaningfulness: of a word, and of a sentence.

Let us begin with the criteria for the meaningfulness of a word. For a word to be meaningful, it must meet two conditions, according to Carnap. First, the syntax of the word must be fixed; that is, one must be able to indicate its way of occurring in an elementary (i.e., simplest possible) sentence. Suppose the word is 'stone.' Since we can determine its manner of occurring in sentences of the form 'x is a stone,' it passes the test. Second, if 'S' is an elementary sentence containing the word, we must be able to answer the question: "What sentence is 'S' deducible from, and what sentences are deducible from 'S'?" Let us apply this to 'arthropod.' According to Carnap, (P), 'This thing x is an arthropod' is deducible from: (a) 'x is an animal,' (b) 'x has a segmented body,' and (c) 'x has jointed legs.' Also (a), (b), and (c) are deducible from (P). Third, the sentences represented by 'a,' 'b,' and 'c' must be protocol, or observational, sentences; they must refer to the immediately given.

We may now turn to Carnap's criteria for a sentence. Since pseudo-statements either contain meaningless words or violate rules of syntax, it follows that, in order for any sentence to be meaningful, every word in it must be meaningful, and the sentence must be syntactically correct. By this Carnap means that a sentence must not violate either the rules of syntax in the ordinary sense or what he calls category rules.

[3] Rudolf Carnap, "The Elimination of Metaphysics through the Logical Analysis of Language," in Ayer, ed., *Logical Positivism*, 60-81.

Thus 'Caesar is and' is meaningless because of a syntactical violation; 'Caesar is a prime number' is meaningless due to its violating a category rule. Carnap points out that these criteria hold only for empirical statements. Tautologies and contradictions are significant by other (formal) criteria.

We may now schematize Carnap's two criteria of meaningfulness (of a word and of a sentence). Let us add a few more abbreviations: 'W' for 'word,' and 'ES' for 'elementary sentence.'

I.   W is M $\equiv$ (1) The syntax of W is fixed; its way of occurring in its simplest ES is determined. *And*

(2) One must be able to specify what Ss ES is deducible from, and what Ss are deducible from ES. *And*

(3) The Ss in (2) must be observation Ss.

II.   S is M $\equiv$ (1) Every W in S is M. *And*

(2) S is syntactically correct and violates no category rule.

We may now turn to one of the most famous attempts to formulate a criterion of meaningfulness, that of A. J. Ayer in *Language, Truth, and Logic*.[4] Ayer, too, begins his discussion by stating that the traditional disputes of philosophy (especially of metaphysics) are all unwarranted because the assertions contained in them are all meaningless. Ayer proposes to overthrow metaphysics by showing that all metaphysical assertions are nonsensical, and that, as a matter of logic, metaphysics is impossible. How is this to be done? By formulating a criterion of meaningfulness and showing that any assertion which does not conform to the criterion is meaningless. The criterion again is one of verifiability. Ayer first presents a rough formulation of the criterion (p. 35) which may be schematized as follows ('x' stands for any individual):

S is M for x $\equiv$ x knows how to verify S.

$\equiv$ x knows what observations would allow one to accept S as true or reject it as false.

Ayer, too, accepts verifiability in principle as sufficient. He also makes a distinction between verifiability in the strong and in the weak sense. Let 'V' mean 'verifiable.' Then

---

[4] A. J. Ayer, *Language, Truth, and Logic,* 2nd ed. (New York: Dover, 1946), Ch. 1. (See also the first article in this section.)

S is V (strong) $\equiv$ its truth value can be conclusively established
in experience.

S is V (weak) $\equiv$ it is possible for experience to render it probable.

A common synonym for 'verifiable in the weak sense' is 'confirmable.'

Ayer then presents his first precise formulation of the criterion (pp. 38-39):

> Let us call a proposition which records an actual or possible observa-
> tion an experiential proposition. Then we may say that it is the
> mark of a genuine factual proposition, not that it should be equiva-
> lent to an experiential proposition, or any finite number of experi-
> ential propositions, but simply that some experiential proposition
> can be deduced from it in conjunction with certain other premises
> without being deducible from those other premises alone.

We note that, for Ayer, the criterion applies to propositions, and it is
clear throughout the chapter that propositions are what sentences express. Let us introduce further abbreviations. Let 'S' designate the
proposition which is to be tested by the criterion (the one whose meaningfulness is in doubt); 'E,' an experiential proposition (one which
records an actual or possible observation); and 'P,' other premises.
Then Ayer's criterion may be schematized:

$$\text{S is M} \equiv (S \cdot P) \supset_L E \cdot \sim (P \supset_L E)$$

where '$\supset_L$' designates logical (as opposed to mere material) implication. Note that the criterion is *not* the much stronger: $\text{S is M} \equiv S \equiv_L E$,
or even: $\text{S is M} \equiv (S \cdot P) \equiv_L E$, but only: $(S \cdot P) \supset_L E \cdot \sim (P \supset_L
E)$. Let us take an example. Suppose that 'S' (the proposition to be
tested) is 'All objects heavier than air fall when released.' Then we
may formulate a sentence 'P,' namely, 'This object is heavier than air,'
such that from 'S' and 'P' the observation statement 'E,' 'This object
falls when released,' may be deduced. Since 'S' passed the test, it is
meaningful.

But there is more to Ayer's view than this (even though he does not
make it explicit in Chapter 1). First, what about experiential propositions themselves? They are accepted as meaningful simply by virtue of
the fact that they record possible or actual observation; they do not
have to be put to the deducibility test. But then we must amend Ayer's
criterion:

$$\text{S is M} \equiv (1)\ \text{S is an E, } or$$
$$(2)\ (S \cdot P) \supset_L E \cdot \sim (P \supset_L E).$$

Second, there are actually two criteria of meaningfulness involved here. One is a criterion of factual meaningfulness. This criterion is more perspicuously stated as:

1. S is M $\equiv$ S is V (weak sense).

The second is a criterion of verifiability. It is the criterion given above, namely:

2. S is V (weak) $\equiv$ (1) S is an E, or
$\quad\quad\quad\quad\quad\quad\quad$ (2) (S $\cdot$ P) $\supset_L$ E $\cdot \sim$ (P $\supset_L$ E).

Third, since Ayer also holds a priori statements to be meaningful, there will also be a criterion for their significance. The test is simply that of being a tautology. Finally, if we now consider both factual and non-factual statements as literally, cognitively significant, we must have a criterion which covers both. This will be:

III. S is literally M $\equiv$ (1) S is a tautology, or
$\quad\quad\quad\quad\quad\quad\quad\quad$ (2) S is V (weak).

We have here a much more sophisticated theory than any of its predecessors. But alas, not too long after the publication of Ayer's book, philosophers began to find fault with the criterion. Ayer gives an account of one of the problems with the criterion in the introduction to the second edition of *Language, Truth, and Logic*, written ten years after publication of the first edition. The problem arises in connection with the second part of the criterion of verifiability, for those propositions which are put to the deducibility test. Let 'S' represent 'The Absolute is lazy.' Surely Ayer would not want this to be allowed as meaningful. But from 'S' and 'P,' 'If the Absolute is lazy, then this is white,' there may be deduced the experiential (observation) proposition 'E,' 'This is white.' Hence it follows, by criterion II (2), that 'The Absolute is lazy' is meaningful! In view of such difficulties, Ayer proposes a new, more rigorous criterion on p. 13 (second paragraph). We leave it for the reader to symbolize the criteria of verifiability and meaningfulness and to test the criteria with examples.

Various other criticisms of the criteria of meaningfulness (or cognitive significance) and of the entire program of attempting to formulate such criteria are found in the lucid papers by Marhenke and Hempel below. We shall not attempt to summarize them here, since they are clearly stated by the authors.

Most attempts to formulate an empirical criterion of meaningfulness have had certain features in common. They were essentially verifiability criteria and criteria for the meaningfulness of statements, stated independently of any total theory of language. In his renowned "Testability and Meaning,"[5] Carnap's approach is very different. It consists in formulating or prescribing the limits for an empiricist language (of an idealized sort) by characterizing the undefined (primitive) descriptive terms of the language; the modes of definition and related procedures by which new terms may be introduced; the formation rules by which certain combinations of words are acceptable sentences; and transformation rules, according to which certain sentences may be validly deduced from others. The vocabulary of such a language will also include logical terms. By means of logical terms alone, certain sentences in the language may be characterized as analytic. An empirical sentence is one which is not analytic. Whereas other theories stressed statements and the role of observation statements in a deducibility test, Carnap attempts to formulate a criterion for the meaningfulness of terms. Any descriptive term which is an observational term is taken to be meaningful directly. Other terms must be either definable or reducible to observation terms. Logical terms are formally meaningful. Roughly, the criterion of meaningfulness for the words of the empiricist language, L, may be schematized as:

W is M in L $\equiv$ (1) W is a logical term (defined or primitive).
Or (2) W is:

  (a) a primitive observational term, *or*
  (b) definable via observational terms, *or*
  (c) reducible to observational terms.

However, this theory is not solely a term theory, for the rules of sentence formation specify which sentences are well formed, and hence meaningful. The details of this program are indicated in the first selection from Carnap's work. Schematically, it proceeds as follows. We build a language, L, by starting with a class of meaningful terms. These are the primitives, not definable in terms of other words, but only ostensively definable. The primitives will include some individual constants and some terms designating observable predicates (both properties and relations). A large number of nonprimitive terms can be introduced by processes of definition, either explicit or contextual.

---

[5] Rudolf Carnap, "Testability and Meaning," *Philosophy of Science*, III (1936), 420-68, and IV (1937), 1-40. (Reprinted as monograph by Whitlock's, New Haven, Conn. 1950.)

However, a problem arises in connection with introducing certain terms such as dispositional terms via any processes of definition. This leads Carnap to the notion of reduction sentences as ways of introducing nonprimitive terms in ways which provide partial meaning for those terms. This amounts to a liberalizing of the criterion of cognitive significance. Neither deducibility (of statements) nor strict definability (of terms) function in this modified criterion.

However, even this modified proposal does not suffice as an adequate criterion of cognitive significance, for there are still other terms of science, namely, theoretical constructs, which are held to be meaningful yet cannot be introduced through either definitions or reduction sentences. In "The Methodological Character of Theoretical Concepts,"[6] Carnap works out a program whereby such terms may be introduced as significant terms by the method of postulational (or implicit) definitions. Terms so introduced are related by postulates to other abstract theoretical constructs. At this point, the system is an uninterpreted one. When an interpretation is supplied for certain terms, then via the postulates (and other definitions) the theoretical terms are given empirical significance. It will be obvious to the reader of this important paper of Carnap's that we have gone a long way from the criteria of meaningfulness put forth in the early 1930's.

SELECTED READINGS

Ayer, A. J. "Demonstration of the Impossibility of Metaphysics." *Mind*, XLIII, 171 (1934), 335-46. Reprinted in *A Modern Introduction to Philosophy*, ed. P. Edwards and A. Pap. New York: Macmillan, 1957, 684-93.
———. "The Principle of Verifiability." *Mind*, XLV (1936), 199-203.
———. *Language, Truth, and Logic*. 2nd ed. New York: Dover, 1950. Introduction, "The Principle of Verification," 5-16; Ch. 1, "The Elimination of Metaphysics," 33-46.
Berlin, I. "Verification." *Proceedings of the Aristotelian Society*, XXXIX (1938-39), 225-48.
Bridgman, P. W. "The Operational Aspect of Meaning." *Synthese*, VII, 1 and 2 (1950-51), 251-59.
Carnap, Rudolf. "The Elimination of Metaphysics through the Logical Analysis of Language." *Erkenntnis* (1931-32). Reprinted in *Logical Positivism*, ed. A. J. Ayer, New York: Macmillan–Free Press, 1959, 60-82.
———. "Truth and Confirmation" (from two works, 1936?). Reprinted in *Readings in Philosophical Analysis*, ed. H. Feigl and W. Sellars. New York: Appleton-Century-Crofts, 1949, 119-27.

[6] In *Minnesota Studies in the Philosophy of Science*, I, ed. Herbert Feigl and Michael Scriven (Minneapolis: University of Minnesota Press, 1956), 38-76.

———. "Testability and Meaning." *Philosophy of Science,* III (1936), 420-68; IV (1937), 1-40. (Republished in monograph form by Whitlock's, New Haven, Conn., 1950.) Reprinted in *Readings in the Philosophy of Science,* ed. H. Feigl and M. Brodbeck. New York: Appleton-Century-Crofts, 1953.

———. "Empiricism, Semantics and Ontology." *Revue Internationale de Philosophie,* 1950. Reprinted in *Readings in the Philosophy of Science,* ed. N. Wiener (New York: Charles Scribner's Sons, 1953), 509-22.

———. "The Methodological Character of Theoretical Concepts." *Minnesota Studies in the Philosophy of Science,* I. Minneapolis: University of Minnesota Press, 1956, 38-76.

Ducasse, C. J. "Verification, Verifiability and Meaningfulness." *Journal of Philosophy,* XXXII (1936), 230-36.

Evans, J. L. "On Meaning and Verification." *Mind,* LXII (1953), 1-19.

Feigl, H. "Confirmability and Confirmation." *Revue Internationale de Philosophie,* V (1951), 268-79. Reprinted in *Readings in the Philosophy of Science,* ed. N. Weiner, 522-30.

Ewing, A. C. "Meaninglessness." *Mind,* XLVI (1937), 347-64. Reprinted in *A Modern Introduction to Philosophy,* ed. P. Edwards and A. Pap. New York: Macmillan, 1957, 705-15.

Hempel, C. G. "The Empiricist Criterion of Meaning." *Revue Internationale de Philosophie,* 1950. Reprinted in *Logical Positivism,* ed. A. J. Ayer. New York: Macmillan–Free Press, 1959, 108-32.

———. "The Criterion of Cognitive Significance." *Proceedings of the American Academy of Arts and Sciences,* LXXX, 1 (1951), 61-77.

———. "The Theoretician's Dilemma." *Minnesota Studies in the Philosophy of Science,* II. Minneapolis: University of Minnesota Press, 1958, 37-99.

Lazerowitz, M. "The Positivist's Use of Nonsense." *The Structure of Metaphysics.* London, 1955.

Lewis, C. I. "Experience and Meaning." *Philosophical Review,* XLIII (1934), 125-46. Reprinted in *Readings in Philosophical Analysis,* ed. H. Feigl and W. Sellars. New York: Appleton-Century-Crofts, 1949, 128-45.

Marhenke, Paul. "The Criterion of Significance." *Proceedings and Addresses of the American Philosophical Association,* 1950. Reprinted in Leonard Linsky, *Semantics and the Philosophy of Language.* Urbana: University of Illinois Press, 1952, 139-59.

Nagel, Ernest. "Verifiability, Truth and Verification." *Journal of Philosophy,* XXXI (1934), 141-48. Reprinted in his *Logic without Metaphysics.* New York: 1956, 143-52.

Reichenbach, H. "The Verifiability Theory of Meaning." In *Readings in the Philosophy of Science,* ed. H. Feigl and M. Brodbeck. New York: Appleton-Century-Crofts, 1953.

Rynin, D. "Vindication of L*G*C*L P*S*T*V*S*M." *Proceedings and Addresses of the American Philosophical Association,* XXX (1957), 45-67.

Schlick, M. "The Turning Point in Philosophy." *Erkenntnis,* 1930-31. Reprinted in *Logical Positivism,* ed. A. J. Ayer. New York: Macmillan–Free Press, 1959, 53-59.

———. "The Future of Philosophy." Published in *Philosophy of College of Pacific,* 1932.

———. "Positivism and Realism." *Erkenntnis,* 1932-33. Reprinted in *Logical Positivism,* ed. A. J. Ayer. New York: Macmillan–Free Press, 1959, 82-107.

————. "Meaning and Verification." *Philosophical Review,* XLV (1936), 339-69. Reprinted in part in *Readings in Philosophical Analysis,* ed. H. Feigl and W. Sellars, New York: Appleton-Century-Crofts, 1949, 146-70.

Stace, W. T. "Metaphysics and Meaning." *Mind,* XLIV (1935), 417-38.

————. "Positivism." *Mind,* LIII (1944), 215-37.

Waismann, F. "Verifiability." In *Logic and Language,* ed. A. Flew. Oxford: Blackwell, 1951, 117-44.

Wisdom, J. "Metaphysics and Verification." *Mind,* XLVII (1938), 452-98.

1

The Elimination of Metaphysics

A. J. AYER

From *Language, Truth and Logic* by Alfred Jules Ayer, Dover Publications, Inc., New York, 1946. Reprinted through the kind permission of the publisher.

CHAPTER I

THE ELIMINATION OF METAPHYSICS

The traditional disputes of philosophers are, for the most part, as unwarranted as they are unfruitful. The surest way to end them is to establish beyond question what should be the purpose and method of a philosophical enquiry. And this is by no means so difficult a task as the history of philosophy would lead one to suppose. For if there are any questions which science leaves it to philosophy to answer, a straightforward process of elimination must lead to their discovery.

We may begin by criticising the metaphysical thesis that philosophy affords us knowledge of a reality transcending the world of science and common sense. Later on, when we come to define metaphysics and account for its existence, we shall find that it is possible to be a metaphysician without believing in a transcendent reality; for we shall see that many metaphysical utterances are due to the commission of logical errors, rather than to a conscious desire on the part of their authors to go beyond the limits of experience. But it is convenient for us to take the case of those who believe that it is possible to have knowledge of a transcendent reality as a starting-point for our discussion. The arguments which we use to refute them will subsequently be found to apply to the whole of metaphysics.

One way of attacking a metaphysician who claimed to have knowledge of a reality which transcended the phenomenal world would be to enquire from what premises his propositions were deduced. Must he not begin, as other men do, with the evidence of his senses? And if so, what valid process of reasoning can possibly lead him to the conception of a transcendent reality? Surely from empirical premises nothing whatsoever concerning the properties, or even the existence, of anything super-empirical can legitimately be inferred. But this objection would be met by a denial on the part of the metaphysician that his assertions were ultimately based on the evidence of his senses. He would say that he was endowed with a faculty of intellectual intuition which

33

enabled him to know facts that could not be known through sense-experience. And even if it could be shown that he was relying on empirical premises, and that his venture into a non-empirical world was therefore logically unjustified, it would not follow that the assertions which he made concerning this non-empirical world could not be true. For the fact that a conclusion does not follow from its putative premise is not sufficient to show that it is false. Consequently one cannot overthrow a system of transcendent metaphysics merely by criticising the way in which it comes into being. What is required is rather a criticism of the nature of the actual statements which comprise it. And this is the line of argument which we shall, in fact, pursue. For we shall maintain that no statement which refers to a "reality" transcending the limits of all possible sense-experience can possibly have any literal significance; from which it must follow that the labours of those who have striven to describe such a reality have all been devoted to the production of nonsense.

It may be suggested that this is a proposition which has already been proved by Kant. But although Kant also condemned transcendent metaphysics, he did so on different grounds. For he said that the human understanding was so constituted that it lost itself in contradictions when it ventured out beyond the limits of possible experience and attempted to deal with things in themselves. And thus he made the impossibility of a transcendent metaphysic not, as we do, a matter of logic, but a matter of fact. He asserted, not that our minds could not conceivably have had the power of penetrating beyond the phenomenal world, but merely that they were in fact devoid of it. And this leads the critic to ask how, if it is possible to know only what lies within the bounds of sense-experience, the author can be justified in asserting that real things do exist beyond, and how he can tell what are the boundaries beyond which the human understanding may not venture, unless he succeeds in passing them himself. As Wittgenstein says, "in order to draw a limit to thinking, we should have to think both sides of this limit,"[1] a truth to which Bradley gives a special twist in maintaining that the man who is ready to prove that metaphysics is impossible is a brother metaphysician with a rival theory of his own.[2]

[1] *Tractatus Logico-Philosophicus*, Preface.
[2] Bradley, *Appearance and Reality*, 2nd ed., p. 1.

Whatever force these objections may have against the Kantian doctrine, they have none whatsoever against the thesis that I am about to set forth. It cannot here be said that the author is himself overstepping the barrier he maintains to be impassable. For the fruitlessness of attempting to transcend the limits of possible sense-experience will be deduced, not from a psychological hypothesis concerning the actual constitution of the human mind, but from the rule which determines the literal significance of language. Our charge against the metaphysician is not that he attempts to employ the understanding in a field where it cannot profitably venture, but that he produces sentences which fail to conform to the conditions under which alone a sentence can be literally significant. Nor are we ourselves obliged to talk nonsense in order to show that all sentences of a certain type are necessarily devoid of literal significance. We need only formulate the criterion which enables us to test whether a sentence expresses a genuine proposition about a matter of fact, and then point out that the sentences under consideration fail to satisfy it. And this we shall now proceed to do. We shall first of all formulate the criterion in somewhat vague terms, and then give the explanations which are necessary to render it precise.

The criterion which we use to test the genuineness of apparent statements of fact is the criterion of verifiability. We say that a sentence is factually significant to any given person, if, and only if, he knows how to verify the proposition which it purports to express—that is, if he knows what observations would lead him, under certain conditions, to accept the proposition as being true, or reject it as being false. If, on the other hand, the putative proposition is of such a character that the assumption of its truth, or falsehood, is consistent with any assumption whatsoever concerning the nature of his future experience, then, as far as he is concerned, it is, if not a tautology, a mere pseudo-proposition. The sentence expressing it may be emotionally significant to him; but it is not literally significant. And with regard to questions the procedure is the same. We enquire in every case what observations would lead us to answer the question, one way or the other; and, if none can be discovered, we must conclude that the sentence under consideration does not, as far as we are concerned, express a genuine question, however strongly its grammatical appearance may suggest that it does.

35

As the adoption of this procedure is an essential factor in the argument of this book, it needs to be examined in detail.

In the first place, it is necessary to draw a distinction between practical verifiability, and verifiability in principle. Plainly we all understand, in many cases believe, propositions which we have not in fact taken steps to verify. Many of these are propositions which we could verify if we took enough trouble. But there remain a number of significant propositions, concerning matters of fact, which we could not verify even if we chose; simply because we lack the practical means of placing ourselves in the situation where the relevant observations could be made. A simple and familiar example of such a proposition is the proposition that there are mountains on the farther side of the moon.[1] No rocket has yet been invented which would enable me to go and look at the farther side of the moon, so that I am unable to decide the matter by actual observation. But I do know what observations would decide it for me, if, as is theoretically conceivable, I were once in a position to make them. And therefore I say that the proposition is verifiable in principle, if not in practice, and is accordingly significant. On the other hand, such a metaphysical pseudo-proposition as "the Absolute enters into, but is itself incapable of, evolution and progress,"[2] is not even in principle verifiable. For one cannot conceive of an observation which would enable one to determine whether the Absolute did, or did not, enter into evolution and progress. Of course it is possible that the author of such a remark is using English words in a way in which they are not commonly used by English-speaking people, and that he does, in fact, intend to assert something which could be empirically verified. But until he makes us understand how the proposition that he wishes to express would be verified, he fails to communicate anything to us. And if he admits, as I think the author of the remark in question would have admitted, that his words were not intended to express either a tautology or a proposition which was capable, at least in principle, of being verified, then it follows that he has made an utterance which has no literal significance even for himself.

A further distinction which we must make is the distinction

[1] This example has been used by Professor Schlick to illustrate the same point.

[2] A remark taken at random from *Appearance and Reality,* by F. H. Bradley.

36

between the "strong" and the "weak" sense of the term "verifiable." A proposition is said to be verifiable, in the strong sense of the term, if, and only if, its truth could be conclusively established in experience. But it is verifiable, in the weak sense, if it is possible for experience to render it probable. In which sense are we using the term when we say that a putative proposition is genuine only if it is verifiable?

It seems to me that if we adopt conclusive verifiability as our criterion of significance, as some positivists have proposed,[1] our argument will prove too much. Consider, for example, the case of general propositions of law—such propositions, namely, as "arsenic is poisonous"; "all men are mortal"; "a body tends to expand when it is heated." It is of the very nature of these propositions that their truth cannot be established with certainty by any finite series of observations. But if it is recognised that such general propositions of law are designed to cover an infinite number of cases, then it must be admitted that they cannot, even in principle, be verified conclusively. And then, if we adopt conclusive verifiability as our criterion of significance, we are logically obliged to treat these general propositions of law in the same fashion as we treat the statements of the metaphysician.

In face of this difficulty, some positivists[2] have adopted the heroic course of saying that these general propositions are indeed pieces of nonsense, albeit an essentially important type of nonsense. But here the introduction of the term "important" is simply an attempt to hedge. It serves only to mark the authors' recognition that their view is somewhat too paradoxical, without in any way removing the paradox. Besides, the difficulty is not confined to the case of general propositions of law, though it is there revealed most plainly. It is hardly less obvious in the case of propositions about the remote past. For it must surely be admitted that, however strong the evidence in favour of historical statements may be, their truth can never become more than highly probable. And to maintain that they also constituted an important, or unimportant, type of nonsense would be unplausible, to say the very least. Indeed, it will be our contention

[1] e.g. M. Schlick, "Positivismus und Realismus," *Erkenntnis*, Vol. I, 1930. F. Waismann, "Logische Analyse des Warscheinlichkeitsbegriffs," *Erkenntnis*, Vol. I, 1930.

[2] e.g. M. Schlick, "Die Kausalität in der gegenwärtigen Physik," *Naturwissenschaft*, Vol. 19, 1931.

that no proposition, other than a tautology, can possibly be anything more than a probable hypothesis. And if this is correct, the principle that a sentence can be factually significant only if it expresses what is conclusively verifiable is self-stultifying as a criterion of significance. For it leads to the conclusion that it is impossible to make a significant statement of fact at all.

Nor can we accept the suggestion that a sentence should be allowed to be factually significant if, and only if, it expresses something which is definitely confutable by experience.[1] Those who adopt this course assume that, although no finite series of observations is ever sufficient to establish the truth of a hypothesis beyond all possibility of doubt, there are crucial cases in which a single observation, or series of observations, can definitely confute it. But, as we shall show later on, this assumption is false. A hypothesis cannot be conclusively confuted any more than it can be conclusively verified. For when we take the occurrence of certain observations as proof that a given hypothesis is false, we presuppose the existence of certain conditions. And though, in any given case, it may be extremely improbable that this assumption is false, it is not logically impossible. We shall see that there need be no self-contradiction in holding that some of the relevant circumstances are other than we have taken them to be, and consequently that the hypothesis has not really broken down. And if it is not the case that any hypothesis can be definitely confuted, we cannot hold that the genuineness of a proposition depends on the possibility of its definite confutation.

Accordingly, we fall back on the weaker sense of verification. We say that the question that must be asked about any putative statement of fact is not, Would any observations make its truth or falsehood logically certain? but simply, Would any observations be relevant to the determination of its truth or falsehood? And it is only if a negative answer is given to this second question that we conclude that the statement under consideration is nonsensical.

To make our position clearer, we may formulate it in another way. Let us call a proposition which records an actual or possible observation an experiential proposition. Then we may say that it is the mark of a genuine factual proposition, not that it should be equivalent to an experiential proposition, or any finite number

[1] This has been proposed by Karl Popper in his *Logik der Forschung*.

of experiential propositions, but simply that some experiential propositions can be deduced from it in conjunction with certain other premises without being deducible from those other premises alone.[1]

This criterion seems liberal enough. In contrast to the principle of conclusive verifiability, it clearly does not deny significance to general propositions or to propositions about the past. Let us see what kinds of assertion it rules out.

A good example of the kind of utterance that is condemned by our criterion as being not even false but nonsensical would be the assertion that the world of sense-experience was altogether unreal. It must, of course, be admitted that our senses do sometimes deceive us. We may, as the result of having certain sensations, expect certain other sensations to be obtainable which are, in fact, not obtainable. But, in all such cases, it is further sense-experience that informs us of the mistakes that arise out of sense-experience. We say that the senses sometimes deceive us, just because the expectations to which our sense-experiences give rise do not always accord with what we subsequently experience. That is, we rely on our senses to substantiate or confute the judgements which are based on our sensations. And therefore the fact that our perceptual judgements are sometimes found to be erroneous has not the slightest tendency to show that the world of sense-experience is unreal. And, indeed, it is plain that no conceivable observation, or series of observations, could have any tendency to show that the world revealed to us by sense-experience was unreal. Consequently, anyone who condemns the sensible world as a world of mere appearance, as opposed to reality, is saying something which, according to our criterion of significance, is literally nonsensical.

An example of a controversy which the application of our criterion obliges us to condemn as fictitious is provided by those who dispute concerning the number of substances that there are in the world. For it is admitted both by monists, who maintain that reality is one substance, and by pluralists, who maintain that reality is many, that it is impossible to imagine any empirical situation which would be relevant to the solution of their dispute. But if we are told that no possible observation could give any

---

[1] This is an over-simplified statement, which is not literally correct. I give what I believe to be the correct formulation in the Introduction, p. 13.

probability either to the assertion that reality was one substance or to the assertion that it was many, then we must conclude that neither assertion is significant. We shall see later on[1] that there are genuine logical and empirical questions involved in the dispute between monists and pluralists. But the metaphysical question concerning "substance" is ruled out by our criterion as spurious.

A similar treatment must be accorded to the controversy between realists and idealists, in its metaphysical aspect. A simple illustration, which I have made use of in a similar argument elsewhere,[2] will help to demonstrate this. Let us suppose that a picture is discovered and the suggestion made that it was painted by Goya. There is a definite procedure for dealing with such a question. The experts examine the picture to see in what way it resembles the accredited works of Goya, and to see if it bears any marks which are characteristic of a forgery; they look up contemporary records for evidence of the existence of such a picture, and so on. In the end, they may still disagree, but each one knows what empirical evidence would go to confirm or discredit his opinion. Suppose, now, that these men have studied philosophy, and some of them proceed to maintain that this picture is a set of ideas in the perceiver's mind, or in God's mind, others that it is objectively real. What possible experience could any of them have which would be relevant to the solution of this dispute one way or the other? In the ordinary sense of the term "real," in which it is opposed to "illusory," the reality of the picture is not in doubt. The disputants have satisfied themselves that the picture is real, in this sense, by obtaining a correlated series of sensations of sight and sensations of touch. Is there any similar process by which they could discover whether the picture was real, in the sense in which the term "real" is opposed to "ideal"? Clearly there is none. But, if that is so, the problem is fictitious according to our criterion. This does not mean that the realist-idealist controversy may be dismissed without further ado. For it can legitimately be regarded as a dispute concerning the analysis of existential propositions, and so as involving a logical problem which, as we shall see, can be definitively solved.[3] What we have just shown is that the question at issue between idealists and

[1] In Chapter VIII.
[2] Vide "Demonstration of the Impossibility of Metaphysics," *Mind*, 1934, p. 339.
[3] Vide Chapter VIII.

40

realists becomes fictitious when, as is often the case, it is given a metaphysical interpretation.

There is no need for us to give further examples of the operation of our criterion of significance. For our object is merely to show that philosophy, as a genuine branch of knowledge, must be distinguished from metaphysics. We are not now concerned with the historical question how much of what has traditionally passed for philosophy is actually metaphysical. We shall, however, point out later on that the majority of the "great philosophers" of the past were not essentially metaphysicians, and thus reassure those who would otherwise be prevented from adopting our criterion by considerations of piety.

As to the validity of the verification principle, in the form in which we have stated it, a demonstration will be given in the course of this book. For it will be shown that all propositions which have factual content are empirical hypotheses; and that the function of an empirical hypothesis is to provide a rule for the anticipation of experience.[1] And this means that every empirical hypothesis must be relevant to some actual, or possible, experience, so that a statement which is not relevant to any experience is not an empirical hypothesis, and accordingly has no factual content. But this is precisely what the principle of verifiability asserts.

It should be mentioned here that the fact that the utterances of the metaphysician are nonsensical does not follow simply from the fact that they are devoid of factual content. It follows from that fact, together with the fact that they are not *a priori* propositions. And in assuming that they are not *a priori* propositions, we are once again anticipating the conclusions of a later chapter in this book.[2] For it will be shown there that *a priori* propositions, which have always been attractive to philosophers on account of their certainty, owe this certainty to the fact that they are tautologies. We may accordingly define a metaphysical sentence as a sentence which purports to express a genuine proposition, but does, in fact, express neither a tautology nor an empirical hypothesis. And as tautologies and empirical hypotheses form the entire class of significant propositions, we are justified in concluding that all metaphysical assertions are nonsensical. Our next task is to show how they come to be made.

[1] Vide Chapter V.   [2] Chapter IV.

The use of the term "substance," to which we have already referred, provides us with a good example of the way in which metaphysics mostly comes to be written. It happens to be the case that we cannot, in our language, refer to the sensible properties of a thing without introducing a word or phrase which appears to stand for the thing itself as opposed to anything which may be said about it. And, as a result of this, those who are infected by the primitive superstition that to every name a single real entity must correspond assume that it is necessary to distinguish logically between the thing itself and any, or all, of its sensible properties. And so they employ the term "substance" to refer to the thing itself. But from the fact that we happen to employ a single word to refer to a thing, and make that word the grammatical subject of the sentences in which we refer to the sensible appearances of the thing, it does not by any means follow that the thing itself is a "simple entity," or that it cannot be defined in terms of the totality of its appearances. It is true that in talking of "its" appearances we appear to distinguish the thing from the appearances, but that is simply an accident of linguistic usage. Logical analysis shows that what makes these "appearances" the "appearances of" the same thing is not their relationship to an entity other than themselves, but their relationship to one another. The metaphysician fails to see this because he is misled by a superficial grammatical feature of his language.

A simpler and clearer instance of the way in which a consideration of grammar leads to metaphysics is the case of the metaphysical concept of Being. The origin of our temptation to raise questions about Being, which no conceivable experience would enable us to answer, lies in the fact that, in our language, sentences which express existential propositions and sentences which express attributive propositions may be of the same grammatical form. For instance, the sentences "Martyrs exist" and "Martyrs suffer" both consist of a noun followed by an intransitive verb, and the fact that they have grammatically the same appearance leads one to assume that they are of the same logical type. It is seen that in the proposition "Martyrs suffer," the members of a certain species are credited with a certain attribute, and it is sometimes assumed that the same thing is true of such a proposition as "Martyrs exist." If this were actually the case, it would, indeed, be as legitimate to speculate about the Being of martyrs

42

as it is to speculate about their suffering. But, as Kant pointed out,[1] existence is not an attribute. For, when we ascribe an attribute to a thing, we covertly assert that it exists: so that if existence were itself an attribute, it would follow that all positive existential propositions were tautologies, and all negative existential propositions self-contradictory; and this is not the case.[2] So that those who raise questions about Being which are based on the assumption that existence is an attribute are guilty of following grammar beyond the boundaries of sense.

A similar mistake has been made in connection with such propositions as "Unicorns are fictitious." Here again the fact that there is a superficial grammatical resemblance between the English sentences "Dogs are faithful" and "Unicorns are fictitious," and between the corresponding sentences in other languages, creates the assumption that they are of the same logical type. Dogs must exist in order to have the property of being faithful, and so it is held that unless unicorns in some way existed they could not have the property of being fictitious. But, as it is plainly self-contradictory to say that fictitious objects exist, the device is adopted of saying that they are real in some non-empirical sense—that they have a mode of real being which is different from the mode of being of existent things. But since there is no way of testing whether an object is real in this sense, as there is for testing whether it is real in the ordinary sense, the assertion that fictitious objects have a special non-empirical mode of real being is devoid of all literal significance. It comes to be made as a result of the assumption that being fictitious is an attribute. And this is a fallacy of the same order as the fallacy of supposing that existence is an attribute, and it can be exposed in the same way.

In general, the postulation of real non-existent entities results from the superstition, just now referred to, that, to every word or phrase that can be the grammatical subject of a sentence, there must somewhere be a real entity corresponding. For as there is no place in the empirical world for many of these "entities," a special non-empirical world is invoked to house them. To this error must be attributed, not only the utterances of a Heidegger,

[1] Vide *The Critique of Pure Reason*, "Transcendental Dialectic," Book II, Chapter iii, section 4.

[2] This argument is well stated by John Wisdom, *Interpretation and Analysis*, pp. 62, 63.

43

who bases his metaphysics on the assumption that "Nothing" is a name which is used to denote something peculiarly mysterious,[1] but also the prevalence of such problems as those concerning the reality of propositions and universals whose senselessness, though less obvious, is no less complete.

These few examples afford a sufficient indication of the way in which most metaphysical assertions come to be formulated. They show how easy it is to write sentences which are literally non-sensical without seeing that they are nonsensical. And thus we see that the view that a number of the traditional "problems of philosophy" are metaphysical, and consequently fictitious, does not involve any incredible assumptions about the psychology of philosophers.

Among those who recognise that if philosophy is to be accounted a genuine branch of knowledge it must be defined in such a way as to distinguish it from metaphysics, it is fashionable to speak of the metaphysician as a kind of misplaced poet. As his statements have no literal meaning, they are not subject to any criteria of truth or falsehood: but they may still serve to express, or arouse, emotion, and thus be subject to ethical or æsthetic standards. And it is suggested that they may have considerable value, as means of moral inspiration, or even as works of art. In this way, an attempt is made to compensate the metaphysician for his extrusion from philosophy.[2]

I am afraid that this compensation is hardly in accordance with his deserts. The view that the metaphysician is to be reckoned among the poets appears to rest on the assumption that both talk nonsense. But this assumption is false. In the vast majority of cases the sentences which are produced by poets do have literal meaning. The difference between the man who uses language scientifically and the man who uses it emotively is not that the one produces sentences which are incapable of arousing emotion, and the other sentences which have no sense, but that the one is primarily concerned with the expression of true propositions, the other with the creation of a work of art. Thus, if a work of science

---

[1] Vide *Was ist Metaphysik*, by Heidegger: criticised by Rudolf Carnap in his "Überwindung der Metaphysik durch logische Analyse der Sprache," *Erkenntnis*, Vol. II, 1932.

[2] For a discussion of this point, see also C. A. Mace, "Representation and Expression," *Analysis*, Vol. I, No. 3; and "Metaphysics and Emotive Language," *Analysis*, Vol. II, Nos. 1 and 2.

contains true and important propositions, its value as a work of science will hardly be diminished by the fact that they are inelegantly expressed. And similarly, a work of art is not necessarily the worse for the fact that all the propositions comprising it are literally false. But to say that many literary works are largely composed of falsehoods, is not to say that they are composed of pseudo-propositions. It is, in fact, very rare for a literary artist to produce sentences which have no literal meaning. And where this does occur, the sentences are carefully chosen for their rhythm and balance. If the author writes nonsense, it is because he considers it most suitable for bringing about the effects for which his writing is designed.

The metaphysician, on the other hand, does not intend to write nonsense. He lapses into it through being deceived by grammar, or through committing errors of reasoning, such as that which leads to the view that the sensible world is unreal. But it is not the mark of a poet simply to make mistakes of this sort. There are some, indeed, who would see in the fact that the metaphysician's utterances are senseless a reason against the view that they have æsthetic value. And, without going so far as this, we may safely say that it does not constitute a reason for it.

It is true, however, that although the greater part of metaphysics is merely the embodiment of humdrum errors, there remain a number of metaphysical passages which are the work of genuine mystical feeling; and they may more plausibly be held to have moral or æsthetic value. But, as far as we are concerned, the distinction between the kind of metaphysics that is produced by a philosopher who has been duped by grammar, and the kind that is produced by a mystic who is trying to express the inexpressible, is of no great importance: what is important to us is to realise that even the utterances of the metaphysician who is attempting to expound a vision are literally senseless; so that henceforth we may pursue our philosophical researches with as little regard for them as for the more inglorious kind of metaphysics which comes from a failure to understand the workings of our language.

2

Verifiability and Meaningfulness

A. J. AYER

From *Language, Truth and Logic* by Alfred Jules Ayer, Dover Publications, Inc., New York, 1946. Reprinted through the kind permission of the publisher.

INTRODUCTION

In the ten years that have passed since *Language, Truth and Logic* was first published, I have come to see that the questions with which it deals are not in all respects so simple as it makes them appear; but I still believe that the point of view which it expresses is substantially correct. Being in every sense a young man's book, it was written with more passion than most philosophers allow themselves to show, at any rate in their published work, and while this probably helped to secure it a larger audience than it might have had otherwise, I think now that much of its argument would have been more persuasive if it had not been presented in so harsh a form. It would, however, be very difficult for me to alter the tone of the book without extensively re-writing it, and the fact that, for reasons not wholly dependent upon its merits, it has achieved something of the status of a text-book is, I hope, a sufficient justification for re-printing it as it stands. At the same time, there are a number of points that seem to me to call for some further explanation, and I shall accordingly devote the remainder of this new introduction to commenting briefly upon them.

THE PRINCIPLE OF VERIFICATION

The principle of verification is supposed to furnish a criterion by which it can be determined whether or not a sentence is literally meaningful. A simple way to formulate it would be to say that a sentence had literal meaning if and only if the proposition it expressed was either analytic or empirically verifiable. To this, however, it might be objected that unless a sentence was literally meaningful it would not express a proposition;[1] for it is commonly assumed that every proposition is either true or false, and to say that a sentence expressed what was either true or false would entail saying that it was literally meaningful. Accordingly, if the principle of verification were formulated in

[1] Vide M. Lazerowitz, "The Principle of Verifiability," *Mind*, 1937, pp. 372–8.

this way, it might be argued not only that it was incomplete as a criterion of meaning, since it would not cover the case of sentences which did not express any propositions at all, but also that it was otiose, on the ground that the question which it was designed to answer must already have been answered before the principle could be applied. It will be seen that when I introduce the principle in this book I try to avoid this difficulty by speaking of "putative propositions" and of the proposition which a sentence "purports to express"; but this device is not satisfactory. For, in the first place, the use of words like "putative" and "purports" seems to bring in psychological considerations into which I do not wish to enter, and secondly, in the case where the "putative proposition" is neither analytic nor empirically verifiable, there would, according to this way of speaking, appear to be nothing that the sentence in question could properly be said to express. But if a sentence expresses nothing there seems to be a contradiction in saying that what it expresses is empirically unverifiable; for even if the sentence is adjudged on this ground to be meaningless, the reference to "what it expresses" appears still to imply that something is expressed.

This is, however, no more than a terminological difficulty, and there are various ways in which it might be met. One of them would be to make the criterion of verifiability apply directly to sentences, and so eliminate the reference to propositions altogether. This would, indeed, run counter to ordinary usage, since one would not normally say of a sentence, as opposed to a proposition, that it was capable of being verified, or, for that matter, that it was either true or false; but it might be argued that such a departure from ordinary usage was justified, if it could be shown to have some practical advantage. The fact is, however, that the practical advantage seems to lie on the other side. For while it is true that the use of the word "proposition" does not enable us to say anything that we could not, in principle, say without it, it does fulfil an important function; for it makes it possible to express what is valid not merely for a particular sentence s but for any sentence to which s is logically equivalent. Thus, if I assert, for example, that the proposition p is entailed by the proposition q I am indeed claiming implicitly that the English sentence s which expresses p can be validly derived from the English sentence r which expresses q, but this is not

6

the whole of my claim. For, if I am right, it will also follow that any sentence, whether of the English or any other language, that is equivalent to *s* can be validly derived, in the language in question, from any sentence that is equivalent to *r*; and it is this that my use of the word "proposition" indicates. Admittedly, we could decide to use the word "sentence" in the way in which we now use the word "proposition," but this would not be conducive to clarity, particularly as the word "sentence" is already ambiguous. Thus, in a case of repetition, it can be said either that there are two different sentences or that the same sentence has been formulated twice. It is in the latter sense that I have so far been using the word, but the other usage is equally legitimate. In either usage, a sentence which was expressed in English would be accounted a different sentence from its French equivalent, but this would not hold good for the new usage of the word "sentence" that we should be introducing if we substituted "sentence" for "proposition." For in that case we should have to say that the English expression and its French equivalent were different formulations of the same sentence. We might indeed be justified in increasing the ambiguity of the word "sentence" in this way if we thereby avoided any of the difficulties that have been thought to be attached to the use of the word "proposition"; but I do not think that this is to be achieved by the mere substitution of one verbal token for another. Accordingly, I conclude that this technical use of the word "sentence," though legitimate in itself, would be likely to promote confusion, without securing us any compensatory advantage.

A second way of meeting our original difficulty would be to extend the use of the word "proposition," so that anything that could properly be called a sentence would be said to express a proposition, whether or not the sentence was literally meaningful. This course would have the advantage of simplicity, but it is open to two objections. The first is that it would involve a departure from current philosophical usage; and the second is that it would oblige us to give up the rule that every proposition is to be accounted either true or false. For while, if we adopted this new usage, we should still be able to say that anything that was either true or false was a proposition, the converse would no longer hold good; for a proposition would be neither true nor

7

false if it was expressed by a sentence which was literally meaning-less. I do not myself think that these objections are very serious, but they are perhaps sufficiently so to make it advisable to solve our terminological problem in some other way.

The solution that I prefer is to introduce a new technical term; and for this purpose I shall make use of the familiar word "state-ment," though I shall perhaps be using it in a slightly unfamiliar sense. Thus I propose that any form of words that is gram-matically significant shall be held to constitute a sentence, and that every indicative sentence, whether it is literally meaningful or not, shall be regarded as expressing a statement. Furthermore, any two sentences which are mutually translatable will be said to express the same statement. The word "proposition," on the other hand, will be reserved for what is expressed by sentences which are literally meaningful. Thus, the class of propositions becomes, in this usage, a sub-class of the class of statements, and one way of describing the use of the principle of verification would be to say that it provided a means of determining when an indicative sentence expressed a proposition, or, in other words, of distinguishing the statements that belonged to the class of propositions from those that did not.

It should be remarked that this decision to say that sentences express statements involves nothing more than the adoption of a verbal convention; and the proof of this is that the question, "What do sentences express?" to which it provides an answer is not a factual question. To ask of any particular sentence what it is that it expresses may, indeed, be to put a factual question; and one way of answering it would be to produce another sentence which was a translation of the first. But if the general question, "What do sentences express?" is to be interpreted factually, all that can be said in answer is that, since it is not the case that all sentences are equivalent, there is not any one thing that they all express. At the same time, it is useful to have a means of re-ferring indefinitely to "what sentences express" in cases where the sentences themselves are not particularly specified; and this purpose is served by the introduction of the word "statement" as a technical term. Accordingly, in saying that sentences express statements, we are indicating how this technical term is to be understood, but we are not thereby conveying any factual in-formation in the sense in which we should be conveying factual

8

information if the question we were answering was empirical. This may, indeed, seem a point too obvious to be worth making; but the question, "What do sentences express?" is closely analogous to the question, "What do sentences mean?" and, as I have tried to show elsewhere,[1] the question, "What do sentences mean?" has been a source of confusion to philosophers because they have mistakenly thought it to be factual. To say that indicative sentences mean propositions is indeed legitimate, just as it is legitimate to say that they express statements. But what we are doing, in giving answers of this kind, is to lay down conventional definitions; and it is important that these conventional definitions should not be confused with statements of empirical fact.

Returning now to the principle of verification, we may, for the sake of brevity, apply it directly to statements rather than to the sentences which express them, and we can then reformulate it by saying that a statement is held to be literally meaningful if and only if it is either analytic or empirically verifiable. But what is to be understood in this context by the term "verifiable"? I do indeed attempt to answer this question in the first chapter of this book; but I have to acknowledge that my answer is not very satisfactory.

To begin with, it will be seen that I distinguish between a "strong" and a "weak" sense of the term "verifiable," and that I explain this distinction by saying that "a proposition is said to be verifiable in the strong sense of the term, if and only if its truth could be conclusively established in experience," but that "it is verifiable, in the weak sense, if it is possible for experience to render it probable." And I then give reasons for deciding that it is only the weak sense of the term that is required by my principle of verification. What I seem, however, to have overlooked is that, as I represent them, these are not two genuine alternatives.[2] For I subsequently go on to argue that all empirical propositions are hypotheses which are continually subject to the test of further experience; and from this it would follow not merely that the truth of any such proposition never was conclusively established but that it never could be; for however

[1] In *The Foundations of Empirical Knowledge*, pp. 92–104.
[2] Vide M. Lazerowitz, "Strong and Weak Verification," *Mind*, 1939, pp. 202–13.

9

strong the evidence in its favour, there would never be a point at which it was impossible for further experience to go against it. But this would mean that my "strong" sense of the term "verifiable" had no possible application, and in that case there was no need for me to qualify the other sense of "verifiable" as weak; for on my own showing it was the only sense in which any proposition could conceivably be verified.

If I do not now draw this conclusion, it is because I have come to think that there is a class of empirical propositions of which it is permissible to say that they can be verified conclusively. It is characteristic of these propositions, which I have elsewhere[1] called "basic propositions," that they refer solely to the content of a single experience, and what may be said to verify them conclusively is the occurrence of the experience to which they uniquely refer. Furthermore, I should now agree with those who say that propositions of this kind are "incorrigible," assuming that what is meant by their being incorrigible is that it is impossible to be mistaken about them except in a verbal sense. In a verbal sense, indeed, it is always possible to misdescribe one's experience; but if one intends to do no more than record what is experienced without relating it to anything else, it is not possible to be factually mistaken; and the reason for this is that one is making no claim that any further fact could confute. It is, in short, a case of "nothing venture, nothing lose." It is, however, equally a case of "nothing venture, nothing win," since the mere recording of one's present experience does not serve to convey any information either to any other person or indeed to oneself; for in knowing a basic proposition to be true one obtains no further knowledge than what is already afforded by the occurrence of the relevant experience. Admittedly, the form of words that is used to express a basic proposition may be understood to express something that is informative both to another person and to oneself, but when it is so understood it no longer expresses a basic proposition. It was for this reason, indeed, that I maintained, in the fifth chapter of this book, that there could not be such things as basic propositions, in the sense in which I am now using the term; for the burden of my argument was that no synthetic proposition could be purely ostensive. My reasoning on

[1] "Verification and Experience," *Proceedings of the Aristotelian Society*, Vol. XXXVII; cf. also *The Foundations of Empirical Knowledge*, pp. 80–4.

this point was not in itself incorrect, but I think that I mistook its purport. For I seem not to have perceived that what I was really doing was to suggest a motive for refusing to apply the term "proposition" to statements that "directly recorded an immediate experience"; and this is a terminological point which is not of any great importance.

Whether or not one chooses to include basic statements in the class of empirical propositions, and so to admit that some empirical propositions can be conclusively verified, it will remain true that the vast majority of the propositions that people actually express are neither themselves basic statements, nor deducible from any finite set of basic statements. Consequently, if the principle of verification is to be seriously considered as a criterion of meaning, it must be interpreted in such a way as to admit statements that are not so strongly verifiable as basic statements are supposed to be. But how then is the word "verifiable" to be understood?

It will be seen that, in this book, I begin by suggesting that a statement is "weakly" verifiable, and therefore meaningful, according to my criterion, if "some possible sense-experience would be relevant to the determination of its truth or falsehood." But, as I recognize, this itself requires interpretation; for the word "relevant" is uncomfortably vague. Accordingly, I put forward a second version of my principle, which I shall restate here in slightly different terms, using the phrase "observation-statement," in place of "experiential proposition," to designate a statement "which records an actual or possible observation." In this version, then, the principle is that a statement is verifiable, and consequently meaningful, if some observation-statement can be deduced from it in conjunction with certain other premises, without being deducible from those other premises alone.

I say of this criterion that it "seems liberal enough," but in fact it is far too liberal, since it allows meaning to any statement whatsoever. For, given any statement "S" and an observation-statement "O," "O" follows from "S" and "if S then O" without following from "if S then O" alone. Thus, the statements "the Absolute is lazy" and "if the Absolute is lazy, this is white" jointly entail the observation-statement "this is white," and since "this is white" does not follow from either of these premises, taken

11

by itself, both of them satisfy my criterion of meaning. Furthermore, this would hold good for any other piece of nonsense that one cared to put, as an example, in place of "the Absolute is lazy," provided only that it had the grammatical form of an indicative sentence. But a criterion of meaning that allows such latitude as this is evidently unacceptable.[1]

It may be remarked that the same objection applies to the proposal that we should take the possibility of falsification as our criterion. For, given any statement "S" and any observation-statement "O", "O" will be incompatible with the conjunction of "S" and "if S then not O." We could indeed avoid the difficulty, in either case, by leaving out the stipulation about the other premises. But as this would involve the exclusion of all hypotheticals from the class of empirical propositions, we should escape from making our criteria too liberal only at the cost of making them too stringent.

Another difficulty which I overlooked in my original attempt to formulate the principle of verification is that most empirical propositions are in some degree vague. Thus, as I have remarked elsewhere,[2] what is required to verify a statement about a material thing is never the occurrence of precisely this or precisely that sense-content, but only the occurrence of one or other of the sense-contents that fall within a fairly indefinite range. We do indeed test any such statement by making observations which consist in the occurrence of particular sense-contents; but, for any test that we actually carry out, there is always an indefinite number of other tests, differing to some extent in respect either of their conditions or their results, that would have served the same purpose. And this means that there is never any set of observation-statements of which it can truly be said that precisely they are entailed by any given statement about a material thing.

Nevertheless, it is only by the occurrence of some sense-content, and consequently by the truth of some observation-statement, that any statement about a material thing is actually verified; and from this it follows that every significant statement about a material thing can be represented as entailing a disjunction of observation-statements, although the terms of this disjunction,

[1] Vide I. Berlin, "Verifiability in Principle," *Proceedings of the Aristotelian Society*, Vol. XXXIX.

[2] *The Foundations of Empirical Knowledge*, pp. 240–1.

being infinite, can not be enumerated in detail. Consequently, I do not think that we need be troubled by the difficulty about vagueness, so long as it is understood that when we speak of the "entailment" of observation-statements, what we are considering to be deducible from the premises in question is not any particular observation-statement, but only one or other of a set of such statements, where the defining characteristic of the set is that all its members refer to sense-contents that fall within a certain specifiable range.

There remains the more serious objection that my criterion, as it stands, allows meaning to any indicative statement whatsoever. To meet this, I shall emend it as follows. I propose to say that a statement is directly verifiable if it is either itself an observation-statement, or is such that in conjunction with one or more observation-statements it entails at least one observation-statement which is not deducible from these other premises alone; and I propose to say that a statement is indirectly verifiable if it satisfies the following conditions: first, that in conjunction with certain other premises it entails one or more directly verifiable statements which are not deducible from these other premises alone; and secondly, that these other premises do not include any statement that is not either analytic, or directly verifiable, or capable of being independently established as indirectly verifiable. And I can now reformulate the principle of verification as requiring of a literally meaningful statement, which is not analytic, that it should be either directly or indirectly verifiable, in the foregoing sense.

It may be remarked that in giving my account of the conditions in which a statement is to be considered indirectly verifiable, I have explicitly put in the proviso that the "other premises" may include analytic statements; and my reason for doing this is that I intend in this way to allow for the case of scientific theories which are expressed in terms that do not themselves designate anything observable. For while the statements that contain these terms may not appear to describe anything that anyone could ever observe, a "dictionary" may be provided by means of which they can be transformed into statements that are verifiable; and the statements which constitute the dictionary can be regarded as analytic. Were this not so, there would be nothing to choose between such scientific theories and those that I should dismiss

13

as metaphysical; but I take it to be characteristic of the meta-physician, in my somewhat pejorative sense of the term, not only that his statements do not describe anything that is capable, even in principle, of being observed, but also that no dictionary is provided by means of which they can be transformed into state-ments that are directly or indirectly verifiable.

Metaphysical statements, in my sense of the term, are excluded also by the older empiricist principle that no statement is literally meaningful unless it describes what could be experienced, where the criterion of what could be experienced is that it should be something of the same kind as actually has been experienced.[1] But, apart from its lack of precision, this empiricist principle has, to my mind, the defect of imposing too harsh a condition upon the form of scientific theories; for it would seem to imply that it was illegitimate to introduce any term that did not itself designate something observable. The principle of verification, on the other hand, is, as I have tried to show, more liberal in this respect, and in view of the use that is actually made of scientific theories which the other would rule out, I think that the more liberal criterion is to be preferred.

It has sometimes been assumed by my critics that I take the principle of verification to imply that no statement can be evid-ence for another unless it is a part of its meaning; but this is not the case. Thus, to make use of a simple illustration, the statement that I have blood on my coat may, in certain circumstances, con-firm the hypothesis that I have committed a murder, but it is not part of the meaning of the statement that I have committed a murder that I should have blood upon my coat, nor, as I under-stand it, does the principle of verification imply that it is. For one statement may be evidence for another, and still neither itself express a necessary condition of the truth of this other statement, nor belong to any set of statements which determines a range within which such a necessary condition falls; and it is only in

[1] cf. Bertrand Russell, *The Problems of Philosophy*, p. 91: "Every proposition which we can understand must be composed wholly of constituents with which we are acquainted." And, if I understand him correctly, this is what Professor W. T. Stace has in mind when he speaks of a "Principle of Observable Kinds." Vide his "Positivism," *Mind*, 1944. Stace argues that the principle of verifica-tion "rests upon" the principle of observable kinds, but this is a mistake. It is true that every statement that is allowed to be meaningful by the principle of observable kinds is also allowed to be meaningful by the principle of verification: but the converse does not hold.

14

these cases that the principle of verification yields the conclusion that the one statement is part of the meaning of the other. Thus, from the fact that it is only by the making of some observation that any statement about a material thing can be directly verified it follows, according to the principle of verification, that every such statement contains some observation-statement or other as part of its meaning, and it follows also that, although its generality may prevent any finite set of observation-statements from exhausting its meaning, it does not contain anything as part of its meaning that cannot be represented as an observation-statement; but there may still be many observation-statements that are relevant to its truth or falsehood without being part of its meaning at all. Again, a person who affirms the existence of a deity may try to support his contention by appealing to the facts of religious experience; but it does not follow from this that the factual meaning of his statement is wholly contained in the propositions by which these religious experiences are described. For there may be other empirical facts that he would also consider to be relevant; and it is possible that the descriptions of these other empirical facts can more properly be regarded as containing the factual meaning of his statement than the descriptions of the religious experiences. At the same time, if one accepts the principle of verification, one must hold that his statement does not have any other factual meaning than what is contained in at least some of the relevant empirical propositions; and that if it is so interpreted that no possible experience could go to verify it, it does not have any factual meaning at ail.

In putting forward the principle of verification as a criterion of meaning, I do not overlook the fact that the word "meaning" is commonly used in a variety of senses, and I do not wish to deny that in some of these senses a statement may properly be said to be meaningful even though it is neither analytic nor empirically verifiable. I should, however, claim that there was at least one proper use of the word "meaning" in which it would be incorrect to say that a statement was meaningful unless it satisfied the principle of verification; and I have, perhaps tendentiously, used the expression "literal meaning" to distinguish this use from the others, while applying the expression "factual meaning" to the case of statements which satisfy my criterion without being analytic. Furthermore, I suggest that it is only if it is literally

15

meaningful, in this sense, that a statement can properly be said to be either true or false. Thus, while I wish the principle of verification itself to be regarded, not as an empirical hypothesis,[1] but as a definition, it is not supposed to be entirely arbitrary. It is indeed open to anyone to adopt a different criterion of meaning and so to produce an alternative definition which may very well correspond to one of the ways in which the word "meaning" is commonly used. And if a statement satisfied such a criterion, there is, no doubt, some proper use of the word "understanding" in which it would be capable of being understood. Nevertheless, I think that, unless it satisfied the principle of verification, it would not be capable of being understood in the sense in which either scientific hypotheses or common-sense statements are habitually understood. I confess, however, that it now seems to me unlikely that any metaphysician would yield to a claim of this kind; and although I should still defend the use of the criterion of verifiability as a methodological principle, I realize that for the effective elimination of metaphysics it needs to be supported by detailed analyses of particular metaphysical arguments.

16

3

The Criterion of Significance

PAUL MARHENKE

Reprinted with the kind permission of Karl Marhenke and the editor from *Proceedings and Addresses of the American Philosophical Association*, XXIII (1950), 1-21.

The Criterion of Significance[1]

PAUL MARHENKE

A CRITERION OF SIGNIFICANCE IS A STATEMENT TO THE EFFECT THAT A sentence is significant if it satisfies such and such conditions, and that it is meaningless if it does not satisfy the specified conditions. When one examines the various formulations of this criterion, it is not always clear whether the criterion is intended as a definition of the term 'significant sentence,' or whether it is intended as a generalization about significant sentences. If the criterion is intended as a definition the conditions referred to are the defining properties of a significant sentence. Thus, a sentence is often said to be significant if and only if it expresses a proposition. This formulation of the criterion is perhaps intended as a definition of the term "significant sentence," rather than as a generalization about significant sentences. If the criterion is intended as a generalization, it specifies some property that belongs to all significant sentences and only to such sentences. When the criterion of significance is formulated as the thesis that a sentence is significant if and only if it is verifiable, this thesis is perhaps intended as a generalization about significant sentences rather than as a definition.

The formulation of a criterion of significance in the sense of a generalization about significant sentences can get under way only if we already know how to distinguish between significant and meaningless sentences. Assuming that we know how to divide any given group of sentences into significant and meaningless sentences, the initial step in the formulation of this generalization is the ascertainment of the common properties of the sentences in the two groups. And assuming that these have been found, we may next find it possible to select a subset of the common properties of the significant sentences which is not also a subset of the common properties of the meaningless sentences. This subset can then be used in the formulation of a criterion of significance, and any sentence that was not used in the formulation of the criterion can be subjected to the test provided by the criterion. The sentence is significant if it has all the properties belonging to the subset, otherwise meaningless.

---

[1]Presidential address delivered before the twenty-third annual meeting of the Pacific Division of the American Philosophical Association at Mills College, Oakland, California, December 27, 28, 29, 1949.

It is theoretically possible to find a correct generalization of this sort, if we know how to distinguish between significant and meaningless sentences. We can make this distinction if we have a definition of significance, and if we can determine for every sentence whether or not it has the defining properties of a significant sentence. But we can also make this distinction if the notion of significance is taken as primitive. To be sure, it may not be possible to determine by simple inspection whether or not a given sentence is significant. But we may nevertheless be able to make this determination indirectly by showing that the sentence can or cannot be transformed into a significant sentence. The criterion we use in making this determination may be formulated in several alternative ways. (1) A sentence is significant if and only if it is translatable into a significant sentence. (2) A sentence is significant if and only if it is a member of a class of synonymous sentences. (3) A sentence is significant if and only if it is well-formed or transformable into a well-formed sentence. This criterion presupposes that certain sentences are known to be significant. Now if we have a definition of significance or a criterion of the sort just described, we can separate sense from nonsense, and we can next attack the problem of finding a criterion of significance in the sense of a generalization that is true of significant sentences and only of such sentences. If we are successful in finding one or more generalizations of this kind, we can subsequently degrade one of these generalizations to the status of a definition. Once the common properties of significant and meaningless sentences have been ascertained, we may find that the notion of significance is definable, even if our original classification of sentences into significant and meaningless was made on the supposition that significance is a primitive notion.

It would be very desirable if we had a criterion of significance either in the sense of a definition or in the sense of a true generalization about all significant sentences. But such a definition or generalization has not yet been found. It will be maintained in this paper that the criteria of significance that have been proposed suffer from two defects. (1) If they are intended as definitions of significance they are either inadequate or else reducible to the criterion for which significance is a primitive notion. (2) If they are intended as generalizations about the class of significant sentences, they are false. It will be maintained instead that the criterion of significance in its present form amounts, roughly speaking, to the statement that a sentence is significant if and only if

THE CRITERION OF SIGNIFICANCE

it is transformable into a significant sentence. This is the criterion which is in fact always used when we seek to determine whether or not a sentence is significant.

In order to see how we arrive at the decision that a sentence is significant or meaningless, let us review first some of the necessary conditions that do not presuppose the notion of significance. For this purpose we need to consider only declarative sentences. Sentences other than declarative may be ignored, because an imperative, optative, or interrogative sentence is significant or meaningless only if its declarative prototype is significant or meaningless. A declarative sentence in a natural language, such as English, is a string of words such that every word, with the possible exception of certain proper names, belongs to the language in question. If the string includes words, aside from proper names, that do not belong to the language, it is not a sentence in that language, unless the definitions of these words have also been supplied, i.e., unless these words can be replaced by their defined equivalents. Though every sentence is a string of words, not every string of words is a sentence, for a sentence may be either grammatical or ungrammatical, and some strings of words are neither. A sentence is ungrammatical if it resembles, in a certain degree, a correctly constructed sentence. How great a departure from the grammatical norm is permissible before a string of words ceases to be an ungrammatical sentence we do not need to decide; we may suppose that any string of words is an acceptable sentence if a grammarian finds it possible to restore it to grammatical correctness. Now, though compliance with the rules of grammar is not a necessary condition of significance, the transformability of an ungrammatical sentence into one that is grammatically sound is a necessary condition of significance. A string of words that fails to satisfy this condition is not a sentence and hence meaningless. In other words, if a sentence is significant, it must be constructed in accordance with the grammatical rules or else it must be transformable into a sentence that satisfies these rules. A string of words may also fail to be a sentence under the foregoing characterization if there is a violation of the rules of orthography. If a string of this nature can not be transformed into a sentence, grammatical or ungrammatical, by restoring the offending words to orthographic perfection, it is meaningless. In other words, if a sentence is significant, the words of the sentence satisfy the rules of orthography or else it is transformable into a sentence whose component words do satisfy these rules.

The two conditions mentioned are, I think, sufficiently trivial to be acceptable as necessary conditions of significance without further argument. These conditions assure us only that a string of words that resists grammatical and orthographic correction is nonsensical. If a sentence is significant, the grammatical and orthographic defects can always be removed, provided we know what the intended meaning is. We shall therefore use the term 'sentence' henceforth as a synonym for the term 'grammatically correct sentence.' Since a sentence may be grammatically and orthographically correct without being significant, a significant sentence has to satisfy further conditions that are stronger than these two. The necessary condition of significance I propose to examine next is as trivial as these two, but, I think, will not be found acceptable without argument.

The condition I have in mind is one that is imposed whenever we encounter a sentence whose significance we question. If a sentence is significant, we require that it be translatable into the ordinary idiom. The ordinary idiom may be characterized, somewhat vaguely it must be admitted, as the idiom we use in communicating with one another. It is the idiom in which most conversations are conducted and in which almost all books are written. Translatability into this idiom is a necessary condition of significance, because we have but one recourse when we are asked to clarify the meaning of a sentence that is not in this idiom. It would not be to the purpose to answer the question by translating the sentence into another sentence of the same idiom, for its meaning, if it has one, would not thereby become any clearer. The problem can be met only, if at all, by translating the sentence into the ordinary idiom. But since translatability into this idiom is only a necessary condition of significance, there is no guarantee that the result of the translation is a significant sentence. Russell's nonsense sentence "Quadruplicity drinks procrastination" is a sentence in the ordinary idiom. The sentence happens to be formulated in English, but it is a simple matter to produce its translation in the ordinary idiom of French or German. Moreover, this sentence can easily be transformed into another sentence in the ordinary idiom of English by replacing "Quadruplicity" and "Procrastination" by their defined equivalents. These translations are of course in every instance as nonsensical as the original sentence.

The objection may now be made that the requirement of translatability into the ordinary idiom is too strong, and that this requirement should be replaced by the weaker condition of translatability into

THE CRITERION OF SIGNIFICANCE

some other idiom. It is undeniable that often only this weaker condition is imposed when a sentence is put to the test of significance. A metaphysician, for instance, may satisfy himself that the statements of a rival metaphysician are intelligible only if he finds it possible to translate them into his own idiom. However, if a sentence is translatable into the private idiom of a metaphysician, it is also translatable into the public idiom in which communication takes place. Once we grant that a sentence is significant only if it is translatable into some other idiom, we also grant that it is significant only if it is translatable into the ordinary idiom. For if the sentence is found translatable because its meaning is known, then this meaning can also be expressed in the ordinary idiom. The objection is therefore without force. Many commentators on the works of metaphysicians appear to take the view, as a matter of fact, that the stronger condition is a necessary condition of significance. Thus, when McTaggart reaches Hegel's statement that "the Various is the Difference which is merely posited, the Difference which is no Difference," he offers the following translation into the ordinary idiom:

What is meant by this? I conceive that he means that in this category there is no special connexion of any thing with any other thing. The relation may fairly be said to be one of Indifference, if no thing has any connection with one other except that which it has to all others. And this Indifference, I conceive, arises as follows. We are now dealing with Likenesses and Unlikenesses. But everything is, as we have seen, Unlike every other thing. And it is also Like every other thing, for in any possible group we can, as we have seen, find a common quality. Thus under this category everything has exactly the same relation to everything else. For it is both Like and Unlike everything else.[2]

The works of Hegel have attracted commentators because this philosopher has written thousands of sentences that are not in the ordinary idiom. The commentators attempt to extract the cognitive meaning of these sentences by translating them into a more familiar idiom, though often with results that are satisfactory, as regards intelligibility, only to themselves. Hegel's famous statement "Being and Nothing are one and the same" is undeniably in need of clarification, as Hegel himself admitted. But his own explanation is not in the ordinary idiom, since Hegel uses the terms "the being" and "the nothing" as designative expressions, while the ordinary idiom does not countenance the use of these expressions as designative. It would be unreasonable to conclude, on this ground alone, that the statement is nonsense. But if it is

---

[2]McTaggart, A Commentary on Hegel's Logic, p. 112.

not, its cognitive content can not be appraised until it is translated into the ordinary idiom.

There is a widespread conviction, which is particularly prevalent among logical positivists, that metaphysical statements, such as the one we quoted from Hegel's Logic, are nonsense. In defense of metaphysics it is often said that such statements are intelligible, but that they create the impression that they are unintelligible, because they are expressed in an unfamiliar idiom. Their meaning is revealed only to those who have mastered the idiom. To the uninitiated they appear to be unintelligible, because their meaning is obscure and recondite. If this is the correct explanation of the belief that metaphysical statements are unintelligible, the charge of unintelligibility can easily be disproved by translating these statements into the ordinary idiom. Anyone who has mastered the esoteric idiom and knows what is being said is *ipso facto* in a position to communicate his knowledge in the language he shares with the rest of us. The requirement of translatability is often rejected on the ground that a sentence can not always be translated without loss or change of meaning. Thus it has often been alleged that a work such as Hegel's *Wissenschaft der Logik* is untranslatable. If this allegation means that this work can not be translated literally into French or English without first inventing an esoteric French or English vocabulary, it is unquestionably correct. No one knows how to translate this work literally into the ordinary idiom of these languages, just as no one knows how to translate it literally into the ordinary idiom of the German language. But if the allegation means that one can say things in German that can not be said in another language, it can easily be refuted. For as soon as one has said what can be said only in German, the required translation can at once be produced. The objection therefore has no merit whatsoever. If the proposed translation of a sentence is rejected as inaccurate or incorrect, it is always possible to improve or correct it. A translation that fails to duplicate the meaning of the original sentence can always be corrected as soon as the difference in meaning is known. There is of course a trivial sense in which no sentence is translatable into a sentence either of the same or of a different language. For the causal and particularly the emotive effects of a sentence are different from the effects of its translation, these differences being determined, in part at least, by the differences in the words alone. Translatability of a sentence requires only that its cognitive meaning be reproducible, if it has one; it does not require that its effects on a hearer or reader be reproducible as well.

THE CRITERION OF SIGNIFICANCE

One who attempts the solution of the problem of translating a work on metaphysics into the ordinary idiom has to be able to eliminate the technical terms that are used in the work, and, if their definitions have not been given, he has to be able to reconstruct these through an investigation of the sentential contexts in which these terms occur. The technical terms are the terms that are not found in the ordinary vocabulary, and, besides these, all the terms that occur in sentential contexts in which they never occur in the ordinary idiom. He must also be able to replace the terms that are used metaphorically by terms that have literal meaning, for the proposed translation is intended to duplicate only the cognitive meanings of the sentences and not also their emotive or poetic overtones. The problem of translating a work on metaphysics is thus in some respects similar to the problem of deciphering a work that has been written in code. The problem of breaking the code is attacked by taking a part of the work and then replacing the code words by words that have the effect of breaking this part up into intelligible sentences. The correct key has been found if the remaining parts of the work likewise break up into intelligible sentences by using this key. But if the key makes nonsense of the remainder, and this is perhaps the fate of most keys to the secrets of metaphysics, we have nevertheless no guarantee that the correct key has not been found, since translatability is only a necessary condition of significance. The correct key turns sentence into sentence and hence nonsense into nonsense.

That translatability is at least a necessary condition of significance is shown by the fact that we answer a question of the form "What does the sentence S mean?" by producing some sentence we believe to be synonymous with S. If you do not know what a given sentence means you ask someone who does know, and he answers you by translating the sentence into one that has the same meaning. This question is answered in exactly the same way in which a dictionary answers the question "What does the word W mean?" The dictionary specifies the meaning of a given word by means of other words. Hence, if you are ignorant of the meannigs of all words, the dictionary is of no help, and similarly, if you are ignorant of the meanings of all sentences, the meaning of a given sentence can not be explained to you. The procedure we use in explaining the meaning of a sentence suggests that a necessary and sufficient condition of significance is obtained by simply strengthening the requirement of translatability: a sentence is significant if and only if it is translatable into a significant sentence. In one sense of the term "criterion" this condition is of course not a criterion of significance. For if a criterion is formulated with the intention of providing us with a method by which we can determine whether or not a given sentence is significant, then the notion of significance can not itself be used in the formulation of such a criterion. A criterion must enable us to make this determination without the prior knowledge that any sentence is significant or meaningless. We shall now turn to the examination of two formulations of the criterion that appear to answer to this description. One of these specifies the necessary and sufficient condition of significance by means of the concept of a proposition: a sentence is significant if and only if it expresses a proposition. The other specifies it by means of the concept of verifiability: a sentence is significant if and only if it is verifiable.

The first of these formulations is based on the view that a significant sentence is related to an entity which is the significance or meaning of the sentence. This entity is the proposition expressed by the sentence. The existence of the entity demanded by this view can of course be guaranteed by defining the phrase "the proposition expressed by S" by means of the phrase "the class of sentences that are synomymous with S." However, the proponents of the view under consideration do not reckon with the possibility of defining the former phrase by means of terms that refer to linguistic entities; they assume, rather, that this phrase designates an extra-linguistic entity. Some philosophers believe that the propositions expressed by sentences are psychical or psycho-physical occurrences, others that they are of the nature of Platonic universals and thus non-physical and non-psychical. Now if there are propositions and if sentences express them, and if we can identify the proposition a sentence expresses whenever such a sentence is significant, then we can decide whether or not a given sentence is significant without the prior knowledge that it is significant or meaningless. But if we are forced to make this decision independently of the fact, if it is a fact, that the sentence does or does not express a proposition, it is useless to tell us that all significant sentences and only such sentences express propositions. For this characteristic of significant sentences can not be used to distinguish sense from nonsense, if we do not know how to determine whether a sentence possesses it.

The most recent version of the view that propositions are psycho-physical entities is due to Russell. Propositions, according to Russell, are to be defined as "psychological and physiological occurrences of certain sorts—complex images, expectations, etc. Such occurrences are

THE CRITERION OF SIGNIFICANCE

expressed by sentences.[3] But nonsense can also cause the occurrence of complex images and expectations, and it therefore becomes necessary to differentiate the kinds of images and expectations that are expressed by significant from the images and expectations that are expressed by meaningless sentences. Russell dismisses this problem with the declaration that "the exact psychological definition of propositions is irrelevant to logic and theory of knowledge."[4] Russell finds it necessary to look for an extra-linguistic entity as the significance of a sentence in the first instance, because he thinks that the syntactical rules of significance are arbitrary unless we can find a reason for them. Apparently he thinks that this reason is to be found in the psychological and physiological occurrences that are expressed by sentences. Now perhaps there is a difference between the psychological and physiological effects that are expressed by significant and by meaningless sentences, but if there is one Russell has certainly not found it. The problem whose solution is to lead him to the discovery of the proposition is formulated by Russell in two ways. (1) "What do we believe when we believe something?" (2) "When a number of people all believe that there is going to be an explosion, what have they in common?" There is only one conceivable kind of answer that can be given to the first question, and that is the kind of answer that is customarily given. Depending on what we take to be the import of the question "What do you believe when you believe there is going to be an explosion?", we give one or the other of the following answers: (1) There is going to be an explosion; (2) I believe there is going to be an explosion; (3) When I believe there is going to be an explosion, I believe there is going to be an explosion. In each case the answer is given by formulating a sentence. To the second question "What is common to a number of people who believe that there is going to be an explosion?", Russell proposes the following answer: "A certain state of tension, which will be discharged when the explosion occurs, but, if their belief was false, will continue for some time, and then give place to surprise."[5] But this answer can not be quite correct. We can not rest satisfied with it because the psychological and physiological states of people who hear about an impending explosion are not the same. Even when the conditions are otherwise the same, people react in different ways to such information. And when the conditions are not the same, the state of tension aroused in a man who knows he is within one hundred yards

---

[3]Russell, An Inquiry into Meaning and Truth, p. 237.
[4]Loc cit., p. 237.   [5]Inquiry, p. 223.

of the impending explosion is quite different from the state of tension of a man who knows that the site of the explosion is one hundred miles away. Russell is quite well aware of such differences, but he thinks that they are probably only differences of degree.[6] As a matter of fact, the degree of the state of tension may be so low that the state is undetectable, again by his own admission: "When I believe something less exciting—that tomorrow's 'Times' will contain a weather forecast, or that Caesar crossed the Rubicon—I cannot observe any such occurrences in myself."[7] But if the state of tension may be of such low degree as to be undetectable, this state of tension, i.e., the proposition expressed by a sentence, can not be used for differentiating between sense and nonsense. Every significant sentence may express a proposition, as Russell claims, but this fact does not help us to distinguish significant from nonsensical sentences. The majority of sentences that come before us are too uninteresting and too unexciting; if any of them do express propositions these are too feeble to be observable. Russell's justification of the rules of syntax must hence be considered as a failure. In view of Russell's demand for a justification of these rules, he might have been expected to show that a given sentence is significant by showing that it expresses a proposition. But he never actually uses this procedure. Instead he shows that a sentence is significant by showing that it can be transformed into a significant sentence, i.e., into a sentence that is constructed in accordance with the syntactical rules.

The view that propositions are non-physical and non-psychic entities is the orthodox form of the proposition theory. The chief defect of this theory is that it forces us to hold that propositions belong to a realm of being that is inaccessible to inspection. A sentence does not come before us with the proposition it expresses, if the sentence is significant. Hence how are we going to determine, in the instance of a given sentence, whether or not it expresses a proposition, and, if we decide that it does, how are we going to determine the proposition it expresses? When we are in doubt whether a given sentence is significant, the doubt can not be removed by finding out whether or not it expresses a proposition. The criterion of significance of the proposition theory is formally similar to the criterion we use in determining whether or not a man is married. In the instance of a man, we can remove any doubt regarding his marital status by producing his wife. When we are in

---

[6]Cf. Inquiry, p. 225.
[7]Inquiry, p. 224.

THE CRITERION OF SIGNIFICANCE

doubt whether a sentence is significant, the doubt can not be similarly resolved by producing the proposition it expresses. In order to resolve the doubt concerning a sentence, we are limited to an examination of the sentence and its logical relations to other sentences.

There is a variant of the criterion of significance of the proposition theory that appears to be immune at least to the objection that propositions are removed to an inaccessible realm of being. This variant may be formulated as follows: a sentence is significant if and only if the sentence would designate a fact if the sentence were true. Aside from the fact that this criterion presupposes that we can know, independently of the condition stipulated by the criterion, that a sentence is significant, this being contained in the supposition that the sentence is true, this formulation of the criterion is objectionable on the following additional grounds. The view that sentences are designative expressions and that they designate facts is presumably based on the analogy between proper names and noun-clauses, i.e., clauses in which sentences occur as fragmentary expressions. But this analogy is defective. On the one hand, a proper name can not be eliminated from a sentence without replacing it by an expression, another proper name for instance, that performs the same semantical function. Noun-clauses, on the other hand, are not resistant to elimination. A sentence containing a noun-clause can usually be replaced by a synonymous sentence without replacing this noun-clause by another noun-clause. We have therefore no more reason to suppose that sentences designate facts than that they express propositions. The criterion moreover forces us to distinguish the facts designated by true sentences from the would-be facts designated by false sentences. These would-be facts are indistinguishable from the propositions which the proponents of this theory of significance would like to repudiate. If sentences are designative expressions, then false sentences certainly do not designate facts, if facts, whatever they may be, belong to the accessible realm of being. We can no more provide a false sentence with a fact, than we can provide a spinster with a husband by defining this personage as the man she would have been married to if she had married him.

If propositions were given with the sentences that express them, the criterion of significance of the proposition theory would be an adequate test of significance. But since only one member of this relation is ever given, this criterion must be rejected as inadequate. If the criterion is taken as a definition, it is inadequate, because the defining property can not be used in the identification of sentences as significant or meaningless. And if it is taken as a generalization, it is at best an untestable hypothesis. On the proposition theory the decision that a sentence is significant should be based on the antecedent ground that the sentence expresses a proposition. Instead, the doctrine of the proposition theory that certain sentences express propositions is based on the antecedent ground that these sentences are significant.

We come now to the much debated verifiability criterion of logical positivism. This criterion has appeared in innumerable formulations in the last twenty-five years, but we shall limit this examination to the more or less official versions of Schlick and of Carnap. An early formulation of the criterion is given by Schlick in the following terms: "It is impossible to specify the meaning of an assertion otherwise than by describing the state of affairs that must obtain if the assertion is to be true."[8] From this formulation it appears that a sentence is significant if it is translatable into a significant sentence. To take only one example, let us apply Schlick's test to the sentence "Caesar crossed the Rubicon." In the instance of this sentence we can all doubtlessly describe the state of affairs that must have obtained if the sentence is true. Presumably what is here wanted as a description of the state of affairs is not the sentence "Caesar crossed the Rubicon," though this sentence describes the state of affairs in question quite adequately, but rather some other sentence which uses a different set of words but describes the same state of affairs. We may offer the sentence "Caesar went from one bank of the Rubicon to the other" as a description of the state of affairs that must have obtained if and only if Caesar crossed the Rubicon. According to Schlick's own statement, then, the criterion of significance amounts to the assertion that a sentence is significant if it is possible to formulate another sentence which is synonymous with the given sentence. Schlick himself does not say that the second sentence must be significant, but this is of course included in the demand that this sentence be the description of a state of affairs.

Schlick appears to think that the criterion he has formulated is equivalent to the following: A sentence is significant if and only if it is possible to specify for every descriptive word that occurs in it a definitional chain (or a set of such chains) whose last link is an ostensive definition. For he says: "In order to find the meaning of a sentence we have to transform it by the introduction of successive definitions

---

[8]Erkenntnis, v. 3, p. 6.
[9]*Loc. cit.,* p. 7.

THE CRITERION OF SIGNIFICANCE

until finally it contains only words that are not further defined, but whose meanings can be given only by direct ostension."[9] We have observed previously that the condition that is here formulated is only a necessary condition of significance, unless we add the further proviso that the transformed sentence be significant. That the criterion as it stands is only a necessary condition of significance becomes obvious when we consider that Russell's nonsense sentence "Quadruplicity drinks procrastination" can easily be transformed into a sentence that contains only ostensively defined terms. But this sentence is not thereby transformed into a significant sentence.

Schlick's second formulation of the criterion may be rendered as follows: A sentence is significant if and only if it is possible to specify the circumstances under which the sentence is true.[10] This formulation is evidently equivalent to the first. For the specification of the circumstances under which a sentence is true is effected by means of sentences. The only circumstance that is at all relevant to the truth of the sentence "Caesar crossed the Rubicon" is the circumstance that Caesar did cross the Rubicon, and the only method known to man of specifying this circumstance is the formulation of a sentence such as the sentence "Caesar crossed the Rubicon" or of some other sentence synonymous with this sentence. There is another version of the foregoing formulation of the criterion in which the notion of verifiability is used. A sentence is significant if and only if it is verifiable, and it is verifiable if it is possible to give a description of the conditions under which it is true as well as of those under which it is false.[11] The property of verifiability that is mentioned in this formulation has nothing to do with verification. To say that a sentence is verifiable is simply a shorthand way of saying that it is possible to give a description of the conditions under which the sentence is true and false respectively.

Schlick's third formulation of the criterion also makes use of the notion of verifiability. But here we get a different account of what is meant by "verifiability." A sentence is significant if and only if it is verifiable, and to say that it is verifiable is to say that it is logically possible to verify it. Schlick says that "a fact or a process is logically possible if it can be *described*, i.e., if the sentence which is supposed to describe it obeys the rules of grammar we have stipulated in our language."[12] If Schlick were now called upon to show that a given sen-

---

[10]*Loc. cit.*, p. 7.
[11]Schlick, Gesammelte Aufsaetze, p. 340.
[12]*Loc. cit.*, p. 348.

tence is verifiable, we would expect him to show that the procedure of verifying the sentence is logically possible, i.e., that the procedure of verifying the sentence can be described. But this he fails to do. He considers the sentence "Rivers flow uphill," but instead of demonstrating the logical possibility of verifying this sentence, he demonstrates the logical possibility of rivers flowing uphill. It is logically possible that rivers flow uphill, because the sentence is not self-contradictory. Schlick does not say how he determines that a sentence is not self-contradictory. He apparently holds that this determination is made by examining its logical form. However, a sentence that is not self-contradictory in form may nevertheless be nonsensical. Neither the sentence S nor the sentences that describe the procedure of verifying S may have the logical form of a contradiction. But this is no guarantee that these sentences are not nonsense. Schlick's test therefore comes to nothing, because in order to apply it we must know in advance that the sentence S is significant.

Verifiability is a dispositional property of a sentence. The decision that a given sentence is verifiable is based on exactly the same sort of considerations on which one bases the decision that a sample of a given substance has a specified dispositional property. Let us take an example. The label on a bottle identifies its contents as ether and it adds the warning that ether is highly inflammable. This dispositional property is attributed to the sample before us, because of the law that ether is easily set on fire when exposed to an open flame. The law asserts an invariable connection between the defining properties of ether and another property. The dispositional property of inflammability is correctly attributed to the contents of the bottle if (i) the law is correct and (ii) the bottle contains ether. We show that a given sentence has the property of verifiability in exactly the same way. We establish (i) a law to the effect that sentences of a specified kind have invariably been verified under specified circumstances and (ii) that the sentence before us is a sentence of this kind. These two conditions are undoubtedly satisfied by sentences of many different kinds. Sentences about last year's arrivals and departures of ships in San Francisco Harbor are verifiable in the sense specified, because we can verify a sentence of this kind whenever we please by looking up the shipping news in a newspaper. Sentences about next week's weather are also verifiable in this sense, because sentences of this kind are invariably verified simply by waiting until next week's weather is here to be scrutinized. Though verifiability in this sense is a sufficient condition of significance, it is

14

THE CRITERION OF SIGNIFICANCE

certainly not a necessary condition. If it were a necessary condition, we would have to know that every significant sentence is verifiable. There is no law to the effect that significant sentences have always been verified whenever we chose to ascertain whether one of these sentences is true. The sentence "Caesar was shaved by his barber on the morning of the day he crossed the Rubicon" is significant, but not verifiable. There are a great many sentences about Caesar, but very few of these have ever been verified. Now if the term "verifiability" is understood in the foregoing sense, Schlick's statement[13] that one can not start verifying a sentence until one has established the possibility of its verification, i.e., its verifiability, is exactly parallel to the statement that one can not start burning the ether in the bottle until one has esablished its inflammability. The demand that we first establish that a sentence is verifiable before we start verifying it is as ridiculous as the demand that we first establish that a substance is inflammable before we start burning it. If no one had ever set any substance on fire he would never have learned that some substances are inflammable, and if no one had ever verified a sentence he would never have learned that some sentences are verifiable.

The criterion of significance has so far been formulated by Schlick simply as a test of significance. We must now consider a formulation of the criterion which does not merely specify the conditions a significant sentence must satisfy, but beyond this tells us what the meaning of the sentence is. The formulation reads as follows: "Stating the meaning of a sentence amounts to stating the rules according to which the sentence is to be used, and this is the same as stating the way in which it can be verified. The meaning of a proposition is the method of its verification."[14] One wonders whether Schlick, and with him many other logical positivists who have repeated the slogan that the meaning of a sentence is the method of its verification, was quite clear in his own mind as to the meaning of the term 'method' when the meaning of a sentence is identified with the method of its verification. A method of verification is a procedure one selects for the purpose of verifying a sentence. Thus I verify the sentence "This is vinegar" by smelling the bottle or by reading the label. But the sentence obviously does not mean smelling the bottle or reading the label. It might be objected that this interpretation of the slogan is a gross misinterpreta-

---

[13]*Loc. cit.,* p. 347.
[14]*Loc. cit.,* p. 340.

tion. That this objection is without force becomes quite plain when Schlick takes occasion to refute an opponent who maintains that statements about the future are meaningless under the verifiability criterion on the ground that such statements are not verifiable. In this refutation Schlick is fully conscious of the meaning of the term "method of verification." He repels the attack and wins an easy victory by telling the opponent that statements about the future are verified by waiting for the event to happen and that waiting is a legitimate method of verification.[15] Schlick apparently never noticed that all statements about future events must be synonymous, if we should choose to verify them by waiting, and if the meaning of a statement is identical with the method of its verification.

In so far as Schlick has established a connection between the meaning of a sentence and its verifiability, he uses the term "verifiable" simply as a synonym for "transformable into a significant sentence." If, however, the term "verifiability" is understood in the ordinary sense as the possibility of describing a method by which the truth-value of a sentence may be ascertained, then verifiability is not a test of significance. For a method of testing, i.e., the test sentences, can be formulated only if we know the meaning of the sentence we are going to test. In other words, the decision that the sentence is significant must be made in advance of the testing.

Carnap's formulation of the verifiability criterion is essentially the same as Schlick's, and we shall therefore deal with it rather briefly. Although Carnap has repudiated the criterion in its original form on the ground that sentences are only confirmable and not verifiable, he nevertheless agrees with Schlick that the meaning of a sentence is linked to its verification. The answers to the two questions "What is the meaning of the sentence S?" and "How is the sentence S verified?", he says, are closely connected. Regarding this connection he makes the following guarded statement: "In a certain sense, there is only one answer to the two questions. If we know what it would be for a given sentence to be found true, then we would know what its meaning is. And if for two sentences the conditions under which we would have to take them as true are the same, then they have the same meaning. Thus the meaning of a sentence is in a certain sense identical with the way we determine its truth or falsehood."[16] Let us ask whether what

---

[15]*Loc. cit.*, p. 445.

[16]Philosophy of Science, v. 3, p. 420.

THE CRITERION OF SIGNIFICANCE

Carnap says about the close connection between the answers to the two questions "What is the meaning of the sentence S?" and "How is the sentence S verified?" is true. If someone were to ask me these questions with reference to the sentence "Caesar transivit Rubiconem flumen" my answers would be far from identical. I would answer the first question by translating it into English, and the second by referring my interlocutor to a book on Roman history. It can not have been Carnap's intention to maintain the absurd thesis that the answers one ordinarily gives to these two questions are the same or even closely connected. We must therefore suppose that he had a different type of answer in mind when he wrote that the answers to the two questions are in a certain sense identical. In order to discover the type of answer Carnap requires, let us frame the question about the verification of a sentence in the idiom he proposes: "What would it be for the sentence 'The dog lies under the table' to be found true?" I can think of only one answer: "That would be to find the dog lying under the table." If a sentence is true and if I find it true, I can report to you what I found true only by means of a sentence, either by means of the sentence I found true or a synonymous sentence. Hence, if Carnap means that a sentence is verifiable, and therefore significant if it is possible to specify the conditions under which the sentence is true, his criterion of significance is identical with the criterion of translatability, since the specification of these conditions consists in the formulation of another sentence, synonymous with the given sentence. But if Carnap means that a sentence is significant if and only if it is possible to find evidence which either confirms or refutes the sentence, then the thesis that meaning and verifiability are identical or closely connected must be rejected. For I can not know that something is evidence for or against a sentence unless I know what the sentence means.

Carnap follows Schlick also in producing a variant of the slogan that the meaning of a sentence is the method of its verification. "The meaning of a sentence," he says, "is in a certain sense identical with the way in which we determine its truth or falsehood." Carnap never reveals whether the identity hinges on the sense we give to "way" or whether it hinges on the sense we give to "meaning," or whether perhaps it hinges on some peculiar sense of both of these terms. In any case, if "way" is understood in the same way in which Schlick understands "method" then the slogan is nonsense. But if Carnap means that a sentence is significant if and only if a test method can be formulated by which the sentence can be confirmed or refuted, then the

17

AMERICAN PHILOSOPHICAL ASSOCIATION

slogan is merely false, on the ground that the formulation of such a method presupposes that the meaning of the sentence is known.

We have seen that the logical positivists use the term "verifiable" in both an improper and a proper sense. In the improper sense, a sentence is said to be verifiable when it is possible to transform the sentence into a significant sentence. In the proper sense it is said to be verifiable when it is possible to formulate the observation sentences that would verify the sentence if the sentence were true. But the possibility of formulating these observation sentences presupposes that the decision that the sentence is significant has already been made. You can not devise an observation test until you know the meaning of the sentence you are going to test.

That the question whether a sentence is verifiable can be raised only after the decision that the sentence is significant has already been made becomes especially clear when one examines Ayer's definition of the term "verifiable": the sentence S is verifiable if and only if there is some sentence R and an observation sentence O such that O is deducible from S and R, but is not deducible from S alone nor from R alone. This definition presupposes that the sentences S, R, and O are all significant, for the rules of deduction apply to significant sentences only. If, however, the rules of deduction apply to nonsense also, then every sentence is verifiable and hence significant under the definition Ayer proposes. Ayer has sought to remedy this defect by revising the definition. But the revised form suffers from the same defect as the original: either the sentence that is tested by means of the criterion is known to be significant independently of the criterion or else every sentence is significant.[17]

If a sentence can not be shown to be significant otherwise than by showing that it is convertible into a significant sentence, we may expect this criterion to be used as the test of significance even by those philosophers whose official criterion would indicate a different procedure. This expectation is fully confirmed by an examination of the text. Russell never demonstrates that an apparently nonsensical sentence is significant by finding the proposition the sentence expresses. He always makes this demonstration by showing that the sentence is transformable into a significant sentence. Thus he decides that the sentence "The sound of a trombone is blue" is significant, because this sentence asserts the identity of two objects that have different names. The sentence is

---

[17]Ayer, *Language, Truth and Logic*, p. 11 sq.

THE CRITERION OF SIGNIFICANCE

thus merely false, but not nonsensical. Again he shows that the paradox to which the sentence "I am lying" gives rise, on the hypothesis that it is significant, can be avoided, if this sentence is regarded as an infinite conjunction of the sentences "I am asserting a false sentence of the first order," "I am asserting a false sentence of the second order," etc. The resulting translation is again merely false.[18] In one of his examples Russell considers the result of translating the sentence "Quadruplicity drinks procrastination" when the word "Quadruplicity" is replaced by its defined equivalent "That property of a propositional function which consists in being true for exactly four values of the variable," and he wonders how we know that the resulting translation is nonsense.[19] On his own theory it should not be too difficult to remove any doubt on this subject: you investigate the body and find out whether the resulting sentence expresses a proposition. If you fail to detect the complex images and expectations which are the components of propositions, you may be sure that the sentence is nonsense. Russell never avails himself of this procedure. The procedure would indeed be quite useless, even if it were feasible to investigate the body, since nonsense is as prolific in the production of complex images and expectations as the soundest sense.

Carnap holds that a sentence is significant when it is possible to formulate an observation sentence by which the sentence in question can be tested. But he never uses this test when he determines whether or not a sentence is significant. Like Russell he uses the test of translatability. Carnap shows how this test operates in his paper on the repudiation of metaphysics. In this paper he is concerned with showing that a great many of the sentences that occur in Heidegger's *Was ist Metaphysik?* are pseudo-sentences. These sentences are shown to be pseudo-sentences, not by applying the criterion of verifiability, or, as Carnap now prefers, of confirmability, but by showing that these sentences can not be transformed into significant sentences of the ordinary idiom.

In order to see on what grounds the metaphysical sentences of Heidegger are repudiated, it is necessary to translate some of these sentences into English. If we have to do violence to the English language in making these translations, this is unavoidable, since Heidegger had to do violence to the German language when he constructed the

---

[18]Inquiry, p. 218.
[19]Inquiry, p. 222.

originals. Heidegger begins by defining the domain of metaphysics. Science, he says, is concerned with the exploration of the real and aside from that with nothing. He then immediately asks the question which is the theme of his paper "How about this nothing?". Since science has preëmpted the realm of the real, there is nothing left for metaphysics but the exploration of the nothing. The question is then followed by sentences of which the following are typical:

> Why are we concerned about this nothing? The nothing is rejected by science and sacrificed as the unreal. Science wants to have nothing to do with the nothing. What is the nothing? Does the nothing exist only because the not, i.e., negation, exists? Or do negation and the not exist only because the nothing exists? We maintain: The nothing is more primitive than the not and negation. We know the nothing. The nothing is the simple negation of the totality of being. Anxiety reveals the nothing. The nothing itself nots.

Carnap shows that none of these sentences can be transformed into significant sentences of the natural language. For in this idiom the word "nothing" is not used as a name. When it appears to be used as a name in a sentence, as for instance in the sentence "Outside there is nothing," the sentence is always transformable into the negation of an existential statement. Everyone of Heidegger's sentences in which "the nothing" is used as a designative expression is accordingly nonsensical, since these sentences are not transformable into sentences of this kind. Furthermore, even if it were assumed that the phrase "the nothing" is used as a descriptive phrase in Heidegger's sentence "The nothing exists," the contextual definition of this phrase would have to be so formulated as to yield the sentence "The nothing does not exist" as a logical consequence. Finally, Carnap points out that Heidegger introduces the meaningless verb "to not." This neologism,—the original is likewise a neologism—, appears in Heidegger's sentences without having been previously defined and can therefore not be eliminated from the sentences in which it occurs. The sentence "The nothing nots" is therefore nonsensical for a two-fold reason. Carnap concludes that Heidegger's sentences can not be constructed in a logically correct language.

A sentence is thus condemned as nonsensical by Carnap not because it is not verifiable, but because it can not be transformed into a significant sentence of the natural language or of a logically correct language which takes the place of the latter. The criterion Carnap actually uses may thus be formulated as follows: A sentence is significant if and only if it is transformable into a significant sentence of standard logical form. A sentence is of standard logical form when it is either

THE CRITERION OF SIGNIFICANCE

a simple sentence or else constructible from sentences of that kind by truth-functional composition and quantification, and it is moreover significant if and only if the simple components from which the sentence is constructed are themselves significant. The conditions a sentence in standard logical form must satisfy in order to be significant are thus specified in such a way that one can decide in a finite number of steps whether or not the sentence is significant. In other words, when we examine a sentence in standard logical form with the view of determining whether it satisfies the conditions of a significant sentence, we are finally led back to the simple sentences from which the given sentence was constructed. And unless these are significant, the original sentence is not significant.

In the absence of a criterion of significance, either in the sense of a definition or a generalization, we are forced, at the present time, to take significance, with respect to simple sentences, e.g., atomic sentences, as a primitive notion. The decision whether or not a sentence not of this form is significant is made by a recursion procedure. For the simple sentences to which we are led by this procedure we have no test of significance. The criterion of significance for sentences of this form has yet to be discovered.

University of California

4

Empiricist Criteria of Cognitive Significance: Problems and Changes

CARL G. HEMPEL

4. EMPIRICIST CRITERIA

OF COGNITIVE SIGNIFICANCE:

PROBLEMS AND CHANGES

1. THE GENERAL EMPIRICIST CONCEPTION OF COGNITIVE AND EMPIRICAL SIGNIFICANCE

It is a basic principle of contemporary empiricism that a sentence makes a cognitively significant assertion, and thus can be said to be either true or false, if and only if either (1) it is analytic or contradictory—in which case it is said to have purely logical meaning or significance—or else (2) it is capable, at least potentially, of test by experiential evidence—in which case it is said to have empirical meaning or significance. The basic tenet of this principle, and especially of its second part, the so-called testability criterion of empirical meaning (or better: meaningfulness), is not peculiar to empiricism alone: it is characteristic also of contemporary operationism, and in a sense of pragmatism as well; for the pragmatist maxim that a difference must make a difference to be a difference may well be construed as insisting that a verbal difference between two sentences must make a difference in experiential implications if it is to reflect a difference in meaning.

How this general conception of cognitively significant discourse led to the rejection, as devoid of logical and empirical meaning, of various formulations in speculative metaphysics, and even of certain hypotheses offered within

This essay combines, with certain omissions and some other changes, the contents of two articles: "Problems and Changes in the Empiricist Criterion of Meaning," *Revue Internationale de Philosophie* No. 11, pp. 41–63 (January, 1950); and "The Concept of Cognitive Significance: A Reconsideration," *Proceedings of the American Academy of Arts and Sciences* 80, No. 1, pp. 61–77 (1951). This material is reprinted with kind permission of the Director of *Revue Internationale de Philosophie* and of the American Academy of Arts and Sciences.

empirical science, is too well known to require recounting. I think that the general intent of the empiricist criterion of meaning is basically sound, and that notwithstanding much oversimplification in its use, its critical application has been, on the whole, enlightening and salutary. I feel less confident, however, about the possibility of restating the general idea in the form of precise and general criteria which establish sharp dividing lines (a) between statements of purely logical and statements of empirical significance, and (b) between those sentences which do have cognitive significance and those which do not.

In the present paper, I propose to reconsider these distinctions as conceived in recent empiricism, and to point out some of the difficulties they present. The discussion will concern mainly the second of the two distinctions; in regard to the first, I shall limit myself to a few brief remarks.

2. THE EARLIER TESTABILITY CRITERIA OF MEANING AND THEIR SHORTCOMINGS

Let us note first that any general criterion of cognitive significance will have to meet certain requirements if it is to be at all acceptable. Of these, we note one, which we shall consider here as expressing a necessary, though by no means sufficient, *condition of adequacy* for criteria of cognitive significance.

(A) If under a given criterion of cognitive significance, a sentence N is nonsignificant, then so must be all truth-functional compound sentences in which N occurs nonvacuously as a component. For if N cannot be significantly assigned a truth value, then it is impossible to assign truth values to the compound sentences containing N; hence, they should be qualified as nonsignificant as well.

We note two corollaries of requirement (A):

(A1) If under a given criterion of cognitive significance, a sentence S is nonsignificant, then so must be its negation, $\sim S$.

(A2) If under a given criterion of cognitive significance, a sentence N is nonsignificant, then so must be any conjunction $N \cdot S$ and any disjunction $N v S$, no matter whether S is significant under the given criterion or not.

We now turn to the initial attempts made in recent empiricism to establish general criteria of cognitive significance. Those attempts were governed by the consideration that a sentence, to make an empirical assertion must be capable of being borne out by, or conflicting with, phenomena which are potentially capable of being directly observed. Sentences describing such potentially observable phenomena—no matter whether the latter do actually occur or not—may be called observation sentences. More specifically, an *observation sentence* might be construed as a sentence—no matter whether true or false—which asserts or denies that a specified object, or group of objects, of macroscopic size has a particular *observable characteristic*, i.e., a characteristic whose presence or absence can, under favorable circumstances, be ascertained by direct observation.[1]

The task of setting up criteria of empirical significance is thus transformed into the problem of characterizing in a precise manner the relationship which obtains between a hypothesis and one or more observation sentences whenever the phenomena described by the latter either confirm or disconfirm the hypothesis in question. The ability of a given sentence to enter into that relationship to some set of observation sentences would then characterize its testability-in-principle, and thus its empirical significance. Let us now briefly examine the major attempts that have been made to obtain criteria of significance in this manner.

One of the earliest criteria is expressed in the so-called *verifiability requirement*. According to it, a sentence is empirically significant if and only if it is not analytic and is capable, at least in principle, of complete verification by observational evidence; i.e., if observational evidence can be described which, if actually obtained, would conclusively establish the truth of the sentence.[2] With the

1. Observation sentences of this kind belong to what Carnap has called the thing-language, cf., e.g., (1938), pp. 52-53. That they are adequate to formulate the data which serve as the basis for empirical tests is clear in particular for the intersubjective testing procedures used in science as well as in large areas of empirical inquiry on the common-sense level. In epistemological discussions, it is frequently assumed that the ultimate evidence for beliefs about empirical matters consists in perceptions and sensations whose description calls for a phenomenalistic type of language. The specific problems connected with the phenomenalistic approach cannot be discussed here; but it should be mentioned that at any rate all the critical considerations presented in this article in regard to the testability criterion are applicable, *mutatis mutandis*, to the case of a phenomenalistic basis as well.

2. Originally, the permissible evidence was meant to be restricted to what is observable by the speaker and perhaps his fellow beings during their life times. Thus construed, the criterion rules out, as cognitively meaningless, all statements about the distant future or the remote past, as has been pointed out, among others, by Ayer (1946), chapter I; by Pap (1949), chapter 13, esp. pp. 333 ff.; and by Russell (1948), pp. 445-47. This difficulty is avoided, however, if we permit the evidence to consist of any finite set of "logically possible observation data", each of them formulated in an observation sentence. Thus, e.g., the sentence S_1, "The tongue of the largest dinosaur in New York's Museum of Natural History was blue or black" is completely verifiable in our sense; for it is a logical consequence of the sentence S_2, "The tongue of the largest dinosaur in New York's Museum of Natural History was blue"; and this is an observation sentence, in the sense just indicated.

And if the concept of *verifiability in principle* and the more general concept of *confirmability in principle*, which will be considered later, are construed as referring to *logically possible evidence* as expressed by observation sentences, then it follows similarly that the class of statements which are verifiable, or at least confirmable, in principle include such assertions as that the planet Neptune and the Antarctic Continent existed before they were discovered, and that atomic warfare, if not checked, will lead to the extermination of this planet. The objections which Russell (1948), pp. 445 and 447, raises against the verifiability criterion by reference to those examples do not apply therefore if the criterion is understood in the manner here suggested.

(continued overleaf)

help of the concept of observation sentence, we can restate this requirement as follows: A sentence S has empirical meaning if and only if it is possible to indicate a finite set of observation sentences, $O_1, O_2, \ldots, O_n$, such that if these are true, then S is necessarily true, too. As stated, however, this condition is satisfied also if S is an analytic sentence or if the given observation sentences are logically incompatible with each other. By the following formulation, we rule these cases out and at the same time express the intended criterion more precisely: (2.1) REQUIREMENT OF COMPLETE VERIFIABILITY IN PRINCIPLE. A sentence has empirical meaning if and only if it is not analytic and follows logically from some finite and logically consistent class of observation sentences.[3] These observation sentences need not be true, for what the criterion is to explicate is testability by "potentially observable phenomena," or testability "in principle."

In accordance with the general conception of cognitive significance outlined earlier, a sentence will now be classified as cognitively significant if either it is analytic or contradictory, or it satisfies the verifiability requirement.

This criterion, however, has several serious defects. One of them has been noted by several writers:

a. Let us assume that the properties of being a stork and of being red-legged

---

3. As has frequently been emphasized in the empiricist literature, the term "verifiability" is to indicate, of course, the conceivability, or better, the logical possibility, of evidence of an observational kind which, if actually encountered, would constitute conclusive evidence for the given sentence; it is not intended to mean the technical possibility of performing the tests needed to obtain such evidence, and even less the possibility of actually finding directly observable phenomena which constitute conclusive evidence for that sentence—which would be tantamount to the actual existence of such evidence and would thus imply the truth of the given sentence. Analogous remarks apply to the terms "falsifiability" and "confirmability". This point has clearly been disregarded in some critical discussions of the verifiability criterion. Thus, e.g., Russell (1948), p. 448 construes verifiability as the actual existence of a set of conclusively verifying occurrences. This conception, which has never been advocated by any logical empiricist, must naturally turn out to be inadequate since according to it the empirical meaningfulness of a sentence could not be established without gathering empirical evidence, and moreover enough of it to permit a conclusive proof of the sentence in question! It is not surprising, therefore, that his extraordinary interpretation of verifiability leads Russell to the conclusion: "In fact, that a proposition is verifiable is itself not verifiable" (*l.c.*). Actually, under the empiricist interpretation of complete verifiability, any statement asserting the verifiability of some sentence S whose text is quoted, is either analytic or contradictory; for the decision whether there exists a class of observation sentences which entail S, i.e., whether such observation sentences can be formulated, no matter whether they are true or false—that decision is a purely logical matter.

Incidentally, statements of the kind mentioned by Russell, which are not actually verifiable by any human being, were explicitly recognized as cognitively significant already by Schlick (1936), Part V, who argued that the impossibility of verifying them was "merely empirical." The characterization of verifiability with the help of the concept of observation sentence as suggested here might serve as a more explicit and rigorous statement of that conception.

are both observable characteristics, and that the former does not logically entail the latter. Then the sentence

(S1)   All storks are red-legged

is neither analytic nor contradictory; and clearly, it is not deducible from a finite set of observation sentences. Hence, under the contemplated criterion, S1 is devoid of empirical significance; and so are all other sentences purporting to express universal regularities or general laws. And since sentences of this type constitute an integral part of scientific theories, the verifiability requirement must be regarded as overly restrictive in this respect.

Similarly, the criterion disqualifies all sentences such as 'For any substance there exists some solvent', which contain both universal and existential quantifiers (i.e., occurrences of the terms 'all' and 'some' or their equivalents); for no sentences of this kind can be logically deduced from any finite set of observation sentences.

Two further defects of the verifiability requirement do not seem to have been widely noticed:

b. As is readily seen, the negation of S1

(∼S1)   There exists at least one stork that is not red-legged

is deducible from any two observation sentences of the type 'a is a stork' and 'a is not red-legged'. Hence, ∼S1 is cognitively significant under our criterion, but S1 is not, and this constitutes a violation of condition (A1).

c. Let S be a sentence which does, and N a sentence which does not satisfy the verifiability requirement. Then S is deducible from some set of observation sentences; hence, by a familiar rule of logic, SvN is deducible from the same set, and therefore cognitively significant according to our criterion. This violates condition (A2) above.[4]

Strictly analogous considerations apply to an alternative criterion, which

---

4. The arguments here adduced against the verifiability criterion also prove the inadequacy of a view closely related to it, namely that two sentences have the same cognitive significance if any set of observation sentences which would verify one of them would also verify the other, and conversely. Thus, e.g., under this criterion, any two general laws would have to be assigned the same cognitive significance, for no general law is verified by any set of observation sentences. The view just referred to must be clearly distinguished from a position which Russell examines in his critical discussion of the positivistic meaning criterion. It is "the theory that two propositions whose verified consequences are identical have the same significance" (1948), p. 448. This view is untenable indeed, for what consequences of a statement have actually been verified at a given time is obviously a matter of historical accident which cannot possibly serve to establish identity of cognitive significance. But I am not aware that any logical empiricist ever subscribed to that "theory."

makes complete falsifiability in principle the defining characteristic of empirical significance. Let us formulate this criterion as follows:

(2.2) REQUIREMENT OF COMPLETE FALSIFIABILITY IN PRINCIPLE. A sentence has empirical meaning if and only if its negation is not analytic and follows logically from some finite logically consistent class of observation sentences.

This criterion qualifies a sentence as empirically meaningful if its negation satisfies the requirement of complete verifiability; as it is to be expected, it is therefore inadequate on similar grounds as the latter:

(a) It denies cognitive significance to purely existential hypotheses, such as 'There exists at least one unicorn', and all sentences whose formulation calls for mixed—i.e., universal and existential—quantification, such as 'For every compound there exists some solvent', for none of these can possibly be conclusively falsified by a finite number of observation sentences.

(b) If 'P' is an observation predicate, then the assertion that all things have the property P is qualified as significant, but its negation, being equivalent to a purely existential hypothesis, is disqualified [cf. (a)]. Hence, criterion (2.2) gives rise to the same dilemma as (2.1).

(c) If a sentence S is completely falsifiable whereas N is a sentence which is not, then their conjunction, $S \cdot N$ (i.e., the expression obtained by connecting the two sentences by the word 'and') is completely falsifiable; for if the negation of S is entailed by a class of observation sentences, then the negation of $S \cdot N$ is, *a fortiori*, entailed by the same class. Thus, the criterion allows empirical significance to many sentences which an adequate empiricist criterion should rule out, such as 'All swans are white and the absolute is perfect.'

In sum, then, interpretations of the testability criterion in terms of complete verifiability or of complete falsifiability are inadequate because they are overly restrictive in one direction and overly inclusive in another, and because both of them violate the fundamental requirement A.

Several attempts have been made to avoid these difficulties by construing the testability criterion as demanding merely a partial and possibly indirect confirmability of empirical hypotheses by observational evidence.

A formulation suggested by Ayer[5] is characteristic of these attempts to set up a clear and sufficiently comprehensive criterion of confirmability. It states, in effect, that a sentence S has empirical import if from S in conjunction with suitable subsidiary hypotheses it is possible to derive observation sentences which are not derivable from the subsidiary hypotheses alone.

This condition is suggested by a closer consideration of the logical structure of

---

5. (1936, 1946), Chap. I. The case against the requirements of verifiability and of falsifiability, and in favor of a requirement of partial confirmability and disconfirmability, is very clearly presented also by Pap (1949), chapter 13.

scientific testing; but it is much too liberal as it stands. Indeed, as Ayer himself has pointed out in the second edition of his book, *Language , Truth, and Logic*,[6] his criterion allows empirical import to any sentence whatever. Thus, e.g., if S is the sentence 'The absolute is perfect', it suffices to choose as a subsidiary hypothesis the sentence 'If the absolute is perfect then this apple is red' in order to make possible the deduction of the observation sentence 'This apple is red', which clearly does not follow from the subsidiary hypothesis alone.

To meet this objection, Ayer proposed a modified version of his testability criterion. In effect, the modification restricts the subsidiary hypotheses mentioned in the previous version to sentences which either are analytic or can independently be shown to be testable in the sense of the modified criterion.[7]

But it can readily be shown that this new criterion, like the requirement of complete falsifiability, allows empirical significance to any conjunction $S \cdot N$, where S satisfies Ayer's criterion while N is a sentence such as 'The absolute is perfect', which is to be disqualified by that criterion. Indeed, whatever consequences can be deduced from S with the help of permissible subsidiary hypotheses can also be deduced from $S \cdot N$ by means of the same subsidiary hypotheses; and as Ayer's new criterion is formulated essentially in terms of the deducibility of a certain type of consequence from the given sentence, it countenances $S \cdot N$ together with S. Another difficulty has been pointed out by Church, who has shown[8] that if there are any three observation sentences none of which alone entails any of the others, then it follows for any sentence S whatsoever that either it or its denial has empirical import according to Ayer's revised criterion.

All the criteria considered so far attempt to explicate the concept of empirical significance by specifying certain logical connections which must obtain between a significant sentence and suitable observation sentences. It seems now that this type of approach offers little hope for the attainment of precise criteria of meaningfulness: this conclusion is suggested by the preceding survey of some representative attempts, and it receives additional support from certain further considerations, some of which will be presented in the following sections.

3. CHARACTERIZATION OF SIGNIFICANT SENTENCES BY CRITERIA FOR THEIR CONSTITUENT TERMS

An alternative procedure suggests itself which again seems to reflect well

6. (1946), 2d ed., pp. 11-12.

7. This restriction is expressed in recursive form and involves no vicious circle. For the full statement of Ayer's criterion, see Ayer (1946), p. 13.

8. Church (1949). An alternative criterion recently suggested by O'Connor (1950) as a revision of Ayer's formulation is subject to a slight variant of Church's stricture: It can be shown that if there are three observation sentences none of which entails any of the others, and if S is any noncompound sentence, then either S or $\sim S$ is significant under O'Connor's criterion.

the general viewpoint of empiricism: It might be possible to characterize cognitively significant sentences by certain conditions which their constituent terms have to satisfy. Specifically, it would seem reasonable to say that all extralogical terms[9] in a significant sentence must have experiential reference, and that therefore their meanings must be capable of explication by reference to observables exclusively.[10] In order to exhibit certain analogies between this approach and the previous one, we adopt the following terminological conventions:

Any term that may occur in a cognitively significant sentence will be called a *cognitively significant term*. Furthermore, we shall understand by an *observation term* any term which either (a) is an *observation predicate*, i.e., signifies some observable characteristic (as do the terms 'blue', 'warm', 'soft', 'coincident with', 'of greater apparent brightness than') or (b) names some physical object of macroscopic size (as do the terms 'the needle of this instrument', 'the Moon', 'Krakatoa Volcano', 'Greenwich, England', 'Julius Caesar').

Now while the testability criteria of meaning aimed at characterizing the cognitively significant sentences by means of certain inferential connections in which they must stand to some observation sentences, the alternative approach under consideration would instead try to specify the vocabulary that may be used in forming significant sentences. This vocabulary, the class of significant terms, would be characterized by the condition that each of its elements is either a logical term or else a term with empirical significance; in the latter case, it has to stand in certain definitional or explicative connections to some observation terms. This approach certainly avoids any violations of our earlier conditions of adequacy. Thus, e.g., if S is a significant sentence, i.e., contains cognitively significant terms only, then so is its denial, since the denial sign, and its verbal equivalents, belong to the vocabulary of logic and are thus significant. Again, if N is a sentence containing a non-significant term, then so is any compound sentence which contains N.

But this is not sufficient, of course. Rather, we shall now have to consider a crucial question analogous to that raised by the previous approach: Precisely how are the logical connections between empirically significant terms and observation terms to be construed if an adequate criterion of cognitive significance is to result? Let us consider some possibilities.

9. An extralogical term is one that does not belong to the specific vocabulary of logic. The following phrases, and those definable by means of them, are typical examples of logical terms: 'not', 'or', 'if...then', 'all', 'some', '... is an element of class...'. Whether it is possible to make a sharp theoretical distinction between logical and extra-logical terms is a controversial issue related to the problem of discriminating between analytic and synthetic sentences. For the purpose at hand, we may simply assume that the logical vocabulary is given by enumeration.

10. For a detailed exposition and critical discussion of this idea, see H. Feigl's stimulating and enlightening article (1950).

(3.1) The simplest criterion that suggests itself might be called the *requirement of definability*. It would demand that any term with empirical significance must be explicitly definable by means of observation terms.

This criterion would seem to accord well with the maxim of operationism that all significant terms of empirical science must be introduced by operational definitions. However, the requirement of definability is vastly too restrictive, for many important terms of scientific and even pre-scientific discourse cannot be explicitly defined by means of observation terms.

In fact, as Carnap[11] has pointed out, an attempt to provide explicit definitions in terms of observables encounters serious difficulties as soon as disposition terms, such as 'soluble', 'malleable', 'electric conductor', etc., have to be accounted for; and many of these occur even on the pre-scientific level of discourse.

Consider, for example, the word 'fragile'. One might try to define it by saying that an object x is fragile if and only if it satisfies the following condition: If at any time t the object is sharply struck, then it breaks at that time. But if the statement connectives in this phrasing are construed truth-functionally, so that the definition can be symbolized by

$$(D) \qquad Fx \equiv (t) \, (Sxt \supset Bxt)$$

then the predicate 'F' thus defined does not have the intended meaning. For let a be any object which is not fragile (e.g., a raindrop or a rubber band), but which happens not to be sharply struck at any time throughout its existence. Then 'Sat' is false and hence '$Sat \supset Bat$' is true for all values of 't'; consequently, 'Fa' is true though a is not fragile.

To remedy this defect, one might construe the phrase 'if... then...' in the original definiens as having a more restrictive meaning than the truth-functional conditional. This meaning might be suggested by the subjunctive phrasing 'If x were to be sharply struck at any time t, then x would break at t.' But a satisfactory elaboration of this construal would require a clarification of the meaning and the logic of counterfactual and subjunctive conditionals, which is a thorny problem.[12]

An alternative procedure was suggested by Carnap in his theory of reduction sentences.[13] These are sentences which, unlike definitions, specify the meaning of a term only conditionally or partially. The term 'fragile', for example, might be introduced by the following reduction sentence:

$$(R) \qquad (x) \, (t) \, [Sxt \supset (Fx \equiv Bxt)]$$

---

11. Cf. (1936-37), especially section 7.

12. On this subject, see for example Langford (1941); Lewis (1946), pp. 210-30; Chisholm (1946); Goodman (1947); Reichenbach (1947), Chapter VIII; Hempel and Oppenheim (1948), Part III; Popper (1949); and especially Goodman's further analysis (1955).

13. Cf. Carnap, *loc. cit.* note 11. For a brief elementary presentation of the main idea, see Carnap (1938), Part III. The sentence R here formulated for the predicate 'F' illustrates only the simplest type of reduction sentence, the so-called bilateral reduction sentence.

which specifies that if x is sharply struck at any time t, then x is fragile if and only if x breaks at t.

Our earlier difficulty is now avoided, for if a is a nonfragile object that is never sharply struck, then that expression in R which follows the quantifiers is true of a; but this does not imply that 'Fa' is true. But the reduction sentence R specifies the meaning of 'F' only for application to those objects which meet the "test condition" of being sharply struck at some time; for these it states that fragility then amounts to breaking. For objects that fail to meet the test condition, the meaning of 'F' is left undetermined. In this sense, reduction sentences have the character of partial or conditional definitions.

Reduction sentences provide a satisfactory interpretation of the experiential import of a large class of disposition terms and permit a more adequate formulation of so-called operational definitions, which, in general, are not complete definitions at all. These considerations suggest a greatly liberalized alternative to the requirement of definability:

(3.2) *The requirement of reducibility*. Every term with empirical significance must be capable of introduction, on the basis of observation terms, through chains of reduction sentences.

This requirement is characteristic of the liberalized versions of positivism and physicalism which, since about 1936, have superseded the older, overly narrow conception of a full definability of all terms of empirical science by means of observables,[14] and it avoids many of the shortcomings of the latter. Yet, reduction sentences do not seem to offer an adequate means for the introduction of the central terms of advanced scientific theories, often referred to as theoretical constructs. This is indicated by the following considerations: A chain of reduction sentences provides a necessary and a sufficient condition for the applicability of the term it introduces. (When the two conditions coincide, the chain is tantamount to an explicit definition.) But now take, for example, the concept of length as used in classical physical theory. Here, the length in centimeters of the distance between two points may assume any positive real number as its value; yet it is clearly impossible to formulate, by means of observation terms, a sufficient condition for the applicability of such expressions as 'having a length of $\sqrt{2}$ cm' and 'having a length of $\sqrt{2} + 10^{-100}$ cm'; for such conditions would provide a possibility for discrimination, in observational terms, between two lengths which differ by only 10^{-100} cm.[15]

14. Cf. the analysis in Carnap (1936-37), especially section 15; also see the briefer presentation of the liberalized point of view in Carnap (1938).

15. (Added in 1964.) This is not strictly correct. For a more circumspect statement, see note 12 in "A Logical Appraisal of Operationism" and the fuller discussion in section 7 of the essay "The Theoretician's Dilemma." Both of these pieces are reprinted in the present volume.

It would be ill-advised to argue that for this reason, we ought to permit only such values of the magnitude, length, as permit the statement of sufficient conditions in terms of observables. For this would rule out, among others, all irrational numbers and would prevent us from assigning, to the diagonal of a square with sides of length 1, the length $\sqrt{2}$, which is required by Euclidean geometry. Hence, the principles of Euclidean geometry would not be universally applicable in physics. Similarly, the principles of the calculus would become inapplicable, and the system of scientific theory as we know it today would be reduced to a clumsy, unmanageable torso. This, then, is no way of meeting the difficulty. Rather, we shall have to analyze more closely the function of constructs in scientific theories, with a view to obtaining through such an analysis a more adequate characterization of cognitively significant terms.

Theoretical constructs occur in the formulation of scientific theories. These may be conceived of, in their advanced stages, as being stated in the form of deductively developed axiomatized systems. Classical mechanics, or Euclidean or some Non-Euclidean form of geometry in physical interpretation, present examples of such systems. The extralogical terms used in a theory of this kind may be divided, in familiar manner, into primitive or basic terms, which are not defined within the theory, and defined terms, which are explicitly defined by means of the primitives. Thus, e.g., in Hilbert's axiomatization of Euclidean geometry, the terms 'point', 'straight line', 'between' are among the primitives, while 'line segment', 'angle', 'triangle', 'length' are among the defined terms. The basic and the defined terms together with the terms of logic constitute the vocabulary out of which all the sentences of the theory are constructed. The latter are divided, in an axiomatic presentation, into primitive statements (also called postulates or basic statements) which, in the theory, are not derived from any other statements, and derived ones, which are obtained by logical deduction from the primitive statements.

From its primitive terms and sentences, an axiomatized theory can be developed by means of purely formal principles of definition and deduction, without any consideration of the empirical significance of its extralogical terms. Indeed, this is the standard procedure employed in the axiomatic development of uninterpreted mathematical theories such as those of abstract groups or rings or lattices, or any form of pure (i.e., noninterpreted) geometry.

However, a deductively developed system of this sort can constitute a scientific theory only if it has received an empirical interpretation[16] which

---

16. The interpretation of formal theories has been studied extensively by Reichenbach, especially in his pioneer analyses of space and time in classical and in relativistic physics. He describes such interpretation as the establishment of *coordinating definitions* (Zuordnungsdefinitionen) for certain terms of the formal theory. See, for example, Reichenbach (1928). More recently,

(continued overleaf)

renders it relevant to the phenomena of our experience. Such interpretation is given by assigning a meaning, in terms of observables, to certain terms or sentences of the formalized theory. Frequently, an interpretation is given not for the primitive terms or statements but rather for some of the terms definable by means of the primitives, or for some of the sentences deducible from the postulates.[17] Furthermore, interpretation may amount to only a partial assignment of meaning. Thus, e.g., the rules for the measurement of length by means of a standard rod may be considered as providing a *partial* empirical interpretation for the term 'the length, in centimeters, of interval *i*', or alternatively, for some sentences of the form 'the length of interval *i* is *r* centimeters'. For the method is applicable only to intervals of a certain medium size, and even for the latter it does not constitute a full interpretation since the use of a standard rod does not constitute the only way of determining length: various alternative procedures are available involving the measurement of other magnitudes which are connected, by general laws, with the length that is to be determined.

This last observation, concerning the possibility of an indirect measurement of length by virtue of certain laws, suggests an important reminder. It is not correct to speak, as is often done, of "the experiential meaning" of a term or a sentence in isolation. In the language of science, and for similar reasons even in pre-scientific discourse, a single statement usually has no experiential implications. A single sentence in a scientific theory does not, as a rule, entail any observation sentences; consequences asserting the occurrence of certain observable phenomena can be derived from it only by conjoining it with a set of other, subsidiary, hypotheses. Of the latter, some will usually be observation sentences, others will be previously accepted theoretical statements. Thus, e.g., the relativistic theory of the deflection of light rays in the gravitational field of the sun entails assertions about observable phenomena only if it is conjoined with a considerable body of astronomical and optical theory as well as a large number of specific statements about the instruments used in those observations of solar eclipses which serve to test the hypothesis in question.

Hence, the phrase, 'the experiential meaning of expression *E*' is elliptical: What

---

17. A somewhat fuller account of this type of interpretation may be found in Carnap (1939), §24. The articles by Spence (1944) and by MacCorquodale and Meehl (1948) provide enlightening illustrations of the use of theoretical constructs in a field outside that of the physical sciences, and of the difficulties encountered in an attempt to analyze in detail their function and interpretation.

Northrop [cf. (1947), Chap. VII, and also the detailed study of the use of deductively formulated theories in science, ibid., Chaps. IV, V, VI] and H. Margenau [cf., for example, (1935)] have discussed certain aspects of this process under the title of *epistemic correlation*.

a given expression "means" in regard to potential empirical data is relative to two factors, namely:

    I. *the linguistic framework L* to which the expression belongs. Its rules determine, in particular, what sentences—observational or otherwise—may be inferred from a given statement or class of statements;

    II. the theoretical context in which the expression occurs, i.e., the class of those statements in *L* which are available as subsidiary hypotheses.

Thus, the sentence formulating Newton's law of gravitation has no experiential meaning by itself; but when used in a language whose logical apparatus permits the development of the calculus, and when combined with a suitable system of other hypotheses—including sentences which connect some of the theoretical terms with observation terms and thus establish a partial interpretation—then it has a bearing on observable phenomena in a large variety of fields. Analogous considerations are applicable to the term 'gravitational field', for example. It can be considered as having experiential meaning only within the context of a theory, which must be at least partially interpreted; and the experiential meaning of the term—as expressed, say, in the form of operational criteria for its application—will depend again on the theoretical system at hand, and on the logical characteristics of the language within which it is formulated.

4. COGNITIVE SIGNIFICANCE AS A CHARACTERISTIC OF INTERPRETED SYSTEMS

The preceding considerations point to the conclusion that a satisfactory criterion of cognitive significance cannot be reached through the second avenue of approach here considered, namely by means of specific requirements for the terms which make up significant sentences. This result accords with a general characteristic of scientific (and, in principle, even pre-scientific) theorizing: Theory formation and concept formation go hand in hand; neither can be carried on successfully in isolation from the other.

If, therefore, cognitive significance can be attributed to anything, then only to entire theoretical systems formulated in a language with a well-determined structure And the decisive mark of cognitive significance in such a system appears to be the existence of an interpretation for it in terms of observables. Such an interpretation might be formulated, for example, by means of conditional or biconditional sentences connecting nonobservational terms of the system with observation terms in the given language; the latter as well as the connecting sentences may or may not belong to the theoretical system.

But the requirement of partial interpretation is extremely liberal; it is satisfied, for example, by the system consisting of contemporary physical theory combined with some set of principles of speculative metaphysics, even if the latter have no empirical interpretation at all. Within the total system, these metaphysical principles play the role of what K. Reach and also O. Neurath liked to call *isolated sentences:* They are neither purely formal truths or falsehoods, demonstrable or refutable by means of the logical rules of the given language system; nor do they have any experiential bearing; i.e., their omission from the theoretical system would have no effect on its explanatory and predictive power in regard to potentially observable phenomena (i.e., the kind of phenomena described by observation sentences). Should we not, therefore, require that a cognitively significant system contain no isolated sentences? The following criterion suggests itself:

(4.1) A theoretical system is cognitively significant if and only if it is partially interpreted to at least such an extent that none of its primitive sentences is isolated.

But this requirement may bar from a theoretical system certain sentences which might well be viewed as permissible and indeed desirable. By way of a simple illustration, let us assume that our theoretical system *T* contains the primitive sentence

$$(S1) \qquad (x) [P_1x \supset (Qx \equiv P_2x)]$$

where 'P_1' and 'P_2' are observation predicates in the given language *L*, while '*Q*' functions in *T* somewhat in the manner of a theoretical construct and occurs in only one primitive sentence of *T*, namely *S1*. Now *S1* is not a truth or falsehood of formal logic; and furthermore, if *S1* is omitted from the set of primitive sentences of *T*, then the resulting system, *T'*, possesses exactly the same systematic, i.e., explanatory and predictive, power as *T*. Our contemplated criterion would therefore qualify *S1* as an isolated sentence which has to be eliminated—excised by means of Occam's razor, as it were—if the theoretical system at hand is to be cognitively significant.

But it is possible to take a much more liberal view of *S1* by treating it as a partial definition for the theoretical term '*Q*'. Thus conceived, *S1* specifies that in all cases where the observable characteristic P_1 is present, '*Q*' is applicable if and only if the observable characteristic P_2 is present as well. In fact, *S1* is an instance of those partial, or conditional, definitions which Carnap calls bilateral reduction sentences. These sentences are explicitly qualified by Carnap as analytic (though not, of course, as truths of formal logic), essentially on the ground that all their consequences which are expressible by means of observation predicates (and logical terms) alone are truths of formal logic.[18]

Let us pursue this line of thought a little further. This will lead us to some observations on analytic sentences and then back to the question of the adequacy of (4.1).

18. Cf. Carnap (1936–37), especially sections 8 and 10.

Suppose that we add to our system T the further sentence

$$(S2) \qquad (x)[P_3x \supset (Qx \equiv P_4x)]$$

where 'P_3', 'P_4' are additional observation predicates. Then, on the view that "every bilateral reduction sentence is analytic", [19] S2 would be analytic as well as S1. Yet, the two sentences jointly entail non-analytic consequences which are expressible in terms of observation predicates alone, such as[20]

$$(O) \qquad (x)\,[\sim(P_1x \cdot P_2x \cdot Px_3 \cdot \sim P_4x) \cdot \sim(P_1x \cdot \sim P_2x \cdot P_3x \cdot P_4x)]$$

But one would hardly want to admit the consequence that the conjunction of two analytic sentences may be synthetic. Hence if the concept of analyticity can be applied at all to the sentences of interpreted deductive systems, then it will have to be relativized with respect to the theoretical context at hand. Thus, e.g., S1 might be qualified as analytic relative to the system T, whose remaining postulates do not contain the term 'Q', but as synthetic relative to the system T enriched by S2. Strictly speaking, the concept of analyticity has to be relativized also in regard to the rules of the language at hand, for the latter determine what observational or other consequences are entailed by a given sentence. This need for at least a twofold relativization of the concept of analyticity was almost to be expected in view of those considerations which required the same twofold relativization for the concept of experiential meaning of a sentence.

If, on the other hand, we decide not to permit S1 in the role of a partial definition and instead reject it as an isolated sentence, then we are led to an analogous conclusion: Whether a sentence is isolated or not will depend on the linguistic frame and on the theoretical context at hand: While S1 is isolated relative to T (and the language in which both are formulated), it acquires definite experiential implications when T is enlarged by S2.

Thus we find, on the level of interpreted theoretical systems, a peculiar rapprochement, and partial fusion, of some of the problems pertaining to the concepts of cognitive significance and of analyticity: Both concepts need to be relativized; and a large class of sentences may be viewed, apparently with equal right, as analytic in a given context, or as isolated, or nonsignificant, in respect to it.

In addition to barring, as isolated in a given context, certain sentences which could just as well be construed as partial definitions, the criterion (4.1) has another serious defect. Of two logically equivalent formulations of a theoretical system it may qualify one as significant while barring the other as containing

---

19. Carnap (1936–37), p. 452.

20. The sentence O is what Carnap calls the *representative sentence* of the couple consisting of the sentences S1 and S2; see (1936–37), pp. 450–53.

an isolated sentence among its primitives. For assume that a certain theoretical system $T1$ contains among its primitive sentences $S,'$ S'', . . . exactly one, S', which is isolated. Then $T1$ is not significant under (4.1). But now consider the theoretical system $T2$ obtained from $T1$ by replacing the two first primitive sentences, S', S'', by one, namely their conjunction. Then, under our assumptions, none of the primitive sentences of $T2$ is isolated, and $T2$, though equivalent to $T1$, is qualified as significant by (4.1). In order to do justice to the intent of (4.1), we would therefore have to lay down the following stricter requirement:

(4.2) A theoretical system is cognitively significant if and only if it is partially interpreted to such an extent that in no system equivalent to it at least one primitive sentence is isolated.

Let us apply this requirement to some theoretical system whose postulates include the two sentences $S1$ and $S2$ considered before, and whose other postulates do not contain 'Q' at all. Since the sentences $S1$ and $S2$ together entail the sentence O, the set consisting of $S1$ and $S2$ is logically equivalent to the set consisting of $S1$, $S2$ and O. Hence, if we replace the former set by the latter, we obtain a theoretical system equivalent to the given one. In this new system, both $S1$ and $S2$ are isolated since, as can be shown, their removal does not affect the explanatory and predictive power of the system in reference to observable phenomena. To put it intuitively, the systematic power of $S1$ and $S2$ is the same as that of O. Hence, the original system is disqualified by (4.2). From the viewpoint of a strictly sensationalist positivism as perhaps envisaged by Mach, this result might be hailed as a sound repudiation of theories making reference to fictitious entities, and as a strict insistence on theories couched exclusively in terms of observables. But from a contemporary vantage point, we shall have to say that such a procedure overlooks or misjudges the important function of constructs in scientific theory: The history of scientific endeavor shows that if we wish to arrive at precise, comprehensive, and well-confirmed general laws, we have to rise above the level of direct observation. The phenomena directly accessible to our experience are not connected by general laws of great scope and rigor. Theoretical constructs are needed for the formulation of such higher-level laws. One of the most important functions of a well-chosen construct is its potential ability to serve as a constituent in ever new general connections that may be discovered; and to such connections we would blind ourselves if we insisted on banning from scientific theories all those terms and sentences which could be "dispensed with" in the sense indicated in (4.2). In following such a narrowly phenomenalistic or positivistic course, we would deprive ourselves of the tremendous fertility of theoretical constructs, and we would often render the formal structure of the expurgated theory clumsy and inefficient.

Criterion (4.2), then, must be abandoned, and considerations such as those outlined in this paper seem to lend strong support to the conjecture that no adequate alternative to it can be found; i.e., that it is not possible to formulate general and precise criteria which would separate those partially interpreted systems whose isolated sentences might be said to have a significant function from those in which the isolated sentences are, so to speak, mere useless appendages.

We concluded earlier that cognitive significance in the sense intended by recent empiricism and operationism can at best be attributed to sentences forming a theoretical system, and perhaps rather to such systems as wholes. Now, rather than try to replace (4.2) by some alternative, we will have to recognize further that cognitive significance in a system is a matter of degree: Significant systems range from those whose entire extralogical vocabulary consists of observation terms, through theories whose formulation relies heavily on theoretical constructs, on to systems with hardly any bearing on potential empirical findings. Instead of dichotomizing this array into significant and non-significant systems it would seem less arbitrary and more promising to appraise or compare different theoretical systems in regard to such characteristics as these:

  a. the clarity and precision with which the theories are formulated, and with which the logical relationships of their elements to each other and to expressions couched in observational terms have been made explicit;
  b. the systematic, i.e., explanatory and predictive, power of the systems in regard to observable phenomena;
  c. the formal simplicity of the theoretical system with which a certain systematic power is attained;
  d. the extent to which the theories have been confirmed by experiential evidence.

Many of the speculative philosophical approaches to cosmology, biology, or history, for example, would make a poor showing on practically all of these counts and would thus prove no matches to available rival theories, or would be recognized as so unpromising as not to warrant further study or development.

If the procedure here suggested is to be carried out in detail, so as to become applicable also in less obvious cases, then it will be necessary, of course, to develop general standards, and theories pertaining to them, for the appraisal and comparison of theoretical systems in the various respects just mentioned. To what extent this can be done with rigor and precision cannot well be judged in advance. In recent years, a considerable amount of work has been done towards a definition and theory of the concept of degree of confirmation, or logical probability, of a theoretical system;[21] and several contributions have been made towards the

---

21. Cf., for example, Carnap (1945)1 and (1945)2, and especially (1950). Also see Helmer and Oppenheim (1945).

clarification of some of the other ideas referred to above.[22] The continuation of this research represents a challenge for further constructive work in the logical and methodological analysis of scientific knowledge.

22. On simplicity, cf. especially Popper (1935), Chap. V; Reichenbach (1938), § 42; Goodman (1949)1, (1949)2, (1950); on explanatory and predictive power, cf. Hempel and Oppenheim (1948), Part IV.

REFERENCES

Ayer, A. J., *Language, Truth and Logic*, London, 1936; 2nd ed. 1946.

Carnap, R., "Testability and Meaning," *Philosophy of Science*, 3 (1936) and 4 (1937).

Carnap, R., "Logical Foundations of the Unity of Science," in: *International Encyclopedia of Unified Science*, I, 1; Chicago, 1938.

Carnap, R., *Foundations of Logic and Mathematics*, Chicago, 1939.

Carnap, R., "On Inductive Logic," *Philosophy of Science*, 12 (1945). Referred to as (1945)1 in this article.

Carnap, R., "The Two Concepts of Probability," *Philosophy and Phenomenological Research*, 5 (1945). Referred to as (1945)2 in this article.

Carnap, R., *Logical Foundations of Probability*, Chicago, 1950.

Chisholm, R. M., "The Contrary-to-Fact Conditional," *Mind*, 55 (1946).

Church, A., Review of Ayer (1946), *The Journal of Symbolic Logic*, 14 (1949), 52-53.

Feigl, H., "Existential Hypotheses: Realistic vs. Phenomenalistic Interpretations," *Philosophy of Science*, 17 (1950).

Goodman, N., "The Problem of Counterfactual Conditionals," *The Journal of Philosophy*, 44 (1947).

Goodman, N., "The Logical Simplicity of Predicates," *The Journal of Symbolic Logic*, 14 (1949). Referred to as (1949)1 in this article.

Goodman, N., "Some Reflections on the Theory of Systems," *Philosophy and Phenomenological Research*, 9 (1949). Referred to as (1949)2 in this article.

Goodman, N., "An Improvement in the Theory of Simplicity," *The Journal of Symbolic Logic*, 15 (1950).

Goodman, N., *Fact, Fiction, and Forecast*, Cambridge, Massachusetts, 1955.

Helmer, O. and P. Oppenheim, "A Syntactical Definition of Probability and of Degree of Confirmation." *The Journal of Symbolic Logic*, 10 (1945).

Hempel, C. G. and P. Oppenheim, "Studies in the Logic of Explanation," *Philosophy of Science*, 15 (1948). (Reprinted in this volume.)

Langford, C. H., Review in *The Journal of Symbolic Logic*, 6 (1941), 67-68.

Lewis, C. I., *An Analysis of Knowledge and Valuation*, La Salle, Ill., 1946.

MacCorquodale, K. and P. E. Meehl, "On a Distinction Between Hypothetical Constructs and Intervening Variables," *Psychological Review*, 55 (1948).

Margenau, H., "Methodology of Modern Physics," *Philosophy of Science*, 2 (1935).

Northrop, F. S. C., *The Logic of the Sciences and the Humanities*, New York, 1947.

O'Connor, D. J., "Some Consequences of Professor A. J. Ayer's Verification Principle," *Analysis*, 10 (1950).

Pap, A., *Elements of Analytic Philosophy*, New York, 1949.

Popper, K., *Logik der Forschung*, Wien, 1935.

Popper, K., "A Note on Natural Laws and So-Called 'Contrary-to-Fact Conditionals'," *Mind*, 58 (1949).

Reichenbach, H., *Philosophie der Raum-Zeit-Lehre*, Berlin, 1928.

Reichenbach, H., *Elements of Symbolic Logic*, New York, 1947.

Russell, B., *Human Knowledge*, New York, 1948.

Schlick, M., "Meaning and Verification," *Philosophical Review*, 45 (1936). Also reprinted in Feigl, H. and W. Sellars, (eds.) *Readings in Philosophical Analysis*, New York, 1949.

Spence, Kenneth W., "The Nature of Theory Construction in Contemporary Psychology," *Psychological Review*, 51 (1944).

5

The Methodological Character
of Theoretical Concepts

RUDOLF CARNAP

Reprinted with the kind permission of the publisher. Carnap, R., "The Methodological Character of Theoretical Concepts" from *Minnesota Studies in the Philosophy of Science Vol. I,* edited by H. Feigl and M. Scriven, University of Minnesota Press, Minneapolis. © Copyright 1956, University of Minnesota.

———— RUDOLF CARNAP ————

The Methodological Character of
Theoretical Concepts

I. Our Problems

IN DISCUSSIONS on the methodology of science, it is customary and useful to divide the language of science into two parts, the observation
language and the theoretical language. The observation language uses
terms designating observable properties and relations for the description of observable things or events. The theoretical language, on the
other hand, contains terms which may refer to unobservable events, unobservable aspects or features of events, e.g., to micro-particles like
electrons or atoms, to the electromagnetic field or the gravitational field
in physics, to drives and potentials of various kinds in psychology, etc.
In this article I shall try to clarify the nature of the theoretical language
and its relation to the observation language. The observation language
will be briefly described in Section 2 of this paper. Then a more detailed
account of the theoretical language and the connections between the
two languages will be given in Sections III–V.

One of the main topics will be the problem of a criterion of significance for the theoretical language, i.e., exact conditions which terms
and sentences of the theoretical language must fulfill in order to have
a positive function for the explanation and prediction of observable
events and thus to be acceptable as empirically meaningful. I shall leave
aside the problem of a criterion of significance for the observation language, because there seem to be hardly any points of serious disagreement among philosophers today with respect to this problem, at least
if the observation language is understood in the narrow sense indicated
above. On the other hand, the problem for the theoretical language is
a very serious one. There are not only disagreements with respect to
the exact location of the boundary line between the meaningful and the
meaningless, but some philosophers are doubtful about the very possi-

38

THEORETICAL CONCEPTS

bility of drawing any boundary line. It is true that empiricists today generally agree that certain criteria previously proposed were too narrow; for example, the requirement that all theoretical terms should be definable on the basis of those of the observation language and that all theoretical sentences should be translatable into the observation language. We are at present aware that these requirements are too strong because the rules connecting the two languages (which we shall call "rules of correspondence") can give only a partial interpretation for the theoretical language. From this fact, some philosophers draw the conclusion that, once the earlier criteria are liberalized, we shall find a continuous line from terms which are closely connected with observations, e.g., 'mass' and 'temperature,' through more remote terms like 'electromagnetic field' and 'psi-function' in physics, to those terms which have no specifiable connection with observable events, e.g., terms in speculative metaphysics; therefore, meaningfulness seems to them merely a matter of degree. This skeptical position is maintained also by some empiricists; Hempel, for instance, has given clear and forceful arguments for this view (see his articles, (14) and (15)). Although he still regards the basic idea of the empiricist meaning criterion as sound, he believes that deep-going modifications are necessary. First, the question of meaningfulness cannot, in his opinion, be raised for any single term or sentence but only for the whole system consisting of the theory, expressed in the theoretical language, and the correspondence rules. And secondly, even for this system as a whole, he thinks that no sharp distinction between meaningful and meaningless can be drawn; we may, at best, say something about its degree of confirmation on the basis of the available observational evidence, or about the degree of its explanatory or predictive power for observable events.

The skeptics do not, of course, deny that we can draw an exact boundary line if we want to. But they doubt whether any boundary line is an adequate explication of the distinction which empiricists had originally in mind. They believe that, if any boundary line is drawn, it will be more or less arbitrary; and, moreover, that it will turn out to be either too narrow or too wide. That it is too narrow means that some terms or sentences are excluded which are accepted by scientists as meaningful; that it is too wide means that some terms or sentences are included which scientifically thinking men would not accept as meaningful.

My attitude is more optimistic than that of the skeptics. I believe

39

Rudolf Carnap

that, also in the theoretical language, it is possible to draw an adequate boundary line which separates the scientifically meaningful from the meaningless. I shall propose criteria of significance; the criterion for theoretical terms will be formulated in Section VI, and the question of its adequacy will be examined in Section VII; the criterion for theoretical sentences will be given in Section VIII.

Two alternative forms for the introduction of scientific concepts into our two-language system will be explained and their comparative usefulness examined (Sections IX and X). One kind is that of theoretical concepts introduced into the theoretical language by postulates. The other kind I call "disposition concepts." They may be introduced into an extended observation language. Concepts defined by so-called operational definitions and the so-called intervening variables belong to this kind. I shall try to show that the introduction in the form of theoretical concepts is a more useful method because it allows greater freedom in the choice of conceptual forms; moreover, it seems more in accord with the way the scientists actually use their concepts.

In the last section, I discuss briefly the possibilities and advantages of the use of theoretical concepts in psychology.

II. The Observation Language L_o

The total language of science, L, is considered as consisting of two parts, the observation language L_o and the theoretical language L_T. I shall here briefly indicate the nature of L_o; the later discussion will chiefly concern L_T and its relations to L_o. Without actually specifying it, we assume that the logical structure of L_o is given. This would include a specification of the primitive constants, divided into logical and descriptive (i.e., nonlogical) constants. Let the observational vocabulary V_o be the class of the descriptive constants of L_o. Further, for each language part the admitted types of variables are specified. In L_o, it may suffice to use only individual variables, with observable events (including thing-moments) taken as individuals. Then rules of formation, which specify the admitted forms of sentences, and rules of logical deduction are given.

Let us imagine that L_o is used by a certain language community as a means of communication, and that all sentences of L_o are understood by all members of the group in the same sense. Thus a complete interpretation of L_o is given.

40

THEORETICAL CONCEPTS

The terms of V_o are predicates designating observable properties of events or things (e.g., "blue," "hot," "large," etc.) or observable relations between them (e.g., "x is warmer than y," "x is contiguous to y," etc.).

Some philosophers have proposed certain principles which restrict either the forms of expression or the procedures of deduction in "the language," in order to make sure that everything said in the language is completely meaningful. It seems to me that the justification of such requirements depends upon the purpose for which the language in question is used. Since L_o is intended for the description of observable events and therefore is meant to be completely interpreted, the requirements, or at least some of them, seem to have merit. Let us consider the most important requirements that have been proposed for some or any language L.

1. Requirement of *observability* for the primitive descriptive terms.
2. Requirements of various degrees of strictness for the nonprimitive descriptive terms.
   (a) Explicit *definability*.
   (b) *Reducibility* by conditional definitions (e.g., by reduction sentences as proposed in (5)).
3. Requirement of *nominalism*: the values of the variables must be concrete, observable entities (e.g., observable events, things, or thing-moments).
4. Requirement of *finitism*, in one of three forms of increasing strictness:
   (a) The rules of the language L do not state or imply that the basic domain (the range of values of the individual variables) is infinite. In technical terms, L has at least one finite model.
   (b) L has only finite models.
   (c) There is a finite number n such that no model contains more than n individuals.
5. Requirement of *constructivism*: every value of any variable of L is designated by an expression in L.
6. Requirement of *extensionality*. The language contains only truth-functional connectives, no terms for logical or causal modalities (necessity, possibility, etc.).

Any language fulfilling these requirements is more directly and more completely understandable than languages transgressing these limitations. However, for the language as a whole, the requirements are not justified; we shall reject them later for the theoretical language L_T.

41

Rudolf Carnap

Since then we have in the part L_T all the freedom of expression desired, we may well accept some or all of these requirements for L_0.

We have already accepted requirements 1 and 3. The decision about requirement 2 depends upon our intention concerning disposition terms (e.g., "soluble," "fragile," "flexible"). We shall not include them in L_0 itself; thus L_0 is here taken as a *restricted observation language* fulfilling the stronger requirement 2(a). Later (in Section IX) the possibility of an extended observation language L'_0, which allows the introduction of disposition terms, will be explained. Another method consists in representing the disposition concepts by theoretical terms in L_T (Section X).

The weakest requirement 4(a) of finitism is fulfilled in L_0. Therefore it is easily possible to satisfy requirement 5. Further, we take L_0 as an extensional language; thus requirement 6 is fulfilled.

III. The Theoretical Language L_T

The primitive constants of L_T are, like those of L_0, divided into logical and descriptive constants. Let the theoretical vocabulary V_T be the class of the descriptive primitive constants of L_T. We shall often call these constants simply "theoretical terms." (They are often called "theoretical constructs" or "hypothetical constructs." However, since the term "construct" was originally used for explicitly defined terms or concepts, it might be preferable to avoid this term here and use instead the neutral phrase "theoretical term" (or "theoretical primitive"). This use seems to be in better accord with the fact that it is, in general, not possible to give explicit definitions for theoretical terms on the basis of L_0.)

We may take it for granted that L_T contains the usual truth-functional connectives (e.g., for negation and conjunction). Other connectives, e.g., signs for logical modalities (e.g., logical necessity and strict implication) and for causal modalities (e.g., causal necessity and causal implication) may be admitted if desired; but their inclusion would require a considerably more complicated set of rules of logical deduction (as syntactical or semantical rules). The most important remaining problem for the specification of the logical structure concerns the ranges of values for the variables to be admitted in universal and existential quantifiers, and thereby the kinds of entities dealt with in L_T. This problem will be discussed in Section IV.

42

THEORETICAL CONCEPTS

A *theory* is given, consisting of a finite number of *postulates* formulated in L_T. Let T be the conjunction of these postulates. Finally, *correspondence rules C* are given, which connect the terms of V_T with those of V_0. These rules will be explained in Section V.

IV. The Problem of the Admissibility of Theoretical Entities

It seems that the acceptance of the following three conventions C1–C3 is sufficient to make sure that L_T includes all of mathematics that is needed in science and also all kinds of entities that customarily occur in any branch of empirical science.

Conventions about the domain D of entities admitted as values of variables in L_T.

C1. D includes a denumerable subdomain I of entities.
C2. Any ordered n-tuple of entities in D (for any finite n) belongs also to D.
C3. Any class of entities in D belongs also to D.

I shall now indicate briefly how these conventions yield all the customary kinds of entities referred to in scientific theories. To facilitate the understanding, I shall first use the customary way of speaking and the customary terms for certain kinds of entities, and only later add a warning against a possible misinterpretation of these formulations.

First about mathematical entities. Since the subdomain I stipulated in C1 is denumerable, we may regard its elements as the natural numbers 0, 1, 2, etc. If R is any relation whose members belong to D, then R may be construed as a class of ordered pairs of its members. Therefore, according to C2 and C3, R belongs also to D. Now the (positive and negative) integers can, in the usual way, be constructed as relations of natural numbers. Thus, they belong also to D. Analogously, we proceed to rational numbers as relations among integers, to real numbers as classes of rational numbers, and to complex numbers as ordered pairs of real numbers. Furthermore, we obtain classes of numbers of these kinds, relations among them, functions (as special kinds of relations) whose arguments and values are numbers, then classes of functions, functions of functions, etc. Thus D includes all those kinds of entities needed in the purely mathematical part of L_T.

Now we proceed to physics. We assume that L_T is based upon a particular space-time coordinate system; thus the space-time points are ordered quadruples of real numbers and hence, according to C2, belong

43

Rudolf Carnap

to D. A space-time region is a class of space-time points. Any particular physical system of which a physicist may speak, e.g., a material body or a process of radiation, occupies a certain space-time region. When a physicist describes a physical system or a process occurring in it or a momentary state of it, he ascribes values of physical magnitudes (e.g., mass, electric charge, temperature, electromagnetic field intensity, energy, and the like) either to the space-time region as a whole or to its points. The values of a physical magnitude are either real numbers or n-tuples of such. Thus a physical magnitude is a function whose arguments are either space-time points or regions and whose values are either real numbers or n-tuples of such. Thus, on the basis of our conventions, the domain D contains space-time points and regions, physical magnitudes and their values, physical systems and their states. A physical system itself is nothing else than a space-time region characterized in terms of magnitudes. In a similar way, all other entities occurring in physical theories can be shown to belong to D.

Psychological concepts are properties, relations, or quantitative magnitudes ascribed to certain space-time regions (usually human organisms or classes of such). Therefore they belong to the same logical types as concepts of physics, irrespective of the question of their difference in meaning and way of definition. Note that the logical type of a psychological concept is also independent of its methodological nature, e.g., whether based on observation of behavior or on introspection; philosophers seem sometimes not to realize this. Thus the domain D includes also all entities referred to in psychology. The same holds for all social sciences.

We have considered some of the kinds of entities referred to in mathematics, physics, psychology, and the social sciences and have indicated that they belong to the domain D. However, I wish to emphasize here that this talk about the admission of this or that kind of entity as values of variables in L_T is only a way of speaking intended to make the use of L_T, and especially the use of quantified variables in L_T, more easily understandable. Therefore the explanations just given must not be understood as implying that those who accept and use a language of the kind here described are thereby committed to certain "ontological" doctrines in the traditional metaphysical sense. The usual ontological questions about the *"reality"* (in an alleged metaphysical sense) of numbers, classes, space-time points, bodies, minds, etc., are pseudo questions

44

THEORETICAL CONCEPTS

without cognitive content. In contrast to this, there is a good sense of the word "real," viz., that used in everyday language and in science. It may be useful for our present discussion to distinguish two kinds of the meaningful use of "real," viz., the common sense use and the scientific use. Although in actual practice there is no sharp line between these two uses, we may, in view of our partition of the total language L into the two parts L_o and L_T, distinguish between the use of "real" in connection with L_o, and that in connection with L_T. We assume that L_o contains only one kind of variable, and that the values of these variables are possible observable events. In this context, the question of reality can be raised only with respect to possible events. The statement that a specified possible observable event, e.g., that of this valley having been a lake in earlier times, is real means the same as the statement that the sentence of L_o which describes this event is true, and therefore means just the same as this sentence itself: "This valley was a lake."

For a question of reality in connection with L_T, the situation is in certain respects more complicated. If the question concerns the reality of an event described in theoretical terms, the situation is not much different from the earlier one: to accept a statement of reality of this kind is the same as to accept the sentence of L_T describing the event. However, a question about the reality of something like electrons in general (in contradistinction to the question about the reality of a cloud of electrons moving here now in a specified way, which is a question of the former kind) or the electromagnetic field in general is of a different nature. A question of this kind is in itself rather ambiguous. But we can give it a good scientific meaning, e.g., if we agree to understand the acceptance of the reality, say, of the electromagnetic field in the classical sense as the acceptance of a language L_T and in it a term, say 'E,' and a set of postulates T which includes the classical laws of the electromagnetic field (say, the Maxwell equations) as postulates for 'E.' For an observer X to "accept" the postulates of T, means here not simply to take T as an uninterpreted calculus, but to use T together with specified rules of correspondence C for guiding his expectations by deriving predictions about future observable events from observed events with the help of T and C.

I said previously that the elements of the basic domain I may be regarded as natural numbers. But I warned that this remark and the others about real numbers, etc., should not be taken literally but merely

45

Rudolf Carnap

as a didactic help by attaching familiar labels to certain kinds of entities or, to say it in a still more cautious way, to certain kinds of expressions in L_T. Let the expressions corresponding to the domain I be "O," "O'," "O''," etc. To say that "O" designates the number zero, "O'" the number one, etc., gives merely the psychological help of connecting these expressions for the reader with useful associations and images, but should not be regarded as specifying part of the interpretation of L_T. All the interpretation (in the strict sense of this term, i.e., observational interpretation) that can be given for L_T is given in the C-rules, and their function is essentially the interpretation of certain sentences containing descriptive terms, and thereby indirectly the interpretation of the descriptive terms of V_T. On the other hand, the essential service that the expressions "O" etc. give, consists in the fact that they represent a particular kind of structure (viz., a sequence with an initial member but no terminal member). Thus the structure can be uniquely specified but the elements of the structure cannot. Not because we are ignorant of their nature; rather, there is no question of their nature. But then, since the sequence of natural numbers is the most elementary and familiar example of the sequential structure here in question, no harm is done in saying that those expressions designate entities and that these entities are the natural numbers, as long as we are not misled by these formulations into asking metaphysical pseudo questions.

In the earlier discussion of the observation language L_o (Section II), we considered certain restrictive requirements, like those of nominalism, finitism, etc., and found them acceptable. However, the situation with respect to the theoretical language is entirely different. For L_T we do not claim to have a complete interpretation, but only the indirect and partial interpretation given by the correspondence rules. Therefore, we should feel free to choose the logical structure of this language as it best fits our needs for the purpose for which the language is constructed.

Thus here in L_T there is no reason against the three conventions, although their acceptance violates the first five requirements mentioned in Section II. First, before the C-rules are given, L_T, with the postulates T and the rules of deduction, is an uninterpreted calculus. Therefore the earlier requirements cannot be applied to it. We are free in the construction of the calculus; there is no lack of clarity, provided the rules of the calculus are clearly given. Then the C-rules are added. All they do is, in effect, to permit the derivation of certain sentences of L_o from

46

THEORETICAL CONCEPTS

certain sentences of L_T or vice versa. They serve indirectly for derivations of conclusions in L_0, e.g., predictions of observable events, from given premises in L_0, e.g., reports of results found by observation, or for the determination of the probability of a conclusion in L_0 on the basis of given premises in L_0. Since both the premises and the conclusion belong to L_0, which fulfills the restricting requirements, there can be no objection against the use of the C-rules and of L_T, as far as the meaningfulness of the results of the derivation procedure is concerned.

V. The Correspondence Rules C

There is no independent interpretation for L_T. The system T is in itself an uninterpreted postulate system. The terms of V_T obtain only an indirect and incomplete interpretation by the fact that some of them are connected by the rules C with observational terms, and the remaining terms of V_T are connected with the first ones by the postulates of T. Thus it is clear that the rules C are essential; without them the terms of V_T would not have any observational significance. These rules must be such that they connect sentences of L_0 with certain sentences of L_T, for instance, by making a derivation in the one or the other direction possible. The particular form chosen for the rules C is not essential. They might be formulated as rules of inference or as postulates. Since we assume that the logical structure of the language is sufficiently rich to contain all necessary connectives, we may assume that the rules C are formulated as postulates. Let C be the conjunction of these *correspondence postulates*. As an example, we may think of L_T as a language of theoretical physics, based on a space-time coordinate system. Among the rules C there will be some basic ones, concerning space-time designations. They may specify a method for finding the coordinates of any observationally specified location, e.g., the method used by navigators for determining the position (the spatial coordinates: longitude, latitude, and altitude) and time. In other words, these C-rules specify the relation R which holds between any observable location u and the coordinates x, y, z, t, where x, y, z are the spatial coordinates and t is the time coordinate of u. More exactly speaking, the relation R relates to an observable space-time region u, e.g., an observable event or thing, a class u' of coordinate quadruples which may be specified by intervals around the coordinate values x, y, z, t.

On the basis of these C-rules for space-time designations, other C-rules

47

Rudolf Carnap

are given for terms of V_T, e.g., for some simple physical magnitudes like mass, temperature, and the like. These rules are spatiotemporally general, i.e., they hold for any space-time location. They will usually connect only very special kinds of value-distributions of the theoretical magnitude in question with an observable event. For example, a rule might refer to two material bodies u and v (i.e., observable at locations u and v); they must be neither too small nor too large for an observer to see them and to take them in his hands. The rule may connect the theoretical term "mass" with the observable predicate "heavier than" as follows: "If u is heavier than v, the mass of u' (i.e., the mass of the coordinate region u' corresponding to u) is greater than the mass of v'." Another rule may connect the theoretical term "temperature" with the observable predicate "warmer than" in this way: "If u is warmer than v, then the temperature of u' is higher than that of v'."

As these examples show, the C-rules effect a connection only between certain sentences of a very special kind in L_T and sentences in L_o. The earlier view, that for some terms of V_T there could be definitions in terms of V_o, called either 'correlative definitions' (Reichenbach) or 'operational definitions' (Bridgman), has been abandoned by most empiricists as an oversimplification (see Section X). The essential incompleteness of the interpretation of theoretical terms was pointed out in my *Foundations of Logic and Mathematics* (6) and is discussed in detail by Hempel in (15, §3) and (16, §7). Moreover, it cannot be required that there is a C-rule for every term of V_T. If we have C-rules for certain terms, and these terms are connected with other terms by the postulates of T, then these other terms thereby also acquire observational significance. This fact shows that the specification, not only of the rules C, but also of the postulates T, is essential for the problem of meaningfulness. The definition of meaningfulness must be relative to a theory T, because the same term may be meaningful with respect to one theory but meaningless with respect to another.

In order to have a more concrete picture, we may think of the terms of V_T as quantitative physical magnitudes, e.g., functions from space-time-points (or finite space-time-regions) to real numbers (or n-tuples of real numbers). The postulates T may be conceived of as representing the fundamental laws of physics, not other physical statements, however well established. Let us think of the postulates T and the rules C as being completely general with respect to space and time—that is

48

THEORETICAL CONCEPTS

as not containing references to any particular position in space or in time.

In the above examples, the C-rules have the form of universal postulates. A more general form would be that of statistical laws involving the concept of statistical probability (which means roughly, relative frequency in the long run). A postulate of this kind might say, for example, that, if a region has a certain state specified in theoretical terms, then there is a probability of 0.8 that a certain observable event occurs (which means that, on the average, in 80 per cent of those cases this event occurs). Or it might, conversely, state the probability for the theoretical property, with respect to the observable event. Statistical correspondence rules have so far been studied very little. (The probability conception of the psi-functions in quantum mechanics might perhaps be regarded as an example of probabilistic C-rules, as some customary formulations by physicists would suggest. I think, however, that this conception constitutes a probability connection *within* L_T rather than between L_T and L_O. What physicists often call "observable magnitudes," e.g., mass, position, velocity, energy, frequency of waves, and the like, are not "observable" in the sense customary in philosophical discussions of methodology, and therefore belong to the theoretical concepts in our terminology.) For the sake of simplicity, in most of my discussions here I shall think of the C-rules as postulates of universal form.

VI. A Criterion of Significance for Theoretical Terms

My task is to explicate the concept of the empirical meaningfulness of theoretical terms. I shall use "empirical significance" or, for short, "significance" as a technical expression for the desired explication. In preparation for the task of explication, let me try to clarify the explicandum somewhat more, i.e., the concept of empirical meaningfulness in its presystematic sense. Let 'M' be a theoretical term of V_T; it may designate a physical magnitude M. What does it mean for 'M' to be *empirically meaningful?* Roughly speaking, it means that a certain assumption involving the magnitude M makes a difference for the prediction of an observable event. More specifically, there must be a certain sentence S_M about M such that we can infer with its help a sentence S_O in L_O. (The inference may be either deductive, as I shall take it to be in the following discussion, or, more generally, probabilistic.) It is, of course, not required that S_O is derivable from S_M alone.

49

Rudolf Carnap

It is clear that we may use in the deduction the postulates T and the rules C. If now S_M contains not only 'M' but also other terms of V_T, then the fact that S_o is deducible does not prove that 'M' is meaningful, because this fact may just be due to the occurrence of the other terms. Therefore I shall require that S_M contain 'M' as the only term of V_T. Now it may be that any assumption involving only the magnitude M is in itself too weak to lead to an observational consequence, and that we have to add a second assumption S_K containing other terms of V_T but not 'M'. Let K be the class of these other terms. For example, S_M may say that, at a certain space-time point, M has the value 5, and S_K may say that, at the same space-time point or in its surroundings, certain other magnitudes have specified values. If S_o can be deduced from the four premises S_M, S_K, T, and C, while it cannot be deduced from S_K, T, and C alone, then the sentence S_M makes a difference for the prediction of an observable event, and therefore has observational significance. Since 'M' is the only descriptive term in S_M, 'M' itself has observational significance. However, this result must be qualified by a proviso. Since we have used the second assumption S_K involving the terms of K, we have shown only that 'M' is meaningful provided that the terms of K are meaningful. For this reason the definition of the significance of 'M' must be made relative not only to T and C, but also to the class K. 'M' is shown by the indicated procedure to be significant provided the terms of K have been found by a previous examination to be significant. Therefore the terms of V_T must be examined in a serial order. The first terms of V_T must be such that they can be shown to be significant without presupposing the significance of other descriptive terms. This will be the case for certain terms of V_T which are directly connected by C-rules with L_0. Other terms of V_T can then be shown to be significant by using the proved significance of the first terms, and so on. The total V_T can be regarded as significant only if we can show for a certain sequence of its terms that each term is significant relative to the class of the terms preceding it in the sequence.

It is clear that the definition must be relative to T, because the question whether a certain term in L_T is significant cannot possibly be decided without taking into consideration the postulates by which it is introduced. Perhaps the objection might be raised that, if significance is dependent upon T, then any observation of a new fact may compel us to take as nonsignificant a term so far regarded as significant or vice

50

THEORETICAL CONCEPTS

versa. However, it should be noted first that the theory T which is here presupposed in the examination of the significance of a term, contains only the postulates, that is, the fundamental laws of science, and not other scientifically asserted sentences, e.g., those describing single facts. Therefore the class of the terms of L_T admitted as significant is not changed whenever new facts are discovered. This class will generally be changed only when a radical revolution in the system of science is made, especially by the introduction of a new primitive theoretical term and the addition of postulates for that term. And note further that the criterion here proposed is such that, although the whole of the theory T is presupposed in the criterion, the question of significance is still raised for each term separately, not only for the vocabulary V_T as a whole.

On the basis of the preceding considerations, I shall now give definitions for the concept of significance of descriptive terms in the theoretical language. The definition D1 will define the auxiliary concept of *relative significance*, i.e., the significance of 'M' relative to a class K of other terms. Then the concept of significance itself will be defined in D2. According to our previous considerations, the concept of significance must furthermore be relative to the theoretical language L_T, the observation language L_O, the set of postulates T, and the correspondence rules C. We presuppose that the specifications of the languages L_T and L_O contain also a specification of the classes of descriptive terms, that is, V_T and V_O, respectively.

D1. A term 'M' is *significant relative to the class* K *of terms, with respect to* L_T, L_O, T, *and* $C = _{Df}$ the terms of K belong to V_T, 'M' belongs to V_T but not to K, and there are three sentences, S_M and S_K in L_T and S_O in L_O, such that the following conditions are fulfilled:

(a) S_M contains 'M' as the only descriptive term.
(b) The descriptive terms in S_K belong to K.
(c) The conjunction $S_M.S_K.T.C$ is consistent (i.e., not logically false).
(d) S_O is logically implied by the conjunction $S_M.S_K.T.C$.
(e) S_O is not logically implied by $S_K.T.C$.

The condition (c) is only added to assure that the situation described in S_M and S_K is possible, i.e., not excluded by the postulates T and the C-rules; otherwise the condition (d) would be trivially fulfilled.

D2. A term 'M_n' is *significant with respect to* L_T, L_O, T *and* $C = _{Df}$ there is a sequence of terms 'M_1', . . ., 'M_n' of V_T, such that every term 'M_i' $(i = 1, . . ., n)$ is significant relative to the class of those terms which precede it in the sequence, with respect to L_T, L_O, T, and C.

Rudolf Carnap

The sequence of terms referred to in $D2$ must obviously be such that the first term 'M_1' can be shown to be significant without the help of other terms of V_T. In this case 'M_1' satisfies $D1$; the class K is the null class; the sentence S_K contains no descriptive terms; it is logically true and can therefore be omitted. In the simplest case of this kind, 'M_1' occurs in a C-rule, like "mass" and "temperature" in our previous examples. Suppose that the first three terms of our sequence are of the kind described. Then for the fourth term, the sentence S_K may contain any one or all three of these terms. In this way we may proceed, step by step, to other terms, which may be more and more remote from direct observation.

(A slightly stronger criterion might be taken into consideration, obtained by the following modification of $D1$. In addition to the sentence S_M, another sentence S'_M is used, which contains likewise 'M' as the only descriptive term. Then the analogue to condition (c) for S'_M is added, and furthermore the analogue to condition (d) with S'_M taking the place of S_M and the negation of S_o taking the place of S_o. Thus here the assumption S_M leads to an observable consequence, as in $D1$, but another assumption S'_M about M, incompatible with S_M, leads to another observable consequence. However, the simpler criterion stated in $D1$ seems sufficient as a minimum requirement for significance.)

In the informal discussion at the beginning of this section, I have referred to the *deduction* of S_o from certain premises. Correspondingly, $D1$(d) requires that S_o is logically implied by the premises. However, this simple situation holds only if the C-postulates have universal form, as we mostly assume in our discussions. In the more general case that also statistical laws are admitted as C-postulates (see the remark at the end of Section V) and perhaps also as postulates of T, then the result is a probability connection between $S_M.S_K$ on the one hand, and S_o on the other. In this case, the conditions (d) and (e) in $D1$ are to be replaced by the condition that the probability of S_o relative to $S_M.S_K$, presupposing T and C, is different from the probability of S_o relative to S_K alone.

VII. The Adequacy of the Criterion of Significance

The criterion here proposed is admittedly very weak. But this is a result of the development of empiricism in these last decades. The original formulations of the criterion were found to be too strong and too narrow. Therefore, step by step, more liberal formulations were

THEORETICAL CONCEPTS

introduced. Hempel has given in his article (15) a clear survey of this development. One change was the replacement of the principle of verifiability by the weaker requirement of confirmability or testability, as formulated in my paper (5). At the time of that paper, I still believed that all scientific terms could be introduced as disposition terms on the basis of observation terms either by explicit definitions or by so-called reduction sentences, which constitute a kind of conditional definition (see Section X). Today I think, in agreement with most empiricists, that the connection between the observation terms and the terms of theoretical science is much more indirect and weak than it was conceived either in my earlier formulations or in those of operationism. Therefore a criterion of significance for L_T must likewise be very weak.

In discussions of the requirement of confirmability (or, in earlier times, verifiability) the question was sometimes raised whether the possibility of the event which constitutes the confirming evidence was to be understood as logical possibility or as causal possibility (i.e., compatibility with the laws of nature or the laws of a given theory). According to Schlick's conception (22, p. 153) the possibility should be understood in the widest sense, as logical possibility. His main argument was the uncertainty about possibility in an empirical sense. He pointed out that the observer does not know whether certain operations are empirically possible for him or not. For example, he does not know whether he is able to lift this table; he is quite certain that he cannot lift an automobile; but both events are still conceivable and should therefore be regarded as possible evidence. Schlick's point was that a question of significance should never be dependent upon contingent facts.

On the other hand, Reichenbach and I (5, p. 423) maintained the view that logical possibility is not sufficient, but that physical (or, more generally, causal) possibility is required. The question whether a given sentence of L_T is confirmable must be taken as relative to a theory T. In examining such a question, a proposed evidence or a proposed test procedure could certainly not be accepted if they were incompatible with T. For example, on the basis of modern physics, which takes the velocity of light as the maximum signal velocity, any proposed test or evidence involving a signal with a higher velocity could not be accepted as proof of significance. The definition $D1$ is based on this conception. The conjunction $S_M.S_K.T.C$ is required to be consistent by condition (c). Since S_O is logically implied by this conjunction, $S_M.S_K.S_O$ is

53

Rudolf Carnap

compatible with T and C and thus causally possible. However, it is to be noted that causal possibility as here understood is much weaker than the kind of empirical possibility which Schlick had seemed to have in mind. In Schlick's example, neither the lifting of the table nor that of the automobile is excluded by our criterion, because these events are not incompatible with the T (and C); T contains only the fundamental laws of science, while those events are merely excluded by our empirical knowledge of the observer's ability to lift things.

I shall now examine the question of the adequacy of our criterion in more specific terms. Let us consider the case that the vocabulary V_T consists of two parts, V_1 and V_2, such that the terms of V_1 are empirically meaningful, while those of V_2 are entirely devoid of any empirical meaning. To make this presupposition about V_1 and V_2 more specific, we assume the following:

(1) If S_1 and S_2 are any sentences of L such that all descriptive terms of S_1 belong to V_1 or to the observational vocabulary V_0 and those of S_2 to V_2, then neither of the two sentences logically implies the other, unless the implying sentence is logically false or the implied sentence is logically true.

Now a proposed criterion for the significance of terms of V_T should be regarded as too narrow if it excluded a term of V_1, and as too broad if it admitted a term of V_2. It would be adequate only if it were neither too narrow nor too broad.

For example, we might think of V_1 as containing terms of physics, and of V_2 as containing meaningless terms of speculative metaphysics such that the supposition (1) holds.

First let us consider a postulate system T' consisting of two parts, T'_1 and T'_2, T'_1 containing only terms of V_1, and T'_2 only terms of V_2. T'_1 may, for example, consist of fundamental laws of physics, and T'_2 of metaphysical principles. A criterion of significance which is adequate in this special case can easily be given. We call a postulate of a system T an *isolated postulate* if its omission from T does not diminish the class of sentences in L_0 which are deducible from T with the help of the C-rules. Then we take a term of V_T as significant if it occurs in a C-rule or in a non-isolated postulate of T. In the case of the above system T', according to (1), all postulates of T'_2 and no others are isolated; therefore all terms of V_1 and no others fulfill the criterion of significance just mentioned.

54

THEORETICAL CONCEPTS

This criterion is, however, not generally adequate. It would, for example, not work for a theory T'' logically equivalent to T' but such that no postulate of T'' is isolated. Those who are sceptical about the possibility of a criterion of significance for L_T have probably a situation of this kind in mind. (Hempel discusses a similar example.) They believe that it is not possible to give a criterion for postulate systems like T''. However, I think that the criterion for terms proposed in Section VI is adequate for cases of this kind. Consider for the postulate system T'' the sequence of terms which is required in $D2$. This sequence must necessarily begin with physical terms of V_1, because, according to our assumption (1), there are no C-rules for any of the metaphysical terms of V_2. Then the sequence may go on to further physical terms, which are connected with L_0 not directly by C-rules, but indirectly by other physical terms. Now we shall see that the sequence cannot reach any term of V_2; thus our criterion is not too broad for systems like T''. We will show this by an indirect proof. We assume that the sequence reaches terms of V_2; let 'M' be the first term of V_2 in the sequence; hence the preceding terms belong to V_1, and thus are meaningful. 'M' is significant relative to the class K of the preceding terms, with respect to L_T, L_0, T'', and C, in the sense of $D1$. Intuitively speaking, 'M' must then be meaningful, in contradiction to our presupposition about V_2. Our task is, to derive formally a contradiction with the presupposition (1).

According to $D1(d)$:

(2) $S_M.S_K.T''.C \supset S_0$ is logically true.

Now T'' is logically equivalent to T' and thus to $T'_1.T'_2$. Hence we obtain from (2) with a simple transformation:

(3) $S_M.T'_2 \supset U$ is logically true, where U is $S_K.T'_1.C \supset S_0$.

Hence:

(4) $S_M.T'_2$ logically implies U.

Now all descriptive terms in $S_M.T'_2$ belong to V_2, and those in U belong to V_1 or V_0. Thus (4) is in contradiction to (1), because

(5) $S_M.T'_2$ is not logically false (by $D1(c)$), and

(6) U is not logically true (by $D1(e)$).

This shows that the sequence cannot reach the terms of V_2.

55

Rudolf Carnap

We have shown that our criterion is not too broad if the given set of postulates T'' is logically equivalent to a set T' which consists of two parts, one containing only meaningful terms of V_1, the other only meaningless terms of V_2. The situation would be different for a theory T that did not fulfill this condition. In this case, T must include a postulate A such that A contains terms from both V_1 and V_2, but A is not logically equivalent to a conjunction $A_1.A_2$ in which A_1 contains only terms of V_1, and A_2 only terms of V_2. But such a postulate A would express a genuine connection between the occurring terms of V_2 and those of V_1. Therefore these terms of V_2 would not be entirely devoid of empirical meaning, against our assumption.

The result that our criterion of significance is not too broad depends essentially on the following feature of our definitions. We refer in $D2$ to a *sequence* of terms, and we require in effect for the significance of a term 'M' of the sequence that 'M' is significant (in the sense of $D1$) relative to the class K of the terms which precede 'M' in the sequence and which therefore have already been found to be significant. We can easily see that the criterion would become too broad if we were to change $D2$ so as to give up the requirement just mentioned. More specifically, we can show the following. A meaningless term 'M_2' of V_2 can, according to $D1$, be significant relative to a class K which contains, in addition to terms of V_1, also a meaningless term of V_2 different from 'M_2', say 'M'_2.' We shall show this first informally. The decisive point is that now, in distinction to our actual definition $D2$, we can have as the additional assumption S_K a sentence connecting the meaningless term 'M'_2' with a meaningful (physical) term of V_1, say 'M_1.' Now there may be a (metaphysical) postulate A_2 of T which connects M_2 with M'_2. With the help of this postulate, we can derive from the assumption S_M about M_2 alone a sentence about M'_2; from this with the sentence S_K mentioned above a physical sentence about M_1, and from this with a suitable C-rule an observation sentence.

The formal derivation is as follows. We take as a postulate of T:
(A_2) For every space-time point, the value of M'_2 is higher than that of M_2 by one.
We take as an instance of a C-rule:
$$(C_1)\ M_1(a') = 5 \supset S_0,$$

56

THEORETICAL CONCEPTS

where a' is the set of coordinates corresponding to the location a referred to in S_0. Finally we take S_K and S_M as follows:

$$(S_K) \quad M_1(a') = M'_2(a'),$$
$$(S_M) \quad M_2(a') = 4.$$

Now we can derive from S_M with A_2:

(i) $\qquad\qquad\qquad M'_2(a') = 5,$

hence with S_K:

(ii) $\qquad\qquad\qquad M_1 a' = 5,$

and hence with C_1:

(iii) $\qquad\qquad\qquad S_0.$

Thus the condition (d) in $D1$ is fulfilled. Therefore, 'M_2' is significant relative to the class K of the terms 'M_1' and 'M'_2'.

We have just seen that, in the definition of the significance of 'M'
relative to K, we must not admit a meaningless term in K and thereby
in the additional assumption S_K, because otherwise an observation sentence could be derived, leading to a deceptive appearance of significance.
This is indeed excluded by $D2$. However, $D1$ allows other premises for
the derivation which contain meaningless terms, viz., postulates of T.
Not only the postulates which contain the meaningful terms of V_1 and
the term 'M' in question are allowed but also postulates containing any
terms of V_2. Could this not lead to the same false appearance of significance for an actually meaningless term 'M' as the use of meaningless terms in S_K would do? In the above example, S_K connected a meaningless term 'M'_2' with a meaningful term 'M_1', and this fact led to the
undesired result. Now the use of T would lead to the same result if a
postulate of T were to make a connection between those terms. For
example, a postulate might yield as an instance the sentence "$M_1(a') =
M'_2(a')$" which was used as S_K in the earlier example. Thus the same
observation sentence S_0 could be derived from S_M even without the use
of any second assumption S_K. As an alternative, a postulate might state
a connection between 'M'_2' and 'M_1' in a conditional form, which,
though weaker, would likewise make possible a derivation of an observation sentence. Does then the fact that $D1$ permits the use of all postulates T make this definition inadequate? It does not, because the occurrence of a postulate making a genuine connection between a term of V_1
and one of V_2 is excluded by our presupposition that the terms of
V_1 are meaningful and those of V_2 meaningless. By virtue of such a

57

Rudolf Carnap

postulate, the term of V_2 (in the example, 'M'_2') would obtain some measure of empirical meaning, as we observed earlier in this section with reference to the postulate A. The essential difference between the two cases is the following. If a sentence connecting a meaningful term with another term in an inseparable way (e.g., by an equation, a conditional, a disjunction or the like, in distinction to a conjunction, which can be separated into its components) is a postulate or provable on the basis of postulates, then it is stated as holding with physical necessity; therefore it conveys some empirical meaning on the second term. On the other hand, if the same sentence is not provable but is merely used as the additional assumption S_K in *D1*, then it has no such effect; it need not even be true.

The preceding considerations have shown that our criterion of significance, formulated in *D1* and *D2*, is not too liberal. It does not admit a term entirely devoid of empirical meaning. Now we shall consider the question whether the criterion might be too narrow. Suppose that the term 'M' has some empirical meaning. Then it will be possible to derive an observation sentence from a suitable assumption S involving 'M' and other terms. Could it then still happen that our criterion would exclude 'M'? The definitions *D1* and *D2*, while permitting the inclusion of all postulates T and C among the premises for the derivation of the observation sentence, allow in addition only the two sentences S_K and S_M, for which specific restrictions are stated, especially the following:

(1) S_K may contain only terms of V_T which are different from 'M' and have to be significant; hence the following terms are not allowed in S_K:

    (a) terms of V_2,
    (b) terms of V_0,
    (c) The term 'M'.

(2) S_M contains 'M' as the only descriptive term.

We will now examine whether these restrictions are narrower than is necessary and thus might lead to the exclusion of a meaningful term 'M.'

1a. We found earlier that it is necessary to exclude the terms of V_2 from S_K, because otherwise the criterion would become too broad.

1b. Is it necessary to exclude the observational terms V_0 from the premises? Could it not be that, for the derivation of an observational

58

THEORETICAL CONCEPTS

conclusion S_0 from S_M, we need, in addition to T and C and the assumption S_K in theoretical terms, some assumption in observation terms, say S'_0? This might well happen. But then the conditional sentence $S'_0 \supset S_0$ is derivable from the premises specified in $D1$, and this is a sentence in L_0. Thus 'M' would fulfill $D1$, with the conditional sentence taking the place of S_0.

1c and 2. The condition (a) in $D1$ requires that S_M contain 'M' as the only descriptive term. The question might be raised whether this requirement is not too strong. Could not the following situation occur? 'M' and the terms of K are meaningful, and S_0 can indeed be derived with the help of T and C from an assumption S containing no other descriptive terms than 'M' and the terms of K, but S cannot be split up into two sentences S_M and S_K such that S_M contains only 'M' and S_K does not contain 'M.' Let us assume that the sentence S refers to space-time points of a certain spatiotemporal region a'. Then we can form sentences S_M and S_K which fulfill the requirements of $D1$ in the following way. Since S is supposed to be compatible with T and C, there must be a possible distribution of values of M for the space-time points of the region a', which is compatible with T, C, and S. Let 'F' be a logical constant, designating a mathematical function which represents such a value distribution. Then we take the following sentence as S_M: "For every space-time point in a', the value of M is equal to that of F." This sentence S_M is compatible with $T.C.S$. Then we take as S_K the sentence formed from S by replacing the descriptive term 'M' by the logical constant 'F'. Then S_M contains 'M' as the only descriptive term and S_K contains only terms of K. Furthermore, S is logically implied by S_M, and S_K. S_0 is logically implied by $S.T.C.$, according to our assumption, and hence also by $S_M.S_K.T.C.$ Therefore 'M' fulfills the definition $D1$.

Thus we have not found a point in which our criterion is too narrow.

VIII. A Criterion of Significance for Theoretical Sentences

The following two problems are closely connected with each other: first, the problem of a criterion of significance for descriptive constants, and second, the problem of the logical forms to be admitted for sentences. For the theoretical language, the connection between these problems is still closer than for the observation language. In the latter,

Rudolf Carnap

we may decide to have primitive predicates like "blue," "cold," "warmer than," and the like, while we are still undecided as to the forms of sentences, especially of general sentences, and the structure of the logic to be built into the language. On the other hand, if we wish to have terms like "temperature," "electromagnetic field," etc. as primitives in L_T, then we need also the accepted postulates for them, and thus we have to admit real number expressions, general sentences with real number variables, etc.

It seems to me that the best approach to the problem of a criterion of significance for sentences is the following. We look first for solutions to the two problems mentioned above; and then we take the most liberal criterion of significance for sentences which is compatible with those solutions. That is to say, we then accept as a significant sentence any expression that has any of the admitted logical forms and contains only descriptive constants which are significant. (I have used a similar approach for L_0 in (5).) I propose to apply this procedure now to L_T.

A criterion of significance for descriptive terms was given in Section VI. Some of the questions concerning the logical forms of sentences were discussed in Section IV, especially the question of the kinds of variables to be admitted in universal and existential quantifiers. We decided to admit at least those kinds of variables and forms of sentences which are essential for classical mathematics. Without actually specifying here the details of the rules, we shall now assume that the logical forms of sentences have been chosen on the basis of the considerations in Section IV, and that the rules of formation for L_T have been laid down in accordance with this choice. Then, applying the procedure proposed above, we define as follows:

D3. An expression A of L_T is a *significant sentence of* $L_T =_{Df}$
  (a) A satisfies the rules of formation of L_T,
  (b) every descriptive constant in A is a significant term (in the sense of D2).

The procedure used in this definition might perhaps appear as obvious. However, a closer examination shows that this is not the case. In fact, this form of the definition (aside from the question of its content, i.e., the choice of the particular rules of formation and of the particular significance criterion for terms) is not in agreement with certain very narrow criteria of significance which were sometimes proposed. For

60

THEORETICAL CONCEPTS

example, verifiability as a condition for the significance of a sentence was sometimes understood in the strict sense of the actual possibility of carrying out a procedure which would lead either to a verification or a falsification of the sentence. According to this criterion, in contrast to D3, the significance of a sentence is not only dependent upon its logical form and the nature of the descriptive constants occurring in it, but also upon the location in space and time referred to and the development of technology. For example, an empiricist applying this narrow criterion would regard as significant a sentence ascribing an observable property P to a body in his laboratory, while he would reject as nonsignificant another sentence which ascribes the same property to a body not accessible to him or not accessible to any human being, e.g., because of technical difficulties or remoteness in space or time.

However, even at the time of the Vienna Circle, we did not interpret the principle of verifiability in this narrow sense. We emphasized that the principle required, not the actual possibility of determination as true or false, but only the possibility *in principle*. By this qualification we intended to admit cases in which the determination was prevented only by technical limitations or by remoteness in space or time. We accepted, for example, a sentence about a mountain on the other side of the moon as meaningful. We stated the general rule that, if a description of an event in our neighborhood is regarded as meaningful, then an analogous description of an event in prehistoric times, or an event on the earth before there were human beings, or before there were any organisms, or at a future time when human beings will not exist any more, should likewise be accepted as meaningful. On the basis of this conception, the space-time location referred to in a sentence was regarded as irrelevant for the question of meaningfulness; this is in accord with D3.

If D3 is accepted and, in line with our earlier considerations in Section IV, all constants, variables and forms of sentences of classical mathematics are admitted in L_T, then the class of significant sentences of L_T is very comprehensive. We must realize that it includes certain sentences for which no observational evidence can ever be relevant, e.g., the sentence: "The value of the magnitude M at a certain space-time point is a rational number," where 'M' is significant. But every physicist would reject a language of physics so restricted that sentences of this and similar kinds were excluded. He would regard their inclusion as a

Rudolf Carnap

negligible price to be paid for the great convenience of using the whole of classical mathematics. It seems to me that no serious objections can be raised against these sentences, since it is in any case not possible to give an observational interpretation for more than a small part of the sentences of L_T. We should require no more than that for such a magnitude there are certain sentences which have an influence on the prediction of observable events and thus the magnitude itself has some amount of observational meaning.

I wish to emphasize that the proposed criterion for the significance of sentences is not meant to guarantee the fruitfulness of T. If all terms of V_T fulfill $D2$ and the postulates T are in accord with the rules of formation, then these postulates are indeed regarded as significant. But this should by no means be understood as implying that T must then be a scientifically satisfactory theory. T may still contain postulates which are of very little use from a scientific point of view. But the question of scientific fruitfulness of sentences and of a theory should be clearly distinguished from the question of empirical significance. There is no sharp boundary line between fruitful and useless hypotheses or theories: this is rather a matter of degree. It seems even doubtful whether it is possible to formulate in a completely general way a definition of a quantitative degree of fruitfulness of a scientific theory.

It should be noted that the significance criterion for L_T cannot be simply absorbed into the rules of formation. These rules determine only the forms of sentences, not the choice of primitive descriptive terms. The significance of these terms depends on other rules of L_T, viz., the list of postulates T and of C-postulates and the rules of logical deduction, as a glance at the essential condition (d) in $D1$ shows. (The rules of deduction may be given either in a syntactical form, as rules of derivation in a calculus, or in a semantical form, in terms of logical implication. I have used in $D1$ the latter form because it is more comprehensive; it presupposes rules specifying models and ranges, not given in this article.)

IX. Disposition Concepts

Among the descriptive terms which do not belong to the observation language L_o there are two different kinds, which today, in distinction to my previous conception, I should like to regard as essentially different. One kind is that of the theoretical terms, which we have

THEORETICAL CONCEPTS

discussed in detail in this article. The other kind I will call (pure) disposition terms. In my view, they occupy an intermediate position between the observational terms of L_0 and the theoretical terms; they are more closely related to the former than to the latter. The name 'observation language' may be understood in a narrower or in a wider sense; the observation language in the wider sense includes the disposition terms. In this article I take the observation language L_0 in the narrower sense. All primitive predicates in this language designate directly observable properties or relations of observable things or events; and a nonprimitive term is admitted in L_0 only if it can be defined on the basis of the primitive terms by an explicit definition in an extensional form, that is, not involving either logical or causal modalities. The *extended observation language* L'_0 is constructed from the original observation language L_0 by the addition of new terms in a way now to be described. Suppose that there is a general regularity in the behavior of a given thing of such a kind that, whenever the condition S holds for the thing or its environment, the event R occurs at the thing. In this case we shall say that the thing has the disposition to react to S by R, or for short, that it has the property D_{SR}. For example, elasticity is a disposition of this kind; a thing is called elastic if it shows the following regularity: whenever it is slightly deformed and then released (S), it resumes its original form (R). Or, an animal may have the disposition to react to a light in an otherwise dark environment (S), by approaching the light (R). Thus, S is sometimes a stimulus, and R is the response characteristic for the disposition in question (if we allow ourselves to use the terms 'stimulus' and 'response' not only in their literal sense applied to certain processes in organisms, as in the last example, but in a wider sense also to processes with inorganic bodies). When both S and R are specified, then the disposition concept D_{SR} is thereby completely characterized in its meaning. If both S and R can be described in L'_0, then we admit the introduction of the disposition term 'D_{SR}' as a new predicate in L'_0. The introduction of the first disposition terms in L'_0 must be of such a kind that in each case both S and R are expressible in L_0. But once some disposition terms have been introduced in this way, then further disposition terms may be introduced in such a way that S and R are described by using not only the terms of L_0, but also the previously introduced disposition terms of L'_0.

(We will not discuss here the possible forms for the rule by which a

63

Rudolf Carnap

disposition term is introduced on the basis of given S and R. This involves some technicalities which are not necessary for our present discussions. I will only mention two different forms for such rules that have been proposed. The first consists of so-called reduction sentences, which I proposed in (5). They represent a kind of conditional definition which uses only truth-functional connectives, but no modalities. The other method uses an explicit definition of a special form, involving logical and causal modalities; the exact form of definitions of this kind is at present not yet sufficiently clarified, but still under discussion.)

Sometimes multiple dispositions are used: $D_{S_1R_1, S_2R_2, \ldots, S_nR_n}$ is the disposition to react to S_1 by R_1, to S_2 by R_2, . . ., and finally to S_n by R_n. (In (5) I proposed to introduce a concept of this kind by several pairs of reduction sentences.) However, it seems preferable to admit only simple dispositions. Something similar to a multiple disposition can still be expressed by a conjunction of simple dispositions. Bridgman has emphasized that, strictly speaking, for one concept not more than one test procedure must be given. If we specify, say for "electric charge," three test procedures, then thereby we have given operational definitions for three different concepts; they should be designated by three different terms, which are not logically equivalent. As far as disposition concepts are concerned, in distinction to theoretical terms, I would agree with Bridgman in this point.

Let us now consider an important special kind of disposition. Let L''_o be that sublanguage of L'_o, in which the introduction of a disposition term 'D_{SR}' is permitted only if S and R are such that the observer is able to produce the condition S at will (at least in suitable cases), and that he is able to find out by suitable experiments whether the event R does or does not occur. In this case, by specifying S and R, a *test procedure* for the disposition D_{SR} is given. This procedure consists in producing the *test condition* S and then finding out whether or not the *positive test result* R occurs. If the observer finds for a given thing a sufficient number of positive instances, in which S is followed by R, and no negative instances, i.e., S followed by non-R, he may inductively infer that the general regularity holds and thus that the thing possesses the disposition D_{SR}. Let us call a disposition of this kind a "testable disposition." The class of *testable properties* includes observable properties and testable dispositions. All predicates in L''_o designate testable properties. The manipulations by which the experimenter produces the

THEORETICAL CONCEPTS

test condition S are sometimes called *test operations*. The introduction of D_{SR} by a specification of the test operations and the characteristic result R is therefore sometimes called an *operational definition*. There is actually no sharp line between observable properties and testable dispositions. An observable property may be regarded as a simple special case of a testable disposition; for example, the operation for finding out whether a thing is blue or hissing or cold, consists simply in looking or listening or touching the thing, respectively. Nevertheless, in the reconstruction of the language it seems convenient to take some properties, for which the test procedure is extremely simple (as in the three examples just mentioned), as directly observable and use them as primitives in L_0.

The view has often been maintained, especially by empiricists, that only terms of the kind just described, may be regarded as empirically meaningful. Thus testability was taken as a criterion of significance. The *principle of operationism* says that a term is empirically meaningful only if an operational definition can be given for it. The requirements of testability and of operationism as represented by various authors are closely related to each other, differing only in minor details and in emphasis. (In my simplifying account above they even appear as identical.) The principle of operationism, which was first proposed in physics by Bridgman and then applied also in other fields of science, including psychology, had on the whole a healthy effect on the procedures of concept formation used by scientists. The principle has contributed to the clarification of many concepts and has helped to eliminate unclear or even unscientific concepts. On the other hand, we must realize today that the principle is too narrow.

That the requirements of testability and of operationism exclude some empirically meaningful terms, can easily be seen. Suppose that 'S' and 'R' are both testable and hence accepted as meaningful by a scientist who takes testability as a criterion of significance. Since now the meaning of the term 'D_{SR}' is given by the specification of S and R, there cannot be any good reason for him to reject this term as meaningless, even if the condition S cannot be produced at will. In the latter case, D_{SR} is not testable; but S may still occur spontaneously and then, by finding R or non-R, the observer may determine whether or not D_{SR} holds. Thus it seems preferable not to impose the restriction as in L''_0, but to allow the general procedure as in L'_0: we start with observable

Rudolf Carnap

properties and allow the introduction of any disposition D_{SR}, provided that S and R are already expressible in our language L'_o.

(In (5), I gave an example of a meaningful but not testable term (p. 462) of the kind just described. I expressed there (§27) my preference for the more general procedure (as in L'_o) in comparison with that restricted by the requirement of testability (as in L''_o). Later it became clear by the consideration of theoretical concepts (see the next section of this paper) that a far more extensive liberalization of operationism is needed; this was emphasized by Feigl in (7) and (10) and by Hempel in (16) and (17).)

X. The Difference between Theoretical Terms and Pure Disposition Terms

I think today that, for most of the terms in the theoretical part of science and especially in physics, it is more adequate and also more in line with the actual usage of scientists, to reconstruct them as theoretical terms in L_T rather than as disposition terms in L'_o. The choice of the form of reconstruction depends to some extent upon the interpretation which we wish to give to the term, and this interpretation is not uniquely determined by the accepted formulations in science. The same term, say "temperature," may be interpreted, as I do interpret it, in such a way that it cannot be represented in L'_o but only in L_T; and, on the other hand, it may also be interpreted, e.g., by an operationist, in such a way that it fulfills the requirement of operationism. I shall now explain the reasons for my present view, which differs from that stated in (5).

A disposition term like 'D_{SR}' introduced by the general method described in the last section (for L'_o) may be called a "pure disposition term" in order to emphasize that it has the following characteristic features which distinguish it from terms in L_T:

1. The term can be reached from predicates for observable properties by one or more steps of the procedure described.

2. The specified relation between S and R constitutes the whole meaning of the term.

3. The regularity involving S and R, on which the term is based, is meant as universal, i.e., holding without exception.

The first characteristic distinguishes a pure disposition term like 'D_{SR}' from other disposition terms which are analogous to 'D_{SR}' but such that

66

THEORETICAL CONCEPTS

the condition S and the characteristic result R are formulated in L_T rather than in L_O or L'_O. (They might be called "theoretical disposition terms"; we shall not discuss them further.) The second characteristic distinguishes 'D_{SR}' from any theoretical term because the latter is never completely interpreted. In (5) I recognized this "open" character of scientific terms, that is, the incompleteness of their interpretation. At that time I tried to do justice to this openness by admitting the addition of further dispositional rules (in the form of reduction sentences; see my remarks in Section IX above on multiple dispositions). I think now that the openness is more adequately represented in L_T; whenever additional C-rules or additional postulates are given, the interpretation of the term may be strengthened without ever being completed.

The third characteristic leads to the following important consequence: (i) If the thing b has the disposition D_{SR} and the condition S is fulfilled for b, then it follows logically that the result R holds for b.

Therefore:

(ii) If S holds for b, but R does not, then b cannot have the disposition D_{SR}. Thus, from a premise in L'_O not involving D_{SR}, at least a negative sentence about D_{SR} is derivable. For a theoretical term, say 'M,' the situation is different. Let S_M be a sentence containing 'M' as the only descriptive term. In the situation described in $D1$ in Section VI, S_O is derivable from S_M and S_K (with the help of T and C, which may be regarded as belonging to the rules of L_T), and therefore non-S_M is derivable from non-S_O and S_K. Since S_K is not translatable into L_O or L'_O, the situation is here different from that in (ii). It is true that, for a term 'M' occurring in a C-rule, there are sentences S_M and S_O such that S_O is derivable from S_M alone without the need of a second premise S_K; and hence non-S_M is derivable from non-S_O, so that the situation is similar to that in (ii). However, this holds only for sentences of a very special kind. Most of the sentences about M alone, even if 'M' is a term occurring in a C-rule, are such that no C-rule is directly applicable, and therefore the derivation of an observation sentence is more indirect and needs additional premises in L_T, like S_K. Consider, for example, the term "mass," which is one of the physical terms most closely related to observational terms. There may be C-rules for "mass" (see the example in Section V). But no C-rule is directly applicable to a sentence S_M ascribing a certain value of mass to a given body, if the value is either so small that the body is not directly observable or so large that the

67

Rudolf Carnap

observer cannot manipulate the body. (I mentioned in Section V the possibility of probabilistic C-rules. If all C-rules have this form, then no theoretical sentence is deducible from sentences in L_o or L'_o. Thus in a language of this kind, the difference between pure disposition terms and theoretical terms becomes still more striking.)

We have seen that pure disposition terms and theoretical terms are quite different in their logical and methodological characteristics. To which of these two kinds do scientific terms belong? For the terms of theoretical physics, both conceptions are represented among leading physicists. Bridgman interprets them in such a manner that they fulfill the requirement of operationism and thus are essentially pure dispositions. On the other hand, Henry Margenau emphasizes the importance of the method of introducing these terms by postulates and connecting only certain statements involving them with statements about observables; in this conception they are theoretical terms.

It seems to me that the interpretation of scientific terms as pure dispositions cannot easily be reconciled with certain customary ways of using them. According to (ii), the negative result of a test for a disposition must be taken as conclusive proof that the disposition is not present. But a scientist, when confronted with the negative result of a test for a certain concept, will often still maintain that it holds, provided he has sufficient positive evidence to outbalance the one negative result. For example, let I_o be the property of a wire carrying at the time t_o no electric current of more than 0.1 ampere. There are many test procedures for this property, among them one in which the test condition S consists in bringing a magnetic needle near to the wire, and the characteristic result R is the fact that the needle is not deflected from its normal direction by more than a certain amount. Suppose that the observer assumes from the arrangement of the experiment that I_o holds, e.g., because he does not see any of the ordinary sources of a current and he has obtained, in addition, positive results by some other tests for I_o (or for a physically equivalent property). Then it may be that he does not give up the assumption of I_o even if the above mentioned test with S and R leads to a negative result, that is, a strong deflection of the needle. He may maintain I_o because it is possible that the negative result is due to an unnoticed disturbing factor; e.g., the deflection of the needle may be caused by a hidden magnet rather than by a current in the wire. The fact that the scientist still assumes I_o in

68

THEORETICAL CONCEPTS

spite of the negative result, viz., S and non-R, shows that he does not take I_o as the pure disposition D_{SR} characterized by S and R, because, according to (ii), this disposition is logically incompatible with the negative result. The scientist will point out that the test procedure for I_o based on S and R should not be taken as absolutely reliable, but only with the tacit understanding "unless there are disturbing factors" or "provided the environment is in a normal state." Generally, the explicit or implicit inclusion of such an escape clause in the description of a test procedure for a concept M in terms of a condition S and a result R shows that M is not the pure disposition D_{SR}. Also, the name "operational definition" for the description of the test procedure is in this case misleading; a rule for the application of a term that permits possible exceptions should not be called a "definition" because it is obviously not a complete specification of the meaning of the term.

On the other hand, if the term in question, e.g., 'I_o', is a theoretical term, then the description of the test procedure involving S and R may well admit of exceptions in case of unusual disturbing factors. For example, it may be possible to derive from the postulates T, the C-rules, and factual premises about usual circumstances in a laboratory the conclusion that, if there is no strong current, there will not be a strong deflection of the needle, except in the case of unusual circumstances like a magnetic field from another source, a strong current of air, or the like.

Thus, if a scientist has decided to use a certain term 'M' in such a way, that for certain sentences about M, any possible observational results can never be absolutely conclusive evidence but at best evidence yielding a high probability, then the appropriate place for 'M' in a dual-language system like our system L_o-L_T is in L_T rather than in L_o or L'_o.

XI. Psychological Concepts

The method of reconstructing the language of science by the dual schema consisting of the observation language L_o and the theoretical language L_T and the distinction between pure dispositions and theoretical concepts were so far in this article illustrated mostly by examples taken from physics. In the historical development of science, physics was indeed the field in which the method of introducing terms by postulates without a complete interpretation was first used systemati-

69

Rudolf Carnap

cally. The beginning phase of this development may perhaps be seen in the classical mechanics of the eighteenth century; its character became more clearly recognizable in the nineteenth century, especially in the Faraday-Maxwell theory of the electromagnetic field and the kinetic theory of gases. The greatest and most fruitful application is found in the theory of relativity and in quantum theory.

We see at present the beginnings of similar developments in other fields of science, and there can be no doubt that here too the more comprehensive use of this method will lead in time to theories much more powerful for explanation and prediction than those theories which keep close to observables. Also in psychology, in these last decades, more and more concepts were used which show the essential features of theoretical concepts. The germs of this development can sometimes be found in much earlier periods and even, it seems to me, in some prescientific concepts of everyday language, both in the physical and psychological field.

In psychology still more than in physics, the warnings by empiricists and operationists against certain concepts, for which no sufficiently clear rules of use were given, were necessary and useful. On the other hand, perhaps due to the too narrow limitations of the earlier principles of empiricism and operationism, some psychologists became overcautious in the formation of new concepts. Others, whose methodological superego was fortunately not strong enough to restrain them, dared to transgress the accepted limits but felt uneasy about it. Some of my psychologist friends think that we empiricists are responsible for the too narrow restrictions applied by psychologists. Perhaps they overestimate the influence that philosophers have on scientists in general; but maybe we should plead guilty to some extent. All the more should we now emphasize the changed conception which gives much more freedom to the working scientist in the choice of his conceptual tools.

In a way similar to the philosophical tendencies of empiricism and operationism, the psychological movement of Behaviorism had, on the one hand, a very healthful influence because of its emphasis on the observation of behavior as an intersubjective and reliable basis for psychological investigations, while, on the other hand, it imposed too narrow restrictions. First, its total rejection of introspection was unwarranted. Although many of the alleged results of introspection were indeed questionable, a person's awareness of his own state of imagining, feel-

70

THEORETICAL CONCEPTS

ing, etc., must be recognized as a kind of observation, in principle not different from external observation, and therefore as a legitimate source of knowledge, though limited by its subjective character. Secondly, Behaviorism in combination with the philosophical tendencies mentioned led often to the requirement that all psychological concepts must be defined in terms of behavior or behavior dispositions. A psychological concept ascribed to a person X by the investigator Y either as a momentary state or process or as a continuing trait or ability, was thus interpreted as a pure disposition D_{SR} of such a kind that S was a process affecting a sensory organ of X but observable also by Y, and R was a specified kind of behavior, likewise observable by Y. In contrast to this, the interpretation of a psychological concept as a theoretical concept, although it may accept the same behavioristic test procedure based on S and R, does not identify the concept (the state or trait) with the pure disposition D_{SR}. The decisive difference is this: on the basis of the theoretical interpretation, the result of this or of any other test or, generally, of any observations, external or internal, is not regarded as absolutely conclusive evidence for the state in question; it is accepted only as probabilistic evidence, hence at best as a reliable indicator, i.e., one yielding a high probability for the state.

In analogy to what I said in the previous section about physical terms, I wish to emphasize here for psychological terms that their interpretation as pure disposition terms is not in itself objectionable. The question is only whether this interpretation is in accord with the way the psychologist intends to use the term, and whether it is the most useful for the purpose of the whole of psychological theory, which is presumably the explanation and prediction of human behavior. Suppose that the psychologist Y declares that he understands the term "an IQ higher than 130" in the sense of the pure disposition D_{SR} to react to a specified kind of test S by a response of a specified kind R, where S and R are specified in terms of overt behavior. He is free to choose this interpretation provided he is consistent in it and willing to accept its implications. Suppose that he assumes on the basis of ample previous evidence that (at present) the person X has an IQ higher than 130. Then, due to his interpretation, he is compelled to give up the assumption if today the test result is negative, i.e., X's response to the test S is not of the specified kind R. (This follows from (ii) in Section X.) He cannot even re-accept the assumption later when he learns that

71

Rudolf Carnap

during the test X was in a very depressed mood, which, however, he neither admitted on question nor showed in his behavior at the time of the test. Can the psychologist not escape from this embarrassing consequence by saying that X's later admission of his depressed state showed that the condition S was actually not fulfilled? Not easily. There would have to be a rule as part of the specification of S that would enable him to make the exception. Let us consider three possibilities for a rule.

1. Let the rule merely say that, at the time t_o of the test, there must be first a complete lack of any observable sign of a disturbed emotional state at time t_o and second a negative answer to a question about such a state. Here the condition S was actually fulfilled and thus the psychologist has no way out.

2. Let the rule add, moreover, that also at no later time must there be a sign indicating a disturbance at time t_o. In this case, S was indeed not fulfilled. But a test procedure containing a rule of this kind would be practically useless, because it could never be completed before the death of the person.

3. Finally, let the rule refer not to behavioral signs but to the emotional state itself. Here the test procedure is not a strictly behavioristic procedure; I_o is not defined as a behavior disposition.

If, on the other hand, "an IQ higher than 130" is taken as a theoretical term, the situation is entirely different. The same test procedure with S and R may still be accepted. But its specification is no longer regarded as an operational definition of the term. There cannot be a definition of the term on the basis of overt behavior. There may be various test procedures for the same concept. But no result of a single test nor of any number of tests is ever absolutely conclusive, although they may, under favorable circumstances, yield a high probability. Any statement ascribing the term in question to a person on the basis of a given test result may later be corrected in view of new evidence, even if there is no doubt that the test rules S were fulfilled and that the response R was made. If a psychologist accepts this non-conclusive, probabilistic character of a test, as, I suppose, practically all would do, then the concept tested cannot be a pure disposition and is best reconstructed as a theoretical term.

I think that, even on a prescientific level, many people would regard their psychological judgments about other people as in principle always

72

THEORETICAL CONCEPTS

open to correction in view of later observations of their behavior. To the extent that someone is willing to change his judgments in this way, his use of psychological terms might be regarded as a beginning of the development which leads finally to theoretical terms. By the way, it would be interesting to make an empirical investigation of the degree of rigidity and flexibility shown by non-psychologists (including philosophers) in making and changing psychological statements about other people and about themselves. This would give a clearer indication of the nature of their concepts than any answers to direct questions about the concepts.

The distinction between intervening variables and theoretical constructs, often discussed since the article by MacCorquodale and Meehl, seems essentially the same or closely related to our distinction between pure dispositions and theoretical terms. "Theoretical construct" means certainly the same as here "theoretical term", viz., a term which cannot be explicitly defined even in an extended observation language, but is introduced by postulates and not completely interpreted. The intervening variables are said to serve merely for a more convenient formulation of empirical laws and to be such that they can always be eliminated. Therefore it seems that they would be definable in a language similar to our extended observation language L'_o but containing also quantitative terms; thus they seem essentially similar to pure dispositions.

Among empiricists, it was especially Feigl who early recognized and continually emphasized the importance of theoretical laws (which he called "existential hypotheses"; see his (8)). And he showed in particular that in the present phase of psychology the use of theoretical concepts and laws constitutes one of the most important methodological problems and tasks. He made important contributions to the clarification of this problem, especially in his article (10); there he points out the close analogy with the earlier development of physics.

Psychological theories with theoretical terms will no doubt be further developed, probably to a much larger extent than so far. There are good reasons for expecting that a development of this kind will prove to be very fruitful, while without it the possible forms of theory construction are too limited to give a good chance for essential progress. This does not imply that the so-called "molar" approach in terms of observable behavior is to be rejected; on the contrary, this approach will always be

Rudolf Carnap

an essential part of psychological investigation. What is wrong is only the principle which demands a restriction of the psychological method to this approach. The molar approach in psychology has a function similar to that of macrophysics both in the historical development and in present research. In all fields, the study of macro-events is the natural approach in the beginning; it leads to the first explanations of facts by the discovery of general regularities among observable properties ("empirical laws"); and it remains always indispensable as the source of confirming evidence for theories.

In physics great progress was made only by the construction of theories referring to unobservable events and micro-entities (atoms, electrons, etc.). Then it became possible to formulate a relatively small number of fundamental laws as postulates from which many empirical laws, both those already known and new ones, could be derived with the help of suitably constructed correspondence rules. In psychology analogous developments have begun from two different starting points. The one development began with the introspective approach. It proceeded from introspectively observed events (feelings, perceptions, images, beliefs, remembrances, etc.) to unconscious, i.e., introspectively not observable, events. These were first conceived as analogous to the observable events, e.g., unconscious feelings, beliefs, etc. Later also, new kinds of entities were introduced, e.g., drives, complexes, the id, the ego, and the like; however, the laws involving these entities are so far only stated in a qualitative form, which limits their explanatory and still more their predictive power. The other development began with the molar behavioristic approach. It started with a study of observable events of behavior, and then proceeded to dispositions, tendencies, abilities, potentialities for such events, and further to more abstract entities. Here the stage of the first quantitative laws has been reached.

Both these approaches in psychology will probably later converge toward theories of the central nervous system formulated in physiological terms. In this physiological phase of psychology, which has already begun, a more and more prominent role will be given to quantitative concepts and laws referring to micro-states described in terms of cells, molecules, atoms, fields, etc. And finally, micro-physiology may be based on micro-physics. This possibility of constructing finally all of science, including psychology, on the basis of physics, so that all theoretical terms are definable by those of physics and all laws derivable

74

THEORETICAL CONCEPTS

from those of physics, is asserted by the thesis of *physicalism* (in its strong sense). (My recent views on the question of physicalism are not yet represented in my publications. Feigl (11) explains them, describes the historical development of physicalism in our movement, and gives an illuminating discussion of the theses of physicalism and the arguments for them.) By far the greater part of the development of psychology just outlined is, of course, today no more than a program for the future. Views vary a great deal as to the probability and even the possibility of such a development; and many will especially oppose, with either scientific or metaphysical arguments, the possibility of the last step, the assertion of physicalism. My personal impression, in view of the progress made within the last decades in psychology, physiology, the chemistry of complex organic molecules, and certain parts of physics, especially the theory of electronic computers, is that the whole development of psychology from the molar phase through the theoretical, the physiological, and the micro-physiological phases to the final foundation in micro-physics seems today much more probable and much less remote in time than it appeared even thirty years ago.

REFERENCES

1. Bridgman, P. W. *The Logic of Modern Physics.* New York: Macmillan, 1927.
2. Bridgman, P. W. *The Nature of Physical Theory.* Princeton: Princeton Univ. Pr., 1936.
3. Bridgman, P. W. "Operational Analysis," *Philosophy of Science,* 5:114–31 (1938).
4. Bridgman, P. W. "The Nature of Some of Our Physical Concepts," *British Journal for the Philosophy of Science,* 1:257–72 (February 1951); 2:25–44 (May 1951); 2:142–60 (August 1951). Reprinted as a separate monograph by Philosophical Lib., New York, 1952.
5. Carnap, Rudolf. "Testability and Meaning," *Philosophy of Science,* 3:420–68 (1936); 4:1–40 (1937). Reprinted as monograph by Whitlock's, Inc., New Haven, Connecticut, 1950. Parts reprinted in H. Feigl and M. Brodbeck (eds.), *Readings in the Philosophy of Science.* New York: Appleton-Century-Crofts, 1953.
6. Carnap, Rudolf. *Foundations of Logic and Mathematics,* Vol. I, No. 3 of the *International Encyclopedia of Unified Science.* Chicago: Univ. of Chicago Pr., 1939. A part ("The Interpretation of Physics") is reprinted in H. Feigl and M. Brodbeck (eds.), *Readings in the Philosophy of Science,* pp. 309–18. New York: Appleton-Century-Crofts, 1953.
7. Feigl, Herbert. "Operationism and Scientific Method," *Psychological Review,* 52:250–59 (1945). Reprinted, with some alterations, in H. Feigl and W. Sellars (eds.), *Readings in Philosophical Analysis,* pp. 498–509. New York: Appleton-Century-Crofts, 1949.
8. Feigl, Herbert. "Existential Hypotheses: Realistic Vs. Phenomenalistic Interpretations." *Philosophy of Science,* 17:35–62 (1950).

Rudolf Carnap

9. Feigl, Herbert. "Confirmability and Confirmation," *Revue Internationale de Philosophie*, 5:268–79 (1951). Reprinted in P. P. Wiener (ed.), *Readings in Philosophy of Science*, pp. 522–30. New York: Scribner's, 1953.

10. Feigl, Herbert. "Principles and Problems of Theory Construction in Psychology," in W. Dennis (ed.), *Current Trends in Psychological Theory*, pp. 179–213. Pittsburgh: Univ. of Pittsburgh Pr., 1951.

11. Feigl, Herbert. "Physicalism, Unity of Science, and the Foundations of Psychology," in P. A. Schilpp (ed.), *The Philosophy of Rudolf Carnap*. New York: Tudor (forthcoming).

12. Feigl, H., and M. Brodbeck (eds.). *Readings in the Philosophy of Science*. New York: Appleton-Century-Crofts, 1953.

13. Feigl, H., and W. Sellars (eds.). *Readings in Philosophical Analysis*. New York: Appleton-Century-Crofts, 1949.

14. Hempel, C. G. "Problems and Changes in the Empiricist Criterion of Meaning," *Revue Internationale de Philosophie*, 4:41–63 (1950). Reprinted in L. Linsky (ed.), *Semantics and the Philosophy of Language*, pp. 163–85. Urbana: Univ. of Illinois Pr., 1952.

15. Hempel, C. G. "The Concept of Cognitive Significance: A Reconsideration," *Proceedings of the American Academy of Arts and Sciences*, 80:61–77 (1951).

16. Hempel, C. G. *Fundamentals of Concept Formation in the Empirical Sciences*, Vol. II, No. 7 of the *International Encyclopedia of Unified Science*. Chicago: Univ. of Chicago Pr., 1952.

17. Hempel, C. G. "A Logical Appraisal of Operationism," *Scientific Monthly*, 79: 215–20 (1954).

18. Hempel, C. G. "Implications of Carnap's Work for the Philosophy of Science," in P. A. Schilpp (ed.), *The Philosophy of Rudolf Carnap*. New York: Tudor (forthcoming).

19. MacCorquodale, Kenneth, and P. E. Meehl. "On a Distinction Between Hypothetical Constructs and Intervening Variables," *Psychological Review*, 55:95–107 (1948). Reprinted in H. Feigl and M. Brodbeck (eds.), *Readings in the Philosophy of Science*, pp. 596–611. New York: Appleton-Century-Crofts, 1953.

20. Margenau, Henry. *The Nature of Physical Reality*. New York: McGraw-Hill, 1950.

21. Schilpp, P. A. (ed.). *The Philosophy of Rudolf Carnap*. New York: Tudor (forthcoming).

22. Schlick, Moritz. "Meaning and Verification," *Philosophical Review*, 45:339–69 (1936). Reprinted in H. Feigl and W. Sellars (eds.), *Readings in Philosophical Analysis*, pp. 146–74. New York: Appleton-Century-Crofts, 1949.

PART

IV

MEANING AND USE

INTRODUCTION

In Parts II and III we considered separately the problems of meaning and meaningfulness. This division reflects the difference between questions about what words or expressions mean, and the rather different request for a criterion that will specify the conditions under which any word or expression can be said to have meaning. Perhaps theories of meaning are more explicitly tied to ontological commitments than are theories of meaningfulness. In the former, philosophers are concerned with asking questions about the types of objects referred to or denoted by terms. Discussions of meaningfulness, while not indifferent to ontological concerns, focus primarily on language and not on the world with which language deals.

Discussions of reference theories of meaning and of the issues of verification and verifiability figured extensively first in the literature of logical atomism and then in the writings of the logical empiricists. Indeed, it is not an exaggeration to say that a concern with these issues was the most significant single characteristic of the philosophy of the years between the two world wars. Bearing in mind that philosophical movements are richly varied and that exceptions are always near at hand, let us mention some major features of the work of the logical positivists or logical empiricists.

First, and most obviously, particular theories of meaning and meaningfulness were meticulously developed, criticized, and defended. Semantic questions were of primary interest. It was realized that answers to these questions would bear directly upon other philosophical issues, but the application of the consequences of semantic theories to philosophical disputes was often left implicit, or merely indicated in some general way, while the theories themselves were explicitly developed. As we have already pointed out, a major feature of the empiricist program was the elimination of metaphysics. For instance, A. J. Ayer writes:

> An example of a controversy which the application of our criterion obliges us to condemn as fictitious is provided by those who dispute concerning the number of substances that there are in the world. For it is admitted both by monists, who maintain that reality is one substance, and by pluralists, who maintain that reality is many, that it is impossible to imagine any empirical situation which would be relevant to the solution of their dispute. But if we are told that no possible observation could give any probability either to the assertion that reality was one substance, or to the assertion that it was many, then we must conclude that neither assertion is significant.[1]

On the whole, the amount of space and degree of elaboration given to the anti-metaphysical arguments themselves was modest. The embattled metaphysician was likely to maintain that the logical empiricist was himself a kind of metaphysician.

While holding that philosophers who engaged in metaphysics said things that were not literally significant, the logical empiricist was far from maintaining that all philosophical utterances were a kind of nonsense attendant upon a failure to note significant features of language. Quite the contrary. At the very least, what philosophy had to say about the logic and structure of scientific theories and scientific methodology was both meaningful and important. If we extend our view to include the later ideal language philosophers, who acknowledge a debt to both the logical atomists and the logical empiricists, we find an explicit claim to ontological relevance.

There is perhaps one other major theme running through the philosophy of this period to which we should draw the reader's attention. Common to logical atomists, logical empiricists, and ideal language philosophers — in short, to *most* contemporary philosophy — was a distinction which has come to be called simply the analytic-synthetic distinction. Propositions were either analytic (that is, tautologies true by virtue of their form alone) or synthetic. If synthetic, then they were true or false by virtue of some state of affairs in the world. Sentences which did not express either an analytic or a synthetic proposition were taken to be not literally meaningful. As the reader knows from the readings in Part III, at least one reason for holding that a sentence was

---

[1] A. J. Ayer, *Language, Truth, and Logic,* 2nd ed. (New York: Dover, 1946), 39-40.

not meaningful was that the proposition it expressed was not verifiable.

With these very general comments in mind, let us turn now to a discussion of meaning and use. An interest in the intimate relation between the meanings of words and the ways in which they are actually used in particular sorts of situations is the characteristic feature of that movement in philosophy to which the name ordinary language philosophy has been given. Contemporary philosophers, as individuals, have tended to be very resistant to identification with schools or movements of philosophy, arguing that such classification, however useful to the student or historian, tends to cover up significant differences in thought. Still, there *is* a body of philosophical literature amongst the particular examples of which there are startling family resemblances, and to which the name 'ordinary language philosophy' has been given. By talking about the general features of this philosophical movement, we can illustrate both the content and the consequences of the theory which identifies or associates the meanings of words with their use.

At the very beginning, it might be argued, we have made two important mistakes in our exposition. It is really misleading to talk about a theory or doctrine in the normal sense of that term; besides, the alleged theory doesn't identify meaning and use. On the whole we judge it best to let the reader settle this second question for himself after reading the selections in Part IV. However, the philosopher who objects to this description of his views might do so on the grounds that it oversimplifies a very complex situation, and draw our attention to an important passage from Wittgenstein's *Philosophical Investigations:* "For a *large* class of cases — though not for all — in which we employ the word 'meaning' it can be defined thus: the meaning of a word is its use in the language. And the *meaning* of a name is sometimes explained by pointing to its *bearer*."[2]

There are two reasons for denying that it is appropriate to talk about a theory or doctrine of meaning and use. To begin with, one thinks of a theory as a set of general assertions, systematically related and bearing on what is common to a number of particular instances. Further, any theory is valuable to us because it helps us to understand what is truly significant in the many instances that confront us; we assume that what is significant is what is common to the instances. This is exactly why it is misleading to talk about a theory of meaning and

[2] Ludwig Wittgenstein, *Philosophical Investigations* (New York: Macmillan, 1953) 43, author's italics.

use. Under no circumstances do we wish to suggest that all words mean in the same way, or that 'meaning' has one, or a very limited number of meanings. The only thing common to various uses is that they are all uses. What is important is the different ways in which words or phrases are used to say things. Another reason for trying to avoid talk about a theory is to be found in the manner in which references to meaning and use occur in the literature. In the writings of the logical atomists and logical empiricists, more space was given to the development of theories of meaning and meaningfulness than to their application to appropriate problems. When we come to the work of the ordinary language philosophers, this balance seems strikingly reversed. Rather than extensive argument and defense of the thesis, we are more likely to find it exhibited at work, employed in the resolution or dissolution of some philosophical perplexity.

Up to this point we have found it possible to make a distinction between theories of meaning and theories of meaningfulness. We have recognized that to ask questions about what expressions (terms or sentences) mean, and under what conditions they are meaningful, is to ask for answers that direct our attention in divergent (if related) directions. But this distinction is not so clear in the case of meaning and use. The reason is obvious. Suppose we ask what some particular word or phrase means or (mistakenly, we would be told) what sorts of things meanings are. Suppose we ask under what conditions a word or phrase is meaningful. In both of these cases we would be advised to turn our attention in the same direction: to the use of the word or phrase in question in a number of concrete instances.

Before we take up some of the reasons for stressing the intimate connection between meaning and use, we should make two further comments on the way in which this view of meaning has tended to set ordinary language philosophy apart from other language-oriented philosophy. We have pointed out that some philosophers have maintained that their work was quite properly concerned with ontological issues, that clarification of questions in ontology was a legitimate undertaking in philosophy. Most notably, the logical atomists and ideal language philosophers have held some such views. Generally the connection has come through discussions of types of entities denoted by expressions (the logical atomists) or by discussions of the most general features of an ideal language. If a philosopher denies that words or phrases mean by virtue of their denoting different sorts of entities, he will be less likely to understand his work of clarification of meanings as one which also involves the sorting out of the ultimate categories, structures, or components of reality. The second way in which ordinary language philosophy has been set apart from other contemporary movements is in the way it has viewed the philosophical activity itself. Some of its critics have accused it of treating philosophy, and philosophical problems, as a set of very subtle language-induced delusions. Philosophy is a kind of mistake which it is the job of other philosophers to set right — an undertaking which, if gone about in the right way, will be self-liquidating. It is suggested that this is the natural outgrowth of considering philosophical problems as the result of misspeakings or misuses of words. Whether these criticisms are justified or are essentially a caricature of the view, we leave it to the reader to decide.

A detailed argument in favor of the correlation of meaning to use is to be found in Gilbert Ryle's "The Theory of Meaning," with which we have concluded Part II. In that article Ryle outlines the historical development of the theory of meaning and discusses the logical problems and significant oversights that lead eventually to a rejection of reference theories. It is neither appropriate nor necessary to give a complete summary of that article here, but it might be well to point out some of its main features.

Ryle begins with a discussion of J. S. Mill; he shows that Mill was sensitive to certain distinctions which subsequent philosophers failed to observe. First, although he treated nearly all words as names, he does not mean by this merely proper names. "For when Mill calls a word or phrase a 'name,' he is using 'name' not, or not always, quite in the ordinary way. Sometimes he says that for an expression to be a name it must be able to be used as the subject or the predicate of a subject-predicate sentence — which lets in, e.g., adjectives as names."[3]

Second, Mill realized that certain words like 'or' and 'not' and 'never' really cannot be assimilated to names at all. There are obviously no objects to be the meanings of these words, or to be the bearers of these words taken as (proper) names. At the same time, they are clearly not meaningless, which they would be if they were names that named nothing. Ryle's point is that, although Mill made a mistake in the analysis he gave of words of this sort, he was correct in realizing

---

[3] Gilbert Ryle, "The Theory of Meaning," in *Philosophy and Ordinary Language,* ed. Charles E. Caton (Urbana: University of Illinois Press, 1963), 131-32.

"that it is not always the case that for a word to mean something it must denote somebody or some thing."[4]

Perhaps most important was that, although his treatment was not wholly adequate, Mill saw the difference that was later distinguished by Frege between the sense and reference of a term. There may be two descriptive phrases which fit the same thing or person but do not mean the same thing. Consider the expressions, 'The largest building on the Acropolis' and 'The temple to Athena built by Ictinus.' Both name the Parthenon, yet mean different things. Mill developed the theory of denotation and connotation to deal with this problem. As Ryle puts it, "Most words and descriptive phrases do two things at once. They *denote* the things or persons they are, as he unhappily puts it, all the names of. But they also connote or signify the simple or complex attributes by possessing which the thing or person denoted is fitted by the description."[5] Remembering that for Mill predicate expressions are names as well, we can see that to ask for the meaning of the expression, 'The largest building on the Acropolis' is to ask two questions at once. First it asks what is denoted by the expression — in this case, the Parthenon. Second it asks what the properties are by which the thing is described — in this case, the property or complex of properties of being the temple to Athena built by Ictinus. Ryle concludes,

> Mill himself virtually says that according to our ordinary natural notion of meaning it would not be proper to say that, e.g. Sir Winston Churchill [in our example, the Parthenon — the Editors] is the meaning of a word or phrase. We ordinarily understand by 'meaning' not the thing denoted but only what is connoted. That is, Mill virtually reaches the correct conclusions that the meaning of an expression is never the thing or person referred to by means of it; and that descriptive phrases and with one exception, single words, are never names in the sense of 'proper names.'[6]

Ryle goes on to suggest reasons for which we would deny not only that words denote straightforward things like objects and properties, but also more sophisticated entities like classes. We recommend that the reader begin his study of this issue with a careful reading of Ryle's article.

The denial of the denotation theory of meaning might spring from

---

[4] *Ibid.*, 135.
[5] *Ibid.*
[6] *Ibid.*, 136.

motives other than those discussed by Ryle. One of the most detailed attacks upon denotationist theory was set forth by Wittgenstein in his *Philosophical Investigations.* Paul Feyerabend has attempted to summarize the theory under attack, the nature of the criticism, and the consequences for philosophy of that criticism in his paper, "Wittgenstein's *Philosophical Investigations*."[7] This paper opens Part IV. It is of special interest because it offers a concise statement of that alternative theory of meaning which has come to be referred to as the theory of 'meaning as use.' We should note, however, Feyerabend's warning about this new theory, which he calls " 'T' ": "It will turn out that this change cannot be described simply as the change from one *theory* to another, although we shall first introduce 'T' as a new theory of meaning."[8]

Many of the discussions of meaning and use are dominated by a particular conceptual model or paradigm, that of the procedures one would have to follow in order to teach someone the meaning of a word. We find references to such procedures in the opening sections of Wittgenstein's *Philosophical Investigations* and in Austin's "The Meaning of a Word."[9] Let us imagine that we are asked the meaning of the word 'clumsy.' How would we teach our inquirer the meaning of that word? Austin suggests that we would do two different sorts of things, which he calls explaining the syntactics and demonstrating the semantics of the word. First, we would give examples of sentences in which the word 'clumsy' could be used, and sentences where it could not be used. The next step would be to get our questioner either actually to experience or to imagine situations correctly described by sentences containing the word 'clumsy.' Finally, we will repeat this procedure with situations in which it would be incorrect to use sentences containing the word 'clumsy.' We have taught him how and when to use the word.

The essential criterion by which we could determine that someone knew the meaning of a word would be that he always used the word in a syntactically correct way in appropriate situations. When we have taught him to do this, there is nothing else to teach him. Particularly,

[7] Paul Feyerabend, "Wittgenstein's *Philosophical Investigations*," *Philosophical Review,* LXIV (1955), 449-83. Reprinted in *Wittgenstein,* ed. George Pitcher (New York: Doubleday, 1966), 104-50.

[8] Pitcher, ed., *Wittgenstein,* 107.

[9] J. L. Austin, "The Meaning of a Word," in *Philosophical Papers,* ed. J. O. Urmson and G. J. Warnock (Oxford: Clarendon Press, 1961), 23-43.

there is not some *third* element which is the meaning of the word; to know the meaning of a word is to know how to use it.

The rigid division of meaningful assertions into analytic statements and synthetic statements capable of being made true or false by empirical states of affairs struck many philosophers as being clearly too restrictive. Very little reflection is necessary to realize that our language is full of expressions which are neither tautologies nor descriptions of states of affairs, but which are also not meaningless or expressions of emotion. Consider any request, 'Please close the door,' for instance. When we use a sentence of this sort in situations appropriate to it, we are not describing what we are doing (making a request) or asserting that we are doing it. To utter the sentence in question is simply to make a request, and it would be meaningless to ask whether it was true or false. J. L. Austin has called utterances of this sort "performative utterances."

Although quite interesting, Norman Malcolm's "Knowledge of Other Minds" may strike some readers as curiously out of place, since the issues being argued seem more properly epistemological than semantic. We have included it because it illustrates the application of the view of meaning with which we have been concerned in the treatment of a philosophical argument. Note that, at a crucial point in the argument, Malcolm appeals to the notion that to know the meanings of words is not only to say them, but also to perform appropriate actions in conjunction with that saying. The presence of the appropriate actions allows us to recognize an instance of use, as opposed to a mere mouthing.

A philosophical movement without critics would be unfortunate indeed, for it is sharpened and refined in response to vigorous criticism. Gilbert Ryle's "Ordinary Language" is directed at correcting certain misunderstandings of ordinary language philosophy that are the result of misusing terms like 'ordinary,' 'use,' and 'usage' in describing it. Ryle's contribution to the joint paper with Findlay, "Use, Usage, and Meaning," is an attempt to answer the charge that ordinary language philosophy is really not relevant to any philosophical concerns since it deals only with what one can and cannot say in some particular language. By introducing the distinction between language and speech, Ryle tries to make clear that ordinary language philosophers are concerned not with the syntax or grammar of some particular language, but with the logical syntax of any meaningful speech. Here are two short quotations which together neatly illustrate the point: "A so-called rule of logical syntax is what a nonsensical dictum is a breach of."[10] "What is impossible in 'The Cheshire Cat vanished leaving only her grin behind her' is not any piece of intolerably barbarous English."[11]

Findlay's criticism deserves the reader's careful attention. We will point out only one feature of that criticism, which is that the notion of use, as we ordinarily employ it, is really parasitic upon the notion of meaning. It is a condition of our being able to use a term that we know its meaning.

H. P. Grice, in "Meaning,"[12] offers an analysis of two possible meanings of 'meaning.' He admits that the distinction he makes is quite broad and perhaps not exhaustive. Still, he will maintain that by and large all our uses of 'mean' fall into one of two possible groups. He calls the two possible meanings of 'meaning' the natural and the non-natural, corresponding very roughly to "what people are getting at when they display an interest in a distinction between 'natural' and 'conventional' signs."[13]

Grice's analysis of meaning in the sense he calls non-natural depends very heavily on the notion that meaning is not something that words do (or have, in any ultimate sense), but something that speakers do with them. Words do not by themselves have meaning in the non-natural sense; rather, the speaker means something by his use of the word. The sense of meaning in which we might say that words mean something is what Grice calls the natural sense of meaning. This sense of meaning is explicated by reference to what a speaker might have intended by some particular utterance on a particular occasion. Finally, the sense we all have that words have meanings which remain the same on different occasions of their use will be explicated by reference to some set of statements about what speakers in general intend by their use of that word. It is worthwhile considering to what extent Grice's analysis is open to the sort of criticism raised by Findlay in the previous article.

The final selection in Part IV is an excerpt from John Searle's *Speech Acts*.[14] He asks us to consider certain fallacies of which he takes

[10] Gilbert Ryle and J. N. Findlay, "Use, Usage and Meaning," *Proceedings of the Aristotelian Society*, suppl. vol. XXXV (1961), 230.

[11] *Ibid.*, 228.

[12] H. P. Grice, "Meaning," *Philosophical Review*, LXVI (1957), 377-88.

[13] *Ibid.*, 379.

[14] John R. Searle, *Speech Acts* (Cambridge: Cambridge University Press, 1969).

contemporary philosophers to be guilty. In particular, the excerpted selection deals with what Searle calls the assertion fallacy. He lays this and other fallacies at the door of philosophers who had "no general theory of language on which to base their particular conceptual analyses. What they had in place of a general theory were a few slogans, the most prominent of which was the slogan 'meaning is use.' "[15] This brief but trenchant analysis of a possible misdirection of thought through the assimilation of meaning to use touches on several themes introduced in other readings in this part.

SELECTED READINGS

Albritton, R. "On Wittgenstein's Use of the Term Criterion." *Journal of Philosophy,* LVI (1959), 845-57.

Austin, J. L. *How to Do Things with Words.* Ed. J. O. Urmson. New York: Oxford University Press, 1965.

――――. *Sense and Sensibilia.* Reconstructed from the manuscript notes by G. J. Warnock. New York: Oxford University Press, 1964.

Chappell, V. C., ed. *Ordinary Language.* Englewood Cliffs, N.J.: Prentice-Hall, 1964.

Chihara, C. S., and Fodor, J. A. "Operationalism and Ordinary Language: A Critique of Wittgenstein." In *Wittgenstein: The Philosophical Investigations.* Ed. George Pitcher. Garden City, N.Y.: Doubleday, 1966, 384-419.

Malcolm, Norman. "Wittgenstein's Philosophical Investigations." In *Knowledge and Certainty: Essays and Lectures.* Englewood Cliffs, N.J.: Prentice-Hall, 1966. Reprinted in *Wittgenstein: The Philosophical Investigations.* Ed. George Pitcher. Garden City, N.Y.: Doubleday, 1966, 65-103.

Passmore, J. "Wittgenstein and Ordinary Language Philosophy." In *A Hundred Years of Philosophy.* New York: Macmillan, 1957, 425-58.

Rhees, R. "Can There Be a Private Language?" *Proceedings of the Aristotelian Society,* suppl. vol. XXVIII (1954), 77-94.

Strawson, P. F. "Review of Wittgenstein's *Philosophical Investigations.*" *Mind,* LXII (1954), 77-99. Reprinted in *Wittgenstein: The Philosophical Investigations.* Ed. George Pitcher. Garden City, N.Y.: Doubleday, 1966, 22-64.

[15] *Ibid.,* 164.

1

Wittgenstein's Philosophical Investigations

PAUL FEYERABEND

Reprinted with the kind permission of the author and the editor from *The Philosophical Review,* LXIV (1955), 449-83.

WITTGENSTEIN'S *PHILOSOPHICAL INVESTIGATIONS*

IN DISCUSSING this book I shall proceed in the following way: I shall first state a philosophical theory *T*, which is attacked throughout the book. In doing so I shall not use the usual statement of the theory (if there is any) but Wittgenstein's, which may, of course, be an idealization. Secondly, I shall show how the theory is criticized by Wittgenstein—first, using an example (which plays a considerable role in the *Investigations*, but which I have used to present arguments not presented in the book in connection with this example), then discussing in general terms the difficulties revealed by the example. Thirdly, I shall state what seems to be Wittgenstein's own position on the issue. This position will be formulated as a philosophical theory, *T'*, without implying that Wittgenstein intended to develop a philosophical theory (he did not). Finally I shall discuss the relation between the theory stated and Wittgenstein's views on philosophy and I shall end up with a few critical remarks.[1]

For brevity's sake I shall introduce three different types of quotation marks: The usual quotation marks ("...") enclosing Wittgenstein's own words, daggers (†...†) enclosing further developments of his ideas and general remarks, asterisks (*...*), enclosing critical remarks. Text without any of these quotation marks is an abbreviated statement of what Wittgenstein is saying.

I

†The theory criticized is closely related to medieval realism (about universals) and to what has recently been termed "essentialism."[2] The theory, as presented by Wittgenstein, includes the following five main items:

†(1) "Every word has a meaning. This meaning is correlated with the word. It is the object, for which the word stands" (1; 90, 120).[3]

---

[1] Although many different problems are discussed in the *Investigations*, it seems to me that the criticism of *T* (or the assertion of *T'*) is to be regarded as the core of the book. I shall therefore concentrate on elaborating *T* and *T'*, and I shall omit all other problems (if there are any).

[2] Cf. K. R. Popper, *The Open Society and Its Enemies* (Princeton, 1950), I, 31 ff.

[3] Parenthetical references are to the numbered sections of Part I of the *Philosophical Investigations*, unless otherwise indicated.

THE PHILOSOPHICAL REVIEW

Meanings exist independently of whether or not any language is used and which language is used. They are definite, single objects and their order "must be *utterly simple*" (97).

†(2) As compared with this definiteness and purity of meanings (their order "must ... be of the purest crystal" [97]), "the actual use ... seems something muddied" (426). That indicates an imperfection of our language.

†(3) This imperfection gives rise to two different philosophical problems: (a) The philosopher has to find out what a word '*W*' stands for, or, as it is sometimes expressed, he has to discover the *essence* of the object which is designated by '*W*,' when its use in everyday language is taken into account. From the knowledge of the essence of *W* the knowledge of the whole use of '*W*' will follow (264, 362, 449). (b) He has to build an ideal language whose elements are related to the essences in a simple way. The method of finding a solution to problem (a) is analysis. This analysis proceeds from the assumption that "*the essence is hidden from us*" (92) but that it nevertheless " '*must*' be found in reality" (101). However different the methods of analysis may be— analysis of the linguistic usage of '*W*'; phenomenological analysis of *W* ('deepening' of the phenomenon *W*); intellectual intuition of the essence of *W*—the answer to problem (a) "is to be given once for all; and independently of any future experience" (92). The form of this answer is the definition. The definition explains why '*W*' is used in the way it is and why *W* behaves as it does (75; 97, 428, 654). The solution of (b) is presupposed in the solution of (a); for it provides us with the terms in which the definitions that constitute the solution of (a) are to be framed. A definite solution of (b) implies a certain form of problem (a). If it is assumed, e.g., that sentences are word-pictures of facts (291; cf. *Tractatus Logico-Philosophicus* 2.1; 4.04) then 'What is a question?' is to be translated into 'What kind of fact is described by a question? The fact that somebody wants to know whether ..., or the fact that somebody is doubtful as to ..., etc.?'

†(4) Asking how the correctness of a certain analysis may be checked, we get the answer that the essence can be *experienced*. This experience consists in the presence of a mental picture, a sensation, a phenomenon, a feeling, or an inner process of a more ethereal kind (305). 'To grasp the meaning' means the same as 'to have a picture before one's inner eye' and "to have understood the explanation means to have in one's mind an idea of the thing explained, and that is a sample or a picture" (73). The essence of the object denoted, the meaning of the denoting expression (these are one and the same thing; cf. 371, 373)

450

DISCUSSION

follows from an analysis of this picture, of this sensation; it follows from the exhibition of the process in question (thus the essence of sensation follows from an analysis of my present headache [314]). It is the presence of the picture which gives meaning to our words (511, 592), which forces upon us the right use of the word (73, 140, 305, 322, 426, 449), and which enables us to perform correctly an activity (reading, calculating) the essence of which it constitutes (179, 175, 186, 232). Understanding, calculating, thinking, reading, hoping, desiring are, therefore, mental processes.

†(5) From all this it follows that teaching a language means showing the connection between words and meanings (362) and that "learning a language consists in giving names to objects" (253). So far the description of T, as it is implicitly contained in the *Philosophical Investigations*.

III

†In criticizing T, Wittgenstein analyzes $T4$ and in this way shows the impossibility of the program $T3$ as well as the insolubility of the problems connected with this program. That implies that, within T, we shall never be able to know what a certain word 'W' means or whether it has any meaning at all, although we are constantly using that word and although the question how it is to be used does not arise when we are not engaged in philosophical investigations. But did not this paradox arise because we assumed that meanings are objects of a certain kind and that a word is meaningful if and only if it stands for one of those objects; i.e., because we assumed $T1, 2$ to be true? If, on the other hand, we want to abandon $T1, 2$, we meet another difficulty: words have, then, no fixed meaning (79). "But what becomes of logic now? Its rigour seems to be giving way here.—But in that case doesn't logic altogether disappear?—For how can it lose its rigour? Of course not by our bargaining any of its rigour out of it.— The *preconceived idea* of crystalline purity can only be removed by turning our whole examination round" (108); i.e., by changing from T to T'. It will turn out that this change cannot be described simply as the change from one *theory* to another, although we shall first introduce T' as a new theory of meaning.

†Before doing so we have to present Wittgenstein's criticism of T. This criticism is spread throughout the book. It consists of careful analyses of many special cases, the connection between which is not easily apprehended. I have tried to use *one* example instead of many and to present as many arguments as possible by looking at this example

451

from as many sides as possible. All the arguments are Wittgenstein's; some of the applications to the example in question are mine.

IV

†The philosopher is a man who wants to discover the meanings of the expressions of a language or the essences of the things designated by those expressions. Let us see how he proceeds. Let us take, e.g., the word 'reading.' "Reading is here the activity of rendering out loud what is written or printed; and also of writing from dictation, writing out something printed, playing from a score and so on" (156).

(A) †According to T1 we have to assume that the word 'reading' stands for a single object. Now, there is a variety of manifestations of reading: reading the morning paper; reading in order to discover misprints (here one reads slowly, as a beginner would read); reading a paper written in a foreign language that one cannot understand but has learned to pronounce; reading a paper in order to judge the style of the author; reading shorthand, reading *Principia Mathematica*, reading Hebrew sentences (from right to left); reading a score in order to study a part one has to sing; reading a score in order to find out something about the inventiveness of the composer, or to find out how far the composer may have been influenced by other contemporary musicians; reading a score in order to find out whether the understanding of the score is connected with acoustic images or with optical images (which might be a very interesting psychological problem). But this variety, without "any one feature that occurs in all cases of reading" (168), is only a superficial aspect. All these manifestations have something *in common* and it is this common property which makes them manifestations of *reading*. It is also this property that is the essence of reading. The other properties, varying from one manifestation to the other, are accidental. In order to discover the essence we have to strip off the particular coverings which make the various manifestations *different* cases of reading. But in doing so (the reader ought to try for himself!) we find, not that what is essential to reading is hidden beneath the surface of the single case, but that this alleged surface is one case out of a family of cases of reading (164).†

Consider for example the proceedings which we call "games." I mean board-games, card-games, ball-games, Olympic games and so on. What is common to them all?—Don't say : "There *must* be something common or they would not be called 'games' "; but *look and see* whether there is anything common to *all*—for if you look at them you will not see something that is in common to all, but similarities, relationships and a whole series of them at that.... And

DISCUSSION

the result of this examination is : we see a complicated network of similarities overlapping and criss-crossing. ... I can think of no better expression to characterize these similarities than "family-resemblances"; for the various resemblances between members of a family : build, features, colours of eyes, gait, temperament, etc., etc., overlap and criss-cross in the same way.—And I shall say: "games" form a family [66 f].

And in the same way we also use the word 'reading' for a family of cases. And in different circumstances we apply different criteria for a person's reading [164].

‡(B) Looking at the outer manifestations of reading we could not discover the structure suggested by T_1. Instead of an accidental variety centering in a well-defined core we found "a complicated network of similarities" (66). Does that fact refute T_1? Surely not; for a philosopher who wants to defend T_1, there are many possible ways of doing so. He may admit that the *overt behavior* of the person reading does not disclose any well-defined center, but he may add that reading is a *physiological process* of a certain kind. Let us call this process the reading process (RP). Person P is reading if and only if the RP is going on within (the brain or the nervous system of)P. (Cf. 158.) But the difficulties of this assumption are clear. Consider the case of a person who does not look at any printed paper, who is walking up and down, looking out of the window and behaving as if he were expecting somebody to come; but the RP is going on within his brain. Should we take the presence of the reading process as a sufficient criterion for the person's reading, adding perhaps that we had discovered a hitherto unknown case of reading? (Cf. 160.) It is clear that in a case like that we should, rather, alter some physiological hypotheses. If, again, reading is a physiological process, then it certainly makes sense to say that P read 'ali' within 'totalitarianism,' but did not read before he uttered those sounds and did not read afterward either, although anybody who observed the outer behavior of P would be inclined to say that P had been reading the whole time. For it is quite possible that the RP should be present only when P is uttering 'ali' (cf. 157). It seems, however, that it is quite meaningless to hypothesize that in the circumstances described a person was reading only for one second or two, so that his uttering of sounds in the presence of printed paper before or after that period must not be called 'reading.'

‡(C) To the failure of attempts (A) and (B) to discover the essence of reading certain philosophers will answer in the following way: Certainly—that was to be expected.‡ For reading is a *mental process*, and "the one real criterion for anybody's *reading* is the conscious act of

THE PHILOSOPHICAL REVIEW

reading, the act of reading the sounds off from the letters. 'A man surely knows whether he is reading or only pretending to read' "(159) †The idea to which they are alluding is this: Just as the sensation *red* is present when we are looking at a red object, so a specific mental process, the reading process (MRP), is present in the mind when we are reading. The MRP is the object of our analysis of reading, its presence makes our overt behavior a manifestation of reading (etc., as already indicated in $T4$). In short, it is thought that this mental process will enable us to solve problems which we could not solve when considering material processes only: "When our language suggests a body and there is none; there, we should like to say, is a *spirit*" (36). But it will turn out that mental processes are subject to the same kind of criticism as material processes: that neither a material nor a spiritual mechanism enables us to explain how it is that words are meaningful and that their meanings can be known; that in pointing to mental processes we cling to the same scheme of explanation as in the physiological or the behavioristic theory of meaning (considered in the two last sections) without realizing that we are doing so.[4] That can be shown by very simple means: Consider the case of a person who does not look at any printed paper, who is walking up and down, looking out of the window, and behaving as if he were expecting somebody to come; but the MRP is going on in his mind (in his consciousness). Should we take the presence of this mental process as a sufficient criterion for the person's reading, adding, perhaps, that we had discovered a hitherto unknown case of reading? It is clear that we should alter, rather, some psychological hypotheses (the hypothesis that reading is always correlated with the MRP). But the last argument is a simple transformation of the first argument of section (B) with 'MRP' (the mental process which is supposed to be the essence of reading) substituted for 'RP' (the physiological process, which was supposed to be the essence of reading in section B). By this substitution the second argument can be used for the present purpose as well.

†(a) Let us now turn to a more detailed investigation of the matter. Let us first ask whether really *every act of reading is accompanied by the MRP*. A few minutes ago I was reading the newspaper. Do I remember any particular mental process which was present all the time I was reading? I remember that I was expecting a friend (actually I looked at my watch several times) and that I was angry because he did not

---

[4] This point is elaborated in some detail in G. Ryle's *Concept of Mind* (London, 1949), which should not, however, be taken to agree completely with Wittgenstein's ideas.

DISCUSSION

come, although he had promised to do so. I also remember having thought of an excellent performance of *Don Giovanni* which I had seen a few days ago and which had impressed me very much. Then I found a funny misprint and was amused. I also considered whether the milk which I had put on the fire was already boiling, etc. Nevertheless, I was *reading* all the time, and it is quite certain that I was (cf. 171).[†] "But now notice this: While I am [reading] everything is quite simple. I notice nothing *special*; but afterward, when I ask myself what it was that happened, it seems to have been something indescribable. *Afterward* no description satisfies me. It is as if I couldn't believe that I merely looked, made such and such a face and uttered words. But don't I *remember* anything else? No" (cf. 175; "being guided" instead of 'reading'). [†]The same applies to activities such as calculating, drawing a picture, copying a blueprint, etc. I *know* of course that I was reading, but that shows only that my knowledge is not based on the memory of a certain sensation, impression, or the like—because there was no such impression.[†] Compare now another example: Look at the mark ∽ and let a sound occur to you as you do so; utter it—let us assume it is the sound 'u.' [†]Now read the sentence 'Diana is a beautiful girl.' Was it in a different way that the perception of the 'eau' (in 'beautiful') led to the utterance of the sound 'u' in the second case? Of course there was a difference! For I *read* the second sentence whereas I did not read when I uttered the 'u' in the presence of the ∽. But is this difference a difference of mental content, i.e., am I able to discover a specific sensation, impression, or the like which was present in the second case, and missing in the first case, whose presence made the second case a case of *reading*?[†] Of course, there were many differences: In the first case "I had told myself beforehand that I was to let a sound occur to me; there was a certain tension present before the sound came. And I did not say 'u' automatically as I do when I look at the letter U. Further that mark [the ∽] was not *familiar* to me in the way the letters of the alphabet are. I looked at it rather intently and with a certain interest in its shape" (166). But imagine now a person who has the feeling described above in the presence of a normal English text, composed of ordinary letters. Being invited to read, he thinks that he is supposed to utter sounds just as they occur to him— one sound for each letter—and he nevertheless utters all the sounds a normal person would utter when reading the text. "Should we say in such a case that he was not really reading the passage? Should we here allow his sensations to count as the criterion for his reading or not reading?" (160). From the negative answer to this question we have

455

THE PHILOSOPHICAL REVIEW

to conclude that, even if we were able to discover a difference between the way in which the perception of the ∽ leads to the utterance of the sound 'u' and the way in which, e.g., the perception of the 'eau' within 'beautiful' leads to the utterance of the 'u,' this difference—if it is a difference of mental content, of behavior, etc.—cannot be interpreted as justifying the assumption of an essential difference between cases of reading and not reading.[5]

(b) It may be objected to this analysis that the MRP is sometimes present quite distinctly. "Read a page of print and you can see that something special is going on, something highly characteristic" (165). This is true especially where "we make a point of reading slowly—perhaps in order to see what does happen if we read" (170). Thus one could be inclined to say that the MRP is a subconscious process which accompanies *every* case of reading but which can be brought to light only by a special effort.[6]

Answer: (1) Reading with the intention of finding out what happens when we are reading is a special case of reading and as such different from ordinary reading (cf. 170). Nevertheless reading without this intention is also a case of reading, which shows that the reason for calling it a case of *reading* cannot be the presence of a sensation which

---

[5] There are cases of mental disease where the patient talks correctly although with the feeling that somebody is making up the words for him. This is rightly regarded as a case of mental disease and not, as the adherents of the mental-picture theory of meaning would be inclined to say, as a case of inspiration : For one judges from the fact that the person in question *talks correctly*, although with queer sensations. Following Locke, a distinction is usually made between impressions of sensation and impressions of reflection. When Wittgenstein talks of sensations, of feelings, of a "picture in the mind" he seems to mean both. So his investigations are directed against a primitive psychologism (concepts are combinations of impressions of sensation) as well as against a more advanced psychologism (concepts are combinations of impressions of reflection). They are also directed against a presentational realism (concepts are objects of a certain kind, but *having* a concept, or *using* a concept is the same as having an idea in one's mind —i.e., although concepts are not psychological events, their representations in people are), against a theory which Wittgenstein elsewhere described as implying that "logic is the physics of the intellectual realm."

[6] A psychologist or an adherent of the phenomenological method in psychology would be inclined to judge the situation in this way. His intention would to be create a kind of "pure situation" in which a special process comes out quite distinctly. It is then supposed that this process is hidden in every ordinary situation (which is not pure, but) which resembles the pure situation to a certain extent. In the case of reading the pure situation would be: reading plus introspecting in order to find out what is going on. The ordinary situation is: simply reading.

DISCUSSION

—admittedly—is present only in special cases and not in the case discussed. Finally, the description of the MRP cannot be a description of reading in general, for the ordinary case is omitted. We should not be misled by the picture which suggests "that this phenomenon comes in sight 'on close inspection.' If I am supposed to describe how an object looks from far off, I don't make the description more accurate by saying what can be noticed about the object on closer inspection" (171).

†(2) Not every kind of introspection is judged in the same way. It is possible that a person who is supposed to find the MRP by introspection, being tired, should experience and describe quite unusual things while thinking all the time that the task which was set him by the psychologist is being performed by giving these descriptions.[7] No psychologist will welcome such a result. Instead of thinking that new and illuminating facts about reading have been discovered, he will doubt the reliability of the guinea pig. From this we have to conclude once more that the sensations experienced in connection with reading, and even those experienced as the essence of reading by the readers themselves, have nothing whatever to do with the question what reading really is.

†(3) Let us now assume that a reliable observer whom we ask to read attentively and to tell us what happens while he is reading provides us with the following report: 'The utterance is *connected* with seeing the signs, it is as if I were *guided* by the perception of the letters, etc.' (cf. 169, 170, 171). Does he, when answering our question in this way, describe a mental content, as a person who is seeing red and who tells us that he is seeing red describes a mental content? Does he say 'I am being guided by the letters' because the mental content *being guided* is present? Then one would have to conclude that every case of being guided is accompanied by *being guided*, as we assumed at the beginning of section (C) that every case of reading is accompanied by the MRP. But this last assumption has already been refuted, and the other, being completely analogous to it, can be refuted by the same arguments. We have to conclude, therefore, that the possibility of describing the process of reading as a case of being guided does not imply that reading is a mental process, because being guided is not one (cf. 172).[8]

---

[7] An illustrative example for experiences of this kind may be found in B. Russell, *History of Western Philosophy* (New York, 1945), p. 145.

[8] The idea that reading is a single object (in spite of the variety of manifestations demonstrated in Sec. A) is apparently supported by the fact that

THE PHILOSOPHICAL REVIEW

†(c) As already indicated, people usually try to escape from argument (C a) by assuming that the MRP is a subconscious sensation which has to be brought to light by introspection. A different form of the same escape is the following one: The arguments that have been brought forward so far assume that reading and the MRP can be separated from one another. This, however, is not the case : Reading is inseparably connected with the MRP. What occurs separably from reading is not the MRP, but only an erroneous interpretation of something as reading. But how are we to decide whether the MRP itself is present or only something else erroneously interpreted as reading; or, what comes to the same thing, how are we to decide whether we are reading or only believing that we are reading? The given content of consciousness cannot be used for deciding that question, for it is *its* reliability which is to be ascertained. The only possible alternative is to call a sensation a case of the MRP if and only if it is accompanied by reading. But now we assume, contrary to our previous assumption, that we do possess a criterion for reading other than a sensation.

†Another argument against the assumption of a hidden mental content, which may be brought to daylight by introspection or some other mental act, consists in developing the paradoxical consequences of such a view: "How can the process of [reading] have been hidden when I said 'now I am [reading]' *because* I was [reading]?! And if I say it is hidden—then how do I know what I have to look for?" (153; "understanding" replaced by "reading.")[9]

---

one can give a definition like the one we gave at the beginning of Sec. IV, or that one can say that reading is a form of being guided. But let us not be misled by words. For the definition of reading in terms of being guided or the like supports the idea that reading is a single object only if being guided can itself be shown to be a single object. But an analysis similar to the one sketched in Sec. A will show that this is not the case.

One of the main reasons for the wide acceptance of the assumption that it is possible to discover the essence of reading by introspection is the fact that the great number of manifestations of reading is usually not taken into account. Beset by theory T we *think* (173, 66) that acute observation must disclose the essence and that what we find in acute observation is hidden in the ordinary case of reading ($T4$). But our knowledge of the ordinary case is much too sketchy to justify that assumption "A main cause of philosophical disease—a one-sided diet: one nourishes one's thinking with only one kind of example" (593).

[9] The same criticism applies to the method of the phenomenologists. How do they know which phenomenon is the 'right' one? They proceed from the assumption that the essence is not open to general inspection but must be

DISCUSSION

†(d) So far we have shown (by a kind of empirical investigation into the use of the word "reading") that there is not a mental content which is *always* present when a person is reading, and that therefore giving the criterion for a person's reading cannot consist in pointing out a particular mental content. Now we shall show that even if there were a mental content which is present if and only if a person is reading, we could not take this content to be the essence of reading. Let us assume that a mental content is the essence of reading and that a person is reading if and only if this content, namely the MRP, is present. We shall now show that the process characterized by the presence of the MRP cannot be reading.† First of all: If reading is a particular experience "then it becomes quite unimportant whether or not you read according to some generally recognized alphabetical rule" (165). One is reading if and only if he is experiencing the MRP; nothing else is of any importance. That implies, however, that no distinction can be drawn between reading and believing that one is reading (cf. 202), or, to put it in another way, that anybody who believes that he is reading is entitled to infer that he *is* reading. The important task of a teacher would, therefore, consist in schooling the receptivity of his pupils (232), reading would be something like listening to inner voices in the presence of printed paper and acting in accordance with their advice (233). That different people who are reading the same text agree in the sounds they utter would be miraculous (233). †Our assumption that reading is a mental act leads, therefore, to the substitution of miracles for an everyday affair. It leads also to the substitution for a simple process (uttering sounds in the presence of printed paper) of a more complicated one (listening to inner voices in the presence of printed paper) i.e., it misses the aim of explaining the process of *reading*.†10

---

discovered by some kind of analysis which proceeds from an everyday appearance. In the course of this analysis several phenomena appear. How are we to know which one of them is the phenomenon that we were looking for? And if we know the answer to this question, why then is it necessary to analyze at all?

10 In presenting the idea to be criticized we assumed, as in $T4$, that the *MRP* is also the reason for our uttering the sounds we utter. The criticism developed in the text applies also to the idea that in calculating we are guided by intuitions (Descartes' theory): It is said that the perception of '2 + 2' is followed by a nonperceptual mental event which advises us how to behave in the sequel; it whispers, as it were, into our mind's ear, 'Say 4!' But the idea cannot explain why we calculate as we do. For instead of explaining the process of obeying a rule (the rule of the multiplication table) it describes the process of obeying

THE PHILOSOPHICAL REVIEW

(e) But does introducing inner voices really solve our problem—
namely, to explain why people read correctly and to justify our own
reading of a text in a certain way? Usually we simply read off the sound
from the letters. Now we want to be justified, and we think that a mental content might justify our procedure. But if we do not trust the
signs on the paper—then why should we trust the more ethereal
advice of intuition, or of the mental content which is supposed to be
the essence of reading? (232, 233.)

V

†What conclusions are to be drawn from this analysis? First of all:
It appears impossible to discover the essence of a thing in the way that
is usually supposed, i.e., $T4$ seems to be inapplicable. But if that is the
case, the correctness of the analysis can no longer be checked in the
usual way. There is no criterion for deciding whether a statement like
' "A" stands for a' or 'the sentence "p" designates the proposition that
p' is true or not; and there is no way to decide whether a certain sign
is meaningful, either. But usually we are not all troubled by such
questions. We talk and solve (mathematical, physical, economic)
problems without being troubled by the fact that there is apparently
no possibility of deciding whether or not we are acting reasonably,
whether or not we are talking sense. But isn't that rather paradoxical?
Isn't it rather paradoxical to assume that a sign which we constantly
use to convey, as we think, important information is really without
meaning, and that we have no possibility of discovering that fact?
And since its being meaningless apparently does not at all affect its
usefulness in discourse (e.g., for conveying information), doesn't that
show that the presuppositions of the paradox, in particular $T1, 2$, need
reconsideration?[11]

VI

†A great deal of the *Philosophical Investigations* is devoted to this
task.† The phenomena of language are first studied in primitive kinds

---

a kind of inspiration. In the case of an inspiration I *await* direction. But I do
not await inspiration when saying that $2 + 2$ are four (232).

[11] There is another presupposition as well, namely that in Sec. IV *all*
possibilities of experiencing the essence have been considered. Clearly, this
assumption cannot be proved. But one thing is certain: We considered all
possibilities of experiencing the essence which have so far been treated by
philosophers who follow theory T. Cf. H. Gomperz, *Weltanschauungslehre*, II,
140 ff., where medieval realism about concepts is criticized by arguments like
Wittgenstein's. Cf. also n. 23 below.

DISCUSSION

of application "in which one can command a clear view of the aim and functioning of words" (5; 130). The primitive, rudimentary languages which are investigated in the course of these studies are called "*language-games.*" Let us consider one such language-game: It is meant

to serve for communication between a builder A and an assistant B. A is building with building-stones: there are blocks, pillars, slabs and beams. B has to pass the stones, and that in the order in which A needs them. For this purpose they use a language consisting of the words "block," "pillar," "slab," "beam," A calls them out;—B brings the stone which he has learned to bring at such and such a call.—Conceive this as a complete primitive language [2].

Consider first of all how A prepares B for the purpose he is supposed to fulfill. "An important part of the training will consist in the teacher's pointing to the objects, directing the [assistant's] attention to them and at the same time uttering a word, for instance the word 'slab' as he points to that shape" (6; "child" replaced by 'assistant'). This procedure cannot be called an ostensive definition, because the assistant who at the beginning is supposed to be without any knowledge of any language cannot as yet *ask* what the name is (6); which shows that teaching a language can be looked at as "adjusting a mechanism to respond to a certain kind of influence" (497; cf. 5). Finally the assistant is able to play the game, he is able to carry out the orders given to him by the builder A. Let us now imagine that A teaches B more complicated orders—orders which contain color-names, number-words ('4 red slabs!') and even orders which contain what one would be inclined to call descriptions ('Give me the slab lying just in front of you!'), etc.

Now, what do the words of this language *signify?*—What is supposed to shew what they signify, if not the kind of use they have? And we have already described that. So we are asking for the expression "This word signifies *this*" to be made a part of the description. In other words the description ought to take the form "the word ... signifies ... ." ... But assimilating the descriptions of the uses of words in this way cannot make the uses themselves any more like one another. For, as we see, they are absolutely unlike [10].

†Compare, e.g., the way in which the word "four" is used with the way in which the word "slab" is used within the language-game in question. The difference in the uses of the two words comes out most clearly when we compare the procedures by means of which their respective uses are taught. A child who is to count correctly has first to learn the series of numerals by heart; he has then to learn how to apply this knowledge to the case of counting, e.g., the number of

461

THE PHILOSOPHICAL REVIEW

apples in a basket. In doing so, he has to say the series of cardinal
numbers, and for each number he has to take one apple out of the
basket (cf. 1). He has to be careful not to count one apple twice or
to miss an apple. The numeral which according to this procedure is
co-ordinated with the last apple is called 'the number of apples in the
basket.' This is how the use of numerals is taught and how numerals are
used in counting. Compare with this the use of a word like 'slab.' It
is taught by simple ostension: The word 'slab' is repeatedly uttered
in the presence of a slab. Finally the child is able to identify slabs
correctly within the language-game it has been taught. Nothing is
involved which has any similarity to the counting procedure which was
described above. The application of the word itself to a concrete object
is much simpler than the application of a number-word to a collection
whose cardinal number cannot be seen at a glance. This application
does not involve any complicated technique; a person who understands
the meaning of 'slab' is able to apply this word quite immediately.†

Let us now imagine that somebody, following T1, should argue in
this way: It is quite clear: 'slab' signifies slabs and '3' signifies 3 ...
every word in a language signifies something (cf. 3). According to
Wittgenstein, he has

so far said *nothing whatever;* unless [he has] explained exactly *what* distinction
[he] wish[es] to make. (It might be of course that [he] wanted to distinguish
the words of [our] language[-game] from words "without meaning" [13].

Imagine someone's saying: "*All* tools serve to modify something. Thus the
hammer modifies the position of the nail, the saw the shape of the board and
so on."—And what is modified by the rule, the glue-pot, the nails?—"Our
knowledge of the thing's length, the temperature of the glue and the solidity
of the board."—Would anything be gained by this assimilation of expressions?
[14].

VII

†Our example and its interpretation suggest an instrumentalist
theory of language.[12] The orders which A gives to B are instruments in

12 Or an intuitionist (pragmatist, constructivist) theory of language—the
expressions "intuitionist" or "pragmatist" being used in the way in which they
serve to describe one of the present tendencies as regards foundations of mathematics. I am inclined to say—and there is strong evidence in favor of this view—
that Wittgenstein's theory of language can be understood as a constructivist
theory of meaning, i.e., as constructivism applied not only to the meanings of
mathematical expressions but to meanings in general. Cf. Poincaré, *Derniers
pensées* (German edition), pp. 143 ff., and especially Paul Lorenzen, "Konstruk-
tive Begründung der Mathematik," *Math. Zs.*, Bd. LIII (1950), 162 ff. Cf. also
Philosophical Investigations, p. 220: "Let the *proof* teach you *what* was being
proved."

DISCUSSION

getting B to act in a certain way. Their meaning depends on how B is supposed to act in the situations in which they are uttered. It seems reasonable to extend this theory—which is a corollary to T', soon to be described—to language games which contain descriptive sentences as well. The meaning of a descriptive sentence would then consist in its role in certain situations; more generally, within a certain culture (cf. 199, 206, 241, 325, p. 226). Wittgenstein has drawn this consequence—which is another corollary of T':

What we call *"descriptions"* are instruments for particular uses. Think of a machine-drawing [which directs the production of the machine drawn in a certain way], a cross-section, an elevation with measurements, which an engineer has before him. Thinking of a description as a word-picture of facts has something misleading about it: one tends to think only of such pictures as hang on the walls: which seem simply to portray how a thing looks, what it is like. (These pictures are as it were idle) [291].

And quite generally: "Language is an instrument. Its concepts are instruments" (569). This idea has an important consequence. Instruments are described by referring to how they work. There are different kinds of instruments for different purposes. And there is nothing corresponding to the ethereal meanings which, according to T_1, are supposed to make meaningful the use of *all* instruments alike. "Let the use of words teach you their meaning" (p. 220) is to be substituted for T_4—and this now seems to be the new theory, T'. But in order to appreciate the full importance of T' we have first of all to consider the following objections, which seem to be inevitable. In talking, ordering, describing, we certainly use words and get other people to act in a certain way (to revise their plans which we show to be unreasonable, to obey our wishes, to follow a certain route which we point out to them on a map). But the description of the meanings of the elements of a language-game is not exhausted by pointing to the way in which we use those elements and the connection of this use with our actions and other people's. For in uttering the words and the sentences we *mean* something by them, we want to express our thoughts, our wishes, etc. (cf. 501). It is "our *meaning* it that gives sense to the sentence.... And 'meaning it' is something in the sphere of the mind" (358; cf. T_4). What we mean seems to be independent of the way we use our words and the way other people react to our utterances (cf. 205, and again T_4). Moreover, the meanings of our utterances, being hidden beneath the surface of the various ways in which we use their elements, can only be discovered by looking at the mental pictures, the presence of which indicates what we mean by them. A person who wants to understand has, therefore, to grasp this mental picture. "One would like to say: 'Telling brings it about that [somebody else] *knows* that I am in pain [for example]; it produces this mental phenomenon: everything else [in particular whether "he does something further with it as well"—e.g., looks for a physician in order to help me] is inessential to the telling' " (363). "Only in the act of understanding is it meant that we are to do *this*. The *order*—why, that is nothing but sounds, ink-marks" (431). Meaning and understanding are, therefore, mental processes.

†Apparently this idea makes it necessary to give an account of meaning which is independent of the description of the way in which signs are used within a certain language-game. Another great part of the *Philosophical Investigations* is devoted to showing that this is not the case. A careful analysis of the way we use phrases such as 'A intends to ...,' 'A means that ...,' 'A suddenly understands that ...,' shows that in trying to account for this use we are again thrown back on a description of the way we use certain elements of the language-game in which those expressions occur and the connection of this use with our actions and other people's.

VIII

†(A) The meaning we connect with a certain sign is a mental picture. We do not look into the mind of a person in order to find out what he is really saying. We take his utterances *at their face value*, e.g., we assume that, when saying 'I hate you' he is in a state of hating. "If I give anyone an order I feel it to be *quite enough* to give him signs. And I should never say: this is only words. Equally, when I have asked someone something and he gives me an answer (i.e., a sign) I am content—that was what I expected—and I don't raise the objection: but that's a mere answer"(503). On our present view, this attitude is easily shown to be superficial. For it might be that on looking into the speaker's soul (or mind) we discover something quite different, e.g., love in the person who said 'I hate you.'

†Now two questions arise about this procedure. First: Why trust the language of the mind (one wonders what kind of language this may be) when we do not trust the overt language, i.e., the sentence 'I hate you'? (cf., e.g., 74 and all the passages on the interpretation of rules: 197 ff.). For whatever appears to be found in the mind can be interpreted in various ways, once we have decided *not* to proceed as we usually do, i.e., not to take parts of a certain language-game which we are playing at their face-value. Secondly: Let us assume that

DISCUSSION

somebody who really loves a certain person tells her that he hates her.[13] Does this fact make 'I hate you' mean the same as 'I love you'? Or imagine a person, who abounds in slips of the tongue (or is at the moment rather occupied with a difficult problem and so not listening attentively), giving what we consider to be a wrong or an irrelevant answer. Doesn't that reaction of considering his answer as irrelevant show that what he says is thought to be meaningful independently of what he is thinking? For we don't say: 'He certainly gave the right answer; what he said was accompanied by the right thought-processes,' but rather 'He gave a quite irrelevant answer; maybe he didn't understand our question or expressed himself wrongly.' Or "suppose I said 'abcd' and meant: the weather is fine. For as I uttered the signs I had the experience normally had only by someone who had year-in year-out used 'a' in the sense of 'the,' 'b' in the sense of 'weather' and so on. Does 'abcd' now mean: the weather is fine?" (509; cf. 665). How does somebody else find out what I meant by 'abcd'? Of course I can explain to him that 'abcd' means 'the weather is fine'; and I can also indicate how the parts of the first string of signs are related to the parts (the words) of the second string. But it would be a mistake to assume that such an explanation reveals what 'abcd' really means. For from the few words which I intend to be an explanation one cannot yet judge whether an *explanation* has been given or not.

†Of course I *say* ' "abcd" means "the weather is fine" ' or 'By "abcd" I mean "the weather is fine," ' and I have the intention of giving an explanation. But now imagine someone's saying 'Mr. A and Mrs. B loved—I mean lived—together for a long time.'[14] In this case he does not want to give a definition or an explanation according to which 'love' is supposed to mean the same as 'live'; rather, he committed a slip of the tongue and wanted to correct himself. In certain cases this is clear enough. In other cases it follows, e.g., from the fact that 'love' is never again mentioned in connection with Mr. A and Mrs. B, etc. When, therefore, I say, 'By "abcd" I mean "the weather is fine," ' it is not yet certain what the case is, whether I intended to give an explanation, or was just awaking from a kind of trance, or whatever else might be the case. The way 'I mean' is to be interpreted follows from the context in which the whole sentence is uttered and from

---

[13] Psychoanalysis has made rather a misleading use of such cases. It has introduced a picture-language (so-called symbols) and interpreted it in such a way that it is not conceivable how the theory could possibly be refuted.

[14] In Freud's *Vorlesungen über Psychoanalyse* one will find plenty of examples of this kind.

what we find out about the further use of the sign 'abcd' (cf. 686). In order to find out whether 'abcd' really means 'the weather is fine' we have, therefore, to find out how 'abcd' is being used quite independently of any feelings on the part of the person who said 'abcd' and of any explanation given by him. Of course his explanation may be the starting point of a training in the use of a new language in which 'a,' 'b,' 'c,' 'd' really have the meanings indicated. But note now that "abcd" makes sense only within this language-game. I cannot mean 'the weather is fine' by 'abcd' before this language-game has been established. I myself could not possibly connect any sense with 'abcd' before the elements of this sign have become meaningful by being made elements of a certain language-game. And even the fact "that I had the experience normally had only by someone who had year-out year-in used 'a' in the sense of 'the,' 'b' in the sense of 'weather' and so on" (509) could not make them meaningful; I could not even *describe* this experience as I did just now, because such a description does not yet exist.

†We have to conclude that no mere mental effort of a person A can either make a string of signs mean something different from the meaning it has within a certain language-game of which it is part, played by the people who come into contact with A, or justify its being said that *he* means (intends) something different from everybody else who uses it. This seems rather paradoxical. But let us assume for a moment that two people

belonging to a tribe unacquainted with games should sit at a chess-board and go through the moves of a game of chess; and with the appropriate mental accompaniments. And if *we* were to see it we should say they were playing chess. But now imagine a game of chess translated according to certain rules into a series of actions which we do not ordinarily associate with a *game*—say into yells and stamping of feet. And now suppose those two people to yell and stamp instead of playing the form of chess that we are used to; and this in such a way that their procedure is translatable by suitable rules into a game of chess. Should we still be inclined to say they were playing a game? [200].

The decision of this question again depends on the situation. Imagine, e.g., that their yelling and stamping has an important role within a religious ceremony of the tribe. That any change of procedure is said to offend the gods and is treated accordingly (the offenders are killed). In this case neither the possibility of the translation nor the presence of the chess-feelings in the minds of the participants would turn this procedure into a game of chess (although it is also quite possible to imagine a tribe where people who lose games of chess are thought to

DISCUSSION

be hated by the gods and are killed. But in this case a difference will be made between games and religious procedures by the fact, e.g., that only priests are admitted to the latter, or that different expressions are used for describing them, which is missing in our case). On the contrary, the strange mental state of those who are troubled by chess-feelings would be an indication either of insanity (cf. n. 5 above) or of lack of religious feeling.

†Now we can turn round our whole argument and look at the people who are sitting at a chess board and moving the pieces. Are they really playing chess? We see now that the inspection of their minds does not help us: they might be queer people, thinking of chess when they are performing a religious ceremony. Their assertion that they are playing chess, even, is not necessarily helpful, for it might be that they heard the words from somebody else and misinterpreted them to mean sitting in front of the board and making arbitrary moves with the pawns. The fact that they are using a chess board does not help us either, for the board is not essential to the game. What, then, is essential? The fact that they are playing according to certain *rules*, that they follow the rules of the chess game. Applying this result to the meaning of sentences in general we arrive at the idea that "if anyone utters a sentence and *means* or *understands* it he is operating a calculus according to definite rules" (81). Thus in analyzing the concepts of meaning, understanding, thinking, etc., we finally arrived at the concept of *following a rule*. But before turning to that concept we have to get more insight into the concepts just mentioned, and especially into the concept of *intention*.†

(B) It is the "queer thing about *intention*, about the mental process, that the existence of a custom, of a technique, is not necessary to it. That, for example, it is imaginable that two people should play chess in a world in which otherwise no games existed; and even that they should begin a game of chess—and then be interrupted" (205). The underlying idea is the same, as in the case of meaning : just as we can attach meaning to a sign by just connecting its use with a certain image which we voluntarily produce, we can also intend to do something by producing a certain mental picture. But how, we have to ask, is it possible to find out whether or not A, who just announced his intention of playing chess, was really intending to do so? Surely chess is defined by its rules (cf. 205). Should we therefore conclude that the rules of chess were present in the mind of A when he uttered his intention? (205).

†Investigation similar to that of IV Ca above will show that not every act of intending to play chess is accompanied by a special mental

picture which is characteristic of the intention of playing chess. Of course, the intention to play chess is sometimes present quite distinctly (I have not played chess for a long time, I am a keen chess player, and *now* I want to play chess and won't stop looking until I have found a chess board and a suitable partner). But this is only a *special kind* of intending to play chess (cf. IV Cb above); therefore its characteristics cannot be the reason for calling other cases cases of intending to play chess—cases, e.g., in which these characteristics are completely absent. But if we assume, on the other hand, that A has a perfect copy of the rules of chess before his inner eye—must he necessarily follow the features of this copy in such a way that the result will be a game of chess? Is it not possible that he either interprets them in an unusual way, that in going over from the reading of his mental picture to the outer world (the chess board, his actions in front of the chess board), he automatically makes a kind of translation, so that finally he is not doing what one would be inclined to call 'playing chess' (cf. 73, 74, 86, 139, 237)? And should we still say that he is intending to play chess just because, somewhere in the chain of events which in the end lead to his actions, a copy of the rules of chess enters in? Of course, we could *interpret* this copy as we are used to do. But is *he* interpreting it in the same way? And even if he could tell us how he is interpreting it do we know how to take his explanation? We see that "interpretations *by themselves* do not determine meaning" (198). We have simply to wait. And if he really acts in such a way that he regards playing chess—as we understand it—as a fulfillment of his intention, then we may say that he intended to play chess. But if it turned out that he did not know how to play chess or that, apparently intending to play chess, he sat down at the chess board and made irregular moves, we should under certain circumstances conclude that he had wrong ideas as to his intentions. Of course the phrase 'under certain circumstances' has to be inserted. For it is perfectly possible that A, intending to play chess, was introduced to a person he did not like and, with the intention of avoiding playing chess with him, acted as if he did not know the rules of chess or as if he had never intended to play chess. But what has to be criticized is the idea that such a difference might be found out by inspecting his mind (or soul) and by reading off his intention from his mental processes. It is his futher actions (talking included), as well as his personal history, which teach us how we are to take his first utterance— that he intended to play chess. But as it now turns out that our criteria for deciding whether a person, A, intends to play chess or not are "extended in time" (cf. 138), we have to conclude that intending to

DISCUSSION

play chess cannot be a mental event which occurs at a certain time. *Intending is not an experience* (cf. p. 217): it has "no experience-content. For the content (images for instance) which accompany and illustrate [it] are not the ... intending" (p. 217).

†(C) The same applies to understanding.† Let us examine the following kind of language-game (143 ff.): When A gives an order, B has to write down series of signs according to a certain formation-rule. The orders are of the kind "1, 2, 3, ...!" or "2, 4, 6, 8, ...!" or "2, 4, 9, 16, ...!" or "2, 6, 12, 20, 30, 42, ...!" etc. B is supposed to continue the series in a certain way, i.e., he is supposed to write down the series of numerals in the first case, the series of the even numerals in the second case, etc. First of all, A will teach B the rules of the language-game. He will then give orders to B, in order to check B's abilities. He will finally state that B has mastered the system, that he understands it. It should be clear that, when used in this way, 'understanding' cannot signify a mental phenomenon. For we also say that B understands (is master of) the language-game just explained when lying on his bed and sleeping (cf. 148). But the mental-act philosopher is ready with a new expression—he speaks of a *subconscious* mental phenomenon, i.e., he says that B, although dreaming perhaps of beautiful women, is nevertheless subconsciously thinking of the new language game and its rules.

The objections to this idea are obvious. Whether subconscious or not, the alleged thinking-process may or may not determine the actual behavior of B (cf. VIII B, above); i.e., B may not be able to carry out the orders of A although a clever psychologist has found out that the thinking-process which is supposed to accompany his ability to obey the orders is present. We shall not say in this case that B has mastered the game, that we have discovered a special case of mastering the game (cp. IV Cb2, above); we shall simply say that he had not mastered it although he or the psychologist thought he had. This objection being accepted, it might be said that

knowing the game is a state of the mind (perhaps of the brain) by means of which we explain the *manifestations* of that knowledge. Such a state is called a disposition. But there are objections to speaking of a state of the mind here, inasmuch as there ought to be two different criteria for such a state: a knowledge of the construction of the apparatus quite apart from what it does [149].

What the apparatus does is in our case the actual behavior of B when he receives certain orders.

But there is a second way in which the word 'understanding' is used. Understanding in this sense is not meant to be understanding of a game as a whole (understanding the rules of chess, i.e., knowing how to play chess) but understanding the meaning of a particular move within the game, e.g., understanding the order 2, 4, 6, ...! "Let us imagine the following example: A writes series of numbers down, B watches him and tries to find a law for the sequence of numbers. If he succeeds, he exclaims: 'Now I can go on!'—So this capacity, this understanding is something that makes its appearance in a moment" (151), and this suggests that 'understanding,' used in this way, might mean a mental event. But wait: *Do* we find any mental event which is common to all cases of understanding? Imagine that A gave the order 1, 5, 11, 19, 29, ...! to B and that, upon A's arriving at 19, B said, 'I understand.' What happened to B?

Various things may have happened; for example, while A was slowly putting one number after the other, B was occupied with trying various algebraic formulae on the numbers which had been written down. After A had written the number 19, B tried the formula $a_n = n^2 + n - 1$; and the next number confirmed his hypothesis. Or again—B does not think of formulae. He watches A writing his numbers down with a certain feeling of tension and all sorts of vague thoughts go through his head. Finally he asks himself: "What is the series of differences?" He finds the series, 4, 6, 8, 10 and says: Now I can go on.—Or he watches and says "Yes, I know *that* series"—and continues it, just as he could have done if A had written down the series 1, 3, 5, 7, 9.—Or he says nothing at all and simply continues the series. Perhaps he had what may be called the feeling "that's easy!" [151].

We can also imagine the case where nothing at all occurred in B's mind except that he suddenly said "Now I know how to go on"—perhaps with a feeling of relief [179].

But are the processes which I have described here *understanding*? [152].

Is it not possible that a person who has the feelings just described is not able to write down the series as it was meant by A? Should we not be inclined to say that he did not really understand? "The application is still a criterion of understanding" (146). It would, therefore, be quite misleading "to call the words ['Now I can go on'] a 'description of a mental state.'—One might rather call them a 'signal'; and we judge whether it was rightly employed by what he [i.e., B] goes on to do" (180).

†Now let us use this example to discuss intention and meaning as well. What if B, in carrying out the order 2, 4, 6, 8, ...! wrote 1000, 1004, 1008, 1012, etc. (cf. 185)? Of course A will say: 'Don't you see? You ought to write 2, 4, 6, 8, ...!' And if that does not lead to a change in the behavior of B, he will tell him : "What I meant was that [you] should write the next but one number after every number

DISCUSSION

[you] wrote; and from this all those propositions follow in turn" (186). Now several conclusions may be drawn from this situation.† First of all one may be inclined to say that 2, 4, 6, 8, ...! was an incomplete order and that there was clearly a possibility of misunderstanding (cf. a similar argument in 19). For this order reveals so to speak, only an external character of the series to be written down, namely the character that its first members are '2,' '4,' '6,' etc. And the training of B, too, taught him only an external character of all the series, namely, that they began in a certain way. B has therefore to *guess* how to continue, and of course he may hit upon the wrong guess. But the order "take the next but one!" seems to be of a different character. It contains so to speak the whole of the series in a nutshell. Understanding *this* order implies knowing the law of development for the whole series. But let us now investigate how the understanding of this order may be taught. Of course, A has to write down the series 2, 4, 6, 8, ... and has to explain to B what 'next but one' means. He does so by comparing this series with 1, 2, 3, 4, ... and by showing that '4' is the 'next but one to 2,' etc. The explanation will therefore be similar to the explanation of 2, 4, 6, 8, ...! Why, then, should teaching the pupil how to take 'the next but one' remove any possibility of error? On the contrary! We could imagine that B has been taught how to use 2, 4, 6, 8, ...! but that he does not know, what 'the next but one' means. In this case the teacher would have to explain the 'next but one' by referring to 2, 4, 6, 8, ...! and not the other way round. The same applies to algebraic formulae. Consider a 'difficult' series such as 1, 3, 13, 21, 31, 43, ... It is not easily seen how this series might be continued. If we hear that its algebraic formula is $n^2 - n + 1$ we are able to write down the next members at once. But that only shows that we already knew how to apply the algebraic expression, but did not know how to apply 1, 3, 13, 21, 31, 43, ... if the continuation of this series is ordered. It does not show us an essential quality which, so to speak, contains the whole series in a nutshell. For an onlooker who is unacquainted with the formula as well as with the series will have to learn how to apply the formula in developing series. And the methods of teaching this ability will be similar to the methods of teaching 2, 4, 6, 8, ...! (cf. 146).

Let us return now to intention. The existence of algebraic formulae for the description of series is misleading in one way: A cannot write down the whole series in order to make himself understood to B. But he can use an algebraic formula or a simple expression, such as 'take the next but one.' He can write down the formula within a few seconds

THE PHILOSOPHICAL REVIEW

and one is therefore inclined to assume that meaning the series 1, 2, 3, 4, ... *ad infinitum* can be a mental act which occurs within a few seconds.

Here I should first of all like to say: Your idea was that that act of meaning the order had in its own way already traversed all those steps; that when you meant it your mind as it were flew ahead and completed all the steps before you physically arrived at this or that one.—Thus you were inclined to use such expressions as: The steps are *really* already taken, even before I take them in writing or orally or in thought[15] [188].

They "are determined by the algebraic formula" (189). But how? Surely thinking of the formula cannot help us (cf. 146), for one and the same formula may be used for different purposes (think of the different use which is made of the formula $a + b = b + a$ in different parts of mathematics: in class-theory it means the commutativity of class-disjunction; in algebra it is used for expressing the commutativity of algebraic addition; in number theory it is used for expressing a general property of numbers; in lattice-theory it has still another meaning and likewise in group-theory, etc.) The imagining of the formula (if it ever does occur) must be connected with a certain application of the formula in order to provide us with the knowledge of its meaning and with the knowledge of the speaker's intention in using it. And as it is always possible to apply a formula in many different ways we have to observe how it is applied in a particular case, by a particular mathematician, in order to determine his way of using the formula and thus *what he means* when he utters the formula. But the use of a formula is "extended in time" (138). And therefore, since following up this use is one of the criteria we employ to find out what is meant by A when he writes down a certain formula, we cannot say that meaning something is a mental event. "It may now be said: 'The way the formula is meant determines which steps are to be taken.' What is the criterion for the way the formula is meant? It is for example, the kind of way we always use it, the way we are taught to use it" (190).[16]

---

[15] Here is the core of Wittgenstein's criticism of the so-called Cantorian (cf. Poincaré *loc. cit.*) interpretation of mathematics. This criticism (it is developed in detail in his mathematical writings, which are still unpublished—in the *Philosophical Investigations* there are only a few passages, cf. 352) is another corollary of *T'*.

[16] Cf. also 693: " 'When I teach someone the formation of the series ... I surely mean him to write ... at the hundredth place.'—Quite right; you mean it. And evidently without necessarily even thinking of it. This shews you how different the grammar of the verb 'to mean' is from that of 'to think.' And nothing is more wrong-headed than calling meaning a mental activity!"

DISCUSSION

(D) Another criticism of the idea that meaning is a mental activity derives from the fact that sometimes it is calculation that decides the question whether a sentence is meaningful or not. Consider the sentence " 'I have n friends and $n^2 + 2n + 2 = 0$.' Does this sentence make sense?" (513). Assuming that a sentence is made meaningful by connecting its utterance with a certain mental content, we should conclude that there is no difficulty; we have only to look for the mental picture behind it, and that will teach us how to judge. But that is not the case, we are even inclined to say that we do not yet know whether anybody will be able to connect any meaning with the sentence, i.e., according to the theory we are discussing at present, whether anybody is justified in connecting an image with the utterance of this sentence. We have first to find out whether the sentence conforms to certain general rules (the number of friends can neither be negative nor imaginary) and we do so by calculating. We also cannot say at once whether we understand or not; we have first to find out whether there is anything to be understood; i.e., whether we understand or not can again be found out by a process of calculation only. One has, therefore, to realize that "we *calculate*, operate with words and in the course of time turn them sometimes into one picture, sometimes into another" (449).

(E) Result: Meaning, understanding, intending, thinking (and, as we may add—remembering, loving, hoping[17]) are *not mental activities*. The criteria by which we decide whether or not A is thinking of ..., intending to do ..., meaning ..., etc., do not relate only to the moment of the intention, the thought, the understanding. We cannot say "A intended ... because" and point to a process which accompanies his utterances or his (apparently intentional) behavior. "For no *process* could have the consequences of [intending]" (cf. p. 218).

IX

[†]The last section was devoted to the discussion of a possible objection against an instrumentalist theory of language, as it seems to be sugges-

---

[17] "What is a *deep* feeling? Could someone have the feeling of ardent love or hope for the space of one second—*no matter what* preceded or followed this second? What is happening now has significance—in these surroundings. The surroundings [the history of the event included—cf. the words "what preceded"] give it its importance" (583; cf. 572, 584, 591, 614 ff., esp. 638: "If someone says 'For a moment ...' is he really only describing a momentary process?—But not even the whole story was my evidence for saying 'For a moment....' ").

ted by Wittgenstein (cf. Sec. VII). The objection was founded on the idea that words are meaningful because we *mean* something when uttering them, and that quite independently of the way in which those words are used. But it turned out that in deciding whether somebody is really meaning something when uttering a sentence we are thrown back on observation of the way he uses certain elements of speech and that, therefore, an account of meaning can and must be given within the instrumentalist interpretation of language. Meaning is not something that needs consideration *apart* from the description of the way certain expressions are used by the speaker or by other people with whom he is trying to communicate. At the same time a tendency was discovered, namely the tendency "to hypostatize feelings where there are none" (598).[18] No objection to the instrumentalist interpretation seems to be left, but one : When playing a language-game we certainly obey certain *rules*. Thus the idea is suggested "that if anyone utters a sentence and *means* or *understands* it, he is operating a calculus according to definite rules" (81), and the rules seem to be something which *directs* the activities within a language-game, which therefore cannot be described in terms which are useful for describing the working of the language-game itself. It is this idea which we have to treat last. The discussion of this idea in the *Philosophical Investigations* is interwoven with the discussion of the other ideas treated in the book because there are arguments which apply to several ideas at once.†

Assuming that in talking, calculating, etc., we are acting in accordance with certain rules leads at once to the following question: "How am I able to obey a rule?" (217). For, on the one hand, it seems to be the case that "the rule, once stamped with a particular meaning, traces the lines along which it is to be followed through the whole of space ... all the steps are already taken" (219). But "if something of that sort really were the case, how would it help?" (219). For is there not always the possibility of interpreting the rule in a different way? And how are we to know which interpretation is the right one? Once the rule is separated from our activity it seems impossible that it can determine this activity any more. For it may try to make itself known to us by mental events ('grasping' the rule), by a book which contains all rules of the language-game to be played, etc. In any one of those cases we can proceed in many different ways depending on how we interpret, i.e., how we use, the mental picture, the book, etc., in the course of our

---

[18] Cf. 295: "When we look into ourselves as we do philosophy, we often get to see just a picture. A full-blown pictorial representation of our grammar. Not facts; but as it were illustrated turns of speech."

DISCUSSION

further activities (cf. 73, 74, 86, 139, 237). Thus it seems that "any course of action [can] be determined by a rule because every course of action [can] be made out to accord with the rule" (201; "could" replaced by 'can').

But "What this shows is that there is a way of grasping a rule which is *not* an *interpretation*, but which is exhibited in what we call 'obeying the rule' and 'going against it' in actual cases" (201). That will become clear from the following example (cf. 454): "A rule stands there like a sign-post. Does the sign-post leave no doubt open about the way I have to go? Does it show which direction I am to take when I have passed it?" (85). How do I know which direction I have to go? "If that means 'have I reasons?' the answer is: My reasons will soon give out. And then I shall act, without reasons" (211). "When someone whom I am afraid of orders me [to follow the sign-post], I act quickly, with perfect certainty, and the lack of reasons does not trouble me" (212, with "to continue the series" replaced by 'to follow the sign-post'). "When I obey a rule, I do not choose. I obey the rule *blindly*" (219). Let us now assume a land where everybody, on seeing a signpost: →, follows it in this direction: ←, where children are advised to follow the sign-post in the way indicated, where foreigners who are in the habit of going → when they see a signpost like this: → are taught that they are acting wrongly, that '→' means 'go ←.' Should we say that the inhabitants of our imaginary country are misinterpreting the signpost? Obviously this would not be the right description of the situation, for without being related to human activities (language-games included) the signpost is a mere piece of matter and the question as to its *meaning* (and therefore the question as to whether a certain interpretation is the right one) does not arise at all.

Now it is using the signpost in a certain way, i.e., behaving in a certain way in the presence of the signpost, that gives a meaning to it and that separates it from the other parts of nature which are meaningless in the sense that they are not parts of human language-games. But *behaving in this way* is also called *obeying the rules*. "And hence also 'obeying a rule' is a practice. And to *think* one is obeying a rule is not to obey a rule. Hence it is not possible to obey a rule 'privately' : Otherwise thinking one was obeying a rule would be the same thing as obeying it" (202).

Apply this to language-games in general. It follows, that "to obey a rule, to make a report, to give an order, to play a game of chess, are *customs* (uses, institutions)" (199) and "not a hocus-pocus which can be performed only by the soul" (454). "To understand a sentence

475

means to understand a language. To understand a language means to master a technique" (199). And so we are back at the instrumental interpretation of language: "Every sign *by itself* seems dead. *What* gives it life?—In *use* it is *alive*. Is life breathed into it then?—Or is the *use* its life?" (432). And questions of meaning, of understanding, of following a rule are to be treated by taking into account the *use* of signs within a certain language-game.

X

†Thus we arrive at the following result. According to *T* meanings are objects for which words stand. Rules are of a similar ethereal character. Understanding the meanings, grasping the rules, is an activity of the mind, which is the organ for finding our way about in the realm of meaning as the senses are organs for finding our way about in the physical world. We found that either there is no representation of the meanings or the rules in the mind or, assuming that a representation does exist, that it cannot determine the way in which we proceed because there are always many possibilities of interpretation. According to *T'* the meaning of the elements of a language-game emerges from their *use* and that use belongs to a quite different category from a single mental event or a mental process, or any process whatever (cf. p. 196).

†Now a sign can be part of different language-games just as a button can be used in a game of chess (instead of a pawn, e.g., which has been lost) or a game of draughts. Do we try in this case to abstract from the differences between these two kinds of use in order to discover a common quality which will explain to us how it is possible for the button to function both as a pawn and as a piece in draughts? The question does not arise because it seems obvious that the button *changes* its function according to the game within which it is used. But in the case of a language-game, theory *T* seduces us into thinking that the sign '2,' e.g., is in any case of its use within language connected with a single element, its meaning, and that the varieties of its use

('Give me *two* apples!'—as said in a grocery; $\int_0^2 x^3 dx = 4$; 'Two hours

ago I met him in the street'; 'The number of solutions of the equation $x^2 + 5x + 4 = 0$ is *two*') are only a superficial aspect. Once this idea has been dropped, once it has been realized that the meaning of a sign is constituted by its use within a certain language-game, words can be looked at as the button was above. And instead of trying to grasp the *essence* of a thing which is to explain the varieties of the

DISCUSSION

use of the sign which stands for the thing we ought simply to describe the language-game of which the sign is part. "We must do away with all *explanation*, and description alone must take its place" (109). "Our mistake is to look for an explanation where we ought to look at what happened as a 'proto-phenomenon.' That is where we ought to have said: *This language-game is played*" (654). "Look at the language-game as the *primary* thing. And look on the feelings, etc., as you look on a way of regarding the language-game, as interpretation" (656).[19]

†Wittgenstein's position has not yet been described correctly. Wittgenstein was said to hold a theory, T', which emphasizes the instrumental aspect of language and which points to use in a language-game as the essential thing. And describing the language-game, so one is inclined to say, according to the presentation which has been given so far, is the task of philosophy. From that description quite a few philosophical problems will become clear which seemed hopelessly muddled when seen from the point of view of theory T. Philosophy, then, seems to be the theory of language-games (a kind of general syntax or semantics in Carnap's sense) and T' seems to be its most important part. But according to Wittgenstein this assumption would involve a misunderstanding. For the supposed theory of language-games could do no more than enable people to run through the single moves of a game, as a player who is acquainted with the game runs through its moves. But for such a player there is no problem. If he asks, e.g., " 'How do sentences manage to represent?'—the answer must be: 'Don't you know? You certainly see it, when you use them.' For nothing is concealed" (435). Everything "lies open to view" (92; 126). "Philosophy" therefore "may in no way interfere with the actual use of language; it can in the end only describe it ... it leaves everything as it is" (124).

†Let us assume that somebody begins to construct a theory of Language-games. This theory, if formulated in the terms of T', will be thought to serve as an explanation of how meaning is conferred upon single signs by the way in which these signs are incorporated into a language-game. The theory (or description, as it may also be called) will involve a new kind of use of terms such as 'sentence,' 'fact,' 'meaning.' But has a useful explanation or description really been found? We must realize that the supposed theory introduces a *new* use of

---

[19] Note that the idea of an ideal language becomes obsolete as soon as it has been recognized that all language-games are on a par. Vague concepts, e.g. (cf. 71), cannot be regarded as inadmissible any longer. They have a definite function, and that is all we can demand from them.

THE PHILOSOPHICAL REVIEW

'meaning,' 'fact,' 'sentence,' etc. If this use involves even a slight deviation from the use of these words within the language-games to be described (explained) the supposed description in fact involves a change in the phenomenon to be described. But if on the other hand the change is a considerable one (and that is to be expected if one is trying to develop a fully-fledged instrumentalist philosophy of meaning) a new language-game for the expression 'sentence,' 'meaning,' etc., has been established and the task of describing the given language-game is not fulfilled either. Thus "we must do away with all *explanation*" and with *T'* as well. The description, however, which Wittgenstein invites us to give instead of the explanation, consists only in "putting the things before us" (126), and as "everything lies open to view, there is nothing to explain" (126). We might therefore say, rather hyperbolically, that the "language disguises thoughts" of the *Tractatus* (4.002) is now replaced by "language is already thought, nothing is concealed."

†But the situation is not quite as simple as that. For there *are* philosophical systems, philosophical theories; and it needs to be explained how it is that they come into existence if "nothing is concealed."

†In describing how philosophical theories come into being, Wittgenstein refers to the fact that "we *do not command a clear view* of the use of our words" (122). Given the answer that nothing is concealed, "one would like to retort: 'Yes, but it all goes by so quick, and I should like to see it as it were laid open to view" (435). On the other hand, "we remain unconscious of the prodigious diversity of all the everyday language-games because the clothing of our language makes everything alike" (p. 224). "What confuses us is the uniform appearance of words when we hear them spoken or meet them in script and print. For their *application* is not presented to us so clearly" (11). Take the following example: The sentences 'Washington is a city' and 'Two is an even number' are of a similar structure. This suggests that just as in the first case 'Washington' is the name of a real thing, 'two' is the name of a more abstract object, notwithstanding the fact that the uses of the two signs are "absolutely unlike" (10).

In the use of words one might distinguish "surface-grammar" from "depth-grammar." What immediately impresses itself upon us about the use of a word is the way it is used in the construction of the sentence, the part of its use—one might say—that can be taken in by the ear. And now compare the depth-grammar, say of the word "to mean," with what the surface-grammar would lead us to suspect. No wonder that we find it difficult to know our way about [661].

This difficulty is the reason why we resort to philosophical theories.

DISCUSSION

Why we invent theories of meaning. And why we try to conceive an ideal form behind the complexities of our language-games.

†But it is clear "that every sentence in our language 'is in order, as it is.' That is to say, we are not *striving after* an ideal, as if our ordinary vague sentences had not yet got a quite unexceptionable sense ... there must be perfect order even in the vaguest sentence" (98). It should also be clear that the "philosophy of logic speaks of sentences and words in exactly the same sense in which we speak of them in ordinary life, when we say, e.g., 'Here is a Chinese sentence' or 'No, that only looks like writing; it is actually just an ornament' and so on" (108). Thus the proper task of philosophy will be to unmask philosophical theories, to "bring words back from their metaphysical to their everyday use" (116), to destroy the "houses of cards" and to clear up "the ground of language on which they stand." (113). And philosophy becomes a "battle against the bewitchment of our intelligence by means of language" (109). This battle is carried through by "assembling reminders for a particular purpose" (127)—for the purpose of "seeing connexions" (122); and "different therapies" (133), not "*a* philosophical method" (133), are used in order to finish it victoriously.

†But in these therapies the statement of T' (or rather of the several corollaries of T' which have been mentioned so far) plays the most important part. So far we have interpreted the statement of T' as the exposition of a new (instrumentalist, nominalist, or whatever you like to call it) *theory of meaning*. This interpretation is not unreasonable in itself and taken as such it is a very interesting contribution to traditional philosophy (actually I think that everything that is interesting in the book attaches to the treatment of T' in this way). But this interpretation would go against the way in which his book is meant to be used by Wittgenstein. That may be seen from the following considerations: In Section IV the idea was criticized that reading is a mental process. If we stick to T' and interpret it as a theory we cannot understand why the discussion in Section IV should be a *criticism*. For we could argue in the following way: Wittgenstein says that the meaning of a word becomes clear from the way in which it is used within a specific language-game. Let us, therefore, look at the language-game which contains both of the expressions 'reading' and 'mental process,' and in which the sentence occurs 'Reading is a mental process.' Wittgenstein's presentation—so one would be inclined to say—is a description of certain features of this language-game and includes, of course, the remark that 'mental process' as used *in this language-game* has nothing whatever to do with toothaches.

479

†But that is not the right account of what Wittgenstein does. Wittgenstein does criticize—but his criticism is of a particular kind. It is not the kind of criticism which is directed, e.g., against a wrong mathematical calculation. In the latter case the result of the criticism is that a certain sentence is replaced by its negation or by a different sentence. But Wittgenstein does not want his reader to discover that reading is *not* a mental process. For if 'mental process' is used in a metaphysical way in 'reading is a mental process,' it is used just as metaphysically in "reading is not a mental process" (cf. 116). For him "the results of philosophy are the uncovering of one or another piece of plain nonsense and of bumps that the understanding has got by running its head against the limits of language" (119), and his aim is "to teach you to pass from a piece of disguised nonsense to something that is patent nonsense" (464) and in this way to clear up "the ground of language" (119). But that can only mean that "the philosophical problems should *completely* disappear" (133); for if the aim has been reached, "everything lies open to view and there is nothing to explain" (126). This implies that the formulation of T' as used within the critical procedure cannot be interpreted as a new theory of meaning, for it is applied with the intention of making the language-games (e.g., that with 'reading') "lie open to view," i.e., lead to a situation where language-games are simply played, without any question arising as to how it is that words become meaningful as part of a certain language-game, etc. That being so, the formulation of T' loses its function as soon as "*complete clarity*" has been arrived at. But without a function the signs which are part of the formulation of T' are without meaning. Thus one could say of the sentences which are part of T': These sentences "are elucidatory in this way: he who understands me finally recognizes them as senseless ... (He must so to speak, throw away the ladder, after he has climbed up on it.) He must surmount these [sentences] ...; then he sees the world rightly" (*Tractatus* 6.54). And seeing the world rightly means playing the language games without being troubled by philosophical *questions* or by philosophical *problems*.†

XI

*Note, now, that in the preceding section the idea of the essence has been reintroduced. In traditional philosophy the essence was hidden beneath the various ways of describing it. Now it is the "everyday use" (116) that "has to be accepted," "is given" (p. 226); but this

DISCUSSION

everyday use is likewise hidden, beneath the "houses of cards" of philosophical theories (118)[20], and it too has to be brought to light. Just so, traditional philosophers (i.e., the adherents of theory T) tried to bring to light the clear and sharp meanings which were hidden beneath the "muddied" use of the words which stand for them (426). If we assume, now, that in removing those philosophical coverings we finally arrive at "*complete* clarity" (133), we assume that there is a *sharp line* between the "houses of cards" on the one hand and the language-games on which they are built on the other. Now while Wittgenstein usually criticizes the idea that, e.g., "there *must* be something common [to games], or they would not be called 'games'" (66; cf. IV A above) and points to the fact that if we "look and see" (66) we find a "complicated network of similarities overlapping and criss-crossing" (66), he seems to assume, nonetheless, that at least philosophical difficulties have something in common, that there is a definite boundary between the card-houses of philosophy and the solid ground of everyday language, such that it becomes possible to "bring words back from their metaphysical use to their everyday use" (116).

*To Wittgenstein we can apply the comment (which he used to characterize the adherents of T) that "A *picture* held [him] captive" (115). For if it is the use, the practice, which constitutes meaning, if "what has to be accepted, the given, is ... *forms of life*" (p. 226), then one may ask why Wittgenstein tries to eliminate theory T, which certainly must be regarded as a form of life if we look at the way in which it is used by its adherents. Nevertheless Wittgenstein tries to eliminate this theory as well as other philosophical theories. But this attempt can only be justified by assuming that there is a difference between using a sign (playing a language-game) and proceeding according to theory T. The procedures which are connected with theory T are supposed not to be taken as parts of a language-game, they constitute a sham-game which is to be destroyed. How is this attitude to be understood?

*I think we can understand it by looking at the ideas which Wittgenstein has about philosophy (at his "*picture*" of philosophy as one might call it, using his own word). This picture is the picture of the *Tractatus*: "The word 'philosophy' must mean something which stands above or below, not beside the natural sciences" (*Tractatus* 4.111). In the *Investigations* we may replace "natural sciences" by "language-

---

[20] "Language disguises the thought" is the position of the *Tractatus* (4.002). One could say that according to the *Investigations*, the (philosophical) thought disguises language.

THE PHILOSOPHICAL REVIEW

games," and we arrive at: "Philosophy must be something which stands above or below, not beside the language-games"; philosophy *cannot* be a language-game itself; e.g., it cannot be theory *T'*. I submit that this idea is still present in the *Investigations* and that it makes it clear why Wittgenstein, having found that a sign can only be meaningful if it is incorporated into a language-game, cannot admit that there are philosophical theories.[21] This observation (as well as others which have not been mentioned[22]) suggests that the *Investigations* (apart from their substitution of language-games for the one language of the *Tractatus*) are after all not as different from the *Tractatus* as they seem to be at first sight. I am even inclined to say (without being able to substantiate this contention at the moment) that the *Investigations* basically contain an application of the main ideas of the *Tractatus* to several concrete problems, the only difference being the use of language-games instead of the language of the natural sciences which formed the theoretical background of the *Tractatus*.

*Trying to evaluate the book, we might say that the criticisms of *T* and the statement of *T'* which it contains, as well as the application of this theory to the discussion of concrete problems (remembering, obeying an order, the problem of sensation, etc.), are a great achievement, which, however, has its predecessors.[23] *Here we are within traditional philosophy*. But Wittgenstein wants us to see his criticisms in a different light. In the end we should forget them as well as *T*, we should forget philosophy entirely. Although the formulation of what can be regarded as a *theory* (theory *T'*) led us to the proper understanding of our difficulties, it must not be taken as the formulation of a *theory* but only as a proper means of getting rid of our philosophical troubles. *T'* has, therefore, to disappear together with those troubles. This new idea, which is Wittgenstein's own and which can be found in the *Tractatus* as well, is due, first, to the *picture* that philosophy must be

---

[21] There are some passages which seem to contradict this interpretation of Wittgenstein's views, e.g., "If one tried to advance *theses* in philosophy it would never be possible to question them, because everyone would agree to them" (128), according to which philosophical theses are not meaningless, but *trivial*.

[22] Cf. the similarity of "shows itself" in the *Tractatus* and "lies open to view" in the *Investigations*.

[23] Cf., e.g., H. Gomperz, *Weltanschauungslehre*, vol. II, where further references are given; E. Mach, *Erkenntnis u. Irrtum*, 3d ed., pp. 126 ff.; D'Alembert, *Traité de dynamique* (1743); the tenets of the various nominalistic schools, old and new, etc. Cf. also K. Popper's criticism of essentialism, developed as early as 1935.

DISCUSSION

something quite extraordinary and, second, to certain difficulties, already mentioned, which could be solved by taking into account the difference between object-language and meta-language (used by Tarski to get rid of similar difficulties, but never recognized by Wittgenstein [cf. 121]). Using this device we find that the philosophical language games do not necessarily disturb the language-games they are supposed to describe. We also find that philosophy is not necessarily on a level with the language-games it is about. On the contrary, the assumption that the philosophical language-games are on a level with the language-games they deal with leads to contradictions. This solution would not agree with Wittgenstein's, but it would retain several elements of his philosophy: (1) his criticisms of T; (2) his statement of T'; (3) his observation, that language-games may be disturbed by other language-games which are supposed to explain or to describe them. It would, however, interpret the statement of T' as a special theory of meaning and formulate it by taking account of the difference between object-language and meta-language. It would be possible still to have philosophical theories and philosophical problems without being open to Wittgenstein's criticisms, except perhaps the one criticism, that the distinction introduced is purely artificial.*

PAUL FEYERABEND

Vienna

2

The Meaning of a Word

J. L. AUSTIN

Reprinted with the kind permission of the publisher from J. L. Austin, *Philosophical Papers,* edited by J. O. Urmson and G. J. Warnock, Second Edition 1970 (Oxford: The Clarendon Press, 1961, 1970), 55-75.

3

THE MEANING OF A WORD

SPECIMENS OF SENSE

I. I.   What-is-the-meaning-of (the word) 'rat'?
I. II.   What-is-the-meaning-of (the word) 'word'?
I. 2I.   What is a 'rat'?
I. 2II.   What is a 'word'?
I. 22.   What is the 'muzzle' of a rat?
2. I.   What-is-the-meaning-of (the phrase) 'What-is-the-meaning-of'?
2. II.   What-is-the-meaning-of (the sentence) 'What-is-the-meaning-of (the word) "x"?'?

SPECIMENS OF NONSENSE

I. I.   What-is-the-meaning-of a word?
I. II.   What-is-the-meaning-of any word?
I. 12.   What-is-the-meaning-of a word in general?
I. 2I.   What is the-meaning-of-a-word?
I. 2II.   What is the-meaning-of-(the-word)-'rat'?
I. 22.   What is the 'meaning' of a word?
I. 22I.   What is the 'meaning' of (the word) 'rat'?
2. I.   What-is-the-meaning-of (the phrase) 'the-meaning-of-a word'?
2. II.   What-is-the-meaning-of (the sentence) 'What is the-meaning-of-(the-word)-"x"?'?
2. 12.   What-is-the-meaning-of (the sentence) 'What is the "meaning" of "the word" "x"?'?

THE MEANING OF A WORD

THIS paper is about the phrase 'the meaning of a word'. It is divided into three parts, of which the first is the most trite and the second the most muddled: all are too long. In the first, I try to make it clear that the phrase 'the meaning of a word' is, in general, if not always, a dangerous nonsense-phrase. In the other two parts I consider in turn two questions, often asked in philosophy, which clearly need new and careful scrutiny if that facile phrase 'the meaning of a word' is no longer to be permitted to impose upon us.

I

I begin, then, with some remarks about 'the meaning of a word'. I think many persons now see all or part of what I shall say: but not all do, and there is a tendency to forget it, or to get it slightly wrong. In so far as I am merely flogging the converted, I apologize to them.

A preliminary remark. It may justly be urged that, properly speaking, what alone has meaning is a *sentence*. Of course, we can speak quite properly of, for example, 'looking up the meaning of a word' in a dictionary. Nevertheless, it appears that the sense in which a word or a phrase 'has a meaning' is derivative from the sense in which a sentence 'has a meaning': to say a word or a phrase 'has a meaning' is to say that there are sentences in which it occurs which 'have meanings': and to know the meaning which the word or phrase has, is to know the meanings of sentences in which it occurs. All the dictionary can do when we 'look up the meaning of a word' is to suggest aids to the understanding of sentences in which it occurs. Hence it appears correct to say that what 'has meaning' in the primary sense is the sentence. And older philosophers who discussed the problem of 'the meaning of words' tend to fall into *special* errors, avoided by more recent philosophers, who discuss rather the parallel problem of 'the meaning of sentences'. Nevertheless, if we are on our guard, we perhaps need not fall into these special errors, and I propose to overlook them at present.

THE MEANING OF A WORD   57

There are many sorts of sentence in which the words 'the meaning of the word so-and-so' are found, e.g. 'He does not know, or understand, the meaning of the word *handsaw*': 'I shall have to explain to her the meaning of the word *pikestaff*': and so on. I intend to consider primarily the common question, 'What is the meaning of *so-and-so*?' or 'What is the meaning of *the word so-and-so*?'

Suppose that in ordinary life I am asked: 'What is the meaning of the word *racy*?' There are two sorts of thing I may do in response: I may reply *in words*, trying to describe what raciness is and what it is not, to give examples of sentences in which one might use the word *racy*, and of others in which one should not. Let us call this *sort* of thing 'explaining the syntactics' of the word 'racy' in the English language. On the other hand, I might do what we may call 'demonstrating the semantics' of the word, by getting the questioner to *imagine*, or even actually to *experience*, situations which we should describe correctly by means of sentences containing the words 'racy' 'raciness', &c., and again other situations where we should *not* use these words. This is, of course, a simple case: but perhaps the same two *sorts* of procedure would be gone through in the case of at least most ordinary words. And in the same way, if I wished to find out 'whether he understands the meaning of the word *racy*', I should test him at some length in these two ways (which perhaps could not be entirely divorced from each other).

Having asked in this way, and answered, 'What is the meaning of (the word) "rat"?', 'What is the meaning of (the word) "cat"?', 'What is the meaning of (the word) "mat"?', and so on, we then try, being philosophers, to ask the further *general* question, 'What is the meaning of a word?' But there is something spurious about this question. We do not intend to mean by it a certain question which would be perfectly all right, namely, 'What is the meaning of (the word) "word"?': *that* would be no more general than is asking the meaning of the word 'rat', and would be answered in a precisely similar way.

No: we want to ask rather, 'What is the meaning of a-word-in-general?' or 'of *any* word'—not meaning 'any' word *you like to choose*, but rather *no particular* word *at all*, just 'any word'. Now if we pause even for a moment to reflect, this is a perfectly absurd question to be trying to ask. I can only answer a question of the form 'What is the meaning of "*x*"?' if "*x*" is some *particular* word you are asking about. This supposed *general* question is really just a spurious question of a type which commonly arises in philosophy. We may call it the fallacy of asking about 'Nothing-in-particular' which is a practice decried by the plain man, but by the philosopher called 'generalizing' and regarded with some complacency. Many other examples of the fallacy can be found: take, for example, the case of 'reality'—we try to pass from such questions as 'How would you distinguish a real rat from an imaginary rat?' to 'What is a real thing?', a question which merely gives rise to nonsense.

We may expose the error in our present case thus. Instead of asking 'What is the meaning of (the word) "rat"?' we might clearly have asked 'What is a "rat"?' and so on. But if our questions have been put in *that* form, it becomes very difficult to formulate any *general* question which could impose on us for a moment. Perhaps 'What is anything?'? Few philosophers, if perhaps not none, have been foolhardy enough to pose such a question. In the same way, we should not perhaps be tempted to generalize such a question as 'Does he know the meaning of (the word) "rat"?' 'Does he know the meaning of a word?' would be silly.

Faced with the nonsense question 'What is the meaning of a word?', and perhaps dimly recognizing it to be nonsense, we are nevertheless not inclined to give it up. Instead, we transform it in a curious and noteworthy manner. Up to now, we had been asking '*What-is-the-meaning-of* (the word) "rat"?', &c.; and ultimately '*What-is-the-meaning-of* a word?' But now, being baffled, we change so to speak, the hyphenation, and ask 'What is *the-meaning-of-a-word?*' or sometimes, 'What is the

THE MEANING OF A WORD   59

"meaning" of a word?' (1. 22): I shall refer, for brevity's sake, only to the other (1. 21). It is easy to see how very different this question is from the other. At once a crowd of traditional and reassuring answers present themselves: 'a concept', 'an idea', 'an image', 'a class of similar sensa', &c. All of which are equally spurious answers to a pseudo-question. Plunging ahead, however, or rather retracing our steps, we now proceed to ask such questions as 'What is the-meaning-of-(the-word) "rat"?' which is as spurious as 'What-is-the-meaning-of (the word) "rat"?' was genuine. And again we answer 'the idea of a rat' and so forth. How quaint this procedure is, may be seen in the following way. Supposing a plain man puzzled, were to ask me 'What is the meaning of (the word) "muggy"?', and I were to answer, 'The idea or concept of "mugginess"' or 'The class of sensa of which it is correct to say "This is muggy"': the man would stare at me as at an imbecile. And that is sufficiently unusual for me to conclude that that was not at all the sort of answer he expected: nor, in plain English, *can* that question *ever* require that sort of answer.

To show up this pseudo-question, let us take a parallel case, where perhaps no one has yet been deluded, though they well might be. Suppose that I ask 'What is the point of doing so-and-so?' For example, I ask Old Father William 'What is the point of standing on one's head?' He replies in the way we know. Then I follow this up with 'What is the point of balancing an eel on the end of one's nose?' And he explains. Now suppose I ask as my third question 'What is the point of doing *anything*—not anything *in particular*, but just *anything*?' Old Father William would no doubt kick me downstairs without the option. But lesser men, raising this same question and finding no answer, would very likely commit suicide or join the Church. (Luckily, in the case of 'What is the meaning of a word?' the effects are less serious, amounting only to the writing of books.) On the other hand, more adventurous intellects would no doubt take to asking 'What is the-point-of-doing-a-thing?' or 'What is the "point" of doing a thing?':

60   THE MEANING OF A WORD

and then later 'What is the-point-of-eating-suet?' and so on.
Thus we should discover a whole new universe of a kind of
entity called 'points', not previously suspected of existence.

To make the matter clearer, let us consider another case
which is precisely *unlike* the case of 'What is the meaning of?'
I can ask not only the question, 'What is the square root of 4?',
of 8, and so on, but also 'What is the square root of a number?':
which is either nonsense or equivalent to 'What is the "square
root" of a number?' I then give a definition of the 'square root'
of a number, such that, for any given number x, 'the square
root of x' is a definite description of another number y. This
differs from our case in that 'the meaning of p' is not a definite
description of any entity.

The general questions which we want to ask about 'meaning' are best phrased as, 'What-is-the-meaning-of (the phrase)
"what-is-the-meaning-of (the word) 'x'?"?' The *sort* of answer we should get to these quite sensible questions is that
with which I began this discussion: viz. that when I am asked
'What-is-the-meaning-of (the word) "x"?', I naturally reply
by explaining its syntactics and demonstrating its semantics.

All this must seem very obvious, but I wish to point out that
it is fatally easy to forget it: no doubt I shall do so myself many
times in the course of this paper. Even those who see pretty
clearly that 'concepts', 'abstract ideas', and so on are fictitious
entities, which we owe in part to asking questions about 'the
meaning of a word', nevertheless themselves think that there
is something which is 'the meaning of a word'. Thus Mr. Hampshire[1] attacks to some purpose the theory that there is such a
thing as '*the* meaning of a word': what *he* thinks is wrong is
the belief that there is a *single* thing called *the* meaning: 'concepts' are nonsense, and no single particular 'image' can be *the*
meaning of a general word. So, he goes on to say, the meaning
of a word must really be 'a *class* of similar particular ideas'. 'If
we are asked "What does this mean?" we point to (!) a class of

[1] 'Ideas, Propositions and Signs', in the *Proceedings of the Aristotelian Society*,
1939–40.

particular ideas.' But a 'class of particular ideas' is every bit as fictitious an entity as a 'concept' or 'abstract idea'. In the same way Mr. C. W. Morris (in the *Encyclopaedia of Unified Science*) attacks, to some purpose, those who think of 'a meaning' as a definite something which is 'simply located' somewhere: what *he* thinks is wrong is that people think of 'a meaning' as a kind of entity which can be described wholly without reference to the total activity of 'semiosis'. Well and good. Yet he himself makes some of the crudest possible remarks about 'the designatum' of a word: every sign has a designatum, which is not a particular thing but a *kind* of object or *class* of object. Now this is quite as fictitious an entity as any 'Platonic idea': and is due to precisely the same fallacy of looking for 'the meaning (or designatum) of a word'.

Why are we tempted to slip back in this way? Perhaps there are two main reasons. First, there is the curious belief that all words are *names*, i.e. in effect *proper* names, and therefore stand for something or designate it in the way that a proper name does. But this view that general names 'have denotation' in the same way that proper names do, is quite as odd as the view that proper names 'have connotation' in the same way that general names do, which is commonly recognized to lead to error. Secondly, we are afflicted by a more common malady, which is this. When we have given an analysis of a certain sentence, containing a word or phrase '*x*', we often feel inclined to ask, of our analysis, 'What *in it*, is "*x*"?' For example, we give an analysis of 'The State owns this land', in sentences about individual men, their relations and transactions: and then at last we feel inclined to ask: well now, *what*, in all that, *is* the State? And we might answer: the State *is* a collection of individual men united in a certain manner. Or again, when we have analysed the statement 'trees can exist unperceived' into statements about sensing sensa, we still tend to feel uneasy unless we can say *something* '*really does*' 'exist unperceived': hence theories about 'sensibilia' and what not. So in our present case, having given all that is required, viz. an account of

62   THE MEANING OF A WORD

'What-is-the-meaning-of "What is-the-meaning-of (the word) '*x*'?"' we *still* feel tempted, wrongly supposing our original sentence to contain a constituent 'the-meaning-of (the-word)-"*x*"', to ask 'Well now, as it turns out, what *is* the meaning of the word "*x*", after all?' And we answer, 'a class of similar particular ideas' and what not.

Of course, all my account of our motives in this matter may be only a convenient didactic schema: I do not think it is—but I recognize that one should not impute motives, least of all rational motives. Anyhow, what I claim is clear, is that there is *no* simple and handy appendage of a word called 'the meaning of (the word) "*x*"'.

II

I now pass on to the first of the two points which need now a careful scrutiny if we are no longer to be imposed upon by that convenient phrase 'the meaning of a word'. What I shall say here is, I know, not as clear as it should be.

Constantly we ask the question, 'Is *y* the meaning, or *part* of the meaning, or *contained* in the meaning, of *x*?—or is it *not*?' A favourite way of putting the question is to ask, 'Is the judgement "*x* is *y*" analytic or synthetic?' Clearly, we suppose, *y must* be *either* a part of the meaning of *x*, *or* not any part of it. And, if *y is* a part of the meaning of *x*, to say '*x* is not *y*' will be self-contradictory: while if it is *not* a part of the meaning of *x*, to say '*x* is not *y*' will present no difficulty—such a state of affairs will be readily 'conceivable'. This seems to be the merest common sense. And no doubt it *would* be the merest common sense if 'meanings' were things in some ordinary sense which contained parts in some ordinary sense. But they are *not*. Unfortunately, many philosophers who know they are not, still speak as though *y* must either be or not be 'part of the meaning' of *x*. But this is the point: *if* 'explaining the meaning of a word' is really the complicated sort of affair that we have seen it to be, and *if* there is really nothing to call 'the meaning of a word'—*then* phrases like 'part of the meaning of the word *x*' are completely undefined; it is left hanging in the air, we do not know what it means at all. *We are using a working-model which fails to fit the facts that we really wish to talk about.* When we consider what we really do want to talk about, and not the working-model, what would really be meant at all by a judgement being 'analytic or synthetic'? We simply do not know. Of course, we feel inclined to say 'I can easily produce examples of analytic and synthetic judgements; for instance, I should confidently say "Being a professor is *not* part of the meaning of being a man" and so forth.' 'A is A is analytic.' Yes, but it is when we are required to give a *general definition* of what we mean by 'analytic' or 'synthetic', and when we are required to justify our dogma that *every* judgement is either analytic or synthetic, that we find we have, in fact, nothing to fall back upon *except our working-model*. From the start, it is clear that our working-model fails to do justice, for example, to the distinction between syntactics and semantics: for instance, talking about the contradictory of every sentence having to be either self-contradictory or not so, is to talk as though all sentences which we are prohibited from saying were sentences which offended against *syntactical* rules, and could be formally reduced to verbal self-contradictions. But this overlooks all semantical considerations, which philosophers are sadly prone to do. Let us consider two cases of some things which we simply *cannot say*: although they are *not* 'self-contradictory' and although—and this of course is where many will have axes to grind—we cannot possibly be tempted to say that we have 'synthetic *a priori*' knowledge of their contradictions.

Let us begin with a case which, being about *sentences* rather than *words*, is not quite in point, but which may encourage us. Take the well-known sentence 'The cat is on the mat, and I do not believe it'. That seems absurd. On the other hand 'The cat is on the mat, and I believe it' seems trivial. If we were to adopt a customary dichotomy, and to say *either* a proposition *p* implies another proposition *r*, *or p* is perfectly compatible with not-*r*, we should at once in our present case be tempted to say that 'The cat is on the mat' *implies* 'I believe it': hence both the triviality of adding 'and I believe it' and the absurdity of adding 'and I do not believe it'. But of course 'the cat is on the mat' does *not* imply 'Austin believes the cat is on the mat': nor even 'the speaker believes the cat is on the mat'—for the speaker may be lying. The doctrine which is produced in this case is, that not p indeed, but *asserting p* implies 'I (who assert p) believe p'. And here 'implies' must be given a special sense: for of course it is not that 'I assert p' implies (in the ordinary sense) 'I believe p', for I may be lying. It is the sort of sense in which by asking a question I 'imply' that I do not know the answer to it. By asserting p I *give it to be understood* that I believe p.

Now the reason why I cannot say 'The cat is on the mat and I do not believe it' is not that it offends against syntactics in the sense of being in some way 'self-contradictory'. What prevents my saying it, is rather some semantic convention (implicit, of course), about the way we use words *in situations*. What precisely is the account to be given in this case we need not ask. Let us rather notice one significant feature of it. Whereas 'p and I believe it' is somehow trivial, and 'p and I do not believe it' is somehow nonsense, a third sentence 'p and *I might not have* believed it' makes perfectly good sense. Let us call these three sentences Q, not Q, and 'might not Q'. Now what prohibits us from saying 'p' implies 'I believe p' in the ordinary sense of 'implies', is precisely shown by this fact: that although not-Q is (*somehow*) absurd, 'might not Q' is not at all absurd. For in ordinary cases of implications, not merely is not Q absurd, but 'might not Q' is *also* absurd: e.g. 'triangles are figures and triangles have no shape' is no more absurd than 'triangles are figures and triangles might have had no shape'. Consideration of the sentence 'might not Q' will afford a rough test as to whether p 'implies' r in the *ordinary* sense, or in the special sense, of 'implies'.

Bearing this in mind, let us now consider a sentence which, as I claim, cannot possibly be classified as *either* 'analytic' *or*

THE MEANING OF A WORD   65

'synthetic'. I refer to the sentence, 'This *x* exists', where *x* is a sensum, e.g. 'This noise exists'. In endeavouring to classify it, one party would point to the triviality of 'This noise exists', and to the absurdity of 'This noise does not exist'. They would say, therefore, that *existence* is 'part of the meaning of' *this*. But another party would point out, that 'This noise might not have existed' makes perfectly good sense. *They* would say, therefore, that *existence* cannot be 'part of the meaning of' *this*.

Both parties, as we are now in a position to see, would be correct in their *arguments*, but incorrect in their *conclusions*. What seems to be true is that *using the word 'this'* (not: the word 'this') *gives it to be understood that* the sensum referred to 'exists'.

Perhaps, historically, this fact about the sentence-trio, 'This noise exists', 'This noise does not exist', and 'This noise might not have existed', was pointed out before any philosopher had had time to pronounce that 'This noise exists' is analytic, or is synthetic. But such a pronouncement might well have been made: and *to this day*, even when the fact has been pointed out, many philosophers *worry* about the case, supposing the sentence *must* be one or the other but painfully aware of the difficulties in choosing either. I wish to point out that consideration of the analogy between this case and the other, should cure us once and for all of this bogy, and of insisting on classifying sentences as *either* analytic *or* synthetic. It may encourage us to consider again what the facts in their actual complexity really are. (One thing it suggests is a reconsideration of 'Caesar is bald' and similar propositions: but I cannot go into that.)

So far, however, we have scarcely begun in earnest: we have merely felt that initial trepidation, experienced when the firm ground of prejudice begins to slip away beneath the feet. Perhaps there are other cases, or other sorts of cases, where it will not be possible to say either that *y* is a 'part of the meaning' of *x* or that it is not, without being misleading.

Suppose we take the case of 'being thought good by me' and 'being approved of by me'. Are we to rush at this with the dichotomy: *either* 'being approved of by me' *is* part of the

66 THE MEANING OF A WORD

meaning of 'being thought good by me' *or* it is *not*? Is it *obvious* that 'I think *x* good but I do not approve of it' is self-contradictory? Of course it is not *verbally* self-contradictory. That it either is or is not 'really' self-contradictory would seem to be difficult to establish. Of course, we think, it must be one or the other—only 'it's difficult to decide *which*': or 'it depends on how you use the words'. But are those really the difficulties which baffle us? Of course, *if* it were certain that every sentence *must* be either analytic or synthetic, those *must* be the difficulties. But then, it is not certain: no account even of what the distinction means, is given except by reference to our shabby working-model. I suggest that 'I think *x* good but I do not approve of it' may very well be neither self-contradictory nor yet 'perfectly good sense' in the way in which 'I think *x* exciting but I do not approve of it' *is* 'perfectly good sense'.

Perhaps this example does not strike you as awkward. It cannot be expected that all examples will appeal equally to all hearers. Let us take some others. Is 'What is good ought to exist' analytic or synthetic? According to Moore's theory, this must be 'synthetic': yet he constantly in *Principia Ethica* takes its truth for granted. And that illustrates one of the main draw-backs of insisting on saying that a sentence *must* be either analytic or synthetic: you are almost certain to have left on your hands some general sentences which are certainly not analytic but which you find it difficult to conceive being false: i.e. you are landed with 'synthetic *a priori* knowledge'. Take that sentence of ill fame 'Pink is more like red than black'. It is rash to pronounce this 'synthetic *a priori* knowledge' on the ground that 'being more like red than black' is not 'part of the meaning' or 'part of the definition' of 'pink' and that it is not 'conceivable' that pink should be more like black than red: I dare say, so far as those phrases have any clear meaning, that it *is not*: but the question is: *is* the thing therefore 'synthetic' *a priori* knowledge?

Or, again, take some examples from Berkeley: is *extended* 'part of the meaning' of *coloured* or of *shaped*, or *shaped* 'part of the meaning' of *extended*? Is 'est sed non percipitur' self-contradictory (when said of a sensum), or is it not? When we worry thus, is it not worth considering the possibility that we are oversimplifying?

What we are to say in these cases, what even the possibilities are, I do not at present clearly see. (1) Evidently, we must throw away the old working-model as soon as we take account even of the existence of a distinction between syntactics and semantics. (2) But evidently also, our *new* working-model, the supposed 'ideal' language, is in many ways a most inadequate model of any *actual* language: its careful separation of syntactics from semantics, its lists of explicitly formulated rules and conventions, and its careful delimitation of their spheres of operation—all are misleading. An *actual* language has few, if any, explicit conventions, no sharp limits to the spheres of operation of rules, no rigid separation of what is syntactical and what semantical. (3) Finally, I think I can see that there are difficulties about our powers of imagination, and about the curious way in which it is enslaved by words.

To encourage ourselves in the belief that this sort of consideration may play havoc with the distinction 'analytic or synthetic', let us consider a similar and more familiar case. It seems, does it not, perfectly obvious that every proposition must have a contradictory? Yet it does not turn out so. Suppose that I live in harmony and friendship for four years with a cat: and then it delivers a philippic. We ask ourselves, perhaps, 'Is it a real cat? or is it *not* a real cat?' 'Either it *is*, or it *is not*, but we cannot be sure which.' Now actually, that is not so: *neither* 'It is a real cat' *nor* 'it is not a real cat' fits the facts semantically: each is designed for other situations than this one: you could not say the former of something which delivers philippics, nor yet the latter of something which has behaved as this has for four years. There are similar difficulties about choosing between 'This *is* a hallucination' and 'This is *not* a hallucination'. With sound instinct, the plain man turns in such cases to Watson and says 'Well now, *what would you* say?' 'How would you *describe* it? The difficulty is just that: there is *no* short description which is not misleading: the only thing to do, and that can easily be done, is to set out the description of the facts at length. Ordinary language breaks down in extraordinary cases. (In such cases, the cause of the breakdown is semantical.) Now no doubt an *ideal* language would *not* break down, whatever happened. In doing physics, for example, where our language is tightened up in order precisely to describe complicated and unusual cases concisely, we *prepare linguistically for the worst*. In ordinary language we do not: *words fail us*. If we talk as though an ordinary must be like an ideal language, we shall misrepresent the facts.

Consider now 'being extended' and 'being shaped'. In ordinary life we never get into a situation where we learn to say that anything is extended but not shaped nor conversely. We have all learned to use, and have used, the words only in cases where it is correct to use both. Supposing now someone says '*x* is extended but has no shape'. Somehow we cannot see what this 'could mean'—there are no semantic conventions, explicit or implicit, to cover this case: yet it is not prohibited in any way—there are no limiting rules about what we might or might not say *in extraordinary cases*. It is not *merely* the difficulty of imagining or experiencing extraordinary cases, either, which causes worry. There is this too: we can only describe what it is we are trying to imagine, by means of words which precisely describe and evoke the *ordinary* case, which we are trying to think away. Ordinary language *blinkers* the already feeble imagination. It would be difficult, in this way, if I were to say 'Can I think of a case where a man would be neither at home nor not at home?' This is inhibiting, because I think of the *ordinary* case where I ask 'Is he at home?' and get the answer, 'No': when certainly he is not at home. But supposing I happen *first* to think of the situation when I call on him just after he has died: then I see at once it would be wrong to say either. So in our case, the only thing to do is to imagine or experience all kinds of odd situations, and then suddenly round on oneself

THE MEANING OF A WORD   69

and ask: there, *now* would I say that, being extended it must be shaped? A new idiom might in odd cases be demanded.

I should like to say, in concluding this section, that in the course of stressing that we must pay attention to the facts of *actual* language, what we can and cannot say, and *precisely* why, another and converse point takes shape. Although it will not do to force actual language to accord with some preconceived model: it *equally* will not do, having discovered the facts about 'ordinary usage' *to rest content* with that, as though there were nothing more to be discussed and discovered. There may be plenty that might happen and does happen which would need new and better language to describe it in. Very often philosophers are only engaged on this task, when they seem to be perversely using words in a way which makes no sense according to 'ordinary usage'. There may be extraordinary facts, even about our everyday experience, which plain men and plain language overlook.

III

The last, and perhaps least unimportant point I have to make is the following: it seems to me that far more *detailed* attention ought to be given to that celebrated question, the posing of which has given birth to, and still keeps alive, so many erroneous theories, namely: why do we call different things by the same name? In reply to this, the philoprogenitive invent theories of 'universals' and what not: some entity or other to be that of which the 'name' is the name. And in reply to *them*, the more cautious (the 'nominalists') have usually been content to reply simply that: the reason why we call different things by the same name is simply that the things are *similar*: there is nothing *identical* present in them. This reply is inadequate in many respects: it does not, for example, attack the misleading form in which the question is posed, nor sufficiently go into the peculiarities of the word 'similar'. But what I wish to object to in it tonight is rather this: that *it is not in the least true* that all the things which I 'call by the same (general) name' *are* in general 'similar', in any ordinary sense of that much abused word.

It is a most strange thing that 'nominalists' should rest content with this answer. Not merely is it untrue to the facts; but further, if they had examined the facts, which are, in themselves, interesting enough, they could have produced with little trouble a far more formidable case against their opponents. So long as they say the things *are similar*, it will always be open to someone to say: 'Ah yes, similar *in a certain respect*: and that can only be explained by means of universals' (or whatever the name may be that they prefer for that well-tried nostrum): or again to maintain that similarity is only 'intelligible' as partial *identity*: and so on. And even those who are not persuaded entirely, may yet go so far as to allow that the 'similarity' and 'identity' languages are *alternatives*, the choice between which is indifferent. But surely, if it were made evident that we often 'call different things by the same name', and for perfectly 'good reasons',[1] when the things are not even in any ordinary sense 'similar', it will become excessively difficult to maintain that there is something 'identical' present in each—and after all, it is in *refuting* that position that the nominalist is really interested. Not, of course, that we can really *refute* it, or hope to cure those incurables who have long since reached the tertiary stage of universals.

Leaving historical disputes aside, it is a matter of urgency that a doctrine should be developed about the various kinds of good reasons for which we 'call different things[2] by the same name'. This is an absorbing question, but habitually neglected, so far as I know, by philologists as well as by philosophers. Lying in the no man's land between them, it falls between two schools, to develop such a doctrine fully would be very complicated and perhaps tedious: but also very useful in many ways. It demands the study of *actual* languages, *not* ideal ones. That the Polish semanticists have discussed such questions I neither know nor believe. Aristotle did to a quite considerable extent, but scrappily and inexactly.

[1] We are not interested in mere equivocation, of course.
[2] Strictly, *sorts* of things rather than *particular* things.

THE MEANING OF A WORD   71

I shall proceed forthwith simply to give some of the more obvious cases where the reasons for 'calling different sorts of things by the same name' are not to be dismissed lightly as 'similarity'. And show how consideration of these facts may warn us against errors which are constant in philosophy.

  1. A very simple case indeed is one often mentioned by Aristotle: the adjective 'healthy': when I talk of a healthy body and again of a healthy complexion, of healthy exercise: the word is *not* just being used *equivocally*. Aristotle would say it is being used 'paronymously'.[1] In this case there is what we may call a *primary nuclear* sense of 'healthy': the sense in which 'healthy' is used of a healthy body: I call this *nuclear* because it is 'contained as a part' in the other two senses which may be set out as 'productive of healthy bodies' and 'resulting from a healthy body'.

  This is a simple case, easily understood. Yet constantly it is forgotten when we start disputing as to whether a certain word *has* 'two senses' or has *not* two senses. I remember myself disputing as to whether 'exist' has two senses (as used of material objects and again of sensa), or only one: actually we were agreed that 'exist' is used paronymously, only he called that 'having two senses', and I did not. Prichard's paper[2] on ἀγαθόν (in Aristotle) contains a classic instance of misunderstanding about paronymity, and so worrying about whether a word really 'has always the same meaning' or 'has several different meanings'.

  Now are we to be content to say that the exercise, the complexion, and the body are all called 'healthy' 'because they are similar'? Such a remark cannot fail to be misleading. Why make it? And why not direct attention to the important and actual facts?

  2. The next case I shall take is what Aristotle calls 'analogous' terms. When A : B :: X : Y then A and X are often called by

---

  [1] But there are other varieties of paronymity of course.
  [2] 'The Meaning of *ΑΓΑΘΟΝ* in the *Ethics* of Aristotle', by H. A. Prichard. Reprinted in his *Moral Obligation*, Oxford, 1949.

the same name, e.g. the foot of a mountain and the foot of a list. Here there is a good reason for calling the things both 'feet' but are we to say they are 'similar'? Not in any ordinary sense. We may say that the relations in which they stand to B and Y respectively are similar relations. Well and good: but A and X are not the relations in which they stand: and anyone simply told that, in calling A and X both 'feet' I was calling attention to a 'similarity' in them, would probably be misled. Anyhow, it is most necessary to remember that 'similarity' covers such possibilities if it is to do so. (An especially severe case of 'analogy' arises when a term is used, as Aristotle says 'in different categories': e.g. when I talk about 'change' as qualitative change, change of position, place, &c., how far is it true to say these 'changes' are 'similar'?)

3. Another case is where I call B by the same name as A, because it resembles A, C by the same name because it resembles B, D . . . and so on. But ultimately A and, say, D do not resemble each other in any recognizable sense at all. This is a very common case: and the dangers are obvious, when we search for something 'identical' in all of them!

4. Another case which is commonly found is this. Take a word like 'fascist': this originally connotes, say, a great many characteristics at once: say x, y, and z. Now we will use 'fascist' subsequently of things which possess only *one* of these striking characteristics. So that things called 'fascist' in these senses, which we may call 'incomplete' senses, need not be similar at all to each other. This often puzzles us most of all when the original 'complete' sense has been forgotten: compare the various meanings of 'cynicism': we should be puzzled to find the 'similarity' there! Sometimes the 'incompleteness' of the resemblance is coupled with a positive lack of resemblance, so that we invent a phrase to mark it as a warning, e.g. 'cupboard love'.

5. Another better-known case is that of a so-called determinable and its determinates: colour and red, green, blue, &c., or rather 'absolutely specific' reds, greens, blues, &c. Because

THE MEANING OF A WORD   73

this is better known, I shall not discuss it, though I am as a matter of fact rather sceptical about the accounts usually given. Instead, it should be pointed out how common this sort of relationship is and that it should be suspected in cases where we are prone to overlook it. A striking example is the case of 'pleasure': pleasures we may say not merely resemble each other in being pleasant, but also *differ* precisely in the way in which they are pleasant.[1] No greater mistake could be made than the hedonistic mistake (copied by non-hedonists) of thinking that pleasure is always a single similar feeling, somehow isolable from the various activities which 'give rise' to it.

6. Another case which often provides puzzles, is that of words like 'youth' and 'love': which sometimes mean the object loved, or the thing which is youthful, sometimes the passion 'Love' or the quality (?) 'youth'. These cases are of course easy (rather *like* 'healthy'?). But suppose we take the noun 'truth': here is a case where the disagreements between different theorists have largely turned on whether they interpreted this as a name of a substance, of a quality, or of a relation.

7. Lastly, I want to take a specially interesting sort of case, which is perhaps commoner and at the bottom of more muddles than we are aware of. Take the sense in which I talk of a cricket bat and a cricket ball and a cricket umpire. The reason that all are called by the same name is perhaps that each has its part—its *own special* part—to play in the activity called cricketing: it is no good to say that cricket *simply* means 'used in cricket': for we cannot explain what we mean by 'cricket' *except* by explaining the special parts played in cricketing by the bat, ball, &c. Aristotle's suggestion was that the word 'good' might be used in such a way: in which case it is obvious how far astray we should go if we look for a 'definition' of the word 'good' in any ordinary simple sense: or look for the way in which 'good' things are 'similar' to each other, in any ordinary sense. If we tried to find out by such methods what

---

[1] If we say that they are all called 'pleasures' 'because they are similar', we shall overlook this fact.

'cricket' meant, we should very likely conclude that it too was a simple unanalysable supersensible quality.

Another thing that becomes plain from such examples is that the apparently common-sense distinction between 'What is the meaning of the word x' and 'What particular things *are x* and to what degrees?' is not of universal application by any means. The questions cannot be distinguished in such cases. Or a similar case would be some word like 'golfing': it is not sense to ask 'What is the meaning of golfing?' 'What things are golfing?' Though it *is* sense to ask what component activities go to constitute golfing, what implements are used in golfing ('golf' clubs, &c.) and in what ways. Aristotle suggests 'happiness' is a word of this kind: in which case it is evident how far astray we shall go if we treat it as though it were a word like 'whiteness'.

These summarily treated examples are enough to show how essential it is to have a thorough knowledge of the different reasons for which we call different things by the same name, before we can embark confidently on an inquiry. If we rush up with a demand for a definition in the simple manner of Plato or many other philosophers, if we use the rigid dichotomy 'same meaning, different meaning', or 'What x means', as distinguished from 'the things which are x', we shall simply make hashes of things. Perhaps some people are now discussing such questions seriously. All that is to be found in traditional Logics is the mention that there are, besides univocal and equivocal words, 'also analogous words': which, without further explanation, is used to lump together all cases where a word has not always absolutely the same meaning, nor several absolutely different meanings. All that 'similarity' theorists manage is to say that all things called by some one name are similar to some one pattern, or are all more similar to each other than any of them is to anything else; which is *obviously* untrue. Anyone who wishes to see the complexity of the problem, has only got to look in a (good) dictionary under such a word as 'head': the different meanings of the word

THE MEANING OF A WORD 75

'head' will be related to each other in all sorts of different ways at once.

To summarize the contentions of this paper then. Firstly, the phrase 'the meaning of a word' is a spurious phrase. Secondly and consequently, a re-examination is needed of phrases like the two which I discuss, 'being a part of the meaning of' and 'having the same meaning'. On these matters, dogmatists require prodding: although history indeed suggests that it may sometimes be better to let sleeping dogmatists lie.

3

Knowledge of Other Minds

NORMAN MALCOLM

Knowledge of Other Minds

I

I believe that the argument from analogy for the existence of other minds still enjoys more credit than it deserves, and my first aim will be to show that it leads nowhere. J. S. Mill is one of many who have accepted the argument and I take his statement of it as representative. He puts to himself the question, "By what evidence do I know, or by what considerations am I led to believe, that there exist other sentient creatures; that the walking and speaking figures which I see and hear, have sensations and thoughts, or in other words, possess Minds?" His answer is the following:

I conclude that other human beings have feelings like me, because, first, they have bodies like me, which I know, in my own case, to be the antecedent condition of feelings; and because, secondly, they exhibit the acts, and other outward signs, which in my own case I know by experience to be caused by feelings. I am conscious in myself of a series of facts connected by an uniform sequence, of which the beginning is modifications of my body, the middle is feelings, the end is outward demeanor. In the case of other human beings I have the evidence of my senses for the first and last links of the series, but not for the intermediate link. I find, however, that the sequence between the first and last is as regular and constant in those other cases as it is in mine. In my own case I know that the first link produces the last through the intermediate link, and could not pro-

130

KNOWLEDGE OF OTHER MINDS   131

duce it without. Experience, therefore, obliges me to conclude that there must be an intermediate link; which must either be the same in others as in myself, or a different one: I must either believe them to be alive, or to be automatons: and by believing them to be alive, that is, by supposing the link to be of the same nature as in the case of which I have experience, and which is in all other respects similar, I bring other human beings, as phenomena, under the same generalizations which I know by experience to be the true theory of my own existence.[1]

I shall pass by the possible objection that this would be very *weak* inductive reasoning, based as it is on the observation of a single instance. More interesting is the following point: Suppose this reasoning could yield a conclusion of the sort "It is probable that that human figure" (pointing at some person other than oneself) "has thoughts and feelings." Then there is a question as to whether this conclusion can *mean* anything to the philosopher who draws it, because there is a question as to whether the sentence "That human figure has thoughts and feelings" can mean anything to him. Why should this be a question? Because the assumption from which Mill starts is that he has *no criterion* for determining whether another "walking and speaking figure" does or does not have thoughts and feelings. If he had a criterion he could apply it, establishing with certainty that this or that human figure does or does not have feelings (for the only plausible criterion would lie in behavior and circumstances that are open to view), and there would be no call to resort to tenuous analogical reasoning that yields at best a probability. If Mill has no criterion for the existence of feelings other than his own then in that sense he does not understand the sentence "That human figure has feelings" and therefore does not understand the sentence "It is *probable* that that human figure has feelings."

There is a familiar inclination to make the following reply: "Although I have no criterion of verification still I *understand*, for example, the sentence 'He has a pain.' For I understand the meaning of 'I have a pain,' and 'He has a pain' means that he has the *same* thing I have when I have a pain." But this is a fruitless maneuver. If I do not know how to establish that someone has a

---

[1] J. S. Mill, *An Examination of Sir William Hamilton's Philosophy*, 6th ed. (New York: Longmans, Green & Co., Inc., 1889), pp. 243-244.

132   KNOWLEDGE OF OTHER MINDS

pain then I do not know how to establish that he has the *same* as
I have when I have a pain.[2] You cannot improve my understanding of "He has a pain" by this recourse to the notion of "the same,"
unless you give me a criterion for saying that someone *has* the
same as I have. If you can do this you will have no use for the
argument from analogy: and if you cannot then you do not understand the supposed conclusion of that argument. A philosopher
who purports to rely on the analogical argument cannot, I think,
escape this dilemma.

There have been various attempts to repair the argument from
analogy. Mr. Stuart Hampshire has argued [3] that its validity as
a method of inference can be established in the following way:
Others sometimes infer that I am feeling giddy from my behavior.
Now I have direct, non-inferential knowledge, says Hampshire,
of my own feelings. So I can check inferences made about me
against the facts, checking thereby the accuracy of the "methods"
of inference.

All that is required for testing the validity of any method of factual
inference is that each one of us should sometimes be in a position to
confront the conclusions of the doubtful method of inference with
what is known by him to be true independently of the method of
inference in question. Each one of us is certainly in this position in
respect of our common methods of inference about the feelings of
persons other than ourselves, in virtue of the fact that each one of
us is constantly able to compare the results of this type of inference
with what he knows to be true directly and non-inferentially; each
one of us is in the position to make this testing comparison, whenever
he is the designated subject of a statement about feelings and sensations. I, Hampshire, know by what sort of signs I may be misled in
inferring Jones's and Smith's feelings, because I have implicitly noticed
(though probably not formulated) where Jones, Smith and others
generally go wrong in inferring my feelings (*op. cit.*, pp. 4-5).

Presumably I can also note when the inferences of others about
my feelings do not go wrong. Having ascertained the reliability

---

[2] "It is no explanation to say: the supposition that he has a pain is simply
the supposition that he has the same as I. For *that* part of the grammar is
quite clear to me: that is, that one will say that the stove has the same experience as I, *if* one says: it is in pain and I am in pain" (Ludwig Wittgenstein, *Philosophical Investigations* (New York: The Macmillan Company,
1953), sec. 350).

[3] "The Analogy of Feeling," *Mind*, January 1952, pp. 1-12.

KNOWLEDGE OF OTHER MINDS   133

of some inference-procedures I can use them myself, in a guarded way, to draw conclusions about the feelings of others, with a modest but justified confidence in the truth of those conclusions.

My first comment is that Hampshire has apparently forgotten the purpose of the argument from analogy, which is to provide some probability that "the walking and speaking figures which I see and hear, have sensations and thoughts" (Mill). For the reasoning that he describes involves the assumption that other human figures *do* have thoughts and sensations: for they are assumed to *make inferences* about me from *observations* of my behavior. But the philosophical problem of the existence of other minds *is* the problem of whether human figures other than one-self do, among other things, make observations, inferences, and assertions. Hampshire's supposed defense of the argument from analogy is an *ignoratio elenchi*.

If we struck from the reasoning described by Hampshire all assumption of thoughts and sensations in others we should be left with something roughly like this: "When my behavior is such and such there come from nearby human figures the sounds 'He feels giddy.' And generally I do feel giddy at the time. Therefore when another human figure exhibits the same behavior and I say 'He feels giddy,' it is probable that he does feel giddy." But the reference here to the sentence-like sounds coming from other human bodies is irrelevant, since I must not assume that those sounds express inferences. Thus the reasoning becomes simply the classical argument from analogy: "When my behavior is such and such I feel giddy; so probably when another human figure behaves the same way he feels the same way." This argument, again, is caught in the dilemma about the criterion of the *same*.

The version of analogical reasoning offered by Professor H. H. Price[4] is more interesting. He suggests that "one's evidence for the existence of other minds is derived primarily from the understanding of language" (p. 429). His idea is that if another body gives forth noises one understands, like "There's the bus," and if these noises give one new information, this "provides some evidence that the foreign body which uttered the noises is animated

---

[4] "Our Evidence for the Existence of Other Minds," *Philosophy*, XIII (1938), 425-456.

134   KNOWLEDGE OF OTHER MINDS

by a mind like one's own. . . . Suppose I am often in its neighborhood, and it repeatedly produces utterances which I can understand, and which I then proceed to verify for myself. And suppose that this happens in many different kinds of situations. I think that my evidence for believing that this body is animated by a mind like my own would then become very strong" (p. 430). The body from which these informative sounds proceed need not be a human body. "If the rustling of the leaves of an oak formed intelligible words conveying new information to me, and if gorse-bushes made intelligible gestures, I should have evidence that the oak or the gorse-bush was animated by an intelligence like my own" (p. 436). Even if the intelligible and informative sounds did not proceed from a body they would provide evidence for the existence of a (disembodied) mind (p. 435).

Although differing sharply from the classical analogical argument, the reasoning presented by Price is still analogical in form: I know by introspection that when certain combinations of sounds come from me they are "symbols in acts of spontaneous thinking"; therefore similar combinations of sounds, not produced by me, "probably function as instruments to an act of spontaneous thinking, which in this case is not my own" (p. 446). Price says that the reasoning also provides an *explanation* of the otherwise mysterious occurrence of sounds which I understand but did not produce. He anticipates the objection that the hypothesis is nonsensical because unverifiable. "The hypothesis is a perfectly conceivable one," he says, "in the sense that I know very well what the world would have to be like if the hypothesis were true—what sorts of entities there must be in it, and what sorts of events must occur in them. I know from introspection what acts of thinking and perceiving are, and I know what it is for such acts to be combined into the unity of a single mind . . ." (pp. 446-447).

I wish to argue against Price that no amount of intelligible sounds coming from an oak tree or a kitchen table could create any probability that it has sensations and thoughts. The question to be asked is: What would show that a tree or table *understands* the sounds that come from it? We can imagine that useful warnings, true descriptions and predictions, even "replies" to questions, should emanate from a tree, so that it came to be of enormous value to its owner. How should we establish that it understood those sentences? Should we "question" it? Suppose that the tree "said" that there was a vixen in the neighborhood, and we "asked" it "What is a vixen?," and it "replied," "A vixen is a female fox." It might go on to do as well for "female" and "fox." This performance might incline us to say that the tree understood the words, in contrast to the possible case in which it answered "I don't know" or did not answer at all. But would it show that the tree understood the words in the same sense that a person could understand them? With a person such a performance would create a presumption that he could make correct *applications* of the word in question; but not so with a tree. To see this point think of the normal teaching of words (e.g., "spoon," "dog," "red") to a child and how one decides whether he understands them. At a primitive stage of teaching one does not require or expect definitions, but rather that the child should *pick out* reds from blues, dogs from cats, spoons from forks. This involves his looking, pointing, reaching for and going to the right things and not the wrong ones. That a child says "red" when a red thing and "blue" when a blue thing is put before him is indicative of a mastery of those words *only* in conjunction with the other activities of looking, pointing, trying to get, fetching, and carrying. Try to suppose that he says the right words but looks at and reaches for the wrong things. Should we be tempted to say that he has mastered the use of those words? No, indeed. The disparity between words and behavior would make us say that he does not understand the words. In the case of a tree there could be no disparity between its words and its "behavior" because it is logically incapable of behavior of the relevant kind.

Since it has nothing like the human face and body it makes no sense to say of a tree, or an electronic computer, that it is looking or pointing at or fetching something. (Of course one can always *invent* a sense for these expressions.) Therefore it would make no sense to say that it did or did not understand the above words. Trees and computers cannot either pass or fail the tests that a child is put through. They cannot take them. That an object was a source of intelligible sounds or other signs (no matter how sequential) would not be enough by itself to establish that it had thoughts or sensations. How informative sentences and valuable predictions could emanate from a gorse-bush might be a grave scientific problem, but the explanation could never be that the gorse-bush has a mind. Better no explanation than nonsense!

It might be thought that the above difficulty holds only for words whose meaning has a "perceptual content" and that if we imagined, for example, that our gorse-bush produced nothing but pure mathematical propositions we should be justified in attributing thought to it, although not sensation. But suppose there was a remarkable "calculating boy" who could give right answers to arithmetical problems but could not apply numerals to reality in empirical propositions, e.g., he could not *count* any objects. I believe that everyone would be reluctant to say that he *understood* the mathematical signs and truths that he produced. If he could count in the normal way there would not be this reluctance. And "counting in the normal way" involves looking, pointing, reaching, fetching, and so on. That is, it requires the human face and body, and human behavior—or something similar. Things which do not have the human form, or anything like it, not merely do not but *cannot* satisfy the criteria for thinking. I am trying to bring out part of what Wittgenstein meant when he said, "We only say of a human being and what is like one that it thinks" (*Investigations*, sec. 360), and "The human body is the best picture of the human soul" (*ibid.*, p. 178).

I have not yet gone into the most fundamental error of the argument from analogy. It is present whether the argument is the classical one (the analogy between my body and other bodies) or Price's version (the analogy between my language and the noises and signs produced by other things). It is the mistaken assumption that *one learns from one's own case* what thinking, feeling, sensation are. Price gives expression to this assumption when he says: "I know from introspection what acts of thinking and perceiving are . . ." (*op. cit.*, p. 447). It is the most natural assumption for a philosopher to make and indeed seems at first to be the only possibility. Yet Wittgenstein has made us see that it leads first to solipsism and then to nonsense. I shall try to state as briefly as possible how it produces those results.

A philosopher who believes that one must learn what thinking, fear, or pain is "from one's own case," does not believe that the thing to be observed is one's behavior, but rather something "inward." He considers behavior to be related to the inward states and occurrences merely as an accompaniment or possibly an effect. He cannot regard behavior as a *criterion* of psychological phenomena: for if he did he would have no use for the analogical argument (as was said before) and also the priority given to "one's own case" would be pointless. He believes that he notes something in himself that he calls "thinking" or "fear" or "pain," and then he tries to infer the presence of the *same* in others. He should then deal with the question of what his criterion of the *same* in others is. This he cannot do because it is of the essence of his viewpoint to reject circumstances and behavior as a criterion of mental phenomena in others. And what else could serve as a criterion? He ought, therefore, to draw the conclusion that the notion of thinking, fear, or pain in others is in an important sense meaningless. He has no idea of what would count for or against it.[5] "That there should be thinking or pain other than my own is unintelligible," he ought to hold. This would be a rigorous solipsism, and a correct outcome of the assumption that one can know only from one's own case what the mental phenomena are. An equivalent way of putting it would be: "When I say 'I am in pain,' by 'pain' I mean a certain inward state. When I say '*He* is in pain,' by 'pain' I mean *behavior*. I cannot attribute pain to others *in the same sense* that I attribute it to myself."

Some philosophers before Wittgenstein may have seen the solipsistic result of starting from "one's own case." But I believe he is the first to have shown how that starting point destroys itself. This may be presented as follows: One supposes that one inwardly picks out something as thinking or pain and thereafter identifies it whenever it presents itself in the soul. But the question to be pressed is, Does one make *correct* identifications? The proponent of these "private" identifications has nothing to say here. He feels sure that he identifies correctly the occurrences in his soul; but feeling sure is no guarantee of being right. Indeed he has no idea of what being *right* could mean. He does not know

----

[5] One reason why philosophers have not commonly drawn this conclusion may be, as Wittgenstein acutely suggests, that they assume that they have "an infallible paradigm of identity in the identity of a thing with itself" (*Investigations*, sec. 215).

138   KNOWLEDGE OF OTHER MINDS

how to distinguish between actually making correct identifications and being under the impression that he does. (See *Investigations*, secs. 258-9.) Suppose that he identified the emotion of
anxiety as the sensation of pain? Neither he nor anyone else
could know about this "mistake." Perhaps he makes a mistake
every time! Perhaps all of us do! We ought to see now that we are
talking nonsense. We do not know what a *mistake* would be. We
have no standard, no examples, no customary practice, with
which to compare our inner recognitions. The inward identification cannot hit the bull's-eye, or miss it either, because there is
no bull's-eye. When we see that the ideas of correct and incorrect have no application to the supposed inner identification, the
latter notion loses its appearance of sense. Its collapse brings
down both solipsism and the argument from analogy.

II

The destruction of the argument from analogy also destroys
the *problem* for which it was supposed to provide a solution. A
philosopher feels himself in a difficulty about other minds because
he assumes that first of all he is acquainted with mental phenomena "from his own case." What troubles him is how to make the
transition from his own case to the case of others. When his thinking is freed of the illusion of the priority of his own case, then
he is able to look at the familiar facts and to acknowledge that
the circumstances, behavior, and utterances of others actually
are his *criteria* (not merely his evidence) for the existence of their
mental states. Previously this had seemed impossible.

But now he is in danger of flying to the opposite extreme of
behaviorism, which errs by believing that through observation
of one's own circumstances, behavior, and utterances one can find
out that one is thinking or angry. The philosophy of "from one's
own case" and behaviorism, though in a sense opposites, make
the common assumption that the first-person, present-tense psychological statements are verified by self-observation. According
to the "one's own case" philosophy the self-observation cannot be
checked by others; according to behaviorism the self-observation
would be by means of outward criteria that are available to all.
The first position becomes unintelligible; the second is false for
at least many kinds of psychological statements. We are forced

to conclude that the first-person psychological statements are not (or hardly ever) verified by self-observation. It follows that they have no verification at all; for if they had a verification it would have to be by self-observation.

But if sentences like "My head aches" or "I wonder where she is" do not express observations then what do they do? What is the relation between my declaration that my head aches and the fact that my head aches, if the former is not the report of an observation? The perplexity about the existence of *other* minds has, as the result of criticism, turned into a perplexity about the meaning of one's own psychological sentences about oneself. At our starting point it was the sentence "*His* head aches" that posed a problem; but now it is the sentence "*My* head aches" that puzzles us.

One way in which this problem can be put is by the question, "How does *one know when to say* the words 'My head aches'?" The inclination to ask this question can be made acute by imagining a fantastic but not impossible case of a person who has survived to adult years without ever experiencing pain. He is given various sorts of injections to correct this condition, and on receiving one of these one day, he jumps and exclaims, "Now I feel pain!" One wants to ask, "How did he *recognize* the new sensation as a *pain*?"

Let us note that if the man gives an answer (e.g., "I knew it must be pain because of the way I jumped") then he proves by that very fact that he has not mastered the correct use of the words "I feel pain." They cannot be used to state a *conclusion*. In telling us *how* he did it he will convict himself of a misuse. Therefore the question "How did he recognize his sensation?" requests the impossible. The inclination to ask it is evidence of our inability to grasp the fact that the use of this psychological sentence has nothing to do with recognizing or identifying or observing a state of oneself.

The fact that this imagined case produces an especially strong temptation to ask the "How?" question shows that we have the idea that it must be more difficult to give the right name of one's sensation *the first time*. The implication would be that it is not so difficult *after* the first time. Why should this be? Are we thinking that then the man would have a paradigm of pain with which he could compare his sensations and so be in a position to know right off whether a certain sensation was or was not a pain? But the paradigm would be either something "outer" (behavior) or something "inner" (perhaps a memory impression of the sensation). If the former then he is misusing the first-person sentence. If the latter then the question of whether he compared *correctly* the present sensation with the inner paradigm of pain would be without sense. Thus the idea that the use of the first-person sentences can be governed by paradigms must be abandoned. It is another form of our insistent misconception of the first-person sentence as resting somehow on the identification of a psychological state.

These absurdities prove that we must conceive of the first-person psychological sentences in some entirely different light. Wittgenstein presents us with the suggestion that the first-person sentences are to be thought of as similar to the natural nonverbal, behavioral expressions of psychological states. "My leg hurts," for example, is to be assimilated to crying, limping, holding one's leg. This is a bewildering comparison and one's first thought is that two sorts of things could not be more unlike. By saying the sentence one can make a *statement*; it has a *contradictory*; it is *true* or *false*; in saying it one *lies* or *tells the truth*; and so on. None of these things, exactly, can be said of crying, limping, holding one's leg. So how can there be any resemblance? But Wittgenstein knew this when he deliberately likened such a sentence to "the primitive, the natural, expressions" of pain, and said that it is "new pain-behavior" (*ibid.*, sec. 244). This analogy has at least two important merits: first, it breaks the hold on us of the question "How does one *know when to say* 'My leg hurts'?", for in the light of the analogy this will be as nonsensical as the question "How does one know when to cry, limp, or hold one's leg?"; second, it explains how the utterance of a first-person psychological sentence by another person can have *importance* for us, although not as an identification—for in the light of the analogy it will have the same importance as the natural behavior which serves as our preverbal criterion of the psychological states of others.

4

Ordinary Language

GILBERT RYLE

Reprinted with the kind permission of the author and the editor from *The Philosophical Review,* LXII (1953), 167-86.

ORDINARY LANGUAGE

PHILOSOPHERS' arguments have frequently turned on references to what we do and do not say or, more strongly, on what we can and cannot say. Such arguments are present in the writings of Plato and are common in those of Aristotle.

In recent years, some philosophers, having become feverishly exercised about the nature and methodology of their calling, have made much of arguments of this kind. Other philosophers have repudiated them. Their disputes on the merits of these arguments have not been edifying, since both sides have been apt to garble the question. I want to ungarble it.

"ORDINARY"

There is one phrase which recurs in this dispute, the phrase 'the use of ordinary language'. It is often, quite erroneously, taken to be paraphrased by 'ordinary linguistic usage'. Some of the partisans assert that all philosophical questions are questions about the use of ordinary language, or that all philosophical questions are solved or are about to be solved by considering ordinary linguistic usage.

Postponing the examination of the notion of *linguistic usage,* I want to begin by contrasting the phrase 'the use of ordinary language' with the similar-seeming but totally different phrase 'the ordinary use of the expression "..."'. When people speak of the use of ordinary language, the word 'ordinary' is in implicit or explicit contrast with 'out-of-the-way', 'esoteric', 'technical', 'poetical', 'notational' or, sometimes, 'archaic'. 'Ordinary' means 'common', 'current', 'colloquial', 'vernacular', 'natural', 'prosaic', 'non-notational', 'on the tongue of Everyman', and is usually in contrast with dictions which only a few people know how to use, such as the technical terms or artificial symbolisms of lawyers, theologians, economists, philosophers, cartographers, mathematicians, symbolic logicians and players of Royal Tennis. There is no sharp boundary between 'common' and 'uncommon', 'technical' and 'untechnical' or 'old-fashioned' and 'current'. Is 'carburettor' a word in common use or only in rather uncommon use? Is 'purl' on the lips of Every-

THE PHILOSOPHICAL REVIEW

man, or on the lips only of Everywoman? What of 'manslaughter', 'inflation', 'quotient' and 'off-side'? On the other hand, no one would hesitate on which side of this no-man's-land to locate 'isotope' or 'bread', 'material implication' or 'if', 'transfinite cardinal' or 'eleven', 'ween' or 'suppose'. The edges of 'ordinary' are blurred, but usually we are in no doubt whether a diction does or does not belong to ordinary parlance.

But in the other phrase, 'the ordinary use of the expression "..."', 'ordinary' is not in contrast with 'esoteric', 'archaic' or 'specialist', etc. It is in contrast with 'non-stock' or 'non-standard'. We can contrast the stock or standard use of a fish-knife or sphygmomanometer with some non-regulation use of it. The stock use of a fish-knife is to cut up fish with; but it might be used for cutting seed-potatoes or as a heliograph. A sphygmomanometer might, for all I know, be used for checking tyre pressures; but this is not its standard use. Whether an implement or instrument is a common or a specialist one, there remains the distinction between its stock use and non-stock uses of it. If a term is a highly technical term, or a non-technical term, there remains the distinction between its stock use and non-stock uses of it. If a term is a highly technical term, most people will not know its stock use or, *a fortiori,* any non-stock uses of it either, if it has any. If it is a vernacular term, then nearly everyone will know its stock use, and most people will also know some non-stock uses of it, if it has any. There are lots of words, like 'of', 'have' and 'object', which have no one stock use, any more than string, paper, brass and pocket-knives have just one stock use. Lots of words have not got any non-stock uses. 'Sixteen' has, I think, none; nor has 'daffodil'. Nor, maybe, have collar-studs. Non-stock uses of a word are, e.g., metaphorical, hyperbolical, poetical, stretched and deliberately restricted uses of it. Besides contrasting the stock use with certain non-stock uses, we often want to contrast the stock use of an expression with certain alleged, suggested, or recommended uses of it. This is a contrast not between the regular use and irregular uses, but between the regular use and what the regular use is alleged to be or what it is recommended that it should be.

When we speak of the ordinary or stock use of a word we need not be characterising it in any further way, e.g., applauding or

ORDINARY LANGUAGE

recommending it or giving it any testimonial. We need not be appealing to or basing anything on its stock-ness. The words 'ordinary', 'standard' and 'stock' can serve merely to refer to a use, without describing it. They are philosophically colourless and can be easily dispensed with. When we speak of the regular night-watchman, we are merely indicating the night-watchman whom we know independently to be the one usually on the job; we are not yet giving any information about him or paying any tribute to his regularity. When we speak of the standard spelling of a word or the standard gauge of British railway tracks, we are not describing or recommending or countenancing this spelling or this gauge; we are giving a reference to it which we expect our hearers to get without hesitation. Sometimes, naturally, this indication does not work. Sometimes the stock use in one place is different from its stock use in another, as with 'suspenders'. Sometimes, its stock use at one period differs from its stock use at another, as with 'nice'. A dispute about which of two or five uses in the stock use is not a philosophical dispute about any one of those uses. It is therefore philosophically uninteresting, though settlement of it is sometimes requisite for communication between philosophers.

If I want to talk about a non-stock use of a word or fish-knife, it is not enough to try to refer to it by the phrase 'the non-stock use of it', for there may be any number of such non-stock uses. To call my hearer's attention to a particular non-stock use of it, I have to give some description of it, for example, to cite a special context in which the word is known to be used in a non-stock way.

This, though always possible, is not often necessary for the stock use of an expression, although in philosophical debates one is sometimes required to do it, since one's fellow-philosophers are at such pains to pretend that they cannot think what its stock use is—a difficulty which, of course, they forget all about when they are teaching children or foreigners how to use it, and when they are consulting dictionaries.

It is easy now to see that learning or teaching the ordinary or stock use of an expression need not be, though it may be, learning or teaching the use of an ordinary or vernacular expression, just as learning or teaching the standard use of an instrument need not be, though it can be, learning or teaching the use of a household uten-

THE PHILOSOPHICAL REVIEW

sil. Most words and instruments, whether out-of-the-way or common, have their stock uses and may or may not also have non-stock uses as well.

A philosopher who maintained that certain philosophical questions are questions about the ordinary or stock uses of certain expressions would not therefore be committing himself to the view that they are questions about the uses of ordinary or colloquial expressions. He could admit that the noun 'infinitesimals' is not on the lips of Everyman and still maintain that Berkeley was examining the ordinary or stock use of 'infinitesimals', namely the standard way, if not the only way, in which this word was employed by mathematical specialists. Berkeley was not examining the use of a colloquial word; he was examining the regular or standard use of a relatively esoteric word. We are not contradicting ourselves if we say that he was examining the ordinary use of an unordinary expression.

Clearly a lot of philosophical discussions are of this type. In the philosophy of law, biology, physics, mathematics, formal logic, theology, psychology and grammar, technical concepts have to be examined, and these concepts are what are expressed by more or less recherché dictions. Doubtless this examination embodies attempts to elucidate in untechnical terms the technical terms of this or that specialist theory, but this very attempt involves discussing the ordinary or stock uses of these technical terms.

Doubtless, too, study by philosophers of the stock uses of expressions which we all employ has a certain primacy over their study of the stock uses of expressions which only, e.g., scientific or legal specialists employ. These specialists explain to novices the stock uses of their terms of art partly by talking to them in non-esoteric terms; they do not also have to explain to them the stock uses of these non-esoteric terms. Untechnical terminology is, in this way, basic to technical terminologies. Hard cash has this sort of primacy over cheques and bills of exchange—as well as the same inconveniences when large and complex transactions are afoot.

Doubtless, finally, some of the cardinal problems of philosophy are set by the existence of logical tangles not in this as opposed to that branch of specialist theory, but in the thought and the discourse of everyone, specialists and non-specialists alike. The con-

ORDINARY LANGUAGE

cepts of *cause, evidence, knowledge, mistake, ought, can,* etc., are not the perquisites of any particular groups of people. We employ them before we begin to develop or follow specialist theories; and we could not follow or develop such theories unless we could already employ these concepts. They belong to the rudiments of all thinking, including specialist thinking. But it does not follow from this that all philosophical questions are questions about such rudimentary concepts. The architect must indeed be careful about the materials of his building; but it is not only about these that he must be careful.

"USE"

But now for a further point. The phrase 'the ordinary (i.e., stock) use of the expression " . . . " ' is often so spoken that the stress is made to fall on the word 'expression' or else on the word 'ordinary' and the word 'use' is slurred over. The reverse ought to be the case. The operative word is *'use'*.

Hume's question was not about the word 'cause'; it was about the *use* of 'cause'. It was just as much about the *use* of 'Ursache'. For the use of 'cause' is the same as the use of 'Ursache', though 'cause' is not the same word as 'Ursache'. Hume's question was not a question about a bit of the English language in any way in which it was not a question about a bit of the German language. The job done with the English word 'cause' is not an English job, or a continental job. What I do with my Nottingham-made boots— namely walk in them—is not Nottingham-made; but nor is it Leicester-made or Derby-made. The transactions I perform with a sixpenny-bit have neither milled nor unmilled edges; they have no edges at all. We might discuss what I can and cannot do with a sixpenny-bit, namely what I can and cannot buy with it, what change I should and should not give or take for it, and so on; but such a discussion would not be a discussion about the date, ingredients, shape, colour or provenance of the coin. It is a discussion about the purchasing power of this coin, or of any other coin of the same value, and not about *this coin*. It is not a numismatic discussion, but a commercial or financial discussion. Putting the stress on the word 'use' helps to bring out the important fact that the enquiry is an enquiry not into the other features or properties of

THE PHILOSOPHICAL REVIEW

the word or coin or pair of boots, but only into what is done with it, or with anything else with which we do the same thing. That is why it is so misleading to classify philosophical questions as linguistic questions—or as non-linguistic questions.

It is, I think, only in fairly recent years that philosophers have picked up the trick of talking about the use of expressions, and even made a virtue of so talking. Our forefathers, at one time, talked instead of the *concepts* or *ideas* corresponding to expressions. This was in many ways a very convenient idiom, and one which in most situations we do well to retain. It had the drawback, though, that it encouraged people to start Platonic or Lockean hares about the status and provenance of these concepts or ideas. The impression was given that a philosopher who wanted to discuss, say, the concept of *cause* or *infinitesimal* or *remorse* was under some obligation to start by deciding whether concepts have a supramundane, or only a psychological existence; whether they are transcendent intuitables or only private introspectibles.

Later on, when philosophers were in revolt against psychologism in logic, there was a vogue for another idiom, the idiom of talking about the *meanings* of expressions, and the phrase 'the concept of cause' was replaced by the phrase "the meaning of the word 'cause' or of any other with the same meaning". This new idiom was also subject to anti-Platonic and anti-Lockean cavils; but its biggest drawback was a different one. Philosophers and logicians were at that time the victims of a special and erroneous theory about meaning. They construed the verb 'to mean' as standing for a relation between an expression and some other entity. The meaning of an expression was taken to be an entity which had that expression for its name. So studying the meaning of the phrase 'the solar system' was supposed or half-supposed to be the same thing as studying the solar system. It was partly in reaction against this erroneous view that philosophers came to prefer the idiom "the use of the expressions '. . . caused . . .' and '. . . the solar system' ". We are accustomed to talking of the use of safety-pins, bannisters, table-knives, badges and gestures; and this familiar idiom neither connotes nor seems to connote any queer relations to any queer entities. It draws our attention to the teachable procedures and techniques of handling or employing things, without suggesting unwanted correlates.

ORDINARY LANGUAGE

Learning how to manage a canoe-paddle, a traveller's cheque or a postage-stamp, is not being introduced to an extra entity. Nor is learning how to manage the words 'if', 'ought' and 'limit'.

There is another merit in this idiom. Where we can speak of managing, handling and employing we can speak of mismanaging, mishandling and misemploying. There are rules to keep or break, codes to observe or flout. Learning to use expressions, like learning to use coins, stamps, cheques and hockey-sticks, involves learning to do certain things with them and not others; when to do certain things with them, and when not to do them. Among the things that we learn in the process of learning to use linguistic expressions are what we may vaguely call 'rules of logic'; for example, that though Mother and Father can both be tall, they cannot both be taller than one another; or that though uncles can be rich or poor, fat or thin, they cannot be male or female, but only male. Where it would sound unplausible to say that concepts or ideas or meanings might be meaningless or absurd, there is no such unplausibility in asserting that someone might use a certain expression absurdly. An attempted or suggested way of operating with an expression may be logically illegitimate or impossible, but a universal or a state of consciousness or a meaning cannot be logically legitimate or illegitimate.

"USE" AND "UTILITY"

On the other hand there are inconveniences in talking much of the *uses* of expressions. People are liable to construe 'use' in one of the ways which English certainly does permit, namely as a synonym of 'utility' or 'usefulness'. They then suppose that to discuss the use of an expression is to discuss what it is useful for or how useful it is. Sometimes such considerations are philosophically profitable. But it is easy to see that discussing the use (*versus* uselessness) of something is quite different from discussing the use (*versus* misuse) of it, i.e., the way, method or manner of using it. The female driver may learn what is the utility of a sparking-plug, but learning this is not learning how to operate with a sparking-plug. She does not have or lack skills or competences with sparking-plugs, as she does with steering-wheels, coins, words and knives. Her sparking-plugs manage themselves; or, rather, they are not man-

THE PHILOSOPHICAL REVIEW

aged at all. They just function automatically, until they cease to function. They are useful, even indispensable to her. But she does not manage or mismanage them.

Conversely, a person who has learned how to whistle tunes may not find the whistling of tunes at all useful or even pleasant to others or to himself. He manages, or sometimes mismanages his lips, tongue and breath; and, more indirectly, manages or mismanages the notes he produces. He has got the trick of it; he can show us and perhaps even tell us how the trick is performed. But it is a useless trick. The question, How do you use your breath or your lips in whistling? has a positive and complicated answer. The question, What is the use, or utility of whistling? has a negative and simple one. The former is a request for the details of a technique; the latter is not. Questions about the use of an expression are often, though not always, questions about the way to operate with it; not questions about what the employer of it needs it for. They are How-questions, not What-for-questions. This latter sort of question can be asked, but it is seldom necessary to ask it, since the answer is usually obvious. In a foreign country, I do not ask what a centime or a peseta is for; what I do ask is how many of them I have to give for a certain article, or how many of them I am to expect to get in exchange for a half-crown. I want to know what its purchasing power is; not that it is for making purchases with.

"USE" AND "USAGE"

Much more insidious than this confusion between the way of operating with something and its usefulness, is the confusion between a 'use', i.e., a way of operating with something, and a 'usage'. Lots of philosophers, whose dominant good resolution is to discern logico-linguistic differences, talk without qualms as if 'use' and 'usage' were synonyms. This is just a howler; for which there is little excuse except that in the archaic phrase 'use and wont', 'use' could, perhaps, be replaced by 'usage'; that 'used to' does mean 'accustomed to'; and that to be hardly used is to suffer hard usage.

A usage is a custom, practice, fashion or vogue. It can be local or widespread, obsolete or current, rural or urban, vulgar or academic. There cannot be a misusage any more than there can be a

ORDINARY LANGUAGE

miscustom or a misvogue. The methods of discovering linguistic usages are the methods of philologists.

By contrast, a way of operating with a razor blade, a word, a traveller's cheque or a canoe-paddle is a technique, knack or method. Learning it is learning how to do the thing; it is not finding out sociological generalities, not even sociological generalities about other people who do similar or different things with razor blades, words, travellers' cheques or canoe-paddles. Robinson Crusoe might find out for himself how to make and how to throw boomerangs; but this discovery would tell him nothing about those Australian aborigines who do in fact make and use them in the same way. The description of a conjuring-trick is not the description of all the conjurors who perform or have performed that trick. On the contrary, in order to describe the possessors of the trick, we should have already to be able to give some sort of description of the trick itself. Mrs. Beeton tells us how to make omelets; but she gives us no information about Parisian chefs. Baedeker might tell us about Parisian chefs, and tell us which of them make omelets; but if he wanted to tell us how they make omelets, he would have to describe their techniques in the way that Mrs. Beeton describes the technique of making omelets. Descriptions of usages presuppose descriptions of uses, i.e., ways or techniques of doing the thing, the more or less widely prevailing practice of doing which constitutes the usage.

There is an important difference between the employment of boomerangs, bows and arrows, and canoe-paddles on the one hand and the employment of tennis rackets, tug-of-war ropes, coins, stamps and words on the other hand. The latter are instruments of inter-personal, i.e., concerted or competitive actions. Robinson Crusoe might play some games of patience; but he could not play tennis or cricket. So a person who learns to use a tennis racket, a stroke-side oar, a coin or a word is inevitably in a position to notice other people using these things. He cannot master the tricks of such inter-personal transactions without at the same time finding out facts about some other people's employment and misemployment of them; and normally he will learn a good many of the tricks from noticing other people employing them. Even so, learning the knacks is not and does not require making a sociological study. A child

THE PHILOSOPHICAL REVIEW

may learn in the home and the village shop how to use pennies, shillings and pound notes; and his mastery of these slightly complex knacks is not improved by hearing how many people in other places and years have managed and now manage or mismanage their pennies, shillings and pound notes. Perfectly mastering a use is not getting to know everything, or even much, about a usage, even when mastering that use does causally involve finding out a bit about a few other people's practices. We were taught in the nursery how to handle a lot of words; but we were not being taught any historical or sociological generalities about employers of these words. That came later, if it came at all.

Before passing on we should notice one big difference between using canoe-paddles or tennis rackets on the one hand and using postage stamps, safety-pins, coins and words on the other. Tennis rackets are wielded with greater or less skill; even the tennis-champion studies to improve. But, with some unimportant reservations, it is true to say that coins, cheques, stamps, separate words, buttons and shoelaces offer no scope for talent. Either a person knows or he does not know how to use and how not to misuse them. Of course literary composition and argumentation can be more or less skilful; but the essayist or lawyer does not know the meaning of 'rabbit' or 'and' better than Everyman. There is no room here for 'better'. Similarly, the champion chess-player manoeuvres more skilfully than the amateur; but he does not know the permitted moves of the pieces better. They both know them perfectly, or rather they just know them.

Certainly, the cultured chess-player may describe the permitted moves better than does the uncultured chess-player. But he does not make these moves any better. I give change for a half-crown no better than you do. We both just give the correct change. Yet I may describe such transactions more effectively than you can describe them. Knowing how to operate is not knowing how to tell how to operate. This point becomes important when we are discussing, say, the stock way (supposing there is one) of employing the word 'cause'. The doctor knows how to make this use of it as well as anyone, but he may not be able to answer any of the philosopher's enquiries about this way of using it.

In order to avoid these two big confusions, the confusion of 'use'

ORDINARY LANGUAGE

with 'usefulness' and the confusion of 'use' with 'usage', I try now-adays to use, *inter alia*, 'employ' and 'employment' instead of the verb and noun 'use'. So I say this. Philosophers often have to try to describe the stock (or, more rarely, some non-stock) manner or way of employing an expression. Sometimes such an expression belongs to the vernacular; sometimes to some technical vocabulary; sometimes it is betwixt and between. Describing the mode of employment of an expression does not require and is not usually helped by information about the prevalence or unprevalence of this way of employing it. For the philosopher, like other folk, has long since learned how to employ or handle it, and what he is trying to describe is what he himself has learned.

Techniques are not vogues—but they may have vogues. Some of them must have vogues or be current in some other way. For it is no accident that ways of employing words, as of employing coins, stamps and chessmen, *tend* to be identical through a whole community and over a long stretch of time. We want to understand and be understood; and we learn our native tongue from our elders. Even without the pressure of legislation and dictionaries, our vocabularies tend towards uniformity. Fads and idiosyncrasies in these matters impair communication. Fads and idiosyncrasies in matters of postage stamps, coins and the moves of chessmen are ruled out by explicit legislation, and partly analogous conformities are imposed upon many technical vocabularies by such things as drill-manuals and text-books. Notoriously these tendencies towards uniformity have their exceptions. However, as there naturally do exist many pretty widespread and pretty long enduring vocabulary usages, it is sometimes condonable for a philosopher to remind his readers of a mode of employing an expression by alluding to 'what everyone says' or 'what no one says'. The reader considers the mode of employment that he has long since learned and feels strengthened, when told that big battalions are on his side. In fact, of course, this appeal to prevalence is philosophically pointless, besides being philologically risky. What is wanted is, perhaps, the extraction of the logical rules implicitly governing a concept, i.e., a way of operating with an expression (or any other expression that does the same work). It is probable that the use of this expression, to perform this job, is widely current; but whether it is so or not,

THE PHILOSOPHICAL REVIEW

is of no philosophical interest. Job-analysis is not Mass Observation. Nor is it helped by Mass Observation. But Mass Observation sometimes needs the aid of job-analysis.

Before terminating this discussion of the use of the expression 'the use of the expression " ... " ', I want to draw attention to an interesting point. We can ask whether a person knows how to use and how not misuse a certain word. But we cannot ask whether he knows how to use a certain *sentence*. When a block of words has congealed into a phrase we can ask whether he knows how to use the phrase. But when a sequence of words has not yet congealed into a phrase, while we can ask whether he knows how to use its ingredient words, we cannot easily ask whether he knows how to use that sequence. Why can we not even ask whether he knows how to use a certain sentence? For we talk about the meanings of sentences, seemingly just as we talk of the meanings of the words in it; so, if knowing the meaning of a word is knowing how to use it, we might have expected that knowing the meaning of a sentence was knowing how to use the sentence. Yet this glaringly does not go.

A cook uses salt, sugar, flour, beans and bacon in making a pie. She uses, and perhaps misuses, the ingredients. But she does not, in this way, use the pie. Her pie is not an ingredient. In a somewhat different way, the cook uses, and perhaps misuses, a rolling-pin, a fork, a frying-pan and an oven. These are the utensils with which she makes her pie. But the pie is not another utensil. The pie is (well or badly) composed out of the ingredients, by means of the utensils. It is what she used them for; but it cannot be listed in either class of them. Somewhat, but only somewhat, similarly a sentence is (well or badly) constructed out of words. It is what the speaker or writer uses them for. He composes it out of them. His sentence is not itself something which, in this way, he either uses or misuses, either uses or does not use. His composition is not a component of his composition. We can tell a person to say something (e.g., ask a question, give a command or narrate an anecdote), using a specified word or phrase; and he will know what he is being told to do. But if we just tell him to pronounce or write down, by itself, that specified word or phrase, he will see the differ-

ORDINARY LANGUAGE

ence between this order and the other one. For he is not now being told to use, i.e., *incorporate* the word or phrase, but only to pronounce it or write it down. Sentences are things that we say. Words and phrases are what we say things *with*.

There can be dictionaries of words and dictionaries of phrases. But there cannot be dictionaries of sentences. This is not because such dictionaries would have to be infinitely and therefore impracticably long. On the contrary, it is because they could not even begin. Words and phrases are there, in the bin, for people to avail themselves of when they want to say things. But the sayings of these things are not some more things which are there in the bin for people to avail themselves of, when they want to say these things. This fact that words and phrases can, while sentences cannot be misused, since sentences cannot be, in this way, used at all, is quite consistent with the important fact that sentences can be well or ill constructed. We can say things awkwardly or ungrammatically and we can say things which are grammatically proper, but do not make sense.

It follows that there are some radical differences between what is meant by 'the meaning of a word or phrase' and what is meant by 'the meaning of a sentence'. Understanding a word or phrase is knowing how to use it, i.e., make it perform its rôle in a wide range of sentences. But understanding a sentence is not knowing how to make it perform its rôle. The play has not got a rôle.

We are tempted to suppose that the question, How are word-meanings related to sentence-meanings? is a tricky but genuine question, a question, perhaps, rather like, How is the purchasing power of my shilling related to the purchasing power of the contents of my pay-envelope? But this model puts things awry from the start.

If I know the meaning of a word or phrase I know something like a body of unwritten rules, or something like an unwritten code or general recipe. I have learned to use the word correctly in an unlimited variety of different settings. What I know is, in this respect, somewhat like what I know when I know how to use a knight or a pawn at chess. I have learned to put it to its work anywhen and anywhere, if there is work for it to do. But the idea of putting a sentence to its work anywhen and anywhere is fantastic.

THE PHILOSOPHICAL REVIEW

It has not got a rôle which it can perform again and again in different plays. It has not got a rôle at all, any more than a play has a rôle. Knowing what it means is not knowing anything like a code or a body of rules, though it requires knowing the codes or rules governing the use of the words or phrases that make it up. There are general rules and recipes for constructing sentences of certain kinds; but not general rules or recipes for constructing the particular sentence 'Today is Monday'. Knowing the meaning of 'Today is Monday' is not knowing general rules, codes or recipes governing the use of this sentence, since there is no such thing as the utilisation or, therefore, the re-utilisation of this sentence. I expect that this ties up with the fact that sentences and clauses make sense or make no sense, where words neither do nor do not make sense, but only have meanings; and that pretence-sentences can be absurd or nonsensical, where pretence-words are neither absurd nor nonsensical, but only meaningless. I can say stupid things, but words can be neither stupid nor not stupid.

PHILOSOPHY AND ORDINARY LANGUAGE

The vogue of the phrase 'the use of ordinary language' seems to suggest to some people the idea that there exists a philosophical doctrine according to which (a) all philosophical enquiries are concerned with vernacular, as opposed to more or less technical, academic or esoteric terms; and (b) in consequence, all philosophical discussions ought themselves to be couched entirely in vernacular dictions. The inference is fallacious, though its conclusion has some truth in it. Even if it were true, which it is not, that all philosophical problems are concerned with non-technical concepts, i.e., with the mode of employment of vernacular expressions, it would not follow from this (false) premiss that the discussions of these problems must or had better be in jurymen's English, French or German.

From the fact that a philologist studies those English words which stem from Celtic roots, it does not follow that he must or had better say what he has to say about them in words of Celtic origin. From the fact that a psychologist is discussing the psychology of witticisms, it does not follow that he ought to write wittily all or any of the time. Clearly he ought not to write wittily most of the time.

ORDINARY LANGUAGE

Most philosophers have in fact employed a good number of the technical terms of past or contemporary logical theory. We may sometimes wish that they had taken a few more pinches of salt, but we do not reproach them for availing themselves of these technical expedients; we should have deplored their long-windedness if they had tried to do without them.

But enslavement to jargon, whether inherited or invented, is, certainly, a bad quality in any writer, whether he be a philosopher or not. It curtails the number of people who can understand and criticise his writings; so it tends to make his own thinking run in a private groove. The use of avoidable jargons is bad literary manners and bad pedagogic policy, as well as being detrimental to the thinker's own wits.

But this is not peculiar to philosophy. Bureaucrats, judges, theologians, literary critics, bankers and, perhaps above all, psychologists and sociologists would all be well advised to try very hard to write in plain and blunt words. None the less, Hobbes who had this virtue of writing plainly and bluntly was a lesser philosopher than Kant who lacked it; and Plato's later dialogues, though harder to translate, have powers which his early dialogues are without. Nor is the simplicity of his diction in Mill's account of mathematics enough to make us prefer it to the account given by Frege, whose diction is more esoteric.

In short, there is no *a priori* or peculiar obligation laid upon philosophers to refrain from talking esoterically; but there is a general obligation upon all thinkers and writers to try to think and write both as powerfully and as plainly as possible. But plainness of diction and power of thought can vary independently, though it is not common for them to do so.

Incidentally it would be silly to require the language of professional journals to be as exoteric as the language of books. Colleagues can be expected to use and understand one another's terms of art. But books are not written only for colleagues. The judge should not address the jury in the language in which he may address his brother judges. Sometimes, but only sometimes, he may be well advised to address even his brother judges, and himself, in the language in which he should address the jury. It all depends on whether his technical terms are proving to be a help or a hindrance.

THE PHILOSOPHICAL REVIEW

They are likely to be a hindrance when they are legacies from a period in which today's questions were not even envisaged. This is what justifies the regular and salutary rebellions of philosophers against the philosophical jargons of their fathers.

There is another reason why philosophers ought sometimes to eschew other people's technical terms. Even when a philosopher is interesting himself in some of the cardinal concepts of, say, physical theory, he is usually partly concerned to state the logical cross-bearings between the concepts of this theory and the concepts of mathematical, theological, biological or psychological theory. Very often his radical puzzle is that of determining these cross-bearings. When trying to solve puzzles of this sort, he cannot naïvely employ the dictions of either theory. He has to stand back from both theories, and discuss the concepts of both in terms which are propri-etary to neither. He may coin neutral dictions of his own, but for ease of understanding he may prefer the dictions of Everyman. These have this required neutrality, even if they lack that semi-codification which disciplines the terms of art of professionalised thought. Barter-terms are not as well regimented as the terms of the counting-house; but when we have to determine rates of ex-change between different currencies, it is to barter-terms that we may have to turn. Inter-theory negotiations can be and may have to be conducted in pre-theory dictions.

So far I have, I hope, been mollifying rather than provoking. I now want to say two philosophically contentious things.

(a) There is a special reason why philosophers, unlike other professionals and specialists, are constantly jettisoning *in toto* all the technical terms of their own predecessors (save some of the technical terms of formal logic); i.e., why the jargon words of epistemology, ethics, aesthetics, etc., seem to be half-hardy annuals rather than hardy perennials. The reason is this. The experts who use the technical terms of bridge, law, chemistry and plumbing learn to employ these terms partly from official instructions but largely by directly engaging in the special techniques and by directly dealing with the special materials or objects of their specialism. They familiarise themselves with the harness by having to drive their (to us unfamiliar) horses.

But the terms of art of philosophy itself (save for those of formal

ORDINARY LANGUAGE

logic), are not like this. There is no peculiar field of knowledge or adeptness in which philosophers *ex officio* make themselves the experts—except of course the business of philosophising itself. We know by what special sorts of work mastery is acquired of the concepts of *finesse, tort, sulphanilamide* and *valve-seating.* But by what corresponding special sorts of work do philosophers get their supposed corresponding mastery of the concepts of *Cognition, Sensation, Secondary Qualities* and *Essences?* What exercises and predicaments have forced them to learn just how to use and how not to misuse these terms?

Philosopher's arguments which turn on these terms are apt, sooner or later, to start to rotate idly. There is nothing to make them point north rather than nor'-nor'-east. The bridge-player cannot play fast and loose with the concepts of *finesse* and *revoke.* If he tries to make them work in a way palatable to him, they jib. The unofficial terms of everyday discourse are like the official terms of specialisms in this important respect. They too jib, if maltreated. It is no more possible to say that someone knows something to be the case which is not so than it is possible to say that the player of the first card in a game of bridge has revoked. We have had to learn in the hard school of daily life how to deploy the verb 'know'; and we have had to learn at the bridge-table how to deploy the verb 'revoke'. There is no such hard school in which to learn how to deploy the verbs 'cognize' and 'sense'. These go through what motions we care to require of them, which means that they have acquired no discipline of their own at all. So the philosophical arguments, which are supposed to deploy these units, win and lose no fights, since these units have no fight in them. Hence, the appeal from philosophical jargon to the expressions which we have all had to learn to use properly (as the chess-player has had to learn the moves of his pieces) is often one well worth making; where a corresponding appeal to the vocabulary of Everyman from the official parlance of a science, of a game or of law would often, not always, be ridiculous. One contrast of 'ordinary' (in the phrase 'ordinary language') is with 'philosophers' jargon'.

(b) But now for quite a different point and one of considerable contemporary importance. The appeal to what we do and do not say, or can and cannot say, is often stoutly resisted by the protagonists of one special doctrine, and stoutly pressed by its antagonists. This doctrine is the doctrine that philosophical disputes can and should be settled by formalising the warring theses. A theory is formalised when it is translated out of the natural language (untechnical, technical or semi-technical), in which it was originally excogitated, into a deliberately constructed notation, the notation, perhaps of *Principia Mathematica*. The logic of a theoretical position can, it is claimed, be regularised by stretching its non-formal concepts between the topic-neutral logical constants whose conduct in inferences is regulated by set drills. Formalisation will replace logical perplexities by logical problems amenable to known and teachable procedures of calculation. Thus one contrast of 'ordinary' (in the phrase 'ordinary language') is with 'notational'.

Of those to whom this, the formaliser's dream, appears a mere dream (I am one of them), some maintain that the logic of everyday statements and even the logic of the statements of scientists, lawyers, historians and bridge-players cannot in principle be adequately represented by the formulae of formal logic. The so-called logical constants do indeed have, partly by deliberate prescription, their scheduled logical powers; but the non-formal expressions both of everyday discourse and of technical discourse have their own unscheduled logical powers, and these are not reducible without remainder to those of the carefully wired marionettes of formal logic. The title of a novel by A. E. W. Mason 'They Wouldn't be Chessmen' applies well to both the technical and the untechnical expressions of professional and daily life. This is not to say that the examination of the logical behaviour of the terms of non-notational discourse is not assisted by studies in formal logic. Of course it is. So may chess-playing assist generals, though waging campaigns cannot be replaced by playing games of chess.

I do not want here to thrash out this important issue. I want only to show that resistance to one sort of appeal to ordinary language ought to involve championing the programme of formalisation. 'Back to ordinary language' can be (but often is not) the slogan of those who have awoken from the formaliser's dream. This slogan, so used, should be repudiated only by those who hope to replace philosophising by reckoning.

ORDINARY LANGUAGE

VERDICT

Well, then, has philosophy got something to do with the use of expressions or hasn't it? To ask this is simply to ask whether conceptual discussions, i.e., discussions about the concept of, say, *voluntariness, infinitesimals, number* or *cause,* come under the heading of philosophical discussions. Of course they do. They always have done, and they have not stopped doing so now.

Whether we gain more than we lose by sedulously advertising the fact that what we are investigating is the stock way of operating with, say, the word 'cause', depends a good deal on the context of the discussions and the intellectual habits of the people with whom we are discussing it. It is certainly a long-winded way of announcing what we are doing; and inverted commas are certainly vexatious to the eye. But, more important than these nuisances, preoccupation with questions about methods tends to distract us from prosecuting the methods themselves. We run, as a rule, worse, not better, if we think a lot about our feet. So let us, at least on alternate days, speak instead of investigating the concept of *causation.* Or, better still, let us, on those days, not speak of it at all but just do it.

But the more longwinded idiom has some big compensating advantages. If we are enquiring into problems of perception, i.e., discussing questions about the concepts of seeing, hearing and smelling, we may be taken to be tackling the questions of opticians, neuro-physiologists or psychologists, and even fall into this mistake ourselves. It is then salutary to keep on reminding ourselves and one another that what we are after is accounts of how certain words work, namely words like 'see', 'look', 'overlook', 'blind', 'visualise' and lots of other affiliated expressions.

One last point. I have talked in general terms about learning and describing the modes of employment of expressions. But there are many different dimensions of these modes, only some of which are of interest to philosophers. Differences of stylistic elegance, rhetorical persuasiveness, and social propriety need to be considered, but not, save *per accidens,* by philosophers. Churchill would have made a rhetorical blunder if he had said, instead of 'We shall fight them on the beaches . . .', 'We shall fight them on the sands . . .'. 'Sands' would have raised thoughts of children's holidays at Skegness. But

THE PHILOSOPHICAL REVIEW

this kind of misemployment of 'sands' is not the kind of mishandling that interests us. We are interested in the informal logic of the employment of expressions, the nature of the logical howlers that people do or might commit if they strung their words together in certain ways, or, more positively, in the logical force that expressions have as components of theories and as pivots of concrete arguments. That is why, in our discussions, we argue *with* expressions and *about* those expressions in one and the same breath. We are trying to register what we are exhibiting; to codify the very logical codes which we are then and there observing.

GILBERT RYLE

Magdalen College, Oxford

5

Use, Usage and Meaning

GILBERT RYLE AND J. N. FINDLAY

Reprinted with the kind permission of the Editor of The Aristotelian Society from *Proceedings of the Aristotelian Society Supplement,* XXXV (1961), 223-42. © 1961 The Aristotelian Society.

V

USE, USAGE AND MEANING

(1) GILBERT RYLE

IN 1932 Mr. (now Sir) Alan H. Gardiner published *The Theory of Speech and Language* (Clarendon Press). A central theme of his book was what, with some acknowledged verbal artificiality, he labelled the distinction between 'Language' and 'Speech'. I shall draw, develop and apply this distinction in my own way.

A Language, such as the French language, is a stock, fund or deposit of words, constructions, intonations, *cliché* phrases and so on. 'Speech', on the other hand, or 'discourse' can be conscripted to denote the activity or rather the clan of activities of saying things, saying them in French, it may be, or English or some other language. A stock of language-pieces is not a lot of activities, but the fairly lasting wherewithal to conduct them; somewhat as a stock of coins is not a momentary transaction or set of momentary transactions of buying, lending, investing, etc., but is the lasting wherewithal to conduct such transactions. Roughly, as Capital stands to Trade, so Language stands to Speech.

A Language is something to be known, and we get to know it by learning it. We learn it partly by being taught it, and partly by picking it up. For any given part of a language, a learner may not yet have learned that part; or he may have learned it and not forgotten it, or he may have learned it and forgotten it, or he may have half-learned it; or he may have half-forgotten it. A Language is a corpus of teachable things. It is not, of course, a static corpus until it is a dead language. Nor would two teachers of it always agree whether something should be taught as a part of that language. Is French literary style to be taught by teachers of the French Language or by teachers of French Literature? Just when does an acceptable turn of phrase become an idiom? How old can a neologism be? What about slang?

Saying something in a language involves but does not reduce to knowing the requisite pieces of that language. The speaker is here

Symposium by Gilbert Ryle and J. N. Findlay, from *Proceedings of the Aristotelian Society*, Supp. Vol. 35 (1961), pp. 223–42. Reprinted by courtesy of the authors and the Editor of the Aristotelian Society.

and now employing what he had previously acquired and still possesses. He is now in the act of operating with things of which he has,
perhaps for years, been the possessor. The words, constructions,
intonations, etc., that he employs in saying what he says in these
words, constructions, etc., is not another part of that language. It
is a momentary operation *with* parts of that language, just as the
buying or lending that I do with part of my capital is not itself a
part of that capital, but a momentary operation with a part of it.
That, indeed, is what my capital is for, namely, to enable me to make
purchases, benefactions, loans, etc., with parts of it whenever I
wish to do so. It is a set of moderately permanent possibilities of
making particular momentary transactions.

   If I say something in French, then, even though what I say has
never been said before, I do not thereby enlarge the French language,
i.e., increase the amount to be learned by a student of the French
language. The fact that he does not know what I said does not entail
that there is a bit of the French language that he has still to learn.
Dicta made in French are not parts of the French language. They are
things done with parts of the French language. You might utilize the
same parts in saying something identical with or quite different from
what I said. Your act of saying it is not mine, and neither is a part
of the fund on which we both draw. But dicta can notoriously fossilize
into *clichés*. '*Je ne sais quoi*' can now be used as a noun; and '*Rest
and be Thankful*' can be a proper name.

   We are tempted to treat the relation between sentences and words
as akin to the relation between faggots and sticks. But this is entirely
wrong. Words, constructions, etc., are the atoms of a Language;
sentences are the units of Speech. Words, constructions, etc., are what
we have to learn in mastering a language; sentences are what we
produce when we say things. Words have histories; sentences do not,
though their authors do. I must have learned the words that I
utter when I say something with them. I need not, and, with reservations, cannot have learned the sentence that I come out with when I
say something. It is something that I compose, not something that
I have acquired. I am its author, not its employer. Sentences are
not things of which I have a stock or fund. Nor are my buyings and
lendings things of which I have a hoard or purseful.

   In daily life we do not often mention as such the sentences that
people produce. We speak instead of their allegations, complaints,
promises, verdicts, requests, witticisms, confessions and commands.
It is, in the main, people like grammarians, compositors, translators,

amanuenses and editors who need to refer to the things that people say as 'sentences', since they are *ex officio* concerned with such matters as page-space, punctuation, syntax, plagiarisation, and so on. None the less, what they are interested in are instances of someone, actual or imagined, alleging, complaining, warning, joking, etc., though their special concern is with the punctuation of them and not with their humorousness; with their length and not with their truth; with their moods and tenses and not with their relevance or rudeness.

When Caesar said '*Veni; vidi; vici*', he said three things, though he used only three Latin words. Then is '*Vici*' a word or a sentence? The queerness of this disjunctive question is revealing. What Caesar produced, orally or in writing, on a certain day, was a laconic sentence, if a sentence is an instance of someone saying something. In this instance Caesar said something which was true. But he said it using only one Latin word, a word which had long been there for anyone to use anywhen in saying all sorts of considerably different things. The word was not true, or, of course, false either. Caesar boasted '*Vici*', but the dictionary's explanation of the verb '*Vici*' need say nothing about Caesar boasting. What it describes was, perhaps, also used by, *inter alios*, some concussed gladiator asking anxiously '*Vici?*'. The boast '*vici*' was a different sentence from the question '*vici?*', though the authors of both used the same Latin word, of which neither was the inventor. The word '*vici*' was there, in their common fund, to be employed, misemployed or left unemployed by anyone anywhere. The boast '*vici*' and the query '*vici?*' were two momentary speech-acts in which this one word was utilized for saying different things. Our question 'Is "*vici*" a word or a sentence?' was queer because its subject was ambiguous. Was it about a speech-episode, like a boast or a query, or was it about an inflected Latin verb? It was queer also because '... a word or a sentence?' was a disjunction between predicates of quite different categories, on a par with '... a bat or a stroke?'

Is the interrogative sentence '*vici?*' a part of the Latin language? Well, would a student still have some Latin to learn who had never met it? Surely not. What he had learned is enough to enable him to construe it if he should ever meet it. What he construes are employments of Latin words, constructions, etc.; what he must know in order to construe or understand these employments, are the Latin words, inflections, constructions, etc. He must know the word in order to understand the one-word boast or question; but that knowing is not this understanding; what he had long since known is not what he has just understood or misunderstood. As we employ coins to make loans, but do not employ lendings, so we employ words, etc., in order to say things, but we do not employ the sayings of things—or misemploy them or leave them unemployed either. Dictions and dicta belong to different categories. So do roads and journeys; so do gallows and executions.

Sometimes a person tries to say something and fails through ignorance of the language. Perhaps he stops short because he does not know or cannot think of the required words or constructions. Perhaps he does not stop, but produces the wrong word or construction, thinking it to be the right one, and so commits a solecism. Perhaps his failure is of lesser magnitude; he says something unidiomatically or ungrammatically; or he gets the wrong intonation or he mispronounces. Such failures show that he has not completely mastered, say, the French language. In the extended sense of 'rule' in which a rule is anything against which faults are adjudged to be at fault, solecisms, mispronunciations, malapropisms, and unidiomatic and ungrammatical constructions are breaches of the rules of, e.g., the French language. For our purposes we do not need to consider the sources or the status of rules of this kind, or the authorities whose censures our French instructor dreads. Solecisms are in general philosophically uninteresting. Nor, for obvious reasons, do we often commit solecisms, save when young, ill-schooled, abroad or out of our intellectual depth.

The reproof 'You cannot say that and speak good French' is generically different from the reproof 'You cannot say that without absurdity'. The latter is not a comment on the quality of the speaker's French, since it could be true though the speaker had spoken in flawless French, or had not been speaking in French at all, but in English or Greek instead. The comment, if true, would be true of what was said whatever language it was said in, and whether it was said in barbarous or impeccable French or English. A mis-pronunciation or a wrong gender may be a bit of faulty French, but a self-contradiction is not a fault-in-French. Cicero's *non sequiturs* were not lapses from good Latin into bad Latin. His carelessness or incompetence was not linguistic carelessness or incompetence, if we tether the adjective 'linguistic' to the noun 'Language' as this is here being contrasted with 'Speech'.

There is an enormous variety of disparate kinds of faults that we can find or claim to find with things that people say. I can complain, justly or else unjustly, that what you said was tactless, irrelevant, repetitious, false, inaccurate, insubordinate, trite, fallacious, ill-timed, blasphemous, malicious, vapid, uninformative, over-informtive, prejudiced, pedantic, obscure, prudish, provocative, self-contradictory, tautologous, circular or nonsensical and so on indefinitely. Some of these epithets can be appropriate also to behaviour which is not speech-behaviour; some of them cannot. Not one of them could be asserted or denied of any item in an English or French dictionary or Grammar. I can stigmatize what you said with any one of these epithets without even hinting that what you said was faulty in its French or whatever other language you said it in. I grumble at your dictum but not at your mastery of the language that it was made in. There are countless heterogeneous disciplines and corrections which are meant to train people not to commit these Speech-faults. Not one of them belongs to the relatively homogeneous discipline of teaching, say, the French language. Speech-faults are not to be equated with Language-faults. Nothing need be wrong with the paints, brushes and canvas with which a portrait is bungled. Painting badly is not a pot of bad paint.

Logicians and philosophers are, *ex officio*, much concerned with kinds of things that people say or might be tempted to say. Only where there can be fallacies can there be valid inferences, namely in arguments; and only where there can be absurdities can there be non-absurdities, namely in dicta. We are presented with *aporiai* not by the telescope or the trawling-net, but by passages in books or by ripostes in debates. A fallacy or an impossible consequence may indeed have to be presented to us in French or English, etc. But it does not follow from this that what is wrong with it is anything faulty in the French or English in which it is presented. It was no part of the business of our French or English instructors to teach us that if most men wear coats and most men wear waistcoats it does not follow that most men wear both. This is a different sort of lesson and one which we cannot begin until we have already learned to use without solecism 'most', 'and', 'if', etc. There are no French implications or non-implications, so though 'p' may be said in French and 'q' may be said in French, it is nonsense to say 'q does not follow from p in the best French'. Similarly, what is impossible in 'The Cheshire Cat vanished, leaving only her grin behind her' is not any piece of intolerably barbarous English. Carroll's wording of the impossible story could not be improved, and the impossibility of his narrated incident survives translation into any language into which it can be translated. Something was amusingly wrong with what he said, but not with what he said it in.

I have a special reason for harking on this point that what someone says may be fallacious or absurd without being in any measure solecistic; i.e., that some Speech-faults, including some of those which matter to logicians and philosophers, are not and do not carry with them any Language-faults. Some philosophers, oblivious of the distinction between Language and Speech, or between having words, etc., to say things with and saying things with them, give to sentences the kind of treatment that they give to words, and, in particular, assimilate their accounts of what a sentence means to their accounts of what a word means. Equating the notion of the meaning of a word with the notion of the use of that word, they go on without apparent qualms to talking as if the meaning of a sentence could equally well be spoken of as the use of that sentence. We hear, for example, that nonsensical English sentences are sentences that have no use in English; as if sentences could *be* solecisms. Should we expect to hear that a certain argument is henceforth to contain an Undistributed Middle in B.B.C. English?

My last sentence but three, say, is not something with which I once learned how to say things. It *is* my saying something. Nor is an execution something erected to hang people on. It *is* the hanging of somebody. Part of what we learn, in learning the words of a language, is indeed how to employ them. But the act of exercising this acquired competence, i.e., the saying something with them is not in its turn an acquired wherewithal to say things. It neither has nor lacks a use, or, therefore, a use in English.

The famous saying: 'Don't ask for the meaning; ask for the use', might have been and I hope was a piece of advice to philosophers, and not to lexicographers or translators. It advised philosophers, I hope, when wrestling with some *aporia*, to switch their attention from the trouble-giving words in their dormancy as language-pieces or dictionary-items to their utilisations in the actual sayings of things; from their general promises when on the shelf to their particular performances when at work; from their permanent purchasing-power while in the bank to the concrete marketing done yesterday morning with them; in short, from these words *quā* units of a Language to live sentences in which they are being actively employed.

More than this; the famous saying, in association with the idea of Rules of Use, could and I think should have been intended to advise philosophers, when surveying the kinds of live dicta that are or might be made with these trouble-giving words, to consider especially some of the kinds of non-solecistic Speech-faults against which the producer of such live dicta ought to take precautions, e.g., what sorts of dicta could not be significantly made with them, and why; what patterns of argument pivoting on these live dicta would be fallacious, and why; what kinds of verification-procedures would be impertinent, and why; to what kinds of questions such live dicta would be irrelevant, and why; and so on. To be clear about the 'how' of the employment of something we need to be clear also about its 'how not to', and about the reasons for both.

Early in this century Husserl and later Wittgenstein used the illuminating metaphors of 'logical syntax' and 'logical grammar'. Somewhat as, say, indicative verbs used instead of subjunctive verbs render some would-be Latin sentences bad Latin, so certain category-skids and logical howlers render dicta, said in no matter which tongue, nonsensical or absurd. A so-called Rule of Logical Syntax is what a nonsensical dictum is in breach of. But the analogy must not be pressed very far. The rules of Latin syntax are part of what we must learn if we are to be able to produce or construe Latin dicta. They are parts of the equipment to be employed by someone if he is to say either sensible or silly things in decent Latin. The Rules of Logical Syntax, on the other hand, belong not to a Language or to Languages, but to Speech. A person who says something senseless or illogical betrays not ignorance but silliness, muddle-headedness or, in some of the interesting cases, over-cleverness. We find fault not with his schooling in years gone by but with his thinking here and now. He has not forgotten or misremembered any of his lessons; he has operated unwarily or over-ingeniously in his execution of his momentary task. In retrospect he will reproach not his teachers, but himself; and he will reproach himself not for never having known something but for not having been thinking what he was saying yesterday.

The vogue of using 'Language' and 'linguistic' ambivalently both for dictions and for dicta, i.e., both for the words, etc., that we say things in and for what we say in them, helps to blind us to the wholesale inappropriateness of the epithets which fit pieces of language to the sayings of things with those pieces; and to the wholesale and hetero-geneous inappropriatenesses of the variegated epithets which fit things said to the language-pieces and language-patterns that they are said in.

It remains true that philosophers and logicians do have to talk about talk or, to put it in a more Victorian way, to discourse about discourse. But it is not true that they are *ex officio* concerned with what language-teachers are *ex officio* concerned with.

(2) J. N. Findlay

I am in great agreement with what I regard as the substantial points in Professor Ryle's paper. His definition of language I think rather arbitrarily narrow: for him it is a 'stock, fund or deposit of words, constructions, *cliché* phrases and so on'. I should have thought it would be wrong not to include in a language the various syntactical and other *rules* which restrict our employment of the capital of expressions mentioned by Professor Ryle, though perhaps I am wrong in thinking he meant to exclude them. That adjectives must agree with the gender of their substantives in certain cases would certainly be held to be part of the French language, as it is not part of the English. There is also, I think, a further arbitrariness in excluding sentences from *language*, and in making them the units of *speech* which are produced when we say things. I think we can and should distinguish between the sentence *Je ne sais quoi* as a mere possibility permitted by the French language, and the same sentence as used or produced by someone to say something. I can in fact see no good reason why one should not have a narrower and a wider conception of a language. On the narrower conception, a language includes a vocabulary and rules, whereas on the wider conception it includes also *all* the possible sentences that could be framed out of the vocabulary in accordance with the rules. In this sense French or English would include all the permissible sentences that could be framed in it, whether anyone ever uttered or wrote or thought them or not. If this conception of a language makes it absurdly wide, the conception of it as a vocabulary plus rules makes it unduly narrow. Certainly, however, I think we want to distinguish between a sentence as a grammatically permissible word-combination, and the utterance or writing down or silent thinking of that sentence by someone on some occasion to make an allegation, raise a query, express a doubt, etc., etc., and in the latter case I find a language of *use* or *employment* more natural than Professor Ryle's language of *production*. I think therefore that Professor Ryle is legislating rather vexatiously in forbidding us to speak of sentences as parts of language, or to say that such sentences can be *used* by speakers. I do not, however, think that this vexatious piece of legislation is in the forefront of Professor Ryle's intentions.

What Professor Ryle is mainly concerned to do seems to me to be to distinguish between grammatical faults in the use of words in constructing sentences, and faults in what may be called 'logical syntax' or 'logical grammar', which involve the use of words to construct perfectly grammatical sentences, but which none the less violate a deeper set of rules, the rules of sense, the rules of logic, the rules regulating the mutual relations of categories, etc., etc. With all this I am deeply in agreement, because it involves precisely the recognition that different sorts of words, as it were, make different sorts of abstract *cuts* in their subject-matter, or help to execute different sorts of abstract *cuts*—some, as Aristotle might say, tell us *what* things are, others *how* they are, others *how many* they are, others *conjoin*, others *emphasize*, others *bracket*, etc., etc.—and that in making such quite different types of cross-section they become subject to the relations necessarily obtaining among such cross-sections, so that some verbal combinations which are smooth and pretty grammatically none the less make hideous nonsense. Professor Ryle, it seems to me, is here suggesting that it is the relations of different sorts of *meanings* to one another which determine the depth-grammar of words, and that these meanings and their relations are matters that must be *independently* considered if we are to study logical as well as grammatical syntax. If this suggestion is not implicit in his words, perhaps he will explain what sort of abuse of words it is that is logical or depth-grammatical as opposed to merely surface-grammatical abuse. Incidentally, I feel in the contexts invoked by Ryle that it is doubly tempting to talk of the *use* and *abuse* of grammatical sentences. The sentence is there, a fully-fashioned grammatical entity, and it is its use to express a categorially possible combination of meanings which is at times possible and legitimate, whereas at other times there is really only an abuse.

Having expressed my agreement and disagreement with Ryle, I may perhaps allow myself to dwell a little on the famous dictum which he quotes and which has dominated philosophical discussion for the past twenty years: 'Don't ask for the meaning: ask for the use.' I wish to make against it the not often raised objection that the use for which it bids us ask, is of all things the most obscure, the most veiled in philosophical mists, the most remote from detailed determination or application, in the wide range of philosophical concepts. There is, I think, a use of 'use' which is humdrum and ordinary, but in which a study of the use of expressions is of only limited philosophical importance and interest. There is also a use of 'use' characteristic of the later writings of Wittgenstein which is utterly remote from the humdrum and ordinary, and which has won its way into the acceptance of philosophers largely because it has *seemed* to have the clearness and the straightforwardness of the ordinary use. We are all proof against the glozing deceits of words like 'substance', 'being', 'nothingness', 'consciousness', etc., etc.: we at once see that some occasions of their employment are really only abuses—but we are not yet proof against the fascinations exerted by the singular abuses of so ordinary a term as 'use'. When these abuses are exposed, the whole attitude represented by the slogan quoted by Ryle reveals itself as completely without significant basis, which unfortunately puts an end to all but a limited emphasis on 'use' and 'usage' by philosophers. Since the suggestion that use and usage—in some acceptable sense— *are* philosophically very important, certainly underlies Ryle's paper, I need not apologize for irrelevance in proceeding to demolish this suggestion.

The reason why it is absurd to tell us *not* to attend to the meaning of expressions but to concentrate on their use, is perfectly simple: it is that the notion of use, as it ordinarily exists and is used, presupposes the notion of meaning (in its central and paradigmatic sense), and that it cannot therefore be used to elucidate the latter, and much less to replace or to do duty for it. The notion of use is a *wider* notion than the paradigmatic notion of meaning: it covers many *other* things beside the meaning of an expression, but the meaning-function in its paradigmatic sense is certainly *one* of the things it covers, and it is not possible to give a clear account of use without presupposing this function. What I am saying is simply that we cannot fully say, in a great many cases, how an expression is used, without saying what sort of things it is intended to refer to, or to bring to mind, and just how, or in what angle or light, it purports to refer to them, or to bring them to mind. And in cases where it would be wrong and absurd to say that an expression *independently* brought something to mind, or presented it in a certain light, it would none the less be uncontestably right to say that it *helped* to do such things in some definite manner, so that what was brought to mind would be *different*, or *differently presented*, if the expression were not part of our total utterance. Thus if I

make use of the word 'dragon' in a large number of contexts, I use it
to refer to a human being or beings, generally mature and female, and
I use it also to represent such a human being or beings as being
restrictive, uncompromising and somewhat terrifying. And if I *apply*
the term in a certain context I see that to which I apply it in the light
connoted by my words. And if I use the words 'such a' before uttering
the word 'dragon', these words certainly help to suggest that what I
am describing is *very* restrictive, *very* uncompromising and *very* terrifying, i.e., they contribute to the force of my description without
playing an independent part of it. In saying what the use of my
expressions is, I therefore have to say what, in the ordinary diction of
logicians, they denote and connote, what their precise reference is or
what their general scope, or how they contribute to connotation
or denotation, and it is not thought possible to say how many expressions are *used*, without bringing in such connotative and denotative
particulars.

   The notion of use of course goes far *beyond* that of connotation and
denotation, and it is one of the extremely important discoveries of
modern semantics that there are *some* expressions whose use, in
certain contexts, is *not* to connote or denote anything, nor even to
help to do either, but to do such things as give voice to feelings
and wishes, evoke certain attitudes in others, or *perform* certain
formal social acts, e.g., promises, which have certain definite
social consequences, etc., etc. That *not* all expressions, on all
occasions of their *use*, perform the functions of reference or characterization, or assist in such performance, is certainly a discovery
not to be underestimated, which has cleared the deck of much tangled
tackle and many stumbling-blocks. But this kind of *non*-referential,
non-connotative use is parasitic upon a connotative, referential
one, and could hardly exist without it. It is one of Wittgenstein's
more irresponsible fancies that there could be a language composed
only of commands, or *only* of curses, or *only* of greetings. The concept
of use also certainly covers all the hidden *implications* and *suggestions*
which attach to the writing or utterance of a word or a sentence,
but which are not strictly part of what it means or says: thus when
I say 'He did not commit this murder' I may use this sentence to
imply that he committed certain other murders, that I absolutely
believe him to be no murderer, that we live under laws forbidding
the taking of life, etc., etc. But all such implications and suggestions
are likewise dependent upon the function of directly connoting or
denoting something, and are in fact an extension of the same.

Use also obviously covers the mere requirements of accidence and syntax, though these, as Ryle has shown, are mere instrumentalities in the task of significant diction.

What is implicit, however, in the slogan 'Don't ask for the meaning: ask for the use' is not that use covers much *more* than the connotative and denotative functions of language, but that it somehow resumes and completely explains the latter, that we can completely see around and see through talk about the reference and connotation of expressions by taking note of the way people operate with such expressions, how they combine them with other expressions to form sentences, and the varying *circumstances* in which producing such sentences is reckoned appropriate or fully justifiable. This study of verbal manoeuvres, and of appropriate and justifying circumstances, must not, however, be confined to the single instant of utterance: it must point *backwards* to the all-important situations in which use was *learnt* or *taught*, and it must point *forwards* to the innumerable situations in which the utterance in question will again be found *appropriate*, or will be found to be more and more abundantly *justified*. The study of use therefore includes a genealogy and a prognosis of the most indefinite and complex kind, much more extensive than any that occurs in a merely grammatical or philological study. In another respect, however, the slogan gives 'use' an extraordinarily restricted interpretation. The operations involved in use are not to be operations conducted privately in anyone's head, or at least such operations can only be brought into consideration in so far as they can be narrowly tied up with other non-private operations, and the *circumstances* in which such operations are conducted must all be circumstances belonging to what may be called the common public environment, circumstances in which bricks are being assembled into buildings, apples taken from drawers and handed over to customers, railway-signals altered, or hunting expeditions conducted. The sort of change which is a mere change in perspective or in conscious 'light' is *not* among the circumstances mentionable in describing use.

And there is yet another most extraordinary restriction placed upon our account of the *circumstances* in which a word is correctly used: we must not employ the word or its equivalent to explain those circumstances. We must not, e.g., say, that when a man is confronted by three apples in a drawer, or by an apple and another apple and yet another apple, he is then justified in employing the word 'three' in connexion with such apples. The word 'three' may be employed in describing the circumstances justifying countless *other* sorts of utterance, but not the circumstances justifying its *own* employment. In the same way we must never say that it is when a man is confronted by a red object, or has learnt to discriminate its colour, that he is justified in calling it 'red'. Such accounts are held to be wholly trivial and unilluminating, and are moreover held to suggest various deep philosophical fallacies: the belief that meanings exist 'out there' in the things we deal with *before* we find the appropriate words to 'pick them out', or that they exist 'in the mind' or the understanding before we find words to express them. Whatever we suggest by our accounts of use, we must never suggest that there are *pre-existent meanings*. Words enjoy meaning and reference in and by our use of them, and our use cannot be explained in terms of any meaning that antedates the use of words. And since understanding and thinking are defined in terms of the operation with signs, we must never speak as if we could understand or think anything before we dispose of appropriate verbal expressions and have been taught to employ them. The programme of this extreme 'utilitarianism'—as one may perhaps call the use-doctrine—is impressive: it resembles nothing so much as the brave empiricist programme of Locke and Hume, in which no idea was to be admitted into the charmed circle of thought and knowledge without producing a genealogy purer than any required by the Nuremberg laws, exhibiting a proper origin in sensation and reflection, and a derivation from these by approved processes. But, like that brave programme, it faces the crucial objection that it cannot be carried out completely, and that no comprehensive account of use and usage can be given which does not contain some members of impure origin. That the brave programme was hopeless Wittgenstein himself perhaps obscurely realized, when he wrongly said of the *Brown Book*, the most profound and wonderful of his writings, that it was *nichts wert*. But if success, rather than stimulus and provocation, is the criterion of philosophical value, his judgement was entirely justified.

I need not range far nor cite many instances to make plain the totally unilluminating, indeed deeply obfuscating character of attempts to give a complete account of the use of expressions in terms of merely public operations and circumstances. The very conception of a *rule*, central to the 'utilitarianism' in question, abounds in difficulty. For we are expressly told that to follow a rule is not necessarily to be guided by a spoken or written formula, since each such formula admits of interpretation in terms of another formula, and this in terms of another, and so on indefinitely. Nor is the following of a rule to be identified with any sort of inner personal understanding of that rule which can guide one's subsequent performance, since to hold this would be to accept pre-existent meanings resident in the queer medium of the mind. Nor can the following of a rule be identified with one's actual performance up to a point, since this is always compatible with an infinity of rules. In the end it would seem that following a rule must be an ineffable sort of affair: it must be something that can be accomplished in one's *doing* (in this case, speaking), but not effectively spoken *about*. It is something that one can know how *to do* without being able to know how what one does is done. The conception of a linguistic rule has, in fact, all the irretrievable obscurity of the structural resemblance constitutive of meaning in the *Tractatus*, which cannot be expressed but only *shown*. If it is at least *possible* that a rule should at times be understood or grasped in thought, we can understand what it is like to follow it without thought, but if grasping is a function of following, the whole activity of following dissolves in mystery. I do not myself know how it differs from the most arbitrary irregularity except that it mysteriously *feels* right at every stage, and that others, standing at my side, mysteriously agree in such feelings. And if it is hard to throw light on the following of rules in terms of outward circumstances and performances, how much harder it is to say in what lies conformity to an *open* rule, one which is to be applied over and over *indefinitely*. While the *thought* expressed by the phrase 'and so on indefinitely' is most absolutely simple and easy to entertain, it is a thought *logically* impossible to evince adequately in one's performance. Much has been written, from the standpoint of the use-doctrine, about the difference between closed and open games, but the discussion ends up with very much what it started from, that it is a difference in the *spirit* with which the respective games are played. A man, e.g., using an open arithmetic simply has a system or general rule for constructing numerals *indefinitely*. That a spirit is operative in this case I should not care to deny, but that it consorts well with the use-doctrine, or establishes its superiority, I cannot conceive.

Similar difficulties confront us if we consider the use-account of the use of descriptive adjectives like those of colour. We are forbidden to talk of prior colour-differences in objects, or prior colour-discriminations in persons, as this would involve the grave error of positing pre-existent meanings. We are introduced to imaginary tribal activities which involve the picturesque carrying about of charts of colour samples and their comparison with, or imposition on objects, but these it would seem explain little or nothing, since the charts are dispensable and admit moreover of a wrong use. From the use of charts the tribe progresses to the use of colour samples carried somehow in the mind's eye, and ultimately to the mere unhesitant pronouncement, after sufficient training, of certain colour-words in the presence of certain objects. With this pronouncement others as unhesitatingly agree. From the Scylla of holding that 'blue' stands for a discriminable blueness in objects, or expresses an awareness of blueness in one's mind, one proceeds to the Charybdis of saying that those things are blue which we and others agree, and have been trained, to call so. It is plain, of course, that one must have ultimates somewhere, and it is plain also that there are different possibilities of colour-discrimination corresponding to different possibilities of usage: what is *not* plain is why one should prefer such a strange, secondary ultimate as a *use* to the more obvious, understandable ultimates of discriminating thoughts in the mind, or discriminable features in things.

The most superb example of the problem-increasing character of the use-semantics is, however, to be found in its treatment of cases where men use expressions without obvious reference to any palpable feature of the public environment, when they give voice, e.g., to recollections or anticipations, or describe their personal feelings or impressions, or report their fantasies or their dreams. Here the course is followed of attempting to account for such uses by supposing men to be such as *spontaneously* to want to use expressions taught in certain contexts in contexts where their normal justification is absent, and that these non-normal needs, so strangely universal among us, constitute the basis for a new *secondary* set of linguistic usages, where the sole fact that we agree in feeling certain linguistic urges is the sole criterion of their correctness. Thus children perhaps spontaneously run over the names of objects recently presented to them, or can be encouraged to do so without difficulty: meaning can then be given to the *past tense*, and they can learn to say that they *had* a ball, a stick, a rattle, etc. To 'refer to the past' is merely to learn to employ the past tense in such circumstances, an account as amusingly free in presupposing pastness and temporal passage in the *circumstances* of the learning, as it is firm in denying any non-verbal *understanding* of them. Men then spontaneously begin to use the past tense where there is no such recent provocation: we then give a use to talk about 'remembering', particularly if others agree in such spontaneous inclinations. The reference to the past in memory is therefore not the ultimate, mysterious thing that Husserl, Broad and others have supposed it to be: it merely reflects the strange tendency of men to talk preteritively beyond the limits of recency, and the further linkage of this fact with the readings of instruments, the reports of others, and many other observed matters. It may now happen that men waking, from sleep spontaneously talk in the past tense *as if* recalling happenings which no one remembers, and which do not fit in with the observable contemporary state, or with the memory-inclinations of others. The concept of 'dreaming' now makes its *debut* to take care of these extraordinary performances. Malcolm, the admirable exponent of a preposterous analysis, admits[1] that on it dream-language is very odd: it is *as if* one is faithfully recalling something, but one cannot explain this fact by saying that one *did* experience what one is disposed to report, since this would involve an unintelligible hypothesis, one excluded by the guiding assumptions of the doctrine of use. What these queer-nesses surely show is the profound mistakenness somewhere of these guiding assumptions. To make use of a gnostic principle used by Moore in other contexts: we *know* certain facts about meaning much more absolutely than we can be sure of the premises, or the inferential rules, of semantic arguments designed either to establish them, or to explain them away. Obviously we cannot make straight sense of many linguistic usages without postulating just those pre-existent understandings (not confined to matters in the public fore-front) and the possibility of communicating such understandings to others, which it is the whole aim of the use-doctrine to exclude.

The use-doctrine may further be objected to for its profoundly circular, question-begging character. This is a point ably made by Mr. Gellner in a book[2] where some of the most profound criticisms of the use-doctrine and its consequences lie hidden under a some-what popular exterior. To have seen an unacceptable, unargued naturalism behind Wittgenstein's brilliant façade of exposition, is no mean insight. By describing the functioning of linguistic expression exclusively in public and social terms, we at once *go too far* in assuming such approaches to be wholly justified and clear, and we also *do not go far enough* in refusing to recognize aspects of language not fitting an approach of this sort, or in 'proving'

[1] [The reference is to N. Malcolm, *Dreaming* (London, 1959). Ed.]

[2] [E. Gellner, *Words and Things* (London, 1959). Ed.]

them to be misguided or senseless. These two lines of objection really coincide, since it is by turning away from aspects of language it cannot readily accommodate that the use-doctrine is unable to see its own difficulties and obscurities. The use-theorists have dwelt much on the profound subtlety of ordinary language, but they have been far from recognizing *how* subtle it actually is. For it not only uses expressions to point to, or to throw light on, ordinary objects, but it also uses them *reflexly*, in the manner studied in Husserl's *Logische Untersuchungen*, to point to or throw light on its own *meanings*, thereby setting up an order of objects as clear-edged and partial as its normal objects are fuzzy and full, and as delicate in their abstraction as they are indispensable for the higher flights of thought. That a phrase like 'the third door on the right' can be used both straightforwardly to refer to a door, and reflexly to refer to its own meaning, is a truth plain to babes, but occasioning head-aches to the semantically over-wise and prudent. Ordinary speech further, provides us with an instrument for communicating with others about matters public and common, which is also an instrument for purely personal use, in which different observations, different views, different judgements provide much the same complementary parallax, and the same corrective or confirmatory testing as in the interpersonal case. But not only is it thus double in its use, it also manages to incorporate the personal in the public use, and the public in the personal, in a regress pursuable as far as even we choose. Thus we all understand other people's first-person talk by analogy with our own, and its imperfect public intelligibility is also perfectly and publicly intelligible, since everyone makes just such first-person statements in his own case. The manner in which we smoothly swing over from another man's perfectly understood use of the first-person pronoun 'I', and replace it with 'he' in reporting the content of his statement, and expect the other man to do the same in regard to us, as well as the children's games in which these proprieties are amusingly violated: all these show an understanding of the antithesis of contrasted privacies, and of their overcoming in a wider publicity, of which the use-semantics betrays no inkling. In the same manner, ordinary speech has in it the germs of what may be called the Cartesian or the Lockean inversion, the reversal of the ordinary approach from outward things to the mind, into an approach to outer things from the facts of our subjective life. Though the language in which we talk of and to ourselves—the best subject-matter and audience—may have had its *source* in contexts

E

of public ostensibility, it can, by a profitable ingratitude, use the personal language thus painfully acquired to cast doubt upon, or to throw light on, its own origin. We may illuminate our understanding and knowledge of public matters in terms of just those personal experiences and pre-existent understandings which talk about public matters first renders possible. And this personal Cartesian or Lockean story can then achieve the widest publicity, since to have back rooms continuous with those opening on the public square is the most universal, most inescapable of predicaments. It is no doubt by a creative transformation that the rumour of the square penetrates backwards, and is re-echoed in the small back rooms, and it is likewise by a creative transformation that these transformed echoes rejoin the rumour of the square. All this, however, unquestionably happens, and it is the task of a philosophical semantics to make sense of it, and not to declare it unintelligible.

Nothing that has been said in the foregoing is meant to reflect on the painstaking, detailed study of linguistic usage, or the actual manner of its teaching, if used to show how we actually come to mean what we undoubtedly do mean, or to throw light on the complexity and subtlety of our meanings, or to show how we come to be misled into supposing we mean what really conflicts with the 'depth-grammar' of our meanings. Our criticisms are only of a radical use-theory carried to extremes, which constructs fables as to how we might have been taught the meanings of words in order to buttress *a priori* doctrines as to what we *must* or *cannot* mean. If anyone thinks such doctrines archaic and superseded, and so not requiring rebuttal, he is wide of the truth. Wittgenstein's accounts of language-games are so arresting, so novel, so subtle in their detailed development, so daring in their frank embrace of the unplausible, so imbued with intellectual seriousness and earnestness, and so great, finally, in their aesthetic appeal, that it is hard to see through them or around them. They fascinate the philosopher in the same way that Wittgenstein claimed that philosophers were fascinated by the forms of ordinary language, and against such fascination determined steps are necessary. The steps I have taken in this paper may not have been sufficiently subtle, and may have involved certain misunderstandings of detail: I shall hope, at least, to have incited others to do better.

All this should not, of course, be taken as reflecting on the philosophical greatness of Wittgenstein. Wittgenstein is the author of three wholly differing accounts of meaning, all of which merit entire

USE, USAGE AND MEANING   127

rejection: meaning is *not* reduplication of structure, it is *not* verification or verifiability, it is plainly *not* what he meant by 'use'. It is
not these things, though it is of course intimately connected with them
all, but it will be best illuminated by construing further the old
humdrum notions of connotation and denotation, and by seeking
painfully to throw light on the 'thought behind our words', for
which, on account of the peculiar categories it involves, it would
seem that no adequate surrogate has been, or can be, offered. It is,
I surmise, in the 'intentional nature of thought' that the true
solution of the problems of meaning is to be found. But by formulating these three inadequate accounts, Wittgenstein has given the
semantic problem the central place it deserves in philosophy, and
has contributed vastly to its solution. Through his inability to account
satisfactorily for certain linguistic performances, he has indicated
the precise nodes where language makes its various creative leaps and
has thereby given philosophical semantics its opportunity and its
task. Moreover, each of Wittgenstein's frequent rhetorical questions
is such that, if answered in the sense *not* intended by the question, it
will lead to an illuminating result: they are practically all arrows
which, if read in the reverse direction, point unerringly to some
truth. A philosophy of meaning so valuably wrong does not differ
profoundly from one that is systematically right.

6

Meaning

H. P. GRICE

Reprinted with the kind permission of the Author and the Editor from *The Philosophical Review*, LXVI (1957), 377-88.

MEANING

CONSIDER the following sentences:

"Those spots mean (meant) measles."

"Those spots didn't mean anything to me, but to the doctor they meant measles."

"The recent budget means that we shall have a hard year."

(1) I cannot say, "Those spots meant measles, but he hadn't got measles," and I cannot say, "The recent budget means that we shall have a hard year, but we shan't have." That is to say, in cases like the above, *x meant that p* and *x means that p* entail *p*.

(2) I cannot argue from "Those spots mean (meant) measles" to any conclusion about "what is (was) meant by those spots"; for example, I am not entitled to say, "What was meant by those spots was that he had measles." Equally I cannot draw from the statement about the recent budget the conclusion "What is meant by the recent budget is that we shall have a hard year."

(3) I cannot argue from "Those spots meant measles" to any conclusion to the effect that somebody or other meant by those spots so-and-so. *Mutatis mutandis,* the same is true of the sentence about the recent budget.

(4) For none of the above examples can a restatement be found in which the verb "mean" is followed by a sentence or phrase in inverted commas. Thus "Those spots meant measles" cannot be reformulated as "Those spots meant 'measles' " or as "Those spots meant 'he has measles.' "

(5) On the other hand, for all these examples an approximate restatement can be found beginning with the phrase "The fact that . . ."; for example, "The fact that he had those spots meant that he had measles" and "The fact that the recent budget was as it was means that we shall have a hard year."

Now contrast the above sentences with the following:

"Those three rings on the bell (of the bus) mean that the 'bus is full.' "

H. P. GRICE

"That remark, 'Smith couldn't get on without his trouble and strife,' meant that Smith found his wife indispensable."

(1) I can use the first of these and go on to say, "But it isn't in fact full—the conductor has made a mistake"; and I can use the second and go on, "But in fact Smith deserted her seven years ago." That is to say, here *x means that p* and *x meant that p* do not entail *p*.

(2) I can argue from the first to some statement about "what is (was) meant" by the rings on the bell and from the second to some statement about "what is (was) meant" by the quoted remark.

(3) I can argue from the first sentence to the conclusion that somebody (viz., the conductor) meant, or at any rate should have meant, by the rings that the bus is full, and I can argue analogously for the second sentence.

(4) The first sentence can be restated in a form in which the verb "mean" is followed by a phrase in inverted commas, that is, "Those three rings on the bell mean 'the bus is full.'" So also can the second sentence.

(5) Such a sentence as "The fact that the bell has been rung three times means that the bus is full" is not a restatement of the meaning of the first sentence. Both may be true, but they do not have, even approximately, the same meaning.

When the expressions "means," "means something," "means that" are used in the kind of way in which they are used in the first set of sentences, I shall speak of the sense, or senses, in which they are used, as the *natural* sense, or senses, of the expressions in question. When the expressions are used in the kind of way in which they are used in the second set of sentences, I shall speak of the sense, or senses, in which they are used, as the *nonnatural* sense, or senses, of the expressions in question. I shall use the abbreviation "means$_{NN}$" to distinguish the nonnatural sense or senses.

I propose, for convenience, also to include under the head of natural senses of "mean" such senses of "mean" as may be exemplified in sentences of the pattern "*A* means (meant) *to do* so-and-so (by *x*)," where *A* is a human agent. By contrast, as the previous examples show, I include under the head of non-

MEANING

natural senses of "mean" any senses of "mean" found in sentences of the patterns "*A* means (meant) something by *x*" or "*A* means (meant) by *x* that. . . ." (This is overrigid; but it will serve as an indication.)

I do not want to maintain that *all* our uses of "mean" fall easily, obviously, and tidily into one of the two groups I have distinguished; but I think that in most cases we should be at least fairly strongly inclined to assimilate a use of "mean" to one group rather than to the other. The question which now arises is this: "What more can be said about the distinction between the cases where we should say that the word is applied in a natural sense and the cases where we should say that the word is applied in an nonnatural sense?" Asking this question will not of course prohibit us from trying to give an explanation of "meaning$_{NN}$" in terms of one or another natural sense of "mean."

This question about the distinction between natural and non-natural meaning is, I think, what people are getting at when they display an interest in a distinction between "natural" and "conventional" signs. But I think my formulation is better. For some things which can mean$_{NN}$ something are not signs (e.g., words are not), and some are not conventional in any ordinary sense (e.g., certain gestures); while some things which mean naturally are not signs of what they mean (cf. the recent budget example).

I want first to consider briefly, and reject, what I might term a causal type of answer to the question, "What is meaning$_{NN}$?" We might try to say, for instance, more or less with C. L. Stevenson,[1] that for *x* to mean$_{NN}$ something, *x* must have (roughly) a tendency to produce in an audience some attitude (cognitive or otherwise) and a tendency, in the case of a speaker, to *be* produced *by* that attitude, these tendencies being dependent on "an elaborate process of conditioning attending the use of the sign in communication."[2] This clearly will not do.

(1) Let us consider a case where an utterance, if it qualifies at all as meaning$_{NN}$ something, will be of a descriptive or informative kind and the relevant attitude, therefore, will be a cognitive one,

---

[1] *Ethics and Language* (New Haven, 1944), ch. iii.
[2] *Ibid.*, p. 57.

H. P. GRICE

for example, a belief. (I use "utterance" as a neutral word to apply to any candidate for meaning$_{NN}$; it has a convenient act-object ambiguity.) It is no doubt the case that many people have a tendency to put on a tail coat when they think they are about to go to a dance, and it is no doubt also the case that many people, on seeing someone put on a tail coat, would conclude that the person in question was about to go to a dance. Does this satisfy us that putting on a tail coat means$_{NN}$ that one is about to go to a dance (or indeed means$_{NN}$ anything at all)? Obviously not. It is no help to refer to the qualifying phrase "dependent on an elaborate process of conditioning. . . ." For if all this means is that the response to the sight of a tail coat being put on is in some way learned or acquired, it will not exclude the present case from being one of meaning$_{NN}$. But if we have to take seriously the second part of the qualifying phrase ("attending the use of the sign in communication"), then the account of meaning$_{NN}$ is obviously circular. We might just as well say, "*X* has meaning$_{NN}$ if it is used in communication," which, though true, is not helpful.

(2) If this is not enough, there is a difficulty—really the same difficulty, I think—which Stevenson recognizes: how we are to avoid saying, for example, that "Jones is tall" is part of what is meant by "Jones is an athlete," since to tell someone that Jones is an athlete would tend to make him believe that Jones is tall. Stevenson here resorts to invoking linguistic rules, namely, a permissive rule of language that "athletes may be nontall." This amounts to saying that we are not prohibited by rule from speaking of "nontall athletes." But why are we not prohibited? Not because it is not bad grammar, or is not impolite, and so on, but presumably because it is not meaningless (or, if this is too strong, does not in any way violate the rules of meaning for the expressions concerned). But this seems to involve us in another circle. Moreover, one wants to ask why, if it is legitimate to appeal here to rules to distinguish what is meant from what is suggested, this appeal was not made earlier, in the case of groans, for example, to deal with which Stevenson originally introduced the qualifying phrase about dependence on conditioning.

A further deficiency in a causal theory of the type just

MEANING

expounded seems to be that, even if we accept it as it stands, we are furnished with an analysis only of statements about the *standard* meaning, or the meaning in general, of a "sign." No provision is made for dealing with statements about what a particular speaker or writer means by a sign on a particular occasion (which may well diverge from the standard meaning of the sign); nor is it obvious how the theory could be adapted to make such provision. One might even go further in criticism and maintain that the causal theory ignores the fact that the meaning (in general) of a sign needs to be explained in terms of what users of the sign do (or should) mean by it on particular occasions; and so the latter notion, which is unexplained by the causal theory, is in fact the fundamental one. I am sympathetic to this more radical criticism, though I am aware that the point is controversial.

I do not propose to consider any further theories of the "causal-tendency" type. I suspect no such theory could avoid difficulties analogous to those I have outlined without utterly losing its claim to rank as a theory of this type.

I will now try a different and, I hope, more promising line. If we can elucidate the meaning of

"x meant$_{NN}$ something (on a particular occasion)" and
"x meant$_{NN}$ that so-and-so (on a particular occasion)"

and of

"A meant$_{NN}$ something by x (on a particular occasion)" and
"A meant$_{NN}$ by x that so-and-so (on a particular occasion),"

this might reasonably be expected to help us with

"x means$_{NN}$ (timeless) something (that so-and-so),"
"A means$_{NN}$ (timeless) by x something (that so-and-so),"

and with the explication of "means the same as," "understands," "entails," and so on. Let us for the moment pretend that we have to deal only with utterances which might be informative or descriptive.

A first shot would be to suggest that "x meant$_{NN}$ something" would be true if x was intended by its utterer to induce a belief in some "audience" and that to say what the belief was would be to say what x meant$_{NN}$. This will not do. I might leave B's

381

H. P. GRICE

handkerchief near the scene of a murder in order to induce the detective to believe that *B* was the murderer; but we should not want to say that the handkerchief (or my leaving it there) meant$_{NN}$ anything or that I had meant$_{NN}$ by leaving it that *B* was the murderer. Clearly we must at least add that, for *x* to have meant$_{NN}$ anything, not merely must it have been "uttered" with the intention of inducing a certain belief but also the utterer must have intended an "audience" to recognize the intention behind the utterance.

This, though perhaps better, is not good enough. Consider the following cases:

(1) Herod presents Salome with the head of St. John the Baptist on a charger.

(2) Feeling faint, a child lets its mother see how pale it is (hoping that she may draw her own conclusions and help).

(3) I leave the china my daughter has broken lying around for my wife to see.

Here we seem to have cases which satisfy the conditions so far given for meaning$_{NN}$. For example, Herod intended to make Salome believe that St. John the Baptist was dead and no doubt also intended Salome to recognize that he intended her to believe that St. John the Baptist was dead. Similarly for the other cases. Yet I certainly do not think that we should want to say that we have here cases of meaning$_{NN}$.

What we want to find is the difference between, for example, "deliberately and openly letting someone know" and "telling" and between "getting someone to think" and "telling."

The way out is perhaps as follows. Compare the following two cases:

(1) I show Mr. *X* a photograph of Mr. *Y* displaying undue familiarity to Mrs. *X*.

(2) I draw a picture of Mr. *Y* behaving in this manner and show it to Mr. *X*.

I find that I want to deny that in (1) the photograph (or my showing it to Mr. *X*) meant$_{NN}$ anything at all; while I want to assert that in (2) the picture (or my drawing and showing it)

MEANING

meant$_{NN}$ something (that Mr. Y had been unduly unfamiliar), or at least that I had meant$_{NN}$ by it that Mr. Y had been unduly familiar. What is the difference between the two cases? Surely that in case (1) Mr. X's recognition of my intention to make him believe that there is something between Mr. Y and Mrs. X is (more or less) irrelevant to the production of this effect by the photograph. Mr. X would be led by the photograph at least to suspect Mrs. X even if instead of showing it to him I had left it in his room by accident; and I (the photograph shower) would not be unaware of this. But it will make a difference to the effect of my picture on Mr. X whether or not he takes me to be intending to inform him (make him believe something) about Mrs. X, and not to be just doodling or trying to produce a work of art.

But now we seem to be landed in a further difficulty if we accept this account. For consider now, say, frowning. If I frown spontaneously, in the ordinary course of events, someone looking at me may well treat the frown as a natural sign of displeasure. But if I frown deliberately (to convey my displeasure), an onlooker may be expected, provided he recognizes my intention, *still* to conclude that I am displeased. Ought we not then to say, since it could not be expected to make any difference to the onlooker's reaction whether he regards my frown as spontaneous or as intended to be informative, that my frown (deliberate) does *not* mean$_{NN}$ anything? I think this difficulty can be met; for though in general a deliberate frown may have the same effect (as regards inducing belief in my displeasure) as a spontaneous frown, it can be expected to have the same effect only *provided* the audience takes it as intended to convey displeasure. That is, if we take away the recognition of intention, leaving the other circumstances (including the recognition of the frown as deliberate), the belief-producing tendency of the frown must be regarded as being impaired or destroyed.

Perhaps we may sum up what is necessary for A to mean something by x as follows. A must intend to induce by x a belief in an audience, and he must also intend his utterance to be recognized as so intended. But these intentions are not independent; the recognition is intended by A to play its part in inducing the belief, and if it does not do so something will have gone wrong with the fulfillment of A's intentions. Moreover, A's intending that the recognition should play this part implies, I think, that he assumes that there is some chance that it will in fact play this part, that he does not regard it as a foregone conclusion that the belief will be induced in the audience whether or not the intention behind the utterance is recognized. Shortly, perhaps, we may say that "A meant$_{NN}$ something by x" is roughly equivalent to "A uttered x with the intention of inducing a belief by means of the recognition of this intention." (This seems to involve a reflexive paradox, but it does not really do so.)

Now perhaps it is time to drop the pretense that we have to deal only with "informative" cases. Let us start with some examples of imperatives or quasi-imperatives. I have a very avaricious man in my room, and I want him to go; so I throw a pound note out of the window. Is there here any utterance with a meaning$_{NN}$? No, because in behaving as I did, I did not intend his recognition of my purpose to be in any way effective in getting him to go. This is parallel to the photograph case. If on the other hand I had pointed to the door or given him a little push, then my behavior might well be held to constitute a meaningful$_{NN}$ utterance, just because the recognition of my intention would be intended by me to be effective in speeding his departure. Another pair of cases would be (1) a policeman who stops a car by standing in its way and (2) a policeman who stops a car by waving.

Or, to turn briefly to another type of case, if as an examiner I fail a man, I may well cause him distress or indignation or humiliation; and if I am vindictive, I may intend this effect and even intend him to recognize my intention. But I should not be inclined to say that my failing him meant$_{NN}$ anything. On the other hand, if I cut someone in the street I do feel inclined to assimilate this to the cases of meaning$_{NN}$, and this inclination seems to me dependent on the fact that I could not reasonably expect him to be distressed (indignant, humiliated) unless he recognized my intention to affect him in this way. (Cf., if my college stopped my salary altogether I should accuse them of ruining me; if they cut it by 2/6^d I might accuse them of insulting me; with some intermediate amounts I might not know quite what to say.)

MEANING

Perhaps then we may make the following generalizations.

(1) "*A* meant$_{NN}$ something by *x*" is (roughly) equivalent to "*A* intended the utterance of *x* to produce some effect in an audience by means of the recognition of this intention"; and we may add that to ask what *A* meant is to ask for a specification of the intended effect (though, of course, it may not always be possible to get a straight answer involving a "that" clause, for example, "a belief that . . .").

(2) "*x* meant something" is (roughly) equivalent to "Somebody meant$_{NN}$ something by *x*." Here again there will be cases where this will not quite work. I feel inclined to say that (as regards traffic lights) the change to red meant$_{NN}$ that the traffic was to stop; but it would be very unnatural to say, "Somebody (e.g., the Corporation) meant$_{NN}$ by the red-light change that the traffic was to stop." Nevertheless, there seems to be *some* sort of reference to somebody's intentions.

(3) "*x* means$_{NN}$ (timeless) that so-and-so" might as a first shot be equated with some statement or disjunction of statements about what "people" (vague) intend (with qualifications about "recognition") to effect by *x*. I shall have a word to say about this.

Will any kind of intended effect do, or may there be cases where an effect is intended (with the required qualifications) and yet we should not want to talk of meaning$_{NN}$? Suppose I discovered some person so constituted that, when I told him that whenever I grunted in a special way I wanted him to blush or to incur some physical malady, thereafter whenever he recognized the grunt (and with it my intention), he did blush or incur the malady. Should we then want to say that the grunt meant$_{NN}$ something? I do not think so. This points to the fact that for *x* to have meaning$_{NN}$, the intended effect must be something which in some sense is within the control of the audience, or that in some sense of "reason" the recognition of the intention behind *x* is for the audience a reason and not merely a cause. It might look as if there is a sort of pun here ("reason for believing" and "reason for doing"), but I do not think this is serious. For though no doubt from one point of view questions about reasons for believing are questions about evidence and so quite different from questions about reasons for doing, nevertheless to recognize an utterer's intention in uttering *x* (descriptive utterance), to have a reason for believing that so-and-so, is at least quite like "having a motive for" accepting so-and-so. Decisions "that" seem to involve decisions "to" (and this is why we can "refuse to believe" and also be "compelled to believe"). (The "cutting" case needs slightly different treatment, for one cannot in any straight-forward sense "decide" to be offended; but one can refuse to be offended.) It looks then as if the intended effect must be something within the control of the audience, or at least the *sort* of thing which is within its control.

One point before passing to an objection or two. I think it follows that from what I have said about the connection between meaning$_{NN}$ and recognition of intention that (insofar as I am right) only what I may call the primary intention of an utterer is relevant to the meaning$_{NN}$ of an utterance. For if I utter *x*, intending (with the aid of the recognition of this intention) to induce an effect *E*, and intend this effect *E* to lead to a further effect *F*, then insofar as the occurrence of *F* is thought to be dependent solely on *E*, I cannot regard *F* as in the least dependent on recognition of my intention to induce *E*. That is, if (say) I intend to get a man to do something by giving him some infor-mation, it cannot be regarded as relevant to the meaning$_{NN}$ of my utterance to describe what I intend him to do.

Now some question may be raised about my use, fairly free, of such words as "intention" and "recognition." I must disclaim any intention of peopling all our talking life with armies of complicated psychological occurrences. I do not hope to solve any philosophical puzzles about intending, but I do want briefly to argue that no special difficulties are raised by my use of the word "intention" in connection with meaning. First, there will be cases where an utterance is accompanied or preceded by a conscious "plan," or explicit formulation of intention (e.g., I declare how I am going to use *x*, or ask myself how to "get something across"). The presence of such an explicit "plan" obviously counts fairly heavily in favor of the utterer's intention (meaning) being as "planned"; though it is not, I think, con-clusive; for example, a speaker who has declared an intention

MEANING

to use a familiar expression in an unfamiliar way may slip into the familiar use. Similarly in nonlinguistic cases: if we are asking about an agent's intention, a previous expression counts heavily; nevertheless, a man might plan to throw a letter in the dustbin and yet take it to the post; when lifting his hand he might "come to" and say *either* "I didn't intend to do this at all" *or* "I suppose I must have been intending to put it in."

Explicitly formulated linguistic (or quasi-linguistic) intentions are no doubt comparatively rare. In their absence we would seem to rely on very much the same kinds of criteria as we do in the case of nonlinguistic intentions where there is a general usage. An utterer is held to intend to convey what is normally conveyed (or normally intended to be conveyed), and we require a good reason for accepting that a particular use diverges from the general usage (e.g., he never knew or had forgotten the general usage). Similarly in nonlinguistic cases: we are presumed to intend the normal consequences of our actions.

Again, in cases where there is doubt, say, about which of two or more things an utterer intends to convey, we tend to refer to the context (linguistic or otherwise) of the utterance and ask which of the alternatives would be relevant to other things he is saying or doing, or which intention in a particular situation would fit in with some purpose he obviously has (e.g., a man who calls for a "pump" at a fire would not want a bicycle pump). Non-linguistic parallels are obvious: context is a criterion in settling the question of why a man who has just put a cigarette in his mouth has put his hand in his pocket; relevance to an obvious end is a criterion in settling why a man is running away from a bull.

In certain linguistic cases we ask the utterer afterward about his intention, and in a few of these cases (the very difficult ones, like a philosopher asked to explain the meaning of an unclear passage in one of his works), the answer is not based on what he remembers but is more like a decision, a decision about how what he said is to be taken. I cannot find a nonlinguistic parallel here; but the case is so special as not to seem to contribute a vital difference.

All this is very obvious; but surely to show that the criteria

387

MEANING

for judging linguistic intentions are very like the criteria for judging nonlinguistic intentions is to show that linguistic intentions are very like nonlinguistic intentions.

H. P. Grice

St. John's College
Oxford

7

The Assertion Fallacy

JOHN R. SEARLE

Reprinted with the kind permission of the publisher from John R. Searle, *Speech Acts* (Cambridge: Cambridge University Press, 1969), 141-49.

6.3   *The assertion fallacy*

I now turn to the third fallacy, which is closely related to the second and which I shall call *the assertion fallacy*. It is the fallacy of confusing the conditions for the performance of the speech act of assertion with the analysis of the meaning of particular words occurring in certain assertions.

Linguistic philosophers wish to analyze the meaning of such traditionally troublesome concepts as knowledge, memory, or voluntary action. To do this, they look to the *use* of such expressions as "know", "remember", "free", "voluntary", etc. The trouble with this method is that in practice it almost always amounts to asking when we would make assertions of the form, "I know that so and so", or "He remembers such and such", or "He did such and such voluntarily". But then there is no easy way to tell how much their answers to these questions depend on what it is to *make assertions* and how much is due to the concepts the philosopher is trying to analyze.

The philosopher notices that it would be very odd or bizarre to say certain things in certain situations; so he then concludes for that reason that certain concepts are inapplicable to such situations. For example, Wittgenstein points out that under normal conditions, when I have a pain, it would be odd to say, "*I know* I am in pain".[1] Another linguistic philosopher[2] has pointed out that it would be very odd for normal adult Englishmen in ordinary situations to say, "I *remember* my own name", or "I *remember* how to speak English". But they then conclude that these are points about the concepts of knowing and remembering; that these concepts are only applicable under certain conditions. I, on the other hand, shall argue that the reason it would be odd to say such things is that they are too *obvious* to be worth saying. It's obviously true that when I have a pain, I know I have it, and it's equally obvious that I do now remember my own name and also

[1] Ludwig Wittgenstein, *Philosophical Investigations* (New York, 1953), e.g., para. 246.
[2] B. S. Benjamin, 'Remembering', *Mind* (1956); reprinted in Donald F. Gustafson (ed.), *Essays in Philosophical Psychology* (New York, 1964).

Three fallacies in contemporary philosophy

remember how to speak English, and the reason it is odd to announce such things under normal circumstances is precisely because they are too obvious to merit announcing.

But before developing this point in terms of conditions for making assertions, I want to consider some other examples of the same fallacy. Ryle says in the *Concept of Mind*[1] that in their most ordinary employment the adjectives "voluntary" and "involuntary" are used as adjectives applying only to actions which ought not to be done. He says, "In this ordinary use, then, it is absurd to discuss whether satisfactory, correct or admirable performances are voluntary or involuntary".[2]

Austin in his article, "A plea for excuses",[3] has a similar and more general thesis. He says that in the *standard* case covered by *any* normal verb *none* of the range of expressions qualifying actions —expressions such as "voluntary", "intentional", "on purpose", "deliberately", etc.—nor any of their negations are in order. "Only if we do the act named in some *special* way or circumstances different from those in which an act is normally done...is a modifying expression called for, or even in order."[4] He summarizes this thesis in the slogan, "No modification without aberration".[5] Unless the action is aberrant, no modifying concept is applicable.

Extending Ryle's point, Austin notices that it would be odd to *say*, in ordinary circumstances, "I bought my car voluntarily", or "I am writing this book of my own free will", and both philosophers therefore conclude that certain conditions are necessary conditions of the applicability of certain concepts. In each case, as in the cases considered earlier, the author claims that a certain concept or range of concepts is inapplicable to a certain state of affairs because that state of affairs fails to satisfy a condition which the author says is a presupposition of the applicability of the concept. Furthermore, the reasons why these philosophers advance these claims are similar in every case. They notice that in normal situations it would be very odd to *say* such things as, "I remember my own name", "I bought my car voluntarily", "I am writing this of my own free will". They notice that it is appropriate to say these things only under certain conditions, so they then infer that those conditions are conditions for the applicability of such con-

---

[1] G. Ryle, *Concept of Mind* (London, 1949).   [2] G. Ryle, *ibid.* p. 69.
[3] Reprinted in *Philosophical Papers* (Oxford, 1961).
[4] *Ibid.* p. 138.   [5] *Ibid.* p. 137.

142

Assertion fallacy

cepts as *remember, voluntary, free will*, etc., and consequently that they are part of the analysis of these concepts. They thus tacitly assume that the conditions for successfully (and accurately) making the assertion, e.g., that I remember my own name, or that I am writing this book of my own free will, form part of an analysis of the concepts of remembering or free will.

These assumptions have been important methodological principles behind much contemporary philosophizing. In order to show that they are false, I now want to consider certain other things it would be odd to say. Consider the following sentences: "He is breathing", "He has five fingers on his left hand". Now ask yourself under what conditions it would be appropriate to actually *utter* these sentences, to make the assertions that would be made with these sentences, and I think you will agree that in standard or normal situations it would be very odd to utter either of them. Just as it is only appropriate to say, "He remembers his own name", when there is some reason for supposing, e.g., that he might have forgotten his name, so it is odd to say "He is breathing", unless there is some reason to suppose, e.g., that he might have stopped breathing, or at least that our audience might have supposed that he might have stopped breathing, or for some other reason might have needed to be reminded that he is breathing. Similarly, we would not *say* "He has five fingers on his left hand" unless there is some abnormal feature of the situation, e.g., if he has six fingers on his right hand, or if we wish to free him of suspicion of being the four fingered left-handed murderer.

But do these points (about what it would be appropriate to *say*) have anything at all to do with the analysis of the concepts of breathing or fingers? Let us go over this ground carefully. We can construct a whole series of sentences: "He remembers his own name", "He knows that he is in pain", "He bought his car voluntarily", "He is writing this book of his own free will", "He is breathing", "He has five fingers on his left hand". We find that it is only appropriate to utter these sentences as assertions under certain conditions. Only if the situation is aberrant—to use Austin's term—is it appropriate to *say* these things.

Now what is the explanation of this fact? The authors who consider the first examples maintain that the explanation has to do with the concepts of remembering, voluntariness, free will, etc. It seems implausible to suppose that similar explanations would

Three fallacies in contemporary philosophy

work for the concepts breathing, or finger; so I wish to offer the following more general explanation: There are standard or normal situations. People normally remember their own names, know whether or not they are in pain, buy their cars voluntarily, write works of philosophy of their own free will, breathe, and have five fingers per hand. In general, it is inappropriate to assert of a particular standard or normal situation that it is standard or normal unless there is some reason for supposing, or for supposing someone might have supposed, etc., that it might have been non-standard or abnormal. For to remark that it is standard is to suggest that its being standard is in some way remarkable, and to imply or suggest that is often, or in general, to imply or suggest that there is some reason for supposing that it might not have been standard or that the audience might have supposed that it might not be standard or at least that the audience might need to be reminded that it is standard. If a speaker describing a situation knows of no reason why anyone might suppose that the situation is non-standard or aberrant or need to be reminded of its standard character, then asserting that it is standard is simply out of order.

The explanation, then, has nothing to do with the analysis of particular words; it lies in explaining what it is to make an assertion. The assertion—for example, that I remember my own name —is just pointless unless the context warrants it in some way. But that pointlessness has nothing to do with the concept of remembering but with the concept of what it is to make an assertion. The general character of the assertion fallacy, then, is to confuse the conditions for making non-defective assertions with the conditions of applicability of certain concepts. The point is not, "No modification without aberration", but "No remark without remarkableness".

What exactly is the nature of the dispute here? Both sides agree on the existence of certain data, data of the form, "It would be odd or impermissible to say such and such". But there is a disagreement about the explanation of the data. I say the data are to be explained in terms of what in general is involved in making an assertion; the view I am attacking says the data are to be explained in terms of the conditions of applicability of certain concepts. So far the only claims I can make for my analysis are greater simplicity, generality, and perhaps plausibility. But I now wish to

Assertion fallacy

present actual counter-examples to certain of the other analyses to try to refute them more conclusively.

It is argued that the conditions of applicability, i.e. the presuppositions, of certain concepts render certain statements in certain standard conditions neither true nor false. But now notice that the negations or opposites of those statements are not neither true nor false in normal circumstances but simply false. Consider: "He does not now know whether he has a pain", "He does not remember his own name", "He is no longer breathing", "He did not buy his car voluntarily; he was forced to", "He is not writing this book of his own free will; he is being forced to", "He does not have five fingers on his left hand but six", and so on. In standard or normal conditions there is nothing nonsensical about such statements; they are just false, for it is their falsity which renders the situation standard or normal in the relevant respects. But then, if they are false, are not their denials true?

Furthermore, if we get away from very simple examples as we did in the case of the speech act fallacy, we shall see that such concepts are applicable without any conditions of the sort considered. Consider the following examples: "The system of voluntary military recruitment is a total failure in California", "The ability to remember such simple things as one's name and phone number is one of the foundation stones of organized society", "It is more pleasant to do things of one's own free will than to be forced to do them". These sentences contain the words "voluntary", "remember", and "free will", and their utterance would be appropriate without any of the special aberrant conditions the philosophers said were necessary conditions for their applicability. So, just as in the speech act fallacy, the concentration on a few very simple examples of indicative sentences has led to an incorrect analysis.

One might put the point slightly differently. The character of the mistake I am citing is that it confuses conditions of assertability with presuppositions of concepts. Most concepts do indeed have presuppositions which determine the scope of their intelligible applicability. For example, the concept *divisible by seven* is only applicable to (certain kinds of) mathematical entities. For that reason, it is odd to the point of unintelligibility to assert, "The Boer War is divisible by seven". Now it is also odd—in the present normal, non-aberrant context—to assert, "I am writing

Three fallacies in contemporary philosophy

this book of my own free will". But the fact that such an assertion is odd except in abnormal or aberrant situations is not sufficient to show that aberrance or abnormality is a presupposition of the applicability of the concept of doing something freely or of one's own free will in a way that being a numerical entity is a presupposition of the applicability of the concept *divisible by seven*. Of course, "intention", "belief", "know", etc., like most interesting words, do indeed have a complicated network of presuppositions, but the methods of classical linguistic analysis are not always adequate to sort them out and distinguish them from conditions for making non-defective assertions.

6.4 *The origin of the fallacies: meaning as use*

I now want to offer some remarks by way of explanation of how these fallacies came to be committed. Linguistic philosophers of the period I am discussing had no general theory of language on which to base their particular conceptual analyses. What they had in place of a general theory were a few slogans, the most prominent of which was the slogan, "Meaning Is Use". This slogan embodied the belief that the meaning of a word is not to be found by looking for some associated mental entity in an introspective realm, nor by looking for some entity for which it stands, whether abstract or concrete, mental or physical, particular or general, but rather by carefully examining how the word is actually used in the language. As an escape route from traditional Platonic or empiricist or Tractatus-like theories of meaning, the slogan "Meaning Is Use" was quite beneficial. But as a tool of analysis in its own right, the notion of use is so vague that in part it led to the confusions I have been trying to expose. And here I think is how its vagueness generated or helped to generate these confusions.

A philosopher wishes to analyze a particular concept, say knowledge or memory. Following the slogan he looks to the use of the verbs "know" or "remember". To do this he gets a few sentences almost invariably of very simple present tense indicative kind, and asks himself such questions as under what conditions would he utter those sentences, and what speech act would he be performing when he uttered them. But since he lacks any general theory of meaning or of syntax or of speech acts, how is he to interpret the

Origin of the fallacies: meaning as use

answers to these questions once he gets them? In the case of the *assertion fallacy*, certain general conditions for the performance of the speech act of assertion were mistakenly attributed to particular words because it was in the investigation into the use of those words that those results turned up. The slogan gave the philosopher no way of distinguishing between the use of the word and the use of the sentence containing it. The slogan thus further engendered the mistaken conviction that because under certain conditions we don't say such and such, in those conditions *it cannot be the case* that such and such. Applying the slogan, "Meaning Is Use", the philosopher asks himself, "Under what conditions would we *say* that we *remember* such and such or that such and such an act was done voluntarily?" But how is he to know that the answer to those questions does not depend as much on *saying* as it does on the concepts of remembering or voluntariness?

The origin of the *speech act fallacy* is quite similar. The linguistic philosopher takes the question, "What does "good" or "know" mean?" to be the same as, "How is "good" or "know" used?" and confines his discussion to a few simple sentences containing these words. He then finds that in the utterance of those sentences we perform certain speech acts. The slogan, "Meaning Is Use" gives him no way of distinguishing features of the utterance which are due solely to the occurrence of the word he is analyzing from features which are due to other characteristics of the sentences or to other extraneous factors altogether; so he mistakenly concludes that the word "good" by itself is used to perform the speech act of commendation, and having come to that conclusion while examining the so-called *use* of the word "good", he concludes that he has analyzed the meaning of "good", since according to his slogan use and meaning are the same. The transition seems to occur as follows. The philosopher wishes to ask:

1. What does the word *W* mean?

Since meaning is use, he takes that question to be the same as:

2. How is *W* used?

which is then tacitly taken to mean:

3. How is *W* used in simple present tense categorical indicative sentences of the form, e.g., "*X* is *W*".

Three fallacies in contemporary philosophy

and that is taken to be the same question as:

4. How are these sentences containing W used?

which is then taken either as:

5. What illocutionary act is performed in the utterance of such sentences?

or:

6. What are the conditions for the performance of non-defective assertions in the utterance of such sentences? That is, when would we actually say things of the form, "X is W"?

To assume that answers to 5 necessarily give answers to 1 leads to the speech act fallacy; and to assume that answers to 6 necessarily give answers to 1 leads to the assertion fallacy. Both fallacies stem from assuming 1 means the same as 2.

The origin of the *naturalistic fallacy fallacy* is more complicated, but even it—in some of its more current versions—is in part due to the slogan, "Meaning Is Use". Linguistic philosophers of the classical period were much impressed by the fact that certain indicative sentences were not used to describe states of affairs but were used to give evaluations, assessments, ratings, judgments, rankings, etc. Now seeing that the *use*, in this sense of illocutionary force of the utterance of the sentences, was different from the use or illocutionary force of the utterance of certain descriptive sentences, they concluded that the meaning must be such that no set of descriptive statements could entail an evaluative one. But that conclusion does not follow, for from the fact that the point or illocutionary force of uttering a sentence is 'evaluative' it does not, follow that the proposition expressed cannot be entailed by a proposition expressed in the utterance of a sentence the illocutionary force or point of uttering which would be 'descriptive'. The truth conditions of the one proposition may be sufficient for the truth conditions of the other—even though the point of uttering one sentence may be different from the point of uttering the other sentence. The truth conditions of a proposition have been confused with the point or force of uttering a sentence, because the word "use" is so vague as to include both the truth conditions of the proposition expressed and the point or illocutionary force of uttering the corresponding sentence.

As a tool of analysis, the use theory of meaning can provide us

148

Origin of the fallacies: meaning as use

only with certain data, i.e., raw material for philosophical analysis; e.g., that in uttering a sentence of the form, "X is good", one is characteristically praising something, or that the sentence, "I remember my own name", is uttered only under certain conditions and not others. How such data are systematically analyzed, explained, or accounted for will depend on what other views or theories about language we bring to bear on such data, for the use theory does not by itself provide us with the tools for such an analysis and can, indeed (as I have tried to show), engender confusions.

KINDS OF STATEMENTS:[1]
THE ANALYTIC-SYNTHETIC DISTINCTION

INTRODUCTION

A Historical Perspective

From the dawn of philosophy it was recognized that there are two distinct methods for supporting our claim to knowledge. Either we support our judgments by appeal to experience and thereby rule it *a posteriori* knowledge, or we support it by appeal to a set of principles taken to be final on various grounds, such as being self-evident, eternal truths, axiomatic, or the rules of the game, and hence rule it *a priori* knowledge.

Aristotle already recognized certain important features of *a priori* knowledge. First, he held that certain classes of sentences such as sentences expressing the so-called law of identity, the law of contradiction, or the law of excluded middle are *a priori* truths, or what we may call analytic truths. Second, he stated, in effect, that if a sentence is analytic, all sentences of what is called "the same logical form" are also analytic. Since the law of excluded middle, or the law of contradiction, is analytic, any sentences having the same logical form as these are also analytic.

(1) All Spartans are Greeks, or not all Spartans are Greeks.

(2) Apollo is angry or Apollo is not angry.

The above sentences are analytic, having the same logical form as $(x)\ Fx\ \lor — (x)\ Fx$.

---

[1] Throughout this essay we use 'sentence' and 'statement' interchangeably. We are not using 'statement' as a sentence used by the speaker for stating that something is a case. In discussing the issue of analyticity, some philosophers use 'proposition' for the meaning of a sentence or 'judgment' for an asserted proposition. In the context of discussing their views we also make use of their expressions. But let it be understood that here we are interested in truth conditions of declarative sentences (and hence with a bivalent language) and not in their other properties, e.g., that they are put forward for consideration or that they are asserted, etc.

(3) Not both: all Spartans are Greeks and not all Spartans are Greeks.

(4) Not both: Apollo is angry and Apollo is not angry.

The above also are analytic, having the same logical form as $- [(x)Fx \land - (x)Fx]$.

Third, Aristotle saw that certain relations among sentences are valid. This validity holds both in what is called "immediate inference," such as

If A belongs to no B, then B will not belong to any A

or,

If A belongs to some B, then B will belong to some A

and in "syllogistic inference," such as:

If A belongs to no B, but B to some C, it is necessary that A does not belong to some C.

Fourth, Aristotle showed that certain valid arguments are derivable from other valid arguments taken as axioms. As for justification of his axioms, he saw that they cannot be justified *within* the system without circularity. However, he provided some pragmatic reasons against the rejection of certain axioms, arguing, for example, that the rejection of the law of contradiction or of the excluded middle destroys all possibility of discourse.[2] We should note that Aristotle's interest in what we call analytic truths was subsidiary to his main concern with logic. He was mainly interested in the concept of validity and not as such in analyticity, even though he seems to see that the two are related. We may also appreciate their affinity when we see that an argument is valid if its corresponding conditional is analytic, and when we know what characterizes a sentence as analytic.

Gottfried Leibniz made the fundamental distinction between analytic and synthetic truths and made full use of this distinction in his system. He used the terms 'necessary' and 'contingent' rather than 'analytic' and 'synthetic.' According to Leibniz there are two classes of truths: "necessary truths," also called by him the "truths of reason," or "eternal truths"; and "contingent truths," or "truths of fact." He defines each class in terms of either the concept of logical possibility and impossibility or the idea of "possible and actual worlds." He writes:

[2] *The Basic Works of Aristotle,* trans. Richard McKeon (New York: Random House, 1941), *Metaphysics,* 1006ᵃ.

"Truths of reasoning are necessary and their opposite is impossible: truths of fact are contingent and their opposite is possible. When a truth is necessary, its reason can be found by analysis, resolving it into simpler ideas and truths, until we come to those that are primary.... Primary principles ... cannot be proved."[3] Leibniz believed that each type of truth is reducible to some basic truth; he suggested that necessary truths could be reduced to ultimate laws of logic (i.e., the law of identity and its counterpart, the law of contradiction), while the contingent truths are reducible to as many premises as there are experiences.

> The primitive truths, which are known by intuition, are, like the derivative, of two kinds. They are among the truths of reason or the truths of fact. Truths of reason are necessary, and those of fact are contingent. The primitive truths of reason are those which I call by the general name of *identicals,* because it seems that they repeat the same thing, without teaching us anything.[4]

Leibniz also believed that all the propositions of logic, arithmetic, and geometry are necessary, whereas all existential propositions (except the existence of God) are contingent. "The great foundation of mathematics is the principle of contradiction.... And this principle alone suffices for proving all Arithmetic and all Geometry, i.e., all mathematical principles."[5] There is also a suggestion that all necessary truths are essentially hypothetical in a sense that, given certain axioms, some theorems follow of necessity from them. "As for the eternal truths, it is to be observed that at bottom they are all hypothetical, and say in fact: Such a thing being posited, such another thing is."[6]

Leibniz's suggestions that necessary truths are reducible to primitive truths, primitive truths are identities, identities are empty, mathematical truths are reducible to the laws of logic, and the eternal truths are essentially hypothetical, are all revolutionary. Indeed, these theses have such an up-to-date ring that it is tempting to attribute to Leibniz the seeds of many theories of modern logicians. These theses contain the Frege-Russell program of the reduction of mathematics to logic, Witt-

---

[3] All references are to "Extracts from Leibniz," in Bertrand Russell, *A Critical Exposition of the Philosophy of Leibniz* (London: Allen and Unwin, 1949), 207-8. Original reference to G. VI 612 (D. 223 L. 236).

[4] *Ibid.,* 207. Original reference to G. V 343 (N.E. 404).

[5] *Ibid.,* 208. Original reference to G. VII 355 (D. 239).

[6] *Ibid.* Original reference to G. V 428 (N.E. 515).

genstein's idea of the emptiness of tautologies — "A tautology follows from all propositions, it says nothing";[7] "(I know, e.g., nothing about the weather, when I know that it rains or does not rain)"[8] — and the widely held view about the if-then property of mathematical and logical statements.

Leibniz also used the notion of possible and actual worlds in defining necessary and contingent truths. Usually, however, Leibniz defines necessary truth as "one the contradictory of which involves a contradiction." A proposition is a necessary truth if and only if it is true of all possible worlds, whereas it is a contingent truth if it is true of the actual world but not of all possible worlds. Thus the statement "Columbus discovered America" is true of the actual world but false of infinitely many other possible worlds, whereas the statement "Either Columbus discovered America or he didn't" is true of all possible worlds.

Leibniz's idea of defining necessary truth as truth of all possible worlds, though metaphorical, once again sounds new. It is similar to the modern notion of defining logical truth in terms of models, i.e., "Logical truths are those sentences true in every model."[9] Another interesting result of the use of the notion of possible world is that, "instead of employing a simple dichotomy between truth and falsehood, Leibniz in effect relativizes these concepts to possible worlds. Given a sentence and a possible world, the sentence is said to be true or false *of* that possible world."[10]

Despite the modernity of these notions, we should not forget two of the Leibnizean metaphysical beliefs which run counter to modern (and perhaps to some of his own) assertions. One is that every truth, whether necessary or contingent, is provable *a priori*. "Every truth has its proof *a priori* derived from the concept of the terms, notwithstanding it does not always lie in our power to achieve this analysis."[11] The other is his belief in the innateness of the eternal truths: "The whole arithmetic

[7] Ludwig Wittgenstein, *Tractatus* (London: Routledge and Kegan Paul, 1945), 5.142.

[8] *Ibid.*, 4.461.

[9] See "The Recent Polemic," in this volume.

[10] Benson Mates, "Leibniz on Possible Worlds," in *Logic, Methodology and the Philosophy of Science,* ed. B. Van Rootselaar and J. P. Staal (Amsterdam: North Holland, 1968), 508.

[11] Quoted in Gottlob Frege, *The Foundations of Arithmetic,* by J. L. Austin (Oxford: Basil Blackwell, 1950); appeared in Erdmann edition of Leibniz's writings, p. 21. Original reference to G. II 57.

is innate and is in virtual fashion in us,"[12] and "It is not true that everything a man learns is not innate. The truths of number are in us and still they are learned, whether it be by drawing them forth from their source when learning by demonstration (which shows them to be innate). . . ."[13]

Among the classical empiricists John Locke recognized varieties of analytic truths; David Hume formulated certain criteria for distinguishing analytic from synthetic truths, and he made a full use of them throughout his philosophical inquiries. Locke classified sentences (he called them "propositions") into various kinds. Unlike Leibniz, he was not concerned with the idea of analytic truths in relation to the issue of the foundations of logic and mathematics, but he recognized that not all analytic truths are trivial; e.g., some mathematical propositions are analytic and informative.[14]

Locke sorts out "propositions" into three types: first, maxims. The law of identity ("whatever is, is"), the law of contradiction ("it is impossible for the same thing to be and not to be"), and the proposition that "the whole is equal to all its parts," are Locke's examples of maxims. They are, in Locke's view, self-evident, because they are known immediately, without the intervention of any other concept. Though we learn the meaning of each idea through experience, we do not give up these propositions. They are also trivial, since these propositions are just impressive ways of saying "the same is the same," "the same isn't different," or "the whole is the whole, i.e., the sum of its parts."

Second, trifling propositions. Trifling propositions are divided into "purely identical propositions," such as "red is red," which are like maxims self-evident and trivial; and propositions in which "a part of the definition of the word is defined." Locke's examples of the second types are "Lead is a metal" and "All gold is fusible." Such propositions are not self-evident. They are trivial for one who asserts them, only if the asserter knows that the predicate is the part of the definition of the concept. Thus if we know a part of the definition of 'lead' is 'metal,' or of 'gold' is 'fusible,' then what we do know is trivial. But if we don't know what falls under a concept, learning that another

---

[12] *Ibid.*, p. 17. Original reference to Erdmann ed., 195, 208-9.

[13] *Ibid.* Original reference to Erdmann ed., 212.

[14] John Locke, *An Essay Concerning Human Understanding* (London: Everyman's Library, 1947), Bk. IV, Ch. VII.

concept belongs to it is learning something that in some sense is non-trivial.

Using the scholastic concept of real and nominal essences, Locke observes that a well-confirmed strong inductive generalization "real essence" may turn into part of the definition of a concept and turn into a "nominal essence." In his terminology, the mind selects certain ideas which are received from experience and "ties them together with a name."[15] Discovering that the atomic weight of lead is 207.19, we define 'lead' now in terms of this property rather than in terms of its softness or its gray color. Such sentences may be called "post factum necessities."

Third, instructive and necessary propositions. Locke sometimes speaks of certain propositions which are "instructive," neither self-evident nor empty but informative while at the same time unfalsifiable and hence in some sense necessary. He writes:

> We can know the truth, and so may be certain in propositions which affirm something of another, which is a necessary consequence of its precise complex idea, but not contained in it: as that the external angle of all triangles is bigger than either of the opposite internal angles, which relation of the outward angle to either of the opposite internal angles, making no part of the complex idea signified by the name triangle, this is a real truth, and conveys with it instructive real knowledge.[16]

Locke's insight in regard to the nontrivial nature of some analytical sentences is significant. Although he does not elaborate the distinction between trivial and instructive analytic sentences, or the point about the transformation of "real essence" to "nominal essence," or about the method we use to arrive at "instructive propositions" (e.g., geometrical theorems), we should appreciate his foresight that not all analytic truths are tautologies. This point will be elaborated in the sequel.

David Hume is a philosopher who shared Leibniz's distinction between analytic and synthetic truths, and his theory that mathematical propositions fall within the domain of analytic sentences. However, like Locke, he disagreed with Leibniz's metaphysical theories with regard to the innateness of the eternal truths and the possibility of providing *a priori* proof for every true proposition.

---

[15] *Ibid.*, 5.4, Ch. VIII.
[16] *Ibid.*, 18, Bk. IV.

Hume's distinction between analytic or synthetic sentences is made in the *Treatise* in terms of certain relations which depend on their relata and certain relations which are independent of their relata. We may present Hume's distinction in the following manner. Suppose S is a sentence of the form

(x) (y) [xRy].

Substitute "*3*" for 'x,' "*2 + 1*" for 'y,' and "$=$" for 'R.' We then obtain

(S) $3 = 2 + 1$,

which is analytic. And that is because S expresses a true relation which holds between the two mentioned numbers. "As long as our ideas remain the same," Hume says the relation holds.

According to Hume, such relations "are discoverable from mere ideas." Now suppose there is another sentence L of the same form. Let us substitute *arsenic* for 'x,' *death* for 'y,' and *causes* for 'R.' We then obtain

(L) Arsenic causes death,

which is synthetic, because in L, the relation R is nonlogical. There is no logical tie between *arsenic* and *death*. Here we may change the relation without changing the relata. If we change 'R' to *does not cause* (leaving 'x' and 'y' unchanged), we will have another synthetic sentence

(K) Arsenic does not cause death.

Such relations as *cause* or its denial are, according to Hume, discoverable "through experience" and not "from mere ideas." Moreover, Hume argues that since S is analytic, its denial is self-contradictory, whereas L or K being synthetic may be true or false, but denial of either one is not self-contradictory.[17] In the *Enquiries* the same distinction is made by using "relations of ideas" for analytic sentences and "matters of fact" for synthetic sentences. Hume further believed that synthetic truths are known *a posteriori*, through experience, whereas we know analytic truths *a priori* by "mere operation of thought, without dependence on what is anywhere existent in the universe."[18]

If our knowledge consists roughly of conceptual (analytic) or factual

[17] David Hume, *Treatise* (Oxford: Oxford University Press, 1888), 69. For details, see Farhang Zabeeh, *Hume: Precursor of Modern Empiricism*, 2nd rev. ed. (The Hague: Martinus Nijhoff, 1973), Ch. 3, "The Principle of Analyticity."

[18] David Hume, *Enquiries*, ed. L. A. Selby-Bigge (Oxford: Oxford University Press, 1951), 25.

(synthetic) truths, what may we claim for the theological or metaphysical assertions which are of neither kind? They are, Hume says, "nothing but sophistry and illusion."[19]

Kant observed that the life or death of metaphysics hinges upon Hume's verdict that the causal maxim, "Whatever begins to exist must have a cause," is neither an analytic nor a synthetic truth. He observed that Hume's analytic-synthetic dichotomy leaves no place for any metaphysical principle. Cognizant that metaphysics consists altogether of statements similar to the causal principle, he remarks that "since the origin of metaphysics so far as we know its history, nothing has ever happened which might have been more decisive to the fortunes of the science than the attack made upon it by David Hume."[20] To rescue metaphysics, or at least "metaphysics of nature" or what of late has been called "descriptive metaphysics," Kant sought to prove that there are some statements in mathematics and theoretical physics which lie outside the Leibniz-Hume dichotomy of analytic-synthetic sentences. He classified all judgments, i.e., asserted sentences, into the trichotomy of analytic *a priori*, synthetic *a posteriori*, and synthetic *a priori*.

A judgment is *a priori* (from Latin meaning "before") if it is logically independent of all judgments which describe experiences, and it is *a posteriori* (from Latin meaning "after") if it is logically dependent on judgments which describe experiences. On the other hand, a judgment is analytic or synthetic if certain relations hold between the subject and predicate of the proposition. Kant states these relations as such:

> In all judgments in which the relation of a subject to a predicate is thought: this relation is possible in two different ways. Either the predicate B belongs to the subject A, as something which is (covertly) contained in this concept A; or B lies outside the concept A, although it does indeed stand in connexion with it. In the one case I call the judgment *analytic,* and the other *synthetic.*[21]

According to Kant, there are synthetic *a priori* judgments, judgments whose predicates are *not* contained in their subjects and yet which are logically independent of all judgments describing experience.

---

[19] *Ibid.,* 165.

[20] Immanuel Kant, *Prolegomena to Any Future Metaphysics,* trans. John P. Mahaffy (London: Macmillan, 1889), 3.

[21] Immanuel Kant, *Critique of Pure Reason,* trans. S. Körner (Pelican Book, 1955), 33. B. 10.

Kant believed that certain metaphysical presuppositions of the natural sciences and of moral assertions and almost the whole of mathematics fall within the synthetic *a priori* category. He was mostly concerned with synthetic *a priori* judgments, and the problem about the possibility of such judgments is the center of his philosophy.

The problem of the existence of such a category was debated by many philosophers. Not debatable, however, is Kant's definition of analytic and synthetic judgments in terms of certain relations between the subject and the predicate of a proposition; i.e., the metaphorical relation of "containment" is inferior to the Leibniz-Hume one, since it excludes a large class of analytic sentences which are not of the subject-predicate form, namely, a very large class of logico-mathematical relations.

Gottlob Frege observed with Leibniz that the issue of whether a proposition is analytic or synthetic is not the issue about epistemology or psychology of belief-formation; "rather, it is a judgment about the ultimate ground upon which rests the justification for holding it to be true."[22]

If the issue about the nature of a proposition is the issue about the ultimate ground for holding it to be true, and if it is possible to reduce arithmetic to logic, and if logic contains nothing but analytic propositions, then it may be claimed that Kant was wrong insofar as he regarded arithmetic propositions as belonging to the synthetic *a priori* category. Frege, in fact, arrived at this conclusion: "From all the preceding it thus emerged as a very probable conclusion that the truths of Arithmetic are analytic and *a priori,* and we achieved an improvement on the view of Kant."[23] However, Frege thought Kant was right in regarding geometrical truths as synthetic *a priori*. "I consider Kant did a great service in drawing the distinction between synthetic and analytic judgments. In calling the truths of geometry synthetic and *a priori,* he revealed their true nature. . . . If Kant was wrong about Arithmetic, that does not seriously detract, in my opinion, from the value of his work."[24]

Logical empiricists rejected the category of synthetic *a priori*. They accepted the logicism of Frege and Russell and Hilbert's axiomatic

[22] Gottlob Frege, *The Foundations of Arithmetic,* trans. J. L. Austin (Oxford: Blackwell, 1950), 3.
[23] *Ibid.,* 118.
[24] *Ibid.,* 101.

treatment of the Euclidean geometry. The creation of various systems of non-Euclidean geometries strengthen their view that pure mathematics, including pure geometries, is analytic and *a priori*, whereas applied mathematical sentences belong to science, and hence are synthetic *a posteriori*.

The Recent Polemic

The belief that pure mathematics is reducible to logic, or to logic and set theory (logicism), is distinct from the belief that statements of pure mathematics are analytic and *a priori*. Apart from the old logicism of Frege and Russell and its offspring, set-theoretical mathematics, there are other schools whose members are engaged in research in the foundations of mathematics, such as the constructivists and metamathematical schools. They disagree with the old program of the logicism without disagreeing with the belief that statements of pure mathematics are analytic and *a priori*.

This belief presupposes that a clear distinction exists between *a priori* and *a posteriori* sentences on one hand, and between analytic and synthetic sentences on the other hand. The *a priori–a posteriori* dichotomy is less problematic than the analytic-synthetic one.

Taking a hint from Kant, we may define judgments:

> (Def. A) A judgment, i.e., an asserted declarative sentence, is *a priori* if and only if its truth value is logically independent of any judgments which describe experiences.

Thus

$$5 + 5 = 10$$

or

> Necessarily an equiangular triangle is equilateral

are *a priori* judgments, even though they have a kind of dependence on experience. Such dependence, however, is contingent and not logical. The above sentences would be true of a possible world in which there are no straight lines, no intersection of lines, and no countable objects whatsoever.

On the other hand:

> (Def. B) A judgment is *a posteriori* if its truth value could be established either by appeal to experience, or it depends logically on other judgments which describe a particular experience.

Thus

> My heart beats

and

> All non-supported bodies fall downward

are *a posteriori* judgments.

When we come to differentiate analytic from synthetic sentences, we encounter certain problems. Tautologies are traditionally regarded as the clearest case of analytic sentences; they are not only true of all possible worlds (to use Leibniz's expression) or true in every *model* (to use a recent expression), but if a sentence is a tautology, every other sentence having the same logical form is also.

We may define tautology:

> (Def. C) A 'tautology' is a sentence which is true by virtue of the semantic properties of the connectives alone (but not the quantifiers).

Note that by 'connectives' we mean only *logical* expressions such as 'not,' 'or,' 'if-then,' and 'if and only if,' but not 'because,' 'but,' 'although,' etc. The boundary between *logical* and *extra-logical* expressions is somewhat arbitrary; even tautologies are relative to division of expressions into logical and extra-logical expressions.

The sentences

> (1) David Hume was born in 1711 A.D., or David Hume was not born in 1711 A.D.

and

> (2) All men are mortal, or not all men are mortal

are tautologies.

Both (1) and (2) are exact substitution instances of the matrix

> $S \text{ or } \bar{S}$

even though (1) should be rendered

> $P \vee \bar{P}$

and (2) as

> $(x) (Hx \to Mx) \vee {-} (x) (Hx \to Mx).$

(1) and (2) are true by virtue of the semantic properties of 'or' and 'not' alone, and independent of the meanings of all other words in them, including 'all.'

We should note first that there are logically true sentences whose truth depends not only on the semantical properties of the connectives but also on those of the quantifiers, e.g., sentences having the form

$(x) (Fx) \rightarrow Fa$ (the principle of universal instantiation)

or

$Fa \rightarrow (\exists x) Fx$ (the principle of existential generalization).

Second, there are true analytic sentences the truth of which does not rest on semantic properties of the connectives or quantifiers. Thus

(3) No spinster is married,

which is of the form

$(x) (Sx \rightarrow -Mx)$,

is analytic, though its truth cannot be established by appeal to semantic properties of the connectives or quantifiers alone.

Note also that although (3) is true,

(4) No woman is married,

which has the same form as (3), is false. Nonetheless, the truth of (3) does not rest either on its logical structure or on facts. It would be absurd to confirm or disconfirm (3) by sending questionnaires to spinsters in order to establish its truth value; it would be equally absurd to collect data on whether the number of living husbands is exactly the same as the number of living wives (barring polygamy or polyandry).

A question then arises. On what grounds do we count a sentence like (3), or in general a sentence whose truth value is independent of its logical structure and of fact, as analytic? An answer to this question is that such sentences are analytic by virtue of their meanings. Given the dictionary meaning or the usage of 'spinster,' we know that (3) is an analytic truth. 'Spinster' is defined in an English dictionary or used by the English speaker as 'an unmarried woman.' Thus we may arrive at:

(Def. D) S is analytic if and only if S is true by virtue of meanings and independently of fact.

It is also suggested that we may be able to reduce analytic sentences to sentences which are true only by virtue of their logical structures (structures which are obtained by virtue of the semantical properties of the connectives, quantifiers, identity signs, and other logical expressions) by substituting synonyms for synonyms. Let us call this suggestion (DS). Thus

No spinster is married

is reducible to

(5) No unmarried woman is married,

and the latter to

(6) No woman who is not married is married,

which is of the form

No X that is not Y is Y,

which is an analytic truth because of its logical structure.

Suppose for the moment that we accept (Def. D). Do we have to accept also the optimistic suggestion (DS) of reducing analytic sentences which are true by virtue of their meanings and independently of facts to sentences which are true only by virtue of their logical structures?

John Kemeny showed that this claim is too strong. He writes: "While substituting synonyms for synonyms in logically true statements will yield analytically true statements, it is not true that all analytically true statements can be so obtained."[25]

Consider:

(7) No tree is taller than itself,

which is analytic by virtue of its meaning. "Yet there is no conceivable way that this particular statement could be obtained by substituting synonym for synonym in a logically true statement."[26] Substituting 'R' for 'taller than,' (7) turns into

$$(x) - (xRx),$$

which is not logically true, i.e., it does not hold for an arbitrary relation R. Substituting 'R' for 'identical to,' we get the falsehood

(8) No tree is identical to itself.

The main problem is not that of reduction of analytic truths to logical truths, but the prior and deeper problem of defining 'analyticity' by appeal to such concepts as "meaning" or "synonymy."

Quine, in his now classic essay "Two Dogmas of Empiricism" and

[25] John Kemeny, "Analyticity Versus Fuzziness," *Synthese,* XV (1963), 64.
[26] *Ibid.*

in his other work which appeared during twenty years since the appearance of that essay, not only attacks various particular definitions of analyticity, but also questions the validity and utility of the analytic-synthetic dichotomy. He begins by pointing out the inadequacies of various definitions of analyticity given in terms of "meaning," "synonymy," "reduction to logical truths," "true of all possible worlds," "necessary truths," "true under every state description," "true according to the semantical rules of L," etc. He ends up with a more radical thesis concerning revisability of every and all sentences, whether they be simple observation sentences or the so-called eternal truths.

Take (Def. D). Quine objects that the very notions of "meaning" or "intention" are "so elusive, not to say debatable, that there seems little hope of erecting a fruitful science about them."[27] Likewise he objects to (DS) by saying, "We have had to lean on a notion of 'synonymy' which is no less in need of clarification than analyticity itself,"[28] and so to other definitions.

Quine's objections in effect undermine any attempted definition of analyticity by questioning our unquestioned assumptions. For example, in (Def. D) and (DS) we appeal to 'meaning' and 'synonymy,' and we simply assume that the dictionary definition or usage determines whether two or more expressions have "the same meaning" or "are synonymous."

Quine pushes the matter a little further by reminding us that our assumptions need examination. "We cannot for example appeal to a dictionary definition since the lexicographers' definition is a report of an observed synonymy and so is not to be itself regarded as a ground of the synonymy."[29] In fact, Quine carries his anti-analyticity thesis a step further and arrives at a thesis of *radical indeterminacy of translation* of one language to another. Two translators could disagree on a translation and still agree in all speech dispositions, e.g., there is no telling whether this native utterance is to be translated as 'rabbit,' or as 'rabbit-stage.' If there is no guarantee that two people from two different tribes are talking about the same thing when the object presents itself to their senses, when their talk is purely extensional, how can they determine that an expression 'x' in one language means the same as 'y' in another when their talk is intensional? "Can an empiricist

[27] W. V. Quine, "Two Dogmas of Empiricism," *Philosophical Review*, LX (1951), 20-43.
[28] *Ibid.*
[29] *Ibid.*

speak seriously of sameness of meaning of two conditions upon an object x, one stated in the heathen language and one in ours," Quine questions, "when even the singling out of an object x as an object at all for the heathen language is too hopelessly arbitrary?"[30]

Quine is more tolerant about "logical truths." The trouble is not as much with (Def. C), 'tautologies,' or even with definitions of sentences which are true by virtue of their logical forms alone. He tolerates such sentences as

(5) No unmarried woman is married,

which is not merely true but remains so under all reinterpretations of its components other than its logical particles. But he does not tolerate

(3) No spinster is married.

In a reply to critics, he writes:

> Now the notion of logical truth is superior to the notion of analyticity, in that one can make clear sense of it for a full language adequate to science. For, we can just list an adequate vocabulary of logical particles, and then a logical truth as a true sentence in which no words other than logical particles occur essentially.[31]

In "Two Dogmas" Quine also attacks the related dogmas, the so-called verifiability theory of logical empiricists, on the grounds that no statement can be verified or falsified in isolation, i.e., in the absence of a theory, especially in science.

The root of Quine's objection is his pragmatic idea about the nature of any theory. According to this, any sentence embodied in a theory is revisable; hence no sentence, be it the one which is assumed to be true only by virtue of its meaning or the one which is true by virtue of observation, is immune to revision. To assume therefore that there are sentences true of all possible worlds *sub specie aeternitatis* is to be blind to the fact and to uphold a dogma. Quine advocates empiricism without a dogma.

During 1950-60 many essays and some books were written in response to Quine's skepticism about analyticity. It is argued, for example, that the general thesis that no sentence is immune to revision does not carry with itself the thesis that there is no "fundamental cleavage" between analytic and synthetic truths, or that Quine's objections to

---

[30] W. V. Quine, *Ontological Relativity* (New York: Columbia University Press, 1969), 20.

[31] W. V. Quine, "Replies," *Synthese,* XIX (1968), 294.

various definitions are based on certain criteria which could not be satisfied in natural language, or that in fact speakers of language do distinguish between sentences which are true *qua* their meanings and those which are true as a matter of fact. Benson Mates, for example, argues:

> It may easily happen that the conditions of adequacy for a definition are so strong that no adequate definition is possible.... There is some ground for supposing that Quine, too, is employing standards so high that it would be impossible for any definition of "analytic" (or, indeed, of any other term in the natural language) to meet them.[32]

Mates points out that if we insist on defining new words in terms of ones not previously used, the only alternative would be an infinite regress. In a finite language our escape must be either circularity or ostensive definition. But since no adequate definition of abstract concepts such as "analyticity" or "meaning" or "synonymy" could be given by pointing, it is reasonable to expect a certain degree of circularity in defining such concepts.

Richard Martin[33] argues that since natural language is imprecise,[34] i.e., its words are usually ambiguous and there is no algorithm for determining which expressions are well formed and which are not, it is unreasonable to demand a precise definition for 'analyticity' — though a precise definition of 'analyticity' could be given for a formalized language. On the other hand, no single definition could be given which would be applicable to all formalized languages.

On the same line, Kemeny argues that by Quine's criteria we should reject an even more basic distinction that we make in language: "If one is willing to accept Quine's criticism of analytic truth, one must also reject the sharp distinction between true and false."[35]

[32] Benson Mates, "Analytic Sentences," *Philosophical Review*, LX (1951), 529-30.

[33] R. M. Martin, "On Analytic," *Philosophical Studies*, III (1952), 42-47.

[34] The contrast between artificial and natural languages has been stressed by Paul Ziff. He argued that a natural language does not have a static store of word senses, that polysemy rather than monosemy is a characteristic feature of it (for example, out of 70,000 entries listed in the ordinary English dictionary, 40,000 have at least three distinct meanings), and that there are various means of modulating the meanings of words. See Paul Ziff, "Natural and Formal Languages," in *Language and Philosophy*, ed. Sidney Hook (New York: New York University Press, 1969), 223-40.

[35] *Ibid.*, 60.

Grice and Strawson,[36] on the other hand, argue that Quine has failed to shed doubt on the possibility of speakers' making a distinction between analytic and synthetic statements. There is strong evidence that speakers agree, whether a sentence is true by virtue of its meaning or by virtue of facts. Disputes over synthetic sentences eventually lead to questions of fact, whereas disputes over analytic sentences lead to a belief that we do not understand each other. If someone seriously denies the statement 'All tall men are tall,' we are forced to say that we do not know what the other is talking about. The authors argue that this difference in our attitudes with regard to sentences furnishes a partial criterion for recognizing analytic sentences in natural language.

It is also argued that the thesis of essential revisability of any statement is independent of the thesis of essential indistinguishability of analytic from synthetic sentences. We may revise a synthetic statement by admitting a factual error; we may also decide to diverge from use of an expression or give a new role for an old expression or even abandon the whole language by inventing a new one. Nonetheless, the conceptual revisability is distinct from the factual.

None of these arguments seems to have changed Quine's mind. In an essay written in 1968, "Epistemology Naturalized," he writes:

> My rejection of the analyticity notion just means drawing no line between what goes into the mere understanding of the sentences of a language and what else the community sees eye-to-eye on. I doubt that an objective distinction can be made between meaning and such collateral information as is community-wide.[37]

And:

> There is one step toward such a distinction, however, which does make sense: a sentence that is true by mere meanings of words should be expected, at least if it is simple, to be subscribed to by all fluent speakers in the community. Perhaps the controversial notion of analyticity can be dispensed with in our definition of observation sentence, in favor of this straightforward attribute of community-wide acceptance.[38]

At this point we would like to remind the reader of the distinction which is made (and particularly emphasized in this book) among

[36] H. P. Grice and P. F. Strawson, "In Defense of a Dogma," in this volume.
[37] W. V. Quine, *Ontological Relativity*, 86.
[38] *Ibid.*

the three dimensions of the general theory of signs. Remember that the problem about the belief or attitude or intention of the speaker in the community, though relevant to truth or falsity of a sentence, is a problem within the pragmatic dimension of language or speech. By cutting the speaker and the hearer from the sentences used in speech, we may still distinguish the semantic and syntactic properties of those sentences. Even though a lexicographer, by the empirical examination of linguistic usage, may tell us that certain expressions are used by all fluent speakers in the community as having the same meaning, we should still be able to distinguish between those sentences which are true by virtue of their meanings alone and those which are not. Hence the problem of whether a sentence is analytic or synthetic falls within the semantic-synthetic dimension.

Not by appealing to semantic and syntactic regularities alone without taking into the account the pragmatic factors can we always determine the nature of a sentence. But there are good reasons why we need *not* take into account such factors. Wittgenstein in his later work stressed the importance of the pragmatic aspects of linguistic forms. "We should consider the occasion and purpose of these phrases . . . 'War is war' is not an example of the law of identity, either."[39] It is imperative, however, to stress the importance of considering the logical and semantical properties of sentences without considering the occasion of their use. Otherwise no pure logic or pure semantics would be possible. In such inquiries Frege warns us that we must "always separate sharply the psychological from the logical, the objective from the subjective."[40] As Quine himself observes, "The logician's purpose is to put the sentence into a form that admits most efficiently of logical calculation, or shows its implications and conceptual affinities most perspicuously, obviating fallacy and paradox."[41]

We defeat this aim if in the inquiries in logic and semantics we consider also the context of use, the intention of the utterer, and the ambiguity of words which is characteristic of any natural language. Such factors belong to pragmatics (see the introduction to Part I).

There are, as we have observed already, some adequate definitions for 'tautology,' 'logical form,' and 'analyticity' which are available and

---

[39] Ludwig Wittgenstein, *The Philosophical Investigations,* trans. G. E. M. Anscombe (Oxford: Blackwell, 1953), 221.

[40] Gottlob Frege, *The Foundations of Arithmetic,* trans. J. L. Austin, p. x.

[41] W. V. Quine, "Methodological Reflections," *Synthese,* XXI (1969), 386-98.

are employed in natural language with success. Taking a hint from Quine, we may relativize our concept not only of logical truths but also of analytic truths. Relative to a domain of a discourse and our choice of logical particles, we may characterize a sentence as logically true if and only if its truth depends on the semantic properties of these particles alone — and relative to a domain of discourse and our choice of extralogical words, we may characterize a sentence as analytic if and only if its truth value depends on semantic properties of these words alone. We should give up the absolutist view that a sentence is eternally true. These concepts were also defined with precision for a certain formalized language L in terms of truth in a model, e.g., a tautology is a sentence true in all models for L, and a sentence is analytic if it is true in every model for L in which each of the meaning postulates of L is true. A meaning postulate is a sentence of a formalized language which provides meaning relation between predicates of that language.[42]

Students who are interested in a precise definition of such concepts in a formalized language may consult the articles in the selected readings.

SELECTED READINGS

Aune, Bruce. "Is There an Analytic A Priori?" *Journal of Philosophy,* LX (1963), 281-90.

Bar-Hillel, Y. "Bolzano's Definition of Analytic Propositions." *Theoria,* XVI (1950), 91-117.

Ebersole, F. B. "On Certain Confusions in the Analytic-Synthetic Distinction." *Journal of Philosophy,* LIII (1956), 485-94.

Edwards, Paul. "Do Necessary Propositions 'Mean Nothing'?" *Journal of Philosophy,* XLVI (1949), 457-68.

Hamlyn, D. W. "Analytic Truths." *Mind,* LXV (1956), 379-91.

Hampshire, Stuart. "Logical Necessity." *Philosophy,* XXIII (1948), 332-45.

Hanson, N. R. "Justifying Analytic Claims." *Analysis,* XXIII (1963), 103-5.

Hintikka, J. "Are Logical Truths Analytic?" *Philosophical Review,* LXXIV (1965), 178-203.

Kalish, Donald. "Semantics: Truth in a *Model.*" *Encyclopedia of Philosophy,* ed. Paul Edwards, VII. New York: Macmillan–Free Press, 1967, 348-58.

Kemeny, J. G. "Analyticity versus Fuzziness." *Synthese,* XIV (1963), 57-59.

Lazerowitz, Morris. "Necessary and Contingent Truths." *Philosophical Review,* XLV (1936), 268-82.

Malcolm, Norman. "Are Necessary Propositions Really Verbal?" *Mind,* XLIX (1940), 189-203.

---

[42] Rudolf Carnap, "Meaning Postulates," *Meaning and Necessity: A Study in Semantics and Modal Logic* (Chicago: University of Chicago Press, 1951), 222-29.

Martin, R. M. "On Analytic." *Philosophical Studies,* III (1952), 42-47.

Mates, Benson. "Analytic Sentences." *Philosophical Review,* LX (1951), 525-34.

Pap, Arthur. "The Different Kinds of A Priori." *Philosophical Review,* LIII (1944), 465-84.

———. "Logical Nonsense." *Philosophy and Phenomenological Research,* IX (1948), 269-83.

Putnam, Hilary. "The Analytic and the Synthetic." *Minnesota Studies in the Philosophy of Science,* III, eds. H. Feigl and Grover Maxwell. Minneapolis: University of Minnesota Press, 1966.

Quine, W. V. "Carnap and Logical Truth." In *The Philosophy of Rudolf Carnap,* ed. P. A. Schilpp. Evanston, Ill.: Northwestern University Press, 1963, 385-406.

Rynin, D. "The Dogma of Logical Pragmatism." *Mind,* LXV (1956), 379-91.

Sellars, Wilfrid. "Is There a Synthetic A Priori?" *Philosophy of Science* (1953), 121-38. Reprinted in Sellars, *Science, Perception and Reality* (London: Routledge and Kegan Paul, 1963), 298-320.

Stebbing, L. S. "The A Priori." *Proceedings of the Aristotelian Society,* suppl. vol. XII (1933), 178-97.

Tarski, Alfred. "The Concept of Truth in Formalized Languages." In *Logic, Semantics, Metamathematics,* trans. J. H. Woodger (Oxford: Oxford University Press, 1956), 152-278.

Watkins, J. W. N. "Between Analytic and Empirical." *Philosophy,* XXXII (1957), 112-31; XXXIII (1958), 342-55.

White, M. C. "The Analytic and Synthetic: An Untenable Dualism." In *John Dewey: Philosopher of Science and Freedom.* New York: Dial, 1950, 316-36.

1

The A Priori

A. J. AYER

From *Language, Truth and Logic* by Alfred Jules Ayer, Dover Publications, Inc., New York, 1946. Reprinted through the kind permission of the publisher.

CHAPTER IV

THE *A PRIORI*

The view of philosophy which we have adopted may, I think, fairly be described as a form of empiricism. For it is characteristic of an empiricist to eschew metaphysics, on the ground that every factual proposition must refer to sense-experience. And even if the conception of philosophizing as an activity of analysis is not to be discovered in the traditional theories of empiricists, we have seen that it is implicit in their practice. At the same time, it must be made clear that, in calling ourselves empiricists, we are not avowing a belief in any of the psychological doctrines which are commonly associated with empiricism. For, even if these doctrines were valid, their validity would be independent of the validity of any philosophical thesis. It could

1 Introduction to L. Wittgenstein's *Tractatus Logico-Philosophicus*, p. 23.
2 Concerning logical paradoxes, see Russell and Whitehead, *Principia Mathematica*, Introduction, Chapter ii; F. P. Ramsey, *Foundations of Mathematics*, pp. 1–63; and Lewis and Langford, *Symbolic Logic*, Chapter xiii.
3 Vide *Logische Syntax der Sprache*, Parts I and II.

71

be established only by observation, and not by the purely logical considerations upon which our empiricism rests.

Having admitted that we are empiricists, we must now deal with the objection that is commonly brought against all forms of empiricism; the objection, namely, that it is impossible on empiricist principles to account for our knowledge of necessary truths. For, as Hume conclusively showed, no general proposition whose validity is subject to the test of actual experience can ever be logically certain. No matter how often it is verified in practice, there still remains the possibility that it will be confuted on some future occasion. The fact that a law has been substantiated in $n-1$ cases affords no logical guarantee that it will be substantiated in the nth case also, no matter how large we take n to be. And this means that no general proposition referring to a matter of fact can ever be shown to be necessarily and universally true. It can at best be a probable hypothesis. And this, we shall find, applies not only to general propositions, but to all propositions which have a factual content. They can none of them ever become logically certain. This conclusion, which we shall elaborate later on, is one which must be accepted by every consistent empiricist. It is often thought to involve him in complete scepticism; but this is not the case. For the fact that the validity of a proposition cannot be logically guaranteed in no way entails that it is irrational for us to believe it. On the contrary, what is irrational is to look for a guarantee where none can be forthcoming; to demand certainty where probability is all that is obtainable. We have already remarked upon this, in referring to the work of Hume. And we shall make the point clearer when we come to treat of probability, in explaining the use which we make of empirical propositions. We shall discover that there is nothing perverse or paradoxical about the view that all the "truths" of science and common sense are hypotheses; and consequently that the fact that it involves this view constitutes no objection to the empiricist thesis.

Where the empiricist does encounter difficulty is in connection with the truths of formal logic and mathematics. For whereas a scientific generalisation is readily admitted to be fallible, the truths of mathematics and logic appear to everyone to be necessary and certain. But if empiricism is correct no proposition which has a factual content can be necessary or certain. Accordingly

72

the empiricist must deal with the truths of logic and mathematics in one of the two following ways: he must say either that they are not necessary truths, in which case he must account for the universal conviction that they are; or he must say that they have no factual content, and then he must explain how a proposition which is empty of all factual content can be true and useful and surprising.

If neither of these courses proves satisfactory, we shall be obliged to give way to rationalism. We shall be obliged to admit that there are some truths about the world which we can know independently of experience; that there are some properties which we can ascribe to all objects, even though we cannot conceivably observe that all objects have them. And we shall have to accept it as a mysterious inexplicable fact that our thought has this power to reveal to us authoritatively the nature of objects which we have never observed. Or else we must accept the Kantian explanation which, apart from the epistemological difficulties which we have already touched on, only pushes the mystery a stage further back.

It is clear that any such concession to rationalism would upset the main argument of this book. For the admission that there were some facts about the world which could be known independently of experience would be incompatible with our fundamental contention that a sentence says nothing unless it is empirically verifiable. And thus the whole force of our attack on metaphysics would be destroyed. It is vital, therefore, for us to be able to show that one or other of the empiricist accounts of the propositions of logic and mathematics is correct. If we are successful in this, we shall have destroyed the foundations of rationalism. For the fundamental tenet of rationalism is that thought is an independent source of knowledge, and is moreover a more trustworthy source of knowledge than experience; indeed some rationalists have gone so far as to say that thought is the only source of knowledge. And the ground for this view is simply that the only necessary truths about the world which are known to us are known through thought and not through experience. So that if we can show either that the truths in question are not necessary or that they are not "truths about the world," we shall be taking away the support on which rationalism rests. We shall be making good the empiricist contention that there are no "truths of reason" which refer to matters of fact.

The course of maintaining that the truths of logic and mathematics are not necessary or certain was adopted by Mill. He maintained that these propositions were inductive generalizations based on an extremely large number of instances. The fact that the number of supporting instances was so very large accounted, in his view, for our believing these generalizations to be necessarily and universally true. The evidence in their favour was so strong that it seemed incredible to us that a contrary instance should ever arise. Nevertheless it was in principle possible for such generalizations to be confuted. They were highly probable, but, being inductive generalizations, they were not certain. The difference between them and the hypotheses of natural science was a difference in degree and not in kind. Experience gave us very good reason to suppose that a "truth" of mathematics or logic was true universally; but we were not possessed of a guarantee. For these "truths" were only empirical hypotheses which had worked particularly well in the past; and, like all empirical hypotheses, they were theoretically fallible.

I do not think that this solution of the empiricist's difficulty with regard to the propositions of logic and mathematics is acceptable. In discussing it, it is necessary to make a distinction which is perhaps already enshrined in Kant's famous dictum that, although there can be no doubt that all our knowledge begins with experience, it does not follow that it all arises out of experience.[1] When we say that the truths of logic are known independently of experience, we are not of course saying that they are innate, in the sense that we are born knowing them. It is obvious that mathematics and logic have to be learned in the same way as chemistry and history have to be learned. Nor are we denying that the first person to discover a given logical or mathematical truth was led to it by an inductive procedure. It is very probable, for example, that the principle of the syllogism was formulated not before but after the validity of syllogistic reasoning had been observed in a number of particular cases. What we are discussing, however, when we say that logical and mathematical truths are known independently of experience, is not a historical question concerning the way in which these truths were originally discovered, nor a psychological question concerning the way in which each of us comes to learn them, but an epistemological

[1] *Critique of Pure Reason*, 2nd ed., Introduction, section i.

question. The contention of Mill's which we reject is that the propositions of logic and mathematics have the same status as empirical hypotheses; that their validity is determined in the same way. We maintain that they are independent of experience in the sense that they do not owe their validity to empirical verification. We may come to discover them through an inductive process; but once we have apprehended them we see that they are necessarily true, that they hold good for every conceivable instance. And this serves to distinguish them from empirical generalizations. For we know that a proposition whose validity depends upon experience cannot be seen to be necessarily and universally true.

In rejecting Mill's theory, we are obliged to be somewhat dogmatic. We can do no more than state the issue clearly and then trust that his contention will be seen to be discrepant with the relevant logical facts. The following considerations may serve to show that of the two ways of dealing with logic and mathematics which are open to the empiricist, the one which Mill adopted is not the one which is correct.

The best way to substantiate our assertion that the truths of formal logic and pure mathematics are necessarily true is to examine cases in which they might seem to be confuted. It might easily happen, for example, that when I came to count what I had taken to be five pairs of objects, I found that they amounted only to nine. And if I wished to mislead people I might say that on this occasion twice five was not ten. But in that case I should not be using the complex sign "$2 \times 5 = 10$" in the way in which it is ordinarily used. I should be taking it not as the expression of a purely mathematical proposition, but as the expression of an empirical generalization, to the effect that whenever I counted what appeared to me to be five pairs of objects I discovered that they were ten in number. This generalization may very well be false. But if it proved false in a given case, one would not say that the mathematical proposition "$2 \times 5 = 10$" had been confuted. One would say that I was wrong in supposing that there were five pairs of objects to start with, or that one of the objects had been taken away while I was counting, or that two of them had coalesced, or that I had counted wrongly. One would adopt as an explanation whatever empirical hypothesis fitted in best with the accredited facts. The one explanation which would in no

75

circumstances be adopted is that ten is not always the product of two and five.

To take another example: if what appears to be a Euclidean triangle is found by measurement not to have angles totalling 180 degrees, we do not say that we have met with an instance which invalidates the mathematical proposition that the sum of the three angles of a Euclidean triangle is 180 degrees. We say that we have measured wrongly, or, more probably, that the triangle we have been measuring is not Euclidean. And this is our procedure in every case in which a mathematical truth might appear to be confuted. We always preserve its validity by adopting some other explanation of the occurrence.

The same thing applies to the principles of formal logic. We may take an example relating to the so-called law of excluded middle, which states that a proposition must be either true or false, or, in other words, that it is impossible that a proposition and its contradictory should neither of them be true. One might suppose that a proposition of the form "x has stopped doing y" would in certain cases constitute an exception to this law. For instance, if my friend has never yet written to me, it seems fair to say that it is neither true nor false that he has stopped writing to me. But in fact one would refuse to accept such an instance as an invalidation of the law of excluded middle. One would point out that the proposition "My friend has stopped writing to me" is not a simple proposition, but the conjunction of the two propositions "My friend wrote to me in the past" and "My friend does not write to me now": and, furthermore, that the proposition "My friend has not stopped writing to me" is not, as it appears to be, contradictory to "My friend has stopped writing to me," but only contrary to it. For it means "My friend wrote to me in the past, and he still writes to me." When, therefore, we say that such a proposition as "My friend has stopped writing to me" is sometimes neither true nor false, we are speaking inaccurately. For we seem to be saying that neither it nor its contradictory is true. Whereas what we mean, or anyhow should mean, is that neither it nor its apparent contradictory is true. And its apparent contradictory is really only its contrary. Thus we preserve the law of excluded middle by showing that the negating of a sentence does not always yield the contradictory of the proposition originally expressed.

76

There is no need to give further examples. Whatever instance we care to take, we shall always find that the situations in which a logical or mathematical principle might appear to be confuted are accounted for in such a way as to leave the principle unassailed. And this indicates that Mill was wrong in supposing that a situation could arise which would overthrow a mathematical truth. The principles of logic and mathematics are true universally simply because we never allow them to be anything else. And the reason for this is that we cannot abandon them without contradicting ourselves, without sinning against the rules which govern the use of language, and so making our utterances self-stultifying. In other words, the truths of logic and mathematics are analytic propositions or tautologies. In saying this we are making what will be held to be an extremely controversial statement, and we must now proceed to make its implications clear.

The most familiar definition of an analytic proposition, or judgement, as he called it, is that given by Kant. He said[1] that an analytic judgement was one in which the predicate B belonged to the subject A as something which was covertly contained in the concept of A. He contrasted analytic with synthetic judgements, in which the predicate B lay outside the subject A, although it did stand in connection with it. Analytic judgements, he explains, "add nothing through the predicate to the concept of the subject, but merely break it up into those constituent concepts that have all along been thought in it, although confusedly." Synthetic judgements, on the other hand, "add to the concept of the subject a predicate which has not been in any wise thought in it, and which no analysis could possibly extract from it." Kant gives "all bodies are extended" as an example of an analytic judgement, on the ground that the required predicate can be extracted from the concept of "body," "in accordance with the principle of contradiction"; as an example of a synthetic judgement, he gives "all bodies are heavy." He refers also to "$7+5=12$" as a synthetic judgement, on the ground that the concept of twelve is by no means already thought in merely thinking the union of seven and five. And he appears to regard this as tantamount to saying that the judgement does not rest on the principle of contradiction alone. He holds, also, that through analytic judgements our knowledge is not extended as it is

[1] *Critique of Pure Reason*, 2nd ed., Introduction, sections iv and v.

through synthetic judgements. For in analytic judgements "the concept which I already have is merely set forth and made intelligible to me."

I think that this is a fair summary of Kant's account of the distinction between analytic and synthetic propositions, but I do not think that it succeeds in making the distinction clear. For even if we pass over the difficulties which arise out of the use of the vague term "concept," and the unwarranted assumption that every judgement, as well as every German or English sentence, can be said to have a subject and a predicate, there remains still this crucial defect. Kant does not give one straightforward criterion for distinguishing between analytic and synthetic propositions; he gives two distinct criteria, which are by no means equivalent. Thus his ground for holding that the proposition "$7+5 = 12$" is synthetic is, as we have seen, that the subjective intension of "$7+5$" does not comprise the subjective intension of "12"; whereas his ground for holding that "all bodies are extended" is an analytic proposition is that it rests on the principle of contradiction alone. That is, he employs a psychological criterion in the first of these examples, and a logical criterion in the second, and takes their equivalence for granted. But, in fact, a proposition which is synthetic according to the former criterion may very well be analytic according to the latter. For, as we have already pointed out, it is possible for symbols to be synonymous without having the same intensional meaning for anyone: and accordingly from the fact that one can think of the sum of seven and five without necessarily thinking of twelve, it by no means follows that the proposition "$7+5 = 12$" can be denied without self-contradiction. From the rest of his argument, it is clear that it is this logical proposition, and not any psychological proposition, that Kant is really anxious to establish. His use of the psychological criterion leads him to think that he has established it, when he has not.

I think that we can preserve the logical import of Kant's distinction between analytic and synthetic propositions, while avoiding the confusions which mar his actual account of it, if we say that a proposition is analytic when its validity depends solely on the definitions of the symbols it contains, and synthetic when its validity is determined by the facts of experience. Thus, the proposition "There are ants which have established a system of slavery" is a synthetic proposition. For we

78

cannot tell whether it is true or false merely by considering the definitions of the symbols which constitute it. We have to resort to actual observation of the behaviour of ants. On the other hand, the proposition "Either some ants are parasitic or none are" is an analytic proposition. For one need not resort to observation to discover that there either are or are not ants which are parasitic. If one knows what is the function of the words "either," "or," and "not," then one can see that any proposition of the form "Either p is true or p is not true" is valid, independently of experience. Accordingly, all such propositions are analytic.

It is to be noticed that the proposition "Either some ants are parasitic or none are" provides no information whatsoever about the behaviour of ants, or, indeed, about any matter of fact. And this applies to all analytic propositions. They none of them provide any information about any matter of fact. In other words, they are entirely devoid of factual content. And it is for this reason that no experience can confute them.

When we say that analytic propositions are devoid of factual content, and consequently that they say nothing, we are not suggesting that they are senseless in the way that metaphysical utterances are senseless. For, although they give us no information about any empirical situation, they do enlighten us by illustrating the way in which we use certain symbols. Thus if I say, "Nothing can be coloured in different ways at the same time with respect to the same part of itself," I am not saying anything about the properties of any actual thing; but I am not talking nonsense. I am expressing an analytic proposition, which records our determination to call a colour expanse which differs in quality from a neighbouring colour expanse a different part of a given thing. In other words, I am simply calling attention to the implications of a certain linguistic usage. Similarly, in saying that if all Bretons are Frenchmen, and all Frenchmen Europeans, then all Bretons are Europeans, I am not describing any matter of fact. But I am showing that in the statement that all Bretons are Frenchmen, and all Frenchmen Europeans, the further statement that all Bretons are Europeans is implicitly contained. And I am thereby indicating the convention which governs our usage of the words "if" and "all."

We see, then, that there is a sense in which analytic propositions do give us new knowledge. They call attention to linguistic

79

usages, of which we might otherwise not be conscious, and they reveal unsuspected implications in our assertions and beliefs. But we can see also that there is a sense in which they may be said to add nothing to our knowledge. For they tell us only what we may be said to know already. Thus, if I know that the existence of May Queens is a relic of tree-worship, and I discover that May Queens still exist in England, I can employ the tautology "If p implies q, and p is true, q is true" to show that there still exists a relic of tree-worship in England. But in saying that there are still May Queens in England, and that the existence of May Queens is a relic of tree-worship, I have already asserted the existence in England of a relic of tree-worship. The use of the tautology does, indeed, enable me to make this concealed assertion explicit. But it does not provide me with any new knowledge, in the sense in which empirical evidence that the election of May Queens had been forbidden by law would provide me with new knowledge. If one had to set forth all the information one possessed, with regard to matters of fact, one would not write down any analytic propositions. But one would make use of analytic propositions in compiling one's encyclopædia, and would thus come to include propositions which one would otherwise have overlooked. And, besides enabling one to make one's list of information complete, the formulation of analytic propositions would enable one to make sure that the synthetic propositions of which the list was composed formed a self-consistent system. By showing which ways of combining propositions resulted in contradictions, they would prevent one from including incompatible propositions and so making the list self-stultifying. But in so far as we had actually used such words as "all" and "or" and "not" without falling into self-contradiction, we might be said already to know what was revealed in the formulation of analytic propositions illustrating the rules which govern our usage of these logical particles. So that here again we are justified in saying that analytic propositions do not increase our knowledge.

The analytic character of the truths of formal logic was obscured in the traditional logic through its being insufficiently formalized. For in speaking always of judgements, instead of propositions, and introducing irrelevant psychological questions, the traditional logic gave the impression of being concerned in some specially intimate way with the workings of thought. What

80

it was actually concerned with was the formal relationship of classes, as is shown by the fact that all its principles of inference are subsumed in the Boolean class-calculus, which is subsumed in its turn in the propositional calculus of Russell and Whitehead.[1] Their system, expounded in *Principia Mathematica*, makes it clear that formal logic is not concerned with the properties of men's minds, much less with the properties of material objects, but simply with the possibility of combining propositions by means of logical particles into analytic propositions, and with studying the formal relationship of these analytic propositions, in virtue of which one is deducible from another. Their procedure is to exhibit the propositions of formal logic as a deductive system, based on five primitive propositions, subsequently reduced in number to one. Hereby the distinction between logical truths and principles of inference, which was maintained in the Aristotelian logic, very properly disappears. Every principle of inference is put forward as a logical truth and every logical truth can serve as a principle of inference. The three Aristotelian "laws of thought," the law of identity, the law of excluded middle, and the law of non-contradiction, are incorporated in the system, but they are not considered more important than the other analytic propositions. They are not reckoned among the premises of the system. And the system of Russell and Whitehead itself is probably only one among many possible logics, each of which is composed of tautologies as interesting to the logician as the arbitrarily selected Aristotelian "laws of thought."[2]

A point which is not sufficiently brought out by Russell, if indeed it is recognised by him at all, is that every logical proposition is valid in its own right. Its validity does not depend on its being incorporated in a system, and deduced from certain propositions which are taken as self-evident. The construction of systems of logic is useful as a means of discovering and certifying analytic propositions, but it is not in principle essential even for this purpose. For it is possible to conceive of a symbolism in which every analytic proposition could be seen to be analytic in virtue of its form alone.

The fact that the validity of an analytic proposition in no way

[1] Vide Karl Menger, "Die Neue Logik," *Krise und Neuaufbau in den Exakten Wissenschaften*, pp. 94–6; and Lewis and Langford, *Symbolic Logic*, Chapter v.

[2] Vide Lewis and Langford, *Symbolic Logic*, Chapter vii, for an elaboration of this point.

depends on its being deducible from other analytic propositions is our justification for disregarding the question whether the propositions of mathematics are reducible to propositions of formal logic, in the way that Russell supposed.[1] For even if it is the case that the definition of a cardinal number as a class of classes similar to a given class is circular, and it is not possible to reduce mathematical notions to purely logical notions, it will still remain true that the propositions of mathematics are analytic propositions. They will form a special class of analytic propositions, containing special terms, but they will be none the less analytic for that. For the criterion of an analytic proposition is that its validity should follow simply from the definition of the terms contained in it, and this condition is fulfilled by the propositions of pure mathematics.

The mathematical propositions which one might most pardonably suppose to be synthetic are the propositions of geometry. For it is natural for us to think, as Kant thought, that geometry is the study of the properties of physical space, and consequently that its propositions have factual content. And if we believe this, and also recognise that the truths of geometry are necessary and certain, then we may be inclined to accept Kant's hypothesis that space is the form of intuition of our outer sense, a form imposed by us on the matter of sensation, as the only possible explanation of our *a priori* knowledge of these synthetic propositions. But while the view that pure geometry is concerned with physical space was plausible enough in Kant's day, when the geometry of Euclid was the only geometry known, the subsequent invention of non-Euclidean geometries has shown it to be mistaken. We see now that the axioms of a geometry are simply definitions, and that the theorems of a geometry are simply the logical consequences of these definitions.[2] A geometry is not in itself about physical space; in itself it cannot be said to be "about" anything. But we can use a geometry to reason about physical space. That is to say, once we have given the axioms a physical interpretation, we can proceed to apply the theorems to the objects which satisfy the axioms. Whether a geometry can be applied to the actual physical world or not, is an empirical question which falls outside the scope of the geometry itself. There is no sense, therefore, in asking

[1] Vide *Introduction to Mathematical Philosophy*, Chapter ii.
[2] cf. H. Poincaré, *La Science et l'Hypothèse*, Part II, Chapter iii.

which of the various geometries known to us are false and which are true. In so far as they are all free from contradiction, they are all true. What one can ask is which of them is the most useful on any given occasion, which of them can be applied most easily and most fruitfully to an actual empirical situation. But the proposition which states that a certain application of a geometry is possible is not itself a proposition of that geometry. All that the geometry itself tells us is that if anything can be brought under the definitions, it will also satisfy the theorems. It is therefore a purely logical system, and its propositions are purely analytic propositions.

It might be objected that the use made of diagrams in geometrical treatises shows that geometrical reasoning is not purely abstract and logical, but depends on our intuition of the properties of figures. In fact, however, the use of diagrams is not essential to completely rigorous geometry. The diagrams are introduced as an aid to our reason. They provide us with a particular application of the geometry, and so assist us to perceive the more general truth that the axioms of the geometry involve certain consequences. But the fact that most of us need the help of an example to make us aware of those consequences does not show that the relation between them and the axioms is not a purely logical relation. It shows merely that our intellects are unequal to the task of carrying out very abstract processes of reasoning without the assistance of intuition. In other words, it has no bearing on the nature of geometrical propositions, but is simply an empirical fact about ourselves. Moreover, the appeal to intuition, though generally of psychological value, is also a source of danger to the geometer. He is tempted to make assumptions which are accidentally true of the particular figure he is taking as an illustration, but do not follow from his axioms. It has, indeed, been shown that Euclid himself was guilty of this, and consequently that the presence of the figure is essential to some of his proofs.[1] This shows that his system is not, as he presents it, completely rigorous, although of course it can be made so. It does not show that the presence of the figure is essential to a truly rigorous geometrical proof. To suppose that it did would be to take as a necessary feature of all geometries what is really only an incidental defect in one particular geometrical system.

[1] cf. M. Black, *The Nature of Mathematics*, p. 154.

We conclude, then, that the propositions of pure geometry are analytic. And this leads us to reject Kant's hypothesis that geometry deals with the form of intuition of our outer sense. For the ground for this hypothesis was that it alone explained how the propositions of geometry could be both true *a priori* and synthetic: and we have seen that they are not synthetic. Similarly our view that the propositions of arithmetic are not synthetic but analytic leads us to reject the Kantian hypothesis[1] that arithmetic is concerned with our pure intuition of time, the form of our inner sense. And thus we are able to dismiss Kant's transcendental æsthetic without having to bring forward the epistemological difficulties which it is commonly said to involve. For the only argument which can be brought in favour of Kant's theory is that it alone explains certain "facts." And now we have found that the "facts" which it purports to explain are not facts at all. For while it is true that we have *a priori* knowledge of necessary propositions, it is not true, as Kant supposed, that any of these necessary propositions are synthetic. They are without exception analytic propositions, or, in other words, tautologies.

We have already explained how it is that these analytic propositions are necessary and certain. We saw that the reason why they cannot be confuted in experience is that they do not make any assertion about the empirical world. They simply record our determination to use words in a certain fashion. We cannot deny them without infringing the conventions which are presupposed by our very denial, and so falling into self-contradiction. And this is the sole ground of their necessity. As Wittgenstein puts it, our justification for holding that the world could not conceivably disobey the laws of logic is simply that we could not say of an unlogical world how it would look.[2] And just as the validity of an analytic proposition is independent of the nature of the external world, so is it independent of the nature of our minds. It is perfectly conceivable that we should have employed different linguistic conventions from those which we actually do employ. But whatever these conventions might be, the tautologies in which we recorded them would always be necessary. For any denial of them would be self-stultifying.

[1] This hypothesis is not mentioned in the *Critique of Pure Reason*, but was maintained by Kant at an earlier date.

[2] *Tractatus Logico-Philosophicus*, 3·031.

84

We see, then, that there is nothing mysterious about the apo-deictic certainty of logic and mathematics. Our knowledge that no observation can ever confute the proposition "$7+5=12$" depends simply on the fact that the symbolic expression "$7+5$" is synonymous with "12," just as our knowledge that every oculist is an eye-doctor depends on the fact that the symbol "eye-doctor" is synonymous with "oculist." And the same explanation holds good for every other *a priori* truth.

What is mysterious at first sight is that these tautologies should on occasion be so surprising, that there should be in mathematics and logic the possibility of invention and discovery. As Poincaré says: "If all the assertions which mathematics puts forward can be derived from one another by formal logic, mathematics cannot amount to anything more than an immense tautology. Logical inference can teach us nothing essentially new, and if everything is to proceed from the principle of identity, everything must be reducible to it. But can we really allow that these theorems which fill so many books serve no other purpose than to say in a round-about fashion '$A=A$'?"[1] Poincaré finds this incredible. His own theory is that the sense of invention and discovery in mathematics belongs to it in virtue of mathematical induction, the principle that what is true for the number 1, and true for $n+1$ when it is true for n,[2] is true for all numbers. And he claims that this is a synthetic *a priori* principle. It is, in fact, *a priori*, but it is not synthetic. It is a defining principle of the natural numbers, serving to distinguish them from such numbers as the infinite cardinal numbers, to which it cannot be applied.[3] Moreover, we must remember that discoveries can be made, not only in arithmetic, but also in geometry and formal logic, where no use is made of mathematical induction. So that even if Poincaré were right about mathematical induction, he would not have provided a satisfactory explanation of the paradox that a mere body of tautologies can be so interesting and so surprising.

The true explanation is very simple. The power of logic and mathematics to surprise us depends, like their usefulness, on the limitations of our reason. A being whose intellect was infinitely

[1] *La Science et l'Hypothèse*, Part I, Chapter i.

[2] This was wrongly stated in previous editions as "true for n when it is true for $n+1$."

[3] cf. B. Russell's *Introduction to Mathematical Philosophy*, Chapter iii, p. 27.

powerful would take no interest in logic and mathematics.[1] For he would be able to see at a glance everything that his definitions implied, and, accordingly, could never learn anything from logical inference which he was not fully conscious of already. But our intellects are not of this order. It is only a minute proportion of the consequences of our definitions that we are able to detect at a glance. Even so simple a tautology as "$91 \times 79 = 7189$" is beyond the scope of our immediate apprehension. To assure ourselves that "7189" is synonymous with "91×79" we have to resort to calculation, which is simply a process of tautological transformation—that is, a process by which we change the form of expressions without altering their significance. The multiplication tables are rules for carrying out this process in arithmetic, just as the laws of logic are rules for the tautological transformation of sentences expressed in logical symbolism or in ordinary language. As the process of calculation is carried out more or less mechanically, it is easy for us to make a slip and so unwittingly contradict ourselves. And this accounts for the existence of logical and mathematical "falsehoods," which otherwise might appear paradoxical. Clearly the risk of error in logical reasoning is proportionate to the length and the complexity of the process of calculation. And in the same way, the more complex an analytic proposition is, the more chance it has of interesting and surprising us.

It is easy to see that the danger of error in logical reasoning can be minimized by the introduction of symbolic devices, which enable us to express highly complex tautologies in a conveniently simple form. And this gives us an opportunity for the exercise of invention in the pursuit of logical enquiries. For a well-chosen definition will call our attention to analytic truths, which would otherwise have escaped us. And the framing of definitions which are useful and fruitful may well be regarded as a creative act.

Having thus shown that there is no inexplicable paradox involved in the view that the truths of logic and mathematics are all of them analytic, we may safely adopt it as the only satisfactory explanation of their *a priori* necessity. And in adopting it we vindicate the empiricist claim that there can be no *a priori*

---

[1] cf. Hans Hahn, "Logik, Mathematik und Naturerkennen," *Einheitswissenschaft*, Heft II, p. 18. "Ein allwissendes Wesen braucht keine Logik und keine Mathematik."

knowledge of reality. For we show that the truths of pure reason, the propositions which we know to be valid independently of all experience, are so only in virtue of their lack of factual content. To say that a proposition is true *a priori* is to say that it is a tautology. And tautologies, though they may serve to guide us in our empirical search for knowledge, do not in themselves contain any information about any matter of fact.

2

Analytic — Synthetic

FRIEDRICH WAISMANN

Reprinted with the kind permission of the publisher (Basil Blackwell) from *Analysis* (1950), 25-40.

ANALYSIS 10 . 2   DECEMBER 1949

ANALYTIC—SYNTHETIC

I

By FRIEDRICH WAISMANN

1. What is " analytic " ?

KANT says[1] " In all judgments in which there is a relation between subject and predicate . . . that relation can be of two kinds.   Either the predicate B belongs to the subject A as something contained (though covertly) in the concept A ; or B lies outside the sphere of the concept A, though somehow connected with it. In the former case I call the judgment analytical, in the latter synthetical. Analytical judgments (affirmative) are therefore those in which the connection of the predicate with the subject is conceived through identity, while others in which that connection is conceived without identity, may be called synthetical. The former might be called illustrating, the latter expanding judgments, because in the former nothing is added by the predicate to the concept of the subject, but the concept is only divided into its constituent concepts which were always conceived as existing within it, though confusedly ; while the latter add to the concept of the subject a predicate not conceived as existing within it, and not to be extracted from it by any process of mere analysis . . . It is clear from this that our knowledge is in no way extended by analytical judgments, but that all they effect is to put the concepts which we possess into better order and render them more intelligible ".

This definition may seem clear enough ; yet isn't it surprising how easy it is to raise questions which are plainly embarrassing ? What, for instance, is meant by saying that, in an analytic judgment, the concept of the subject is " only *divided into* its constituent concepts " ? Is the subject-term to be regarded as a sort of sum total of its constituent concepts, i.e., of all those which, analytically, can be asserted of it ? This doesn't seem to make sense. Suppose we make a number of analytic judgments such as S is P_1, S is P_2, . . . S is P_n, these being *all* the analytic judgments we can make about this particular subject S. Then, according to Kant, it would seem natural to say that S is thereby " divided ", or " dissolved "[2], into the constituent concepts P_1, P_2 . . . P_n But what meaning are we to attach to this ? Shall we say, e.g.,

---

[1] Critique of Pure Reason : Introduction IV.
[2] In German " *durch Zergliederung zerfallt* " (Critique), " *aufgelost* " (Proleg.).

that S is the collection, or the class, or the totality of all the members $P_1, P_2, \ldots P_n$? To assert of a class any of its member concepts, e.g., to assert of the class $\{P_1, P_2, \ldots P_n\}$ that it is P_1, would be absurd. We don't say of the attributes of a thing that *they*, all of them, have any of these attributes. Take the simplest case in which the class consists of one member only, say P. Then the class consisting of P will be different from P, and to say of this class $\{P\}$ that it is itself P, i.e. that it has the property expressed by " P ", would be self-stultifying, or more accurately, it would be a type-fallacy, landing us in a lot of well-known logical contradictions. So this way is blocked : the relation of S to any of its predicates must be different from the relation of a class to any of its members. In what, then, *does* it consist ? The same difficulty can be brought out in a slightly different way when we ask—What is meant by saying that the predicate is " contained in " the concept of the subject, or is " conceived as existing within it ", or that the former can be " extracted from it "—turns of speech which sound as if they were taken from dentistry ? The word " contain ", even if not taken in its strictly spatial sense " to enclose ", is used in a great many different ways as when I say, " A pound contains 16 ounces ", " This book contains some valuable information ", " The premiss of an inference contains the conclusion ", and the like. In *which* of these senses, then, is the predicate to " be contained in " the notion of the subject ? Perhaps in the sense of our last example, that is, in the sense in which a conclusion is often held to " be contained in " the premiss from which, according to the same view, it can be " extracted " by inference ? That, it seems, is an analogy worth following. But if so, what exactly *is* the relation that holds between the premiss and the conclusion of an inference ? Shall I say, e.g., that whenever I think of the premiss, I *coincidently* think of the conclusion ? That would be glaringly untrue : I may consider the premiss *without* noticing some particular conclusion. (How on earth could a mathematical discovery be thrilling ?) Saying that the latter is " contained in " the former, whatever this may mean, can certainly not be taken to refer to any *psychological* relationship between the two such that thinking of the one is accompanied, or followed, by thinking of the other. No ; in studying the logical relation between the parts of an inference, we are clearly *not* investigating what is actually going on, or what may be going on, in someone's mind. Similarly in our case : to say, in the case of an analytic judgment, that the predicate is " contained in " the concept of the subject can certainly not be taken to mean that whoever thinks of the subject will simultaneously, or a little while later, think of the predicate, or something of this sort. So far our result is mainly negative : we see that the relation can certainly not be a *psychological* one, though we are baffled to say *what* it is. I don't think that these questions are raised wantonly ; they present themselves to anyone who tries to understand clearly what an analytic judgment is. Our difficulty is, at least in part, due to the fact that Kant, when he speaks of " analytic ", is unwittingly using nothing but metaphorical terms, which hint at, and at the same time obscure, what the true relation is. Nor is this the only problem with which we are confronted. Another difficulty arises from the fact that Kant's definition is such as to apply, according to his own words, only to statements of the subject-predicate pattern, ignoring other types—such as relational, and existential statements, let alone mathematical formulae like $7+5=12$ (which Kant, oddly enough, cites as an example of a synthetic judgment). Subject and predicate are, after all, ideas which are borrowed from the grammar of certain word sentences, but which cannot, without destroying the clarity of our ideas, be applied to forms so fundamentally different. In other words, Kant's definition is *too narrow*, a fact we shall do well to keep in mind too.

Attempts have been made to amend Kant's definition. To quote a recent writer on the subject, A. Pap[3] : " Analytic statements . . . may be roughly characterized as statements whose truth *follows* (my italics) from the very meaning of their terms ". Here I immediately come up against a stumbling block : what can be meant by saying that a statement *follows from the very meaning of its terms ?* I should have thought that *one* statement can follow from *another ;* but from the meaning—! Yet, strangely enough, such a view has been taken by no one less than Frege. Criticising the formalist account of mathematics—the view according to which mathematics is but a sort of game played with inkmarks on paper instead of with chessmen on a board— he very emphatically says : " If there were any meaning to be considered, the rules [of this game] could not be arbitrarily laid down. On the contrary, the rules follow necessarily from the meaning of the marks ".[4] Frege's idea seems, roughly, to have been this : If I write down a rule, e.g., the equation " $2+2=4$ ", this may be regarded as a configuration in a game not so very unlike a configuration of chessmen on a board. But then the question of truth and falsehood does not arise. As soon as I

---

[3] " Indubitable Existential Statements ", *Mind*, 1946.
[4] Grundgesetze der Arithmetik, Vol. ii, 1900, p. 158.

come to *know*, however, what the marks " 2 ", " + ", " = ",
" 4 " mean, I am no longer free to choose any configuration I
please to include in my game : the truth of that equation seems
rather to be *grounded in* the meaning of those marks. It would
lead us far to dig down to the roots from which Frege's mistake
springs. One word, however, will not be amiss. Whoever says
that a rule, say, an equation, *follows* from the meaning of its
terms, is bound to make quite clear what he understands by that.
If someone tells me that the rule, " ' John ' is spelt with a capital"
follows from, or is a consequence of, the rule, "Any proper
name is spelt with a capital ", I have no difficulty in understanding what he means. If, on the other hand, he tells me that an
equation follows from the meaning of its terms, or that an
analytic statement is one whose truth follows from the meaning
of its terms, I am absolutely at a loss to make head or tail of it.
One thing, at any rate is clear : as the meaning is not a starting
point for making deductions, " follows ", in this context, can
not mean " logically follows " ; so what *can* it mean ? Queer
that so subtle a mind as Frege should have failed to see that there
is a problem, dropping not the slightest hint as to what he had
in mind.

A different approach is made by M. Schlick.[5] The predicate
"is contained in the concept of the subject ", he says, " can
only mean that it is part of its definition ". This interpretation
has two merits : first, it is not open to the objections we had
to raise against Frege ; and secondly, it can easily be extended
so as to cover other types of judgments. Schlick thus arrives
at the following formulation : A judgment is analytic if the
ground for its truth lies solely in the *definitions* of the terms
which occur in it. " Consequently, one may say with Kant
that analytic judgments rest upon the law of contradiction,
they derive from definitions by means of this law ".[6] What
Schlick obviously has in mind is that a judgment, or a statement,
is analytic if it follows from mere definitions only by logical
inference. Similarly Ewing (*A Short Commentary on Kant's
Critique of Pure Reason,* 1938) : "An analytic judgment is
one which *follows* (my italics) from the definition of its
subject-term."

Before proceeding to deeper lying questions let us see
whether the last two definitions are satisfactory. It undeniably
marks a great advance in them that they refer, not to such
elusive and questionable entities as the " meaning of the terms ",

[5] *Allgemeine Erkenntnislehre,* 1st ed., 1918, p. 97.
[6] *loc. cit.*

but to *definitions*. Before, however, we acquiesce in this view we are bound to ask—Is it really free from any obscurities? Strange as it may seem, when I attend to the question a bit more closely, I become doubtful. If an analytic statement is characterized as one that follows from mere definitions, why is it not itself a definition? A definition behaves in many respects like a rule, e.g., a rule of chess : it is *pre*scriptive rather than *de*scriptive—it tells us how a word, or a symbol, *is* to be used, not what its actual, or predominant, usage is. If I wish to assert that a definition given is in accord with the actual, or the prevailing, use of language, then I am, truly or falsely, making a *statement*, and no longer laying down a mere definition. There are further analogies between a definition and a rule. Thus a definition may be employed in the *learning* of a language in much the same way in which, say, the rules of chess may be employed in learning chess ; a definition may be referred to in order to *justify* a certain use of words in a way similar to that in which a rule of chess may be referred to in order to justify a certain move. A definition, like a rule, can be *set up* at a certain time, and *abandoned*, or *altered*, later on ; it may be *recognized*, or it may not ; a definition, like a rule, can be *observed*, or be *infringed* in practice ; and there are perhaps more such features. In view of this far-reaching analogy it seems very odd that it should break down at one point : what follows from a rule will, generally, be another rule (see the example concerning spelling) ; why, then, is it that what follows from a definition is, not, as one would expect, a *definition*, but an analytic *judgment*? Why suddenly this difference?

Let us first take a look at one or two examples in order to throw some light on the matter. Suppose I define a dragon as a fabulous winged serpent breathing flame, and a serpent, in its turn, as a scaly reptile, then I can derive from these two definitions the sentence "A dragon is a fabulous winged and scaly reptile, breathing flame ", which, to all appearance, might well pass for an alternative definition of " dragon " ; certainly it is not the sort of thing which would be called " analytic ". Again, if I define mephitis as poisonous stench, poisonous as a property that causes harm to life, or death, and stench as a foul smell, I am led on to say that mephitis is a foul smell that causes harm to life, or death—a sentence which, in ordinary circumstances, will be taken by most people as a mere re-wording, or a more explicit form, of the definition.

So far we were considering examples culled from word language. Before jumping to conclusions, let us be cautious and look at different sorts of examples, for instance, from symbolic logic, or from arithmetic. Suppose I start with the following three definitions :—

$$p \supset q . = . \sim p \vee q \quad \text{Df} \tag{1}$$
$$p \vee q . = . \sim p \mid \sim q \quad \text{Df} \tag{2}$$
$$\sim p . = . p \mid p \quad \text{Df} \tag{3}$$

Add to these the theorem

$$\vdash . \sim \sim p . \equiv . p \tag{4}$$

Before consequences from these formulae can be derived, certain rules of inference must first be laid down; let the following ones be chosen :—

(I) The relation expressed by the sign " = " is symmetrical and transitive.

(II) Two equivalent expressions may be substituted for each other in any occurrence.

(III) The statement variables " p ", " q ", etc. may be replaced by other, and possibly complex, statement variables. (Rule of substitution).

Applying these three rules, we may transform $p \supset q$ as follows:

$$p \supset q . =_{(1)} . \sim p \vee q . =_{(2)} \sim \sim p \mid \sim q . =_{(4)} . p \mid \sim q . =_{(3)} p \mid q \mid q .$$

Here each step of the transformation is made according to the rules (I)—(III), and, moreover, in accordance with one of the formulae (1)—(4), as indicated by the subscripts. The transformation yields

$$p \supset q . = . p \mid q \mid q \tag{5}$$

which, in view of our three rules of inference, is a *logical consequence* of (1)—(4). As (5) might have been chosen as a *definition* of the symbol " $\supset$ " in Sheffer's notation, we have exactly the same result as before : what can be derived from definitions (and logical truths), is a definition. If, however, we were to rest content with these examples and enunciate it as a general principle that whatever follows from a definition is a definition, we should be mistaken; as can be seen from the example

$$2 = 1 + 1 \quad \text{Df} \qquad (1)$$
$$3 = 2 + 1 \quad \text{Df} \qquad (2)$$
$$4 = 3 + 1 \quad \text{Df} \qquad (3)$$
$$a+(b+1) = (a+b)+1 \quad \text{Df} \qquad (4) \text{ (recursive definition of}$$
$$\text{addition)}$$

With the help of these four definitions it is easily proved that $4 = 2+2$:

$$4 =_{(3)} 3+1 =_{(2)} (2+1)+1 =_{(4)} 2+(1+1) =_{(1)} 2+2.$$

The result

$$4 = 2+2$$

is, admittedly, derived from mere definitions ; yet to regard it as a *definition* of " 4 " would be most unnatural. Why not regard $8 \times 7 = 56$ as a definition of the number 56 ? Why, indeed, not regard *any* numerical equation as a definition ?

In this way we come to see that it is only in *certain* cases true to say that what follows from a definition is a definition, whereas in other cases it is not. Why this should be so is very puzzling, and we shall have to go into this point more fully. However that may be, the examples adduced are, I think, sufficient to dispose of the view that an analytic statement is one that *follows from the definitions* of its terms.

The true state of affairs can be expressed in a somewhat different way. Instead of saying "A statement is analytic if it *follows* from definitions ", we shall have to say "A statement is analytic if it can, by means of mere definitions, be *turned into a truth of logic*", i.e., if it is *transformable* into such a truth. Consider an example. Suppose I define a planet as a heavenly body moving round the sun. (This is not quite accurate as it fails to distinguish between planets on the one, and asteroids, comets, meteors, etc. on the other hand ; and further because it ignores the fact that some other fixed stars also have planets. For the sake of simplicity let us, however, disregard these complications and keep to the simple definition). If I now say, "All planets move round the sun ", I am making an analytic statement. This statement is such that, in virtue of the definition, it can be *turned* into a logical truth. Indeed, replacing " planet " by its *definiens*, we get "All heavenly bodies which move round the sun move round the sun ", which is precisely the sort of truism one would expect to find in an analytic statement. Although we can see " with the naked eye " that this is a logical truth, we cannot yet identify the skeleton of the sentence in question with some definite logical formula, i.e., we cannot put a finger on the precise spot in PM, or in any other textbook of logic, saying, " *That's* the logical form of the statement." We shall rather have to transform our sentence by a number of steps until the logical skeleton of the proposition it expresses can be seen with perfect clarity. And in doing this, I hope to make an incidental gain—to throw more light on the status of a definition. Up till now the behaviour of a definition must have appeared rather erratic ; we shall understand the deeper reason for this far better when we come to see a definition in its natural setting of similar and related structures. To this end I shall make use of a somewhat new notation which will help to throw this point into relief.

Let p stand for the original sentence, "All planets move round the sun ". The first step is to translate the " all " idiom into

the idiom " there is no such thing that not " ; for instance,
"All men are mortal " can be paraphrased as " There is no man
that is not mortal ". Call this transformation T. Applying T
to the sentence p in the way of an operator, we obtain

Tp = There is no planet that does not move round the sun.
The next step is to put the term " planet " in the place of a
predicate ; let L symbolize this process, and write simply LTp
for L (Tp) :

LTp = There is no thing such that it is a planet that does not
move round the sun. Next eliminate the last restrictive clause
and put it conjunctively (operation R) :

$RLTp$ = There is no thing such that it is a planet and that it
does not move round the sun. According to the principle of
double negation (N), this can be expanded to saying :

$NRLTp$ = There is no thing such that it has not not the
following property : it is a planet, and it does not move round
the sun. Now translate the idiom " there is no such thing that
not" back into the "all", or "whatever"—idiom (transformation T^{-1}) :

$T^{-1}NRLTp$=Whatever a thing may be, it has not the following
    property : it is a planet, and it does not move round the sun.
According to the rule of De Morgan (M) this is further equivalent to

$MT^{-1}NRLTp$=Whatever a thing may be, it has the following
    property : it is not a planet, or it is not the case that it does
    not move round the sun.
Apply N^{-1} (the converse of N) :

$N^{-1}MT^{-1}NRLTp$=Whatever a thing may be, it has the follow-
    ing property : it is not a planet, or it moves round the
    sun.
Now the denial of " If something is a planet, it moves round
the sun " is " Something is a planet, and it does not move round
the sun " ; as the denial of the latter, according to M and N^{-1},
is " Something is not a planet, or it does move round the sun ",
and as the two denials cancel (N^{-1}), this must come to the same
as the first sentence ; which shows that the " if " idiom can be
transformed into the " not " and " or " idiom (I) :

$IN^{-1}MT^{-1}NRLTp$ = Whatever a thing may be, it has the follow-
    ing property : if it is a planet, it does move round the sun.
Let finally D stand for the definition of " planet " ; applying D
as a sort of operator, we get :

$DIN^{-1}MT^{-1}NRLTp$ = Whatever a thing may be it has the
    following property : if it is a heavenly body that moves
    round the sun, then it moves round the sun.

Repeating the R-step yields :

$RDIN^{-1}MT^{-1}NRLTp$=Whatever a thing may be, it has the following property : if it is a heavenly body and if it moves round the sun, then it moves round the sun.

Now at last we have reached the stage where the structure of our statement can be seen to coincide with a quite definite formula in PM, namely, with

$$(x) : \phi x . \psi x . \supset \psi x.$$

In words, whatever has the property ϕ and the property ψ, has the property ψ. This collects together a range of statements, each of which is of the form p. q. $\supset$. q, thus clearly exhibiting its tautologous character. In this way it is finally seen that the statement under consideration is a truth of logic. (In the transformation just carried out only the more important steps have been accounted for ; some of the purely idiomatic steps of paraphrasing have been neglected or telescoped.)[7]

It may seem pedantic, indeed excessively so, to go to such lengths to prove a very trivial thing. However, it helps us to see one point which we should not so easily have seen otherwise, viz. how similar the use of a definition is to that of other tools of transformation. Indeed, in looking back on the whole chain of transformations we have carried out, it becomes clear how near a definition comes to any of the other operators—as far as its *function* goes ; and how unnatural, for this reason, it would be to separate sharply the concept of a definition from that of other transformers.

A word must here be said on the notion of an *operator*. Suppose we consider any logical equivalence, i.e. an expression of the form

$$(. \; . \; . \; .) \equiv (. \; . \; . \; .)$$

As we pass along the equivalence, we are led from one expression to another without change of meaning ; now there are two directions of doing so, from left to right, or from right to left. Correspondingly, each logical equivalence gives rise to a pair of inverse operators, say Ω and Ω^{-1}, each of which can be used for transforming an expression into an equivalent one. Conversely, any such operator may be re-written as an equivalence, read from left to right, or from right to left, as the case may be. In this way operators and equivalences are

---

[7] Thus we have : there is a thing such that=there is something such that=there is at least one thing such that=there are some things such that=at least one thing exists such that=things (or : objects) exist such that, etc. Or again : there is no such thing that= it is not true (or : it is not the case) that there is a thing such that, etc.

---

intimately related. Thus we have the following correspon-
dences :

N : $\qquad p \equiv \sim \sim p$

M : $\qquad \sim (p.q). \equiv . \sim p \vee \sim q$

I : $\qquad p \supset q. \equiv . \sim p \vee q$

T : $\qquad (x). \phi x. \equiv . \sim (\exists x). \sim \phi x$

$\qquad$ etc.

I do not mean to say that an operator *is* an equivalence ;   an
operator is, as observed, rather the *transition* from one expression to another in *accordance with* an equivalence. But as there is
a one-one correspondence between pairs of operators on the
one hand, and equivalences on the other, we shall in future not
always take the trouble to distinguish between the two.

In formal respects it will be observed that two inverse
operators, applied successively, yield identity, in symbols $A A^{-1}$
$= 1$, and further that

$$(A \ B)^{-1} = B^{-1} \ A^{-1}.$$

However, it is not the subject of this paper to construct a
calculus of operators.

A definition fits into the same scheme on the ground that it,
too, can always be written as an equivalence ; thus instead of
defining the term " planet " in the usual way, we might have
laid it down as an equivalence

x is a planet $\equiv x$ is a heavenly body moving round the sun.

Having said all this, we are now in the position to bring to
light the fallacy that lies at the root of Schlick's and Ewing's
definitions of the term "analytic". Two different concepts have
been confused, namely, " to *follow from* a definition " and " to
be logically true *in virtue* of a definition ". The point has been
made quite clear by W.V.O. Quine in an article published 1936.[8]
" What is loosely called a logical consequence of definitions is
therefore more exactly describable as a logical truth definition-
ally abbreviated : a statement which becomes a truth of logic
when *definienda* are replaced by *definientia* ". The same point,
however, was already seen by Frege 1884 when he wrote.[9]
" When a proposition is called . . . analytic in my sense, this is
. . . a judgment about the ultimate ground upon which rests the
justification for holding it to be true. This means that the question is . . . assigned, if the truth concerned is a mathematical one,
to the sphere of mathematics. The problem thus becomes that
of finding the proof of the proposition and of following it up

[8] " Truth by Convention " : *Philosophical Essays for A. N. Whitehead*, p. 92.
[9] *Grundlagen der Arithmetik* trans. Austin § 3.

right back to the primitive truths. (*Urwahrheiten*). If, in carrying out this process, we come only on general logical laws and on definitions, then the truth is an analytic one, with the proviso that we must also take into account all propositions without which any of the definitions would become inadmissible. If, however, it is impossible to give the proof without making use of truths which are not of a general logical character . . . then the proposition is a synthetic one ".

2. Logical and idiomatic equivalence ; definition and substitution licence

In this section we shall consider more closely how logical equivalences, definitions and other operators are related. We have seen how, by means of operators, a certain sentence can be transformed into a truth of logic. In retrospect two points stand out clearly :—(1) The sentence is transformable into such a truth not *only* by means of definitions, but with the material aid of certain other operators ; (2) the definition D behaves, in point of application, *not so differently* from operators such as N, M, I, T, L, R etc. These operators, however, fall into two distinct types which we will call *logical* and *linguistic*, respectively. Thus N, M, I, T are of the first, L and R of the second type. The principle according to which this distinction is made deserves perhaps some attention. The first group consists of those transitions which are valid on *logical* grounds alone. If they are written as equivalences, they become instances of certain logical truths. But the operators of the second group are not purely logical, and cannot be expressed in logical symbols only ; rather it is characteristic of them that they are due to *the way word language is used*. To give an example for the first type, the operator N is the transition along the equivalence (indicated by the arrow).

$$\overrightarrow{p. \equiv \sim \sim p.}$$

and this equivalence is true in virtue of its *logical form ;* and similarly in the cases of $M, I,$ and T. On the other hand, the operator L which enables us to pass from saying " There is a planet that moves round the sun " to " There is a thing such that it is a planet that moves round the sun ", putting the term " planet " in the place of a predicate, will be recognized by any user of the English language as idiomatically correct ; but a logical truth it is not. In fact, it is used to *prepare* the first sentence for symbolization within the frame work of symbolic logic, though it does not go far enough for that ; it's only when we apply the further operator R (which eliminates the last restrictive clause), that we reach a sentence-form which can so be symbolized. From this it appears that the last two operators have a job very different from that of the former ones : they are transitions *within* word language, used, among other things, for re-phrasing a sentence such that it can go into symbols. The equivalence :

There is a plane that moves round the sun ≡ There is a thing such that it is a planet that moves round the sun

is certainly true ; but it is true *neither on empirical nor on logical grounds ;* there is no formula in PM which covers such a case. It is true simply because, *according to the idiomatic use of the English language,* the two sentences come to the same. A *logical* equivalence (such as that linked with *M*) is *always* and *universally* true, irrespective of the language to which it is applied ; an equivalence of the latter sort, if it is true, is true because it is in accordance with the *particular way* in which a *particular language* (such as English) is used, but it holds no place in a universal system of logic. The two groups of equivalences are therefore not of the same standing. And yet *both* sorts are needed for transforming a certain sentence into a truth of logic. That shows that Frege's and Quine's account of the matter is incomplete in an important respect. According to Frege, only *general logical laws* and *definitions* are permitted in testing the analyticity of a proposition ; Quine stresses one thing only, *definitions.* Neither of them seems to have noticed the need for a third kind of processes which are *linguistic* in nature. If we were to limit ourselves to definitions, or to definitions and logical laws, we should never be able to translate the sentence "All planets move round the sun " into a truth of logic. Frege may have been led to the view he has taken by concentrating on mathematics to the exclusion of word language. A definition which is meant to apply to word language also, must obviously allow for other tools of transformation as well.

All this makes it desirable to modify our definition by saying : A statement is analytic if it can, by means of mere definitions, logical and, further, idiomatic (linguistic) operators, be turned into a truth of logic. We proceed now to consider these means separately.

The idea of a logical operator seems sufficiently clear insofar as it is based on that of a logical equivalence. A definition can always be re-written as an equivalence (see example above). However there is an important difference in that a definition is valid in virtue of the way a certain term, e.g., the word " planet", is used in English, without, however, belonging to the body of truths provided once and for all by logic. In this respect a definition is more like an equivalence of the third kind. What is the difference ? If I say that the sentence, " Some planet moves round the sun " expresses the same fact as the sentence, " Something is a planet that moves round the sun ", I am making a statement about the way two phrases are used, viz., I am stating that the two sentences come to the same. This can, if we like, be construed as a *substitution licence* which gives permission to interchange these two locutions. The difference between a definition and a licence of the last sort is this : whereas a definition refers to *one* term only, and usually provides for its elimination from a context, an idiomatic licence applies to *whole sentences*, or clauses of such, or syntactical constructions, offering them as alternative modes of expression. That the dividing line is not an absolutely precise one, that the two sorts rather shade off into one another,—e.g., what B. Russell calls a " definition in use " also refers to a whole phrase —lies only in the nature of things and reflects how closely related, at bottom, the two sorts of licences are. Thus, whereas D is related to a *definitional* equivalence, and N, M, I, T to *logical* equivalences, L and R are related to *idiomatic* ones. By applying any of these three sorts of means, a statement, if it is analytic, is transformable into a logical truth.

In this way we have arrived at a definition, broad enough to be applicable to word language, and at the same time free from the defects which mar the afore-mentioned attempts. In the next section we shall have to consider some doubtful points to which the definition suggested gives rise. But before we do so it will be well go to into some minor points.

Let us consider the relation between a definition and a substitution licence more in detail, for the moment ignoring equivalences of the idiomatic kind. We shall approach this subject by asking first another sort of question : What is the difference between a substitution and a definition ? What, for instance, is the difference between $\dfrac{p \mathbf{v} q}{p}$ and $p \supset q . = . \sim p \mathbf{v} p$ Df ? The former is an instruction saying that $p \mathbf{v} q$ is to be put in the place of p in the context of a *given formula only ;* it is *unidirectional,* i.e. it tells us to replace p by $p \mathbf{v} q$, not $p \mathbf{v} q$ by p, thus making that process *irreversible ;* and it *commands* us to carry out this substitution. The latter permits the substitution of $p \supset q$ by $\sim p \mathbf{v} q$ in *any* context whatever, not just in that of one particular formula ; it allows us to pass *either* from $p \supset q$ to

$\sim p \vee q$, *or* from $\sim p \vee q$ to $p \supset q$, just as we please, making the transition *reversible ;* and, finally, it *permits* it merely without actually instructing us to make it. We may express this briefly by saying that a definition is, not so much a rule (an instruction), as a *licence for re-writing* a sentence, or a formula, by putting *definiens* for *definiendum* and leaving it to us whether we wish to make use of it. In other words, a definition *paves a way* without forcing us to go it.

Similar remarks apply to *any logical* equivalence : we may pass from the one side of it to the other, in any direction and in any context we please ; but we need not do so. Thus every logical equivalence supplies us with a substitution licence for replacing a certain expression by another one. In fact, all the operators which occur in our transformation chain, including the definition, provide us with such licences—further evidence of how closely related they all are.

This way of looking at things has, I submit, the advantage that it makes us see right from the start what matters in logic. It is not so much because of its *truth* that we take an interest in this or that particular equivalence, as because of the *use* we can make of it. What is really of value in a logical equivalence is that it lends itself to a use very similar to that of a definition : it supplies, to say it once more, a substitution licence, and that's in actual fact its more important side. But not *every* substitution licence supplies us with a *definition ;* for a definition must be such as to permit the elimination of one symbol by others. Thus I can make use of the equivalence

$$p \supset q. \equiv . \sim p \vee q$$

in order to define the symbol " $\supset$ " by putting,

$$p \supset q. = . \sim p \vee q \ \ \text{Df}$$

If, however, I were to say

$$\sim \sim p. \equiv . p,$$

I should, it is true, be stating a logical equivalence, but there would be no point in using it as a definition by writing

$$\sim \sim p. = p. \ \ \text{Df}$$

For the latter formula may well serve to eliminate the combination of symbols " $\sim \sim$ ", but not the symbol " $\sim$ " alone, and can, for this reason, not be taken as an explanation of that symbol. Similarly

$$\sim \sim \sim p. \equiv . \sim p,$$

though a perfectly valid equivalence and a substitution licence, would be useless as a definition of the symbol " $\sim$ ".

Shall we, then, demand of a definition that it should allow the complete elimination of one of the symbols? That won't do either. Suppose I define addition recursively by writing

$$a+(b+1) = (a+b)+1 \text{ Df},$$

then the symbol " $+$ " occurs on both sides of the definition; yet it would be a mistake to reject, on this ground, the definition as circular. For the whole point of the formula is that it reduces the addition of a and $b+1$ to the simpler addition of a and b, and, if this process is repeated a suitable number of times, finally to the operation " $+1$ "; thus we can, step by step, reduce $7+5$ to $7+4$, $7+4$ to $7+3$, and so on, until we reach $7+1$; the operation " $+1$ " itself is undefinable in arithmetic, being the simple step of forming the successor of a given number. We may bring this out, perhaps somewhat more clearly, by writing

$$a+S(b) = S(a+b) \text{ Df},$$

i.e., the sum of a and the successor b is the successor of $a+b$. This formula exhibits the general scheme according to which, in any particular case, the sum of two numbers can be defined in terms of " successor "; it is perhaps best characterized as an *instruction for framing particular definitions,* but is commonly itself taken for a definition by recursion. This example shows that a definition *need not* be a licence for eliminating a symbol. And even if a formula *does* permit eliminating a symbol, it need not be a *definition.* Take, for instance, the formula $4 = 2+2$; though it permits the elimination of the symbol " 4 ", it would hardly be recognized as a definition of this number. Thus the condition suggested is neither necessary nor sufficient. Whether conditions can be specified which determine, without any doubt, what a definition is, I do not know. Incidentally, in view of the indefiniteness with which nearly all the terms of word language are used, and the need for leaving, at least, some freedom for adjusting them to new situations which may crop up—would Aristotle have considered the case of a recursive definition?— I doubt the wisdom of pressing for a hard-and-fast rule, which can lead only to a sort of pseudo-precision. It is perhaps better to keep a term like definition flexible and make a decision, if the need arises, only in individual cases without anticipating the issue. That, of course, applies only to *natural* language; in an artificial, formalized language, the matter may be different.

We may sum up the discussion by saying that definitions are substitution licences of a *particular sort* (leaving the sense of this somewhat open), and that every substitution licence can be re-written as an equivalence. It is only when expressed in this way that we can do logical work with definitions, for instance derive consequences from them.

We can now understand—what we failed to understand before—why it is that definitions behave in such a disorderly manner. The point is that a definition, if it is explicit, can be re-phrased as an equivalence. Now from an equivalence another equivalence may be derived by logical inference ; if the latter is such that it can be used as an explanation of one of the symbols involved, it can itself be construed as a definition ; thus it happens that the " logical consequence " of a definition may again be a definition. If, however, the equivalence obtained falls short of this demand, then what follows from a definition will not be a definition. In the former case the procedure by which we " deduce " a definition from another definition involves, strictly speaking, three separate steps : (1) putting the definition in the form of an equivalence, (2) deriving another equivalence from the given one by logical inference, and (3) re-writing the result obtained in (2) as a definition.

3

Two Dogmas of Empiricism

W. V. QUINE

II

TWO DOGMAS OF EMPIRICISM

Modern empiricism has been conditioned in large part by two dogmas. One is a belief in some fundamental cleavage between truths which are *analytic*, or grounded in meanings independently of matters of fact, and truths which are *synthetic*, or grounded in fact. The other dogma is *reductionism*: the belief that each meaningful statement is equivalent to some logical construct upon terms which refer to immediate experience. Both dogmas, I shall argue, are ill-founded. One effect of abandoning them is, as we shall see, a blurring of the supposed boundary between speculative metaphysics and natural science. Another effect is a shift toward pragmatism.

1. Background for Analyticity

Kant's cleavage between analytic and synthetic truths was foreshadowed in Hume's distinction between relations of ideas and matters of fact, and in Leibniz's distinction between truths of reason and truths of fact. Leibniz spoke of the truths of reason as true in all possible worlds. Picturesqueness aside, this is to say that the truths of reason are those which could not possibly be false. In the same vein we hear analytic statements defined as statements whose denials are self-contradictory. But this definition has small explanatory value; for the notion of self-contradictoriness, in the quite broad sense needed for this definition of analyticity, stands in exactly the same need of clarification as does the notion of analyticity itself. The two notions are the two sides of a single dubious coin.

Kant conceived of an analytic statement as one that attributes to its subject no more than is already conceptually contained in the subject. This formulation has two shortcomings: it limits itself to statements of subject-predicate form, and it appeals to a notion of containment which is left at a metaphorical level. But Kant's intent, evident more from the use he makes of the notion of analyticity than from his definition of it, can be restated thus: a statement is analytic when it is true by virtue of meanings and independently of fact. Pursuing this line, let us examine the concept of *meaning* which is presupposed.

Meaning, let us remember, is not to be identified with naming.[1] Frege's example of 'Evening Star' and 'Morning Star', and Russell's of 'Scott' and 'the author of *Waverley*', illustrate that terms can name the same thing but differ in meaning. The distinction between meaning and naming is no less important at the level of abstract terms. The terms '9' and 'the number of the planets' name one and the same abstract entity but presumably must be regarded as unlike in meaning; for astronomical observation was needed, and not mere reflection on meanings, to determine the sameness of the entity in question.

The above examples consist of singular terms, concrete and abstract. With general terms, or predicates, the situation is somewhat different but parallel. Whereas a singular term purports to name an entity, abstract or concrete, a general term does not; but a general term is *true of* an entity, or of each of many, or of none.[2] The class of all entities of which a general term is true is called the *extension* of the term. Now paralleling the contrast between the meaning of a singular term and the entity named, we must distinguish equally between the meaning of a general term and its extension. The general terms 'creature with a heart' and 'creature with kidneys', for example, are perhaps alike in extension but unlike in meaning.

Confusion of meaning with extension, in the case of general terms, is less common than confusion of meaning with naming in the case of singular terms. It is indeed a commonplace in philosophy to oppose intension (or meaning) to extension, or, in a variant vocabulary, connotation to denotation.

[1] See above, p. 9.
[2] See above, p. 10, and below, pp. 107-115.

The Aristotelian notion of essence was the forerunner, no doubt, of the modern notion of intension or meaning. For Aristotle it was essential in men to be rational, accidental to be two-legged. But there is an important difference between this attitude and the doctrine of meaning. From the latter point of view it may indeed be conceded (if only for the sake of argument) that rationality is involved in the meaning of the word 'man' while two-leggedness is not; but two-leggedness may at the same time be viewed as involved in the meaning of 'biped' while rationality is not. Thus from the point of view of the doctrine of meaning it makes no sense to say of the actual individual, who is at once a man and a biped, that his rationality is essential and his two-leggedness accidental or vice versa. Things had essences, for Aristotle, but only linguistic forms have meanings. Meaning is what essence becomes when it is divorced from the object of reference and wedded to the word.

For the theory of meaning a conspicuous question is the nature of its objects: what sort of things are meanings? A felt need for meant entities may derive from an earlier failure to appreciate that meaning and reference are distinct. Once the theory of meaning is sharply separated from the theory of reference, it is a short step to recognizing as the primary business of the theory of meaning simply the synonymy of linguistic forms and the analyticity of statements; meanings themselves, as obscure intermediary entities, may well be abandoned.[3]

The problem of analyticity then confronts us anew. Statements which are analytic by general philosophical acclaim are not, indeed, far to seek. They fall into two classes. Those of the first class, which may be called *logically true*, are typified by:

(1)   No unmarried man is married.

The relevant feature of this example is that it not merely is true as it stands, but remains true under any and all reinterpretations of 'man' and 'married'. If we suppose a prior inventory of *logical* particles, comprising 'no', 'un-', 'not', 'if', 'then', 'and', etc., then in general a logical truth is a statement which is true

---

[3] See above, pp. 11f, and below, pp. 48f.

and remains true under all reinterpretations of its components other than the logical particles.

But there is also a second class of analytic statements, typified by:

(2)   No bachelor is married.

The characteristic of such a statement is that it can be turned into a logical truth by putting synonyms for synonyms; thus (2) can be turned into (1) by putting 'unmarried man' for its synonym 'bachelor'. We still lack a proper characterization of this second class of analytic statements, and therewith of analyticity generally, inasmuch as we have had in the above description to lean on a notion of "synonymy" which is no less in need of clarification than analyticity itself.

In recent years Carnap has tended to explain analyticity by appeal to what he calls state-descriptions.[4] A state-description is any exhaustive assignment of truth values to the atomic, or noncompound, statements of the language. All other statements of the language are, Carnap assumes, built up of their component clauses by means of the familiar logical devices, in such a way that the truth value of any complex statement is fixed for each state-description by specifiable logical laws. A statement is then explained as analytic when it comes out true under every state description. This account is an adaptation of Leibniz's "true in all possible worlds." But note that this version of analyticity serves its purpose only if the atomic statements of the language are, unlike 'John is a bachelor' and 'John is married', mutually independent. Otherwise there would be a state-description which assigned truth to 'John is a bachelor' and to 'John is married', and consequently 'No bachelors are married' would turn out synthetic rather than analytic under the proposed criterion. Thus the criterion of analyticity in terms of state-descriptions serves only for languages devoid of extralogical synonym-pairs, such as 'bachelor' and 'unmarried man'— synonym-pairs of the type which give rise to the "second class" of analytic statements. The criterion in terms of state-descrip-

---

[4] Carnap [3], pp. 9ff; [4], pp. 70ff.

tions is a reconstruction at best of logical truth, not of analyticity.

I do not mean to suggest that Carnap is under any illusions on this point. His simplified model language with its state-descriptions is aimed primarily not at the general problem of analyticity but at another purpose, the clarification of probability and induction. Our problem, however, is analyticity; and here the major difficulty lies not in the first class of analytic statements, the logical truths, but rather in the second class, which depends on the notion of synonymy.

2. Definition

There are those who find it soothing to say that the analytic statements of the second class reduce to those of the first class, the logical truths, by *definition*; 'bachelor', for example, is *defined* as 'unmarried man'. But how de we find that 'bachelor' is defined as 'unmarried man'? Who defined it thus, and when? Are we to appeal to the nearest dictionary, and accept the lexicographer's formulation as law? Clearly this would be to put the cart before the horse. The lexicographer is an empirical scientist, whose business is the recording of antecedent facts; and if he glosses 'bachelor' as 'unmarried man' it is because of his belief that there is a relation of synonymy between those forms, implicit in general or preferred usage prior to his own work. The notion of synonymy presupposed here has still to be clarified, presumably in terms relating to linguistic behavior. Certainly the "definition" which is the lexicographer's report of an observed synonymy cannot be taken as the ground of the synonymy.

Definition is not, indeed, an activity exclusively of philologists. Philosophers and scientists frequently have occasion to "define" a recondite term by paraphrasing it into terms of a more familiar vocabulary. But ordinarily such a definition, like the philologist's, is pure lexicography, affirming a relation of synonymy antecedent to the exposition in hand.

Just what it means to affirm synonymy, just what the interconnections may be which are necessary and sufficient in order that two linguistic forms be properly describable as synonymous, is far from clear; but, whatever these interconnections may be, ordinarily they are grounded in usage. Definitions reporting selected instances of synonymy come then as reports upon usage.

There is also, however, a variant type of definitional activity which does not limit itself to the reporting of preëxisting synonymies. I have in mind what Carnap calls *explication*—an activity to which philosophers are given, and scientists also in their more philosophical moments. In explication the purpose is not merely to paraphrase the definiendum into an outright synonym, but actually to improve upon the definiendum by refining or supplementing its meaning. But even explication, though not merely reporting a preëxisting synonymy between definiendum and definiens, does rest nevertheless on *other* preexisting synonymies. The matter may be viewed as follows. Any word worth explicating has some contexts which, as wholes, are clear and precise enough to be useful; and the purpose of explication is to preserve the usage of these favored contexts while sharpening the usage of other contexts. In order that a given definition be suitable for purposes of explication, therefore, what is required is not that the definiendum in its antecedent usage be synonymous with the definiens, but just that each of these favored contexts of the definiendum, taken as a whole in its antecedent usage, be synonymous with the corresponding context of the definiens.

Two alternative definientia may be equally appropriate for the purposes of a given task of explication and yet not be synonymous with each other; for they may serve interchangeably within the favored contexts but diverge elsewhere. By cleaving to one of these definientia rather than the other, a definition of explicative kind generates, by fiat, a relation of synonymy between definiendum and definiens which did not hold before. But such a definition still owes its explicative function, as seen, to preexisting synonymies.

There does, however, remain still an extreme sort of definition which does not hark back to prior synonymies at all: namely, the explicitly conventional introduction of novel notations for purposes of sheer abbreviation. Here the definiendum becomes synonymous with the definiens simply because it has been created expressly for the purpose of being synonymous with the definiens. Here we have a really transparent case of synonymy created by definition; would that all species of synonymy were as intelligible. For the rest, definition rests on synonymy rather than explaining it.

The word 'definition' has come to have a dangerously reassuring sound, owing no doubt to its frequent occurrence in logical and mathematical writings. We shall do well to digress now into a brief appraisal of the role of definition in formal work.

In logical and mathematical systems either of two mutually antagonistic types of economy may be striven for, and each has its peculiar practical utility. On the one hand we may seek economy of practical expression—ease and brevity in the statement of multifarious relations. This sort of economy calls usually for distinctive concise notations for a wealth of concepts. Second, however, and oppositely, we may seek economy in grammar and vocabulary; we may try to find a minimum of basic concepts such that, once a distinctive notation has been appropriated to each of them, it becomes possible to express any desired further concept by mere combination and iteration of our basic notations. This second sort of economy is impractical in one way, since a poverty in basic idioms tends to a necessary lengthening of discourse. But it is practical in another way: it greatly simplifies theoretical discourse *about* the language, through minimizing the terms and the forms of construction wherein the language consists.

Both sorts of economy, though prima facie incompatible, are valuable in their separate ways. The custom has consequently arisen of combining both sorts of economy by forging in effect two languages, the one a part of the other. The inclusive language, though redundant in grammar and vocabulary, is economical in message lengths, while the part, called primitive notation, is economical in grammar and vocabulary. Whole and part are correlated by rules of translation whereby each idiom not in primitive notation is equated to some complex built up of primitive notation. These rules of translation are the so-called *definitions* which appear in formalized systems. They are best viewed not as adjuncts to one language but as correlations between two languages, the one a part of the other.

But these correlations are not arbitrary. They are supposed to show how the primitive notations can accomplish all purposes, save brevity and convenience, of the redundant language. Hence the definiendum and its definiens may be expected, in each case, to be related in one or another of the three ways lately noted. The definiens may be a faithful paraphrase of the definiendum into the narrower notation, preserving a direct synonymy[5] as of antecedent usage; or the definiens may, in the spirit of explication, improve upon the antecedent usage of the definiendum; or finally, the definiendum may be a newly created notation, newly endowed with meaning here and now.

In formal and informal work alike, thus, we find that definition—except in the extreme case of the explicitly conventional introduction of new notations—hinges on prior relations of synonymy. Recognizing then that the notion of definition does not hold the key to synonymy and analyticity, let us look further into synonymy and say no more of definition.

3. Interchangeability

A natural suggestion, deserving close examination, is that the synonymy of two linguistic forms consists simply in their interchangeability in all contexts without change of truth value —interchangeability, in Leibniz's phrase, *salva veritate*.[6] Note that synonyms so conceived need not even be free from vagueness, as long as the vaguenesses match.

[5] According to an important variant sense of 'definition', the relation preserved may be the weaker relation of mere agreement in reference; see below, p. 132. But definition in this sense is better ignored in the present connection, being irrelevant to the question of synonymy.

[6] Cf. Lewis [1], p. 373.

But it is not quite true that the synonyms 'bachelor' and 'unmarried man' are everywhere interchangeable *salva veritate*. Truths which become false under substitution of 'unmarried man' for 'bachelor' are easily constructed with the help of 'bachelor of arts' or 'bachelor's buttons'; also with the help of quotation, thus:

'Bachelor' has less than ten letters.

Such counterinstances can, however, perhaps be set aside by treating the phrases 'bachelor of arts' and 'bachelor's buttons' and the quotation ' 'bachelor' ' each as a single indivisible word and then stipulating that the interchangeability *salva veritate* which is to be the touchstone of synonymy is not supposed to apply to fragmentary occurrences inside of a word. This account of synonymy, supposing it acceptable on other counts, has indeed the drawback of appealing to a prior conception of "word" which can be counted on to present difficulties of formulation in its turn. Nevertheless some progress might be claimed in having reduced the problem of synonymy to a problem of word-hood. Let us pursue this line a bit, taking "word" for granted.

The question remains whether interchangeability *salva veritate* (apart from occurrences within words) is a strong enough condition for synonymy, or whether, on the contrary, some heteronymous expressions might be thus interchangeable. Now let us be clear that we are not concerned here with synonymy in the sense of complete identity in psychological associations or poetic quality; indeed no two expressions are synonymous in such a sense. We are concerned only with what may be called *cognitive* synonymy. Just what this is cannot be said without successfully finishing the present study; but we know something about it from the need which arose for it in connection with analyticity in §1. The sort of synonymy needed there was merely such that any analytic statement could be turned into a logical truth by putting synonyms for synonyms. Turning the tables and assuming analyticity, indeed, we could explain cognitive synonymy of terms as follows (keeping to the familiar example): to say that 'bachelor' and 'unmarried man' are cognitively synonymous is to say no more nor less than that the statement:

(3)   All and only bachelors are unmarried men

is analytic.[7]

What we need is an account of cognitive synonymy not presupposing analyticity—if we are to explain analyticity conversely with help of cognitive synonymy as undertaken in §1. And indeed such an independent account of cognitive synonymy is at present up for consideration, namely, interchangeability *salva veritate* everywhere except within words. The question before us, to resume the thread at last, is whether such interchangeability is a sufficient condition for cognitive synonymy. We can quickly assure ourselves that it is, by examples of the following sort. The statement:

(4)   Necessarily all and only bachelors are bachelors

is evidently true, even supposing 'necessarily' so narrowly construed as to be truly applicable only to analytic statements. Then, if 'bachelor' and 'unmarried man' are interchangeable *salva veritate*, the result:

(5)   Necessarily all and only bachelors are unmarried men

of putting 'unmarried man' for an occurrence of 'bachelor' in (4) must, like (4), be true. But to say that (5) is true is to say that (3) is analytic, and hence that 'bachelor' and 'unmarried man' are cognitively synonymous.

Let us see what there is about the above argument that gives it its air of hocus-pocus. The condition of interchangeability *salva veritate* varies in its force with variations in the richness of the language at hand. The above argument supposes we are working with a language rich enough to contain the adverb 'necessarily', this adverb being so construed as to yield truth

---

[7] This is cognitive synonymy in a primary, broad sense. Carnap ([3], pp. 56ff) and Lewis ([2], pp. 83ff) have suggested how, once this notion is at hand, a narrower sense of cognitive synonymy which is preferable for some purposes can in turn be derived. But this special ramification of concept-building lies aside from the present purposes and must not be confused with the broad sort of cognitive synonymy here concerned.

when and only when applied to an analytic statement. But can we condone a language which contains such an adverb? Does the adverb really make sense? To suppose that it does is to suppose that we have already made satisfactory sense of 'analytic'. Then what are we so hard at work on right now?

Our argument is not flatly circular, but something like it. It has the form, figuratively speaking, of a closed curve in space.

Interchangeability *salva veritate* is meaningless until relativized to a language whose extent is specified in relevant respects. Suppose now we consider a language containing just the following materials. There is an indefinitely large stock of one-place predicates (for example, 'F' where 'Fx' means that x is a man) and many-place predicates (for example, 'G' where 'Gxy' means that x loves y), mostly having to do with extralogical subject matter. The rest of the language is logical. The atomic sentences consist each of a predicate followed by one or more variables 'x', 'y', etc.; and the complex sentences are built up of the atomic ones by truth functions ('not', 'and', 'or', etc.) and quantification.[8] In effect such a language enjoys the benefits also of descriptions and indeed singular terms generally, these being contextually definable in known ways.[9] Even abstract singular terms naming classes, classes of classes, etc., are contextually definable in case the assumed stock of predicates includes the two-place predicate of class membership.[10] Such a language can be adequate to classical mathematics and indeed to scientific discourse generally, except in so far as the latter involves debatable devices such as contrary-to-fact conditionals or modal adverbs like 'necessarily'.[11] Now a language of this type is extensional, in this sense: any two predicates which agree extensionally (that is, are true of the same objects) are interchangeable *salva veritate*.[12]

[8] Pp. 81ff, below, contain a description of just such a language, except that there happens there to be just one predicate, the two-place predicate 'ϵ'.

[9] See above, pp. 5-8; also below, pp. 85f, 166f.

[10] See below, p. 87.

[11] On such devices see also Essay VIII.

[12] This is the substance of Quine [1], *121.

In an extensional language, therefore, interchangeability *salva veritate* is no assurance of cognitive synonymy of the desired type. That 'bachelor' and 'unmarried man' are interchangeable *salva veritate* in an extensional language assures us of no more than that (3) is true. There is no assurance here that the extensional agreement of 'bachelor' and 'unmarried man' rests on meaning rather than merely on accidental matters of fact, as does the extensional agreement of 'creature with a heart' and 'creature with kidneys'.

For most purposes extensional agreement is the nearest approximation to synonymy we need care about. But the fact remains that extensional agreement falls far short of cognitive synonymy of the type required for explaining analyticity in the manner of §1. The type of cognitive synonymy required there is such as to equate the synonymy of 'bachelor' and 'unmarried man' with the analyticity of (3), not merely with the truth of (3).

So we must recognize that interchangeability *salva veritate*, if construed in relation to an extensional language, is not a sufficient condition of cognitive synonymy in the sense needed for deriving analyticity in the manner of §1. If a language contains an intensional adverb 'necessarily' in the sense lately noted, or other particles to the same effect, then interchangeability *salva veritate* in such a language does afford a sufficient condition of cognitive synonymy; but such a language is intelligible only in so far as the notion of analyticity is already understood in advance.

The effort to explain cognitive synonymy first, for the sake of deriving analyticity from it afterward as in §1, is perhaps the wrong approach. Instead we might try explaining analyticity somehow without appeal to cognitive synonymy. Afterward we could doubtless derive cognitive synonymy from analyticity satisfactorily enough if desired. We have seen that cognitive synonymy of 'bachelor' and 'unmarried man' can be explained as analyticity of (3). The same explanation works for any pair of one-place predicates, of course, and it can be extended in obvious fashion to many-place predicates. Other syntactical categories can also be accommodated in fairly parallel fashion.

Singular terms may be said to be cognitively synonymous when the statement of identity formed by putting '=' between them is analytic. Statements may be said simply to be cognitively synonymous when their biconditional (the result of joining them by 'if and only if') is analytic.[13] If we care to lump all categories into a single formulation, at the expense of assuming again the notion of "word" which was appealed to early in this section, we can describe any two linguistic forms as cognitively synonymous when the two forms are interchangeable (apart from occurrences within "words") *salva* (no longer *veritate* but) *analyticitate*. Certain technical questions arise, indeed, over cases of ambiguity or homonymy; let us not pause for them, however, for we are already digressing. Let us rather turn our backs on the problem of synonymy and address ourselves anew to that of analyticity.

4. Semantical Rules

Analyticity at first seemed most naturally definable by appeal to a realm of meanings. On refinement, the appeal to meanings gave way to an appeal to synonymy or definition. But definition turned out to be a will-o'-the-wisp, and synonymy turned out to be best understood only by dint of a prior appeal to analyticity itself. So we are back at the problem of analyticity.

I do not know whether the statement 'Everything green is extended' is analytic. Now does my indecision over this example really betray an incomplete understanding, an incomplete grasp of the "meanings", of 'green' and 'extended'? I think not. The trouble is not with 'green' or 'extended', but with 'analytic'.

It is often hinted that the difficulty in separating analytic statements from synthetic ones in ordinary language is due to the vagueness of ordinary language and that the distinction is clear when we have a precise artificial language with explicit "semantical rules." This, however, as I shall now attempt to show, is a confusion.

[13] The 'if and only if' itself is intended in the truth functional sense. See Carnap [3], p. 14.

The notion of analyticity about which we are worrying is a purported relation between statements and languages: a statement S is said to be *analytic for* a language L, and the problem is to make sense of this relation generally, that is, for variable 'S' and 'L'. The gravity of this problem is not perceptibly less for artificial languages than for natural ones. The problem of making sense of the idiom 'S is analytic for L', with variable 'S' and 'L', retains its stubbornness even if we limit the range of the variable 'L' to artificial languages. Let me now try to make this point evident.

For artificial languages and semantical rules we look naturally to the writings of Carnap. His semantical rules take various forms, and to make my point I shall have to distinguish certain of the forms. Let us suppose, to begin with, an artificial language L_0 whose semantical rules have the form explicitly of a specification, by recursion or otherwise, of all the analytic statements of L_0. The rules tell us that such and such statements, and only those, are the analytic statements of L_0. Now here the difficulty is simply that the rules contain the word 'analytic', which we do not understand! We understand what expressions the rules attribute analyticity to, but we do not understand what the rules attribute to those expressions. In short, before we can understand a rule which begins 'A statement S is analytic for language L_0 if and only if ...', we must understand the general relative term 'analytic for'; we must understand 'S is analytic for L' where 'S' and 'L' are variables.

Alternatively we may, indeed, view the so-called rule as a conventional definition of a new simple symbol 'analytic-for-L_0', which might better be written untendentiously as 'K' so as not to seem to throw light on the interesting word 'analytic'. Obviously any number of classes K, M, N, etc. of statements of L_0 can be specified for various purposes or for no purpose; what does it mean to say that K, as against M, N, etc., is the class of the "analytic" statements of L_0?

By saying what statements are analytic for L_0 we explain 'analytic-for-L_0' but not 'analytic', not 'analytic for'. We do not begin to explain the idiom 'S is analytic for L' with variable

'*S*' and '*L*', even if we are content to limit the range of '*L*' to the realm of artificial languages.

Actually we do know enough about the intended significance of 'analytic' to know that analytic statements are supposed to be true. Let us then turn to a second form of semantical rule, which says not that such and such statements are analytic but simply that such and such statements are included among the truths. Such a rule is not subject to the criticism of containing the un-understood word 'analytic'; and we may grant for the sake of argument that there is no difficulty over the broader term 'true'. A semantical rule of this second type, a rule of truth, is not supposed to specify all the truths of the language; it merely stipulates, recursively or otherwise, a certain multitude of statements which, along with others unspecified, are to count as true. Such a rule may be conceded to be quite clear. Derivatively, afterward, analyticity can be demarcated thus: a statement is analytic if it is (not merely true but) true according to the semantical rule.

Still there is really no progress. Instead of appealing to an unexplained word 'analytic', we are now appealing to an unexplained phrase 'semantical rule'. Not every true statement which says that the statements of some class are true can count as a semantical rule—otherwise *all* truths would be "analytic" in the sense of being true according to semantical rules. Semantical rules are distinguishable, apparently, only by the fact of appearing on a page under the heading 'Semantical Rules'; and this heading is itself then meaningless.

We can say indeed that a statement is *analytic-for-L_0* if and only if it is true according to such and such specifically appended "semantical rules," but then we find ourselves back at essentially the same case which was originally discussed: '*S* is analytic-for-L_0 if and only if. . . .' Once we seek to explain '*S* is analytic for *L*' generally for variable '*L*' (even allowing limitation of '*L*' to artificial languages), the explanation 'true according to the semantical rules of *L*' is unavailing; for the relative term 'semantical rule of' is as much in need of clarification, at least, as 'analytic for'.

It may be instructive to compare the notion of semantical rule with that of postulate. Relative to a given set of postulates, it is easy to say what a postulate is: it is a member of the set. Relative to a given set of semantical rules, it is equally easy to say what a semantical rule is. But given simply a notation, mathematical or otherwise, and indeed as thoroughly understood a notation as you please in point of the translations or truth conditions of its statements, who can say which of its true statements rank as postulates? Obviously the question is meaningless—as meaningless as asking which points in Ohio are starting points. Any finite (or effectively specifiable infinite) selection of statements (preferably true ones, perhaps) is as much *a* set of postulates as any other. The word 'postulate' is significant only relative to an act of inquiry; we apply the word to a set of statements just in so far as we happen, for the year or the moment, to be thinking of those statements in relation to the statements which can be reached from them by some set of transformations to which we have seen fit to direct our attention. Now the notion of semantical rule is as sensible and meaningful as that of postulate, if conceived in a similarly relative spirit—relative, this time, to one or another particular enterprise of schooling unconversant persons in sufficient conditions for truth of statements of some natural or artificial language L. But from this point of view no one signalization of a subclass of the truths of L is intrinsically more a semantical rule than another; and, if 'analytic' means 'true by semantical rules', no one truth of L is analytic to the exclusion of another.[14]

It might conceivably be protested that an artificial language L (unlike a natural one) is a language in the ordinary sense *plus* a set of explicit semantical rules—the whole constituting, let us say, an ordered pair; and that the semantical rules of L then are specifiable simply as the second component of the pair L. But, by the same token and more simply, we might construe an artificial language L outright as an ordered pair whose second

[14] The foregoing paragraph was not part of the present essay as originally published. It was prompted by Martin (see Bibliography), as was the end of Essay VII.

component is the class of its analytic statements; and then the analytic statements of L become specifiable simply as the statements in the second component of L. Or better still, we might just stop tugging at our bootstraps altogether.

Not all the explanations of analyticity known to Carnap and his readers have been covered explicitly in the above considerations, but the extension to other forms is not hard to see. Just one additional factor should be mentioned which sometimes enters: sometimes the semantical rules are in effect rules of translation into ordinary language, in which case the analytic statements of the artificial language are in effect recognized as such from the analyticity of their specified translations in ordinary language. Here certainly there can be no thought of an illumination of the problem of analyticity from the side of the artificial language.

From the point of view of the problem of analyticity the notion of an artificial language with semantical rules is a *feu follet par excellence*. Semantical rules determining the analytic statements of an artificial language are of interest only in so far as we already understand the notion of analyticity; they are of no help in gaining this understanding.

Appeal to hypothetical languages of an artificially simple kind could conceivably be useful in clarifying analyticity, if the mental or behavioral or cultural factors relevant to analyticity—whatever they may be—were somehow sketched into the simplified model. But a model which takes analyticity merely as an irreducible character is unlikely to throw light on the problem of explicating analyticity.

It is obvious that truth in general depends on both language and extralinguistic fact. The statement 'Brutus killed Caesar' would be false if the world had been different in certain ways, but it would also be false if the word 'killed' happened rather to have the sense of 'begat'. Thus one is tempted to suppose in general that the truth of a statement is somehow analyzable into a linguistic component and a factual component. Given this supposition, it next seems reasonable that in some statements the factual component should be null; and these are the analytic statements. But, for all its a priori reasonableness, a boundary between analytic and synthetic statements simply has not been drawn. That there is such a distinction to be drawn at all is an unempirical dogma of empiricists, a metaphysical article of faith.

5. The Verification Theory and Reductionism

In the course of these somber reflections we have taken a dim view first of the notion of meaning, then of the notion of cognitive synonymy, and finally of the notion of analyticity. But what, it may be asked, of the verification theory of meaning? This phrase has established itself so firmly as a catchword of empiricism that we should be very unscientific indeed not to look beneath it for a possible key to the problem of meaning and the associated problems.

The verification theory of meaning, which has been conspicuous in the literature from Peirce onward, is that the meaning of a statement is the method of empirically confirming or infirming it. An analytic statement is that limiting case which is confirmed no matter what.

As urged in §1, we can as well pass over the question of meanings as entities and move straight to sameness of meaning, or synonymy. Then what the verification theory says is that statements are synonymous if and only if they are alike in point of method of empirical confirmation or infirmation.

This is an account of cognitive synonymy not of linguistic forms generally, but of statements.[15] However, from the concept of synonymy of statements we could derive the concept of synonymy for other linguistic forms, by considerations somewhat similar to those at the end of §3. Assuming the notion of "word," indeed, we could explain any two forms as synonymous when the

---

[15] The doctrine can indeed be formulated with terms rather than statements as the units. Thus Lewis describes the meaning of a term as "*a criterion in mind*, by reference to which one is able to apply or refuse to apply the expression in question in the case of presented, or imagined, things or situations" ([2], p. 133).—For an instructive account of the vicissitudes of the verification theory of meaning, centered however on the question of meaning*fulness* rather than synonymy and analyticity, see Hempel.

putting of the one form for an occurrence of the other in any statement (apart from occurrences within "words") yields a synonymous statement. Finally, given the concept of synonymy thus for linguistic forms generally, we could define analyticity in terms of synonymy and logical truth as in §1. For that matter, we could define analyticity more simply in terms of just synonymy of statements together with logical truth; it is not necessary to appeal to synonymy of linguistic forms other than statements. For a statement may be described as analytic simply when it is synonymous with a logically true statement.

So, if the verification theory can be accepted as an adequate account of statement synonymy, the notion of analyticity is saved after all. However, let us reflect. Statement synonymy is said to be likeness of method of empirical confirmation or infirmation. Just what are these methods which are to be compared for likeness? What, in other words, is the nature of the relation between a statement and the experiences which contribute to or detract from its confirmation?

The most naïve view of the relation is that it is one of direct report. This is *radical reductionism*. Every meaningful statement is held to be translatable into a statement (true or false) about immediate experience. Radical reductionism, in one form or another, well antedates the verification theory of meaning explicitly so called. Thus Locke and Hume held that every idea must either originate directly in sense experience or else be compounded of ideas thus originating; and taking a hint from Tooke we might rephrase this doctrine in semantical jargon by saying that a term, to be significant at all, must be either a name of a sense datum or a compound of such names or an abbreviation of such a compound. So stated, the doctrine remains ambiguous as between sense data as sensory events and sense data as sensory qualities; and it remains vague as to the admissible ways of compounding. Moreover, the doctrine is unnecessarily and intolerably restrictive in the term-by-term critique which it imposes. More reasonably, and without yet exceeding the limits of what I have called radical reductionism, we may take full statements as our significant units—thus demanding that our statements as wholes be translatable into sense-datum language, but not that they be translatable term by term.

This emendation would unquestionably have been welcome to Locke and Hume and Tooke, but historically it had to await an important reorientation in semantics—the reorientation whereby the primary vehicle of meaning came to be seen no longer in the term but in the statement. This reorientation, explicit in Frege ([1], §60), underlies Russell's concept of incomplete symbols defined in use;[16] also it is implicit in the verification theory of meaning, since the objects of verification are statements.

Radical reductionism, conceived now with statements as units, set itself the task of specifying a sense-datum language and showing how to translate the rest of significant discourse, statement by statement, into it. Carnap embarked on this project in the *Aufbau*.

The language which Carnap adopted as his starting point was not a sense-datum language in the narrowest conceivable sense, for it included also the notations of logic, up through higher set theory. In effect it included the whole language of pure mathematics. The ontology implicit in it (that is, the range of values of its variables) embraced not only sensory events but classes, classes of classes, and so on. Empiricists there are who would boggle at such prodigality. Carnap's starting point is very parsimonious, however, in its extralogical or sensory part. In a series of constructions in which he exploits the resources of modern logic with much ingenuity, Carnap succeeds in defining a wide array of important additional sensory concepts which, but for his constructions, one would not have dreamed were definable on so slender a basis. He was the first empiricist who, not content with asserting the reducibility of science to terms of immediate experience, took serious steps toward carrying out the reduction.

If Carnap's starting point is satisfactory, still his construc-

---

16 See above, p. 6.

tions were, as he himself stressed, only a fragment of the full program. The construction of even the simplest statements about the physical world was left in a sketchy state. Carnap's suggestions on this subject were, despite their sketchiness, very suggestive. He explained spatio-temporal point-instants as quadruples of real numbers and envisaged assignment of sense qualities to point-instants according to certain canons. Roughly summarized, the plan was that qualities should be assigned to point-instants in such a way as to achieve the laziest world compatible with our experience. The principle of least action was to be our guide in constructing a world from experience.

Carnap did not seem to recognize, however, that his treatment of physical objects fell short of reduction not merely through sketchiness, but in principle. Statements of the form 'Quality q is at point-instant $x;y;z;t$' were, according to his canons, to be apportioned truth values in such a way as to maximize and minimize certain over-all features, and with growth of experience the truth values were to be progressively revised in the same spirit. I think this is a good schematization (deliberately oversimplified, to be sure) of what science really does; but it provides no indication, not even the sketchiest, of how a statement of the form 'Quality q is at $x;y;z;t$' could ever be translated into Carnap's initial language of sense data and logic. The connective 'is at' remains an added undefined connective; the canons counsel us in its use but not in its elimination.

Carnap seems to have appreciated this point afterward; for in his later writings he abandoned all notion of the translatability of statements about the physical world into statements about immediate experience. Reductionism in its radical form has long since ceased to figure in Carnap's philosophy.

But the dogma of reductionism has, in a subtler and more tenuous form, continued to influence the thought of empiricists. The notion lingers that to each statement, or each synthetic statement, there is associated a unique range of possible sensory events such that the occurrence of any of them would add to the likelihood of truth of the statement, and that there is associated also another unique range of possible sensory events whose occurrence would detract from that likelihood. This notion is of course implicit in the verification theory of meaning.

The dogma of reductionism survives in the supposition that each statement, taken in isolation from its fellows, can admit of confirmation or infirmation at all. My countersuggestion, issuing essentially from Carnap's doctrine of the physical world in the *Aufbau*, is that our statements about the external world face the tribunal of sense experience not individually but only as a corporate body.[17]

The dogma of reductionism, even in its attenuated form, is intimately connected with the other dogma—that there is a cleavage between the analytic and the synthetic. We have found ourselves led, indeed, from the latter problem to the former through the verification theory of meaning. More directly, the one dogma clearly supports the other in this way: as long as it is taken to be significant in general to speak of the confirmation and infirmation of a statement, it seems significant to speak also of a limiting kind of statement which is vacuously confirmed, *ipso facto*, come what may; and such a statement is analytic.

The two dogmas are, indeed, at root identical. We lately reflected that in general the truth of statements does obviously depend both upon language and upon extralinguistic fact; and we noted that this obvious circumstance carries in its train, not logically but all too naturally, a feeling that the truth of a statement is somehow analyzable into a linguistic component and a factual component. The factual component must, if we are empiricists, boil down to a range of confirmatory experiences. In the extreme case where the linguistic component is all that matters, a true statement is analytic. But I hope we are now impressed with how stubbornly the distinction between analytic and synthetic has resisted any straightforward drawing. I am impressed also, apart from prefabricated examples of black and white balls in an urn, with how baffling the problem has always

---

[17] This doctrine was well argued by Duhem, pp. 303-328. Or see Lowinger, pp. 132-140.

been of arriving at any explicit theory of the empirical confirmation of a synthetic statement. My present suggestion is that it is nonsense, and the root of much nonsense, to speak of a linguistic component and a factual component in the truth of any individual statement. Taken collectively, science has its double dependence upon language and experience; but this duality is not significantly traceable into the statements of science taken one by one.

The idea of defining a symbol in use was, as remarked, an advance over the impossible term-by-term empiricism of Locke and Hume. The statement, rather than the term, came with Frege to be recognized as the unit accountable to an empiricist critique. But what I am now urging is that even in taking the statement as unit we have drawn our grid too finely. The unit of empirical significance is the whole of science.

6. Empiricism without the Dogmas

The totality of our so-called knowledge or beliefs, from the most casual matters of geography and history to the profoundest laws of atomic physics or even of pure mathematics and logic, is a man-made fabric which impinges on experience only along the edges. Or, to change the figure, total science is like a field of force whose boundary conditions are experience. A conflict with experience at the periphery occasions readjustments in the interior of the field. Truth values have to be redistributed over some of our statements. Reëvaluation of some statements entails reëvaluation of others, because of their logical interconnections —the logical laws being in turn simply certain further statements of the system, certain further elements of the field. Having reëvaluated one statement we must reëvaluate some others, which may be statements logically connected with the first or may be the statements of logical connections themselves. But the total field is so underdetermined by its boundary conditions, experience, that there is much latitude of choice as to what statements to reëvaluate in the light of any single contrary experience. No particular experiences are linked with any particular statements in the interior of the field, except indirectly through considerations of equilibrium affecting the field as a whole.

If this view is right, it is misleading to speak of the empirical content of an individual statement—especially if it is a statement at all remote from the experiential periphery of the field. Furthermore it becomes folly to seek a boundary between synthetic statements, which hold contingently on experience, and analytic statements, which hold come what may. Any statement can be held true come what may, if we make drastic enough adjustments elsewhere in the system. Even a statement very close to the periphery can be held true in the face of recalcitrant experience by pleading hallucination or by amending certain statements of the kind called logical laws. Conversely, by the same token, no statement is immune to revision. Revision even of the logical law of the excluded middle has been proposed as a means of simplifying quantum mechanics; and what difference is there in principle between such a shift and the shift whereby Kepler superseded Ptolemy, or Einstein Newton, or Darwin Aristotle?

For vividness I have been speaking in terms of varying distances from a sensory periphery. Let me try now to clarify this notion without metaphor. Certain statements, though *about* physical objects and not sense experience, seem peculiarly germane to sense experience—and in a selective way: some statements to some experiences, others to others. Such statements, especially germane to particular experiences, I picture as near the periphery. But in this relation of "germaneness" I envisage nothing more than a loose association reflecting the relative likelihood, in practice, of our choosing one statement rather than another for revision in the event of recalcitrant experience. For example, we can imagine recalcitrant experiences to which we would surely be inclined to accommodate our system by reëvaluating just the statement that there are brick houses on Elm Street, together with related statements on the same topic. We can imagine other recalcitrant experiences to which we would be inclined to accommodate our system by reëvaluating just the statement that there are no centaurs, along with kindred statements. A recalcitrant experience can, I have urged, be accommodated by any of various alternative reëvaluations in various alternative quarters of the total system; but, in the cases which we are now imagining, our natural tendency to disturb the total system as little as possible would lead us to focus our revisions upon these specific statements concerning brick houses or centaurs. These statements are felt, therefore, to have a sharper empirical reference than highly theoretical statements of physics or logic or ontology. The latter statements may be thought of as relatively centrally located within the total network, meaning merely that little preferential connection with any particular sense data obtrudes itself.

As an empiricist I continue to think of the conceptual scheme of science as a tool, ultimately, for predicting future experience in the light of past experience. Physical objects are conceptually imported into the situation as convenient intermediaries—not by definition in terms of experience, but simply as irreducible posits[18] comparable, epistemologically, to the gods of Homer. For my part I do, qua lay physicist, believe in physical objects and not in Homer's gods; and I consider it a scientific error to believe otherwise. But in point of epistemological footing the physical objects and the gods differ only in degree and not in kind. Both sorts of entities enter our conception only as cultural posits. The myth of physical objects is epistemologically superior to most in that it has proved more efficacious than other myths as a device for working a manageable structure into the flux of experience.

Positing does not stop with macroscopic physical objects. Objects at the atomic level are posited to make the laws of macroscopic objects, and ultimately the laws of experience, simpler and more manageable; and we need not expect or demand full definition of atomic and subatomic entities in terms of macroscopic ones, any more than definition of macroscopic

[18] Cf. pp. 17f above.

things in terms of sense data. Science is a continuation of common sense, and it continues the common-sense expedient of swelling ontology to simplify theory.

Physical objects, small and large, are not the only posits. Forces are another example; and indeed we are told nowadays that the boundary between energy and matter is obsolete. Moreover, the abstract entities which are the substance of mathematics—ultimately classes and classes of classes and so on up—are another posit in the same spirit. Epistemologically these are myths on the 'same footing with physical objects and gods, neither better nor worse except for differences in the degree to which they expedite our dealings with sense experiences.

The over-all algebra of rational and irrational numbers is underdetermined by the algebra of rational numbers, but is smoother and more convenient; and it includes the algebra of rational numbers as a jagged or gerrymandered part.[19] Total science, mathematical and natural and human, is similarly but more extremely underdetermined by experience. The edge of the system must be kept squared with experience; the rest, with all its elaborate myths or fictions, has as its objective the simplicity of laws.

Ontological questions, under this view, are on a par with questions of natural science.[20] Consider the question whether to countenance classes as entities. This, as I have argued elsewhere,[21] is the question whether to quantify with respect to variables which take classes as values. Now Carnap [6] has maintained that this is a question not of matters of fact but of choosing a convenient language form, a convenient conceptual scheme or framework for science. With this I agree, but only on the proviso that the same be conceded regarding scientific hypotheses generally. Carnap ([6], p. 32n) has recognized that he is able to preserve a double standard for ontological questions and scientific hypotheses only by assuming an absolute distinc-

---

[19] Cf. p. 18 above.

[20] "L'ontologie fait corps avec la science elle-même et ne peut en être separée." Meyerson, p. 439.

[21] Above, pp. 12f; below, pp. 102ff.

tion between the analytic and the synthetic; and I need not say again that this is a distinction which I reject.[22]

The issue over there being classes seems more a question of convenient conceptual scheme; the issue over there being centaurs, or brick houses on Elm Street, seems more a question of fact. But I have been urging that this difference is only one of degree, and that it turns upon our vaguely pragmatic inclination to adjust one strand of the fabric of science rather than another in accommodating some particular recalcitrant experience. Conservatism figures in such choices, and so does the quest for simplicity.

Carnap, Lewis, and others take a pragmatic stand on the question of choosing between language forms, scientific frameworks; but their pragmatism leaves off at the imagined boundary between the analytic and the synthetic. In repudiating such a boundary I espouse a more thorough pragmatism. Each man is given a scientific heritage plus a continuing barrage of sensory stimulation; and the considerations which guide him in warping his scientific heritage to fit his continuing sensory promptings are, where rational, pragmatic.

[22] For an effective expression of further misgivings over this distinction, see White [2].

4

Two Cornerstones of Empiricism

GUSTAV BERGMANN

Reprinted with the kind permission of the author and the publisher (D. Reidel) from *Synthese*, VIII, 435-52.

TWO CORNERSTONES OF EMPIRICISM [1]

QUINE'S RECENT paper, "Two Dogmas of Empiricism," [2] opens with a historical diagnosis. Modern empiricism is said to have been conditioned in large part by two beliefs. The one, worded as I would word it, holds that an epistemologically significant distinction can be made between the two kinds of truth traditionally spoken of as analytic and synthetic. The other is now also known as the linguistic version of phenomenalism. I agree completely with this diagnosis; but I disagree as completely with the burden of Quine's paper. He argues that the two beliefs are ill founded. I shall attempt to show, in this paper, that they are tenable as well as of strategic importance. Naturally, then, I think of them not as two dogmas but, rather, as two cornerstones of philosophical analysis in the empiricist vein. Yet, the disagreement is neither as crass nor as unsubtle as one might infer from my thus opposing, for the sake of emphasis, thesis and counterthesis. With respect to the first issue: Examining some recent attempts at "justifying" the dichotomy in question, Quine finds them circular, question

[1] This paper was read, as part of a discussion with W. V. Quine, at a meeting sponsored by the Institute for the Unity of Science in Boston, Spring 1951. Subsequently, it appeared in *Synthese*, 8 (June, 1953), 435-52. It is here reprinted by permission.

[2] *Philosophical Review*, 60 (1951), 20-43.

[78]

TWO CORNERSTONES OF EMPIRICISM

begging, or otherwise untenable and inadequate. These criticisms, which make up more than half of the paper, are, in my opinion, most penetrating, admirably lucid, and irrefutable. Also, I share what I believe is their intellectual motive, the rejection of a certain unclear idea of *certainty* that has, from a tangle of historical causes, vexed our philosophical tradition. With respect to the second issue: Whatever we know about the external world is, in varying degrees, subject to doubt. At the one extreme, say, in the case of a novel scientific theory, this is obvious. At the other extreme, I understand and accept the traditional thesis, supported by the traditional arguments, that even a perceptual judgment as simple as 'This is a chair' is not, in principle, beyond doubt. However, this circumstance is counterbalanced by another. In principle we always can and in practice we sometimes do maintain the truth of such judgments in the teeth of what I shall, for brevity's sake, call evidence for their falsehood. I am as impressed as Quine is and as, I take it, most philosophers who think of themselves as empiricists are, with these two pervasive features of our knowledge of the external world. So there is much agreement, negative, as on the first issue, and positive, as on the second. I believe, indeed, that most, if not all disagreements in the empiricist camp have been worn very thin in the discussions of the last decades. We mutually approve of our partial analyses, particularly, alas, of the destructive ones. Nor do we often disagree on the pervasive features of our world that our descriptions of it should portray. What we argue about among ourselves are no longer those analyses and these features but, rather, though sometimes without noticing it, the nature and task of philosophical analysis itself.

This task, as I conceive it, is the solution of the traditional

[79]

THE METAPHYSICS OF LOGICAL POSITIVISM

philosophical problems, the simultaneous solution of all these problems, and nothing but the solution of these problems; or, as some put it, the dissolution of the traditional puzzles. There is much in this on which, among empiricists, I need not touch except *sub figura praeteritionis.* For instance, I shall take it for granted that if the second belief, the one Quine calls reductionism, could be maintained, some familiar problems would be solved or, at least, be on their way toward solution. Similarly, I take it for granted that the linguistic version of this thesis marks a further advance in that it keeps us from becoming entangled with ontological assertions of the classical variety. The label, linguistic version of phenomenalism, which I have chosen in order to identify our concerns with those of others, thus turns out to be captious; so we may prefer to speak of the dissolution of puzzles rather than of the solution of problems. What interests me at the moment is that these are *not* the things we argue about among ourselves. Though we may not always know it, our most fundamental disagreements nowadays are about such matters as how detailed and how accurate, in a sense of 'accurate' which is itself in need of clarification, the "linguistic reconstruction" involved in the reductionist thesis must be. This indicates one group of reasons that make me feel that our intellectual situation is very delicate and, in some sense, peculiar. There are two more such groups; to indicate their nature I shall make use of certain cues I planted.

Let me start from the two features of our knowledge of the external world with which, as I put it, Quine and I are equally impressed. There is also another feature of our experience; I shall call it the third. Some things, such as that we have at the moment a chair percept, we know, whenever

[80]

TWO CORNERSTONES OF EMPIRICISM

we do know them, so that it makes absolutely no sense to say that we may doubt them. If I did not sometimes know some such truths, I could not understand what it means to doubt some others. If it were not for them, I could not understand the word 'true'. Nor could I, without understanding this word, understand what it means to say that the truth of some statements is problematic in the sense that, on the one hand, it can always be doubted and, on the other, always be preserved by certain adjustments in a wider context. Quine does not, in his paper, repudiate this third aspect of our experience. But he says very little about it and he also advocates a *rapprochement* with pragmatism. I must say I am puzzled; for the whole intellectual edifice of pragmatism in its dominant instrumentalist form rests on the emphatic rejection of the third feature. As a historical fact this is beyond dispute; controversial is merely whether it is, as I am prepared to maintain, an irreparable shortcoming of that position.

It has appeared that because of the light they shed on each other our three features are really quite inseparable for the purposes of philosophical analysis. This merely illustrates that very intricate and thorough interdependence of all philosophical problems or puzzles that leads me to speak of cornerstones and of strategy. To add one more metaphor, we must beware lest we weave, if weaving it is, a Penelopean garment. More literally, the task is, as I said before, to dissolve simultaneously all puzzles and, as I now add, to account justly for all those pervasive features of our experience that have attracted the philosopher's attention. Many of our disagreements turn, I think, on whether what one has said about a particular issue fits into such a general pattern. This is my second comment about the situation I

[81]

THE METAPHYSICS OF LOGICAL POSITIVISM

called both delicate and peculiar. Quine's present position leaves the two features both he and I think important serenely secure. Naturally—for are they not his cornerstones? Does not his strategy work from them rather than toward them? Yet I am disturbed by the price he pays and I believe must pay for this. Let us disregard the pitfalls of the material mode and, for the sake of the argument, assume that he does not need to reject the third feature. Even so, I am not willing to say, as he does and I believe must, that the external world is an ontological hypothesis or posit. We may, of course, doubt the truth of 'There are physical objects' in the sense in which a single perceptual judgment is not beyond doubt. In this light, though, all cows are black and we have hardly said anything in particular about that hoary puzzle, the existence of the external world. More important, I don't know what ontological hypotheses are, in a sense that goes beyond the truism I just mentioned, except that we may doubt, as we may doubt so much else, whatever can be said legitimately in the realm of ontology, which is quite a different matter. But surely this will do by way of unsupported assertions. For the moment they may serve as signposts, indicating my strategy as well as my intellectual motives. Later on I shall have to give reasons; and they had better be of the kind which I insist the situation requires.

For my last comment on how we disagree I planted the cue when I spoke of justifying the dichotomy analytic-synthetic. In that sense of the term which has its root in the law and which is the only one I understand, we are not obliged to justify anything, not even, as some still believe, induction. We merely describe the world, for our own peculiar purposes, in our own peculiar way. Justification in

[82]

TWO CORNERSTONES OF EMPIRICISM

the legalistic sense is no more our business than is that other futile and not unrelated quest, the search for some superior kind of certainty. Yet, one part of our task does bear some vague resemblance to that of a man asked to show cause in a court of law. Even there, though, I prefer to speak of *explication* rather than of *justification*. In the case of the dichotomy analytic-synthetic the evidence for a felt differ-ence is as overwhelming as are the arguments in the destruc-tive part of Quine's paper. Thus, caution is in order. Surely, there are some cases where all we can do is to explain how and why our predecessors erred. But whether we can be satisfied with such a negative result is, in each case, a fur-ther question, on which one may disagree. This, I submit, is the third kind of disagreement still to be found among us. To my mind, it is better to fail trying than to give up too soon. With respect to analyticity, I believe there are features of our experience that account for what I just called the felt difference. I propose to point at these features, to locate them correctly, as it were, and to state them justly, showing in this manner that it is not all a misunderstanding, a matter of psychology or, as one says in this case, one of degree. To do this sort of thing for a philosophical distinction is what I mean by explicating it and what some may mean when they speak, at their own peril, of justifying it. I say at their own peril, because the main reason the explication of analyticity proved so elusive was that those who sought it also sought for a certainty that is not to be had and for a justification that is not needed.

Much of what follows depends in part and some of it depends wholly on a technic I shall use and which is, therefore, more than a technic. So I must call attention to this phase of my strategy, though I shall be brief since

[83]

THE METAPHYSICS OF LOGICAL POSITIVISM

the matter is familiar. I have long sided with those who hold that philosophical analysis proceeds properly through the construction of an ideal language. Quine never explicitly embraced this view, but he is I believe not unsympathetic to it and certainly not as violently opposed to it as some of our British friends, the so-called casuists, and their latter-day offspring, the therapeutic linguists. I may hope, then, that I do not obstruct communication when I speak the only language I feel I can speak, with some expectation of clarity and effectiveness, on issues as fundamental as those that are here at stake.

An ideal language or, as I shall sometimes say, disregarding the problems of a possible plurality, the ideal language has three essential characteristics. First, it is a formalism, that is, a system of signs or, if you please, marks on paper designed without reference to anything else but the shapes and the arrangements of these signs themselves. Second, it becomes, upon interpretation, a picture or reconstruction of ordinary English, that is, of those statements we make or would make, if we had occasion to make them, outside the philosopher's study. Third, we can, by discoursing about it, dissolve the philosophical puzzles. One requirement I urged before, that all philosophical problems be solved simultaneously, as it were, is automatically fulfilled if one adopts this method of philosophizing. The idea is, of course, not to have different formalisms for different problems, but one which is complete in that it is a picture of all ordinary English and adequate in that it allows the discursive solution of all puzzles. When we construct the ideal language, in the first step, and when we interpret it, in the second, we speak ordinary English. This is also true for the third step; for in this discourse, which is the heart of the philosophical

[84]

TWO CORNERSTONES OF EMPIRICISM

enterprise, the statements made in the philosopher's study occur merely in quotes, as it were, as our *explicanda*. This emphasis on ordinary, nonphilosophical English reflects what I owe to G. E. Moore. Whoever thinks that the double role it assigns to ordinary English makes the schema vitiatingly circular hunts for an absolute that is not there; I shall not, because I cannot, argue with him. I turn, instead, to two other arguments that can and must be made. The first may produce agreement where there seemed to be disagreement; the second should at least help us to agree that part of our disagreement is a difference in opinion, not as to what is the case, but as to what philosophers ought to do about it.

That we speak in the ordinary course of events the language I call ordinary English is, of course, a matter of fact or, if you please, of empirical fact or, still more pointedly, merely a matter of fact. Surely, there is nothing certain, in any nonordinary sense of 'certain', about this fact. One may even, if one cares to do so, call it an anthropological fact and go on to assert that my conception of philosophy makes it a branch of anthropology. In a sense this is true; only, it is also trivial. Again we have entered a night in which all cows are black. The philosopher's art is, to me, still the art of distinction. We clarify our thought and, incidentally, the historical puzzles by making all the distinctions that can and, therefore, must be made. To emphasize the "anthropological truism" at the expense of such distinctions is not only unhelpful but definitely harmful. Does Quine really think, I wonder, that all a philosopher can do, when he wishes to characterize the sort of thing Quine does in his *Mathematical Logic*, is to call it a study, albeit a rather abstract one, in the psychology of thought and in the sociology of discovery. If he does not think so, in spite of some

[85]

THE METAPHYSICS OF LOGICAL POSITIVISM

anthropological *obiter dicta* that crop up strangely in his most recent papers, then I am once more puzzled by the gesture he makes toward pragmatism; for, that pragmatism not only implicitly neglects but explicitly rejects the distinctions involved is, again, a matter of record.[3] Yet there is another side to the story. Just as distinctions must be made correctly, so there is no truism that is not of strategic importance somewhere. The distinction between the two kinds of truth has so far not been made correctly, or, as I had better say, has not been talked about correctly. The anthropological truism has its part in correcting these errors.

Assume, for the sake of the argument, that I shall succeed in what I have undertaken to do presently, namely, to distinguish in the ideal language two kinds of statements, corresponding to the two kinds of truth, analytic and synthetic. Success would consist, first, in explicating, without using them, the traditional formulae such as that "analytical truths are formal, syntactical, or linguistic, while synthetic truths depend on fact." It consists, second, in demonstrating that the distinction thus established does justice to what I called the felt difference and that it is, as I put it, epistemologically significant in that it is crucial for other clarifications such as, for instance, my second cornerstone or, as Quine has it, dogma. If one can thus successfully explicate the old formulae, then one may, if one wishes, continue to speak of factual and of formal truths, at least occasionally, since for some purposes this nomenclature is indeed quite adequate and very suggestive. But if the circumstances require it, as they do on this occasion, then one can add, consistently and without intellectual embarrassment, that the distinction be-

---

[3] See also M. Brodbeck, "The New Rationalism; Dewey's Theory of Induction," *Journal of Philosophy*, 46 (1949), 781-91.

[86]

TWO CORNERSTONES OF EMPIRICISM

tween factual and formal truths is itself a matter of fact. Naturally, 'fact' occurs here in two different meanings. The first time it marks the relevant distinction; the second time it is used in the sense in which everything is a fact and in which, therefore, nothing is certain in that indefensible sense of 'certain' in which some advocates of the dichotomy analytic-synthetic think that the truths they call formal or linguistic are certain. I note, for later reference, that I just scored for the first time against that sort of certainty. I turn, next, to the other point about the ideal language that needs arguing.

To his client, the future owner, the architect submits a sketch that helps him visualize the style of the building, the order and arrangement of the rooms, their shape and size. To his workmen the architect gives a large number of blueprints specifying all sorts of detail, down to the dimensions of a lintel and, perhaps, even the grain of a wooden panel. Assuming, for the sake of the argument, that we know otherwise what we mean when we call the ideal language a picture or reconstruction of ordinary English, how accurate and how detailed must this picture be? Is it more like the architect's sketch or more like his blueprints? Quine observes, in his discussion of what he calls the second dogma, not only that Carnap's *Aufbau,* whatever else its weaknesses and strengths, is merely a sketch but also, and more important, that no blueprints in support of the linguistic version of phenomenalism are likely ever to come forth. With this I have no quarrel. Disagreement begins when Quine turns his observation into a criticism of my second cornerstone, arguing as he does that since we cannot really reconstruct physical objects we may as well accept them as ontological posits. To coin a phrase for the convenience of

[87]

THE METAPHYSICS OF LOGICAL POSITIVISM

the moment, Quine is a blueprint theorist. I am, emphatically, a sketch theorist. Yet, to repeat, I am as convinced as he is that it is practically impossible to define blueprintwise such words as, say, 'chair' from the kind of inventory of undefined descriptive terms we *Aufbauers* would be willing to accept, say, for instance, a class of predicates referring to qualities of and some spatial and temporal relations among those particulars which it is customary to call sense data. What I maintain not to be impossible, either practically or otherwise, is the reconstruction from such an inventory of such statements as 'a, which was just contiguous with b, is now contiguous with c', where 'a', 'b', and 'c' refer to particulars of the kind just mentioned. If this can be achieved, ·even if only as one usually says for a two-dimensional visual field and within the specious present, much is achieved. For, as I need not explain, this amounts to an analysis or, at least, to an essential part of the analysis, of the idea of a *continuant* and, therefore, of the ideas of *physical identity* and *substance*. A few more such schematic analyses properly related, explicating such notions as the three just mentioned, constitute what I accept as the reconstruction, complete and adequate for all philosophical purposes, of the idea of a *physical object*. This is what I had in mind when I insisted earlier that the task of philosophical analysis is the solution of the philosophical problems and *nothing but* the solution of these problems. What does not pertain to them is detail that need not and should not appear in the sketch.

The issue of the counterfactuals, which attracts now so much attention, provides as good an illustration as any for what I mean by accuracy in this context. Idiomatically accurate translations of the so-called dispositional terms

[88]

TWO CORNERSTONES OF EMPIRICISM

cannot be constructed from nondispositional terms with the syntactical apparatus of logical atomism. This, I take it, has been settled. But we may still disagree and we do, in fact, disagree among ourselves on whether this forces us to abandon the thesis of logical atomism or whether translations as accurate or, if you prefer it that way, as inaccurate as we can give without abandoning it suffice for the purposes of philosophical analysis. The blueprint theorist has no choice. Ideal language or no ideal language, he must give up logical atomism and commit himself, in Quine's terms, to an ontology crowded not only with physical objects but with potentialities and connections of all kinds and levels, really quite an Aristotelian universe. To defend the other alternative, that of accepting this inaccuracy of the ideal language, is not one of the tasks I have set myself in this paper. It is fortunate, though, that, since I am a sketch theorist, I can choose this alternative. For it will soon appear that my explication of analyticity stands and falls with logical atomism, that is, with the thesis that the syntactical categories of the ideal language are, roughly speaking, connectives, individual and predicate variables, quantifiers and constants corresponding to these variables, and nothing else.

Permit me to conclude this topic with an historical conjecture. The present recrudescence of the blueprint theory of reconstruction and of philosophy in general has, I believe, two main causes. The one is the casuists' excessive concern with ordinary English, with the fine shades of meaning which they so cleverly discern in the spoken word and, generally, with linguistics in a sense that has very little, if any, bearing on the philosophical problems. The futility and the futilitarianism into which this tendency has degenerated are only too manifest. The other cause is the wrong kind of

[89]

THE METAPHYSICS OF LOGICAL POSITIVISM

concern with and regard for science that prevailed and still prevails among some groups of empiricists. Science often does and eventually always should deliver blueprints, not sketches. Philosophers, however, in this respect as in all others, are not scientists.

I turn now to the explication of analyticity. Very judiciously, I think, particularly for his critical purposes, Quine distinguishes between two kinds of allegedly analytic truth. Supposing "a prior inventory of *logical* particles" such as the connectives, a truth of the first kind "remains true under all reinterpretations of its components other than the logical particles." A truth of the second kind, such as 'No bachelor is married' is supposedly reducible to the first by replacing some terms, such as 'bachelor' by their "definitions," where 'definition' does not necessarily have the meaning of abbreviation in a formalism. Quine's demonstrations that analyticity cannot be grounded in such ideas of definition, synonymy, and interchangeability are surpassingly brilliant and lucid. It is fortunate, then, that I need not deal with that second kind, for it will soon appear that the ideal language contains only definitions in the harmless sense of abbreviation. As I have already shown in part, the "factual" burden "definitions" carry in other conceptions of reconstruction is, by my strategy, placed elsewhere. For another hint about this strategy, one cannot deny epistemological significance to the distinction between analytic and synthetic truths and grant it to that between *logical* and *descriptive signs*, which is at least implicit in Quine's mention of a prior inventory. One motive for my defending the first dichotomy is that unlike Quine I need, in my ontology, the second. Both 'all' and 'green' are in the ideal language; thus both allness and greenness are, in some sense, in the world. Yet

[90]

TWO CORNERSTONES OF EMPIRICISM

there is a "felt difference" between their modes of being there. This difference I explicate by that between logical and descriptive signs. And this, I believe, was also the intent of the old, inadequate formula according to which logical signs and analytical truths are formal or linguistic.

As a philosopher I am not interested in formalisms as such. So I shall henceforth speak only about that formalism which is as likely a candidate as any for the ideal language, namely, the noncontroversial parts of *Principia Mathematica* supplemented by a sufficiency of (descriptive) constants. In this formalism one can with the familiar results distinguish between the two kinds of signs, formally and yet not trivially as, e.g., by enumeration, but structurally, by means of the formation and transformation rules and, in particular, the rules of substitution. (In itself such a formal distinction is, of course, not epistemologically significant; it becomes so only when it can bear the burden imposed on it in philosophical discourse about the formalism.) Quine,[4] I am well aware, does not favor this particular piece of machinery and minimizes it in his variant of the formalism. However, since his preference seems to stem from his ontological views rather than from his philosophy of logic, to whatever extent these two can be kept apart, and since I follow after all good logical doctrine, I do not think it unfair on my part to proceed as I do.

Consider now that rather limited class of truths known as the tautologies of sentential logic. I shall explicate what sets them apart in two steps. *First,* they remain true, *as far*

[4] W. V. Quine, "Ontology and Ideology," *Philosophical Studies,* 2 (1951), 11-15; G. Bergmann, "A Note on Ontology," *ibid.,* 1 (December, 1950), 89-92, and also pp. 238-42 of this book.

[91]

THE METAPHYSICS OF LOGICAL POSITIVISM

as I know and as a matter of fact, if their descriptive signs are consistently but otherwise arbitrarily replaced by others of the proper syntactical kinds. As far as my campaign against the wrong kind of certainty is concerned, the two qualifications, "as far as I know and as a matter of fact," are of the essence. Here I score for the second time in this campaign. But perhaps one wishing to test my empiricist orthodoxy would now like to ask whether I really agree, then, that one of these substitutions could "conceivably" yield a falsehood. So questioned, I might smile and wonder whether the questioner himself is quite untainted by the heresy known as psychologism. But I would not quibble and I would agree. Yet it remains most remarkable that, having once constructed the ideal language, one can, in fact, recognize the truth of some statements merely by inspecting these statements. This, however, is only half of what must be said; otherwise most any truth could by the proper tricks be made "formal" or "linguistic." I note, then, *second,* that the connectives, which are the only signs that occur nonvacuously in tautologies, have very special properties. They are, in a familiar sense, truth tables; and a sentential compound is a tautology if and only if its truth table exhibits that familiar feature which mathematicians express by saying that the sentential calculus has an adequate matrix representation. Taken together and with what follows, this purely combinatorial, arithmetical schema for the connectives and the vacuous occurrence of all other signs in the tautologies *are* the proper explication of the former being called logical signs and the latter analytic truths.

Not all analytical truths are sentential tautologies. The vacuous occurrence of the descriptive signs is characteristic

[92]

TWO CORNERSTONES OF EMPIRICISM

of all of them. But there are, of course, no truth tables for the so-called functional calculus. Fortunately, their place is taken by the idea of an identical formula. This, too, is a purely combinatorial, arithmetical schema. Originally devised for the lower calculus, it can be extended to the higher types, as Carnap did in *The Logical Syntax of Language*. Everybody familiar with this schema knows that *mutatis mutandis* it does exactly what the truth tables do. This, then, is my explication of analyticity. It has two immediate consequences of strategic import. Applying the technic of identical formulae to the higher types commits one to an extensional ideal language. Since I see no reason to shrink from this commitment, since Quine, too, inclines toward the extensionalist thesis, and since I must limit myself, I shall say no more on this head. Even more fundamentally, I have committed myself to logical atomism. To see this, assume that 'because' in 'I am ill because I smoked too much' corresponds to a primitive sign of the ideal language. If it is a special sign, then my explication of analyticity breaks down because it is not a connective. If it is a substitution instance of a new kind of variable, that is, a syntactical category not known to logical atomism, then I know of no combinatorial schema that does for such variables what the technic of identical formulae does for predicate variables.[5]

I am now ready to turn more exclusively to the problems of the reconstruction. But I should like to show first in an intermediate case the use to which this explication of analyticity can be put. Quine says incidentally that he does not know whether 'Everything green is extended' is analytic.

[5] See also "Logical Atomism, Elementarism, and the Analysis of Value," *Philosophical Studies*, 2 (December, 1951), 85-92, and also pp. 243-54 of this book.

[93]

THE METAPHYSICS OF LOGICAL POSITIVISM

Surely the blur is not due to some blurred notions of synonymy or definition; the idea of defining one of the two descriptive predicates in terms of the other is simply too unreasonable to be taken seriously. So one may, for the sake of the argument, assume that they are both primitive or undefined. From my view, then, it follows immediately that the statement is not analytic. It follows further that whatever tie there is between descriptive characters in such cases, it is not the tie that binds conclusion to premise. Many philosophers would have saved themselves many troubles if they had been able to state this difference justly and clearly instead of lumping it under the notion of entailment. Philosophy, I repeat, is the art of distinction.

In one respect all proponents of an *Aufbau* agree. The undefined descriptive predicates that are, as it were, the basis of the reconstruction are of the kind that has led to the familiar charges of phenomenalism or subjective idealism. Whether this inventory must contain some roots specific to our moral and esthetic experience and to such activities of the Self as knowing and remembering is controversial. Again, the basis needed for the reconstruction of our knowledge of the external world is not controversial, except for some rather technical points which, since they do not concern Quine in his paper, need not concern us in this discussion. So I shall say no more about the basic inventory. The reconstruction itself consists in the designing of definitions for such *definienda* as, say, 'chair'. These are all definitions in the strict and, as I put it before, harmless sense of abbreviation. The procedure is successful, within the limits set by the sketch theory, if and only if (a) we can indicate two classes of statements, *A* and *B*, such that the statements of *B* follow deductively from those of *A* in conjunction with the definitions;

[94]

TWO CORNERSTONES OF EMPIRICISM

(b) the statements of both *A* and *B* correspond to empirical laws we believe to be true; (c) all descriptive terms occurring in *A*-statements belong to the basic inventory; (d) a *B*-statement corresponds to an ordinary statement about the external world. All this is familiar. So I shall limit myself to three comments that are relevant to my purpose.

It is worth noticing, *first,* that the ideal language does not and need not contain terms that are names of particular chairs in the sense in which the individual constants (particulars) it does contain or which may be added to it are the names of, say, sense data. In traditional terms this amounts to a refutation of all kinds of substantialism. 'Chair' itself is, of course, a predicate of the reconstruction. What corresponds to '*This is a chair*' of ordinary English is, roughly, a conjunction of '*This* is a chair percept' and a rather complex statement of lawfulness. 'This' thus stands, roughly, for one or several particulars of the ideal language. To put it as I did once before,[6] when I hear the first bars of a certain piece and exclaim 'This is Haydn's Lark', 'this' refers in the reconstruction to these bars, not to the whole quartet. And one sees, upon a little reflection, that this is just as it ought to be. It follows that existential statements such as 'There are chairs' and, similarly, 'There are physical objects' merely assert that there are particulars of a kind I do know. They may be hypothetical in that the particular which, in a manner of speaking, the bound variable represents is not present. But they are not hypothetical in that they assert the existence of kinds I do not know. One may, of course, define kinds one has never seen exemplified, say, centaurs and mermaids, in terms of kinds one knows. Definition does not, in an obvious and

---

[6] "Remarks on Realism," *Philosophy of Science,* 13 (October, 1946), 261-73, and also pp. 153-75 of this book.

THE METAPHYSICS OF LOGICAL POSITIVISM

familiar sense, involve existence. For the rest I simply do not understand that alleged second meaning of 'hypothesis', the "positing" of a kind unknown. This is why I do not wish to say, as Quine does, that physical objects are hypothetical entities, myths like centaurs and mermaids. And, as I have just shown, one does not need to say it. This unwillingness, caused by that ultimate inability to understand, is probably the main intellectual motive that moves all advocates of philosophy by reconstruction. It certainly is mine.

Second, I wish to call attention to a very neat and clear-cut dichotomy within the reconstruction. There are, on the one hand, the definitions and, on the other, the statements that may be truly made in the terms defined. This merely portrays what is familiar from everyday life and from science. Sometimes we ask what a thing *is;* sometimes what *happens* to it under circumstances. Scientists say that they *describe* the initial and the terminal states of a system and, by means of a process formula or law, *explain* how the latter evolves from the former. There is, however, a meaning of 'meaning' that is quite resistant to these distinctions. In this sense, we know the better what 'apple' means the more we know about apples. This meaning is forever open, growing, or, to use a technical term, holistic. Naturally, it cannot be "formalized," either my way or any other. This is the meaning which once Hegel extolled and which now the pragmatists emphasize at the expense of all others. Quine's professed sympathy with pragmatism is quite consistent in this respect. From where I stand this is another irreparable weakness of that position. I do not know how to speak of a process without speaking of what proceeds. The proverb has it that it is easier to ride a tiger than to descend from it. This tiger I wouldn't even know how to mount. In other words, I be-

[96]

TWO CORNERSTONES OF EMPIRICISM

lieve that if we want to understand the world we cannot help projecting upon it that dichotomy which is so clear cut in the reconstruction, though, to be sure, in doing this we must be as cautious and as judicious as always when we handle that sharp tool, the ideal language. Yet, I do not deny the importance, let alone the existence, of the holistic meaning of 'meaning'; I believe I can even understand the fascination it has for some. I merely insist that the proper place to study it is the science of psychology. Pragmatists, of course, do not wish to distinguish between science and philosophy and Quine now suggests that we follow suit. At any rate, the ideal language cannot and need not portray holistic meaning. This is another of its inevitable inaccuracies.

Third, I am now ready to strike my final blows against the wrong kind of certainty. There are those uncertainties of a general and pervasive nature that arise whenever we speak about the world, and, therefore, when we attempt to project any formalism upon it, or, what amounts to the same thing, upon the ordinary language of common sense and science. These uncertainties I pointed out on earlier occasions. The explication of analyticity is perfectly clear and in this sense certain, in spite of the subtle difficulties that beset the decision whether a sufficiently complicated formula of the ideal language is in fact analytic. These difficulties naturally and quite properly occupy the mathematicians; to introduce them, as some now propose, into the discussion of certainty and analyticity is, I believe, a mistake. Yet, there are some specific uncertainties that spring from the very technic of the reconstruction. We merely draw a sketch and we lose, in drawing it, the holistic meanings. For the solution of the philosophical problems this is an advantage; but when we want to decide whether any given ordinary English state-

[97]

THE METAPHYSICS OF LOGICAL POSITIVISM

ment is analytic, or more precisely, whether its ideal correlate is, then this becomes a limitation, a source of uncertainty. Only, I think this limitation quite natural and so do
not chafe at it. There is the related circumstance, of which
our casuist friends make so much, that in ordinary speech
we use without defining them words whose ideal correlates
would undoubtedly have to be defined. These matters have
been talked to shreds; so I shall say no more about them.
Yet I find it intriguing to observe that much as they otherwise disagree, there is at least this one point of contact between Quine and the casuist linguists. The patterns into
which the relatively few basic ideas group and regroup
themselves are indeed full of surprises. To return to the
peculiar uncertainties of the reconstruction, there is also the
choice of the primitive predicates to be considered. Surely,
this choice is a matter of fact; besides, we make it only
schematically, sketchwise, not blueprintwise. And what appears to be analytic upon one such choice could, conceivably,
be synthetic upon another. But again, this neither puzzles nor
upsets me, since the blur comes not from a blurred notion
of analyticity but from our ignorance in matters of fact, in
a sense in which I can and Quine cannot contrast the factual
with the analytic.

Certainty of the wrong kind, our common enemy, is dead.
I beg a moment's leave to give it a soldier's burial. More
plainly, it will be worth our while to inquire where the reasonable kind of certainty has its place in the reconstruction.
I have long insisted that the ideal language contains the act
pattern, a direct and not merely behavioristic reconstruction
of such sentences as 'I know that...', 'I remember that...'.
This is, of course, quite a story by itself; so I shall merely
remark that if one represents in the ideal language the de-

[98]

TWO CORNERSTONES OF EMPIRICISM

pendent clauses by those particulars which are their names, then the mental verbs become descriptive predicates and the act pattern can, in principle, be reproduced without abandoning either atomism or extensionality. As for the reasonable kind of certainty, to know for certain is, I submit, a species of knowing. Accordingly, the locus of certainty in the reconstruction is the mental verb. I realize that by that special revelation the casuists have received about ordinary English to know simply means to know for certain. Thus they would find it absurd that I might have occasion to say that yesterday I knew for certain what today I know to be false. I think that this is exactly as it should be. To play with a fashionable phrase, this absurdity, or alleged absurdity, is indeed part of the human situation. To accept without analyzing it any other meaning of 'knowing' is to begin where one should end and to prejudge some of the most important issues. We, who do not have to pay this awful price, are yet saved more than one perplexity. We are once and for all rid of that inverted psychologism that makes propositions certain while it is we who are certain about them. We notice, further, that my being certain of something, even if this be an analytic truth, is in the reconstruction expressed by a synthetic sentence. For the mental verbs, we remember, are descriptive predicates. Thus, to be certain of something is a fact among facts, not more certain than some others. We have definitely rid ourselves of all apriorism. Also, we are now in an excellent position to understand why and how our predecessors were misled. It is true enough that when we once know a proposition to be analytic we do, in fact, know this proposition for certain. But, to be sure, this is merely a rather striking fact about analyticity, not part of the explication of this notion. So we see at one glance why the ideas of

[99]

THE METAPHYSICS OF LOGICAL POSITIVISM

certainty and analyticity must be kept separate as well as why they have, in fact, become enmeshed with each other. There is still another class of truths of which we are, in fact, certain, namely, those propositions about sense data of which I said before that it makes no sense to doubt them. I even believe that the certainty of these propositions is part of the attraction which phenomenalism, linguistic or otherwise, had for some. Russell's *Inquiry* is only the last in a long series of documents one could cite in support of this historical conjecture about intellectual motives. Some sought certainty in logic; some sought it in sense data; but, by some quirk of history and the human mind, they unfortunately all sought some superior kind of certainty.

I agree heartily with everything Quine says about meaning and the so-called meaning criterion. This criterion, whatever it may be, is certainly not part of the ideal language but, rather, part of the philosophical discourse about it. It is something to be explicated, not something to be demonstrated; something to strive toward, not something to start from. Nor must it be treated as a premise or a dogma, though it may turn out to be a cornerstone if found to be adequate and, at the same time, of strategic importance. Freed from the unnecessary and confusing reference to verification, this so-called criterion amounts to a choice of the undefined descriptive predicates of the reconstruction and, at least implicitly, of the syntactical apparatus of the ideal language. In this less garish form, which is its own explication, it is also known as the principle of acquaintance, though there, too, the emphasis was usually on the descriptive rather than on the logical inventory. The choice its proponents indicate by means of it is, I believe, for the most part the one I made. In this sense the criterion embraces my two cornerstones or, as Quine

[100]

TWO CORNERSTONES OF EMPIRICISM

has it, my two dogmas. Only, I am not particularly eager to state them in this manner, for I have long discovered that every opportunity to avoid the term 'meaning' in philosophical discussion is nowadays one more opportunity to keep out of trouble and confusion.

The worst of these tangles—though, really, I find it difficult to choose among them—Quine diagnoses with most elegant succinctness as the identification of meaning and reference. One of its stranger fruits is the following argument that is now being made in favor of some sort of realism: 'Dog' is a meaningful word; hence it must have a referent; but dog percepts are, as everyone agrees, different from dogs; hence they are not the referents of 'dog'; hence there are real dogs. The actual arguments are more elaborate; those who make them prefer to speak of electrons rather than of dogs. But that merely adds to the confusion. Since Quine is as skeptical about all this as I am, I should like to remind him whence and why this Trojan horse has been introduced into the philosophical discussion. If one wishes to study language scientifically and with behavioristic methods, then the definition of "meanings" in terms of reference is indeed not only proper but very clever, and, as far as I can judge, probably inevitable. (In introspective psychology it is a confusion. Titchener knew that and explained it well.) With me this alone goes a long way toward showing how wise it is never to blur the differences between science and philosophy. Quine, however, suggests now that this difference, too, is merely one of degree. The pragmatists, of course, would agree. They, at least, are consistent, believing as they do that the proper approach to the *philosophical* study of meaning, as of anything else, is *anthropological*.

Finally, I should like to comment on Quine's and my con-

[101]

THE METAPHYSICS OF LOGICAL POSITIVISM

ceptions of what both he and I call ontology. There are agreements and there are differences. I shall be brief on both, partly because we have aired some of these matters in an earlier discussion.[7] We agree that the old poser about what there is must be treated syntactically, or, as I would have to say, through the syntax of the ideal language. The most fundamental difference is that Quine wishes to reconstruct the old ontological assertions, or some reasonable equivalent of them, in the ideal language. I merely wish to *explicate* them in that informal discourse *about* the ideal language which is in my scheme of things the last and crowning phase of the philosophical enterprise. For instance, I advocate a phenomenalistic reconstruction only because I know of no other way to dissolve all the old puzzles, not because I wish to say that phenomena or, if you please, sense data are the only things that exist; for I believe that if taken literally the old questions and answers make no sense, or, as one said in the salad days in Vienna, that they are meaningless. I really do believe that. In this sense there is no difference between now and then. The difference is that then I would have let it go at that. Now I feel strongly that we can and must explicate these bad questions and answers and that in doing this we can recover or, perhaps, discover some good questions and answers behind them. To me the most interesting of these good questions and, accordingly, the core of the new ontology is: What are the undefined descriptive constants of the ideal language? One reason Quine does not proceed in this manner, is, perhaps, that he does not take as seriously as I do that positivistic turn which Wittgenstein gave to the empirical philosophy when he proclaimed that certain things cannot be said and which I express by insisting that the

[7] See footnote 4.

[102]

TWO CORNERSTONES OF EMPIRICISM

proper way to say them is ordinary discourse about the ideal language. But there is still another reason, which is much subtler.

It seems to me that one who says "There is a drugstore around the corner" hardly says anything about existence in the sense in which the old ontologists tried to say something about it. Yet, Quine's reconstruction of ontology fastens on the existential statements of the ideal language and, in particular, on the existential operator and the variable it binds. Now I do not deny that these operators and variables are of some ontological interest. To observe that the ideal language requires such and such inventory of *logical* signs and categories is to point at a feature one may, in a broader sense, well call ontological. Only, since I can distinguish between logical and descriptive signs, I can also distinguish between this broader sense of ontology and that other one, which I think is the central and traditional one and which is best explicated by the quest for the primitive *descriptive* inventory. Incidentally, this recovers the old distinction between existence and subsistence, or, at least, a large part of it. Quine, on the other hand, cannot in principle distinguish between logical and descriptive signs, or, as I had better say, he cannot attribute epistemological significance to the distinction. For, as we have seen, to do this is virtually the same thing as to attribute such significance to analyticity. To put it as one should not, for the sake of making a point, in Quine's world both logical and descriptive signs designate equally, without further distinction. This, I suggest, is why he is so impressed with the idiomatic accident that we sometimes say 'Centaurs exist' instead of 'There are centaurs'; and this is also that second subtler reason for his conception of ontology.

[103]

THE METAPHYSICS OF LOGICAL POSITIVISM

As for his specific ontological beliefs, if I may again state them as I would, I take him to assert that we must include into the basic inventory certain undefined descriptive predicates, such as the names of kinds of physical objects or 'physical object' itself, though we are not acquainted with any of their exemplifications. This, in turn, leads him to call physical objects myths or ontological hypotheses. That I do not understand this meaning of 'hypothesis', either in ontology or elsewhere, I have said before. Besides, I shun the wrong kind of phenomenalism of which it smacks. I do think that it makes sense to say we are acquainted with physical objects and that we are, in fact, acquainted with them. In the reconstruction, 'physical object' is a predicate defined in terms of what we all agree to be acquainted with; and when I have heard all the tones of a tune and grasped its line, then I have also heard the tune. To repeat, when I insist on what Quine calls reduction, it is not because I do not wish to say or could not say 'There are physical objects', but because I know of no other way to say it intelligibly and of no other path that leads to the simultaneous solution of all philosophical problems. This, I think, also indicates how I would explicate and recover the common-sense core of realism. Quine's present position is not in this sense analytic and untainted by the old ontologies. It hovers uneasily between pragmatism and traditional phenomenalism.

I should like to say, in conclusion, that I believe to have demonstrated at least two of my contentions. I have shown that in one sense the disagreement between Quine and me is as marked as are the differences between the positivist and the pragmatist tempers and between the intellectual and cultural atmospheres in which each thrives. Yet it has also appeared that we agree on virtually all those partial analyses

[104]

TWO CORNERSTONES OF EMPIRICISM

that are the secure fruits of the joint labors of recent and contemporary empiricists. We merely differ on how best to talk about them and how to marshall them into a world view, or, if I may say so among empiricists, into a metaphysics.

[105]

5

In Defense of a Dogma

H. P. GRICE AND P. F. STRAWSON

Reprinted with the kind permission of the authors and the editor from *The Philosophical Review,* LXV (1956), 141-58.

IN DEFENSE OF A DOGMA

IN HIS article "Two Dogmas of Empiricism,"[1] Professor
Quine advances a number of criticisms of the supposed
distinction between analytic and synthetic statements, and of other
associated notions. It is, he says, a distinction which he rejects.[2]
We wish to show that his criticisms of the distinction do not
justify his rejection of it.

There are many ways in which a distinction can be criticized,
and more than one in which it can be rejected. It can be criticized
for not being a sharp distinction (for admitting of cases which
do not fall clearly on either side of it); or on the ground that the
terms in which it is customarily drawn are ambiguous (have more
than one meaning); or on the ground that it is confused (the
different meanings being habitually conflated). Such criticisms
alone would scarcely amount to a rejection of the distinction.
They would, rather, be a prelude to clarification. It is not this
sort of criticism which Quine makes.

Again, a distinction can be criticized on the ground that it is
not useful. It can be said to be useless for certain purposes, or
useless altogether, and, perhaps, pedantic. One who criticizes in
this way may indeed be said to reject a distinction, but in a sense
which also requires him to acknowledge its existence. He simply
declares he can get on without it. But Quine's rejection of the
analytic-synthetic distinction appears to be more radical than
this. He would certainly say he could get on without the distinction, but not in a sense which would commit him to acknowledging
its existence.

Or again, one could criticize the way or ways in which a
distinction is customarily expounded or explained on the ground
that these explanations did not make it really clear. And Quine
certainly makes such criticisms in the case of the analytic-
synthetic distinction.

---

[1] W. V. O. Quine, *From a Logical Point of View* (Cambridge, Mass., 1953),
pp. 20-46.   All references are to page numbers in this book.

[2] Page 46.

141

I

H. P. GRICE AND P. F. STRAWSON

But he does, or seems to do, a great deal more. He declares, or seems to declare, not merely that the distinction is useless or inadequately clarified, but also that it is altogether illusory, that the belief in its existence is a philosophical mistake. "That there is such a distinction to be drawn at all," he says, "is an unempirical dogma of empiricists, a metaphysical article of faith."[3] It is the existence of the distinction that he here calls in question; so his rejection of it would seem to amount to a denial of its existence.

Evidently such a position of extreme skepticism about a distinction is not in general justified merely by criticisms, however just in themselves, of philosophical attempts to clarify it. There are doubtless plenty of distinctions, drawn in philosophy and outside it, which still await adequate philosophical elucidation, but which few would want on this account to declare illusory. Quine's article, however, does not consist wholly, though it does consist largely, in criticizing attempts at elucidation. He does try also to diagnose the causes of the belief in the distinction, and he offers some positive doctrine, acceptance of which he represents as incompatible with this belief. If there is any general prior presumption in favor of the existence of the distinction, it seems that Quine's radical rejection of it must rest quite heavily on this part of his article, since the force of any such presumption is not even impaired by philosophical failures to clarify a distinction so supported.

Is there such a presumption in favor of the distinction's existence? Prima facie, it must be admitted that there is. An appeal to philosophical tradition is perhaps unimpressive and is certainly unnecessary. But it is worth pointing out that Quine's objection is not simply to the words "analytic" and "synthetic," but to a distinction which they are supposed to express, and which at different times philosophers have supposed themselves to be expressing by means of such pairs of words or phrases as "necessary" and "contingent," "a priori" and "empirical," "truth of reason" and "truth of fact"; so Quine is certainly at odds with a philosophical tradition which is long and not wholly disreputable. But there is no need to appeal only to tradition; for there is also present practice. We can appeal, that is, to the fact that those

---

[3] Page 37.

IN DEFENSE OF A DOGMA

who use the terms "analytic" and "synthetic" do to a very considerable extent agree in the applications they make of them. They apply the term "analytic" to more or less the same cases, withhold it from more or less the same cases, and hesitate over more or less the same cases. This agreement extends not only to cases which they have been *taught* so to characterize, but to new cases. In short, "analytic" and "synthetic" have a more or less established philosophical *use*; and this seems to suggest that it is absurd, even senseless, to say that there is no such distinction. For, in general, if a pair of contrasting expressions are habitually and generally used in application to the same cases, *where these cases do not form a closed list*, this is a sufficient condition for saying that there are *kinds* of cases to which the expressions apply; and nothing more is needed for them to mark a distinction.

In view of the possibility of this kind of argument, one may begin to doubt whether Quine really holds the extreme thesis which his words encourage one to attribute to him. It is for this reason that we made the attribution tentative. For on at least one natural interpretation of this extreme thesis, when we say of something true that it is analytic and of another true thing that it is synthetic, it simply never is the case that we thereby mark a distinction between them. And this view seems terribly difficult to reconcile with the fact of an established philosophical usage (i.e., of general agreement in application in an open class). For this reason, Quine's thesis might be better represented not as the thesis that there is *no difference at all* marked by the use of these expressions, but as the thesis that the nature of, and reasons for, the difference or differences are totally misunderstood by those who use the expressions, that the stories they tell themselves *about* the difference are full of illusion.

We think Quine might be prepared to accept this amendment. If so, it could, in the following way, be made the basis of something like an answer to the argument which prompted it. Philosophers are notoriously subject to illusion, and to mistaken theories. Suppose there were a particular mistaken theory about language or knowledge, such that, seen in the light of this theory, some statements (or propositions or sentences) appeared to have a characteristic which no statements really have, or even, perhaps, which it does not make sense to suppose that any statement has, and which no one who was not consciously or subconsciously influenced by this theory would ascribe to any statement. And suppose that there were other statements which, seen in this light, did not appear to have this characteristic, and others again which presented an uncertain appearance. Then philosophers who were under the influence of this theory would tend to mark the supposed presence or absence of this characteristic by a pair of contrasting expressions, say "analytic" and "synthetic." Now in these circumstances it still could not be said that there was no distinction at all being marked by the use of these expressions, for there would be at least the distinction we have just described (the distinction, namely, between those statements which appeared to have and those which appeared to lack a certain characteristic), and there might well be other assignable differences too, which would account for the difference in appearance; but it certainly could be said that *the* difference these philosophers supposed themselves to be marking by the use of the expressions simply did not exist, and perhaps also (supposing the characteristic in question to be one which it was absurd to ascribe to any statement) that these expressions, as so used, were senseless or without meaning. We should only have to suppose that such a mistaken theory was very plausible and attractive, in order to reconcile the fact of an established philosophical usage for a pair of contrasting terms with the claim that *the* distinction which the terms purported to mark did not exist at all, though not with the claim that there simply did not exist a difference of any kind between the classes of statements so characterized. We think that the former claim would probably be sufficient for Quine's purposes. But to establish such a claim on the sort of grounds we have indicated evidently requires a great deal more argument than is involved in showing that certain explanations of a term do not measure up to certain requirements of adequacy in philosophical clarification—and not only more argument, but argument of a very different kind. For it would surely be too harsh to maintain that the *general* presumption is that philosophical distinctions embody the kind of illusion we have described. On the whole, it seems that philosophers are prone to

IN DEFENSE OF A DOGMA

make too few distinctions rather than too many. It is their assimilations, rather than their distinctions, which tend to be spurious.

So far we have argued as if the prior presumption in favor of the existence of the distinction which Quine questions rested solely on the fact of an agreed *philosophical* usage for the terms "analytic" and "synthetic." A presumption with only this basis could no doubt be countered by a strategy such as we have just outlined. But, in fact, if we are to accept Quine's account of the matter, the presumption in question is not only so based. For among the notions which belong to the analyticity-group is one which Quine calls "cognitive synonymy," and in terms of which he allows that the notion of analyticity could at any rate be formally explained. Unfortunately, he adds, the notion of cognitive synonymy is just as unclarified as that of analyticity. To say that two expressions x and y are cognitively synonymous seems to correspond, at any rate roughly, to what we should ordinarily express by saying that x and y have the same meaning or that x means the same as y. If Quine is to be consistent in his adherence to the extreme thesis, then it appears that he must maintain not only that the distinction we suppose ourselves to be marking by the use of the terms "analytic" and "synthetic" does not exist, but also that the distinction we suppose ourselves to be marking by the use of the expressions "means the same as," "does not mean the same as" does not exist either. At least, he must maintain this insofar as the notion of *meaning the same as*, in its application to predicate-expressions, is supposed to differ from and go beyond the notion of *being true of just the same objects as*. (This latter notion—which we might call that of "coextensionality"—he is prepared to allow to be intelligible, though, as he rightly says, it is not sufficient for the explanation of analyticity.) Now since he cannot claim this time that the pair of expressions in question (viz., "means the same," "does not mean the same") is the special property of philosophers, the strategy outlined above of countering the presumption in favor of their marking a genuine distinction is not available here (or is at least enormously less plausible). Yet the denial that the distinction (taken as different from the distinction between the coextensional and the non-

H. P. GRICE AND P. F. STRAWSON

coextensional) really exists, is extremely paradoxical. It involves saying, for example, that anyone who seriously remarks that "bachelor" means the same as "unmarried man" but that "creature with kidneys" does not mean the same as "creature with a heart"—supposing the last two expressions to be coextensional—*either* is not in fact drawing attention to any distinction at all between the relations between the members of each pair of expressions *or* is making a philosophical mistake about the nature of the distinction between them. In either case, what he says, taken as he intends it to be taken, is senseless or absurd. More generally, it involves saying that it is always senseless or absurd to make a statement of the form "Predicates *x* and *y* in fact apply to the same objects, but do not have the same meaning." But the paradox is more violent than this. For we frequently talk of the presence or absence of relations of synonymy between kinds of expressions—e.g., conjunctions, particles of many kinds, whole sentences—where there does not appear to be any obvious substitute for the ordinary notion of synonymy, in the way in which coextensionality is said to be a substitute for synonymy of predicates. Is all such talk meaningless? Is all talk of correct or incorrect *translation* of sentences of one language into sentences of another meaningless? It is hard to believe that it is. But if we do successfully make the effort to believe it, we have still harder renunciations before us. If talk of sentence-synonymy is meaningless, then it seems that talk of sentences having a meaning at all must be meaningless too. For if it made sense to talk of a sentence having a meaning, or meaning something, then presumably it would make sense to ask "What does it mean?" And if it made sense to ask "What does it mean?" of a sentence, then sentence-synonymy could be roughly defined as follows: Two sentences are synonymous if and only if any true answer to the question "What does it mean?" asked of one of them, is a true answer to the same question, asked of the other. We do not, of course, claim any clarifying power for this definition. We want only to point out that if we are to give up the notion of sentence-synonymy as senseless, we must give up the notion of sentence-significance (of a sentence having meaning) as senseless too. But then perhaps we might as well give up the notion of sense.—It seems clear that we

IN DEFENSE OF A DOGMA

have here a typical example of a philosopher's paradox. Instead of examining the actual use that we make of the notion of *meaning the same*, the philosopher measures it by some perhaps inappropriate standard (in this case some standard of clarifiability), and because it falls short of this standard, or seems to do so, denies its reality, declares it illusory.

We have argued so far that there is a strong presumption in favor of the existence of the distinction, or distinctions, which Quine challenges—a presumption resting both on philosophical and on ordinary usage—and that this presumption is not in the least shaken by the fact, if it is a fact, that the distinctions in question have not been, in some sense, adequately clarified. It is perhaps time to look at what Quine's notion of adequate clarification is.

The main theme of his article can be roughly summarized as follows. There is a certain circle or family of expressions, of which "analytic" is one, such that if any one member of the circle could be taken to be satisfactorily understood or explained, then other members of the circle could be verbally, and hence satisfactorily, explained in terms of it. Other members of the family are: "self-contradictory" (in a broad sense), "necessary," "synonymous," "semantical rule," and perhaps (but again in a broad sense) "definition." The list could be added to. Unfortunately each member of the family is in as great need of explanation as any other. We give some sample quotations: "The notion of self-contradictoriness (in the required broad sense of inconsistency) stands in exactly the same need of clarification as does the notion of analyticity itself."[4] Again, Quine speaks of "a notion of synonymy which is in no less need of clarification than analyticity itself."[5] Again, of the adverb "necessarily," as a candidate for use in the explanation of synonymy, he says, "Does the adverb *really make sense?* To suppose that it does is to suppose that we have already *made satisfactory sense* of 'analytic.'"[6] To make "satisfactory sense" of one of these expressions would seem to involve two things. (1) It would seem to involve providing an explanation which does not incorporate any expression belonging to the family-circle. (2) It would seem that the explanation

---

[4] Page 20.   [5] Page 23.   [6] Page 30, our italics.

H. P. GRICE AND P. F. STRAWSON

provided must -be of the same general character as those rejected explanations which do incorporate members of the family-circle (i.e., it must specify some feature common and peculiar to all cases to which, for example, the word "analytic" is to be applied; it must have the same general form as an explanation beginning, "a statement is analytic if and only if . . ."). It is true that Quine does not explicitly state the second requirement; but since he does not even consider the question whether any other kind of explanation would be relevant, it seems reasonable to attribute it to him. If we take these two conditions together, and generalize the result, it would seem that Quine requires of a satisfactory explanation of an expression that it should take the form of a pretty strict definition but should not make use of any member of a group of interdefinable terms to which the expression belongs. We may well begin to feel that a satisfactory explanation is hard to come by. The other element in Quine's position is one we have already commented on in general, before enquiring what (according to him) is to count as a satisfactory explanation. It is the step from "We have not made satisfactory sense (provided a satisfactory explanation) of *x*" to "*x* does not make sense."

It would seem fairly clearly unreasonable to insist *in general* that the availability of a satisfactory explanation in the sense sketched above is a necessary condition of an expression's making sense. It is perhaps dubious whether *any* such explanations can *ever* be given. (The hope that they can be is, or was, the hope of reductive analysis in general.) Even if such explanations can be given in some cases, it would be pretty generally agreed that there other cases in which they cannot. One might think, for example, of the group of expressions which includes "morally wrong," "blameworthy," "breach of moral rules," etc.; or of the group which includes the propositional connectives and the words "true" and "false," "statement," "fact," "denial," "assertion." Few people would want to say that the expressions belonging to either of these groups were senseless on the ground that they have not been formally defined (or even on the ground that it was impossible formally to define them) except in terms of members of the same group. It might, however, be said that while the

IN DEFENSE OF A DOGMA

unavailability of a satisfactory explanation in the special sense described was not a *generally* sufficient reason for declaring that a given expression was senseless, it was a sufficient reason in the case of the expressions of the analyticity group. But anyone who said this would have to advance a reason for discriminating in this way against the expressions of this group. The only plausible reason for being harder on these expressions than on others is a refinement on a consideration which we have already had before us. It starts from the point that "analytic" and "synthetic" themselves are technical philosophical expressions. To the rejoinder that other expressions of the family concerned, such as "means the same as" or "is inconsistent with," or "self-contradictory," are not at all technical expressions, but are common property, the reply would doubtless be that, to qualify for inclusion in the family circle, these expressions have to be used in specially adjusted and precise senses (or pseudo-senses) which they do not ordinarily possess. It is the fact, then, that all the terms belonging to the circle are *either* technical terms *or* ordinary terms used in specially adjusted senses, that might be held to justify us in being particularly suspicious of the claims of members of the circle to have any sense at all, and hence to justify us in requiring them to pass a test for significance which would admittedly be too stringent if generally applied. This point has some force, though we doubt if the special adjustments spoken of are in every case as considerable as it suggests. (This seems particularly doubtful in the case of the word "inconsistent"—a perfectly good member of the nontechnician's meta-logical vocabulary.) But though the point has some force, it does not have whatever force would be required to justify us in insisting that the expressions concerned should pass exactly that test for significance which is in question. The fact, if it is a fact, that the expressions cannot be explained in precisely the way which Quine seems to require, does not mean that they cannot be explained at all. There is no need to try to pass them off as expressing innate ideas. They can be and are explained, though in other and less formal ways than that which Quine considers. (And the fact that they are so explained fits with the facts, first, that there is a generally agreed philosophical use for them, and second, that this use is technical or specially adjusted.) To illustrate the point briefly for one member of the analyticity family. Let us suppose we are trying to explain to someone the notion of *logical impossibility* (a member of the family which Quine presumably regards as no clearer than any of the others) and we decide to do it by bringing out the contrast between logical and natural (or causal) impossibility. We might take as our examples the logical impossibility of a child of three's being an adult, and the natural impossibility of a child of three's understanding Russell's Theory of Types. We might instruct our pupil to imagine two conversations one of which begins by someone (X) making the claim:

(1) "My neighbor's three-year-old child understands Russell's Theory of Types,"

and the other of which begins by someone (Y) making the claim:

(1') "My neighbor's three-year-old child is an adult."

It would not be inappropriate to reply to X, taking the remark as a hyperbole:

(2) "You mean the child is a particularly bright lad."

If X were to say:

(3) "No, I mean what I say—he really does understand it,"

one might be inclined to reply:

(4) "I don't believe you—the thing's impossible."

But if the child were then produced, and did (as one knows he would not) expound the theory correctly, answer questions on it, criticize it, and so on, one would in the end be forced to acknowledge that the claim was literally true and that the child was a prodigy. Now consider one's reaction to Y's claim. To begin with, it might be somewhat similar to the previous case. One might say:

(2') "You mean he's uncommonly sensible or very advanced for his age."

If Y replies:

(3') "No, I mean what I say,"

we might reply:

(4') "Perhaps you mean that he won't grow any more, or that he's a sort of freak, that he's already fully developed."

Y replies:

(5') "No, he's not a freak, he's just an adult."

IN DEFENSE OF A DOGMA

At this stage—or possibly if we are patient, a little later—we shall
be inclined to say that we just don't understand what Y is saying,
and to suspect that he just does not know the meaning of some
of the words he is using. For unless he is prepared to admit that
he is using words in a figurative or unusual sense, we shall say,
not that we don't believe him, but that his words have *no* sense.
And whatever kind of creature is ultimately produced for our
inspection, it will not lead us to say that what Y said was literally
true, but at most to say that we now see what he meant. As a
summary of the difference between the two imaginary conversations, we might say that in both cases we would tend to begin by
supposing that the other speaker was using words in a figurative
or unusual or restricted way; but in the face of his repeated claim
to be speaking literally, it would be appropriate in the first case
to say that we did not believe him and in the second case to say
that we did not understand him. If, like Pascal, we thought it
prudent to prepare against very long chances, we should in the
first case know what to prepare for; in the second, we should have
no idea.

We give this as an example of just one type of informal explanation which we might have recourse to in the case of one notion
of the analyticity group. (We do not wish to suggest it is the only
type.) Further examples, with different though connected types
of treatment, might be necessary to teach our pupil the use of the
notion of logical impossibility in its application to more complicated cases—if indeed he did not pick it up from the one case.
Now of course this type of explanation does not yield a formal
statement of necessary and sufficient conditions for the application
of the notion concerned. So it does not fulfill one of the conditions
which Quine seems to require of a satisfactory explanation. On
the other hand, it does appear to fulfill the other. It breaks out of
the family circle. The distinction in which we ultimately come to
rest is that between not believing something and not understanding something; or between incredulity yielding to conviction,
and incomprehension yielding to comprehension. It would be rash
to maintain **that** *this* distinction does not need clarification; but
it would be absurd to maintain that it does not exist. In the face
of the availability of this informal type of explanation for the

H. P. GRICE AND P. F. STRAWSON

notions of the analyticity group, the fact that they have not received another type of explanation (which it is dubious whether *any* expressions *ever* receive) seems a wholly inadequate ground for the conclusion that the notions are pseudo-notions, that the expressions which purport to express them have no sense. To say this is not to deny that it would be philosophically desirable, and a proper object of philosophical endeavor, to find a more illuminating general characterization of the notions of this group than any that has been so far given. But the question of how, if at all, this can be done is quite irrelevant to the question of whether or not the expressions which belong to the circle have an intelligible use and mark genuine distinctions.

So far we have tried to show that sections 1 to 4 of Quine's article—the burden of which is that the notions of the analyticity group have not been satisfactorily explained—do not establish the extreme thesis for which he appears to be arguing. It remains to be seen whether sections 5 and 6, in which diagnosis and positive theory are offered, are any more successful. But before we turn to them, there are two further points worth making which arise out of the first two sections.

(1) One concerns what Quine says about *definition* and *synonymy*. He remarks that definition does not, as some have supposed, "hold the key to synonymy and analyticity," since "definition—except in the extreme case of the explicitly conventional introduction of new notations—hinges on prior relations of synonymy."[7] But now consider what he says of these extreme cases. He says: "Here the definiendum becomes synonymous with the definiens simply because it has been expressly created for the purpose of being synonymous with the definiens. Here we have a really transparent case of synonymy created by definition; would that all species of synonymy were as intelligible." Now if we are to take these words of Quine seriously, then his position *as a whole* is incoherent. It is like the position of a man to whom we are trying to explain, say, the idea of one thing fitting into another thing, or two things fitting together, and who says: "I can understand what it means to say that one thing fits into another, or that two things fit together, in the case where one was specially made

---

[7] Page 27.

IN DEFENSE OF A DOGMA

to fit the other; but I cannot understand what it means to say this in any other case." Perhaps we should not take Quine's words here too seriously. But if not, then we have the right to ask him exactly what state of affairs he thinks *is* brought about by explicit definition, what relation between expressions *is* established by this procedure, and why he thinks it unintelligible to suggest that the same (or a closely analogous) state of affairs, or relation, should exist in the absence of this procedure. For our part, we should be inclined to take Quine's words (or some of them) seriously, and reverse his conclusions; and maintain that the notion of synonymy by explicit convention would be unintelligible if the notion of synonymy by usage were not presupposed. There cannot be law where there is no custom, or rules where there are not practices (though perhaps we can understand better what a practice is by looking at a rule).

(2) The second point arises out of a paragraph on page 32 of Quine's book. We quote:

I do not know whether the statement "Everything green is extended" is analytic. Now does my indecision over this example really betray an incomplete understanding, an incomplete grasp, of the "meanings" of "green" and "extended"? I think not. The trouble is not with "green" or "extended," but with "analytic."

If, as Quine says, the trouble is with "analytic," then the trouble should doubtless disappear when "analytic" is removed. So let us remove it, and replace it with a word which Quine himself has contrasted favorably with "analytic" in respect of perspicuity— the word "true." Does the indecision at once disappear? We think not. The indecision over "analytic" (and equally, in this case, the indecision over "true") arises, of course, from a further indecision: viz., that which we feel when confronted with such questions as "Should we count a *point* of green light as *extended* or not?" As is frequent enough in such cases, the hesitation arises from the fact that the boundaries of application of words are not determined by usage in all possible directions. But the example Quine has chosen is particularly unfortunate for his thesis, in that it is only too evident that our hesitations are not *here* attributable to obscurities in "analytic." It would be possible to choose other examples in which we should hesitate between "analytic" and "synthetic" and have few qualms about "true." But no more in these cases than in the sample case does the hesitation necessarily imply any obscurity in the notion of analyticity; since the hesitation would be sufficiently accounted for by the same or a similar kind of indeterminacy in the relations between the words occurring within the statement about which the question, whether it is analytic or synthetic, is raised.

Let us now consider briefly Quine's positive theory of the relations between the statements we accept as true or reject as false on the one hand and the "experiences" in the light of which we do this accepting and rejecting on the other. This theory is boldly sketched rather than precisely stated.[8] We shall merely extract from it two assertions, one of which Quine clearly takes to be incompatible with acceptance of the distinction between analytic and synthetic statements, and the other of which he regards as barring one way to an explanation of that distinction. We shall seek to show that the first assertion is not incompatible with acceptance of the distinction, but is, on the contrary, most intelligibly interpreted in a way quite consistent with it, and that the second assertion leaves the way open to just the kind of explanation which Quine thinks it precludes. The two assertions are the following:

(1) It is an illusion to suppose that there is any class of accepted statements the members of which are in principle "immune from revision" in the light of experience, i.e., any that we accept as true and must continue to accept as true whatever happens.

(2) It is an illusion to suppose that an individual statement, taken in isolation from its fellows, can admit of confirmation or disconfirmation at all. There is no particular statement such that a particular experience or set of experiences decides once for all whether that statement is true or false, independently of our attitudes to all other statements.

The apparent connection between these two doctrines may be summed up as follows. Whatever our experience may be, it is in principle possible to hold on to, or reject, any particular statement we like, so long as we are prepared to make extensive enough

---

[8] Cf. pages 37-46.

IN DEFENSE OF A DOGMA

revisions elsewhere in our system of beliefs. In practice our choices are governed largely by considerations of convenience: we wish our system to be as simple as possible, but we also wish disturbances to it, as it exists, to be as small as possible.

The apparent relevance of these doctrines to the analytic-synthetic distinction is obvious in the first case, less so in the second.

(1) Since it is an illusion to suppose that the characteristic of immunity in principle from revision, come what may, belongs, or could belong, to any statement, it is an illusion to suppose that there is a distinction to be drawn between statements which possess this characteristic and statements which lack it. Yet, Quine suggests, this is precisely the distinction which those who use the terms "analytic" and "synthetic" suppose themselves to be drawing. Quine's view would perhaps also be (though he does not explicitly say this in the article under consideration) that those who believe in the distinction are inclined at least sometimes to mistake the characteristic of strongly resisting revision (which belongs to beliefs very centrally situated in the system) for the mythical characteristic of total immunity from revision.

(2) The connection between the second doctrine and the analytic-synthetic distinction runs, according to Quine, through the verification theory of meaning. He says: "If the verification theory can be accepted as an adequate account of statement synonymy, the notion of analyticity is saved after all."[9] For, in the first place, two statements might be said to be synonymous if and only if any experiences which contribute to, or detract from, the confirmation of one contribute to, or detract from, the confirmation of the other, to the same degree; and, in the second place, synonymy could be used to explain analyticity. But, Quine seems to argue, acceptance of any such account of synonymy can only rest on the mistaken belief that individual statements, taken in isolation from their fellows, can admit of confirmation or disconfirmation at all. As soon as we give up the idea of a set of experiential truth-conditions for each statement taken separately, we must give up the idea of explaining synonymy in terms of identity of such sets.

---

[9] Page 38.

Now to show that the relations between these doctrines and the analytic-synthetic distinction are not as Quine supposes. Let us take the second doctrine first. It is easy to see that acceptance of the second doctrine would not compel one to abandon, but only to revise, the suggested explanation of synonymy. Quine does not deny that individual statements are regarded as confirmed or disconfirmed, are in fact rejected or accepted, in the light of experience. He denies only that these relations between single statements and experience hold independently of our attitudes to *other* statements. He means that experience can confirm or disconfirm an individual statement, only given certain assumptions about the truth or falsity of other statements. When we are faced with a "recalcitrant experience," he says, we always have a choice of what statements to amend. What we have to renounce is determined by what we are anxious to keep. This view, however, requires only a slight modification of the definition of statement-synonymy in terms of confirmation and disconfirmation. All we have to say now is that two statements are synonymous if and only if any experiences which, *on certain assumptions about the truth-values of other statements*, confirm or disconfirm one of the pair, also, *on the same assumptions*, confirm or disconfirm the other to the same degree. More generally, Quine wishes to substitute for what he conceives to be an oversimple picture of the confirmation-relations between particular statements and particular experiences, the idea of a looser relation which he calls "germaneness" (p. 43). But however loosely "germaneness" is to be understood, it would apparently continue to make sense to speak of two statements as standing in the same germaneness-relation to the same particular experiences. So Quine's views are not only consistent with, but even suggest, an amended account of statement-synonymy along these lines. We are not, of course, concerned to defend such an account, or even to state it with any precision. We are only concerned to show that acceptance of Quine's doctrine of empirical confirmation does not, as he says it does, entail giving up the attempt to define statement-synonymy in terms of confirmation.

Now for the doctrine that there is no statement which is in principle immune from revision, no statement which might not

IN DEFENSE OF A DOGMA

be given up in the face of experience. Acceptance of this doctrine is quite consistent with adherence to the distinction between analytic and synthetic statements. Only, the adherent of *this* distinction must also insist on another; on the distinction between that kind of giving up which consists in merely admitting falsity, and that kind of giving up which involves changing or dropping a concept or set of concepts. Any form of words at one time held to express something true may, no doubt, at another time, come to be held to express something false. But it is not only philosophers who would distinguish between the case where this happens as the result of a change of opinion solely as to matters of fact, and the case where this happens at least partly as a result of a shift in the sense of the words. Where such a shift in the sense of the words is a necessary condition of the change in truth-value, then the adherent of the distinction will say that the form of words in question changes from expressing an analytic statement to express-ing a synthetic statement. We are not now concerned, or called upon, to elaborate an adequate theory of conceptual revision, any more than we were called upon, just now, to elaborate an adequate theory of synonymy. If we can make sense of the idea that the same form of words, taken in one way (or bearing one sense), may express something true, and taken in another way (or bearing another sense), may express something false, then we can make sense of the idea of conceptual revision. And if we can make sense of this idea, then we can perfectly well preserve the distinction between the analytic and the synthetic, while conced-ing to Quine the revisability-in-principle of everything we say. As for the idea that the same form of words, taken in different ways, may bear different senses and perhaps be used to say things with different truth-values, the onus of showing that this is somehow a mistaken or confused idea rests squarely on Quine. The point of substance (or one of them) that Quine is making, by this emphasis on revisability, is that there is no absolute necessity about the adoption or use of any conceptual scheme whatever, or, more narrowly and in terms that he would reject, that there is no analytic proposition such that we *must* have lin-guistic forms bearing just the sense required to express that pro-position. But it is one thing to admit this, and quite another thing

157

IN DEFENSE OF A DOGMA

to say that there are no necessities within any conceptual scheme we adopt or use, or, more narrowly again, that there are no linguistic forms which do express analytic propositions.

The adherent of the analytic-synthetic distinction may go further and admit that there may be cases (particularly perhaps in the field of science) where it would be pointless to press the question whether a change in the attributed truth-value of a statement represented a conceptual revision or not, and correspondingly pointless to press the analytic-synthetic distinction. We cannot quote such cases, but this inability may well be the result of ignorance of the sciences. In any case, the existence, if they do exist, of statements about which it is pointless to press the question whether they are analytic or synthetic, does not entail the nonexistence of statements which are clearly classifiable in one or other of these ways and of statements our hesitation over which has different sources, such as the possibility of alternative interpretations of the linguistic forms in which they are express ed

This concludes our examination of Quine's article. It will be evident that our purpose has been wholly negative. We have aimed to show merely that Quine's case against the existence of the analytic-synthetic distinction is not made out. His article has two parts. In one of them, the notions of the analyticity group are criticized on the ground that they have not been adequately explained. In the other, a positive theory of truth is outlined, purporting to be incompatible with views to which believers in the analytic-synthetic distinction either must be, or are likely to be, committed. In fact, we have contended, no single point is established which those who accept the notions of the analyticity group would feel any strain in accommodating in their own system of beliefs. This is not to deny that many of the points raised are of the first importance in connection with the problem of giving a satisfactory general account of analyticity and related concepts. We are here only criticizing the contention that these points justify the rejection, as illusory, of the analytic-synthetic distinction and the notions which belong to the same family.

H. P. GRICE AND P. F. STRAWSON

Oxford University

PART
VI

TRUTH

INTRODUCTION

The problem of truth has many aspects, to which varying answers have been given. As Alan R. White has pointed out,[1] the questions 'What is truth?' and 'What is the truth?' are distinct. The second asks what things are true, whereas the first asks what it means to say that such things are true. The second is significant only with regard to particular subject matter, such as one of the sciences; the first is independent of any application to a specific field or discipline. There is an additional problem as to how one can discover truth(s) in a given area; this problem is linked to only the second of the above two questions and is primarily of concern to scientists, historians, etc. The first problem is the one which is crucial to philosophy. What is truth? Or, as some have put it, what is the nature of truth?[2]

Throughout the history of philosophy three traditional theories of truth have been distinguished: the correspondence theory, which had its origin in Aristotle; the coherence theory, which seems to be implicitly held by the seventeenth-century Rationalists and nineteenth-century Idealists; and the pragmatic theory, which was put forth by American philosophers such as C. S. Peirce and William James. In addition to these, we find in the works of contemporary philosophers several other theories which have been advocated and which are related to one or the other of the traditional theories, or which stem from a reaction to one or all of the latter. These are usually referred to as the logical superfluity theory, the semantic theory, and the nondescriptive theory.

1. The Traditional Theories

In his *Metaphysics*[3] Aristotle writes: "To say of what is that it is not, or of what is not that it is, is false, while to say of what is that it is,

---

[1] Alan R. White, *Truth* (Garden City, N.Y.: Doubleday, 1970), ix.
[2] *Ibid.*
[3] T, 7, 27.

or of what is not that it is not, is true." This passage has been interpreted by many as expressing or being a precursor of the correspondence theory of truth, which has been summed up as follows: the truth of a sentence (statement, proposition) consists in its correspondence to (or agreement with) reality (or a fact). There have been many controversies as to whether sentences, statements, propositions, or something else can properly be said to be true, and regarding the correct interpretation of the crucial terms 'correspondence' and 'fact.' We shall not attempt to deal with all these problems here. We refer the reader to some of the works listed in the selected readings, and to an extended discussion by G. E. Moore in *Some Main Problems of Philosophy*.[4]

The coherence theory of truth is commonly attributed to such philosophers as Spinoza, Hegel, and Bradley. A variant of it can be found in the writings of twentieth-century logical empiricists, such as Neurath and Hempel. According to the coherence theory, the truth of a proposition (judgment, belief) consists in its cohering with other propositions (judgments, etc.). The metaphysical philosophers who supported this theory seem to have held that nothing can be properly called true unless it fits into a single and totally comprehensive account of the universe, which itself is a rational and coherent system. For logical empiricists, the system with which all true statements must cohere is that which has been accepted by the scientists of a given contemporary culture. Again, many difficulties and problems arise which have been discussed by Bertrand Russell, Alan R. White, and others. (See selected readings.)

The pragmatic theory of truth was espoused in various forms by C. S. Peirce, William James, John Dewey, and F. C. S. Schiller. Using the term 'idea' to refer to any belief or statement, James accepts the view that truth consists in the agreement of an idea with reality. However, he finds this formulation to be misleading or uninformative. He advocates the thesis that the truth of an idea means its power to "work." Hence we may formulate the pragmatic theory thus: the truth of an idea (belief, etc.) consists in its working, or leading to satisfactory consequences, or being useful. "You can say of [any truth] then either that 'it is useful because it is true' or that 'it is true because it is use-

---

[4] G. E. Moore, *Some Main Problems of Philosophy* (London: Routledge and Kegan Paul, 1953), Chs. 3, 14-17.

ful.' "[5] For a critical appraisal of this position, we refer the reader to the selected readings and especially to G. E. Moore's essay, "Professor James' 'Pragmatism.' "[6]

2. Recent Theories

Correspondence and correspondence-like theories

A theory of truth along more traditional lines is a correspondence theory when it more or less conforms to the formula: if x corresponds to y, then x is true. Schematically, $Cxy \supset Tx$. For convenience, we will refer to this formula or one like it as simply CF. As CF now stands, it states that Cxy is a sufficient condition of x being true. For greater latitude, a correspondence theory need not conform to a formula in which Cxy is a sufficient condition; all that is needed is conformity to a formula in which Cxy is *some* condition. Thus to speak of CF is to speak of a formula in which Cxy is some condition of Tx. Furthermore, as CF now stands, there is no assumed interpretation of its variables; these are obtained *ex hypothesi*. Again, the correspondence relation occurs only nominally in CF; it remains unanalyzed or undefined. When we speak of a correspondence relation, often we only signify its nominal occurrence in Cxy or in CF as a whole; the analysis or definition is also obtained, for the most part, *ex hypothesi*. That relation is a function of the pair (or more) of things that one, *ex hypothesi*, interprets x and y with. However a philosopher might analyze or define the correspondence relation (or the expression 'corresponds to'), it is a function of the pair of things which are said to correspond.

The more recent correspondence or correspondence-like theories of truth (not to exclude necessarily those less recent) are such theories which ostensibly interpret x and y semantically. X and y are said to be interpreted semantically in the broadest sense when the domains of x and y are or seem to be elements of language and elements of the world respectively,[7] such that (it is hoped) $x \neq y$. Most correspondence theories are semantic in this general sense.

[5] William James, *Pragmatism* (New York, 1907), Ch. VI.

[6] G. E. Moore, "Professor James' 'Pragmatism,' " in *Philosophical Studies* (London: Routledge and Kegan Paul, 1922).

[7] This characterization holds good in different ways; here, under the relation of correspondence. For Tarski, who propounds no true correspondence relation in his theory, it holds good, among other relations, under the relation of satisfaction. See A. Tarski, "The Semantic Conception of Truth," in *Philosophy and Phenomenological Research*, IV (1944), 345.

Looking over the various theories of truth which may be subsumable under the head of correspondence, we find those that are (a) loosely correspondence and loosely semantic, (b) truly correspondence and loosely semantic, (c) truly correspondence and truly semantic, and (d) loosely correspondence and truly semantic. Perhaps Wittgenstein's theory, propounded in his *Tractatus*,[8] fits situation (a). Austin's revised correspondence theory fits (c).[9] And perhaps Tarski's semantic theory fits (d).[10]

A theory of truth that fits (a-c) more rather than less conforms to CF. Tarski's theory that fits (d) more rather than less does not conform to CF, if indeed it conforms at all. The set (a-c) are generally and for the most part correctly thought of as fact-linked or fact-committed theories of truth. We may simply refer to them as the fact set. Tarski's theory is to be distinguished from them in that his theory is not fact-committed, at least not in any obvious way. It is associated in (d) with the preceding three because of Davidson's construction on Tarski's theory. Tarski's theory deserves to be called a correspondence theory, for various reasons which are sustained on his analysis of "facts" and Tarski's semantic notion of "satisfaction." The reader is advised to consult Davidson on this point. Strawson's performative theory, later to be reviewed, fits no situation (a-d).

To say that a theory is a member of the fact set is to say simply that y is invariably interpreted as a domain for facts. "Facts" are reckoned in this interpretation to be genuine elements of the world, such that $x \neq y$. Since the correspondence relation is a function of the interpretation of x and y, if y is a fact, then if the relation is ostensibly semantic, Cxy is ostensibly a semantic relation between x (some language sequence) and "facts" — such as between statements and "facts." A correspondence theory need not be exclusively committed to "facts" for y, but may only include "facts" among other things as entries for y, such as happens in Austin's theory.

With such preliminaries disposed of, we may now approach and

[8] Ludwig Wittgenstein, *Tractatus Logico-Philosophicus* (London: Routledge and Kegan Paul, 1961).

[9] J. Austin, "Truth," in *Philosophical Papers* (London: Oxford University Press, 1961).

[10] The basis for this classification derives from Davidson's argument and is as valid a classification as Davidson's argument is plausible. See D. Davidson, "True to the Facts," in *Journal of Philosophy*, LXVI (1969), 758 — an article also included in this volume.

consider the sorts of difficulties and problems which many philosophers believe correspondence theories are prone to.

Lines of criticism of some correspondence theories

We shall assume here that the correspondence theories in question belong to the fact set, as is most often assumed. Once we have surveyed the standard lines of criticism taken to the set over-all, we will move on to Austin's revised theory of correspondence, seeing how his revised theory might circumvent the standard lines of criticism.

There are two interwoven lines of criticism. First, it is charged, any formula of the sort CF in which y is interpreted as a "fact" can be reduced to one that states something trivial or truistic (tautologous). Therefore Cxy, for any analysis of the correspondence relation, is no real, working condition of truth. Second, for any analysis of correspondence, if y is a "fact," then either Cxy makes no sense as a semantic relation, or it makes no sense as any significant relation (save, vacuously, self-identity).

The grounds for the first line of criticism are as follows. In order to identify just which "fact" is to be entered into y, that particular "fact" can only be obtained on the assumption that x is already true (for reasons other than x "corresponds to a fact"). The "fact" and the statement of its issuance are held to be indistinguishable. Hence a "fact" is a pseudo-element of the world and is a quasi-linguistic entity.[11] X $\neq$ y does not stand up, and its not standing up has been called "the identity crisis" of correspondence theories. There can be no formula for which y is interpreted as a "fact" such that Cxy (for any analysis of the correspondence relation) is anything other than a vacuous condition of x being true.

This charge relates to a line of criticism that goes in a different direction: "correspondence" makes no sense if y is a "fact," either as a semantic relation or as any other significant relation. Let us pursue this second line further, using Wittgenstein's theory as an example.

In his account of truth in the *Tractatus* Wittgenstein declares, "Propositions are true or false only by being pictures of reality."[12] This and his remarks at 2.11 permit us to suppose his theory is a member

[11] See P. F. Strawson, "Truth," in *Proceedings of the Aristotelian Society*, suppl. vol. XXIV (1950), 133-45.
[12] Wittgenstein, *Tractatus*, 69 and elsewhere.

of the fact set. By saying that his theory fits (a), we are assuming that 'picture of' is one possible way of defining 'corresponds to.' Assuming that to be the case, then *being a picture of* is a function of the sort of things propositions and facts are. We may ask whether it makes sense to say that a proposition is a "picture of a fact." This is a disputed case, as against standard cases — such as, for example, photographs being pictures of (photographs of) subjects or landscapes. If facts seem queer as subjects, or propositions as photographs, then "pictures of facts" seem queer as pictures. If, as some have said, a proposition is what a sentence or statement means, then whatever is meant by 'picture of' must be such that propositions (meanings) fill the bill. What is more, whatever sort of thing x is, it will be the sort of thing that it makes sense to call true. The disputed case in this regard is part of a wider controversy which need not concern us here.[13]

To summarize, there are two lines of criticism that can be taken against correspondence theories: the identity crisis and the disputed case.

Austin's revised correspondence theory of truth

According to Austin, "A statement is said to be true when the historic state of affairs to which it is correlated by the demonstrative conventions (the one to which it 'refers') is of a type with which the sentence used in making it is correlated by the descriptive conventions."[14] In unpacking this rather compendious formula, we find CF in a more elaborate form. The correspondence relation is analyzed as two semantic relations: C^1x_1y, putatively, a demonstrative or referring relation; and C^2x_2z, putatively, a descriptive relation. CF in this revision states schematically: $(C^1x_1y \cdot C^2x_2z) \supset Tx_1$.[15] With this formula and Aus-

---

[13] A larger controversy is entered here which might affect any theory of truth. Are *sentences* true (Tarski)? Are *statements* true (Austin)? Neither? What? See White, *Truth*, Ch. 1. The answer in part awaits analysis of the linguistic unit in question, as for instance Tarski defining a sentence as "a sentential function which contains no free variables." See Tarski, "The Semantic Conception of Truth," *Philosophy and Phenomenological Research*, IV (1944), 353, and in this volume.

[14] Austin, "Truth," 90.

[15] Actually this is not the complete formula. Following out the quoted passage faithfully, we should obtain $[(C^1x_1y \cdot C^2x_2z) \equiv Kyz] \supset Tx_1$, where 'Kyz' = 'x is of the type y.' Or with Austin's full analysis, 'Kyz' = 'x is sufficiently like those standard states of affairs, y.' 'My cat is asleep' correlates demonstratively to some particular, actual state of affairs, and it correlates descriptively to something like (generally or standardly) *cats being asleep*. But given the right side of the biconditional, for given values of y and z, it does not follow that the values for x are

tin's adjacent remarks, we may construct the following table of interpretations:

> x: a sequence of words (utterance, locution)
>> x_1: a sequence of words as a *statement*
>> x_2: the same sequence as a *sentence*
>
> y: 1) a historical situation, state of affairs, fact
>>> ('historical' = 'temporally coordinated')
>> 2) a historical event
>> 3) a historical thing
>
> z: 1) a type of situation, state of affairs (paradigm of meaning?)
>> 2) a type of event
>> 3) a type of thing.

With these interpretations, let us examine the relations they are said to enter into. Apart from anything else, we should acknowledge that C^1x_1y and C^2x_2z are metastatements, putatively expressing semantic rules or conditions concerning certain sequences of words. The first has roughly to do with the relation-through-convention of reference. The second has roughly to do with the relation-through-convention of description. C^1x_1y seems to say that as x (a statement) is used demonstratively (referringly), there is a historical situation, event, or thing it is to correlate to. C^2x_2z seems to say that as x (a sentence) is used descriptively, there is a type of situation, event, or thing it is to correlate to.

Still, the expressions 'correlate demonstratively to' and 'correlate descriptively to' are difficult to understand because of what Austin provides as interpretations of x, y, and z. Largely for the same reason, it is not altogether plain just what sort of conditions C^1x_1y and C^2x_2z state as conditions of Tx_1.

Pursuing the matter further, what is difficult about C^1x_1y, just to single out one of the correspondence relations, is that it seems to permit something as complex as x itself to be a bona fide element of the world, something that even may be "referred to." So if x is 'My cat is napping,' then the historical situation or state of affairs that Austin allows is the complex element in the world, *a cat napping*. It would seem outwardly

---

derivable, since the language for x is, as Austin says, arbitrary. For illumination and criticism of this point, see P. F. Strawson's "Truth: A Reconsideration of Austin's Views," in *Philosophical Quarterly*, XV (1965), 202. The working part of the formula goes into C^1x_1y and C^2x_2z, and so we have omitted Kyz.

that what Austin means by 'historical situation' or 'state of affairs' is very much like "fact" in the sense that "fact" has been usually understood. Warnock argues that Austin's "fact" — just as much as any object, only a more abstract kind of object — is entitled to a place in the world. The reader is advised to consult Warnock's article for clarification of that point.[16]

But if Austin's is a fact set theory, even in part, of the sort vulnerable to the lines of criticism that any correspondence theory is vulnerable to, his formula continues to have trouble making a smooth go of it. First, with "facts," he faces the "identity crisis." Second, if "demonstrative correlation" is literally a referring relation, then, since it seems that the whole of x "refers," his referring becomes something of a disputed case against standard cases of referring. We are inclined to think that only certain words in x, e.g., 'my cat,' have the function of referring — not the entire sequence of words as C^1x_1y suggests.

Something one might do to get Austin out of that imbroglio is intimated by Strawson.[17] We may account for C^1x_1y in this way. When 'My cat is napping' is uttered by me at a certain time, that utterance by virtue of being mine at the time I uttered it coordinates with the "relevant fact." This points to a hypothesis. If one utters 'My cat is napping' at a certain time, there generally exists at that time a fact (now adding C^2x_2z) of the sort which 'My cat is napping' (as might be uttered by anyone under similar circumstances at any time) standardly describes. It does not seem certain that Austin would approve of such a construction on his views. In any case, this account only reflects again the difficulties Austin's theory has without it. How is one to explain how a certain fact is relevant and the alleged coordination of utterances with it? Perhaps it is as Warnock urges: one simply looks.[18]

This account maintains the same drawback that is present in the formula, in that it asserts, all the same, the existence of some fact in the condition of x being true. This strikes philosophers, notably Strawson, as just another way of saying that x is true.[19] Hence we recur to the

[16] See G. J. Warnock, "Truth and Correspondence," in *Knowledge and Experience*, ed. C. D. Rollins (Pittsburgh: University of Pittsburgh Press, 1963). See also Warnock's "A Problem about Truth," in *Truth*, ed. G. Pitcher (Englewood Cliffs, N.J.: Prentice-Hall, 1964).

[17] Intimated, but not expressly suggested. See Strawson's "Truth: A Reconsideration of Austin's Views."

[18] Warnock, "Truth and Correspondence."

[19] Strawson, "Truth," in Pitcher, ed., *Truth*, 44-50. For rebuttal, see Austin's "Unfair to Facts," in *Philosophical Papers*.

inevitable triviality. Once we have the relevant fact, it appears that the demonstrative correlation simply turns idly in the formula.

There are still other measures open to us. One of these follows Warnock's approach. We leave this for the reader to investigate. Another measure is again suggested by Strawson, but the measure is so severe as to pretty much debilitate Austin's formula.

Strawson contends that y, if it is anything, should be an object or event.[20] And if C^1x_1y means anything, it means that certain words of x have the job of referring to the sorts of things standardly referred to.[21] In 'My cat is napping,' 'my cat' refers to a certain cat. C^2x_1z, on the other hand, merely contains the descriptive part, 'napping.' Both together say either that a certain object referred to fits the description accorded to it or that certain words must refer and certain others must describe. There is an important difference between these two alternatives, which, by the way, substantially alter the formula. First, to its credit, with objects we do not get into the identity crisis, nor do we run into any disputed case of reference. But then, C^1x_1y and C^2x_2z may or may not be the sufficient condition of x being true. As necessary conditions only, the formula would merely maintain that in order for x to be true, x refers and describes what it refers to — the last of the alternatives above. In this event, the formula is false for all x's if there are statements which do not refer, e.g., 'All swine are contemptible.'[22] If not false, then the formula is impermissively restricted in scope. If the two relations are enrolled as sufficient conditions, then, with the first alternative, to say that a certain object fits the description applied to it is to tacitly claim success. And that, it seems, is virtually to assert x is true. We acquire the unwanted tautology once again.

Tarski's semantic theory

Tarski's theory of truth[23] advances in severity from a germ formula (T) to its fully augmented form (T') as follows:

   (T) X is true if and only if p;
   (T') X is true in L if and only if p.

[20] Strawson, "Truth," in Pitcher, ed., *Truth*.

[21] This means in 'My cat is napping,' 'napping' is excluded from the world of referable things. But still it is not clear, to take Warnock's side, whether gerundive substantives do not refer, e.g., 'My cat's napping was not surprising then.'

[22] For how this may be accommodated in Austin's theory, see Warnock's "Truth and Correspondence."

[23] Tarski, "The Semantic Conception of Truth."

(T) is Tarski's "criterion of material adequacy," which vis-à-vis (T')
may be viewed informally simply as a paradigm. (T') takes (T) to its
formal terminus. The wider philosophical consequences of (T') are
far more radical than the consequences of (T).

In (T), and also in (T'), Tarski like Austin takes 'true' to be a
metalinguistic predicate assignable to sentences of an object language.
Since 'true' is predicated of sentences as objects, the sentences that are
true are only mentioned by name or some other way. 'X' is replaced
by a name or orthographical description of a certain sentence; 'p' is
replaced by the sentence whose name appears in 'X.' The entry for
'p' is a sentence of the object language, and is used in (T). Otherwise
the name of the sentence, and the expressions 'true' and 'if and only if,'
are being used in the metalanguage. As an instance of (T), we may
obtain: 'Snow is white' is true if and only if snow is white. Since 'if
and only if' marks for logical equivalence, this instance (or, *mutatis
mutandis,* any other instance of [T]) states that if 'Snow is white' is
assertable in the object language, then ' 'Snow is white' is true' is
assertable in the metalanguage and vice versa. Nothing more or less
is said in (T). The grounds for asserting some sentence of 'p,' which
would be grounds logically independent of what is correspondingly
assertable in the metalanguage, are grounds independent of the paradigm. Assuming that the paradigm, as Tarski claims, explicates in part
the meaning of 'true,' then those independent grounds are also independent of the meaning of 'true.' This rules out, importantly, any
condition of factuality (and also verificational criteria) as relevant to
the matter of a sentence being true. But it also rules out as relevant
any linguistic conditions of use regarding the sentences of the everyday
sort in the object language. Criteria of reference, for example, do not
on (T) attach to the matter of some sentence being true.[24]

(T') is much more in keeping with Tarski's primary theoretic intentions. It follows out his program of formalized semantics and meets
a central objective: to formulate a definition of truth such that paradoxes like the liar paradox cannot be generated. Two key provisions
must be complied with. First, the metalanguage must be richer
and of a higher logical type than the object language, and it is to be
exactly specified and formalized. Through a recursive type of definition,

---

[24] Donald Davidson sketches out a way in which such conditions of use for
ordinary sentences may be fitted ino Tarski's theory. See Davidson's "True to the
Facts," 756-57.

whether any x is a sentence in the object language, L, can be deter-mined in a finite number of steps.[25] Since L will include sentences of any logical complexity desired, (T′) has a scope that is apparently unavailable to correspondence theories. But (T′), on the other hand, restricts truth as a semantic concept only to members of L. Since L is an artificial language, truth is then restricted to artificial languages. On this score, the philosophical import of (T′) is unmistakable. As White observes with alarm, "Tarksi's theory reaches the disheartening conclusion that no adequate definition of truth can be given for every-day or colloquial languages. . . ."[26]

Comparing Tarski's theory with correspondence theory, on the credit side of the ledger, Tarski's theory avoids all the difficulties that beset any correspondence theory, and it can boast of a scope which is lacking in correspondence theories. However, the tautological nature of (T) points to Ramsey's redundancy thesis, to be noted below. So whereas CF is overly committed,[27] philosophers have claimed that Tarski's formula is overly noncommittal and that it is at bottom philosophically neutral. In fact, Black calls this theory a "no theory" theory of truth.[28] This may or may not be a criticism of Tarski's theory, that it may fail to satisfy us philosophically. Counterargument to Tarski's view is per-haps more forcefully pressed by Strawson.

Strawson's "performative" theory of truth[29]

In order to better understand Strawson's own theory of truth, we must first examine his objections to the semantic theory of truth. Straw-son proceeds on the assumption (presumably founded on paradigm case argument) that 'true' is not applied to sentences; for, he holds, truth is not any sort of property at all. But he allows that 'is true if and only if' may be applied to sentences *in the sense that* (taking his cue from Carnap) it is synonymous with 'means that'; such expres-sions may genuinely occur in metastatements about sentences. However,

[25] For amplification and criticism of this point and other related points, see Max Black, "The Semantic Definition of Truth," *Analysis,* VIII (1948).

[26] White, *Truth,* 95.

[27] In light of Davidson's arguments, fact-packing in the end is not packing in too much, but packing in nothing at all. See his "True to the Facts," 752-53. And, of course, if CF turns out to be tautologous, "packing in too much" means some-thing more like begging the question.

[28] Black, "The Semantic Definition of Truth," 62.

[29] Strawson, "Truth," *Analysis,* IX (1949).

such metastatements are neither truly tautologies nor truly contingent. According to Strawson, ' 'The monarch is deceased' is true if and only if [means that] the king is dead' is a legitimate, contingent metastatement. But in this respect, ' 'Snow is white' is true if and only if Snow is white' is not a legitimate, contingent metastatement. Is it then a tautology? Strawson argues that it is not; for if one were to say ' 'The monarch is deceased' does not mean that the king is dead,' one wouldn't be saying anything self-contradictory. Strawson concludes that Tarski's (T) is a "degenerate case" of a contingent metastatement. He further concludes,

> To read the degenerate cases, then, as specification, or parts, of some ideal defining formula for the phrase 'is true' is to separate the phrase from the context which alone confers this meta-linguistic use upon it, and to regard the result as a model for the general use of 'is true.' It is to be committed to the mistake of supposing that the phrase 'is true' is normally (or strictly) used as a meta-linguistic predicate.[30]

Strawson's own analysis of truth hinges on two considerations: 'x is true' and 'x,' both being statements, are assertively equivalent; but 'x is true' means more than 'x' alone does. In the former, Strawson is agreeing with Ramsey (and that part of Tarski's theory that accords with Ramsey's thesis), but only up to a point. And in the latter he goes beyond Ramsey, while agreeing with Tarski to this extent, that 'x is true' adverts to 'x,' 'x' being a statement made or one about to be made. Ramsey held that 'x is true' and 'x' are assertively equivalent; hence 'is true' is redundant or logically superfluous — but it may mark for rhetorical emphasis.[31]

Rather than treat 'is true' as a meta-linguistic predicate, and rather than treat it as perhaps marking for rhetorical emphasis, Strawson resorts to an analysis in which 'is true' marks for reassertion and an illocutionary act. Thus if I say that what you have stated is true, then I talk about what you talk about (not about your statement), and I agree with what you say. Agreement is expressed in illocutionary acts, such as concessives, admitives, endorsives, etc. Importantly, no conditions are tacked on, either such as those in correspondence theory or the formal ones in the semantic theory (yet there might be criteria for

[30] *Ibid.*, 88.

[31] See F. P. Ramsey, "Facts and Propositions," *Proceedings of the Aristotelian Society*, VIII (1927).

success regarding the relevant illocutionary acts). Strawson, like Tarski, leaves only for fringe interest the matter of grounds for agreement, but they are extraneous to his analysis.

SELECTED READINGS

Acton, H. B. "The Correspondence Theory of Truth." *Proceedings of the Aristotelian Society,* XXXV (1935), 177-94.

Adams, G. P. "Truth, Discourse and Reality." In *The Problem of Truth,* ed. G. P. Adams, J. Loewenberg, and S. C. Pepper, University of California Publications in Philosophy no. 10, Berkeley, 1928.

Austin, J. L. "Truth." *Proceedings of the Aristotelian Society,* suppl. vol. XXIV (1950), 111-28.

――――. "How to Do Things with Words." Oxford: Oxford University Press, 1962.

Ayer, A. J. "The Criterion of Truth." *Analysis,* III (1935).

――――. "Truth by Convention." *Analysis,* IV (1936), 17-22.

――――. "Truth." *Revue Internationale de Philosophie,* VII (1953), 183-200.

――――. "Truth." In *The Concept of a Person* (London: Macmillan, 1963), Ch. 6.

Black, Max. "Truth by Convention." *Analysis,* IV (1937).

――――. "The Semantic Definition of Truth." *Analysis,* VIII (1948), 49-63.

Cohen, L. J. "Mr. Strawson's Analysis of Truth." *Analysis,* X (1950), 136-40.

Cousin, D. R. "Truth." *Proceedings of the Aristotelian Society,* XXIV (1950), 157-72.

Ducasse, C. J. "Is a Fact a True Proposition? A Reply." *Journal of Philosophy,* XXXIX (1942), 132-36.

――――. "Propositions, Truth and the Ultimate Criterion of Truth." *Philosophy and Phenomenological Research,* IV (1943-44), 317-40.

――――. "Facts, Truth and Knowledge." *Philosophy and Phenomenological Research,* V (1944-45), 320-32.

Dummett, M. "Truth." *Proceedings of the Aristotelian Society,* LIX (1959), 141-62.

Ezorsky, G. "Truth in Context." *Journal of Philosophy,* LX (1963), 113-35.

Greenwood, D. *Truth and Meaning.* New York, 1957.

Harre, R. " '. . . is true'." *Australasian Journal of Philosophy,* XXXV (1957), 119-24.

Honderich, T. "Truth: Austin, Strawson, Warnock." In *Studies in Logical Theory, American Philosophical Quarterly,* Monograph Series no. 2 (1968), 125-37.

James, William. "Pragmatism's Conception of Truth." *Journal of Philosophy,* 4 (1907), 396-406.

Kalish, D. "Meaning and Truth." *University of California Publications in Philosophy* (1950).

Khatchadourian, H. "Truth as Appraisal." *Mind,* LXXI (1962), 387-91.

Kincade, J. "On the Performatory Theory of Truth." *Mind,* LXVII (1958), 394-98.

Körner, S. "Truth as a Predicate." *Analysis,* XV (1955), 106-9.

Lewy, C. "Truth and Significance." *Analysis,* VIII (1947).

Mayo, B. "Truth as Appraisal." *Mind,* LXVIII (1959), 80-86.

Nagel, Ernest. "Truth and Knowledge of Truth." *Philosophy and Phenomenological Research,* V (1944-45), 50-68.

Pap, A. "Note on the 'Semantic' and the 'Absolute' Concept of Truth." *Philosophical Studies,* III (1952), 1-8.

———. "Propositions, Sentences and the Semantic Definition of Truth." *Theoria,* XX (1954), 23-35.

Perkins, M. "Notes on the Pragmatic Theory of Truth." *Journal of Philosophy,* XLIX (1952), 573-87.

Pitcher, G., ed. *Truth.* Englewood Cliffs, N.J.: Prentice-Hall, 1964, 1-15.

Pole, D. "A Note on Truth." *Analysis,* XXVIII (1967), 56-58.

Popper, Karl. "A Note on Tarski's Definition of Truth." *Mind,* LXIV (1955).

Pratt, J. B. "Truth and Its Verification." *Journal of Philosophy,* IV (1907), 320-24.

———. "Truth and Ideas." *Journal of Philosophy,* V (1908), 122-31.

Prior, A. N. "The Correspondence Theory of Truth." In *Encyclopedia of Philosophy,* II, ed. P. Edwards (New York: Macmillan, 1967), 223-32.

Ratner, J. "The Correspondence Theory of Truth." *Journal of Philosophy,* XXXII (1935), 141-52.

Richman, R. J. "Truth and Verifiability: A Reply to Mr. Perkins." *Journal of Philosophy,* L (1953), 807-11.

Russell, Bertrand. *An Inquiry into Meaning and Truth.* London: Allen and Unwin, 1940.

Scheer, R. K. "Verification and the Performatory Theory of Truth." *Mind,* LXIX (1960), 568.

Sellars, Wilfrid. " 'True' as Contextually Implying Correspondence." *Journal of Philosophy,* LVI (1959), 717-22.

———. "A Correspondence Theory of Truth." *Journal of Philosophy,* LIX (1962), 29-56.

Strawson, P. F. "Truth." *Analysis,* IX (1949), 83-97.

———. "Truth." *Proceedings of the Aristotelian Society,* suppl. vol. XXIV (1950), 129-56.

"A Problem about Truth — A Reply to Mr. Warnock." In *Truth,* ed. G. Pitcher. Englewood Cliffs, N.J.: Prentice-Hall, 1964, 68-84.

———. "Truth: A Reconsideration of Austin's Views." *Philosophical Quarterly,* XV (1965), 289-301.

Tarski, A. "The Concept of Truth in Formalised Languages" (1936). Reprinted in *Logic, Semantics, Metamathematics,* trans. J. H. Woodger (Oxford: Oxford University Press, 1956), 152-278.

———. "The Semantic Conception of Truth." *Philosophy and Phenomenological Research,* IV (1943-44), 341-75.

Thomson, J. F. "A Note on Truth." *Analysis,* IX (1949), 67-72.

Ushenko, A. "A Note on the Semantic Conception of Truth." *Philosophy and Phenomenological Research,* V (1944-45), 104-7.

Walsh, W. H. "A Note on Truth." *Mind,* LXI (1952), 72-74.

Warnock, G. J. "Truth and Correspondence." In *Knowledge and Experience,* ed. C. D. Rollins. Pittsburgh: University of Pittsburgh Press, 1962, 11-20.

———. "A Problem about Truth." In *Truth,* ed. G. Pitcher. Englewood Cliffs, N.J.: Prentice-Hall, 1964, 54-67.

White, A. R. "Truth as Appraisal." *Mind,* LXVI (1957), 318-30.

———. " 'True' and 'Truly'." *Nous,* II (1968), 247-51.

1

The Semantic Conception of Truth

ALFRED TARSKI

Reprinted with the kind permission of the editor from *Philosophy and Phenomenological Research,* IV, 3 (1944), 341-75.

THE SEMANTIC CONCEPTION OF TRUTH

AND THE FOUNDATIONS OF SEMANTICS

This paper consists of two parts; the first has an expository character, and the second is rather polemical.

In the first part I want to summarize in an informal way the main results of my investigations concerning the definition of truth and the more general problem of the foundations of semantics. These results have been embodied in a work which appeared in print several years ago.[1] Although my investigations concern concepts dealt with in classical philosophy, they happen to be comparatively little known in philosophical circles, perhaps because of their strictly technical character. For this reason I hope I shall be excused for taking up the matter once again.[2]

Since my work was published, various objections, of unequal value, have been raised to my investigations; some of these appeared in print, and others were made in public and private discussions in which I took part.[3] In the second part of the paper I should like to express my views regarding these objections. I hope that the remarks which will be made in this context will not be considered as purely polemical in character, but will be found to contain some constructive contributions to the subject.

In the second part of the paper I have made extensive use of material graciously put at my disposal by Dr. Marja Kokoszyńska (University of Lwów). I am especially indebted and grateful to Professors Ernest Nagel (Columbia University) and David Rynin (University of California, Berkeley) for their help in preparing the final text and for various critical remarks.

I. EXPOSITION

1. THE MAIN PROBLEM—A SATISFACTORY DEFINITION OF TRUTH. Our discussion will be centered around the notion[4] of *truth*. The main problem is that of giving a *satisfactory definition* of this notion, i.e., a definition which is *materially adequate* and *formally correct*. But such a formulation of the problem, because of its generality, cannot be considered unequivocal, and requires some further comments.

In order to avoid any ambiguity, we must first specify the conditions under which the definition of truth will be considered adequate from the material point of view. The desired definition does not aim to specify the meaning of a familiar word used to denote a novel notion; on the contrary, it aims to catch hold of the actual meaning of an old notion. We must then characterize this notion precisely enough to enable anyone to determine whether the definition actually fulfills its task.

Secondly, we must determine on what the formal correctness of the definition depends. Thus, we must specify the words or concepts which we wish to use in defining the notion of truth; and we must also give the formal rules to which the definition should conform. Speaking more generally, we must describe the formal structure of the language in which the definition will be given.

The discussion of these points will occupy a considerable portion of the first part of the paper.

2. THE EXTENSION OF THE TERM "TRUE." We begin with some remarks regarding the extension of the concept of truth which we have in mind here.

The predicate *"true"* is sometimes used to refer to psychological phenomena such as judgments or beliefs, sometimes to certain physical objects, namely, linguistic expressions and specifically sentences, and sometimes to certain ideal entities called "propositions." By "sentence" we understand here what is usually meant in grammar by "declarative sentence"; as regards the term "proposition," its meaning is notoriously a subject of lengthy disputations by various philosophers and logicians, and it seems never to have been made quite clear and unambiguous. For several reasons it appears most convenient to *apply the term "true" to sentences*, and we shall follow this course.[5]

Consequently, we must always relate the notion of truth, like that of a sentence, to a specific language; for it is obvious that the same expression which is a true sentence in one language can be false or meaningless in another.

Of course, the fact that we are interested here primarily in the notion of truth for sentences does not exclude the possibility of a subsequent extension of this notion to other kinds of objects.

3. THE MEANING OF THE TERM "TRUE." Much more serious difficulties are connected with the problem of the meaning (or the intension) of the concept of truth.

The word *"true,"* like other words from our everyday language, is certainly not unambiguous. And it does not seem to me that the philosophers who have discussed this concept have helped to diminish its ambiguity. In works and discussions of philosophers we meet many different conceptions of truth and falsity, and we must indicate which conception will be the basis of our discussion.

We should like our definition to do justice to the intuitions which adhere to the *classical Aristotelian conception of truth*—intuitions which find their expression in the well-known words of Aristotle's *Metaphysics*:

*To say of what is that it is not, or of what is not that it is, is false, while
to say of what is that it is, or of what is not that it is not, is true.*

If we wished to adapt ourselves to modern philosophical terminology,
we could perhaps express this conception by means of the familiar formula:

The truth of a sentence consists in its agreement with (or correspondence to) reality.

(For a theory of truth which is to be based upon the latter formulation the
term "correspondence theory" has been suggested.)

If, on the other hand, we should decide to extend the popular usage of
the term *"designate"* by applying it not only to names, but also to sentences, and if we agreed to speak of the designata of sentences as "states
of affairs," we could possibly use for the same purpose the following
phrase:

A sentence is true if it designates an existing state of affairs.[6]

However, all these formulations can lead to various misunderstandings,
for none of them is sufficiently precise and clear (though this applies
much less to the original Aristotelian formulation than to either of the
others); at any rate, none of them can be considered a satisfactory definition of truth. It is up to us to look for a more precise expression of our
intuitions.

4. A CRITERION FOR THE MATERIAL ADEQUACY OF THE DEFINITION.[7]
Let us start with a concrete example. Consider the sentence *"snow is
white."* We ask the question under what conditions this sentence is true
or false. It seems clear that if we base ourselves on the classical conception of truth, we shall say that the sentence is true if snow is white, and
that it is false if snow is not white. Thus, if the definition of truth is to
conform to our conception, it must imply the following equivalence:

The sentence "snow is white" is true if, and only if, snow is white.

Let me point out that the phrase *"snow is white"* occurs on the left
side of this equivalence in quotation marks, and on the right without
quotation marks. On the right side we have the sentence itself, and on
the left the name of the sentence. Employing the medieval logical terminology we could also say that on the right side the words *"snow is white"*
occur in *suppositio formalis*, and on the left in *suppositio materialis*. It is
hardly necessary to explain why we must have the name of the sentence,
and not the sentence itself, on the left side of the equivalence. For, in the
first place, from the point of view of the grammar of our language, an
expression of the form *"X is true"* will not become a meaningful sentence
if we replace in it 'X' by a sentence or by anything other than a name—

344   Philosophy and Phenomenological Research

since the subject of a sentence may be only a noun or an expression functioning like a noun.   And, in the second place, the fundamental conventions regarding the use of any language require that in any utterance we make about an object it is the name of the object which must be employed, and not the object itself.   In consequence, if we wish to say something about a sentence, for example, that it is true, we must use the name of this sentence, and not the sentence itself.[8]

It may be added that enclosing a sentence in quotation marks is by no means the only way of forming its name.   For instance, by assuming the usual order of letters in our alphabet, we can use the following expression as the name (the description) of the sentence "*snow is white*":

the sentence constituted by three words, the first of which consists of the 19th, 14th, 15th, and 23rd letters, the second of the 9th and 19th letters, and the third of the 23rd, 8th, 9th, 20th, and 5th letters of the English alphabet.

We shall now generalize the procedure which we have applied above. Let us consider an arbitrary sentence; we shall replace it by the letter '*p.*'   We form the name of this sentence and we replace it by another letter, say '*X.*'   We ask now what is the logical relation between the two sentences "*X is true*" and '*p.*'   It is clear that from the point of view of our basic conception of truth these sentences are equivalent.   In other words, the following equivalence holds:

(T)   *X is true if, and only if, p.*

We shall call any such equivalence (with '*p*' replaced by any sentence of the language to which the word "*true*" refers, and 'X' replaced by a name of this sentence) an "*equivalence of the form* (T)."

Now at last we are able to put into a precise form the conditions under which we will consider the usage and the definition of the term "*true*" as adequate from the material point of view: we wish to use the term "*true*" in such a way that all equivalences of the form (T) can be asserted, and *we shall call a definition of truth "adequate" if all these equivalences follow from it.*

It should be emphasized that neither the expression (T) itself (which is not a sentence, but only a schema of a sentence) nor any particular instance of the form (T) can be regarded as a definition of truth.   We can only say that every equivalence of the form (T) obtained by replacing '*p*' by a particular sentence, and 'X' by a name of this sentence, may be considered a partial definition of truth, which explains wherein the truth of this one individual sentence consists.   The general definition has to be, in a certain sense, a logical conjunction of all these partial definitions.

(The last remark calls for some comments.   A language may admit the construction of infinitely many sentences; and thus the number of partial definitions of truth referring to sentences of such a language will also be infinite. Hence to give our remark a precise sense we should have to explain what is meant by a "logical conjunction of infinitely many sentences"; but this would lead us too far into technical problems of modern logic.)

5. TRUTH AS A SEMANTIC CONCEPT. I should like to propose the name *"the semantic conception of truth"* for the conception of truth which has just been discussed.

Semantics is a discipline which, speaking loosely, *deals with certain relations between expressions of a language and the objects* (or "states of affairs") *"referred to" by those expressions.* As typical examples of semantic concepts we may mention the concepts of *designation, satisfaction,* and *definition* as these occur in the following examples:

the expression "the father of his country" designates (denotes) George Washington;

snow satisfies the sentential function (the condition) "x is white";

the equation "2·x = 1" defines (uniquely determines) the number 1/2.

While the words *"designates," "satisfies,"* and *"defines"* express relations (between certain expressions and the objects "referred to" by these expressions), the word *"true"* is of a different logical nature: it expresses a property (or denotes a class) of certain expressions, viz., of sentences. However, it is easily seen that all the formulations which were given earlier and which aimed to explain the meaning of this word (cf. Sections 3 and 4) referred not only to sentences themselves, but also to objects "talked about" by these sentences, or possibly to "states of affairs" described by them. And, moreover, it turns out that the simplest and the most natural way of obtaining an exact definition of truth is one which involves the use of other semantic notions, e.g., the notion of satisfaction. It is for these reasons that we count the concept of truth which is discussed here among the concepts of semantics, and the problem of defining truth proves to be closely related to the more general problem of setting up the foundations of theoretical semantics.

It is perhaps worth while saying that semantics as it is conceived in this paper (and in former papers of the author) is a sober and modest discipline which has no pretensions of being a universal patent-medicine for all the ills and diseases of mankind, whether imaginary or real. You will not find in semantics any remedy for decayed teeth or illusions of grandeur or class conflicts. Nor is semantics a device for establishing that everyone except the speaker and his friends is speaking nonsense.

From antiquity to the present day the concepts of semantics have played an important role in the discussions of philosophers, logicians, and philologists. Nevertheless, these concepts have been treated for a long time with a certain amount of suspicion. From a historical standpoint, this suspicion is to be regarded as completely justified. For although the meaning of semantic concepts as they are used in everyday language seems to be rather clear and understandable, still all attempts to characterize this meaning in a general and exact way miscarried. And what is worse, various arguments in which these concepts were involved, and which seemed otherwise quite correct and based upon apparently obvious premises, led frequently to paradoxes and antinomies. It is sufficient to mention here the *antinomy of the liar*, Richard's *antinomy of definability* (by means of a finite number of words), and Grelling-Nelson's *antinomy of heterological terms.*[9]

I believe that the method which is outlined in this paper helps to overcome these difficulties and assures the possibility of a consistent use of semantic concepts.

6. LANGUAGES WITH A SPECIFIED STRUCTURE. Because of the possible occurrence of antinomies, the problem of specifying the formal structure and the vocabulary of a language in which definitions of semantic concepts are to be given becomes especially acute; and we turn now to this problem.

There are certain general conditions under which the structure of a language is regarded as *exactly specified*. Thus, to specify the structure of a language, we must characterize unambiguously the class of those words and expressions which are to be considered *meaningful*. In particular, we must indicate all words which we decide to use without defining them, and which are called *"undefined* (or *primitive) terms"*; and we must give the so-called *rules of definition* for introducing new or *defined terms*. Furthermore, we must set up criteria for distinguishing within the class of expressions those which we call *"sentences."* Finally, we must formulate the conditions under which a sentence of the language can be *asserted*. In particular, we must indicate all *axioms* (or *primitive sentences*), i.e., those sentences which we decide to assert without proof; and we must give the so-called *rules of inference* (or *rules of proof*) by means of which we can deduce new asserted sentences from other sentences which have been previously asserted. Axioms, as well as sentences deduced from them by means of rules of inference, are referred to as *"theorems"* or *"provable sentences."*

If in specifying the structure of a language we refer exclusively to the form of the expressions involved, the language is said to be *formalized*. In such a language theorems are the only sentences which can be asserted.

At the present time the only languages with a specified structure are the formalized languages of various systems of deductive logic, possibly enriched by the introduction of certain non-logical terms. However, the field of application of these languages is rather comprehensive; we are able, theoretically, to develop in them various branches of science, for instance, mathematics and theoretical physics.

(On the other hand, we can imagine the construction of languages which have an exactly specified structure without being formalized. In such a language the assertability of sentences, for instance, may depend not always on their form, but sometimes on other, non-linguistic factors. It would be interesting and important actually to construct a language of this type, and specifically one which would prove to be sufficient for the development of a comprehensive branch of empirial science; for this would justify the hope that languages with specified structure could finally replace everyday language in scientific discourse.)

The problem of the definition of truth obtains a precise meaning and can be solved in a rigorous way only for those languages whose structure has been exactly specified. For other languages—thus, for all natural, "spoken" languages—the meaning of the problem is more or less vague, and its solution can have only an approximate character. Roughly speaking, the approximation consists in replacing a natural language (or a portion of it in which we are interested) by one whose structure is exactly specified, and which diverges from the given language "as little as possible."

7. THE ANTINOMY OF THE LIAR. In order to discover some of the more specific conditions which must be satisfied by languages in which (or for which) the definition of truth is to be given, it will be advisable to begin with a discussion of that antinomy which directly involves the notion of truth, namely, the antinomy of the liar.

To obtain this antinomy in a perspicuous form,[10] consider the following sentence:

> *The sentence printed in this paper on p. 347, l. 31, is not true.*

For brevity we shall replace the sentence just stated by the letter '*s*.'

According to our convention concerning the adequate usage of the term "*true*," we assert the following equivalence of the form (T):

(1) '*s*' *is true if, and only if, the sentence printed in this paper on p. 347, l. 31, is not true.*

On the other hand, keeping in mind the meaning of the symbol '*s*,' we establish empirically the following fact:

(2) '*s*' *is identical with the sentence printed in this paper on p. 347, l. 31.*

348   PHILOSOPHY AND PHENOMENOLOGICAL RESEARCH

Now, by a familiar law from the theory of identity (Leibniz's law), it follows from (2) that we may replace in (1) the expression *"the sentence printed in this paper on p. 347, l. 31"* by the symbol *" 's.' "* We thus obtain what follows:

(3)   *'s' is true if, and only if, 's' is not true.*

In this way we have arrived at an obvious contradiction.

In my judgment, it would be quite wrong and dangerous from the standpoint of scientific progress to depreciate the importance of this and other antinomies, and to treat them as jokes or sophistries. It is a fact that we are here in the presence of an absurdity, that we have been compelled to assert a false sentence (since (3), as an equivalence between two contradictory sentences, is necessarily false). If we take our work seriously, we cannot be reconciled with this fact. We must discover its cause, that is to say, we must analyze premises upon which the antinomy is based; we must then reject at least one of these premises, and we must investigate the consequences which this has for the whole domain of our research.

It should be emphasized that antinomies have played a preeminent role in establishing the foundations of modern deductive sciences. And just as class-theoretical antinomies, and in particular Russell's antinomy (of the class of all classes that are not members of themselves), were the starting point for the successful attempts at a consistent formalization of logic and mathematics, so the antinomy of the liar and other semantic antinomies give rise to the construction of theoretical semantics. ·

8. THE INCONSISTENCY OF SEMANTICALLY CLOSED LANGUAGES.[7] If we now analyze the assumptions which lead to the antinomy of the liar, we notice the following:

(I) We have implicitly assumed that the language in which the antinomy is constructed contains, in addition to its expressions, also the names of these expressions, as well as semantic terms such as the term *"true"* referring to sentences of this language; we have also assumed that all sentences which determine the adequate usage of this term can be asserted in the language. A language with these properties will be called *"semantically closed."*

(II) We have assumed that in this language the ordinary laws of logic hold.

(III) We have assumed that we can formulate and assert in our language an empirical premise such as the statement (2) which has occurred in our argument.

It turns out that the assumption (III) is not essential, for it is possible to reconstruct the antinomy of the liar without its help.[11]   But the assumptions (I) and (II) prove essential. Since every language which satisfies both of these assumptions is inconsistent, we must reject at least one of them.

It would be superfluous to stress here the consequences of rejecting the assumption (II), that is, of changing our logic (supposing this were possible) even in its more elementary and fundamental parts. We thus consider only the possibility of rejecting the assumption (I).   Accordingly, we decide *not to use any language which is semantically closed* in the sense given.

This restriction would of course be unacceptable for those who, for reasons which are not clear to me, believe that there is only one "genuine" language (or, at least, that all "genuine" languages are mutually translatable).   However, this restriction does not affect the needs or interests of science in any essential way. The languages (either the formalized languages or—what is more frequently the case—the portions of everyday language) which are used in scientific discourse do not have to be semantically closed. This is obvious in case linguistic phenomena and, in particular, semantic notions do not enter in any way into the subject-matter of a science; for in such a case the language of this science does not have to be provided with any semantic terms at all. However, we shall see in the next section how semantically closed languages can be dispensed with even in those scientific discussions in which semantic notions are essentially involved.

The problem arises as to the position of everyday language with regard to this point. At first blush it would seem that this language satisfies both assumptions (I) and (II), and that therefore it must be inconsistent. But actually the case is not so simple. Our everyday language is certainly not one with an exactly specified structure. We do not know precisely which expressions are sentences, and we know even to a smaller degree which sentences are to be taken as assertible. Thus the problem of consistency has no exact meaning with respect to this language. We may at best only risk the guess that a language whose structure has been exactly specified and which resembles our everyday language as closely as possible would be inconsistent.

9. OBJECT-LANGUAGE AND META-LANGUAGE. Since we have agreed not to employ semantically closed languages, we have to use two different languages in discussing the problem of the definition of truth and, more generally, any problems in the field of semantics. The first of these languages is the language which is "talked about" and which is the subject-matter of the whole discussion; the definition of truth which we are seeking

applies to the sentences of this language. The second is the language in which we "talk about" the first language, and in terms of which we wish, in particular, to construct the definition of truth for the first language. We shall refer to the first language as *"the object-language,"* and to the second as *"the meta-language."*

It should be noticed that these terms "object-language" and "meta-language" have only a relative sense. If, for instance, we become interested in the notion of truth applying to sentences, not of our original object-language, but of its meta-language, the latter becomes automatically the object-language of our discussion; and in order to define truth for this language, we have to go to a new meta-language—so to speak, to a meta-language of a higher level. In this way we arrive at a whole hierarchy of languages.

The vocabulary of the meta-language is to a large extent determined by previously stated conditions under which a definition of truth will be considered materially adequate. This definition, as we recall, has to imply all equivalences of the form (T):

(T) X *is true if, and only if, p.*

The definition itself and all the equivalences implied by it are to be formulated in the meta-language. On the other hand, the symbol 'p' in (T) stands for an arbitrary sentence of our object-language. Hence it follows that every sentence which occurs in the object-language must also occur in the meta-language; in other words, the meta-language must contain the object-language as a part. This is at any rate necessary for the proof of the adequacy of the definition—even though the definition itself can sometimes be formulated in a less comprehensive meta-language which does not satisfy this requirement.

(The requirement in question can be somewhat modified, for it suffices to assume that the object-language can be translated into the meta-language; this necessitates a certain change in the interpretation of the symbol 'p' in (T). In all that follows we shall ignore the possibility of this modification.)

Furthermore, the symbol 'X' in (T) represents the name of the sentence which 'p' stands for. We see therefore that the meta-language must be rich enough to provide possibilities of constructing a name for every sentence of the object-language.

In addition, the meta-language must obviously contain terms of a general logical character, such as the expression "if, and only if."[12]

It is desirable for the meta-language not to contain any undefined terms except such as are involved explicitly or implicitly in the remarks above, i.e.: terms of the object-language; terms referring to the form of the expressions of the object-language, and used in building names for these expressions; and terms of logic. In particular, we desire *semantic terms* (referring to the object-language) *to be introduced into the meta-language only by definition*. For, if this postulate is satisfied, the definition of truth, or of any other semantic concept, will fulfill what we intuitively expect from every definition; that is, it will explain the meaning of the term being defined in terms whose meaning appears to be completely clear and unequivocal. And, moreover, we have then a kind of guarantee that the use of semantic concepts will not involve us in any contradictions.

We have no further requirements as to the formal structure of the object-language and the meta-language; we assume that it is similar to that of other formalized languages known at the present time. In particular, we assume that the usual formal rules of definition are observed in the meta-language.

10. CONDITIONS FOR A POSITIVE SOLUTION OF THE MAIN PROBLEM. Now, we have already a clear idea both of the conditions of material adequacy to which the definition of truth is subjected, and of the formal structure of the language in which this definition is to be constructed. Under these circumstances the problem of the definition of truth acquires the character of a definite problem of a purely deductive nature.

The solution of the problem, however, is by no means obvious, and I would not attempt to give it in detail without using the whole machinery of contemporary logic. Here I shall confine myself to a rough outline of the solution and to the discussion of certain points of a more general interest which are involved in it.

The solution turns out to be sometimes positive, sometimes negative. This depends upon some formal relations between the object-language and its meta-language; or, more specifically, upon the fact whether the meta-language in its logical part is "*essentially richer*" than the object-language or not. It is not easy to give a general and precise definition of this notion of "essential richness." If we restrict ourselves to languages based on the logical theory of types, the condition for the meta-language to be "essentially richer" than the object-language is that it contain variables of a higher logical type than those of the object-language.

If the condition of "essential richness" is not satisfied, it can usually be shown that an interpretation of the meta-language in the object-language is possible; that is to say, with any given term of the meta-language a well-determined term of the object-language can be correlated in such a way that the assertible sentences of the one language turn out to be correlated with assertible sentences of the other. As a result of this interpretation, the hypothesis that a satisfactory definition of truth has been formulated in the meta-language turns out to imply the possibility of reconstructing in that language the antinomy of the liar; and this in turn forces us to reject the hypothesis in question.

(The fact that the meta-language, in its non-logical part, is ordinarily more comprehensive than the object-language does not affect the possibility of interpreting the former in the latter. For example, the names of expressions of the object-language occur in the meta-language, though for the most part they do not occur in the object-language itself; but, nevertheless, it may be possible to interpret these names in terms of the object-language.)

Thus we see that the condition of "essential richness" is necessary for the possibility of a satisfactory definition of truth in the meta-language. If we want to develop the theory of truth in a meta-language which does not satisfy this condition, we must give up the idea of defining truth with the exclusive help of those terms which were indicated above (in Section 8). We have then to include the term *"true,"* or some other semantic term, in the list of undefined terms of the meta-language, and to express fundamental properties of the notion of truth in a series of axioms. There is nothing essentially wrong in such an axiomatic procedure, and it may prove useful for various purposes.[13]

It turns out, however, that this procedure can be avoided. For *the condition of the "essential richness" of the meta-language proves to be, not only necessary, but also sufficient for the construction of a satisfactory definition of truth;* i.e., if the meta-language satisfies this condition, the notion of truth can be defined in it. We shall now indicate in general terms how this construction can be carried through.

11. THE CONSTRUCTION (IN OUTLINE) OF THE DEFINITION.[14] A definition of truth can be obtained in a very simple way from that of another semantic notion, namely, of the notion of *satisfaction*.

Satisfaction is a relation between arbitrary objects and certain expressions called *"sentential functions."* These are expressions like *"x is white,"* *"x is greater than y,"* etc. Their formal structure is analogous to that of sentences; however, they may contain the so-called free variables (like 'x' and 'y' in *"x is greater than y"*), which cannot occur in sentences.

In defining the notion of a sentential function in formalized languages, we usually apply what is called a "recursive procedure"; i.e., we first describe sentential functions of the simplest structure (which ordinarily presents no difficulty), and then we indicate the operations by means of which compound functions can be constructed from simpler ones. Such an operation may consist, for instance, in forming the logical disjunction or conjunction of two given functions, i.e., by combining them by the

Semantic Conception of Truth   353

word *"or"* or *"and."*   A sentence can now be defined simply as a sentential function which contains no free variables.

As regards the notion of satisfaction, we might try to define it by saying that given objects satisfy a given function if the latter becomes a true sentence when we replace in it free variables by names of given objects.   In this sense, for example, snow satisfies the sentential function *"x is white"* since the sentence *"snow is white"* is true.   However, apart from other difficulties, this method is not available to us, for we want to use the notion of satisfaction in defining truth.

To obtain a definition of satisfaction we have rather to apply again a recursive procedure.   We indicate which objects satisfy the simplest sentential functions; and then we state the conditions under which given objects satisfy a compound function—assuming that we know which objects satisfy the simpler functions from which the compound one has been constructed.   Thus, for instance, we say that given numbers satisfy the logical disjunction *"x is greater than y or x is equal to y"* if they satisfy at least one of the functions *"x is greater than y"* or *"x is equal to y."*

Once the general definition of satisfaction is obtained, we notice that it applies automatically also to those special sentential functions which contain no free variables, i.e., to sentences.   It turns out that for a sentence only two cases are possible: a sentence is either satisfied by all objects, or by no objects.   Hence we arrive at a definition of truth and falsehood simply by saying that *a sentence is true if it is satisfied by all objects, and false otherwise.*[15]

(It may seem strange that we have chosen a roundabout way of defining the truth of a sentence, instead of trying to apply, for instance, a direct recursive procedure.   The reason is that compound sentences are constructed from simpler sentential functions, but not always from simpler sentences; hence no general recursive method is known which applies specifically to sentences.)

From this rough outline it is not clear where and how the assumption of the "essential richness" of the meta-language is involved in the discussion; this becomes clear only when the construction is carried through in a detailed and formal way.[16]

12. CONSEQUENCES OF THE DEFINITION.   The definition of truth which was outlined above has many interesting consequences.

In the first place, the definition proves to be not only formally correct, but also materially adequate (in the sense established in Section 4); in other words, it implies all equivalences of the form (T).   In this connection it is important to notice that the conditions for the material adequacy of the definition determine uniquely the extension of the term *"true."*

354   Philosophy and Phenomenological Research

Therefore, every definition of truth which is materially adequate would necessarily be equivalent to that actually constructed. The semantic conception of truth gives us, so to speak, no possibility of choice between various non-equivalent definitions of this notion.

Moreover, we can deduce from our definition various laws of a general nature. In particular, we can prove with its help the *laws of contradiction and of excluded middle*, which are so characteristic of the Aristotelian conception of truth; i.e., we can show that one and only one of any two contradictory sentences is true. These semantic laws should not be identified with the related logical laws of contradiction and excluded middle; the latter belong to the sentential calculus, i.e., to the most elementary part of logic, and do not involve the term *"true"* at all.

Further important results can be obtained by applying the theory of truth to formalized languages of a certain very comprehensive class of mathematical disciplines; only disciplines of an elementary character and a very elementary logical structure are excluded from this class. It turns out that for a discipline of this class *the notion of truth never coincides with that of provability;* for all provable sentences are true, but there are true sentences which are not provable.[17] Hence it follows further that every such discipline is consistent, but incomplete; that is to say, of any two contradictory sentences at most one is provable, and—what is more—there exists a pair of contradictory sentences neither of which is provable.[18]

13. EXTENSION OF THE RESULTS TO OTHER SEMANTIC NOTIONS.   Most of the results at which we arrived in the preceding sections in discussing the notion of truth can be extended with appropriate changes to other semantic notions, for instance, to the notion of satisfaction (involved in our previous discussion), and to those of *designation* and *definition*.

Each of these notions can be analyzed along the lines followed in the analysis of truth. Thus, criteria for an adequate usage of these notions can be established; it can be shown that each of these notions, when used in a semantically closed language according to those criteria, leads necessarily to a contradiction;[19] a distinction between the object-language and the meta-language becomes again indispensable; and the "essential richness" of the meta-language proves in each case to be a necessary and sufficient condition for a satisfactory definition of the notion involved. Hence the results obtained in discussing one particular semantic notion apply to the general problem of the foundations of theoretical semantics.

Within theoretical semantics we can define and study some further notions, whose intuitive content is more involved and whose semantic origin is less obvious; we have in mind, for instance, the important notions of *consequence, synonymity,* and *meaning*.[20]

We have concerned ourselves here with the theory of semantic notions related to an individual object-language (although no specific properties of this language have been involved in our arguments). However, we could also consider the problem of developing *general semantics* which applies to a comprehensive class of object-languages. A considerable part of our previous remarks can be extended to this general problem; however, certain new difficulties arise in this connection, which will not be discussed here. I shall merely observe that the axiomatic method (mentioned in Section 10) may prove the most appropriate for the treatment of the problem.[21]

II. POLEMICAL REMARKS

14. IS THE SEMANTIC CONCEPTION OF TRUTH THE "RIGHT" ONE? I should like to begin the polemical part of the paper with some general remarks.

I hope nothing which is said here will be interpreted as a claim that the semantic conception of truth is the "right" or indeed the "only possible" one. I do not have the slightest intention to contribute in any way to those endless, often violent discussions on the subject: "What is the right conception of truth?"[22] I must confess I do not understand what is at stake in such disputes; for the problem itself is so vague that no definite solution is possible. In fact, it seems to me that the sense in which the phrase "the right conception" is used has never been made clear. In most cases one gets the impression that the phrase is used in an almost mystical sense based upon the belief that every word has only one "real" meaning (a kind of Platonic or Aristotelian idea), and that all the competing conceptions really attempt to catch hold of this one meaning; since, however, they contradict each other, only one attempt can be successful, and hence only one conception is the "right" one.

Disputes of this type are by no means restricted to the notion of truth. They occur in all domains where—instead of an exact, scientific terminology—common language with its vagueness and ambiguity is used; and they are always meaningless, and therefore in vain.

It seems to me obvious that the only rational approach to such problems would be the following: We should reconcile ourselves with the fact that we are confronted, not with one concept, but with several different concepts which are denoted by one word; we should try to make these concepts as clear as possible (by means of definition, or of an axiomatic procedure, or in some other way); to avoid further confusions, we should agree to use different terms for different concepts; and then we may proceed to a quiet and systematic study of all concepts involved, which will exhibit their main properties and mutual relations.

Referring specifically to the notion of truth, it is undoubtedly the case that in philosophical discussions—and perhaps also in everyday usage—

some incipient conceptions of this notion can be found that differ essentially from the classical one (of which the semantic conception is but a modernized form). In fact, various conceptions of this sort have been discussed in the literature, for instance, the pragmatic conception, the coherence theory, etc.[6]

It seems to me that none of these conceptions have been put so far in an intelligible and unequivocal form. This may change, however; a time may come when we find ourselves confronted with several incompatible, but equally clear and precise, conceptions of truth. It will then become necessary to abandon the ambiguous usage of the word *"true,"* and to introduce several terms instead, each to denote a different notion. Personally, I should not feel hurt if a future world congress of the "theoreticians of truth" should decide—by a majority of votes—to reserve the word *"true"* for one of the non-classical conceptions, and should suggest another word, say, *"frue,"* for the conception considered here. But I cannot imagine that anybody could present cogent arguments to the effect that the semantic conception is "wrong" and should be entirely abandoned.

15. FORMAL CORRECTNESS OF THE SUGGESTED DEFINITION OF TRUTH. The specific objections which have been raised to my investigations can be divided into several groups; each of these will be discussed separately.

I think that practically all these objections apply, not to the special definition I have given, but to the semantic conception of truth in general. Even those which were leveled against the definition actually constructed could be related to any other definition which conforms to this conception.

This holds, in particular, for those objections which concern the formal correctness of the definition. I have heard a few objections of this kind; however, I doubt very much whether anyone of them can be treated seriously.

As a typical example let me quote in substance such an objection.[23] In formulating the definition we use necessarily sentential connectives, i.e., expressions like *"if . . . , then," "or,"* etc. They occur in the definiens; and one of them, namely, the phrase *"if, and only if"* is usually employed to combine the definiendum with the definiens. However, it is well known that the meaning of sentential connectives is explained in logic with the help of the words *"true"* and *"false";* for instance, we say that an equivalence, i.e., a sentence of the form *"p if, and only if, q,"* is true if either both of its members, i.e., the sentences represented by 'p' and 'q,' are true or both are false. Hence the definition of truth involves a vicious circle.

If this objection were valid, no formally correct definition of truth would be possible; for we are unable to formulate any compound sentence without using sentential connectives, or other logical terms defined with their help. Fortunately, the situation is not so bad.

It is undoubtedly the case that a strictly deductive development of logic is often preceded by certain statements explaining the conditions under which sentences of the form "*if p, then q,*" etc., are considered true or false. (Such explanations are often given schematically, by means of the so-called truth-tables.) However, these statements are outside of the system of logic, and should not be regarded as definitions of the terms involved. They are not formulated in the language of the system, but constitute rather special consequences of the definition of truth given in the meta-language. Moreover, these statements do not influence the deductive development of logic in any way. For in such a development we do not discuss the question whether a given sentence is true, we are only interested in the problem whether it is provable.[24]

On the other hand, the moment we find ourselves within the deductive system of logic—or of any discipline based upon logic, e.g., of semantics— we either treat sentential connectives as undefined terms, or else we define them by means of other sentential connectives, but never by means of semantic terms like "*true*" or "*false.*" For instance, if we agree to regard the expressions "*not*" and "*if . . . , then*" (and possibly also "*if, and only if*") as undefined terms, we can define the term "*or*" by stating that a sentence of the form "*p or q*" is equivalent to the corresponding sentence of the form "*if not p, then q.*" The definition can be formulated, e.g., in the following way:

$$(p \text{ or } q) \text{ if, and only if, } (\text{if not } p, \text{ then } q).$$

This definition obviously contains no semantic terms.

However, a vicious circle in definition arises only when the definiens contains either the term to be defined itself, or other terms defined with its help. Thus we clearly see that the use of sentential connectives in defining the semantic term "*true*" does not involve any circle.

I should like to mention a further objection which I have found in the literature and which seems also to concern the formal correctness, if not of the definition of truth itself, then at least of the arguments which lead to this definition.[25]

The author of this objection mistakenly regards scheme (T) (from Section 4) as a definition of truth. He charges this alleged definition with "inadmissible brevity, i.e., incompleteness," which "does not give us the means of deciding whether by 'equivalence' is meant a logical-formal, or a non-logical and also structurally non-describable relation." To remove this "defect" he suggests supplementing (T) in one of the two following ways:

(T′)   *X is true if, and only if, p is true,*

or

(T″)   *X is true if, and only if, p is the case (i.e., if what p states is the case).*

358   PHILOSOPHY AND PHENOMENOLOGICAL RESEARCH

Then he discusses these two new "definitions," which are supposedly free from the old, formal "defect," but which turn out to be unsatisfactory for other, non-formal reasons.

This new objection seems to arise from a misunderstanding concerning the nature of sentential connectives (and thus to be somehow related to that previously discussed). The author of the objection does not seem to realize that the phrase "*if, and only if*" (in opposition to such phrases as "*are equivalent*" or "*is equivalent to*") expresses no relation between sentences at all since it does not combine names of sentences.

In general, the whole argument is based upon an obvious confusion between sentences and their names. It suffices to point out that —in contradistinction to (T)—schemata (T′) and (T″) do not give any meaningful expressions if we replace in them '*p*' by a sentence; for the phrases "*p is true*" and "*p is the case*" (i.e., "*what p states is the case*") become meaningless if '*p*' is replaced by a sentence, and not by the name of a sentence (cf. Section 4).[26]

While the author of the objection considers schema (T) "inadmissible brief," I am inclined, on my part, to regard schemata (T′) and (T″) as "inadmissibly long." And I think even that I can rigorously prove this statement on the basis of the following definition: An expression is said to be "inadmissibly long" if (i) it is meaningless, and (ii) it has been obtained from a meaningful expression by inserting superfluous words.

16. REDUNDANCY OF SEMANTIC TERMS—THEIR POSSIBLE ELIMINATION. The objection I am going to discuss now no longer concerns the formal correctness of the definition, but is still concerned with certain formal features of the semantic conception of truth.

We have seen that this conception essentially consists in regarding the sentence "*X is true*" as equivalent to the sentence denoted by '*X*' (where '*X*' stands for a name of a sentence of the object-language). Consequently, the term "*true*" when occurring in a simple sentence of the form "*X is true*" can easily be eliminated, and the sentence itself, which belongs to the meta-language, can be replaced by an equivalent sentence of the object-language; and the same applies to compound sentences provided the term "*true*" occurs in them exclusively as a part of the expressions of the form "*X is true.*"

Some people have therefore urged that the term "*true*" in the semantic sense can always be eliminated, and that for this reason the semantic conception of truth is altogether sterile and useless. And since the same considerations apply to other semantic notions, the conclusion has been drawn that semantics as a whole is a purely verbal game and at best only a harmless hobby.

But the matter is not quite so simple.[27]   The sort of elimination here discussed cannot always be made.   It cannot be done in the case of universal statements which express the fact that all sentences of a certain type are true, or that all true sentences have a certain property.   For instance, we can prove in the theory of truth the following statement:

All consequences of true sentences are true.

However, we cannot get rid here of the word *"true"* in the simple manner contemplated.

Again, even in the case of particular sentences having the form *"X is true"* such a simple elimination cannot always be made.   In fact, the elimination is possible only in those cases in which the name of the sentence which is said to be true occurs in a form that enables us to reconstruct the sentence itself.   For example, our present historical knowledge does not give us any possibility of eliminating the word *"true"* from the following sentence:

The first sentence written by Plato is true.

Of course, since we have a definition for truth and since every definition enables us to replace the definiendum by its definiens, an elimination of the term *"true"* in its semantic sense is always theoretically possible.   But this would not be the kind of simple elimination discused above, and it would not result in the replacement of a sentence in the meta-language by a sentence in the object-language.

If, however, anyone continues to urge that—because of the theoretical possibility of eliminating the word *"true"* on the basis of its definition— the concept of truth is sterile, he must accept the further conclusion that all defined notions are sterile.   But this outcome is so absurd and so unsound historically that any comment on it is unnecessary.   In fact, I am rather inclined to agree with those who maintain that the moments of greatest creative advancement in science frequently coincide with the introduction of new notions by means of definition.

17. CONFORMITY OF THE SEMANTIC CONCEPTION OF TRUTH WITH PHILOSOPHICAL AND COMMON-SENSE USAGE.   The question has been raised whether the semantic conception of truth can indeed be regarded as a precise form of the old, classical conception of this notion.

Various formulations of the classical conception were quoted in the early part of this paper (Section 3).   I must repeat that in my judgment none of them is quite precise and clear.   Accordingly, the only sure way of settling the question would be to confront the authors of those statements with our new formulation, and to ask them whether it agrees with their intentions. Unfortunately, this method is impractical since they died quite some time ago.

As far as my own opinion is concerned, I do not have any doubts that our formulation does conform to the intuitive content of that of Aristotle. I am less certain regarding the later formulations of the classical conception, for they are very vague indeed.[28]

Furthermore, some doubts have been expressed whether the semantic conception does reflect the notion of truth in its common-sense and everyday usage. I clearly realize (as I already indicated) that the common meaning of the word *"true"*—as that of any other word of everyday language—is to some extent vague, and that its usage more or less fluctuates. Hence the problem of assigning to this word a fixed and exact meaning is relatively unspecified, and every solution of this problem implies necessarily a certain deviation from the practice of everyday language.

In spite of all this, I happen to believe that the semantic conception does conform to a very considerable extent with the common-sense usage— although I readily admit I may be mistaken. What is more to the point, however, I believe that the issue raised can be settled scientifically, though of course not by a deductive procedure, but with the help of the statistical questionnaire method. As a matter of fact, such research has been carried on, and some of the results have been reported at congresses and in part published.[29]

I should like to emphasize that in my opinion such investigations must be conducted with the utmost care. Thus, if we ask a highschool boy, or even an adult intelligent man having no special philosophical training, whether he regards a sentence to be true if it agrees with reality, or if it designates an existing state of affairs, it may simply turn out that he does not understand the question; in consequence his response, whatever it may be, will be of no value for us. But his answer to the question whether he would admit that the sentence *"it is snowing"* could be true although it is not snowing, or could be false although it is snowing, would naturally be very significant for our problem.

Therefore, I was by no means surprised to learn (in a discussion devoted to these problems) that in a group of people who were questioned only 15% agreed that *"true"* means for them *"agreeing with reality,"* while 90% agreed that a sentence such as *"it is snowing"* is true if, and only if, it is snowing. Thus, a great majority of these people seemed to reject the classical conception of truth in its "philosophical" formulation, while accepting the same conception when formulated in plain words (waiving the question whether the use of the phrase "the same conception" is here justified).

18. THE DEFINITION IN ITS RELATION TO "THE PHILOSOPHICAL PROBLEM OF TRUTH" AND TO VARIOUS EPISTEMOLOGICAL TRENDS. I have heard it remarked that the formal definition of truth has nothing to do with "the philosophical problem of truth."[30] However, nobody has ever pointed out to me in an intelligible way just what this problem is. I have been informed in this connection that my definition, though it states necessary and sufficient conditions for a sentence to be true, does not really grasp the "essence" of this concept. Since I have never been able to understand what the "essence" of a concept is, I must be excused from discussing this point any longer.

In general, I do not believe that there is such a thing as "the philosophical problem of truth." I do believe that there are various intelligible and interesting (but not necessarily philosophical) problems concerning the notion of truth, but I also believe that they can be exactly formulated and possibly solved only on the basis of a precise conception of this notion.

While on the one hand the definition of truth has been blamed for not being philosophical enough, on the other a series of objections have been raised charging this definition with serious philosophical implications, always of a very undesirable nature. I shall discuss now one special objection of this type; another group of such objections will be dealt with in the next section.

It has been claimed that—due to the fact that a sentence like "snow is white" is taken to be semantically true if snow is *in fact* white (italics by the critic)—logic finds itself involved in a most uncritical realism.[31]

If there were an opportunity to discuss the objection with its author, I should raise two points. First, I should ask him to drop the words "*in fact*," which do not occur in the original formulation and which are misleading, even if they do not affect the content. For these words convey the impression that the semantic conception of truth is intended to establish the conditions under which we are warranted in asserting any given sentence, and in particular any empirical sentence. However, a moment's reflection shows that this impression is merely an illusion; and I think that the author of the objection falls victim to the illusion which he himself created.

In fact, the semantic definition of truth implies nothing regarding the conditions under which a sentence like (1):

(1)   *snow is white*

can be asserted. It implies only that, whenever we assert or reject this sentence, we must be ready to assert or reject the correlated sentence (2):

(2)   *the sentence "snow is white" is true.*

Thus, we may accept the semantic conception of truth without giving up any epistemological attitude we may have had; we may remain naive realists, critical realists or idealists, empiricists or metaphysicians—whatever we were before. The semantic conception is completely neutral toward all these issues.

In the second place, I should try to get some information regarding the conception of truth which (in the opinion of the author of the objection) does not involve logic in a most naive realism. I would gather that this conception must be incompatible with the semantic one. Thus, there must be sentences which are true in one of these conceptions without being true in the other. Assume, e.g., the sentence (1) to be of this kind. The truth of this sentence in the semantic conception is determined by an equivalence of the form (T):

The sentence "snow is white" is true if, and only if, snow is white.

Hence in the new conception we must reject this equivalence, and consequently we must assume its denial:

The sentence "snow is white" is true if, and only if, snow is not white (or perhaps: *snow, in fact, is not white*).

This sounds somewhat paradoxical. I do not regard such a consequence of the new conception as absurd; but I am a little fearful that someone in the future may charge this conception with involving logic in a "most sophisticated kind of irrealism." At any rate, it seems to me important to realize that every conception of truth which is incompatible with the semantic one carries with it consequences of this type.

I have dwelt a little on this whole question, not because the objection discussed seems to me very significant, but because certain points which have arisen in the discussion should be taken into account by all those who for various epistemological reasons are inclined to reject the semantic conception of truth.

19. alleged metaphysical elements in semantics. The semantic conception of truth has been charged several times with involving certain metaphysical elements. Objections of this sort have been made to apply not only to the theory of truth, but to the whole domain of theoretical semantics.[32]

I do not intend to discuss the general problem whether the introduction of a metaphysical element into a science is at all objectionable. The only point which will interest me here is whether and in what sense metaphysics is involved in the subject of our present discussion.

The whole question obviously depends upon what one understands by

Semantic Conception of Truth   363

"metaphysics." Unfortunately, this notion is extremely vague and equivocal. When listening to discussions in this subject, sometimes one gets the impression that the term "metaphysical" has lost any objective meaning, and is merely used as a kind of professional philosophical invective.

For some people metaphysics is a general theory of objects (ontology)— a discipline which is to be developed in a purely empirical way, and which differs from other empirical sciences only by its generality. I do not know whether such a discipline actually exists (some cynics claim that it is customary in philosophy to baptize unborn children); but I think that in any case metaphysics in this conception is not objectionable to anybody, and has hardly any connections with semantics.

For the most part, however, the term "metaphysical" is used as directly opposed—in one sense or another—to the term "empirical"; at any rate, it is used in this way by those people who are distressed by the thought that any metaphysical elements might have managed to creep into science. This general conception of metaphysics assumes several more specific forms.

Thus, some people take it to be symptomatic of a metaphysical element in a science when methods of inquiry are employed which are neither deductive nor empirical. However, no trace of this symptom can be found in the development of semantics (unless some metaphysical elements are involved in the object-language to which the semantic notions refer). In particular, the semantics of formalized languages is constructed in a purely deductive way.

Others maintain that the metaphysical character of a science depends mainly on its vocabulary and, more specifically, on its primitive terms. Thus, a term is said to be metaphysical if it is neither logical nor mathematical, and if it is not associated with an empirical procedure which enables us to decide whether a thing is denoted by this term or not. With respect to such a view of metaphysics it is sufficient to recall that a metalanguage includes only three kinds of undefined terms: (i) terms taken from logic, (ii) terms of the corresponding object-language, and (iii) names of expressions in the object-language. It is thus obvious that no metaphysical undefined terms occur in the meta-language (again, unless such terms appear in the object-language itself).

There are, however, some who believe that, even if no metaphysical terms occur among the primitive terms of a language, they may be introduced by definitions; namely, by those definitions which fail to provide us with general criteria for deciding whether an object falls under the defined concept. It is argued that the term "*true*" is of this kind, since no universal criterion of truth follows immediately from the definition of this term, and since it is generally believed (and in a certain sense can even be proved)

364   Philosophy and Phenomenological Research

that such a criterion will never be found.   This comment on the actual
character of the notion of truth seems to be perfectly just.   However,
it should be noticed that the notion of truth does not differ in this respect
from many notions in logic, mathematics, and theoretical parts of various
empirical sciences, e.g., in theoretical physics.

In general, it must be said that if the term "metaphysical" is employed
in so wide a sense as to embrace certain notions (or methods) of logic,
mathematics, or empirical sciences, it will apply *a fortiori* to those of
semantics.   In fact, as we know from Part I of the paper, in developing
the semantics of a language we use all the notions of this language, and we
apply even a stronger logical apparatus than that which is used in the
language itself.   On the other hand, however, I can summarize the arguments given above by stating that in no interpretation of the term "metaphysical" which is familiar and more or less intelligible to me does semantics
involve any metaphysical elements peculiar to itself.

I should like to make one final remark in connection with this group of
objections.   The history of science shows many instances of concepts
which were judged metaphysical (in a loose, but in any case derogatory
sense of this term) before their meaning was made precise; however, once
they received a rigorous, formal definition, the distrust in them evaporated.
As typical examples we may mention the concepts of negative and imaginary numbers in mathematics.   I hope a similar fate awaits the concept of
truth and other semantic concepts; and it seems to me, therefore, that those
who have distrusted them because of their alleged metaphysical implications should welcome the fact that precise definitions of these concepts are
now available.   If in consequence semantic concepts lose philosophical
interest, they will only share the fate of many other concepts of science,
and this need give rise to no regret.

20. applicability of semantics to special empirical sciences.
We come to the last and perhaps the most important group of objections.
Some strong doubts have been expressed whether semantic notions find or
can find applications in various domains of intellectual activity.   For
the most part such doubts have concerned the applicability of semantics
to the field of empirical science—either to special sciences or to the general
methodology of this field; although similar skepticism has been expressed
regarding possible applications of semantics to mathematical sciences and
their methodology.

I believe that it is possible to allay these doubts to a certain extent, and
that some optimism with respect to the potential value of semantics for
various domains of thought is not without ground.

To justify this optimism, it suffices I think to stress two rather obvious points. First, the development of a theory which formulates a precise definition of a notion and establishes its general properties provides *eo ipso* a firmer basis for all discussions in which this notion is involved; and, therefore, it cannot be irrelevant for anyone who uses this notion, and desires to do so in a conscious and consistent way. Secondly, semantic notions are actually involved in various branches of science, and in particular of empirical science.

The fact that in empirical research we are concerned only with natural languages and that theoretical semantics applies to these languages only with certain approximation, does not affect the problem essentially. However, it has undoubtedly this effect that progress in semantics will have but a delayed and somewhat limited influence in this field. The situation with which we are confronted here does not differ essentially from that which arises when we apply laws of logic to arguments in everyday life—or, generally, when we attempt to apply a theoretical science to empirical problems.

Semantic notions are undoubtedly involved, to a larger or smaller degree, in psychology, sociology, and in practically all the humanities. Thus, a psychologist defines the so-called intelligence quotient in terms of the numbers of *true* (right) and *false* (wrong) answers given by a person to certain questions; for a historian of culture the range of objects for which a human race in successive stages of its development possesses adequate *designations* may be a topic of great significance; a student of literature may be strongly interested in the problem whether a given author always uses two given words with the same *meaning*. Examples of this kind can be multiplied indefinitely.

The most natural and promising domain for the applications of theoretical semantics is clearly linguistics—the empirical study of natural languages. Certain parts of this science are even referred to as "semantics," sometimes with an additional qualification. Thus, this name is occasionally given to that portion of grammar which attempts to classify all words of a language into parts of speech, according to what the words mean or designate. The study of the evolution of meanings in the historical development of a language is sometimes called "historical semantics." In general, the totality of investigations on semantic relations which occur in a natural language is referred to as "descriptive semantics." The relation between theoretical and descriptive semantics is analogous to that between pure and applied mathematics, or perhaps to that between theoretical and empirical physics; the role of formalized languages in semantics can be roughly compared to that of isolated systems in physics.

It is perhaps unnecessary to say that semantics cannot find any direct applications in natural sciences such as physics, biology, etc.; for in none of these sciences are we concerned with linguistic phenomena, and even less with semantic relations between linguistic expressions and objects to which these expressions refer.   We shall see, however, in the next section that semantics may have a kind of indirect influence even on those sciences in which semantic notions are not directly involved.

21. APPLICABILITY OF SEMANTICS TO THE METHODOLOGY OF EMPIRICAL SCIENCE.   Besides linguistics, another important domain for possible applications of semantics is the methodology of science; this term is used here in a broad sense so as to embrace the theory of science in general. Independent of whether a science is conceived merely as a system of statements or as a totality of certain statements and human activities, the study of scientific language constitutes an essential part of the methodological discussion of a science.   And it seems to me clear that any tendency to eliminate semantic notions (like those of truth and designation) from this discussion would make it fragmentary and inadequate.[33]   Moreover, there is no reason for such a tendency today, once the main difficulties in using semantic terms have been overcome.   The semantics of scientific language should be simply included as a part in the methodology of science.

I am by no means inclined to charge methodology and, in particular, semantics—whether theoretical or descriptive—with the task of clarifying the meanings of all scientific terms.   This task is left to those sciences in which the terms are used, and is actually fulfilled by them (in the same way in which, e.g., the task of clarifying the meaning of the term *"true"* is left to, and fulfilled by, semantics).   There may be, however, certain special problems of this sort in which a methodological approach is desirable or indeed necessary (perhaps, the problem of the notion of causality is a good example here); and in a methodological discussion of such problems semantic notions may play an essential role.   Thus, semantics may have some bearing on any science whatsoever.

The question arises whether semantics can be helpful in solving general and, so to speak, classical problems of methodology.   I should like to discuss here with some detail a special, though very important, aspect of this question.

One of the main problems of the methodology of empirical science consists in establishing conditions under which an empirical theory or hypothesis should be regarded as acceptable.   This notion of acceptability must be relativized to a given stage of the development of a science (or to a given amount of presupposed knowledge).   In other words, we may consider it as provided with a time coefficient; for a theory which is acceptable today may become untenable tomorrow as a result of new scientific discoveries.

It seems *a priori* very plausible that the acceptability of a theory somehow depends on the truth of its sentences, and that consequently a methodologist in his (so far rather unsuccessful) attempts at making the notion of acceptability precise, can expect some help from the semantic theory of truth. Hence we ask the question: Are there any postulates which can be reasonably imposed on acceptable theories and which involve the notion of truth? And, in particular, we ask whether the following postulate is a reasonable one:

An acceptable theory cannot contain (or imply) any false sentences.

The answer to the last question is clearly negative. For, first of all, we are practically sure, on the basis of our historical experience, that every empirical theory which is accepted today will sooner or later be rejected and replaced by another theory. It is also very probable that the new theory will be incompatible with the old one; i.e., will imply a sentence which is contradictory to one of the sentences contained in the old theory. Hence, at least one of the two theories must include false sentences, in spite of the fact that each of them is accepted at a certain time. Secondly, the postulate in question could hardly ever be satisfied in practice; for we do not know, and are very unlikely to find, any criteria of truth which enable us to show that no sentence of an empirical theory is false.

The postulate in question could be at most regarded as the expression of an ideal limit for successively more adequate theories in a given field of research; but this hardly can be given any precise meaning.

Nevertheless, it seems to me that there is an important postulate which can be reasonably imposed on acceptable empirical theories and which involves the notion of truth. It is closely related to the one just discussed, but is essentially weaker. Remembering that the notion of acceptability is provided with a time coefficient, we can give this postulate the following form:

As soon as we succeed in showing that an empirical theory contains (or implies) false sentences, it cannot be any longer considered acceptable.

In support of this postulate, I should like to make the following remarks.

I believe everybody agrees that one of the reasons which may compel us to reject an empirical theory is the proof of its inconsistency: a theory becomes untenable if we succeed in deriving from it two contradictory sentences. Now we can ask what are the usual motives for rejecting a theory on such grounds. Persons who are acquainted with modern logic are inclined to answer this question in the following way: A well-known logical law shows that a theory which enables us to derive two contradictory sentences enables us also to derive every sentence; therefore, such a theory is trivial and deprived of any scientific interest.

I have some doubts whether this answer contains an adequate analysis of the situation. I think that people who do not know modern logic are as little inclined to accept an inconsistent theory as those who are thoroughly familiar with it; and probably this applies even to those who regard (as some still do) the logical law on which the argument is based as a highly controversial issue, and almost as a paradox. I do not think that our attitude toward an inconsistent theory would change even if we decided for some reasons to weaken our system of logic so as to deprive ourselves of the possibility of deriving every sentence from any two contradictory sentences.

It seems to me that the real reason of our attitude is a different one: We know (if only intuitively) that an inconsistent theory must contain false sentences; and we are not inclined to regard as acceptable any theory which has been shown to contain such sentences.

There are various methods of showing that a given theory includes false sentences. Some of them are based upon purely logical properties of the theory involved; the method just discussed (i.e., the proof of inconsistency) is not the sole method of this type, but is the simplest one, and the one which is most frequently applied in practice. With the help of certain assumptions regarding the truth of empirical sentences, we can obtain methods to the same effect which are no longer of a purely logical nature. If we decide to accept the general postulate suggested above, then a successful application of any such method will make the theory untenable.

22. APPLICATIONS OF SEMANTICS TO DEDUCTIVE SCIENCE. As regards the applicability of semantics to mathematical sciences and their methodology, i.e., to meta-mathematics, we are in a much more favorable position than in the case of empirical sciences. For, instead of advancing reasons which justify some hopes for the future (and thus making a kind of pro-semantics propaganda), we are able to point out concrete results already achieved.

Doubts continue to be expressed whether the notion of a true sentence—as distinct from that of a provable sentence—can have any significance for mathematical disciplines and play any part in a methodological discussion of mathematics. It seems to me, however, that just this notion of a true sentence constitutes a most valuable contribution to meta-mathematics by semantics. We already possess a series of interesting meta-mathematical results gained with the help of the theory of truth. These results concern the mutual relations between the notion of truth and that of provability; establish new properties of the latter notion (which, as well known, is one of the basic notions of meta-mathematics); and throw some light on the fundamental problems of consistency and completeness. The most significant among these results have been briefly discussed in Section 12.[34]

Furthermore, by applying the method of semantics we can adequately define several important meta-mathematical notions which have been used so far only in an intuitive way—such as, e.g., the notion of definability or that of a model of an axiom system; and thus we can undertake a systematic study of these notions. In particular, the investigations on definability have already brought some interesting results, and promise even more in the future.[35]

We have discussed the applications of semantics only to meta-mathematics, and not to mathematics proper. However, this distinction between mathematics and meta-mathematics is rather unimportant. For meta-mathematics is itself a deductive discipline and hence, from a certain point of view, a part of mathematics; and it is well known that—due to the formal character of deductive method—the results obtained in one deductive discipline can be automatically extended to any other discipline in which the given one finds an interpretation. Thus, for example, all meta-mathematical results can be interpreted as results of number theory. Also from a practical point of view there is no clear-cut line between meta-mathematics and mathematics proper; for instance, the investigations on definability could be included in either of these domains.

23. FINAL REMARKS. I should like to conclude this discussion with some general and rather loose remarks concerning the whole question of the evaluation of scientific achievements in terms of their applicability. I must confess I have various doubts in this connection.

Being a mathematician (as well as a logician, and perhaps a philosopher of a sort), I have had the opportunity to attend many discussions between specialists in mathematics, where the problem of applications is especially acute, and I have noticed on several occasions the following phenomenon: If a mathematician wishes to disparage the work of one of his colleagues, say, A, the most effective method he finds for doing this is to ask where the results can be applied. The hard pressed man, with his back against the wall, finally unearths the researches of another mathematician B as the locus of the application of his own results. If next B is plagued with a similar question, he will refer to another mathematician C. After a few steps of this kind we find ourselves referred back to the researches of A, and in this way the chain closes.

Speaking more seriously, I do not wish to deny that the value of a man's work may be increased by its implications for the research of others and for practice. But I believe, nevertheless, that it is inimical to the progress of science to measure the importance of any research exclusively or chiefly in terms of its usefulness and applicability. We know from the history of science that many important results and discoveries have had to wait centuries before they were applied in any field. And, in my opinion, there are

370   Philosophy and Phenomenological Research

also other important factors which cannot be disregarded in determining the value of a scientific work.   It seems to me that there is a special domain of very profound and strong human needs related to scientific research, which are similar in many ways to aesthetic and perhaps religious needs. And it also seems to me that the satisfaction of these needs should be considered an important task of research.   Hence, I believe, the question of the value of any research cannot be adequately answered without taking into account the intellectual satisfaction which the results of that research bring to those who understand it and care for it.   It may be unpopular and out-of-date to say—but I do not think that a scientific result which gives us a better understanding of the world and makes it more harmonious in our eyes should be held in lower esteem than, say, an invention which reduces the cost of paving roads, or improves household plumbing.

It is clear that the remarks just made become pointless if the word "application" is used in a very wide and liberal sense.   It is perhaps not less obvious that nothing follows from these general remarks concerning the specific topics which have been discussed in this paper; and I really do not know whether research in semantics stands to gain or lose by introducing the standard of value I have suggested.

Notes

[1] Compare Tarski [2] (see bibliography at the end of the paper).   This work may be consulted for a more detailed and formal presentation of the subject of the paper, especially of the material included in Sections 6 and 9–13.   It contains also references to my earlier publications on the problems of semantics (a communication in Polish, 1930; the article Tarski [1] in French, 1931; a communication in German, 1932; and a book in Polish, 1933).   The expository part of the present paper is related in its character to Tarski [3].   My investigations on the notion of truth and on theoretical semantics have been reviewed or discussed in Hofstadter [1], Juhos [1], Kokoszyńska [1] and [2], Kotarbiński [2], Scholz [1], Weinberg [1], *et al.*

[2] It may be hoped that the interest in theoretical semantics will now increase, as a result of the recent publication of the important work Carnap [2].

[3] This applies, in particular, to public discussions during the I. International Congress for the Unity of Science (Paris, 1935) and the Conference of International Congresses for the Unity of Science (Paris, 1937); cf., e.g., Neurath [1] and Gonseth [1].

[4] The words "notion" and "concept" are used in this paper with all of the vagueness and ambiguity with which they occur in philosophical literature.   Thus, sometimes they refer simply to a term, sometimes to what is meant by a term, and in other cases to what is denoted by a term.   Sometimes it is irrelevant which of these interpretations is meant; and in certain cases perhaps none of them applies adequately. While on principle I share the tendency to avoid these words in any exact discussion, I did not consider it necessary to do so in this informal presentation.

[5] For our present purposes it is somewhat more convenient to understand by "expressions," "sentences," etc., not individual inscriptions, but classes of inscriptions of similar form (thus, not individual physical things, but classes of such things).

SEMANTIC CONCEPTION OF TRUTH   371

⁶ For the Aristotelian formulation see Aristotle [1], Γ, 7, 27.   The other two formulations are very common in the literature, but I do not know with whom they originate.   A critical discussion of various conceptions of truth can be found, e.g., in Kotarbiński [1] (so far available only in Polish), pp. 123 ff., and Russell [1], pp. 362 ff.

⁷ For most of the remarks contained in Sections 4 and 8, I am indebted to the late S. Leśniewski who developed them in his unpublished lectures in the University of Warsaw (in 1919 and later).   However, Leśniewski did not anticipate the possibility of a rigorous development of the theory of truth, and still less of a definition of this notion; hence, while indicating equivalences of the form (T) as premisses in the antinomy of the liar, he did not conceive them as any sufficient conditions for an adequate usage (or definition) of the notion of truth.   Also the remarks in Section 8 regarding the occurrence of an empirical premiss in the antinomy of the liar, and the possibility of eliminating this premiss, do not originate with him.

⁸ In connection with various logical and methodological problems involved in this paper the reader may consult Tarski [6].

⁹ The antinomy of the liar (ascribed to Eubulides or Epimenides) is discussed here in Sections 7 and 8.   For the antinomy of definability (due to J. Richard) see, e.g., Hilbert-Bernays [1], vol. 2, pp. 263 ff.; for the antinomy of heterological terms see Grelling-Nelson [1], p. 307.

¹⁰ Due to Professor J. Łukasiewicz (University of Warsaw).

¹¹ This can roughly be done in the following way.   Let S be any sentence beginning with the words *"Every sentence."*   We correlate with S a new sentence S^* by subjecting S to the following two modifications: we replace in S the first word, *"Every,"* by *"The"*; and we insert after the second word, *"sentence,"* the whole sentence S enclosed in quotation marks.   Let us agree to call the sentence S "(self-)applicable" or "non-(self-)applicable" dependent on whether the correlated sentence S^* is true or false.   Now consider the following sentence:

Every sentence is non-applicable.

It can easily be shown that the sentence just stated must be both applicable and non-applicable; hence a contradiction.   It may not be quite clear in what sense this formulation of the antinomy does not involve an empirical premiss; however, I shall not elaborate on this point.

¹² The terms "logic" and "logical" are used in this paper in a broad sense, which has become almost traditional in the last decades; logic is assumed here to comprehend the whole theory of classes and relations (i.e., the mathematical theory of sets).   For many different reasons I am personally inclined to use the term "logic" in a much narrower sense, so as to apply it only to what is sometimes called "elementary logic," i.e., to the sentential calculus and the (restricted) predicate calculus.

¹³ Cf. here, however, Tarski [3], pp. 5 f.

¹⁴ The method of construction we are going to outline can be applied—with appropriate changes—to all formalized languages that are known at the present time; although it does not follow that a language could not be constructed to which this method would not apply.

¹⁵ In carrying through this idea a certain technical difficulty arises.   A sentential function may contain an arbitrary number of free variables; and the logical nature of the notion of satisfaction varies with this number.   Thus, the notion in question when applied to functions with one variable is a binary relation between these functions and single objects; when applied to functions with two variables it becomes a ternary relation between functions and couples of objects; and so on.   Hence, strictly

372   Philosophy and Phenomenological Research

speaking, we are confronted, not with one notion of satisfaction, but with infinitely many notions; and it turns out that these notions cannot be defined independently of each other, but must all be introduced simultaneously.

To overcome this difficulty, we employ the mathematical notion of an infinite sequence (or, possibly, of a finite sequence with an arbitrary number of terms). We agree to regard satisfaction, not as a many-termed relation between sentential functions and an indefinite number of objects, but as a binary relation between functions and sequences of objects. Under this assumption the formulation of a general and precise definition of satisfaction no longer presents any difficulty; and a true sentence can now be defined as one which is satisfied by every sequence.

[16] To define recursively the notion of satisfaction, we have to apply a certain form of recursive definition which is not admitted in the object-language. Hence the "essential richness" of the meta-language may simply consist in admitting this type of definition. On the other hand, a general method is known which makes it possible to eliminate all recursive definitions and to replace them by normal, explicit ones. If we try to apply this method to the definition of satisfaction, we see that we have either to introduce into the meta-language variables of a higher logical type than those which occur in the object-language; or else to assume axiomatically in the meta-language the existence of classes that are more comprehensive than all those whose existence can be established in the object-language. See here Tarski [2], pp. 393 ff., and Tarski [5], p. 110.

[17] Due to the development of modern logic, the notion of mathematical proof has undergone a far-reaching simplification. A sentence of a given formalized discipline is provable if it can be obtained from the axioms of this discipline by applying certain simple and purely formal rules of inference, such as those of detachment and substitution. Hence to show that all provable sentences are true, it suffices to prove that all the sentences accepted as axioms are true, and that the rules of inference when applied to true sentences yield new true sentences; and this usually presents no difficulty.

On the other hand, in view of the elementary nature of the notion of provability, a precise definition of this notion requires only rather simple logical devices. In most cases, those logical devices which are available in the formalized discipline itself (to which the notion of provability is related) are more than sufficient for this purpose. We know, however, that as regards the definition of truth just the opposite holds. Hence, as a rule, the notions of truth and provability cannot coincide; and since every provable sentence is true, there must be true sentences which are not provable.

[18] Thus the theory of truth provides us with a general method for consistency proofs for formalized mathematical disciplines. It can be easily realized, however, that a consistency proof obtained by this method may possess some intuitive value—i.e., may convince us, or strengthen our belief, that the discipline under consideration is actually consistent—only in case we succeed in defining truth in terms of a meta-language which does not contain the object-language as a part (cf. here a remark in Section 9). For only in this case the deductive assumptions of the meta-language may be intuitively simpler and more obvious than those of the object-language—even though the condition of "essential richness" will be formally satisfied. Cf. here also Tarski [3], p. 7.

The incompleteness of a comprehensive class of formalized disciplines constitutes the essential content of a fundamental theorem of K. Gödel; cf. Gödel [1], pp. 187 ff. The explanation of the fact that the theory of truth leads so directly to Gödel's theorem is rather simple. In deriving Gödel's result from the theory of truth we make

Semantic Conception of Truth   373

an essential use of the fact that the definition of truth cannot be given in a meta-language which is only as "rich" as the object-language (cf. note 17); however, in establishing this fact, a method of reasoning has been applied which is very closely related to that used (for the first time) by Gödel. It may be added that Gödel was clearly guided in his proof by certain intuitive considerations regarding the notion of truth, although this notion does not occur in the proof explicitly; cf. Gödel [1], pp. 174 f.

[19] The notions of designation and definition lead respectively to the antinomies of Grelling-Nelson and Richard (cf. note 9). To obtain an antinomy for the notion of satisfaction, we construct the following expression:

The sentential function X does not satisfy X.

A contradiction arises when we consider the question whether this expression, which is clearly a sentential function, satisfies itself or not.

[20] All notions mentioned in this section can be defined in terms of satisfaction. We can say, e.g., that a given term designates a given object if this object satisfies the sentential function "x is identical with T" where 'T' stands for the given term. Similarly, a sentential function is said to define a given object if the latter is the only object which satisfies this function. For a definition of consequence see Tarski [4], and for that of synonymity—Carnap [2].

[21] General semantics is the subject of Carnap [2]. Cf. here also remarks in Tarski [2], pp. 388 f.

[22] Cf. various quotations in Ness [1], pp. 13 f.

[23] The names of persons who have raised objections will not be quoted here, unless their objections have appeared in print.

[24] It should be emphasized, however, that as regards the question of an alleged vicious circle the situation would not change even if we took a different point of view, represented, e.g., in Carnap [2]; i.e., if we regarded the specification of conditions under which sentences of a language are true as an essential part of the description of this language. On the other hand, it may be noticed that the point of view represented in the text does not exclude the possibility of using truth-tables in a deductive development of logic. However, these tables are to be regarded then merely as a formal instrument for checking the provability of certain sentences; and the symbols 'T' and 'F' which occur in them and which are usually considered abbreviations of "*true*" and "*false*" should not be interpreted in any intuitive way.

[25] Cf. Juhos [1]. I must admit that I do not clearly understand von Juhos' objections and do not know how to classify them; therefore, I confine myself here to certain points of a formal character. Von Juhos does not seem to know my definition of truth; he refers only to an informal presentation in Tarski [3] where the definition has not been given at all. If he knew the actual definition, he would have to change his argument. However, I have no doubt that he would discover in this definition some "defects" as well. For he believes he has proved that "on ground of principle it is impossible to give such a definition at all."

[26] The phrases "*p is true*" and "*p is the case*" (or better "*it is true that p*" and "*it is the case that p*") are sometimes used in informal discussions, mainly for stylistic reasons; but they are considered then as synonymous with the sentence represented by 'p'. On the other hand, as far as I understand the situation, the phrases in question cannot be used by von Juhos synonymously with 'p'; for otherwise the replacement of (T) by (T') or (T'') would not constitute any "improvement."

[27] Cf. the discussion of this problem in Kokoszyńska [1], pp. 161 ff.

374   PHILOSOPHY AND PHENOMENOLOGICAL RESEARCH

[28] Most authors who have discussed my work on the notion of truth are of the opinion that my definition does conform with the classical conception of this notion; see, e.g., Kotarbiński [2] and Scholz [1].

[29] Cf. Ness [1]. Unfortunately, the results of that part of Ness' research which is especially relevant for our problem are not discussed in his book; compare p. 148, footnote 1.

[30] Though I have heard this opinion several times, I have seen it in print only once and, curiously enough, in a work which does not have a philosophical character—in fact, in Hilbert-Bernays [1], vol. II, p. 269 (where, by the way, it is not expressed as any kind of objection). On the other hand, I have not found any remark to this effect in discussions of my work by professional philosophers (cf. note 1).

[31] Cf. Gonseth [1], pp. 187 f.

[32] See Nagel [1], and Nagel [2], pp. 471 f. A remark which goes, perhaps, in the same direction is also to be found in Weinberg [1], p. 77; cf., however, his earlier remarks, pp. 75 f.

[33] Such a tendency was evident in earlier works of Carnap (see, e.g., Carnap [1], especially Part V) and in writings of other members of Vienna Circle. Cf. here Kokoszyńska [1] and Weinberg [1].

[34] For other results obtained with the help of the theory of truth see Gödel [2]; Tarski [2], pp. 401 ff.; and Tarski [5], pp. 111 f.

[35] An object—e.g., a number or a set of numbers—is said to be definable (in a given formalism) if there is a sentential function which defines it; cf. note 20. Thus, the term "definable," though of a meta-mathematical (semantic) origin, is purely mathematical as to its extension, for it expresses a property (denotes a class) of mathematical objects. In consequence, the notion of definability can be re-defined in purely mathematical terms, though not within the formalized discipline to which this notion refers; however, the fundamental idea of the definition remains unchanged. Cf. here—also for further bibliographic references—Tarski [1]; various other results concerning definability can also be found in the literature, e.g., in Hilbert-Bernays [1], vol. I, pp. 354 ff., 369 ff., 456 ff., etc., and in Lindenbaum-Tarski [1]. It may be noticed that the term "definable" is sometimes used in another, meta-mathematical (but not semantic), sense; this occurs, for instance, when we say that that a term is definable in other terms (on the basis of a given axiom system). For a definition of a model of an axiom system see Tarski [4].

BIBLIOGRAPHY

Only the books and articles actually referred to in the paper will be listed here.

Aristotle [1]. *Metaphysica.* (*Works*, vol. VIII.) English translation by W. D. Ross. Oxford, 1908.

Carnap, R. [1]. *Logical Syntax of Language.* London and New York, 1937.

Carnap, R. [2]. *Introduction to Semantics.* Cambridge, 1942.

Gödel, K. [1]. "Über formal unentscheidbare Sätze der *Principia Mathematica* und verwandter Systeme, I." *Monatshefte für Mathematik und Physik*, vol. XXXVIII, 1931, pp. 173–198.

Gödel, K. [2]. "Über die Länge von Beweisen." *Ergebnisse eines mathematischen Kolloquiums*, vol. VII, 1936, pp. 23–24.

Gonseth, F. [1]. "Le Congrès Descartes. Questions de Philosophie scientifique." *Revue thomiste*, vol. XLIV, 1938, pp. 183–193.

Grelling, K., and Nelson, L. [1]. "Bemerkungen zu den Paradoxien von Russell

SEMANTIC CONCEPTION OF TRUTH   375

und Burali-Forti." *Abhandlungen der Fries'schen Schule*, vol. II (new series), 1908, pp. 301–334.

Hofstadter, A. [1]. "On Semantic Problems." *The Journal of Philosophy*, vol. XXXV, 1938, pp. 225–232.

Hilbert, D., and Bernays, P. [1]. *Grundlagen der Mathematik*. 2 vols. Berlin, 1934–1939.

Juhos, B. von. [1]. "The Truth of Empirical Statements." *Analysis*, vol. IV, 1937, pp. 65–70.

Kokoszyńska, M. [1]. "Über den absoluten Wahrheitsbegriff und einige andere semantische Begriffe." *Erkenntnis*, vol. VI, 1936, pp. 143–165.

Kokoszyńska, M. [2]. "Syntax, Semantik und Wissenschaftslogik." *Actes du Congrès International de Philosophie Scientifique*, vol. III, Paris, 1936, pp. 9–14.

Kotarbiński, T. [1]. *Elementy teorji poznania, logiki formalnej i metodologji nauk*. (*Elements of Epistemology, Formal Logic, and the Methodology of Sciences*, in Polish.) Lwów, 1929.

Kotarbiński, T. [2]. "W sprawie pojęcia prawdy." ("*Concerning the Concept of Truth*," in Polish.) *Przegląd filozoficzny,* vol. XXXVII, pp. 85–91.

Lindenbaum, A., and Tarski, A. [1]. "Über die Beschränktheit der Ausdrucksmittel deduktiver Theorien." *Ergebnisse eines mathematischen Kolloquiums*, vol. VII, 1936, pp. 15–23.

Nagel, E. [1]. Review of Hofstadter [1]. *The Journal of Symbolic Logic*, vol. III, 1938, p. 90.

Nagel, E. [2]. Review of Carnap [2]. *The Journal of Philosophy*, vol. XXXIX, 1942, pp. 468–473.

Ness, A. [1]. " 'Truth' As Conceived by Those Who Are Not Professional Philosophers." *Skrifter utgitt av Det Norske Videnskaps-Akademi i Oslo, II. Hist.-Filos. Klasse*, vol. IV, Oslo, 1938.

Neurath, O. [1]. "Erster Internationaler Kongress für Einheit der Wissenschaft in Paris 1935." *Erkenntnis*, vol. V, 1935, pp. 377–406.

Russell, B. [1]. *An Inquiry Into Meaning and Truth*. New York, 1940.

Scholz, H. [1]. Review of *Studia philosophica*, vol. I. *Deutsche Literaturzeitung*, vol. LVIII, 1937, pp. 1914–1917.

Tarski, A. [1]. "Sur les ensembles définissables de nombres réels. I." *Fundamenta mathematicae*, vol. XVII, 1931, pp. 210–239.

Tarski, A. [2]. "Der Wahrheitsbegriff in den formalisierten Sprachen." (German translation of a book in Polish, 1933.) *Studia philosophica*, vol. I, 1935, pp. 261–405.

Tarski, A. [3]. "Grundlegung der wissenschaftlichen Semantik." *Actes du Congrès International de Philosophie Scientifique*, vol. III, Paris, 1936, pp. 1–8.

Tarski, A. [4]. "Über den Begriff der logischen Folgerung." *Actes du Congrès International de Philosophie Scientifique*, vol. VII, Paris, 1937, pp. 1–11.

Tarski, A. [5]. "On Undecidable Statements in Enlarged Systems of Logic and the Concept of Truth." *The Journal of Symbolic Logic*, vol. IV, 1939, pp. 105–112.

Tarski, A. [6]. *Introduction to Logic*. New York, 1941.

Weinberg, J. [1]. Review of *Studia philosophica*, vol. I. *The Philosophical Review*, vol. XLVII, pp. 70–77.

ALFRED TARSKI.

UNIVERSITY OF CALIFORNIA, BERKELEY.

2

Truth

P. F. STRAWSON

Reprinted with the kind permission of the publisher (Basil Blackwell) from *Analysis,* IX (1949), 83-97.

ANALYSIS 9 . 6   JUNE 1949

TRUTH

By P. F. Strawson

IN the following discussion, I confine myself to the question of the truth of empirical statements. My positive thesis is an elaboration of what was said, a long time ago, by F. P. Ramsey.[1] My negative purpose is the criticism of a current misconception —the Semantic or Meta-linguistic Theory of Truth—which seems to me to repeat, in a new way, some old mistakes. In so far as this theory is simply a contribution to the construction of artificial languages, and is not intended to be regarded as relevant to the use of actual languages, I am not concerned with it. But I think the theory has been claimed by some, and it has certainly been thought by many, to throw light on the actual use of the word ' true ' ; or (which I take to be the same claim) on the philosophical problem of truth. I think it *does* throw some light ; but I think it is also seriously misleading. Nothing that follows, however, is to be taken as implying that the word ' true ' is *never* used in the way described by the semantic theory. It is certainly so used for some technical purposes, and may sometimes be so used for non-technical purposes as well ; though I know of no such non-technical purposes.

I

In recent discussions of truth, one or both of two theses are commonly maintained. These are :

First, any sentence beginning ' It is true that . . .' does not change its assertive meaning when the phrase ' It is true that ' is omitted. More generally, to say that an assertion is true is not to make any further assertion at all ; it is to make the same assertion. This I shall call Thesis 1.

Second, to say that a statement is true is to make a statement about a sentence of a given language, viz., the language in which the first statement was made. It is (in other and more technical terms) to make a statement in a meta-language ascribing the semantic property of truth (or the semantic predicate ' true ') to a sentence in an object-language. The object-sentence concerned should strictly be written in inverted commas to make it clear that we are talking *about the sentence* ; and the phrase ' is true ' should strictly be followed by some such phrase as ' in L ', where ' L ' designates the object-language concerned. This I shall call Thesis 2.

[1] Ramsey, *Foundations of Mathematics*. pp. 142–143.

84   ANALYSIS

Of these two thesis, the first is true, but inadequate ; the second is false, but important. The first thesis is right in what it asserts, and wrong in what it suggests. The second thesis is wrong in what it asserts, but right in what it implies. The first thesis is right in asserting that to say that a statement is true is not to make a further statement ; but wrong in suggesting that to say that a statement is true is not to do something different from, or additional to, just making the statement. The second thesis is right in implying that to say that a statement is true is to do something different from just making the statement ; but wrong in asserting that this ' something different ' consists in making a further statement, viz. a statement about a sentence.

Although both theses are sometimes maintained by the same philosopher, it is easy to see that they cannot both be correct. For if it is true that to say (1) " Moths fly by night " is to make the same assertion as to say (2) " It is true that moths fly by night ", then it is false that to say (2) is to say anything about the English sentence " Moths fly by night " ; i.e. false that (2) ought strictly to be written " ' Moths fly by night ' is true in English ". If to say (2) is to make the same assertion as to say (1), then to say (2) cannot be to say anything about an English sentence ; for to say (1) is not to say anything about an English sentence, but is to say something about moths.

Independently of this, one sees how misleading it is to say that the phrase ' . . . is true ' is used to talk *about sentences,* by comparing it with other phrases which certainly are used to talk about sentences (or words, or phrases). For example, someone says, in French, " Il pleuve " ; and someone else corrects him, saying : " ' Il pleuve ' is *incorrect* French. ' Il pleut ' is the right way of saying it ". Or, criticising the style of a passage, someone says : " The sentence ' . . . . ' is *badly expressed.*" Similarly, one may ask what a sentence *means,* or say that a sentence is *ungrammatical, misspelt, a poor translation.* In all these cases, it is natural to say that one is talking *about a sentence.* If any statement of this kind were correctly translated into any language at all, the sentence which was being discussed would re-appear, quoted and untranslated, in the translation of the statement as a whole. Otherwise the translation would be incorrect. But it is perfectly obvious that a correct translation of any statement containing the phrase ' is true ' (used as it is ordinarily used) never contains a quoted and untranslated sentence to which the phrase " is true ' was *applied* in the original sentence. The phrase ' is true ' is not *applied to* sentences ; for it is not *applied to* anything.

Truth is not a property of symbols ; for it is not a property.

II

The habit of calling truth a ' semantic ' concept (' true ' a ' semantical predicate ') does not lessen the confusion involved in saying that ' true ' is a predicate of sentences ; but it helps to indicate a possible source of the confusion. I shall digress briefly to explore this source. For light on the use of the word ' semantic ', I quote the following from Carnap's ' Introduction to Semantics ' (p. 22) :

> " By a *semantical system* we understand a system of rules, formulated in a meta-language and referring to an object-language, of such a kind that the rules determine a *truth-condition* for every sentence of the object-language. . . . To formulate it in another way : the rules determine the *meaning* or *sense* of the sentences."

It will be noticed that the expressions ' truth-condition ' and ' meaning ' are used synonymously. And this suggests that even if there is no use of the phrase ' is true ' in which that phrase is correctly applied to (used to talk about) sentences, there is, or might be, a use of the phrase ' is true if and only if ', in which *this* phrase is correctly applied to (used to talk about) sentences ; a use, namely, in which this phrase would be synonymous with the phrase ' means that ' ; which certainly *is* used to talk about sentences. Suppose, for example, that we wish to give information about the meaning of the sentence " The monarch is deceased ". We can do this by making the following meta-statement :

(i) " The monarch is deceased " means that the king is dead. Here we put the sentence " The monarch is deceased " in inverted commas to indicate that we are talking about this sentence. We are making a meta-statement. And the meta-statement is contingent, for it is a contingent matter that the sentence in question has this meaning in English, or, indeed, that it has any meaning at all. To be quite strict, we perhaps ought to write it :

(ia) " The monarch is deceased " in English means that the king is dead.

If we were to translate this meta-statement into another language, none of the expressions occurring in it would remain unchanged except the quoted sentence " The monarch is deceased ". That would remain unchanged ; otherwise the translation would be incorrect. Now the suggestion is that we might, without unintelligibility, give the same information in exactly the same way, except that we should replace the phrase ' mean that ' with the phrase ' is true if and only if ' obtaining the contingent meta-statement :

86   ANALYSIS

(ii) " The monarch is deceased " is true if and only if the king is dead
or, more strictly :

(iia) " The monarch is deceased " is true in English if and only if the king is dead.

This seems to be an intelligible procedure. All that I have said of statements (i) and (ia) will apply to statements (ii) and (iia) ; we shall be using the phrase ' is true if and only if ', in a contingent statement, to talk about a sentence. Now consider a degenerate case of such meta-statements : the case exemplified in the sentences :

(iii) " The monarch is deceased " means (in English) that the monarch is deceased.

(iv) " The monarch is deceased " is true (in English) if and only the monarch is deceased.

It is difficult, and, perhaps, for the present purpose, not very important, to decide what status to assign to such sentences as these. Considerations which might tempt us to describe them firmly as true, contingent meta-statements are the following :

(*a*) Although they are of no use for telling us what the quoted sentence means, they do give us some information about it. They do at any rate indicate that the quoted sentence has some meaning in English.[1] And this is a contingent matter.

(*b*) These statements could be obtained from the non-degenerate cases by a quite legitimate process of translation, inference and retranslation. (Or, more simply, their correct translation into, say, French would undoubtedly yield a contingent meta-statement).

(*c*) It is a contingent matter that any sentence means what it does mean, expresses the proposition it does express.[2]

Although these considerations are decisive against calling (iii) and (iv) ' logically necessary ',[3] they are very inadequate grounds for calling them, without qualification, ' true and contingent '. For what contingent matter do they state? If we answer, taking the hint from (*a*), that they state merely that the

[1] One can imagine another use for statements (iii) and (iv) ; e.g. if the object-language were written, and the meta-language spoken, English.

[2] Cf. Lewy, " Truth and Significance," ANALYSIS, Vol. 8, No. 2.

[3] We might be tempted to call (iii) and (iv) " necessary ", because it seems self-contradictory to say :
(iiia) " The monarch is deceased " does not mean in English that the monarch is deceased.
But this would be a mistake. To say that a sentence both has some meaning or other and has no meaning at all would be to say something self-contradictory. To say that a sentence both has and has not some particular, specified meaning would be to say something self-contradictory. But (iiia) does neither of these things. The form of (iii) is appropriate to assigning, and that of (iiia) to withholding, some specific meaning. But since (iii) does not assign, (iiia) does not withhold, any specific meaning. (iiia) is not a self-contradictory, nor a false, contingent, statement ; but a pseudo-statement.

TRUTH 87

quoted sentence has some meaning in English, then their form (the use of the expression ' means that ') is utterly misleading. If we demand what contingent matter they state, which falls under the head of (*c*), no answer is possible. One cannot *state* what a sentence means without the help of another sentence.

For these reasons, I propose to continue to refer to statements (or pseudo-statements) like (iii) and (iv) not as necessary, nor as contingent, but simply as ' degenerate cases ' of contingent meta-statements of the type of (i) and (ii). The point is not in itself important ; though it is important that no confusion should arise from it.

The next step is to notice the deceptive similarity of the use of the phrase ' if and only if ' in this type of contingent meta-statement to its use in expressions which are not contingent statements, but necessary or defining formulae. An example of such a formula would be :

The monarch is deceased if and only if the king is dead.

Here the phrase ' is true ' does not occur ; and no part of this expression is in inverted commas. The formula itself does not give us information about the meaning of the sentence " The monarch is deceased ", though the statement that it *was* a necessary formula *would* give us such information. Now the similarity of the use of the phrase ' if and only if ' in these necessary formulae to its use as *part* of the phrase ' is true if and only if ' in contingent meta-statements, may have constituted a strong temptation to split the degenerate cases of such meta-statements down the middle, and to regard what follows the phrase ' if and only if ' as the definiens of what precedes it ; i.e. of the phrase " the sentence ' . . . . ' is true (in L) " ; to regard, for example, the whole expression (iii).

    " The monarch is deceased " is true if and only if the monarch
       is deceased.

as a specification or consequence or part[1] of a general definition of " . . . . is true " (or of " . . . is true in L "). And this we in fact find ; i.e. we find it said that a satisfactory general definition of truth must have as its consequences such expressions as the following :[2]

    (v) " To-day is Monday " is true if and only if to-day is Monday.

---

[1] E.g. Tarski, in *The Semantic Conception of Truth*, ' Philosophy and Phenomenological Research ', Vol. 4, 1943–44, p. 344, says :

" Every equivalence of the form (T) [(T) X is true if and only if p] obtained by replacing ' p ' by a particular sentence and ' X ' by a name of this sentence, may be considered a partial definition of truth, which explains wherein the truth of this one individual sentence consists. The general definition has to be, in a certain sense, a logical conjunction of all these partial definitions."

[2] Cf. M. Black, expounding and criticising Tarski, in ANALYSIS, Vol. 8, No. 4, p. 51.

88   ANALYSIS

(vi) " London is a City " is true if and only if London is a City. Now we have seen that such statements as (v) and (vi) are degenerate cases of those contingent meta-statements of the type of (ii), which make use of the phrase ' *is true if and only if* ' as a synonym for ' *means that* '. It is only *as a part of the former phrase* that the expression ' *is true* ' is used, in such statements, to talk about sentences. To read the degenerate cases, then, as specification, or parts, of some ideal defining formula for the phrase ' is true ' is to separate the phrase from the context which alone confers this meta-linguistic use upon it, and to regard the result as a model for the general use of ' is true '. It is to be committed to the mistake of supposing that the phrase ' is true ' is normally (or strictly) used as a meta-linguistic predicate. Thus misinterpreted, as defining formulae, such expressions as (v) are both fascinating and misleading. They mislead because, as we have seen, they crystallise the false Thesis 2. They fascinate because they seem to point to the true Thesis 1 ; for part of the expression to be defined (namely, the combination of quotation-marks and the phrase is ' true ') *disappears* in the definiens without being replaced by anything else. (How odd it is, incidentally, to call this definition-by-disappearance ' definition '!). In this way, the view that ' true ' is assertively redundant is represented as somehow combined with, and dependent upon, the view that ' true ' is a meta-linguistic predicate of sentences. We may express, then, the main contention of the semantic theory as follows : to say that a statement is true is not to say something further *about the subject-matter* of the statement, but is to say the same thing about the subject-matter of the statement, *by means of a further statement, namely a statement about a sentence.* Now I said that Thesis 1 is true. A fortiori, a modification of Thesis 1 is true, which I shall call Thesis 1A, and which runs as follows :

To say that a statement is true is not to say something further about the subject-matter of the statement, but, in so far as it is to say anything about that subject-matter, is to say the same thing about it.

Now Thesis 1A, but not Thesis 1, is compatible with Thesis 2. The semantic theory consists in the joint assertion of 1A and 2. I suggest that the semantic theory borrows a lot of its plausibility from the truth of 1A. We swallow 2 for the sake of 1A. I now wish to show that the unmodified thesis 1 is true, and that we therefore can and must assert 1A while rejecting 2 and, therefore, rejecting the semantic theory.

As for the muddle I have described above—the muddle of reading a degenerate case of contingent statements meta-lin-

TRUTH   89

guistically employing the phrase *is true if and only if*, as a pseudo-defining-formula of which the definiendum consists of a quoted sentence followed by the phrase *is true*—I do not claim that this muddle represents the genesis of the semantic theory ; but I do think that it, too, may have contributed to the plausibility of the theory.

III

The best way of showing that Thesis 1 is true is to correct its inadequacy. The best way of correcting its inadequacy is to discover the further reasons which have led to Thesis 2. To bring out those features of the situation which lead to the mistake of saying that the word 'true' is used meta-linguistically (to talk about sentences), I want first to compare the use of 'true' with that of 'Yes'. If you and I have been sitting together in silence for some time, and I suddenly say 'Yes', you would, perhaps, look at me with surprise and answer " I didn't say anything ". Of course, a man may say 'Yes' to himself ; and this will be a sign that he has resolved a doubt in his own mind, or come to a decision. But the normal use of 'Yes' is to answer : and where no question is asked, no answer can be given. Suppose you now ask : "Was Jones there?" and I say 'Yes' ; there seems no temptation whatever to say that, in so answering, I am *talking about* the English sentence "Was Jones there ?" So, in the case of 'Yes', we have a word of which the normal use requires some linguistic occasion (a question), without there being any temptation at all to say that it is used to *talk about* the sentence of which the utterance is the occasion for its use. There is indeed a temptation to go further in the opposite direction and say that in answering 'Yes' I am not talking *about* anything, not making any assertion, at all ; but simply answering. In a way, this is correct ; but in a way, it's wrong. For it would be perfectly correct for you, reporting our dialogue, to say of me : " He said Jones was there ". So of the ordinary use of 'Yes', we may say : first, that it demands a linguistic occasion, namely the asking of a question ; second, that it is not used meta-linguistically, to talk about the question, but to answer it ; third, that in so far as we are making an assertion at all in using it, the content of the assertion is the same as the content of the question. Now imagine a possible, and perhaps vulgarly current, use of the expression ' Ditto '. You make an assertion, and I say ' Ditto '. In so far as I assert anything, talk. about anything, I talk about and assert what you talk about and assert. Of course—and this points to the inadequacy of Thesis 1 and the reason for the meta-linguistic error—to say ' Ditto ' is not *the same as* to make the statement in question ; for, whereas I might have made the statement before anyone else had spoken, it would be meaningless for me to say ' Ditto ' before anyone else had spoken. ' Ditto ', like ' Yes ', requires a linguistic occasion. But again, and largely, I think, because the expression ' Ditto ' does not consist of a grammatical subject and a grammatical predicate, there is absolutely no temptation to say that in thus using ' Ditto ', I should be talking *about the sentence* you used, and the utterance of which was the linguistic occasion for my use of this expression. I am not talking about what you said (the noise you made, or the sentence you spoke, or the proposition you expressed). I am agreeing with, endorsing, underwriting what you said ; and, unless you had said something, I couldn't perform *these* activities, though I could *make the assertion* you made. Now the expression ' That's true ' sometimes functions in just the way in which I have suggested the expression ' Ditto ' might function. A says " Jones was there " and B says ' That's true ' ; and C, reporting the conversation, can correctly say : " Both A and B said that Jones was there ". But the point is that B couldn't have said that Jones was there in the way he *did* say it, (i.e. by the use of the expression ' That's true '), unless A had previously uttered the *sentence* " Jones was there ", or some equivalent sentence. It is, perhaps, *this* fact about the use (*this* use) of the word ' true ', together with the old prejudice that any indicative sentence must describe (be ' about ') something, which encourages those who have become chary of saying that truth is a property of propositions to say instead that in using the word ' true ', we are talking about sentences. (What I have said about the use of ' That's true ' applies, of course, with suitable alterations, to the use of ' That's false ').

Now those who assert that ' true ' is a predicate of sentences have not, in general, considered these simple cases of the use of ' true ' (and ' false '), but the more puzzling cases which lead, or seem to lead, to paradoxes : such as the case where someone utters the isolated sentence " What I am saying now is false ", or writes on an otherwise clean blackboard the sentence " Every statement on this blackboard is false ". The solution on meta-linguistic lines is to treat these sentences as making statements of the second order to the effect :

(1) that there is some statement of the first order written on the blackboard (or said by me now) ;
and (2) that any first-order statement written on the blackboard (or said by me now) is false.

By means of this distinction of orders, the distinction between meta and object-language, the puzzling sentences are

TRUTH   91

said no longer to engender contradictions : either they are simply false, since the existential part of what they assert is false ; or, alternatively, leaving out the existential part of the analysis, and treating them solely as hypotheticals, they are seen to be vacuously true, since no first-order statements occur. This solution is formally successful in avoiding the apparent contra-dictions. But it seems to me to achieve this success only by repeating the fundamental mistake from which the contradictions themselves arise, and also, and consequently, involving the difficulties mentioned at the beginning of this paper. That is, first, it involves the view that to say that a statement is true (or false) is to make a further, second-order, statement (thus contradicting Thesis 1) ; and, second, it (usually) involves the unplausibility of saying that this second-order statement is *about* a sentence or sentences. Now the point of the previous discussion of the actual use of ' Yes ', the possible use of ' Ditto ' and the actual use of ' That's true ' is to show that these expedients are unnecessary. When no-one has spoken, and I say ' Ditto ', I am not making a false statement to the effect that something true has been said, nor a true statement to the effect that nothing false has been said. I am not making a statement at all ; but producing a pointless utterance. When somebody has made an assertion previously, my saying ' Ditto ' acquires a point, has an occasion : and, if you like, you may say that I am now making a statement, repeating, in a manner, what the speaker said. But I am not making an additional statement, a meta-statement. It would perhaps be better to say that my utterance is not a statement at all, but a linguistic per-formance for which in the first case there was not, and in the second case there was, an occasion : so that in the first case it was a spurious, and in the second case a genuine, perfomance. Similarly, the words ' true ' and ' false ' normally require, as an occasion for their significant use, that somebody should have made, be making or be about to make (utter or write), some statement. (The making of the statement need not precede the use of ' true ' : it may follow it as in the case of the expression " It is true that . . . "—a form of words I shall discuss later). But in all cases the indicative clause of which the grammatical predicate is the phrase ' is true ' does not in itself make any kind of statement at all (not even a meta-statement), and *a fortiori* cannot make the statement, the making of which is required as the occasion for the significant use of the words ' true ' or ' false '. This is not, as it stands, quite accurate. For an indica-tive sentence of which the grammatical predicate is the phrase ' is true ' may sometimes, as I shall shortly show, be used to make an implicit meta-statement. But when this is so, the phrase 'is true' plays no part in the making of this meta-statement. The phrase 'is true' *never* has a statement-making role. And when this is seen, the paradoxes vanish without the need for the meta-linguistic machinery; or at least without the need for regarding the words 'true' and 'false" as part of that machinery. The paradoxes arise on the assumption that the words 'true' and 'false' can be used to make first-order assertions. They are formally solved by the declaration that these words can be used only to make second-order assertions. Both paradoxes and solution disappear on the more radical assumption that they are not used to make assertions of any order, are not used to make assertions at all.

I said, however, that indicative sentences of which the grammatical predicate is the phrase 'is true' or the phrase 'is false' may be used to make an implicit meta-statement, in the making of which these phrases themselves play no part. To elucidate this, consider the following sentences :

(1) What I am saying now is false
(2) All statements made in English are false
(3) What the policeman said is true.

It is certainly not incorrect to regard each of these sentences as implicitly making an *existential* meta-statement, which does not involve the words 'true' or 'false'. The implicit meta-statements in these cases might be written as follows :

(1a) I have just made (am about to make) a statement
(2a) Some statements are made in English
(3a) The policeman made a statement.

These are all second-order assertive sentences to the effect that there are some first-order assertive sentences, uttered (*a*) by me, (*b*) in English, (*c*) by the policeman.

These second-order assertive sentences we can regard as part of the analysis of the sentences (1), (2) and (3). Obviously they are not the whole of their analysis. The sentence "The policeman made a statement " clearly has not the same use as the sentence " What the policeman said is true ". To utter the second is to do something more than to assert the first. What is this additional performance ? Consider the circumstances in which we might use the expression " What the policeman said is true ". Instead of using this expression, I might have *repeated* the policeman's story. In this case, I shall be said to have *confirmed* what the policeman said. I might, however, have made exactly the same set of statements as I made in repeating his story, but have made them *before* the policeman spoke. In this case, though the assertions I have made are no different, I have not done what I did in the other case, namely ' confirmed his story '. So to confirm his story is not to say anything further, *about* his story, or the sentences he used in telling it, though it is to do something that cannot be done unless he has told his story. Now, unlike the confirming narrative which I might have told, the sentence " What the policeman said is true " has no use *except* to confirm the policeman's story[1] ; but like the confirming narrative, the sentence does not say anything further *about* the policeman's story or the sentences he used in telling it. It is a device for confirming the story without telling it again. So, in general, in using such expressions, we are confirming, underwriting, admitting, agreeing with, what somebody has said ; but (except where we are implicitly making an existential meta-statement, in making which the phrase ' is true ' plays no part), we are not making any assertion additional to theirs ; and are *never* using ' is true ' to talk *about* something which is *what they said*, or the sentences they used in saying it. To complete the analysis, then, of the entire sentence (3) " What the policeman said is true ", we have to add, to the existential meta-assertion, a phrase which is not assertive, but (if I may borrow Mr. Austin's word) performatory.[2] We might, e.g., offer, as a complete analysis of one case, the expression : " The policeman made a statement. I confirm it " ; where, in uttering the words " I confirm it ", I am not describing something I do, but *doing* something.[3] There is, then, a difference between the more complicated cases in which the phrase ' is true ' is preceded by a descriptive phrase, and the simpler sentences (e.g. ' That's true ') in which the phrase ' is true ' is preceded by a demonstrative. The former may be regarded as involving an implicit meta-statement, while the latter are purely confirmatory (or purely ' admittive '). But in neither sort of case has the phrase ' is true ' any assertive (or meta-assertive) function.

There may still be some uneasiness felt at the denial that the phrase ' is true ' has any assertive, or descriptive, function. Partially to allay this uneasiness, I will again say something familiar, that I have said already : that is, that when I say ' That's true ' in response to your statement, I am in a manner making an assertion, namely the assertion you made ; describing something, namely what you described. But pointing this out is quite consistent with saying that ' That's true ' makes no statement in its own right. It makes no meta-statement. If

---

[1] This needs qualification. Uttered by a witness, the sentence is a *confirmation* ; wrung from the culprit, it is an *admission*. No doubt there are other cases.

[2] Cf. J. L. Austin, ' Other Minds ', P.S.A. Supp. Vol. XX, pp. 169–175 for an account of some words of this class.

[3] Cf. also ' I admit it '. To *say* this *is* to make an admission.

94   ANALYSIS

there is any residual uneasiness, it ought not to be allayed. For
its source is the ancient prejudice that any indicative sentence is,
or makes,[1] a statement. I call it a prejudice : we could, instead,
make it a criterion. And there would even be no harm in adopting this criterion for 'statement', if we could simultaneously
divorce the word, in this strictly grammatical use, from its
logic in other uses : from that logic which leads us, given a
'statement', to enquire : What is it about ? What does it
describe ? What property, or what relation, does it assert to
belong to, or hold between, what entity or entities ? Asking
these questions when confronted with such a sentence as
"What Pascal said is true ", we are led to look for the entity
which is *what Pascal said* ; looking with cautious, contemporary
eyes, we find only his words ; and so are induced to say that, in
using this expression, we are talking about the French sentences
he wrote or spoke. It is, then, the out-of-date desire that the
phrase 'is true' should be some kind of a descriptive phrase,
that leads to the up-to-date suggestion that the word 'true' is a
second-level predicate of first-level sentences. More important
than simply to reject *this* view is to have the right reason for
rejecting it : the reason, namely, that the phrase 'is true' is
not descriptive at all. If we persist that it describes (is about)
something, while denying that it describes (is about) sentences,
we shall be left with the old, general questions about the nature
of, and tests for, truth, about the nature of the entities related
by the truth-relation, and so on. Better than asking "What is
the criterion of truth ? " is to ask : "What are the grounds for
agreement ? "—for those we see to be not less various than the
subjects on which an agreed opinion can be reached. And this
will perhaps also discourage us from seeking to mark the
difference between one kind of utterance and another by saying,
for example, " Ethical utterances are not true or false ". It is
correct to say that utterances of any kind are true or false, if it is
correct usage to signify agreement or disagreement with such
utterances by means of the *expressions* 'true' or 'false'.

Of course, the formula that I have adopted in the discussion
of one use of 'true' is not immune from another variant of
that argument from grammar which leads to treating 'true' as a
descriptive word. Someone might say : in order for you to
confirm anything, there must be some *object* of this activity; a
sentence or a proposition: and to perform this activity upon
this object is nothing other than to assert that the object has the

---

[1] Throughout I have used such mild barbarisms as " This sentence makes a statement "
as shorthand for such expressions as " Anyone who uttered this sentence would be making
a statement ".

property, stands in the relation, referred to by the word ' true '. Anyone who says this is misled partly by the fact that the verb ' confirm ' takes a grammatical object ; and partly by the fact that the linguistic performance (of ' confirming ') requires, not an object, but an *occasion*—a fact which I declared to be the misunderstood element of truth in the semantic theory. Even this assertion—that there must be, or be thought to be, some kind of sign-occasion for the significant, or genuine, use of the word ' true '—is not quite correct, if it means that some spoken or written utterance must occur, or be thought to occur. For it would not be incorrect, though it would be unusual, to say : " What you are thinking is true " ; when nothing has been said. (But, then, a conversation *can* be carried on by glances and nods).

IV

In philosophical discussion of this whole subject, very little attention has been paid to the actual use of ' true '. And I want to conclude by distinguishing some of its normal uses in a little more detail. The uses mentioned so far I was tempted to call ' performatory '. But this is a misnomer. A performatory word, in Austin's sense, I take to be a verb, the use of which, in the first person present indicative, seems to describe some activity of the speaker, but in fact *is* that activity. Clearly the use of ' is true ' does not seem to describe any activity of the speaker ; it *has seemed* to describe a sentence, a proposition, or statement. The point of using Austin's word at all is the fact that the phrase ' is true ' can sometimes be replaced,[1] without any important change in meaning, by some such phrase as " I confirm it ", which is performatory in the strict sense. I shall take the substitute performatory word as a title for each of these cases ; and shall speak, e.g., of the ' confirmatory ' or ' admissive ' use of ' true '. What commends the word as, e.g., a confirmatory device is its economy. By its means we can confirm without repeating.

The word has other, equally non-descriptive, uses. A familiar one is its use in sentences which begin with the phrase " It's true that ", followed by a clause, followed by the word ' but ', followed by another clause. It has been pointed to me that the words " It's true that . . . but . . . " could, in these sentences, be replaced by the word ' Although ' ; or, alternatively, by the words " I concede that . . . but . . ." This use of the phrase, then, is concessive. The inappropriateness of the meta-linguistic treatment seems peculiarly apparent here.

[1] Of course, not *simply* replaced. Other verbal changes would be necessary.

96   ANALYSIS

The purely confirmatory use is probably no more common
than other uses which look much the same, but which are, I
think, distinct. A man may make an assertion to you, not wanting you to confirm it, to remove the doubt of others or his own ;
but wanting to know that you share his belief, or his attitude.
If, in this case, you say ' That's true ', you are not *saying*, but
indicating, that you do share his belief. It seems to me natural
to describe this simply as ' agreeing '. Again, it seems to me
that we very often use the phrase ' That's true ' to express, not
only agreement with what is said, but also our sense of its
novelty and force. We register the impact of what is said, much
as we might register it by saying : " I never thought of that ".
Contrast the ironical ' very true ' with which we sometimes
rudely greet the obvious. The use of ' true ' here is effectively
ironical just because we normally use it to express agreement
when our agreement is in doubt, or to register a sense of revelation. Sometimes, in sentences beginning " Is it true that . . .? "
or " So it's true that . . . ", we could preserve the expressive
quality of the utterance by substituting the adverb ' really ' for
the quoted phrases, at an appropriate point in the sentence ; to
convey, as they do, incredulity or surprise.

No doubt, the word has other functions ; but those I have
mentioned are probably as common as any. The important
• point is that the performance of these functions (and, I suspect,
of all other non-technical jobs the word may do) does not involve
the use of a meta-linguistic predicate; and that we *could*, with no
very great violence to our language, perform them without the
need for any expression which *seems* (as ' is true ' seems) to make
a statement. For instance, the substitution of ' although ' for
" It's true that . . . but . . . " is an obvious way of dealing with
the concessive use ; an extension of the practice of the inarticu-
late election-candidate whose speech consisted of " Ditto to
Mr. X " might deal with the confirmatory and, partly, with the
expressive uses ; and so on. The selection of the substitute-
expressions would of course be governed by the propagandist
consideration that they should provide the minimum encouragement to anyone anxious to mistake them for statement-making
phrases, or descriptive words.

One last point : a suggestion on the reasons why the puzzle
about truth has commonly got entangled with the puzzle about
certainty. It is above all when a doubt has been raised, when
mistakes or deceit seem possible ; when the need for confirmation is felt ; that we tend to make use of those certifying
words of which ' true ' is one and of which others are ' certain ',
' know ', ' prove ', ' establish ', ' validate ', ' confirm ', ' evi-

dence' and so on. So that the question " What is the nature of truth ? " leads naturally to the question " What are the tests for truth ? ", and this, in its turn, to the question " What are the conditions of certainty ? " The historical or judicial search for truth is the search for the evidence which will set doubt at rest. The philosophical endeavour to characterise truth *in general* has tended to become the endeavour to characterise that which *in general* sets doubt at rest ; really and finally at rest. Where you find the indubitable, there you find the true. And this metaphysical road branches into different paths, at the end of one of which you find the Atomic Fact, and, at the end of another, the Absolute.

Finally, I will repeat that in saying that the word ' true ' has not in itself any assertive function, I am not of course saying that a sentence like " His statement is true " is incorrect. Of course the word ' statement ' may be the grammatical subject of a sentence of which the phrase ' is true ' is the grammatical predicate. Nor am I recommending that we drop this usage. But for the usage, there would be no problem.

University College, Oxford.

3

Truth and Correspondence

G. J. WARNOCK

Reprinted with the kind permission of the publisher from C. D. Rollins, ed., *Knowledge and Experience* (Pittsburgh: University of Pittsburgh Press, 1963), 11-20.

TRUTH AND CORRESPONDENCE

G. J. WARNOCK

1. As philosophical theories go, the so-called Correspondence Theory of Truth has had a pretty long life, and I hope I am not alone in thinking that it is not dead yet. It has, indeed, quite recently been pronounced dead. In 1950 the late J. L. Austin propounded what has been called a "purified version" of the theory, in reply to which Mr. P. F. Strawson contended—with, I think it has been widely supposed, conclusive success—that the theory could not be purified: it needed to be interred.[1] However, it is not clear to me that Mr. Strawson's grounds for saying this were conclusive; so that the Correspondence Theory is not yet, in my view, a plainly dead duck. In this paper I shall consider some of the objections which have been or which might be urged against it.

Austin's "purified version" runs briefly as follows. Let us take it, he says, that it is statements which primarily or centrally are said to be true or untrue. It is then, he thinks, correct to say—so correct indeed as to be somewhat platitudinous—that a statement's being true consists in its "correspondence" to something "in the world"— the expression 'the world' here being used to designate quite generally the subject-matter of possible statement-making discourse. Where purification is called for is not, he thinks, in saying this much, but only in going on to give an account of what is to be understood here by the term 'correspondence.' What is it for a statement to "correspond to" something in the world?

To this question Austin offers an answer in two stages. Consider for example the words 'The corn is green.' There are in the first place, Austin says, "descriptive conventions" by which these words are "correlated" with a certain *type* of situation, or state of affairs, to be found (perhaps) in the world; and, roughly speaking, to know what these conventions are is to know what the English sentence

[1] See Symposium on Truth, Aristotelian Society Supplementary Volume XXIV, 1950, pp. 111–172; also J. L. Austin, *Philosophical Papers*, Oxford, 1961, pp. 85–101. Perhaps I should mention here that the present paper examines some points not examined in another (not yet published) paper dealing with the same cluster of issues: in particular I consider there, and do not consider here, the question whether it is, as Mr. Strawson has argued, mistaken in principle to suppose that one who says that what someone has said is true thereby makes a statement about a statement, or a further assertion about an assertion, or says something about what the (other) speaker has said. I believe, for reasons too lengthy to be rehearsed here, that this very natural supposition is not mistaken. But besides this there are, of course, many other issues of interest, importance, and relevance not touched on in the pages that follow.

12   TRUTH AND CORRESPONDENCE

'The corn is green' means. But second, there are also "demonstrative conventions" correlating, not the words but particular utterances of the words, with particular—in Austin's term "historic"—situations or states of affairs to be found at particular times or places in the world; and to know what these conventions are is to be in a position to know (given the context of utterance) what *particular* state of affairs one who says on some occasion that the corn is green, is alluding to. The statement that the corn is green is said to be true, then, when it corresponds to something in the world in the following sense: the words 'The corn is green,' as uttered on some particular occasion, are correlated by the demonstrative conventions with a historic situation or state of affairs which is of the type with which, in the language, the words 'The corn is green' are correlated by the descriptive conventions.[2]

2. Now this account of the matter, which Austin evidently regarded as rather obviously correct, has in fact been objected to on a good many grounds. Let us first take this one. Austin's account, it might be said, offers to elucidate the notion of truth in terms of the correspondence of statements to something "in the world"; but it does not actually do this. If we consider the statement that the corn is green, we see that there is indeed something in the world to which the words 'the corn' could (not very felicitously) be said to correspond —namely, that corn which the speaker refers to, which his statement is about. But there is actually nothing at all in the world with which the statement *as a whole* could be said to correspond, in the way in which the referring expression 'the corn' could be said to correspond to the corn. To put it rather roughly: only objects (such as corn) are genuinely in the world; those entities, "situations" or "states of affairs," to which in Austin's account true statements are said to correspond are plainly not, however, objects, and hence are not in the world.

Now this objection aims, it may be, at a serious point; but there is surely not very much in what it actually says. For it is surely both quite good sense and perfectly good English to speak, say, of the political situation in Cuba in 1959, or of the state of affairs in my cornfield at the end of May 1962; and do we not here have places and dates used, quite naturally, to identify particular situations or states of affairs? How could this be done, if they were not in any sense at all in space or time? A state of affairs, no doubt, is not an object, and does not have a neatly bounded place in the world *just as* an object typically does; but is this the only sense in which anything can be said to be in the world? Suppose I were to say that one-party dictatorships are sometimes very popular; would it not be

[2] See J. L. Austin, *Philosophical Papers*, p. 90.

quite proper for a sceptical interlocutor to ask where in the world such a state of affairs is to be found? And might I not answer quite properly, even truly perhaps, "In Cuba, for instance"? There does not appear to me to be any better reason for denying that situations, say, can be in the world than there would be for denying that reflections, say, can be in mirrors. The expression 'the situation in Cuba' is not indeed exactly analogous with the expression 'the house in Cuba,' just as the expression 'the reflection in the mirror' is not exactly analogous with the expression 'the glass in the mirror.' But what this seems to show is only that 'in' has somewhat different uses.

3. It might more seriously be objected, however, that to look, as Austin does, for something "in the world" to which a true statement as a whole can be said to correspond is inevitably to reduce one's account of truth to triviality, to the status of a wholly unilluminating *pseudo*-account. The most natural candidate, so Mr. Strawson has argued, for the role of that in the world to which a true statement corresponds is "a fact." But to say that a true statement corresponds to a fact is to say practically nothing; for there is no way of identifying a fact except as that which some true statement states; so that to say that a true statement corresponds to a fact is in effect to produce the markedly unenlivening tautology that a true statement states what that statement, if it is true, does state.

This objection, however, is not as it stands strictly applicable to what Austin says. For his account of truth does not employ the term 'fact'; it employs the terms 'situation' and 'state of affairs.' Does this difference matter? I am inclined to think, though with some trepidation and uncertainty, that it does.

I take it that the nerve of the objection to the use, in this context, of the expression 'fact' is that, in Mr. Strawson's worlds, 'fact' is wedded to 'that'-clauses.[3] The fact with which, if with any, the statement that the corn is green is correlated is the fact that the corn is green; but this fact is simply what the statement states, or what one who makes that statement alleges. The fact that the corn is green does not "make" the statement that the corn is green true or untrue; for, on the one hand, if the statement is not true, there is no such fact; while, on the other hand, if the statement is true, then that there is such a fact is quite trivially analytic. As we expressed it a moment ago, there is no way of identifying a fact except as that which some true statement states, or as that which some person states in making a true statement; so that here we have absolutely no explanatory leverage.

[3] It should be noted that Austin had questions to raise about this. See *Philosophical Papers*, pp. 102–122.

But the case is surely otherwise with states of affairs. If I hear someone say that the corn is green, then certainly, if I understand his words, I know what sort or "type" of state of affairs he is alleging to obtain; but there also arises the further question, what *particular* state of affairs his utterance alludes to. Well, I learn, let us say, that he is alluding to the state of affairs currently obtaining in my hundred-acre field. So far, so good; but it does not of course follow from any of this that what he says is true, or again untrue. To determine that question I may need to go to my hundred-acre field and examine the state of affairs there obtaining; and what I observe there may "make" what he says true—or, of course, it may not. Whereas, one might say, a statement is related to a fact not at all if it is false, and trivially if it is true, it may be related to, "correlated" with, a particular state of affairs and be in fact *either* true *or* false *of* that state of affairs; and the "type" of that state of affairs is what "makes" it true or false. I do not see in this either an impropriety, or a triviality. To put it succinctly, Austin's account embodies, what doubtless talk of "correspondence with facts" undesirably obscures, the distinction between meaning ("descriptive conventions") and reference ("demonstrative conventions"); and I cannot suppose that anyone would wish to hold either that this distinction is not important, or that it is not of central relevance to the question what it is for a statement to be true.

Again, it has been said that facts are "*quasi*-linguistic" entities, and for that reason unsuited to illuminate the nature of truth; but, if I know what this means, it would seem that the same thing is *not* true of situations. Facts, I suppose, might be said to be "linguistic" for such reasons as these: people *state* facts, much as they state (say) propositions; facts are, much as (say) statements are, very often *about* things; we refer to a fact, as we refer to what someone said, with a 'that'-clause. The fact that there are tigers in India is a fact about the fauna of India, and is what someone states who says truly that there are tigers there. But situations are not, like facts, stated; they may be, like tables, described. They cannot, as facts can, be said to be "about" anything. The expression 'the situation that . . .' is not admissible English. It appears, then, that if the term 'fact' is objectionable in this connection, it at least cannot be for just the same reasons that the terms 'situation' and 'state of affairs' are objectionable; a new case, if there is one, would need to be made out against them.

4. But, it may next be urged, though the distinction between meaning and reference is doubtless of importance, Austin's mode of stating and employing it is nevertheless infelicitous. There fall, I think, to be considered here two objections—objections which, if I am right, rather neatly cancel each other out.

(i) What would we ordinarily say that a statement, or one who utters a statement, refers to? To what the statement is about. What then is the statement that the corn is green about? Surely it is about the corn—in particular, let us suppose, about the corn now standing in my hundred-acre field. All this seems very clear: and would it not be vastly preferable to state the matter in this way, rather than to nominate, as Austin does, so relatively perplexing an entity as the *state of affairs* in my hundred-acre field as that with which the statement is "demonstratively correlated"? The expressions 'situation' and 'state of affairs' are certainly vague and perhaps obscure in significance; situations and states of affairs are somewhat abstract entities; and what reason is there for bringing them in at this point, rather than such familiar objects as corn, cats, cabbages, and kings —the *things* in the world that from time to time we refer to, or talk about? We do, indeed, sometimes refer to situations, as in 'The situation in my hundred-acre field is deteriorating daily'; but should not this very special case be distinguished from that of such earthier, less abstract locutions as 'The corn is green'?

I think, however, that it is not difficult to see a reason for Austin's choice of terminology at this point. It seems perfectly proper to say in general, though admittedly in somewhat distressingly abstract terms, that one who makes a statement thereby says that some state of affairs obtains, and that whether or not his statement is true is a matter of whether or not the particular state of affairs he alludes to is of the character, kind, or type of which, in his utterance, he says that it is. It is, by contrast, plainly not possible to say in general, even though the terms be less alarmingly abstract, that one who makes a statement thereby says something about some thing or things to which he refers; for this is true, of course, only of statements of a certain sort, namely, those which do happen to be about, or to refer to, some particular thing or things. If I say, for instance, that there are no green dogs, I allude presumably to the present state of affairs in the animal kingdom; but I do not refer to green dogs, nor to any other dogs, or animals, or even objects. Thus, while the terminology of 'situations' and 'states of affairs' may justly be thought to have the demerit of abstractness, and even of some measure of obscurity, it may be held to have the compensating virtue, for the present purpose, of general applicability.

(ii) Consideration of this latter objection disposes also, I believe, of the next one. It has been urged by Mr. Strawson against Austin's account that it is, among other things, undesirably narrow in its range of application; by implying, as Austin does, that all stating involves both "demonstration" and "description," does he not implicitly restrict his account to that particular variety of stating which does consist in saying something about some particular thing or things? Does it not appear that he has overlooked the existence of

16   TRUTH AND CORRESPONDENCE

statements in which nothing (in particular) is referred to, no object is talked about?

But it will be evident, I think, that there is a misunderstanding here. For, as we have just seen, Austin's words are so chosen as precisely to avoid the restrictiveness with which he is thus charged. Mr. Strawson evidently took Austin to be claiming, or perhaps to be inadvertently implying, that every statement must involve demonstrative conventions in the sense that it must refer to, or be about, some individual thing (object, event, etc.) or things, as 'The cat is white' refers to or is about this particular cat. This would indeed be pretty intolerably restrictive; and it would indeed be pertinent to object to this claim, or this implication, that 'There are white cats' is an evident counter-example, since of course in making the statement that there are white cats I do not allude to any white cats in particular, and could not properly be asked *which* white cats I am saying that there are. But the fact is that Austin's account does not actually have the implication which Mr. Strawson claims to find in it. For that with which a statement is, in Austin's sense, correlated by demonstrative conventions is never a particular thing or things—not, for instance, a particular cat; but rather a particular situation or state of affairs—for instance, the particular situation of some cat's being (or possibly not being) white. It is plain that this is a substantially different matter; for one thing, it is plain that two or more statements about a cat might all refer, in Mr. Strawson's sense, to the same thing, namely the same cat, while being demonstratively correlated, in Austin's sense, with quite different things, namely two or more different states of affairs in the presumably quite varied life-history of the cat.

5. In saying, then, or implying that all stating involves both demonstrative and descriptive conventions, Austin is not espousing the certainly most restrictive and unappealing doctrine that all statements must be about, must refer to, some individual thing or things. However, the question does of course still arise whether or not, when we have cleared this misunderstanding out of the way, it is actually correct to imply, as he does, that "demonstrative conventions" are involved in the making of *any* true statement. There remain, I think, serious grounds on which this might be questioned.

Let us ask, then, this question: what does Austin's assumption of the general necessity of both demonstrative and descriptive conventions presuppose? What would have to be the case for it to be true? Well, what his view presupposes, I believe, is this: that any statement is such that (i) it is possible for states of affairs in the world either to be or not be of the "type" which it asserts to obtain; and also such that (ii) we might, at least in principle, come across states of affairs whose being of that type would not establish its truth, and whose not being of that type would not establish its falsehood. For in the case of any statement satisfying these conditions, since there will be in the world states of affairs not *relevant* to its truth or falsehood, the question whether it is true or false must raise the prior question what particular state of affairs is being alluded to, and thus may relevantly be investigated; and to answer this question we must make use of demonstrative conventions. For example: cats may in general be either white or not white; and further, when I state on some particular occasion that the cat is white, there will be some cats whose whiteness does not establish that my statement is true, and some cats whose tabbiness, say, does not establish that it is false. Thus, if we are to consider profitably whether or not my statement that the cat is white is true, we need to be apprised, by way of the appropriate demonstrative conventions, what particular state of affairs—roughly, which cat when—it would be to the point for us to take a look at.

The question now arises, then, whether it can be held that statements in general must satisfy the above two conditions. Well, I think this much at any rate can be said: that any statement must satisfy these conditions, *if* we are ever to be in a position to pronounce it to be true on empirical grounds. It is fairly obvious, I think, that this is so. For if we are to be in a position to pronounce statements to be true on empirical grounds, we must do so by investigation of the appropriate states of affairs in the world; but, however many such states of affairs we might investigate, it seems reasonable to suppose that there would always be indefinitely many that we have not investigated; and thus, if our investigations are ever to reach a point at which we are entitled to pronounce our statements to be true, it appears that we must be entitled, at some point, to hold as not relevant the indefinitely many further states of affairs which we have not investigated. But, if we are to do this, we must of course be in a position to say that a statement relates to *this* state, or *these* states, of affairs and *not* to others; and to be in a position to say this is to rely on "demonstrative conventions" in Austin's sense.

6. Thus Austin's "purified version" of the Correspondence Theory is not, in my submission, grossly and intolerably restricted in its range of application in the way that Mr. Strawson has suggested—restricted, that is, roughly speaking to the special case of subject-predicate statements about individual things. The restriction actually implied by its incorporation into his account of truth of *both* demonstrative *and* descriptive conventions is, rather, that his account fits the case only of utterances which, in principle at least, we could be in a position to pronounce to be true on empirical grounds. But here a rather important question very naturally arises which, I regret

B

to say, I have no notion how to answer. I can set up the pieces, so to speak, but I don't know what moves to make, and am not doing much more, in the rest of this paper, than appealing for help.

The difficulty is this. One may, I think, very naturally feel that Austin's account, even if not too narrow in the extreme way that Mr. Strawson suggests, is nevertheless too narrow; for surely there are a good many kinds of utterances to which his account has at least no obvious or natural application, but which are yet, very often and very naturally, said to be true. There are, first of all, analytic statements, or theorems in logic, or in mathematics; these of course are not asserted on empirical grounds, and there is no question here of our needing to know which "states of affairs in the world" would be relevant to their truth or falsity, since none would be so relevant; but surely we do often apply to them the predicate 'true.' Then too, what about the case of quite general statements of natural law? If I say, for instance, that metals expand when heated, I do not mean, and would not be taken to mean, that this state of affairs obtains in some particular part or parts of the world, or over certain particular stretches of the world's history; there can be no place, surely, for "demonstrative conventions" here, since my statement is of unrestricted generality; but can it not be said to be *true* that metals expand when heated?

Now, in defence of Austin's account against this objection, it might conceivably be argued that the cases here brought up, which his account of truth certainly does not appear to cater for, are not counter-examples since they are not examples of truths. An analytic proposition, it might be argued, is not true or false, but either necessary or impossible; a well-proved proposition in logic or in mathematics is not true but valid, not a truth but a theorem: that metals expand when heated can be said to be strongly confirmed, to be much-tested and not falsified, but not to be true. Yet it will probably be felt, and with some reason, that to take this line would be somewhat high-handed. After all we do speak often enough of necessary truth, or of truths of logic; and if we accept some well-confirmed statement of natural law, we find it entirely natural to say that it is true. It might possibly be argued that these ways of speaking are in some ways undesirable, undiscriminating, potentially misleading, or whatnot; but on what grounds could it be declared that to speak as we thus do is flatly wrong?

The next defensive move, then, which suggests itself is to hold that, although it is perfectly permissible or proper to apply the predicate 'true' to, for instance, theorems in logic or formulations of natural law, the "sense" of the word in such applications is different, or even, more ambitiously perhaps, that its meaning is different. I am inclined to think, though I am by no means sure, that Austin would have said this. At any rate the view underlying, and probably indeed required for the tenability of, his account of truth seems to be that there is what might be called a central or primary use of 'true'— namely its use in application to utterances made, and pronounced to be true or false, on empirical grounds, in the light of the relevant states of affairs in the world; that the (purified) Correspondence Theory of truth quite rightly concentrates on, and characterizes in a general way, this central use; but that the word 'true' may also be used in other contexts than these, in "senses" more or less different and remote from its central or primary meaning, and calling for elucidation in more or less different terms.[4]

As to the merits of this view, however, I feel both very uncertain, and regrettably helpless. On the one hand, there seems a good deal to be said for the view that 'true,' like 'good,' should not be represented as having different senses, or meanings, in its different occurrences; though of course the grounds on which, or criteria by which, it is applied must be admitted to be different, and indeed of different kinds, in different cases. If so, it would follow that a general account of what 'true' means ought to fit the cases equally of, for instance, contingent and necessary truths. But on the other hand, one may feel that the analogy with 'good' is perhaps not a sound one here—that the shift from contingent to necessary truth is greater than, or somehow different in character from, the shifts from, say, evaluating apples to evaluating arguments, and is in fact radical enough to justify our speaking of a shift to another "sense." But perhaps my uncertainty about which way to go here is simply evidence of the fact that I have not—has anybody?—a theory about "senses" of words in the light of which such an uncertainty could be resolved. Without a doctrine, perhaps, one can do nothing here but fumble around, more or less persuasively but still inconclusively.

At the moment, at any rate, I think I cannot do more than propose that this question in particular needs further investigation. If it were decided that 'true' in all its uses, or at least in all its uses in application to things written or said or otherwise uttered, is to be

---

[4] What Austin says in his paper is carefully guarded on this point, indeed deliberately non-committal. "When is a statement not a statement? When it is a formula in a calculus: when it is a performatory utterance: when it is a value-judgment: when it is a definition: when it is part of a work of fiction. . . . It is a matter for decision how far we should continue to call such masqueraders 'statements' at all, and how widely we should be prepared to extend the uses of 'true' and 'false' in 'different senses'. My own feeling is that it is better, when once a masquerader has been unmasked, *not* to call it a statement and *not* to say it is true or false." See *Philosophical Papers*, p. 99. But this position, carefully guarded though it is, seems doubtfully tenable; for it seems to have been decided already, *omnium consensu*, that, for instance, theorems in a calculus may be said to be true; and it is not clear to me how, even if we withold from them the appellation of "statements", they could be held only to "masquerade" as truths. I believe, then, that Austin would have been obliged, in some cases at least, to countenance what he envisages as an "extension" of the uses of 'true' and 'false', in "different senses".

regarded as strictly univocal, then it would follow that the Correspondence Theory of Truth, even in Austin's (and perhaps in any other) "purified version," is too restricted, and so not acceptable as a general account of truth. But if we allow ourselves the luxury of different "senses," then the Correspondence Theory has, so far as I can see, a still undefeated claim to be considered a sound account, so far as it goes, of the central sense, or of one of the more central senses. I should have liked to come to some more definite or more ambitious conclusion than this, but have not, I fear, been able to see my way to doing so. I do not at present see how we are to decide whether, in for instance the sentences 'It's true that he is bald' and 'That a triangle has three sides is true,' the word 'true' should or should not be said to have different senses. I should be glad to be told.

4

True to the Facts

DONALD DAVIDSON

Reprinted with the kind permission of the author and the editor from *The Journal of Philosophy*, LXVI, No. 21 (1969), 748-64.

748 THE JOURNAL OF PHILOSOPHY

TRUE TO THE FACTS *

A TRUE statement is a statement that is true to the facts. This remark seems to embody the same sort of obvious and essential wisdom about truth as the following about motherhood: a mother is a person who is the mother of someone. The *property* of being a mother is explained by the *relation* between a woman and her child; similarly, the suggestion runs, the property of being true is to be explained by a relation between a statement and something else. Without prejudice to the question what the something else might be, or what word or phrase best expresses the relation (of being true to, corresponding to, picturing), I shall take the license of calling any view of this kind a *correspondence theory* of truth.

Correspondence theories rest on what appears to be an ineluctable if simple idea, but they have not done well under examination. The chief difficulty is in finding a notion of fact that explains anything, that does not lapse, when spelled out, into the trivial or the empty. Recent discussion is thus mainly concerned with deciding whether some form of correspondence is true and trivial (". . . the theory of truth is a series of truisms" [1]) or, in so far as it is not confused, simply empty ("The correspondence theory requires, not purification, but elimination" [2]). Those who have discussed the semantic concept of truth in connection with correspondence theories have typically ruled the semantic concept either irrelevant or trivial.

In this paper I defend a version of the correspondence theory. I think truth can be explained by appeal to a relation between language and the world, and that analysis of that relation yields insight into how, by uttering sentences, we sometimes manage to say what is true. The semantic concept of truth, as first systematically expounded by Tarski,[3] will play a crucial role in the defense.

* To be presented in an APA symposium on Truth, December 28, 1969; see James F. Thomson, "Truth-bearers and the Trouble about Propositions," this JOURNAL, LXVI, 21 (Nov. 6, 1969): 737–747.

I have benefited greatly from discussions with John Wallace and from reading an unpublished paper in which he argues that the concept of satisfaction (which may be viewed as a form of correspondence) emerges in *any* theory of truth that meets certain desirable demands.

My research was supported by the National Science Foundation and the Center for Advanced Study in the Behavioral Sciences.

1, 2 J. L. Austin and P. F. Strawson, symposium on "Truth," *Aristotelian Society Supplementary Volume XXIV* (1950), reprinted in George Pitcher, ed., *Truth* (Englewood Cliffs, N.J.: Prentice-Hall, 1964). The quoted remarks are from Austin and Strawson respectively, and appear on pages 21 and 32 of Pitcher.

3 Alfred Tarski, "The Concept of Truth in Formalized Languages," in *Logic, Semantics, Metamathematics* (New York: Oxford, 1956).

It might be possible to prove that any theory or definition of truth meeting plausible standards necessarily contained conceptual resources adequate to define a sense of correspondence. My project is less ambitious: I shall be satisfied if I can find a natural interpretation of the relation of correspondence that helps explain truth. Clearly it is consistent with the success of this attempt that there be a formula for eliminating phrases like 'it is true that' and 'is true' from many or all contexts: correspondence and redundancy theories do not necessarily conflict. Nevertheless, we may find instruction concerning the role of correspondence by asking how well we can do in systematically replacing sentences with truth-words or phrases by sentences without.

The sentence

(1) The statement that French is the official language of Mauritius is true.

is materially equivalent to 'French is the official language of Mauritius'; and the same might be said for any two sentences similarly related. This encourages the thought that the words that bed the embedded sentence in (1) represent an identity truth function, the same in power as double negation, but lacking significant articulation. On this suggestion, it would be no more than a freak of grammar that (1) consists of a complex singular term and a predicate.

The trouble with the double-negation theory of truth is that it applies only to sentences, like (1) and 'It is true that $2 + 2 = 5$', that have embedded sentences. The theory cannot cope directly with

(2) The Pythagorean theorem is true.
(3) Nothing Aristotle said is true.

We might retain the double-negation theory as applied to (1) while reserving (2) and (3) for separate treatment. But it is hardly plausible that the words 'is true' have different meanings in these different cases, especially since there seem to be simple inferences connecting sentences of the two sorts. Thus from (2) and 'The Pythagorean theorem is the statement that the square on the hypotenuse is equal to the sum of the squares on the other two sides' we can infer 'The statement that the square on the hypotenuse is equal to the sum of the squares on the other two sides is true'.

It is tempting to think that the double-negation theory can somehow be extended to cover the likes of (2) and (3). The reasoning might go this way: the double-negation theory tells us there is a sentence that expresses every statement. But then (2) holds just in case there is a true sentence that expresses the Pythagorean theorem, and (3) holds in case no true sentence expresses something Aristotle said. The seeming need, in this explanation, to use the word 'true' will be shown harmless by rendering (2) and (3) thus:

(2′)   (*p*)(the statement that $p =$ the Pythagorean theorem $\rightarrow p$)
(3′) $-(\exists p)$(Aristotle said that $p \cdot p$)

We are now pursuing a line that diverges from the simple double-negation theory by accepting an ontology of statements, and by introducing quantification into positions that can be occupied by sentences. Not that the variables in (2′) and (3′) range over statements; it is rather expressions of the sort flanking the identity sign in (2′) that refer to statements. In the double-negation theory, putative reference to statements and putative predication of truth were absorbed into a grammatically complex, but logically simple, expression, a truth-functional sentential connective. By contrast, the present theory allows us to view 'is true' as a genuine predicate. It provides a principle, namely

(4)   (*p*)(the statement that *p* is true $\leftrightarrow p$)

that leads to sentences free of the predicate 'is true' and logically equivalent to sentences containing it. Here, truth is not explained away as something that can be predicated of statements, but explained.

Explained, that is, if we understand (2′), (3′), and (4). But do we? The trouble is in the variables. Since the variables replace sentences both as they feature after words like 'Aristotle said that' and in truth-functional contexts, the range of the variables must be entities that sentences may be construed as naming in both such uses. But there are very strong reasons, as Frege pointed out, for supposing that if sentences, when standing alone or in truth-functional contexts, name anything, then all true sentences name the same thing.[4] This would force us to conclude that the statement that *p* is identical with the statement that *q* whenever *p* and *q* are both true; presumably an unacceptable result.

In a brief, and often mentioned, passage F. P. Ramsey puts forward a theory similar to, or identical with, the one just discussed. He observes that sentences like (2′), (3′), and (4) cannot be convincingly read in English without introducing the words 'is true' at the end, but seems to see this as a quirk, or even defect, of the language

[4] Gottlob Frege, "On Sense and Reference," reprinted in *Translations from the Philosophical Writings of Gottlob Frege*, edited and translated by Peter Geach and Max Black (New York: Oxford, 1952), pp. 62–63.

(we add 'is true' because we forget 'p' already contains a "variable" verb).[5] Ramsey then says

> This may perhaps be made clearer by supposing for a moment that only one form of proposition is in question, say the relational form aRb; then 'He is always right' could be expressed by 'For all a, R, b, if he asserts aRb, then aRb', to which 'is true' would be an obviously superfluous addition. When all forms of proposition are included the analysis is more complicated but not essentially different (17).

I think we must assume that Ramsey wants the variables 'a' and 'b' to range over individuals of some sort, and 'R' over (two-place) relations. So his version of 'He is always right' would be more fully expressed by 'For all a, R, b, if he asserts that a has R to b, then a has R to b'. Clearly, if "all forms of proposition" are included, the analysis must be recursive in character, for the forms of propositions follow the (logical) forms of sentences, and of these there are an infinite number. There is no reason to suppose, then, that Ramsey's analysis could be completed in a way that did not essentially parallel Tarski's method for defining truth. Tarski's method, however, introduces (as I shall argue) something like the notion of correspondence, and this is just what the theories we have been exploring were supposed to avoid. Paradox may also be a problem for Ramsey's recursive project. Where a theory based on the principle of (4) can always informally plead that a term of the form 'the statement that p' fails to name when a troublesome sentence replaces 'p', a theory that runs systematically through the sentences of a language will need to appeal to a more mechanical device to avoid contradiction. One wonders what conviction Ramsey's claim that "there really is no separate problem of truth" would carry after his analysis was carried to completion.

I have said nothing whatsoever about the purposes served in (non-philosophical) conversation by uttering sentences containing 'true' and cognates. No doubt the idea that remarks about truth typically are used to express agreement, to emphasize conviction or authority, to save repetition, or to shift responsibility, would gain support if it could be shown that truth-words can always be eliminated without cognitive loss by application of a simple formula. Nevertheless, I would hold that theories about the extralinguistic aims with which sentences are issued are logically independent of the question what they mean; and it is the latter with which I am concerned.

---

[5] F. P. Ramsey, "Facts and Propositions," *Aristotelian Society Supplementary Volume VII* (July 1927). The passage under discussion is reprinted in Pitcher, *op. cit.*, pp. 16–17.

We have failed to find a satisfactory theory to back the thesis that attributions of truth to statements are redundant; but even if it could be shown (as it has not been) that no such theory is possible, this would not suffice to establish the correspondence theory. So let us consider more directly the prospects for an account of truth in terms of correspondence.

It is facts correspondence to which is said to make statements true. It is natural, then, to turn to talk of facts for help. Not much can be learned from sentences like

(5) The statement that Thika is in Kenya corresponds to the facts.

or such variants as 'It is a fact that Thika is in Kenya', 'That Thika is in Kenya is a fact', and 'Thika is in Kenya, and that's a fact'. Whether or not we accept the view that correspondence to facts explains truth, (5) and its kin say no more than 'The statement that Thika is in Kenya is true' (or 'It is true that . . .' or '. . . , and that's the truth', etc.). If (5) is to take on independent interest, it will be because we are able to give an account of facts and correspondence that does not circle back immediately to truth. Such an account would enable us to make sense of sentences with this form:

(6) The statement that p corresponds to the fact that q.

The step to truth would be simple: a statement is true if there is a fact to which it corresponds. [(5) could be rewritten 'the statement that Thika is in Kenya corresponds to a fact'.]

When does (6) hold? Certainly when 'p' and 'q' are replaced by the same sentence; after that the difficulties set in. The statement that Naples is farther north than Red Bluff corresponds to the fact that Naples is farther north than Red Bluff, but also, it would seem, to the fact that Red Bluff is farther south than Naples (perhaps these are the same fact). Also to the fact that Red Bluff is farther south than the largest Italian city within thirty miles of Ischia. When we reflect that Naples is the city that satisfies this description: it is the largest city within thirty miles of Ischia, and such that London is in England, then we begin to suspect that if a statement corresponds to one fact, it corresponds to all. ('Corresponds to the *facts*' may be right in the end.) Indeed, employing principles implicit in our examples, it is easy to confirm the suspicion. The principles are that if a statement corresponds to the fact described by an expression of the form 'the fact that p', then it corresponds to the fact described by 'the fact that q' provided 'p' and 'q' are logically equivalent sentences, or one differs from the other in that a singular term has been replaced by a coextensive singular term. The confirming argument is this. Let '*s*' abbreviate some true sentence. Then surely the statement that *s* corresponds to the fact that *s*. But we may substitute for the second '*s*' the logically equivalent '(the *x* such that *x* is identical with Diogenes and *s*) is identical with (the *x* such that *x* is identical with Diogenes)'. Applying the principle that we may substitute coextensive singular terms, we can substitute '*t*' for '*s*' in the last quoted sentence, provided '*t*' is true. Finally, reversing the first step we conclude that the statement that *s* corresponds to the fact that *t*, where '*s*' and '*t*' are any true sentences.[6]

Since aside from matters of correspondence no way of distinguishing facts has been proposed, and this test fails to uncover a single difference, we may read the result of our argument as showing that there is exactly one fact. Descriptions like 'the fact that there are stupas in Nepal', if they describe at all, describe the same thing: The Great Fact. No point remains in distinguishing among various names of The Great Fact when written after 'corresponds to'; we may as well settle for the single phrase 'corresponds to The Great Fact'. This unalterable predicate carries with it a redundant whiff of ontology, but beyond this there is apparently no telling it apart from 'is true'.

The argument that led to this conclusion could be thwarted by refusing to accept the principles on which it was based. And one can certainly imagine constructing facts in ways that might reflect some of our feeling for the problem without leading to ontological collapse. From the point of view of the theory of truth, however, all such constructions seem doomed by the following difficulty. Suppose, to leave the frying pan of extensionality for the fires of intension, we distinguish facts as finely as statements. Of course, not every statement has its fact; only the true ones do. But then, unless we find another way to pick out facts, we cannot hope to explain truth by appeal to them.[7]

Talk about facts reduces to predication of truth in the contexts we have considered; this might be called the *redundancy theory* of facts. Predications of truth, on the other hand, have not proved so easy to eliminate. If there is no comfort for redundancy theories of

---

6 Frege used essentially this reasoning to prove that sentences alike in truth value must have the same reference. For further discussion of the argument, and some surprising applications, see John Wallace, "Propositional Attitudes and Identity," this JOURNAL, LXVI, 6 (Mar. 27, 1969): 145–152.

7 A similar point is made by P. F. Strawson, "Truth: A Reconsideration of Austin's Views," *The Philosophical Quarterly*, xv, 61 (October 1965): 289–301, p. 295.

truth in this, neither is there encouragement for correspondence theories.

I think there is a fairly simple explanation for our frustration: we have so far left language out of account. Statements are true or false because of the words used in making them, and it is words that have interesting, detailed, conventional connections with the world. Any serious theory of truth must therefore deal with these connections, and it is here if anywhere that the notion of correspondence can find some purchase. We have been restricting ourselves to ways of specifying statements that make no apparent mention of words. Thus 'Jones's statement that the cat is on the mat' irretrievably washes out reference to the particulars of Jones's language that might support a nontrivial account of truth, and the same may be thought to hold for the 'the statement that p' idiom generally.

Discussions of truth may have avoided the linguistic turn because it is obvious that truth cannot be pinned on sentences; but if this has been a motive, it is a confused one. Sentences cannot be true or false because if they were we should have to say that 'Je suis Titania' was true (spoken or sung by Titania), false (spoken by anyone else), and neither (uttered by someone with no French). What this familiar argument shows is not that we must stop talking of sentences and truth in the same breath, but that we must breathe a little deeper and talk also of the time the sentence is uttered, and its utterer. Truth (in a given natural language) is not a property of sentences; it is a relation between sentences, speakers, and dates. To view it thus is not to turn away from language to speechless eternal entities like propositions, statements, and assertions, but to relate language with the occasions of truth in a way that invites the construction of a theory.

The last two paragraphs may suggest that if we are to have a competent theory about truth we must abandon the view that statements are the proper vehicles of truth. But this is not so. If I am right, theories of truth must characterize or define a three-place predicate 'T s,u,t'. It will not matter to the theory whether we read this predicate 'sentence s is true (as English) for speaker u at time t' or 'the statement expressed by sentence s (as English) by speaker u at t is true'. Those who believe we must, for further reasons, retain statements as truth vehicles will find the second formulation, with its complex singular term ('the statement . . .') and one-place predicate ('is true') more perspicuous, while those who (with me) think we can get along without statements may prefer the more austere first formulation. But either party may talk either way; the difference comes out only when the talk is seen in the light of a comprehensive theory. Whether that theory requires an ontology of statements is not settled, I think, by the matters under discussion.

There are excellent reasons for not predicating truth of sentences, but these reasons do not apply to speech acts, utterances, or tokens. It has been argued, and convincingly, that we do not generally, or perhaps ever, say of a speech act, utterance, or token, that it was true.[8] This hardly shows why we *ought* not to call these entities (if they exist) true. No confusion would result if we said that the particular speaking of a sentence was true just in case it was used on that occasion to make a true statement; and similarly for tokens and utterances. According to Strawson,

> "My statement" may be either what I say or my saying it. My saying something is certainly an episode. What I say is not. It is the latter, not the former, we declare to be true.[9]

I'm not sure a statement is ever a speech act, but in any case we may accept the conclusion that speech acts are not said to be true. But what follows? Certainly not that we cannot explain what it is to make a true statement in terms of the conventional relations between words and things that hold when the words are used by particular agents on particular occasions. For although 'my statement' may not refer, at least when truth is in question, to a speech act, still it may succeed in identifying its statement only by relating it to a speech act. (What makes it "my" statement?)

If someone speaking English utters the sentence 'The sun is over the yardarm', under what conditions has he made the statement that the sun is over the yardarm? One range of answers might include such provisions as that he intended to convey to his hearers the impression that he believed the sun was over the yardarm, that he was authorized by his status to issue information about the location of the sun, etc. Thinking along these lines, one might maintain that, if the speaker had no thought of the location of the sun, and wanted to announce that it was time for a drink, then he *didn't* make the statement that the sun is over the yardarm. But there is also a sense of making a statement in which we would say, even under conditions of the sort just mentioned, that the man had ("literally") made the statement that the sun was over the yardarm, and that what he said was ("literally") true provided the sun was over the yardarm at the time he spoke, even though he had no rea-

8 See R. Cartwright, "Propositions," in R. J. Butler, ed., *Analytical Philosophy* (New York: Barnes & Noble, 1962).
9 P. F. Strawson, "Truth," p. 33 in Pitcher.

son to believe it, and didn't care if it were true. In such cases, we are interested not in what the person meant by uttering the sentence, but what the sentence, as uttered, meant. Both of these notions of meaning are relative to the circumstances of performance, but in the second case we abstract away from the extralinguistic intentions of the speaker. Communication by language is communication by way of literal meaning; so there must be the literal sense of making a statement if there are others. The theory of truth deals with the literal sense. (Of course this point deserves to be discussed at much greater length.)

Cleaving to the literal, then, someone speaking English will make a true statement by uttering the sentence 'It's Tuesday' if and only if it is Tuesday in his vicinity at the time he speaks. The example invites generalization: every instance of the following schema will be a truth about truth when 's' is replaced by a description of a sentence of English and 'p' is replaced by a sentence that gives the conditions under which the described sentence is true:

(7) Sentence s is true (as English) for speaker u at time t if and only if p.

(An alternative schema apparently attributing truth to statements could be substituted.) Even if we restrict the descriptions we substitute for 's' to some stylized vocabulary of syntax, we may assume that there is a true sentence of the form of (7) for each English sentence. The totality of such sentences uniquely determines the extension of the three-place predicate of (7) (the relativized truth-predicate). We seem here on the verge of a theory of truth; yet nothing like correspondence is in sight. The reason may be, however, that we are *only* on the verge of a theory. Schema (7) tells us what a theory of truth should encompass, but it is not such a theory itself, and does not suggest how such a theory can be contrived. Schema (7) is meant to play for English a role analogous to that played for an artificial language by a similar schema in Tarski's convention T.[10] The role is that of providing a test of the adequacy of a theory of truth: an acceptable theory must entail a true sentence of the form of (7) no matter what sentence of English is described by the canonical expression that replaces 's'.

Schema (7) lacks an elegant feature of its analogue in the *Wahrheitsbegriff*. Tarski, not concerned with languages with indexical elements, can use this simple formula: 's is true (in L) if and only if p' where the sentence substituted for 'p' is the sentence described by the expression that replaces 's', if the metalanguage contains the

[10] Tarski, *op. cit.*, pp. 187, 188.

object language; otherwise it translates that sentence in some straightforward sense. This uncomplicated formula cannot be ours; for when there are indexical terms (demonstratives, tenses), what goes for '*p*' cannot in general be what '*s*' names or a translation of it, as witness the example in the first sentence of the preceding paragraph. The elaboration called for to state (7) in explicit syntactic terms would be considerable, but there is no reason to think it impossible since what replaces '*p*' must be systematically related to the sentence described by the replacement of '*s*' by the rules that govern the use of indexical terms in English.

If the indicative sentences of English comprised just a finite number of elementary sentences and truth-functional compounds of them, it would be easy to give a recursive characterization of truth by providing a sentence of the form of (7) for each elementary sentence, and giving a rule corresponding to each sentential connective. This strategy breaks down, however, as soon as we allow predicates of arbitrary complexity to be built up using variables and connectives, as in quantification or complex singular terms; and it is just here that the theory of truth becomes interesting. Let us concentrate on quantificational structure at the expense of singular terms, not only because the latter are arguably dispensable while the former is not, but also because the point to be made will come through more simply. The problem presented by quantificational structure for a recursive theory of truth is, of course, that, although sentences of any finite length can be constructed from a small supply of variables, connectives, predicates, and quantifiers, none of the parts of a sentence needs to be a sentence in turn; therefore the truth of a complex sentence cannot in general be accounted for in terms of the truth of its parts.

Tarski taught us to appreciate the problem, and he gave an ingenious solution. The solution depends on first characterizing a relation called *satisfaction* and then defining truth by means of it. The entities that are satisfied are sentences both open and closed; the satisfiers are functions that map the variables of the object language onto the entities over which they range—almost everything, if the language is English.[11] A function satisfies an unstructured *n*-place predicate with variables in its *n* places if the predicate is *true of* the entities (in order) that the function assigns to those variables. So if '*x* loves *y*' is an open sentence of the simplest kind, a function f satisfies it just in case the entity that f assigns to '*x*'

---

[11] Tarski's satisfiers are infinite sequences, not functions. The reader in search of precision and deeper understanding cannot be too strongly urged to study Tarski's "The Concept of Truth in Formalized Languages."

loves the entity that f assigns to 'y'. The recursive characterization of satisfaction must run through every primitive predicate in turn. It copes with connectives in the obvious way: thus a conjunction of two sentences s and t (open or closed) is satisfied by f provided f satisfies s and f satisfies t. The universal quantification of an open sentence s with respect to a variable v is satisfied by f in case f, and every other function like f except in what it assigns to v, satisfies s. (The previous sentence works with 'existential' replacing 'universal' and 'or some' replacing 'and every'.) Whether or not a particular function satisfies a sentence depends entirely on what entities it assigns to the free variables of the sentence. So if the sentence has no free variables—if it is a closed, or genuine, sentence—then it must be satisfied by every function or by none. And, as is clear from the details of the recursion, those closed sentences which are satisfied by all functions are true; those which are satisfied by none are false. [I assume throughout that satisfaction, like truth, is relativized in the style of (7).]

The semantic concept of truth as developed by Tarski deserves to be called a correspondence theory because of the part played by the concept of satisfaction; for clearly what has been done is that the property of being true has been explained, and nontrivially, in terms of a relation between language and something else. The relation, satisfaction, is not, it must be allowed, exactly what intuition expected of correspondence; and the functions or sequences that satisfy may not seem much like facts. In part the contrast is due to a special feature of variables: just because they refer to no particular individual, satisfaction must consider arbitrary assignments of entities to variables (our functions). If we thought of proper names instead, satisfiers could be more nearly the ordinary objects of our talk—namely, ordered n-tuples of such. Thus 'Dolores loves Dagmar' would be satisfied by Dolores and Dagmar (in that order), provided Dolores loved Dagmar. I suppose Dolores and Dagmar (in that order) is not a fact either—the fact that verifies 'Dolores loves Dagmar' should somehow include the loving. This "somehow" has always been the nemesis of theories of truth based on facts. So the present point isn't that 's is satisfied by all functions' means exactly what we thought 's corresponds to the facts' meant, only that the two phrases have this in common: both intend to express a relation between language and the world, and both are equivalent to 's is true' when s is a (closed) sentence.

The comparison between correspondence theories that exploit the concept of satisfaction and those which rest on correspondence to facts is at its best with sentences without free variables. The parallel even extends, if we accept Frege's argument about the extensions of sentences, to the conclusion that true sentences cannot be told apart in point of what they correspond to (the facts, The Great Fact) or are satisfied by (all functions, sequences). But Tarski's strategy can afford this sameness in the finished product where the strategy of facts cannot, because satisfaction of closed sentences is explained in terms of satisfaction of sentences both open and closed, whereas it is only closed sentences that traditionally have corresponding facts. Since different assignments of entities to variables satisfy different open sentences and since closed sentences are constructed from open, truth is reached, in the semantic approach, by different routes for different sentences. All true sentences end up in the same place, but there are different stories about how they got there; a semantic theory of truth tells the story for a particular sentence by running through the steps of the recursive account of satisfaction appropriate to the sentence. And the story constitutes a proof of a theorem in the form of an instance of schema (7).

The strategy of facts can provide no such instructive variety. Since all true sentences have the same relation to the facts, an explanation of the truth of a sentence on the basis of its relations to other (closed) sentences must, if it sticks to the facts, begin where it ends.

Seen in retrospect, the failure of correspondence theories of truth based on the notion of fact traces back to a common source: the desire to include in the entity to which a true sentence corresponds not only the objects the sentence is "about" (another idea full of trouble) but also whatever it is the sentence says about them. One well-explored consequence is that it becomes difficult to describe the fact that verifies a sentence except by using that sentence itself. The other consequence is that the relation of correspondence (or "picturing") seems to have direct application to only the simplest sentences ('Dolores loves Dagmar'). This prompts fact-theorists to try to explain the truth of all sentences in terms of the truth of the simplest and hence in particular to interpret quantification as mere shorthand for conjunctions or alternations (perhaps infinite in length) of the simplest sentences. The irony is that, insofar as we can see quantification in this light, there is no real need for anything like correspondence. It is only when we are forced to take generality as an essential addition to the conceptual resources of predication and the compounding of sentences, and not reducible to them, that we appreciate the uses of a sophisticated correspondence theory. Theory of truth based on satisfaction is instructive

partly because it is less ambitious about what it packs into the entities to which sentences correspond: in such a theory, these entities
are no more than arbitrary pairings of the objects over which the
variables of the language range with those variables. Relative simplicity in the objects is offset by the trouble it takes to explain the
relation between them and sentences, for every truth-relevant feature
of every sentence must be taken into account in describing satisfaction. The payoff is clear: in explaining truth in terms of satisfaction, all the conceptual resources of the language in relation to its
ontology are brought to bear.

Talk of sentences', or better, statements', being true to, or corresponding to, the facts is of course as harmless as talk of truth.
Even the suggestion in these phrases that truth is owed to a relation
between language and the world can, I have argued, be justified.
The strategy of facts, against which I have just been inveighing, is
something else: a philosophical theory, and a bad one. It would be
a shame to discredit all correspondence theories, and in particular
Tarski's semantical approach, through thinking they must share
the inadequacies of the usual attempts to explain truth on the basis
of facts.

The assumption that all correspondence theories must use the
strategy of facts is at least understandable and, given the vagaries
of philosophical usage, could be considered true by fiat. There is
less excuse for the widespread misunderstanding of the role of formulas like (7) in the semantical approach. The following example
is no worse than many that could be quoted:

> . . . unless there is more to the "correspondence" insisted on by clas-
> sical correspondence theories of truth than is captured by the formu-
> lations of current semantic theory and unless this more can be shown
> to be an essential property of truth (or, at least, of a significant variety
> of truths), then the battle over correspondence, instead of being *won*
> by correspondence theorists, has shown itself to be a *Scheinstreit*. For,
> as has often been noted, the formula
>
>   'Snow is white' (in our language) is true ≡ Snow is white
> is viewed with the greatest equanimity by pragmatist and coherentist
> alike. If the "correspondence" of the correspondence theorist amounts
> to nothing more than is illustrated by such equivalences, then, while
> pragmatist and coherentist may hope to make important points, . . .
> nothing further would remain to be said about "truth and correspon-
> dence." [12]

[12] Wilfrid Sellars, "Truth and 'Correspondence'," this JOURNAL, LIX, 2 (Jan. 18,
1962): 29–56, p. 29. The quoted passage is on p. 197 of the article as reprinted
in *Science, Perception and Reality* (New York: Humanities Press, 1963).

Whether or not there is more to the semantic approach to truth than Sellars is ready to allow, it may be the case that no battle is won, or even joined, between correspondence theories and others. My trouble with this passage hinges on its assumption that a sentence like ' "Snow is white" is true if and only if snow is white' (even when properly relativized and with a structural description in place of the quotation) in itself provides a clue to what is unique to the semantical approach. Of course, as Sellars says, such sentences are neutral ground; it is just for this reason that Tarski hopes everyone can agree that an adequate theory or definition of truth must entail all sentences of this form. There is no trace of the notion of correspondence in these sentences, no relational predicate that expresses a relation between sentences and what they are about. Where such a relation, satisfaction, *does* come into play is in the elaboration of a nontrivial theory capable of meeting the test of entailing all those neutral snowbound trivialities.

I would like now and by way of conclusion to mention briefly two of the many kinds of obstacle that must be overcome if we are to have a comprehensive theory of truth for a natural language. First, it is certainly reasonable to wonder to what extent it will ever be possible to treat a natural language as a formal system, and even more to question whether the resources of the semantical method can begin to encompass such common phenomena as adverbial modification, attributive adjectives, talk of propositional attitudes, of causality, of obligation, and all the rest. At present we do not even have a satisfactory semantics for singular terms, and on this matter many others hang. Still, a degree of optimism is justified. Until Frege, serious semantics was largely limited to predication and the truth-functional compounding of sentences. By abstracting quantificational structure from what had seemed a jungle of pronouns, quantifiers, connectives, and articles, Frege showed how an astonishingly powerful fragment of natural language could be semantically tamed. Indeed, it may still turn out that this fragment will prove, with ingenuity, to be the whole. Meanwhile, promising work goes on in many directions, enlarging the resources of formal semantics, extending the application of known resources, and providing the complex and detailed rules necessary to give a revealing description of the structure of natural language. Whatever range the semantic theory of truth ultimately turns out to have, we may welcome the insight that comes where we understand language well enough to apply it.

The second difficulty is on another level: we have suggested how it might be possible to interpret attributions of truth to statements or to sentences relativized to occasions of use, but only in contexts of the sort provided by the left branch of (7). We have given no indication of how the analysis could be extended to apply to sentences like

(8) It is true that it is raining.
(9) The statement that it is raining is true.

Here is how we might try to meet the case of (8). We have, we are supposing, a theory of truth-in-English with truth treated as a relation between a sentence, a speaker, and a time. [The alternative version in terms of statements would apply to (9).] The problem, then, is to find natural counterparts of these elements in (8). A speaker of (8) speaks the words 'it is raining', thus performing an act that embodies a particular sentence, has its speaker, and its time. A reference to this act can therefore serve as a reference to the three items needed to apply the theory of truth. The reference we can think of as having been boiled down into the demonstrative 'that' of (8) and (9). A long-winded version of (8) might, then, go like this. First (reversing the order for clarity) I say 'It's raining'. Then I say '*That* speech act embodied a sentence which, spoken by me now, is true'. On this analysis, an utterance of (8) or (9) consists of two logically (semantically) independent speech acts, one of which contains a demonstrative reference to the other. An interesting feature of these utterances is that one is true if the other is; perhaps this confirms an insight of the redundancy theory.

A further problem is raised by

(10) Peter's statement that Paul is hirsute is true.

Following the suggestion made for (8) and (9), the analysis of (10) should be 'Paul is hirsute. That is true, and Peter said (stated) it'. The 'that', as before, refers to an act of speaking, and now the 'it' picks up the same reference. What is needed to complete the account is a paratactic analysis of indirect discourse that interprets an utterance by a speaker u of 'Peter said that Paul is hirsute' as composed of an utterance of 'Paul is hirsute' and another utterance ('Peter said that') that relates Peter in a certain way to u's utterance of 'Paul is hirsute'. The relation in question can, perhaps, be made intelligible by appeal to the notion of *samesaying*: if u says what is true when he says 'Peter said that', it is because, by saying 'Paul is hirsute', he has made Peter and himself samesayers.[13]

---

[13] I say more about this analysis of indirect discourse in "On Saying That," *Synthèse*, XIX, 1/2 (December 1968): 130–146.

One may, of course, insist that the relation of samesaying (which holds between speech acts) can be understood only by reference to a third entity: a statement, meaning, or proposition. Nothing I have written here bears on this question, except indirectly, by showing that, with respect to the problems at hand, no need arises for such entities. Is this simply the result of neglecting troublesome cases? Consider, as a final example,

(11) Peter said something true.

This cannot be rendered, 'Some (past) utterance of Peter's makes us samesayers', for I may not have said, or know how to say, the appropriate thing. Nor will it help to try 'Some utterance of Peter's embodied a sentence true under the circumstances'. This fails because (11) does not tell what language Peter spoke, and the concept of truth with which we are dealing is necessarily limited to a specific, known, language. Not knowing what his language is, we cannot make sense of 'true-in-his-language'.

What we can hope to make sense of, I think, is the idea of a sentence in another tongue being the *translation* of a sentence of English. Given this idea, it becomes natural to see (11) as meaning something like 'Peter uttered a sentence that translates a sentence of English true under the circumstances'. The exact nature of the counterfactual assumption barely concealed in this analysis depends on the details of the theory of truth (for English) as relativized to occasions of utterance. In any case, we seem required to understand what someone else would mean by a sentence of our language if he spoke our language. But difficult as this concept is, it is hard to see how communication can exist without it.

The conclusion I would tentatively draw is this. We can get away from what seems to be talk of the (absolute) truth of timeless statements if we accept truth as relativized to occasions of speech, and a strong notion of translation. The switch may create more problems than it solves. But they are, I think, the right problems: providing a detailed account of the semantics of natural language, and devising a theory of translation that does not depend upon, but rather founds, whatever there is to the concept of meaning.

Strawson describes Austin's "purified version of the correspondence theory of truth" in this way:

> His . . . theory is, roughly, that to say that a statement is true is to say that a certain speech-episode is related in a certain conventional way to something in the world exclusive of itself (32).

It is this theory Strawson has in mind when he says, "The correspondence theory requires, not purification, but elimination." I would not want to defend the details of Austin's conception of correspondence, and many of the points I have made against the strategy of facts echo Strawson's criticisms. But the debilities of particular formulations of the correspondence theory ought not be held against the theory. If I am right, then by appealing to Tarski's semantical conception of truth we can defend a theory that almost exactly fits Strawson's description of Austin's "purified version of the correspondence theory of truth." And this theory deserves, not elimination, but elaboration.

DONALD DAVIDSON

Princeton University
Center for Advanced Study in the Behavioral Sciences

VII

MODALITIES

INTRODUCTION

The issue of modality is clearly connected with the issue of analyticity. The problem of the logical relation between the concept of modality and analyticity and their interdefinability will be touched on later in this introduction. We suggest, therefore, that students who are interested in modality consult our introduction to Part V.

Briefly, modality is concerned with the issue of usage and meaning of concepts such as necessity, non-necessity, possibility, impossibility, and contingency. To single out these concepts, to investigate their semantic properties, and to indicate the context of their use are the first steps towards the construction of modal logic. Modal logic is the extension of elementary logic (technically, that part of symbolic logic in which the existential and universal quantifiers are applied only to individuals and not also to classes of individuals) to a logic in which modal concepts are used.

We may thus separate the semantic (descriptive) aspects of modality from the syntactic or formal aspects of modal logic, which is concerned with the problems of determination of truth value, quantification, derivation of sentences governed by modal operators, and finally with the problem of consistency and completeness of modal systems (though the problem of semantic interpretation of modal logics does belong to modal logic).

In our discussion of analyticity we have observed that some philosophers made use of the concept of necessity and its counterpart, possibility, in order to characterize a sentence as analytic or synthetic. Leibniz, for example, characterizes analytic truth as necessary truth, "one the contradictory of which involves a contradiction," or alternatively as a sentence true of all possible worlds; he sees synthetic truth as contingent truth, true of the actual world. Hume also sometimes

761

speaks of "absolute necessity" of "propositions that are proved by intuition or demonstration," or the absence of it "in reasoning from causation and concerning matters of fact."[1]

We may express this view and show the kinship between necessity and analyticity by saying that the modal operator 'necessarily' in general governs S, if S is analytic, whereas 'possibly' governs S, if S is synthetic. This view of necessity is akin to the medieval notion of *de dicto* necessities. It is also compatible with Quine's views that "being necessarily or possibly . . . is in general not a trait of the object concerned, but depends on the manner of referring to the object,"[2] and that "necessity resides in the way in which we say things, and not in the things we talk about."[3] This, however, is oversimplification. There are other usages of 'necessarily' which deviate from our general rule. We speak also of "physical necessities," which echoes the Aristotelian theory of essentialism and is akin to the medieval *de re* necessities. Philosophers have spoken also of moral necessities and categorical imperatives.

There are at least three contexts governed by 'necessarily': (1) necessarily "An equilateral triangle is equiangular," where the modal operator governs an analytic sentence; (2) necessarily "given the earth's atmosphere, all nonsupported bodies fall downward," where the modal governs a synthetic sentence; and (3) necessarily "Smith is obligated to pay his debt (excluding certain excusable conditions)," where the modal governs an optative sentence. We may now expand our concept of necessity by dividing it into the following classes.

Let S be a sentence, then:

(A) 'It is logically necessary that S' is true $\equiv$ S is a theorem of a deductive system.

(B) 'It is physically necessary that S' is true $\equiv$ S is deducible from a certain class of physical laws.

(C) 'It is ethically necessary that S' is true $\equiv$ S is deducible from a certain class of ethical laws.[4]

Sentences which satisfy definitions (A) and (B) are said to be in the alethic modes, and those which satisfy (C) in the deontic modes.

---

[1] David Hume, *Treatise* (Oxford: Oxford University Press, 1888), 95.

[2] W. V. Quine, *From a Logical Point of View* (Cambridge: Harvard University Press, 1953), p. 148.

[3] *Ibid.*

[4] These are adapted from Richard Montague, "Logical Necessity, Physical Necessity, Ethics and Quantifiers," *Inquiry*, IV (1966), 259-69, with modification.

Given these definitions, we observe that (1) is true since 'S' is a theorem of Euclidean geometry; (2) is true since 'S' is deducible from Newton's law of motion; and (3) is true since 'S' is deducible from an ethical law which states certain obligations.

In each case we observe that the truths of (1), (2), and (3) are relative to their axioms. If S is deducible from L, we say that S is necessary. We do not, however, commit ourselves that L is necessary. We should distinguish between what the medievals call *necessitas consequentiae* and *necessitas consequentis,* or what we may call necessity of the axioms and the necessity of theorems, relative to their respective axioms.

We express the above point by using the sign '$\Box$' for modal operator necessary as

(D) $\Box (P \to P)$
(E) $P \to \Box P$

Clearly the axioms of deductive systems are not necessary in the same sense as their respective theorems.

We may reject the necessity of Euclid's axioms, or the law of motion, or Kant's categorical imperative, without rejecting the necessity of their theorems. Indeed, if we accept Leibniz's suggestion that "the eternal truths . . . at bottom . . . are all hypothetical and say in fact: such a thing being posited, such another thing is," we may as well reject the necessity of every axiom. As a matter of fact, Hume argued against attributing necessity to any law of nature, even though supported by the strongest inductive evidence. Einstein's famous quip about laws of nature being true until further notice is the echo of Hume's battle cry, "There are no necessary connections of matters of fact."

Turning now to the nature of axioms of logic and mathematics, it has been argued that, since the idea of self-evidence of axioms is discredited, it makes no sense to ask whether the axioms are necessary truths or even whether they are true — though under a semantic interpretation axioms may turn out to be true of some objects or of others.

Likewise, the necessity of ethical laws is questioned by saying that, if we regard certain moral maxims as being unconditionally binding, we may turn out to be blind to certain other moral imperatives which are incompatible with the former. For example, accepting the Kantian injunction that one should never lie, we might increase the amount of suffering in the world.

By giving up the attribution of necessity to every axiom of any system, be it logical, physical, or ethical, and restricting its application to the theorems of these systems, we may deprive some other necessary truths of being so regarded. Since there are classes of true assertions in the elementary arithmetic of natural numbers whose truths are not derivable from any particular set of axioms (Gödel), we should not identify necessary truths with derivable truths alone. It has been shown that there are nonderivable but nonetheless necessary truths.

In discussing the issue of analyticity, we have shown likewise that we may not identify analytic truths with logical truths. If we consider analytic truths as necessary truths, we should note also that there are sets of such truths which are not derivable from axioms of logic. We should note the limitation of defining 'necessity' in terms of derivability as in (A), (B), and (C).

Given that we know which class of sentences is governed by the modal operator 'necessary,' we may define other modal concepts in terms of that operator.

Let

'$\square$ P' designate *necessary P*

then

'$\square \overline{P}$' designate *impossible P*

'$- \square \overline{P}$' designate *possible P*

'$- \square P \wedge \sim \square \overline{P}$ designate *contingent P*

'$- \square P$' designate *non-necessary P*

'$\square P \vee \square \overline{P}$' designate *non-contingent P*.[5]

By virtue of such definitional transformation we obtain simplicity and economy in modal logic.

It could easily be shown that the appearance of a modal operator in front of a sentence changes the truth value of that sentence. Consider:

(4) Snow is white
(5) Possibly 'Snow is white'
(6) Necessarily 'If snow is white, then snow is white'
(7) Necessarily 'Snow is white.'

(4) is a synthetic truth; (5) is a modal truth, since (4) is a synthetic truth and is governed by a proper operator. (6) is also a modal truth,

---

[5] These are adapted with some modification from Rudolf Carnap, *Meaning and Necessity* (Chicago: University of Chicago Press, 1955), 173.

since the sentence governed by the proper operator is logically true; (7) is a modal falsehood, since a wrong modal governs the synthetic sentence.

Modal logic, as we said, is concerned with logical relationships holding among sentences with modal operators; with the quantification into context of such sentences (in cases where these sentences fall under predicate calculus and identity); with the problems of semantic interpretation; and finally with the problem of consistency and completeness of modal logic.

The expansion of elementary logic into modal logic is regarded by many logicians as both necessary and desirable. It has been argued that modal logic may be used where elementary logic will not do. For example, we may formulate certain logical relations holding between law sentences or law-like sentences and counterfactual sentences supporting these laws in modal logic; or certain meta-ethical assertions, such as the Kantian view that necessarily what is obligatory must be possible, may be formulated in deontic logic. The idea that logic need not limit itself to declarative sentences — sentences which are true or false (bivalent) alone — and may investigate the logic of optative assertions and validity of certain meta-ethical inferences is new, exciting, and to some extent has been fulfilled.

There are some indications that Aristotle, the creator of logic, was aware of modal inferences. There are indeed certain modal inferences considered by the medievals. The first system of modal logic was developed by C. I. Lewis in 1932. Carnap in 1946 developed the first semantic account of modality.[6] Since then various systems of semantics for modal logic have been constructed by logicians.

It should be mentioned, however, that Quine in various articles launched many criticisms of modal logic. He showed that certain established theses in neoclassical logic (such as the vital distinction between use and mention, or principles of identity, substitutivity, and extensionality) are disrupted when quantification is used in modal logic, and that modal logic accommodates certain metaphysical views, e.g., Aristotelian essentialism. Aristotelian essentialism is the doctrine that some of the attributes of an object, independently of the language in which the object is referred to, may be essential to the object and others

[6] Rudolf Carnap, "Modalities and Quantification," *Journal of Symbolic Logic,* IV (1946), 33-36.

may be accidental, e.g., a man is essentially rational and accidentally two-legged.

Despite Quine's objections, various systems of semantics for modal logic were constructed. We are not concerned with modal logic or with its formal semantics as such. Suffice it to mention that there are systems of modal logic and that there are semantic interpretations for such systems which escape Quine's objections to the use-mention confusion, unwelcome results of quantification into modal contexts, and commitment to essentialism. It has been shown, for example, that in a range of modal systems for which Kripke has provided semantics, no essential sentence is a theorem.

Let us conclude by citing a significant comment of Quine on the notion of possible world and its contribution to the semantics of modal logic.

> The notion of possible world did indeed contribute to the semantics of modal logic, and it behooves us to recognize the nature of its contribution: it led to Kripke's precocious and significant theory of models of modal logic. Models afford consistency proofs; also they have heuristic value; but they do not constitute explication. Models, however clear they be in themselves, may leave us still at a loss for the primary, intended interpretation. When modal logic has been paraphrased in terms of such notions as possible world or rigid designator, where the displaced fog settles is on the question when to identify objects between worlds, or when to treat a designator as rigid, or where to attribute metaphysical necessity.[7]

We advise students who are interested in problems of modal logic to consider articles in this part, as well as those listed in the selected readings.

SELECTED READINGS

Carnap, Rudolf. *Meaning and Necessity.* 2nd ed. Chicago: University of Chicago Press, 1947.

Davidson, Donald, and Herman, G., eds. *Semantics of Natural Language.* Dordrecht: Reidel, 1971.

Fenstad, J. E., ed. *Proceedings of the Second Scandinavian Logic Symposium.* Amsterdam: North Holland, 1971, V, 405.

Hilpinen, Risto, ed. *Deontic Logic: Introductory and Systematic Readings.* Dordrecht: Reidel; New York: Humanities Press, 1971, VI, 182.

[7] Review of *Identity and Individuation*, ed. Milton K. Munitz (New York: N.Y.U. Press, 1972); *Journal of Philosophy*, LXIX, no. H (September 7, 1972), 492-93.

Hintikka, Jaakko. "Existential Presuppositions and Existential Commitments." *Journal of Philosophy,* LVI (1959), 125-37.

——. "Modality and Quantification." *Theoria,* XXVII (1961), 119-28.

——. *Knowledge and Belief.* Ithaca, N.Y.: Cornell University Press, 1962.

——. "The Modes of Modality." *Acta Philosophica Fennica,* XVI (1963), 65-81.

——. *Models for Modalities: Selected Essays.* Amsterdam: Reidel; New York: Humanities Press, 1969, VII, 220.

Kneale, N. "Logical and Metaphysical Necessity." *Proceedings of the Aristotelian Society,* XXXVIII (1937-38).

Kripke, Saul A. "Semantical Analyses of Modal Logic." *Journal of Symbolic Logic,* XXIV (1959), 323-24.

——. "Semantical Considerations on Modal Logic." *Acta Philosophica Fennica,* XVI (1963), 83-94.

Marcus, Ruth Barcan. "Modalities and Intensional Languages." *Synthese,* XII, 4 (1961), 303-22.

Montague, Richard. "Logical Necessity, Physical Necessity, Ethics and Quantifiers." *Inquiry,* IV (1966), 259-67.

Parsons, T. "Essentialism in Quantified Modal Logic." *Nous,* II (1967), 253-68.

Prior, A. N. *Time and Modality.* London: Oxford University Press, 1963.

——. *Formal Logic.* London: Oxford University Press, 1962.

——. "Modality and Quantification." *Journal of Symbolic Logic,* XXI (1956), 60-62.

Quine, W. V. *From a Logical Point of View.* Cambridge: Harvard University Press, 1953.

——. "Three Grades of Modal Involvement," in *The Ways of Paradox.* New York: Random House, 1966, 174-84.

Smullyan, A. F. "Modality and Description." *Journal of Symbolic Logic,* XIII (1948), 31-37.

Von Wright, G. *An Essay in Modal Logic.* Amsterdam: North Holland, 1951.

1

Modalities

RUDOLF CARNAP

Reprinted with the kind permission of the publisher from R. Carnap, *Meaning and Necessity,* second edition (Chicago: The University of Chicago Press, 1959), Chapter 5, 173-77. © 1947 and 1956 by The University of Chicago.

CHAPTER V

ON THE LOGIC OF MODALITIES

In this chapter we study logical modalities like necessity, possibility, impossibility. We introduce 'N' as a symbol of necessity; the other modal concepts, including necessary implication and necessary equivalence, can be defined with its help. The modal system S_2 is constructed by adding 'N' to our previous system S_1 (§ 39); and the semantical rules for S_2 are stated (§ 41). An analysis of the variables occurring in modal sentences shows that they have to be interpreted as referring to intensions (§ 40); hence a translation in words must be given either in terms of intensions (in the metalanguage M) or in neutral terms (in M') (§ 43). Quine's views on the possibility of combining modalities and variables are discussed (§ 44). Finally, the main results of the discussions in this book are briefly summarized (§ 45).

§ 39. Logical Modalities

We form the modal system S_2 from our earlier system S_1 by the addition of the modal sign 'N' for logical necessity. We regard a proposition as necessary if any sentence expressing it is L-true. Other modalities can be defined in terms of necessity, for example, impossibility, possibility, contingency. With the help of 'N', we define symbols for necessary implication and necessary equivalence; the latter symbol may be regarded as an identity sign for intensions.

In the earlier chapters, modal sentences have sometimes been taken as examples, especially sentences about necessity or possibility, either in words (for instance, in §§ 30 and 31) or in symbols (for instance, § 11, Example II). We use 'N' as a sign for logical necessity; 'N(A)' is the symbolic notation for 'it is (logically) necessary that A'.

Quite a number of different systems of modal logic have been constructed, by C. I. Lewis (see Bibliography) and others.[1] These systems differ from one another in their basic assumptions concerning modalities. There is, for instance, the question of whether all sentences of the form 'Np ⊃ NNp' are true, in words: 'if it is necessary that p, then it is necessary that it is necessary that p'. Some of the systems give an affirmative answer to this question, other systems give a negative answer or leave it undecided. Not only do logicians disagree among themselves on this question, but sometimes also one logician constructs systems which differ in this point, probably because he is doubtful whether he should regard the sentences mentioned as true or false. There are several further points of

[1] For bibliographical references up to 1938, see Church's bibliography in *Journal of Symbolic Logic*, Vols. I and III; the pertinent references are listed in III, 199 ("Modality") and 202 ("Strict Implication").

difference between the systems. All these differences are, I think, due to the fact that the concept of logical necessity is not sufficiently clear; it can, for instance, be conceived in such a way that the sentences mentioned are true, but also in another way such that they, or some of them, are false.

Our task will be to find clear and exact concepts to replace the vague concepts of the modalities as used in common language and in traditional logic. In other words, we are looking for explicata for the modalities. It seems to me that a simple and convenient way of explication consists in basing the modalities on the semantical L-concepts. The concept of logical necessity, as explicandum, seems to be commonly understood in such a way that it applies to a proposition p if and only if the truth of p is based on purely logical reasons and is not dependent upon the contingency of facts; in other words, if the assumption of not-p would lead to a logical contradiction, independent of facts. Thus we see a close similarity between two explicanda, the logical necessity of a proposition and the logical truth of a sentence. Now for the latter concept we possess an exact explicatum in the semantical concept of L-truth, defined on the basis of the concepts of state-description and range (2-2). Therefore, the most natural way seems to me to take as the explicatum for logical necessity that property of propositions which corresponds to the L-truth of sentences. Accordingly, we lay down the following convention for 'N':

39-1. For any sentence '. . .', 'N(. . .)' is true if and only if '. . .' is L-true.

We shall construct the system S_2 by adding to the system S_1 the sign 'N' with suitable rules such that the convention just stated is fulfilled (§ 41). This convention may be regarded as a rule of truth for the full sentences of 'N'. S_2 thus contains all the signs and the sentences of S_1.

On the basis of our interpretation of 'N', as given by the convention 39-1, the old controversies can be solved. Suppose that 'L-true in S_2' is defined in such a way that our earlier convention 2-1, which says that a sentence is L-true if and only if it is true in virtue of the semantical rules alone, independently of any extra-linguistic facts, is fulfilled. Let 'A' be an abbreviation for an L-true sentence in S_2 (for example, 'Hs $V \sim$ Hs'). Then 'N(A)' is true, according to 39-1. And, moreover, it is L-true, because its truth is established by the semantical rules which determine the truth and thereby the L-truth of 'A', together with the semantical rule for 'N', say 39-1. Thus, generally, if 'N(. . .)' is true, then 'NN(. . .)' is true; hence any sentence of the form 'N$p \supset$ NNp' is true. This constitutes an affirmative answer to the controversial question mentioned in the beginning. It can be shown in a similar way that every sentence of the

§ 39. LOGICAL MODALITIES 175

form '$\sim Np \supset N \sim Np$' is true. This settles another one of the controversial questions.[2]

This analysis leads to the result that, if '$N(\ldots)$' is true, it is L-true; and if it is false, it is L-false; hence:

39-2. Every sentence of the form '$N(\ldots)$' is L-determinate.

Therefore, the convention 39-1 may be replaced by the following more specific one:

39-3. For any sentence '$\ldots$' in S_2, '$N(\ldots)$' is L-true if '$\ldots$' is L-true; and otherwise '$N(\ldots)$' is L-false.

On the basis of the concept of logical necessity, the other logical modalities can easily be defined, as is well known. For example, 'p is impossible' means 'non-p is necessary'; 'p is contingent' means 'p is neither necessary nor impossible'; 'p is possible' means 'p is not impossible' (we adopt this interpretation in agreement with the majority of contemporary logicians, in distinction to other philosophers who use 'possible' in the sense of our 'contingent'). Let us use the diamond, '$\Diamond$', as a sign of possibility; we define it on the basis of 'N':

39-4. *Abbreviation.* '$\Diamond(\ldots)$' for '$\sim N \sim(\ldots)$'.

It would also be possible to take '$\Diamond$' as primitive, as Lewis does, and then to define '$N(\ldots)$' by '$\sim \Diamond \sim(\ldots)$'.

There are six modalities, that is, purely modal properties of propositions (as distinguished from mixed modal properties, for instance, contingent truth, see 30-1). The accompanying table shows how they can be

THE SIX MODALITIES

Modal Property of a Proposition	With 'N'	With '$\Diamond$'	Semantical Property of a Sentence
Necessary.......	Np	$\sim \Diamond \sim p$	L-true
Impossible......	$N \sim p$	$\sim \Diamond p$	L-false
Contingent......	$\sim Np \cdot \sim N \sim p$	$\Diamond \sim p \cdot \Diamond p$	Factual
Non-necessary...	$\sim Np$	$\Diamond \sim p$	Non-L-true
Possible.........	$\sim N \sim p$	$\Diamond p$	Non-L-false
Noncontingent..	$Np \vee N \sim p$	$\sim \Diamond \sim p \vee \sim \Diamond p$	L-determinate

expressed in terms of 'N' and in terms of '$\Diamond$'. The last column gives the corresponding semantical concepts; a proposition has one of the modal

---

[2] The two questions and the reasons for our affirmative answers are discussed in more detail in [Modalities], § 1.

properties if and only if any sentence expressing the proposition has the corresponding semantical property.

Every proposition with respect to a given system S is either necessary or impossible or contingent. This classification is, according to our inter-pretation of the modalities, analogous to the classification of the sentences of S into the three classes of L-true, L-false, and factual sentences. There is, however, one important difference between the two classifications. The number of L-true sentences may be infinite, and it is, indeed, infinite for each of the systems discussed in this book. On the other hand, there is only one necessary proposition, because all L-true sentences are L-equiva-lent with one another and hence have the same intension. [This result holds only for that use of the term 'proposition' which is based on L-equivalence as the condition of identity. It is, of course, possible to choose a stronger requirement for identity, for instance, intensional isomorphism. In this case the intensional structures are called 'propositions'. And their number is infinite.] Likewise, there is only one impossible proposition, be-cause all L-false sentences are L-equivalent. But the number of con-tingent propositions (with respect to a system with an infinite number of individuals) is infinite, like that of factual sentences.

It should be noted that the two sentences 'N(A)' and 'the sentence 'A' is L-true in S_2' correspond to each other merely in the sense that, if one of them is true, the other must also be true; in other words, they are L-equivalent (assuming that L-terms are defined in a suitable way so as to apply also to the metalanguage). This correspondence cannot be used as a *definition* for 'N', because the second sentence belongs, not to the object language S_2 as the first one does, but to the metalanguage M. The second sentence is not even a *translation* of the first in the strict sense which requires not only L-equivalence but intensional isomorphism (§ 14). If M contains the modal term 'necessary', then 'N(A)' can be translated into M by a sentence of the form 'it is necessary that . . .' (where '. . .' is the translation of 'A'). If M contains no modal terms, then there is no strict translation for 'N(A)'. But the correspondence stated makes it possible in any case to give an *interpretation* for 'N(A)' in M with the help of the concept of L-truth, for example, by laying down the truth-rule, 39-1.

On the basis of 'N', we introduce two further modal signs for modal relations between propositions:

39-5. *Abbreviation.* Let '. . .' and '- - -' be sentences in S_2. '. . . $\sqsupset$ - - -' for 'N(. . . $\supset$ - - -)'.

§ 40. MODALITIES AND VARIABLES   177

39-6. *Abbreviation.* Let '. . .' and '- - -' be any designators in S_2 (sentences or otherwise). '. . . $\equiv$ - - -' for 'N(. . . $\equiv$ - - -)'.

Thus '$\supset$' is a sign for necessary implication between propositions (Lewis' strict implication). The symbol '$\equiv$' is a sign for necessary equivalence. The sign '$\equiv$' in S_2 is the analogue to the term 'L-equivalent' in its non-semantical use in M (5-4) or M' (§ 34), where it designates a relation between intensions, not between designators. When standing between sentences, it corresponds to Lewis' sign '$=$' for strict equivalence. We have seen earlier that '$\equiv$', standing between designators of any type, is a sign for the identity of extensions (see remark on 5-3). Here in S_2, '$\equiv$' is, similarly, a sign for the identity of intensions. For example, 'H $\equiv$ RA' is short for 'N(H $\equiv$ RA)'. Hence, according to the rule 39-1, 'H $\equiv$ RA' is true if and only if 'H $\equiv$ RA' is L-true, hence if and only if 'H' and 'RA' are L-equivalent, in other words, have the same intension.

We have earlier formulated the two principles of interchangeability (12-1 and 12-2). For the first principle we have given, in addition to the chief formulation in semantical terms (12-1a), alternative formulations with the help of sentences of the object language containing '$\equiv$' (12-1b and c). Now, with the help of '$\equiv$', we can provide analogous formulations for the second principle. The following theorems 39-7b and c, which may be added to 12-2a as 12-2b and c, follow from 12-2a because $\mathfrak{A}_j$ and $\mathfrak{A}_k$ are L-equivalent if and only if $\mathfrak{A}_j \equiv \mathfrak{A}_k$ is true.

Second Principle of Interchangeability (alternative formulations):

39-7. Under the conditions of 12-2, the following holds:

> **b.** (12-2b). $(\mathfrak{A}_j \equiv \mathfrak{A}_k) \supset (. . \mathfrak{A}_j . . \equiv . . \mathfrak{A}_k . .)$ is true (in S).
>
> **c.** (12-2c). Suppose the system S contains variables for which $\mathfrak{A}_j$ and $\mathfrak{A}_k$ are substitutable, say 'u' and 'v'; then '$(u)(v)\left[(u \equiv v) \supset (. . u . . \equiv . . v . .)\right]$' is true (in S).

2

Reference and Modality

W. V. QUINE

VIII

REFERENCE AND MODALITY

1

One of the fundamental principles governing identity is that of *substitutivity*—or, as it might well be called, that of *indiscernibility of identicals*. It provides that, *given a true statement of identity, one of its two terms may be substituted for the other in any true statement and the result will be true*. It is easy to find cases contrary to this principle. For example, the statements:

(1)   Giorgione = Barbarelli,

(2)   Giorgione was so-called because of his size

are true; however, replacement of the name 'Giorgione' by the name 'Barbarelli' turns (2) into the falsehood:

Barbarelli was so-called because of his size.

Furthermore, the statements:

(3)   Cicero = Tully,

(4)   'Cicero' contains six letters

are true, but replacement of the first name by the second turns (4) false. Yet the basis of the principle of substitutivity appears quite solid; whatever can be said about the person Cicero (or Giorgione) should be equally true of the person Tully (or Barbarelli), this being the same person.

In the case of (4), this paradox resolves itself immediately. The fact is that (4) is not a statement about the person Cicero, but simply about the word 'Cicero'. The principle of substitutivity should not be extended to contexts in which the name to be supplanted occurs without referring simply to the object. Failure of substitutivity reveals merely that the occurrence to be supplanted is not *purely referential*,[1] that is, that the statement depends not only on the object but on the form of the name. For it is clear that whatever can be affirmed about the object remains true when we refer to the object by any other name.

An expression which consists of another expression between single quotes constitutes a name of that other expression; and it is clear that the occurrence of that other expression or a part of it, within the context of quotes, is not in general referential. In particular, the occurrence of the personal name within the context of quotes in (4) is not referential, not subject to the substitutivity principle. The personal name occurs there merely as a fragment of a longer name which contains, beside this fragment, the two quotation marks. To make a substitution upon a personal name, within such a context, would be no more justifiable than to make a substitution upon the term 'cat' within the context 'cattle'.

The example (2) is a little more subtle, for it is a statement about a man and not merely about his name. It was the man, not his name, that was called so and so because of his size. Nevertheless, the failure of substitutivity shows that the occurrence of the personal name in (2) is not *purely* referential. It is easy in fact to translate (2) into another statement which contains two occurrences of the name, one purely referential and the other not:

(5)   Giorgione was called 'Giorgione' because of his size.

The first occurrence is purely referential. Substitution on the basis of (1) converts (5) into another statement equally true:

Barbarelli was called 'Giorgione' because of his size.

The second occurrence of the personal name is no more referential than any other occurrence within a context of quotes.

----

[1] Frege [3] spoke of *direct* (*gerade*) and *oblique* (*ungerade*) occurrences, and used substitutivity of identity as a criterion just as here.

It would not be quite accurate to conclude that an occurrence of a name within single quotes is *never* referential. Consider the statements:

(6)   'Giorgione played chess' is true,

(7)   'Giorgione' named a chess player,

each of which is true or false according as the quotationless statement:

(8)   Giorgione played chess

is true or false. Our criterion of referential occurrence makes the occurrence of the name 'Giorgione' in (8) referential, and must make the occurrences of 'Giorgione' in (6) and (7) referential by the same token, despite the presence of single quotes in (6) and (7). The point about quotation is not that it must destroy referential occurrence, but that it can (and ordinarily does) destroy referential occurrence. The examples (6) and (7) are exceptional in that the special predicates 'is true' and 'named' have the effect of undoing the single quotes—as is evident on comparison of (6) and (7) with (8).

To get an example of another common type of statement in which names do not occur referentially, consider any person who is called Philip and satisfies the condition:

(9)   Philip is unaware that Tully denounced Catiline,

or perhaps the condition:

(10)   Philip believes that Tegucigalpa is in Nicaragua.

Substitution on the basis of (3) transforms (9) into the statement:

(11)   Philip is unaware that Cicero denounced Catiline,

no doubt false. Substitution on the basis of the true identity:

Tegucigalpa = capital of Honduras

transforms the truth (10) likewise into the falsehood:

(12) Philip believes that the capital of Honduras is in Nicaragua.

We see therefore that the occurrences of the names 'Tully' and 'Tegucigalpa' in (9)-(10) are not purely referential.

In this there is a fundamental contrast between (9), or (10), and:

> Crassus heard Tully denounce Catiline.

This statement affirms a relation between three persons, and the persons remain so related independently of the names applied to them. But (9) cannot be considered simply as affirming a relation between three persons, nor (10) a relation between person, city, and country—at least not so long as we interpret our words in such a way as to admit (9) and (10) as true and (11) and (12) as false.

Some readers may wish to construe unawareness and belief as relations between persons and statements, thus writing (9) and (10) in the manner:

(13)   Philip is unaware of 'Tully denounced Catiline',

(14)   Philip believes 'Tegucigalpa is in Nicaragua',

in order to put within a context of single quotes every not purely referential occurrence of a name. Church [5] argues against this. In so doing he exploits the concept of analyticity, concerning which we have felt misgivings (pp. 23-37 above); still his argument cannot be set lightly aside, nor are we required here to take a stand on the matter. Suffice it to say that there is certainly no *need* to reconstrue (9)-(10) in the manner (13)-(14). What *is* imperative is to observe merely that the contexts 'is unaware that . . .' and 'believes that . . .' *resemble* the context of the single quotes in this respect: a name may occur referentially in a statement S and yet not occur referentially in a longer statement which is formed by embedding S in the context 'is unaware that . . .' or 'believes that . . .'. To sum up the situation in a word, we may speak of the contexts 'is unaware that . . .' and 'believes that . . .' as *referentially opaque.*[2] The same is true of the contexts 'knows that . . .', 'says that . . .', 'doubts that

---

[2] This term is roughly the opposite of Russell's 'transparent' as he uses it in his Appendix C to *Principia*, 2d ed., vol. 1.

. . .', 'is surprised that . . .', etc. It would be tidy but unnecessary to force all referentially opaque contexts into the quotational mold; alternatively we can recognize quotation as one referentially opaque context among many.

It will next be shown that referential opacity afflicts also the so-called *modal* contexts 'Necessarily . . .' and 'Possibly . . .', at least when those are given the sense of *strict* necessity and possibility as in Lewis's modal logic.[3] According to the strict sense of 'necessarily' and 'possibly', these statements would be regarded as true:

(15)   9 is necessarily greater than 7,

(16)   Necessarily if there is life on the Evening Star then there is life on the Evening Star,

(17)   The number of planets is possibly less than 7,

and these as false:

(18)   The number of planets is necessarily greater than 7,

(19)   Necessarily if there is life on the Evening Star then there is life on the Morning Star,

(20)   9 is possibly less than 7.

The general idea of strict modalities is based on the putative notion of *analyticity* as follows: a statement of the form 'Necessarily . . .' is true if and only if the component statement which 'necessarily' governs is analytic, and a statement of the form 'Possibly . . .' is false if and only if the negation of the component statement which 'possibly' governs is analytic. Thus (15)-(17) could be paraphrased as follows:

(21)   '9 > 7' is analytic,

(22)   'If there is life on the Evening Star then there is life on the Evening Star' is analytic,

(23)   'The number of planets is not less than 7' is not analytic,

and correspondingly for (18)-(20).

   [3] Lewis, [1], Ch. 5; Lewis and Langford, pp. 78-89, 120-166.

That the contexts 'Necessarily . . .' and 'Possibly . . .' are referentially opaque can now be quickly seen; for substitution on the basis of the true identities:

(24)   The number of planets $= 9$,

(25)   The Evening Star $=$ the Morning Star

turns the truths (15)-(17) into the falsehoods (18)-(20).

Note that the fact that (15)-(17) are equivalent to (21)-(23), and the fact that '9' and 'Evening Star' and 'the number of planets' occur within quotations in (21)-(23), would not of themselves have justified us in concluding that '9' and 'Evening Star' and 'the number of planets' occur irreferentially in (15)-(17). To argue thus would be like citing the equivalence of (8) to (6) and (7) as evidence that 'Giorgione' occurs irreferentially in (8). What shows the occurrences of '9', 'Evening Star', and 'the number of planets' to be irreferential in (15)-(17) (and in (18)-(20)) is the fact that substitution by (24)-(25) turns the truths (15)-(17) into falsehoods (and the falsehoods (18)-(20) into truths).

Some, it was remarked, may like to think of (9) and (10) as receiving their more fundamental expression in (13) and (14). In the same spirit, many will like to think of (15)-(17) as receiving their more fundamental expression in (21)-(23).[4] But this again is unnecessary. We would certainly not think of (6) and (7) as somehow more basic than (8), and we need not view (21)-(23) as more basic than (15)-(17). What is important is to appreciate that the contexts 'Necessarily . . .' and 'Possibly . . .' are, like quotation and 'is unaware that . . .' and 'believes that . . .', referentially opaque.

2

The phenomenon of referential opacity has just now been explained by appeal to the behavior of singular terms. But singular terms are eliminable, we know (cf. pp. 7f, 85, 166f), by paraphrase. Ultimately the objects referred to in a theory are

[4] Cf. Carnap [2], pp. 245-259.

to be accounted not as the things named by the singular terms, but as the values of the variables of quantification. So, if referential opacity is an infirmity worth worrying about, it must show symptoms in connection with quantification as well as in connection with singular terms.[5] Let us then turn our attention to quantification.

The connection between naming and quantification is implicit in the operation whereby, from 'Socrates is mortal', we infer '$(\exists x)(x$ is mortal)', that is, 'Something is mortal'. This is the operation which was spoken of earlier (p. 120) as *existential generalization*, except that we now have a singular term 'Socrates' where we then had a free variable. The idea behind such inference is that whatever is true of the object named by a given singular term is true of something; and clearly the inference loses its justification when the singular term in question does not happen to name. From:

There is no such thing as Pegasus,

for example, we do not infer:

$(\exists x)$(there is no such thing as x),

that is, 'There is something which there is no such thing as', or 'There is something which there is not'.

Such inference is of course equally unwarranted in the case of an irreferential occurrence of any substantive. From (2), existential generalization would lead to:

$(\exists x)(x$ was so-called because of its size),

that is, 'Something was so-called because of its size'. This is clearly meaningless, there being no longer any suitable antecedent for 'so-called'. Note, in contrast, that existential generalization with respect to the purely referential occurrence in (5) yields the sound conclusion:

$(\exists x)(x$ was called 'Giorgione' because of its size),

that is, 'Something was called 'Giorgione' because of its size'.

[5] Substantially this point was made by Church [3].

The logical operation of *universal instantiation* is that whereby we infer from 'Everything is itself', for example, or in symbols '$(x)(x = x)$', the conclusion that Socrates = Socrates. This and existential generalization are two aspects of a single principle; for instead of saying that '$(x)(x = x)$' implies 'Socrates = Socrates', we could as well say that the denial 'Socrates $\neq$ Socrates' implies '$(\exists x)(x \neq x)$'. The principle embodied in these two operations is the link between quantifications and the singular statements that are related to them as instances. Yet it is a principle only by courtesy. It holds only in the case where a term names and, furthermore, occurs referentially. It is simply the logical content of the idea that a given occurrence is referential. The principle is, for this reason, anomalous as an adjunct to the purely logical theory of quantification. Hence the logical importance of the fact that all singular terms, aside from the variables that serve as pronouns in connection with quantifiers, are dispensable and eliminable by paraphrase.[6]

We saw just now how the referentially opaque context (2) fared under existential generalization. Let us see what happens to our other referentially opaque contexts. Applied to the occurrence of the personal name in (4), existential generalization would lead us to:

(26) $(\exists x)('x'$ contains six letters),

that is:

(27) There is something such that 'it' contains six letters,

or perhaps:

(28)   'Something' contains six letters.

Now the expression:

'x' contains six letters

[6] See above, pp. 7f, 13, and below, pp. 166f. Note that existential generalization as of p. 120 does belong to pure quantification theory, for it has to do with free variables rather than singular terms. The same is true of a correlative use of universal instantiation, such as is embodied in R2 of Essay V.

means simply:

The 24th letter of the alphabet contains six letters.

In (26) the occurrence of the letter within the context of quotes is as irrelevant to the quantifier that precedes it as is the occurrence of the same letter in the context 'six'. (26) consists merely of a falsehood preceded by an irrelevant quantifier. (27) is similar; its part:

'it' contains six letters

is false, and the prefix 'there is something such that' is irrelevant. (28), again, is false—if by 'contains six' we mean 'contains exactly six'.

It is less obvious, and correspondingly more important to recognize, that existential generalization is unwarranted likewise in the case of (9) and (10). Applied to (9), it leads to:

($\exists x$)(Philip is unaware that x denounced Catiline),

that is:

(29)   Something is such that Philip is unaware that it denounced Catiline.

What is this object, that denounced Catiline without Philip's having become aware of the fact? Tully, that is, Cicero? But to suppose this would conflict with the fact that (11) is false.

Note that (29) is not to be confused with:

Philip is unaware that ($\exists x$)(x denounced Catiline),

which, though it happens to be false, is quite straightforward and in no danger of being inferred by existential generalization from (9).

Now the difficulty involved in the apparent consequence (29) of (9) recurs when we try to apply existential generalization to modal statements. The apparent consequences:

(30)   ($\exists x$)(x is necessarily greater than 7),

(31)   ($\exists x$)(necessarily if there is life on the Evening Star then there is life on x)

of (15) and (16) raise the same questions as did (29). What is this number which, according to (30), is necessarily greater than 7? According to (15), from which (30) was inferred, it was 9, that is, the number of planets; but to suppose this would conflict with the fact that (18) is false. In a word, to be necessarily greater than 7 is not a trait of a number, but depends on the manner of referring to the number. Again, what is the thing x whose existence is affirmed in (31)? According to (16), from which (31) was inferred, it was the Evening Star, that is, the Morning Star; but to suppose this would conflict with the fact that (19) is false. Being necessarily or possibly thus and so is in general not a trait of the object concerned, but depends on the manner of referring to the object.

Note that (30) and (31) are not to be confused with:

Necessarily $(\exists x)(x > 7)$,

Necessarily $(\exists x)$(if there is life on the Evening Star then there is life on x),

which present no problem of interpretation comparable to that presented by (30) and (31). The difference may be accentuated by a change of example: in a game of a type admitting of no tie it is necessary that some one of the players will win, but there is no one player of whom it may be said to be necessary that he win.

We had seen, in the preceding section, how referential opacity manifests itself in connection with singular terms; and the task which we then set ourselves at the beginning of this section was to see how referential opacity manifests itself in connection rather with variables of quantification. The answer is now apparent: if to a referentially opaque context of a variable we apply a quantifier, with the intention that it govern that variable from outside the referentially opaque context, then what we commonly end up with is unintended sense or nonsense of the type (26)–(31). In a word, we cannot in general properly *quantify into* referentially opaque contexts.

The context of quotation and the further contexts '. . . was so called', 'is unaware that . . .', 'believes that . . .', 'Necessarily . . .', and 'Possibly . . .' were found referentially opaque in the preceding section by consideration of the failure of substitutivity of identity as applied to singular terms. In the present section these contexts have been found referentially opaque by a criterion having to do no longer with singular terms, but with the miscarriage of quantification. The reader may feel, indeed, that in this second criterion we have not really got away from singular terms after all; for the discrediting of the quantifications (29)-(31) turned still on an expository interplay between the singular terms 'Tully' and 'Cicero', '9' and 'the number of planets', 'Evening Star' and 'Morning Star'. Actually, though, this expository reversion to our old singular terms is avoidable, as may now be illustrated by re-arguing the meaninglessness of (30) in another way. Whatever is greater than 7 is a number, and any given number x greater than 7 can be uniquely determined by any of various conditions, some of which have '$x > 7$' as a *necessary* consequence and some of which do not. One and the same number x is uniquely determined by the condition:

$$(32) \qquad x = \sqrt{x} + \sqrt{x} + \sqrt{x} \neq \sqrt{x}$$

and by the condition:

(33)   There are exactly x planets,

but (32) has '$x > 7$' as a necessary consequence while (33) does not. *Necessary* greaterness than 7 makes no sense as applied to a *number* x; necessity attaches only to the connection between '$x > 7$' and the particular method (32), as opposed to (33), of specifying x.

Similarly, (31) was meaningless because the sort of thing x which fulfills the condition:

(34)   If there is life on the Evening Star then there is life on x,

namely, a physical object, can be uniquely determined by any of various conditions, not all of which have (34) as a necessary consequence. *Necessary* fulfillment of (34) makes no sense as applied to a physical object x; necessity attaches, at best, only to the connection between (34) and one or another particular means of specifying x.

The importance of recognizing referential opacity is not easily overstressed. We saw in §1 that referential opacity can obstruct substitutivity of identity. We now see that it also can interrupt quantification: quantifiers outside a referentially opaque construction need have no bearing on variables inside it. This again is obvious in the case of quotation, as witness the grotesque example:

$$(\exists x)(\text{'\textit{six}'} \text{ contains '}x\text{'}).$$

3

We see from (30)-(31) how a quantifier applied to a modal sentence may lead simply to nonsense. Nonsense is indeed mere absence of sense, and can always be remedied by arbitrarily assigning some sense. But the important point to observe is that granted an understanding of the modalities (through uncritical acceptance, for the sake of argument, of the underlying notion of analyticity), and given an understanding of quantification ordinarily so called, we do not come out automatically with any meaning for quantified modal sentences such as (30)-(31). This point must be taken into account by anyone who undertakes to work out laws for a quantified modal logic.

The root of the trouble was the referential opacity of modal contexts. But referential opacity depends in part on the ontology accepted, that is, on what objects are admitted as possible objects of reference. This may be seen most readily by reverting for a while to the point of view of §1, where referential opacity was explained in terms of failure of interchangeability of names which name the same object. Suppose now we were to repudiate all objects which, like 9 and the planet Venus, or Evening Star, are nameable by names which fail of interchangeability in modal contexts. To do so would be to sweep away all examples indicative of the opacity of modal contexts.

But what objects would remain in a thus purified universe? An object x must, to survive, meet this condition: if S is a statement containing a referential occurrence of a name of x, and S' is formed from S by substituting any different name of x, then S and S' not only must be alike in truth value as they stand, but must stay alike in truth value even when 'necessarily' or 'possibly' is prefixed. Equivalently: putting one name of x for another in any analytic statement must yield an analytic statement. Equivalently: any two names of x must be synonymous.[7]

Thus the planet Venus as a material object is ruled out by the possession of heteronymous names 'Venus', 'Evening Star', 'Morning Star'. Corresponding to these three names we must, if modal contexts are not to be referentially opaque, recognize three objects rather than one—perhaps the Venus-concept, the Evening-Star-concept, and the Morning-Star-concept.

Similarly 9, as a unique whole number between 8 and 10, is ruled out by the possession of heteronymous names '9' and 'the number of the planets'. Corresponding to these two names we must, if modal contexts are not to be referentially opaque, recognize two objects rather than one; perhaps the 9-concept and the number-of-planets-concept. These concepts are not numbers, for the one is neither identical with nor less than nor greater than the other.

The requirement that any two names of x be synonymous might be seen as a restriction not on the admissible objects x, but on the admissible vocabulary of singular terms. So much the worse, then, for this way of phrasing the requirement; we have here simply one more manifestation of the superficiality of treating ontological questions from the vantage point of singular terms. The real insight, in danger now of being obscured, was rather this: necessity does not properly apply to the fulfillment of conditions by *objects* (such as the ball of rock which is Venus, or the number which numbers the planets), apart from special ways of specifying them. This point was most conveniently brought out by consideration of singular terms, but it is not abrogated by their elimination. Let us now review the matter from the point of view of quantification rather than singular terms.

---

[7] See above, p. 32. Synonymy of names does not mean merely naming the same thing; it means that the statement of identity formed of the two names is analytic.

From the point of view of quantification, the referential opacity of modal contexts was reflected in the meaninglessness of such quantifications as (30)–(31). The crux of the trouble with (30) is that a number x may be uniquely determined by each of two conditions, for example, (32) and (33), which are not necessarily, that is, analytically, equivalent to each other. But suppose now we were to repudiate all such objects and retain only objects x such that *any two conditions uniquely determining x are analytically equivalent.* All examples such as (30)–(31), illustrative of the referential opacity of modal contexts, would then be swept away. It would come to make sense in general to say that there is an object which, independently of any particular means of specifying it, is necessarily thus and so. It would become legitimate, in short, to quantify into modal contexts.

Our examples suggest no objection to quantifying into modal contexts as long as the values of any variables thus quantified are limited to *intensional objects.* This limitation would mean allowing, for purposes of such quantification anyway, not classes but only class-concepts or attributes, it being understood that two open sentences which determine the same class still determine distinct attributes unless they are analytically equivalent. It would mean allowing, for purposes of such quantification, not numbers but only some sort of concepts which are related to the numbers in a many-one way. Further it would mean allowing, for purposes of such quantification, no concrete objects but only what Frege [3] called senses of names, and Carnap [3] and Church have called individual concepts. It is a drawback of such an ontology that the principle of individuation of its entities rests invariably on the putative notion of synonymy, or analyticity.

Actually, even granted these dubious entities, we can quickly see that the expedient of limiting the values of variables to them is after all a mistaken one. It does not relieve the original difficulty over quantifying into modal contexts; on the contrary, examples quite as disturbing as the old ones can be adduced within the realm of intensional objects. For, where

A is any intensional object, say an attribute, and 'p' stands for an arbitrary true sentence, clearly

$$(35) \qquad A = (\imath x)[p \cdot (x = A)].$$

Yet, if the true sentence represented by 'p' is not analytic, then neither is (35), and its sides are no more interchangeable in modal contexts than are 'Evening Star' and 'Morning Star', or '9' and 'the number of the planets'.

Or, to state the point without recourse to singular terms, it is that the requirement lately italicized — "any two conditions uniquely determining x are analytically equivalent" — is not assured merely by taking x as an intensional object. For, think of 'Fx' as any condition uniquely determining x, and think of 'p' as any nonanalytic truth. Then '$p \cdot Fx$' uniquely determines x but is not analytically equivalent to 'Fx', even though x be an intensional object.

It was in my 1943 paper that I first objected to quantifying into modal contexts, and it was in his review of it that Church proposed the remedy of limiting the variables thus quantified to intensional values. This remedy, which I have just now represented as mistaken, seemed all right at the time. Carnap [3] adopted it in an extreme form, limiting the range of his variables to intensional objects throughout his system. He did not indeed describe his procedure thus; he complicated the picture by propounding a curious double interpretation of variables. But I have argued[8] that this complicating device has no essential bearing and is better put aside.

By the time Church came to propound an intensional logic of his own [6], he perhaps appreciated that quantification into modal contexts could not after all be legitimized simply by limiting the thus quantified variables to intensional values. Anyway his departures are more radical. Instead of a necessity operator attachable to sentences, he has a necessity predicate attachable to complex names of certain intensional objects called propositions. What makes this departure more serious than it sounds

[8] In a criticism which Carnap generously included in his [3], pp. 196f.

is that the constants and variables occurring in a sentence do not recur in Church's name of the corresponding proposition. Thus the interplay, usual in modal logic, between occurrences of expressions outside modal contexts and recurrences of them inside modal contexts, is ill reflected in Church's system. Perhaps we should not call it a system of modal logic; Church generally did not. Anyway let my continuing discussion be understood as relating to modal logics only in the narrower sense, where the modal operator attaches to sentences.

Church [4] and Carnap tried — unsuccessfully, I have just argued — to meet my criticism of quantified modal logic by restricting the values of their variables. Arthur Smullyan took the alternative course of challenging my criticism itself. His argument depends on positing a fundamental division of names into proper names and (overt or covert) descriptions, such that proper names which name the same object are always synonymous. (Cf. (38) below.) He observes, quite rightly on these assumptions, that any examples which, like (15)–(20) and (24)–(25), show failure of substitutivity of identity in modal contexts, must exploit some descriptions rather than just proper names. Then he undertakes to adjust matters by propounding, in connection with modal contexts, an alteration of Russell's familiar logic of descriptions.[9] As stressed in the preceding section, however, referential opacity remains to be reckoned with even when descriptions and other singular terms are eliminated altogether.

Nevertheless, the only hope of sustaining quantified modal logic lies in adopting a course that resembles Smullyan's, rather than Church [4] and Carnap [3], in this way: it must overrule my objection. It must consist in arguing or deciding that quantification into modal contexts makes sense even though any

[9] Russell's theory of descriptions, in its original formulation, involved distinctions of so-called 'scope.' Change in the scope of a description was indifferent to the truth value of any statement, however, unless the description failed to name. This indifference was important to the fulfillment, by Russell's theory, of its purpose as an analysis or surrogate of the practical idiom of singular description. On the other hand, Smullyan allows difference of scope to affect truth value even in cases where the description concerned succeeds in naming.

value of the variable of such a quantification be determinable by conditions that are not analytically equivalent to each other. The only hope lies in accepting the situation illustrated by (32) and (33) and insisting, despite it, that the object x in question is necessarily greater than 7. This means adopting an invidious attitude toward certain ways of uniquely specifying x, for example (33), and favoring other ways, for example (32), as somehow better revealing the "essence" of the object. Consequences of (32) can, from such a point of view, be looked upon as necessarily true of the object which is 9 (and is the number of the planets), while some consequences of (33) are rated still as only contingently true of that object.

Evidently this reversion to Aristotelian essentialism (cf. p. 22) is required if quantification into modal contexts is to be insisted on. An object, of itself and by whatever name or none, must be seen as having some of its traits necessarily and others contingently, despite the fact that the latter traits follow just as analytically from some ways of specifying the object as the former traits do from other ways of specifying it. In fact, we can see pretty directly that any quantified modal logic is bound to show such favoritism among the traits of an object; for surely it will be held, for each thing x, on the one hand that

$$(36) \qquad\qquad \text{necessarily } (x = x)$$

and on the other hand that

$$(37) \qquad\qquad \sim \text{necessarily } [p \cdot (x = x)] \,,$$

where 'p' stands for an arbitrary contingent truth.

Essentialism is abruptly at variance with the idea, favored by Carnap, Lewis, and others, of explaining necessity by analyticity (cf. p. 143). For the appeal to analyticity can pretend to distinguish essential and accidental traits of an object only relative to how the object is specified, not absolutely. Yet the champion of quantified modal logic must settle for essentialism.

Limiting the values of his variables is neither necessary nor sufficient to justify quantifying the variables into modal contexts. Limiting their values can, however, still have this purpose in conjunction with his essentialism: if he wants to limit his essentialism to special sorts of objects, he must correspondingly limit the values of the variables which he quantifies into modal contexts.

The system presented in Miss Barcan's pioneer papers on quantified modal logic differed from the systems of Carnap and Church in imposing no special limitations on the values of variables. That she was prepared, moreover, to accept the essentialist presuppositions seems rather hinted in her theorem:

$$(38) \qquad (x)(y)\{(x = y) \supset [\text{necessarily } (x = y)]\} \,,$$

for this is as if to say that some at least (and in fact at most; cf. '$p \cdot Fx$') of the traits that determine an object do so necessarily. The modal logic in Fitch [1] follows Miss Barcan on both points. Note incidentally that (38) follows directly from (36) and a law of substitutivity of identity for variables:

$$(x)(y)[(x = y \cdot Fx) \supset Fy] \,.$$

The upshot of these reflections is meant to be that the way to do quantified modal logic, if at all, is to accept Aristotelian essentialism. To defend Aristotelian essentialism, however, is not part of my plan. Such a philosophy is as unreasonable by my lights as it is by Carnap's or Lewis's. And in conclusion I say, as Carnap and Lewis have not: so much the worse for quantified modal logic. By implication, so much the worse for unquantified modal logic as well; for, if we do not propose to quantify across the necessity operator, the use of that operator ceases to have any clear advantage over merely quoting a sentence and saying that it is analytic.

4

The worries introduced by the logical modalities are introduced also by the admission of attributes (as opposed to classes). The idiom 'the attribute of being thus and so' is referentially opaque, as may be seen, for example, from the fact that the true statement:

(39)   The attribute of exceeding 9 = the attribute of exceeding 9

goes over into the falsehood:

> The attribute of exceeding the number of the planets =
> the attribute of exceeding 9

under substitution according to the true identity (24). Moreover, existential generalization of (39) would lead to:

(40) $(\exists x)$(the attribute of exceeding x = the attribute of
exceeding 9)

which resists coherent interpretation just as did the existential
generalizations (29)–(31) of (9), (15), and (16). Quantification
of a sentence which contains the variable of quantification
within a context of the form 'the attribute of . . .' is exactly on a
par with quantification of a modal sentence.

Attributes, as remarked earlier, are individuated by this
principle: two open sentences which determine the same class
do not determine the same attribute unless they are analytically
equivalent. Now another popular sort of intensional entity is
the *proposition*. Propositions are conceived in relation to statements as attributes are conceived in relation to open sentences:
two statements determine the same proposition just in case they
are analytically equivalent. The foregoing strictures on attributes obviously apply equally to propositions. The truth:

(41)   The proposition that $9 > 7$ = the proposition that $9 > 7$

goes over into the falsehood:

> The proposition that the number of the planets > 7 = the
> proposition that $9 > 7$.

under substitution according to (24). Existential generalization
of (41) yields a result comparable to (29)–(31) and (40).

Most of the logicians, semanticists, and analytical philosophers who discourse freely of attributes, propositions, or logical
modalities betray failure to appreciate that they thereby imply
a metaphysical position which they themselves would scarcely
condone. It is noteworthy that in *Principia Mathematica*, where
attributes were nominally admitted as entities, all actual con-

texts occurring in the course of formal work are such as could be fulfilled as well by classes as by attributes. All actual contexts are *extensional* in the sense of page 30 above. The authors of *Principia Mathematica* thus adhered in practice to a principle of extensionality which they did not espouse in theory. If their practice had been otherwise, we might have been brought sooner to an appreciation of the urgency of the principle.

We have seen how modal sentences, attribute terms, and proposition terms conflict with the nonessentialist view of the universe. It must be kept in mind that those expressions create such conflict only when they are quantified into, that is, when they are put under a quantifier and themselves contain the variable of quantification. We are familiar with the fact (illustrated by (26) above) that a quotation cannot contain an effectively free variable, reachable by an outside quantifier. If we preserve a similar attitude toward modalities, attribute terms, and proposition terms, we may then make free use of them without any misgivings of the present urgent kind.

What has been said of modality in these pages relates only to strict modality. For other sorts, for example, physical necessity and possibility, the first problem would be to formulate the notions clearly and exactly. Afterward we could investigate whether such modalities, like the strict ones, cannot be quantified into without precipitating an ontological crisis. The question concerns intimately the practical use of language. It concerns, for example, the use of the contrary-to-fact conditional within a quantification; for it is reasonable to suppose that the contrary-to-fact conditional reduces to the form 'Necessarily, if p then q' in some sense of necessity. Upon the contrary-to-fact conditional depends in turn, for example, this definition of solubility in water: To say that an object is soluble in water is to say that it would dissolve if it were in water. In discussions of physics, naturally, we need quantifications containing the clause 'x is soluble in water', or the equivalent in words; but, according to the definition suggested, we should then have to admit within quantifications the expression 'if x were in water then x would dissolve', that is, 'necessarily if x is in water then

x dissolves'. Yet we do not know whether there is a suitable sense of 'necessarily' into which we can so quantify.[10]

Any way of imbedding statements within statements, whether based on some notion of "necessity" or, for example, on a notion of "probability" as in Reichenbach, must be carefully examined in relation to its susceptibility to quantification. Perhaps the only useful modes of statement composition susceptible to unrestricted quantification are the truth functions. Happily, no other mode of statement composition is needed, at any rate, in mathematics; and mathematics, significantly, is the branch of science whose needs are most clearly understood.

Let us return, for a final sweeping observation, to our first test of referential opacity, namely, failure of substitutivity of identity; and let us suppose that we are dealing with a theory in which (a) *logically* equivalent formulas are interchangeable in all contexts *salva veritate* and (b) the logic of classes is at hand.[11] For such a theory it can be shown that *any* mode of statement composition, other than the truth functions, is referentially opaque. For, let ϕ and ψ be any statements alike in truth value, and let $\Phi(\phi)$ be any true statement containing ϕ as a part. What is to be shown is that $\Phi(\psi)$ will also be true, unless the context represented by 'Φ' is referentially opaque. Now the class named by $\hat{\alpha}\phi$ is either V or Λ, according as ϕ is true or false; for remember that ϕ is a statement, devoid of free α. (If the notation $\hat{\alpha}\phi$ without recurrence of α seems puzzling, read it as $\hat{\alpha}(\alpha = \alpha \cdot \phi)$.) Moreover ϕ is logically equivalent to $\hat{\alpha}\phi = $ V. Hence, by (a), since $\Phi(\phi)$ is true, so is $\Phi(\hat{\alpha}\phi = $ V). But $\hat{\alpha}\phi$ and $\hat{\alpha}\psi$ name one and the same class, since ϕ and ψ are alike in truth value. Then, since $\Phi(\hat{\alpha}\phi = $ V) is true, so is $\Phi(\hat{\alpha}\psi = $ V) unless the context represented by 'Φ' is referentially opaque. But if $\Phi(\hat{\alpha}\psi = $ V) is true, then so in turn is $\Phi(\psi)$, by (a).

[10] For a theory of disposition terms, like 'soluble', see Carnap [5].
[11] See above, pp. 27, 87.

3

Semantical Considerations on Modal Logic

SAUL A. KRIPKE

Reprinted with the kind permission of the editor from *Acta Philosophica Fennica,* XVI (1963), 83-94.

Semantical Considerations on Modal Logic

Saul A. Kripke

This paper gives an exposition of some features of a semantical theory of modal logics [1]. For a certain quantified extension of S5, this theory was presented in [1], and it has been summarized in [2]. The present paper will concentrate on one aspect of the theory — the introduction of quantifiers — and it will restrict itself in the main to one method of achieving this end. The emphasis of the paper will be purely semantical, and hence it will omit the use of semantic tableaux, which is essential to a full presentation of the theory. (For these, see [1] and [11].) Proofs, also, will largely be suppressed.

We consider four modal systems. Formulae A, B, C, ... are built out of atomic formulae P, Q, R, ..., using the connectives $\wedge$, $\sim$, and $\square$. The system M has the following axiom schemes and rules:

A1. $\square A \supset A$
A2. $\square (A \supset B) \supset . \square A \supset \square B$
R1. $A, A \supset B \mid B$
R2. $A \mid \square A$

If we add the following axiom scheme, we get S4:

$\square A \supset \square \square A$

We get the *Brouwersche* system if we add to M:

$A \supset \square \lozenge A$

S5, if we add:

$\lozenge A \supset \square \lozenge A$

---

[1] The theory given here has points of contact with many authors: For lists of these, see [11] and Hintikka [6]. The authors closest to the present theory appear to be Hintikka and Kanger. The present treatment of quantification, however, is unique as far as I know, although it derives some inspiration from acquaintance with the very different methods of Prior and Hintikka.

Modal systems whose theorems are closed under the rules R1 and R2, and include all theorems of M, are called "normal". Although we have developed a theory which applies to such non-normal systems as Lewis's S2 and S3, we will restrict ourselves here to normal systems.

To get a semantics for modal logic, we introduce the notion of a (normal) *model structure*. A model structure (m.s.) is an ordered triple $(\mathbf{G}, \mathbf{K}, \mathbf{R})$ where $\mathbf{K}$ is a set, $\mathbf{R}$ is a reflexive relation on $\mathbf{K}$, and $\mathbf{G} \, \varepsilon \, \mathbf{K}$. Intuitively, we look at matters thus: $\mathbf{K}$ is the set of all "possible worlds;" $\mathbf{G}$ is the "real world." If $\mathbf{H}_1$ and $\mathbf{H}_2$ are two worlds, $\mathbf{H}_1 \, \mathbf{R} \, \mathbf{H}_2$ means intuitively that $\mathbf{H}_2$ is "possible relative to" $\mathbf{H}_1$; *i.e.*, that every proposition *true* in $\mathbf{H}_2$ is *possible* in $\mathbf{H}_1$. Clearly, then, the relation $\mathbf{R}$ should indeed be reflexive; every world $\mathbf{H}$ is *possible* relative to itself, since every proposition *true* in $\mathbf{H}$ is, *a fortiori*, possible in $\mathbf{H}$. Reflexivity is thus an intuitively natural requirement. We may impose additional requirements, corresponding to various "reduction axioms" of modal logic: If $\mathbf{R}$ is transitive, we call $(\mathbf{G}, \mathbf{K}, \mathbf{R})$ an S4-m.s.; if $\mathbf{R}$ is symmetric, $(\mathbf{G}, \mathbf{K}, \mathbf{R})$ is a *Brouwersche* m.s.; and if $\mathbf{R}$ is an equivalence relation, we call $(\mathbf{G}, \mathbf{K}, \mathbf{R})$ an S5-m.s. A model structure without restriction is also called an M-model structure.

To complete the picture, we need the notion of *model*. Given a model structure $(\mathbf{G}, \mathbf{K}, \mathbf{R})$, a *model* assigns to each atomic formula (propositional variable) P a truth-value $\mathbf{T}$ or $\mathbf{F}$ in each world $\mathbf{H} \, \varepsilon \, \mathbf{K}$. Formally, a *model* φ on a m.s. $(\mathbf{G}, \mathbf{K}, \mathbf{R})$ is a binary function $\varphi(P, \mathbf{H})$, where P varies over atomic formulae and $\mathbf{H}$ varies over elements of $\mathbf{K}$, whose range is the set $\{\mathbf{T}, \mathbf{F}\}$. Given a model, we can define the assignments of truth-values to non-atomic formulae by induction. Assume $\varphi(A, \mathbf{H})$ and $\varphi(B, \mathbf{H})$ have already been defined for all $\mathbf{H} \, \varepsilon \, \mathbf{K}$. Then if $\varphi(A, \mathbf{H}) = \varphi(B, \mathbf{H}) = \mathbf{T}$, define $\varphi(A \wedge B, \mathbf{H}) = \mathbf{T}$; otherwise, $\varphi(A \wedge B, \mathbf{H}) = \mathbf{F}$. $\varphi(\sim A, \mathbf{H})$ is defined to be $\mathbf{F}$ iff $\varphi(A, \mathbf{H}) = \mathbf{T}$; otherwise, $\varphi(\sim A, \mathbf{H}) = \mathbf{T}$. Finally, we define $\varphi(\square A, \mathbf{H}) = \mathbf{T}$ iff $\varphi(A, \mathbf{H}') = \mathbf{T}$ for every $\mathbf{H}' \, \varepsilon \, \mathbf{K}$ such that $\mathbf{H} \, \mathbf{R} \, \mathbf{H}'$; otherwise, $\varphi(\square A, \mathbf{H}) = \mathbf{F}$. Intuitively, this says that A is necessary in $\mathbf{H}$ iff A is true in all worlds $\mathbf{H}'$ possible relative to $\mathbf{H}$.

Completeness theorem. $\vdash A$ in M (S4, S5, the *Brouwersche* system) if and only if $\varphi(A, \mathbf{G}) = \mathbf{T}$ for every model φ on an M- (S4-, S5-, *Brouwersche*) model structure $(\mathbf{G}, \mathbf{K}, \mathbf{R})$.

(For a proof, see [11].)

This completeness theorem equates the syntactical notion of *provability* in a modal system with a semantical notion of *validity*.

The rest of this paper concerns, with the exception of some concluding remarks, the introduction of quantifiers. To do this, we must associate with each world a domain of individuals, the individuals that exist in that world. Formally, we define a *quantificational model structure* (q.m.s.) as a model structure (**G**, **K**, **R**), together with a function ψ which assigns to each **H** ε **K** a set $\psi(\mathbf{H})$, called the *domain* of **H**. Intuitively $\psi(\mathbf{H})$ is the set of all individuals existing in **H**. Notice, of course, that $\psi(\mathbf{H})$ need not be the same set for different arguments **H**, just as, intuitively, in worlds other than the real one, some actually existing individuals may be absent, while new individuals, like Pegasus, may appear.

We may then add, to the symbols of modal logic, an infinite list of individual variables x, y, z, . . . , and, for each nonnegative integer n, a list of n-adic predicate letters P^n, Q^n, . . . , where the superscripts will sometimes be understood from the context. We count propositional variables (atomic formulae) as "0-adic" predicate letters. We then build up well-formed formulae in the usual manner, and can now prepare ourselves to define a quantificational *model*.

To define a quantificational model, we must extend the original notion, which assigned a truth-value to each atomic formula in each world. Analogously, we must suppose that in each world a given n-adic predicate letter determines a certain set of ordered n-tuples, its *extension* in that world. Consider, for example, the case of a monadic predicate letter $P(x)$. We would like to say that, in the world **H**, the predicate $P(x)$ is true of some individuals in ψ (**H**) and false of others; formally, we would say that, relative to certain assignments of elements of $\psi(\mathbf{H})$ to x, $\varphi(P(x), \mathbf{H}) = \mathbf{T}$ and relative to others $\varphi(P(x), \mathbf{H}) = \mathbf{F}$. The set of all individuals of which P is true is called the *extension* of P in **H**. But there is a problem: should $\varphi(P(x), \mathbf{H})$ be given a truth-value when x is assigned a value in the domain of some *other* world **H'**, and not in the domain of **H**? Intuitively, suppose $P(x)$ means "x is bald" — are we to assign a truth-value to the substitution instance "Sherlock Holmes is bald"? Holmes does not exist, but in other states of affairs, he would have existed. Should we assign a definite truth-value to the statement that he is bald, or not? Frege [3] and Strawson [4] would not assign the statement a truth-value; Russell [5] would [1]. For the purposes of modal logic we hold that different

---

[1] Russell, however, would conclude that "Sherlock Holmes" is therefore not a genuine name; and Frege would eliminate such empty names by an artifact.

answers to this question represent alternative *conventions*. All are tenable. The only existing discussions of this problem I have seen — those of Hintikka [6] and Prior [7] — adopt the Frege-Strawson view. This view necessarily must lead to some modification of the usual modal logic. The reason is that the semantics for modal propositional logic, which we have already given, assumed that every formula must take a truth-value in each world; and now, for a formula $A(x)$ containing a free variable x, the Frege-Strawson view requires that it not be given a truth-value in a world **H** when the variable x is assigned an individual not in the domain of that world. We thus can no longer expect that the original laws of modal propositional logic hold for statements containing free variables, and are faced with an option: either revise modal propositional logic or restrict the rule of substitution. Prior does the former, Hintikka the latter. There are further alternatives the Frege-Strawson choice involves: Should we take $\square A$ (in **H**) to mean that A is *true* in all possible worlds (relative to **H**), or just *not false* in any such world? The second alternative merely demands that A be either true or lack a truth-value in each world. Prior, in his system Q, in effect admits both types of necessity, one as "L" and the other as "NMN". A similar question arises for conjunction: if A is false and B has no truth-value, should we take $A \wedge B$ to be false or truth-valueless?

In a full statement of the semantical theory, we would explore all these variants of the Frege-Strawson view. Here we will take the other option, and assume that a statement containing free variables has a truth-value in each world for every assignment to its free variables [1]. Formally, we state the matter as follows: Let $\mathbf{U} = \bigcup_{H \, \varepsilon \, K} \psi(\mathbf{H})$. $\mathbf{U}^n$ is the nth Cartesian product of $\mathbf{U}$ with itself. We define a quantificational *model* on a q.m.s. (**G, K, R**) as a binary

---

[1] It is natural to assume that an *atomic* predicate should be *false* in a world **H** of all those individuals not existing in that world; that is, that the extension of a predicate letter must consist of actually existing individuals. We can do this by requiring semantically that $\varphi(P^n, \mathbf{H})$ be a subset of $[\psi(\mathbf{H})]^n$; the semantical treatment below would otherwise suffice without change. We would have to add to the axiom system below all closures of formulae of the form $P^n(x_1, \ldots, x_n) \wedge (y)A(y) . \supset . A(x_i) \; (1 \leq i \leq n)$. We have chosen not to do this because the rule of substitution would no longer hold; theorems would hold for atomic formulae which would not hold when the atomic formulae are replaced by arbitrary formulae. (This answers a question of Putnam and Kalmar.)

function $\varphi(P^n, \mathbf{H})$, where the first variable ranges over n-adic predicate letters, for arbitrary n, and $\mathbf{H}$ ranges over elements of $\mathbf{K}$. If $n = 0$, $\varphi(P^n, \mathbf{H}) = \mathbf{T}$ or $\mathbf{F}$; if $n \geq 1$, $\varphi(P^n, \mathbf{H})$ is a subset of $\mathbf{U}^n$. We now define, inductively, for every formula A and $\mathbf{H} \, \varepsilon \, \mathbf{K}$, a truth-value $\varphi(A, \mathbf{H})$, relative to a given assignment of elements of $\mathbf{U}$ to the free variables of A. The case of a propositional variable is obvious. For an atomic formula $P^n(x_1, \ldots, x_n)$, where P^n is an n-adic predicate letter and $n \geq 1$, given an assignment of elements $a_1, \ldots, a_n$ of $\mathbf{U}$ to $x_1, \ldots, x_n$, we define $\varphi(P^n(x_1, \ldots, x_n),$ $\mathbf{H}) = \mathbf{T}$ if the n-tuple $(a_1, \ldots, a_n)$ is a member of $\varphi(P^n, \mathbf{H})$; otherwise, $\varphi(P^n(x_1, \ldots, x_n), \mathbf{H}) = \mathbf{F}$, relative to the given assignment. Given these assignments for atomic formulae, we can build up the assignments for complex formulae by induction. The induction steps for the propositional connectives $\wedge$, $\sim$, $\square$, have already been given. Assume we have a formula $A(x, y_1, \ldots, y_n)$, where x and the y_i are the only free variables present, and that a truth-value $\varphi(A(x, y_1, \ldots, y_n), \mathbf{H})$ has been defined for each assignment to the free variables of $A(x, y_1, \ldots, y_n)$. Then we define $\varphi((x)A$ $(x, y_1, \ldots, y_n), \mathbf{H}) = \mathbf{T}$ relative to an assignment of $b_1, \ldots, b_n$ to $y_1, \ldots, y_n$ (where the b_i are elements of $\mathbf{U}$), if $\varphi((A(x, y_1, \ldots, y_n),$ $\mathbf{H}) = \mathbf{T}$ for every assignment of $a, b_1, \ldots, b_n$ to $x, y_1, \ldots, y_n$, respectively, where $a \, \varepsilon \, \psi(\mathbf{H})$; otherwise, $\varphi((x)A(x, y_1, \ldots, y_n),$ $\mathbf{H}) = \mathbf{F}$ relative to the given assignment. Notice that the restriction $a \, \varepsilon \, \psi(\mathbf{H})$ means that, in $\mathbf{H}$, we quantify only over the objects actually existing in $\mathbf{H}$.

To illustrate the semantics, we give counterexamples to two familiar proposals for laws of modal quantification theory — the "Barcan formula" $(x)\square A(x) \supset \square (x)A(x)$ and its converse $\square (x)A(x) \supset (x)\square A(x)$. For each we consider a model structure $(\mathbf{G}, \mathbf{K}, \boldsymbol{R})$, where $\mathbf{K} = \{\mathbf{G}, \mathbf{H}\}$, $\mathbf{G} \neq \mathbf{H}$, and $\boldsymbol{R}$ is simply the Cartesian product $\mathbf{K}^2$. Clearly $\boldsymbol{R}$ is reflexive, transitive, and symmetric, so our considerations apply even to S5.

For the Barcan formula, we extend $(\mathbf{G}, \mathbf{K}, \boldsymbol{R})$ to a quantificational model structure by defining $\psi(\mathbf{G}) = \{a\}$, $\psi(\mathbf{H}) = \{a, b\}$, where a and b are distinct. We then define, for a monadic predicate letter P, a model φ in which $\varphi(P, \mathbf{G}) = \{a\}$, $\varphi(P, \mathbf{H}) = \{a\}$. Then clearly $\square P(x)$ is true in $\mathbf{G}$ when x is assigned a; and since a is the only object in the domain of $\mathbf{G}$, so is $(x)\square P(x)$. But, $(x)P(x)$ is clearly false in $\mathbf{H}$ (for $\varphi(P(x), \mathbf{H}) = \mathbf{F}$ when x is assigned b), and hence $\square(x)P(x)$ is false in $\mathbf{G}$. So we have a counterexample to the Barcan formula. Notice that this counterexample is quite independent of whether b is assigned a truth-value in **G** or not, so also it applies to the systems of Hintikka and Prior. Such counterexamples can be disallowed, and the Barcan formula reinstated, only if we require a model structure to satisfy the condition that $\psi(\mathbf{H'}) \subseteq \psi(\mathbf{H})$ whenever $\mathbf{H} \, R \, \mathbf{H'}$ $(\mathbf{H}, \mathbf{H'} \, \varepsilon \, \mathbf{K})$.

For the converse of the Barcan formula, set $\psi(\mathbf{G}) = \{a, b\}$, $\psi(\mathbf{H}) = \{a\}$, where again $a \neq b$. Define $\varphi(P, \mathbf{G}) = \{a, b\}$, $\varphi(P, \mathbf{H}) = \{a\}$, where P is a given monadic predicate letter. Then clearly $(x)P(x)$ holds in both **G** and **H,** so that $\varphi(\Box(x)P(x), \mathbf{G}) = \mathbf{T}$. But $\varphi(P\,(x), \mathbf{H}) = \mathbf{F}$ when x is assigned b, so that, when x is assigned $\varphi(\Box P(x), \mathbf{G}) = \mathbf{F}$. Hence $\varphi((x)\Box P(x), \mathbf{G}) = \mathbf{F,}$ and we have the desired counterexample to the converse of the Barcan formula. This counterexample, however, depends on asserting that, in **H,** $P(x)$ is actually *false* when x is assigned b; it might thus disappear if, for this assignment, $P(x)$ were declared to lack truth-value in **H.** In this case, we will still have a counterexample if we require a necessary statement to be *true* in all possible worlds (Prior's "*L*"), but not if we merely require that it never be false (Prior's "*NMN*"). On our present convention, we can eliminate the counterexample only by requiring, for each q.m.s., that $\psi\,(\mathbf{H}) \subseteq \psi\,(\mathbf{H'})$ whenever $\mathbf{H} \, R \, \mathbf{H'}$.

These counterexamples lead to a peculiar difficulty: We have given countermodels, in quantified S5, to both the Barcan formula and its converse. Yet Prior appears to have shown in [8] that the Barcan formula is derivable in quantified S5; and the converse seems derivable even in quantified M by the following argument:

    (A) $(x)A(x) \supset A(y)$ (by quantification theory)

    (B) $\Box \, ((x)A(x) \supset A(y))$ (by necessitation)

    (C) $\Box \, ((x)A(x) \supset A(y)) \supset \Box(x)A(x) \supset \Box \, A(y)$ (Axiom A2)

    (D) $\Box \, (x)A(x) \supset \Box \, A(y)$ (from (B) and (C))

    (E) $(y) \, (\Box \, (x)A(x) \supset \Box \, A(y))$ (generalizing on (D))

    (F) $\Box \, (x)A(x) \supset (y) \, \Box \, A(y)$ (by quantification theory, and (E))

We seem to have derived the conclusion using principles that should all be valid in the model-theory. Actually, the flaw lies in the application of necessitation to (A). In a formula like (A), we give the free variables the generality interpretation: [1] When (A) is asserted as a theorem, it abbreviates assertion of its ordinary universal closure

(A') $(y) ((x)A(x) \supset A(y))$

Now if we applied necessitation to (A'), we would get

(B') $\Box\ (y) ((x)A(x) \supset A(y))$

On the other hand, (B) itself is interpreted as asserting

(B'') $(y)\ \Box\ ((x)A(x) \supset A(y))$

To infer (B'') from (B'), we would need a law of the form $\Box\ (y)C(y) \supset (y)\Box C(y)$, which is just the converse Barcan formula that we are trying to prove. In fact, it is readily checked that (B'') fails in the countermodel given above for the converse Barcan formula, if we replace $A(x)$ by $P(x)$.

We can avoid this sort of difficulty if, following Quine [15], we formulate quantification theory so that only *closed* formulae are asserted. Assertion of formulae containing free variables is at best a convenience; assertion of $A(x)$ with free x can always be replaced by assertion of $(x)A(x)$.

If A is a formula containing free variables, we define a *closure* of A to be any formula without free variables obtained by prefixing universal quantifiers and necessity signs, in any order, to A. We then define the axioms of quantified M to be the closures of the following schemata:

(0) Truth-functional tautologies
(1) $\Box\ A \supset A$
(2) $\Box\ (A \supset B) . \supset . \Box\ A \supset \Box\ B$
(3) $A \supset (x)A$, where x is not free in A.
(4) $(x) (A \supset B) . \supset . (x)A \supset (x)B$
(5) $(y) ((x)A(x) \supset A(y))$

---

[1] It is not asserted that the generality interpretation of theorems with free variables is the only possible one. One might wish a formula A to be provable iff, for each model φ, $\varphi(A, \mathbf{G}) = \mathbf{T}$ for every assignment to the free variables of A. But then $(x)A(x) \supset A(y)$ will not be a theorem; in fact, in the countermodel above to the Barcan formula, $\varphi ((x)P(x) \supset P(y), \mathbf{G}) = \mathbf{F}$ if y is assigned b. Thus quantification theory would have to be revised along the lines of [9] or [10]. This procedure has much to recommend it, but we have not adopted it since we wished to show that the difficulty can be solved without revising quantification theory or modal propositional logic.

The rule of inference is detachment for material implication. Necessitation can be obtained as a derived rule.

To obtain quantified extensions of S4, S5, the *Brouwersche* system, simply add to the axiom schemata all closures of the appropriate reduction axiom.

The systems we have obtained have the following properties: They are a straightforward extension of the modal propositional logics, without the modifications of Prior's Q; the rule of substitution holds without restriction, unlike Hintikka's presentation; and nevertheless neither the Barcan formula nor its converse is derivable. Further, all the laws of quantification theory — modified to admit the empty domain — hold. The semantical completeness theorem we gave for modal propositional logic can be extended to the new systems.

We can introduce *existence as a predicate* in the present system if we like. Semantically, existence is a monadic predicate $E(x)$ satisfying, for each model φ on a m.s. $(\mathbf{G}, \mathbf{K}, \boldsymbol{R})$, the identity $\varphi\,(E, \mathbf{H}) = \psi\,(\mathbf{H})$ for every $\mathbf{H}\,\varepsilon\,\mathbf{K}$. Axiomatically, we can introduce it through the postulation of closures of formulae of the form: $(x)A(x) \wedge E(y)$. $\supset$. $A(y)$, and $(x)E(x)$. The predicate P used above in the counterexample to the converse Barcan formula can now be recognized as simply existence. This fact shows how existence differs from the tautological predicate $A(x)\,\mathrm{v} \sim A(x)$ even though $\square(x)E(x)$ is provable. For although $(x)\,\square\,(A(x)\,\mathrm{v} \sim A(x))$ is valid, $(x)\square E(x)$ is not; although it is necessary that every thing exists, it does not follow that everything has the property of necessary existence.

We can introduce identity semantically in the model theory by defining $x = y$ to be true in a world $\mathbf{H}$ when x and y are assigned the same value and otherwise false; existence could then be defined in terms of identity, by stipulating that $E(x)$ means $(\exists y)\,(x = y)$. For reasons not given here, a broader theory of identity could be obtained if we complicated the notion of quantificational model structure.

We conclude with some brief and sketchy remarks on the "provability" interpretations of modal logics, which we give in each case for propositional calculus only. The reader will have obtained the main point of this paper if he omits this section. Provability interpretations are based on a desire to adjoin a necessity operator to a formal system, say Peano arithmetic, in such a way that, for any formula A of the system, $\square\,A$ will be interpreted as true iff A is provable in the system. It has been argued that such "provability" interpretations of a modal operator are dispensable in favor of a provability *predicate*, attaching to the Gödel number of A; but Professor Montague's contribution to the present volume casts at least some doubt on this viewpoint.

Let us consider the formal system **PA** of Peano arithmetic, as formalized in Kleene [12]. We adjoin to the formation rules operators $\wedge$, $\sim$, and $\square$ (the conjunction and negation adjoined are to be distinct from those of the original system), operating on closed formulae only. In the model theory we gave above, we took atomic formulae to be propositional variables, or predicate letters followed by parenthesized individual variables; here we take them to be simply the closed well-formed formulae of **PA** (*not* just the atomic formulae of **PA**). We define a model structure $(\mathbf{G}, \mathbf{K}, \mathbf{R})$, where $\mathbf{K}$ is the set of all distinct (non-isomorphic) countable models of **PA**, $\mathbf{G}$ is the standard model in the natural numbers, and $\mathbf{R}$ is the Cartesian product $\mathbf{K}^2$. We define a model φ by requiring that, for any atomic formula P and $\mathbf{H} \varepsilon \mathbf{K}$, $\varphi(P, \mathbf{H}) = \mathbf{T}$ $(\mathbf{F})$ iff P is true (false) in the model $\mathbf{H}$. (Remember, P is a wff of **PA**, and $\mathbf{H}$ is a countable model of **PA**.) We then build up the evaluation for compound formulae as before. [1] To say that A is true is to say it is true in the real world $\mathbf{G}$; and, for any atomic P, $\varphi(\square P, \mathbf{G}) = \mathbf{T}$ iff P is provable in **PA**. (Notice that $\varphi(P, \mathbf{G}) = \mathbf{T}$ iff P is true in the intuitive sense.) Since $(\mathbf{G}, \mathbf{K}, \mathbf{R})$ is an S5-m.s., all the laws of S5 will be valid on this interpretation; and we can show that *only* the laws of S5 are generally valid. (For example, if P is Gödel's undecidable formula, $\varphi(\square P$ v $\square \sim P, \mathbf{G}) = \mathbf{F}$, which is a counterexample to the "law" $\square A$ v $\square \sim A$.)

Another provability interpretation is the following: Again we take the atomic formulae to be the closed wffs of **PA**, and then build up new formulae using the adjoined connectives $\wedge$, $\sim$, and $\square$.

---

[1] It may be protested that **PA** already contain symbols for conjunction and negation, say "&" and "¬"; so why do we adjoin new symbols "$\wedge$" and "$\sim$"? The answer is that if P and Q are atomic formulae, then P & Q is *also* atomic in the present sense, since it is well-formed in **PA**; but $P \wedge Q$ is not. In order to be able to apply the previous theory, in which the conjunction of atomic formulae is not atomic, we need "$\wedge$". Nevertheless, for any $\mathbf{H} \varepsilon \mathbf{K}$ and atomic P and Q, $\varphi(P \& Q, \mathbf{H}) = \varphi(P \wedge Q, \mathbf{H})$, so that confusion of "&" with "$\wedge$" causes no harm in practice. Similar remarks apply to negation, and to the provability interpretation of S4 in the next paragraph.

Let $\mathbf{K}$ be the set of all ordered pairs $(\mathbf{E}, \alpha)$, where $\mathbf{E}$ is a consistent extension of $\mathbf{PA}$, and α is a (countable) model of the system $\mathbf{E}$. Let $\mathbf{G} = (\mathbf{PA}, \alpha_0)$, where α_0 is the standard model of $\mathbf{PA}$. We say $(\mathbf{E}, \alpha) \, \boldsymbol{R} \, (\mathbf{E}', \alpha')$, where $(\mathbf{E}, \alpha)$ and $(\mathbf{E}', \alpha')$ are in $\mathbf{K}$, iff $\mathbf{E}'$ is an extension of $\mathbf{E}$. For atomic P, define $\varphi(P, (\mathbf{E}, \alpha)) = \mathbf{T}$ $(\mathbf{F})$ iff P is true (false) in α. Then we can show, for atomic P, that $\varphi(\square \, P, (\mathbf{E}, \alpha)) = \mathbf{T}$ iff P is provable in $\mathbf{E}$; in particular, $\varphi(\square \, P, \mathbf{G}) = \mathbf{T}$ iff P is provable in $\mathbf{PA}$. Since $(\mathbf{G}, \mathbf{K}, \boldsymbol{R})$ is an S4-m.s., all the laws of S4 hold. But not all the laws of S5 hold; if P is Gödel's undecidable formula, $\varphi((\sim \square \, P \supset \square \sim \square \, P), \mathbf{G}) = \mathbf{F}$. But some laws are valid which are not provable in S4; in particular, we can prove for any A, $\varphi(\square \sim \square \, (\Diamond \, A \wedge \Diamond \sim A), \mathbf{G}) = \mathbf{T}$, which yields the theorems of McKinsey's S4.1 (cf. [13]). By suitable modifications this difficulty could be removed; but we do not go into the matter here.

Similar interpretations of M and the *Brouwersche* system could be stated; but, in the present writer's opinion, they have less interest than those given above. We mention one more class of provability interpretations, the "reflexive" extensions of $\mathbf{PA}$. Let $\mathbf{E}$ be a formal system containing $\mathbf{PA}$, and whose well-formed formulae are formed out of the closed formulae of $\mathbf{PA}$ by use of the connectives &, ¬, and $\square$. (I say " & " and "¬" to indicate that I am using the same conjunction and negation as in $\mathbf{PA}$ itself, not introducing new ones. See footnote 1, p. 91.) Then $\mathbf{E}$ is called a reflexive extension of $\mathbf{PA}$ iff: (1) It is an inessential extension of $\mathbf{PA}$; (2) $\square \, A$ is provable in $\mathbf{E}$ iff A is; (3) there is a valuation α, mapping the closed formulae of $\mathbf{E}$ into the set $\{\mathbf{T}, \mathbf{F}\}$, such that conjunction and negation obey the usual truth tables, all the true closed formulae of $\mathbf{PA}$ get the value $\mathbf{T}$, $\alpha(\square \, A) = \mathbf{T}$ iff A is provable in $\mathbf{E}$, and all the theorems of $\mathbf{E}$ get the value $\mathbf{T}$. It can be shown that there are reflexive extensions of $\mathbf{PA}$ containing the axioms of S4 or even S4.1, but none containing S5.

Finally, we remark that, using the usual mapping of intuitionistic logic into S4, we can get a model theory for the intuitionistic predicate calculus. We will not give this model theory here, but instead will mention, for propositional calculus only, a particular useful interpretation of intuitionistic logic that results from the model theory. Let $\mathbf{E}$ be any consistent extension of $\mathbf{PA}$. We say a formula P of $\mathbf{PA}$ is *verified* in $\mathbf{E}$ iff it is provable in $\mathbf{E}$. We take the closed wffs P of $\mathbf{PA}$ as atomic, and build formulae out of them using the intuitionistic connectives $\wedge$, $\vee$, ¬, and $\supset$. We then stipulate inductively: $A \wedge B$ is verified in $\mathbf{E}$ iff A and B are; $A \vee B$ is verified in **E** iff A or B is; $\neg A$ is verified in **E** iff there is no consistent extension of **E** verifying A; $A \supset B$ is verified in **E** iff every consistent extension **E**′ of **E** verifying A also verifies B.

Then every instance of a law of intuitionistic logic is verified in **PA**; but, e.g., $A \vee \neg A$ is not, if A is the Gödel undecidable formula. In future work, we will extend this interpretation further, and show that using it we can find an interpretation for Kreisel's system FC of absolutely free choice sequences (cf. [14]). It is clear, incidentally, that **PA** can be replaced in the provability interpretations of S4 and S5 by any truth functional system (i.e., by any system whose models determine each closed formula as true or false); while the interpretation of intuitionism applies to any formal system whatsoever.

Harvard University.

References

[1] SAUL A. KRIPKE. *A completeness theorem in modal logic.* **The journal of symbolic logic,** vol. 24 (1959), pp. 1—15.

[2] SAUL A. KRIPKE. *Semantical analysis of modal logic* (abstract). **The journal of symbolic logic,** vol. 24 (1959), pp. 323—324.

[3] GOTTLOB FREGE. *Über Sinn und Bedeutung.* **Zeitschrift für Philosophie und philosophische Kritik,** vol. 100 (1892), pp. 25—50. English translations in P. Geach and M. Black, **Translations from the philosophical writings of Gottlob Frege,** Basil Blackwell, Oxford 1952, and in H. Feigl and W. Sellars (ed.), **Readings in philosophical analysis,** Appleton-Century-Crofts, Inc., New York 1949.

[4] P. F. STRAWSON. *On referring.* **Mind,** n. s., vol. 59 (1950), pp. 320—344.

[5] BERTRAND RUSSELL. *On denoting.* **Mind,** n. s., vol. 14 (1905), pp. 479—493.

[6] JAAKKO HINTIKKA. *Modality and quantification.* **Theoria** (Lund), vol. 27 (1961), pp. 119—128.

[7] A. N. PRIOR. **Time and modality.** Clarendon Press, Oxford 1957, VIII + 148 pp.

[8] A. N. PRIOR. *Modality and quantification in S5.* **The journal of symbolic logic,** vol. 21 (1956), pp. 60—62.

[9] JAAKKO HINTIKKA. *Existential presuppositions and existential commitments.* **The journal of philosophy,** vol. 56 (1959), pp. 125—137.

[10] HUGUES LEBLANC and THEODORE HAILPERIN. *Nondesignating singular terms.* **Philosophical review,** vol. 68 (1959), pp. 239—243.

[11] SAUL A. KRIPKE. *Semantical analysis of modal logic I.* **Zeitschrift für mathematische Logik und Grundlagen der Mathematik,** vol. 9 (1963), pp. 67—96.

[12] STEPHEN C. KLEENE. **Introduction to metamathematics.** D. Van Nostrand, New York 1952, x + 550 pp.

[13] J. C. C. McKINSEY. *On the syntactical construction of systems of modal logic.* **The journal of symbolic logic,** vol. 10 (1945), pp. 83—94.

[14] G. KREISEL. *A remark on free choice sequences and the topological completeness proofs.* **The journal of symbolic logic,** vol. 23 (1958), pp. 369—388.

[15] W. VAN O. QUINE. **Mathematical logic.** Harvard University Press, Cambridge, Mass., 1940; second ed., revised, 1951, xii + 346 pp.

4

Quine on Modality

DAGFINN FØLLESDAL

Reprinted with the kind permission of the publisher (D. Reidel) from *Synthese,* XIX (1968), 147-57.

DAGFINN FØLLESDAL

QUINE ON MODALITY

Over the past thirty-two years, Quine has presented a number of arguments against the modalities, his criticism culminating in *Word and Object*. During the same period, modal logic has flourished as never before, and a number of semantic systems for the different modalities have been proposed, apparently quite unencumbered by Quine's criticism. What is even more remarkable, Quine's arguments have very rarely been discussed or even referred to by the proponents of modal logic, and the few who have discussed them, have all taken exception to them. What, then, is the current status of the modalities and of Quine's arguments against them?

Quine has concentrated his criticism on the logical modalities. He has argued that all attempts to draw an epistemologically relevant distinction between logical, or, more broadly, linguistic truth and factual truth have been unsuccessful, and he has developed, in *Word and Object*, a theory of language according to which there is no such distinction to be drawn. Quine has further argued that the fundamental unclarity of such a distinction becomes particularly apparent when it is applied to *open* sentences, that is sentences which contain pronouns or variables that purport to refer back to objects mentioned outside of the modal context.

According to Quine, it is difficult to make any sense of such sentences, in particular it is unclear what the objects are, if any, that are referred to in modal contexts. Consider, for example,

(1) $(\exists x)\, N(x > 7)$

"Would 9, that is, the number of planets, be one of the numbers necessarily greater than 7?" Quine has asked[1], pointing out that such an affirmation would be true in the form

(2) $N(9 > 7)$

and false in the form

(3)   N (the number of planets > 1)

147

Synthese 19 (1968–69) 147–157. © *D. Reidel Publishing Co., Dordrecht - Holland*

DAGFINN FØLLESDAL

The difficulty, according to Quine, is due to the modal context's being referentially opaque; 'the number of planets' cannot be substituted for '9' in (2) *salva veritate* although the two expressions refer to the same object. In order to make sense of quantification, Quine concludes, the positions of the variables have to be referential in the sentence following the quantifier, names which refer to the same object must be interchangeable in these positions, or, in other words, whatever is asserted in this open sentence to be true of an object in our universe of discourse, must be true of it regardless of how it is referred to. That is, whatever predicate '*F*' stands for, simple or complex, in order for quantification to make sense,

$$(4) \qquad (x)(y)(x = y \supset . Fx \supset Fy)$$

must be true (Quine's thesis).

Is it then possible to make sense of quantifying into modal contexts? As observed by Quine[2], the difficulties connected with quantification into modal contexts would vanish if one were to exclude from one's universe of discourse all objects that can be uniquely specified in ways which are not necessarily equivalent to one another and retain only objects x such that any two conditions uniquely determining x are necessarily equivalent, i.e. such that:

$$(5) \qquad (y)(Fy \equiv . y = x).(y)(Gy \equiv . y = x). \supset N(y)(Fy \equiv Gy)$$

However, as Quine points out in *From a Logical Point of View* (1st ed., pp. 152–153), (5) has consequences which some modal logicians might be reluctant to accept, for example:

$$(x)(y)(x = y \supset N(x = y))$$

that is, all identities are necessary.

In *Word and Object*, Quine draws a further, disastrous consequence from (5), viz. the consequence that every true sentence is necessarily true, or

$$p \supset Np$$

Since the converse holds, too, this means that modal distinctions collapse; the whole point of the modalities vanishes.

148

QUINE ON MODALITY

Is then Quine's criticism of the modalities decisive?

The few proponents of the modalities who have discussed Quine's arguments, all argue that his criticism is ill-founded; usually they reject Quine's basic thesis, that the positions of the quantified variables have to be referential.

Thus Church, in his review of Quine's 'Notes on Existence and Necessity'[3], argues that modal contexts are referentially opaque, but that this does not prevent variables within modal contexts from referring to a quantifier anterior to the context, provided that the variables have an intensional range – a range, for instance, composed of attributes rather than classes.

However, merely restricting the range of the variables does not help one out of the difficulties; nothing is presupposed about the range of the variables in Quine's arguments, which are unaffected by any restriction on variables.

The crucial part of Church's review is his reference to Frege's ideas concerning sense, denotation and oblique occurrences. In his later article 'A Formulation of the Logic of Sense and Denotation' (1951)[4], Church makes ingenious use of these ideas to develop a system where one quantifies into necessity contexts without this leading to any collapse of modal distinctions. In this system the variables take intensions as values in necessity-contexts, but what saves the system is not that the variables are thus restricted, but that the positions of the variables are referential. There are no opaque constructions in the system. Its necessity operator notwithstanding, it is therefore not a modal, i.e. non-extensional system, and it is not evidence against Quine's thesis that one cannot quantify into referentially opaque contexts. Church has rather shown how to handle the logical modalities without making use of opaque contexts.

Carnap, in *Meaning and Necessity*[5], argues that although modal contexts are referentially opaque, one can make sense of quantification into such contexts by help of his method of extension and intension.

Now, if one interprets the variables as ranging over intensions, then Carnap's quantification into modal contexts makes good sense. However, this is just what one should expect if Quine is right, for if two expressions, 'a' and 'b', refer to the same intension, that is, if $a \equiv b$, then they can be substituted for one another in all contexts in Carnap's system (S_2). That is, the positions of the variables are referential, and substitutivity and

149

DAGFINN FØLLESDAL

quantification go together after all, just as was required by Quine. However, if one tries to interpret the variables as ranging over extensions, i.e. entities individuated by the relation '$\equiv$', then, as argued by Quine in a statement included by Carnap in *Meaning and Necessity*, pp. 196–197, quantification ceases to make sense; Quine's questions concerning what the objects are over which we quantify, again become embarrassing.

Hence there seems to be good reason in Carnap's system, too, to accept Quine's thesis that substitutivity and quantification go together. However, one may wonder, what then happens with modal distinctions? Do they collapse?

As a matter of fact, '$p \equiv Np$' is not derivable in Carnap's system. However, what prevents it from being derivable is a restriction which Carnap puts on definite descriptions in his system, to the effect that no description may contain a modal operator. No justification is given for this restriction; all Carnap says is that "in order to avoid certain complications, which cannot be explained here, it seems advisable to admit in S_2 only descriptions which do not contain 'N'".[6] If one lifts the restriction, one sees what these complications are: modal distinctions collapse. As long as Carnap has not given a semantic justification for his restriction on descriptions, therefore, it seems that he has not succeeded in giving a satisfactory semantics for the modalities.

Hintikka is the third and last main proponent of modal logic who has taken exception to Quine's thesis. Like Church and Carnap, Hintikka has argued that quantification into opaque contexts can be interpreted in such a way as to make sense.[7] As a matter of fact, Hintikka's semantics does make sense if the values of the variables are taken to be expressions, i.e. singular terms that are substituted for the variables. However, Hintikka does not intend to give this kind of 'substitutional' interpretation of quantification. He wants, and I think rightly, the values of his variables to be "real, fullfledged individuals".[8] However, if this is to be the case, it is unclear what the objects are over which Hintikka quantifies, unless he supplements his semantics in such a way that Quine's thesis becomes valid in it. As far as I know, Hintikka has accepted this, and no longer rejects Quine's thesis.[9] It seems, therefore, that those modal logicians who have taken exception to Quine's thesis have not succeeded in refuting it. They have presented semantics for quantified modal logic in which Quine's thesis is claimed not to hold. But, as we have seen, all of these semantics

150

QUINE ON MODALITY

are such that in so far as Quine's thesis does not come out valid in them, it is unclear what the objects are over which one quantifies.

Do we then have to give up the modalities? It seems to me that we cannot. Quine's argument, leading up to the collapse of modal distinctions, is simply too disastrous to be right.

For although the argument in *Word and Object* is directed against the logical modalities, it can easily be paralleled for the other modalities. In fact, by reasoning exactly parallel to that on pp. 198–199 of *Word and Object* one can show that any attempt to single out from the class of all true sentences a proper subclass of sentences is doomed to failure if:

(i) One has a standard system of quantification theory with identity and definite descriptions. (If descriptions are treated in the Frege-Carnapian way, and not defined contextually, one must in addition require that the universe contain at least one object which is necessarily distinct from the object which is selected as descriptum for all descriptions that do not satisfy the condition of uniqueness.)

(ii) One permits quantification into the members of the subclass from outside.

Whenever (i) and (ii) are satisfied one can prove that the subclass coincides with the full class, that is, it cannot be a proper subclass; the distinction one was trying to make between the two classes is eradicated.

This means that if Quine's conclusion in *Word and Object* is unavoidable, then any attempt to build up adequate theories of causation, counterfactuals, probability, preference, knowledge, belief, action, duty, responsibility, rightness, goodness, etc. must be given up since, presumably, any such theory would require quantification into open sentences of this kind from outside.

The mere fact that Quine's conclusion has these disastrous consequences indicates that there must be a way of avoiding it.

However, as we saw, all attempts to reject Quine's thesis have been unsuccessful, and it seems that what one has to do is to accept the thesis and still find a way of avoiding Quine's calamitous conclusion, that is one must find a semantics for modal contexts according to which these contexts are at the same time *referentially transparent* (as required for quantification) and *extensionally opaque*; that is, co-extensional expressions must not be interchangeable (since such interchangeability would

151

DAGFINN FØLLESDAL

amount precisely to the collapse of modal distinctions warned against by Quine).

From this it is immediately clear that a satisfactory semantics for the modalities must distinguish between expressions which refer (singular terms) and expressions which have extension (general terms and sentences, the extension of a sentence being its truth value). This means that a Fregean semantics, according to which all expressions are treated on a par as referring expressions cannot be a satisfactory semantics for modal logic.[10] Neither can a Carnapian semantics in which all expressions are treated indiscriminately as having extensions. In neither of these two systems can one get the required combination of referential transparency and extensional opacity. (Of course, this does not affect the adequacy of these semantics for extensional contexts, where no such combination of transparency and opacity is needed, and where a unitary treatment of the various kinds of expressions brings about simplifications.) It is instructive to note that Church's Frege-inspired system of sense and denotation, as we noted earlier, contains no opaque contexts.

However, does distinguishing between expressions which refer and expressions which have extension generate the possibility of contexts which are at the same time referentially transparent and extensionally opaque? In order to get a clearer view of the situation, I shall now, following Quine[11], define the notion of a referentially transparent construction, and similarly that of an extensionally transparent construction.

As a preliminary to this, let us first define the notion of a referential *position* or occurrence, of a singular term, and an extensional position of a general term or sentence. Depending on whether the containing expression is a singular term or a general term or sentence, we have four cases to consider, which can be put together in the following definition:

DEF. 1: A *position* of a $\begin{Bmatrix} \text{singular term} \\ \text{general term or sentence} \end{Bmatrix}$ in an expression is $\begin{Bmatrix} \text{referential} \\ \text{extensional} \end{Bmatrix}$ if and only if any $\begin{Bmatrix} \text{singular term} \\ \text{general term or sentence} \end{Bmatrix}$ that occurs in that position can be replaced by a $\begin{Bmatrix} \text{co-referential} \\ \text{co-extensional} \end{Bmatrix}$ expression without the containing expression changing its reference (if the containing expression is a singular term) or extension (if the containing expression is a general term or sentence).

152

QUINE ON MODALITY

With this definition at hand we can now define the notion of a referentially transparent *construction* and, parallel to it, an extensionally transparent construction:

DEF. 2: A *construction*, or mode of containment, is $\left\{ \begin{array}{l} \text{referentially} \\ \text{extensionally} \end{array} \right\}$ transparent if and only if for every expression which may be an ingredient in the construction, every position which is $\left\{ \begin{array}{l} \text{referential} \\ \text{extensional} \end{array} \right\}$ in the ingredient expression is $\left\{ \begin{array}{l} \text{referential} \\ \text{extensional} \end{array} \right\}$ in the product of the construction (i.e. in the expression that results when the construction is applied to the ingredient).

Constructions that are not referentially (extensionally) transparent are called referentially (extensionally) opaque.

Thus, for example, truth-functional negation is an extensionally transparent construction. For, consider '$\sim p$': if an expression is in referential position in the ingredient 'p', it will remain in extensional position in the product, i.e. in '$\sim p$'. Similarly for the other truth-functional and quantificational constructions.

The modal constructions are obviously extensionally opaque. For an expression which is in extensional position with respect to a sentence 'p' need not be in an extensional position in 'Np'; a trivial example is the sentence 'p' itself, which is in extensional position with respect to itself, but is not in extensional position in 'Np', if modal distinctions are not to collapse.

Our question now is: Can the modal constructions be referentially transparent?

One can show that *every referentially transparent construction on singular terms has to be extensionally transparent*. The proof is as follows:

Let

(i) Φ be a construction on singular terms (e.g. '$\{...\}$', (unit class), where the three dots stand for any singular term)

(ii) Φ be referentially transparent

(iii) t and t' be general terms and $\Psi(t)$ an ingredient of the construction Φ. ($\Psi(t)$ is hence a singular term, according to (i).)

153

DAGFINN FØLLESDAL

Let further

(iv) t and t' be co-extensional.

and

(v)   the position of t in $\Psi(t)$ be extensional.

Then, by (iii), (iv), and (v)

(vi)   the expressions $\Psi(t)$ and $\Psi(t')$ are co-referential

Then, since obviously every singular term is in a referential position with respect to itself, we may conclude from (vi) by (ii) that

(vii) $\Phi(\Psi(t))$ and $\Phi(\Psi(t'))$ are co-extensional (or co-referential, if Φ is a construction which produces singular terms).

So, it is impossible to have a construction on singular terms which is at the same time referentially transparent and extensionally opaque.

By a parallel argument one can also prove that every extensionally transparent construction on general terms or sentences is referentially transparent.

If we could now prove that every referentially transparent construction on *general* terms or sentences is extensionally transparent, we would have vindicated Quine; the impossibility of a semantics for quantified modal logic would follow as a mere logical consequence from Quine's thesis.

However, the above type of proof does not carry over to this case, and no other proof can be given either, for as a matter of fact there are referentially transparent constructions on general terms or sentences that are extensionally opaque.

One can arrive at such constructions in various ways, as one sees if one looks into the reasons why the proof does not carry over to this case and observes what additional assumptions would be needed for it to go through. As obviously has to be the case, granting the truth of Quine's thesis every satisfactory approach to quantified modal logic that has been or will ever be proposed must be found among these ways.

The oldest and at the same time one of the simplest methods is to treat all troublesome singular terms as descriptions and eliminate them contextually. In 1942, in his review of Quine's 'Whitehead and the Rise of Modern Logic', Church observed that this gives an immediate reply to

QUINE ON MODALITY

Quine's objection that the substitutivity of identity breaks down in the example concerning the number of planets and 9: Both in *Principia Mathematica* and in Quine's own *Mathematical Logic*

... the translation into symbolic notation of the phrase 'the number of planets' would render it either as a description or as a class abstract, and in either case it would be construed contextually; any formal deduction must refer to the unabbreviated forms of the sentences in question, and the unabbreviated form of the first sentence is found actually to contain no name of the number 9.[12]

In 1947, in his review of Quine's 'The Problem of Interpreting Modal logic'[13] and more fully in his article 'Modality and Description' (1948), Arthur F. Smullyan has argued that the modalities need not involve paradox either in connection with substitution or with quantification "when they are referred to a system in which descriptions and class abstracts are contextually defined".[14] This course has been followed by Marcus[15], Fitch[16], and Myhill[17] and several later writers. The relevance of distinguishing between quantifiable variables and constant singular terms was noted by Quine in 'Three Grades of Modal Involvement' (1953), pp. 79–80, in *From a Logical Point of View* (1953), p. 154, and in 'Reply to Professor Marcus' (1962), p. 101. It was also noted by Montague in 'Logical Necessity, Physical Necessity, Ethics, and Quantifiers' (1955, published 1960), p. 266.[18] In that article, Montague also presents semantics for the logical, physical and deontic modalities in which he shows that (4) is valid.

So, although Quine's thesis seems to be valid in spite of the criticism which has been directed against it, the disastrous collapse of modal distinctions warned against by Quine can be avoided.

I shall end my paper with two minor remarks.

(1) One of Quine's points concerning the modalities has been that quantified modal logic commits one to essentialism, i.e. the view that

an object, of itself and by whatever name or none, must be seen as having some of its traits necessarily and others contingently, despite the fact that the latter traits follow just as analytically from some ways of specifying the objects as the former do from other ways of specifying it.[19]

Now, this follows from our previous observations. For we have seen that given Quine's thesis, if one wants to quantify into modal contexts without having modal distinctions collapse, then these contexts have to be referentially transparent and extensionally opaque. And essentialism is just this

155

DAGFINN FØLLESDAL

combination of referential transparency and extensional opacity: whatever is true of an object is true of it regardless of how it is referred to (referential transparency), and among the predicates true of an object, some are necessarily true of it, others only accidentally (extensional opacity).

However, it should also be observed that given a way of obtaining contexts that are referentially transparent and extensionally opaque, there are no more problems with essentialism than with unquantified modal logic. If the modal operators make sense when applied to closed sentences, then they make sense when applied to open sentences, too. To make sense of essentialism and to make sense of open sentences with a modal operator prefixed are one and the same problem, and a solution to the one is a solution to the other.

This brings me to my second and final remark:

(2) Since the formal semantic problems that turn up in connection with quantification into modal contexts can be solved, this means that the modalities cannot be rejected for purely formal reasons. The modalities can be made *formally* respectable, free from logical difficulties. It seems, therefore, that if one is to take exception to the modalities, it has to be on metaphysical or epistemological grounds, and not on logical ones. This applies to all the non-extensional contexts I mentioned earlier, those that occur in ethics and in natural science as well as the logical modalities.

However, in addition to the formal arguments I have discussed and which I have indicated how to overcome, Quine has directed a number of general epistemological arguments against one particular kind of modalities, the *logical* modalities, arguing in 'Two Dogmas of Empiricism', *Word and Object*, and several of his other writings that the logical necessity- and possibility-operators, even when applied to *closed* sentences, do not make sense. As long as these arguments have not been met, it seems that the other modalities, for example the physical, epistemic, and deontic ones, are better off than the logical modalities.

REFERENCES

[1] 'Notes on Existence and Necessity', *Journal of Philosophy* **40** (1943) 124. See also *From a Logical Point of View*, Harvard University Press, Cambridge, Mass., 1953 (2nd ed., 1961. Paperback: Harper Torchbooks, New York 1963), p. 148. In 'Whitehead and the Rise of Modern Logic', in *The Philosophy of Alfred North Whitehead*

QUINE ON MODALITY

(P. A. Schilpp, ed.), Northwestern University Press, Evanston and Chicago 1941, p. 142 n., Quine uses the same example to illustrate the breakdown of the substitutivity of identity in modal contexts.

[2] *From a Logical Point of View*, p. 152; *Word and Object*, pp. 197–198.

[3] Alonzo Church, Review of Quine's 'Notes on Existence and Necessity', in *Journal of Symbolic Logic* **8** (1943) 45–47.

[4] Alonzo Church, 'A Formulation of the Logic of Sense and Denotation', in *Structure, Method, and Meaning: Essays in Honor of Henry M. Sheffer* (ed. by Paul Henle, H.M. Kallen, and S.K. Langer), Liberal Arts Press, New York, 1951, pp. 3–24.

[5] Rudolf Carnap, *Meaning and Necessity*, University of Chicago Press, Chicago, 1947 (2nd. ed., with supplements, 1956).

[6] *Meaning and Necessity*, p. 184.

[7] Mainly in 'The Modes of Modality', *Acta Philosophica Fennica* **16** (1963) 65–81. Cf. also 'Modality as Referential Multiplicity', *Ajatus* **20** (1957) 49–64, 'Modality and Quantification', *Theoria* **27** (1961) 119–128, and 'Studies in the Logic of Existence and Necessity', *The Monist* **50** (1966) 55–76.

[8] Jaakko Hintikka, 'Individuals, Possible Worlds, and Epistemic Logic', *Noûs* **1** (1967) 38; cf. also Hintikka, 'Modality as Referential Multiplicity', p. 61.

[9] Cp. Hintikka, 'Individuals, Possible Worlds, and Epistemic Logic', pp. 55ff.

[10] Again, Church's logic of sense and denotation is not what I call a modal logic, since it has no opaque constructions.

[11] *Word and Object*, § 30 and § 31.

[12] Alonzo Church, Review of Quine's 'Whitehead and the Rise of Modern Logic', *Journal of Symbolic Logic* **7** (1942) 101.

[13] Arthur F. Smullyan, Review of Quine's 'The Problem of Interpreting Modal Logic', *Journal of Symbolic Logic* **12** (1947) 139–141.

[14] Arthur F. Smullyan, 'Modality and Description', *Journal of Symbolic Logic* **13** (1948) 35.

[15] Ruth Barcan Marcus, Review of Smullyan's 'Modality and Description', *Journal of Symbolic Logic* **13** (1948) 149–150.

[16] Frederic B. Fitch, 'The Problem of the Morning Star and the Evening Star', *Philosophy of Science* **16** (1949) 137–141.

[17] John Myhill, 'Problems arising in the Formalization of Intensional Logic', *Logique et Analyse* **1** (1958) 74–83.

[18] Richard Montague, 'Logical Necessity, Physical Necessity, Ethics, and Quantifiers', *Inquiry* **3** (1960) 259–269. (Delivered before the Annual Spring Conference in Philosophy, UCLA, May, 1955.)

[19] *From a Logical Point of View*, 2nd ed., p. 155. Cf. also 'Three Grades of Modal Involvement' (1953), p. 80, and 'Reply to Professor Marcus', p. 104.

5

The Problem of Interpreting Modal Logic

W. V. QUINE

Reprinted with the kind permission of the publisher, The Association for Symbolic Logic, from *The Journal of Symbolic Logic*, XII (1947), 42-48.

THE JOURNAL OF SYMBOLIC LOGIC
Volume 12, Number 2, June 1947

THE PROBLEM OF INTERPRETING MODAL LOGIC

W. V. QUINE

There are logicians, myself among them, to whom the ideas of modal logic (e. g. Lewis's) are not intuitively clear until explained in non-modal terms.   But so long as modal logic stops short of quantification theory, it is possible (as I shall indicate in §2) to provide somewhat the type of explanation desired.   When modal logic is extended (as by Miss Barcan[1]) to include quantification theory, on the other hand, serious obstacles to interpretation are encountered—particularly if one cares to avoid a curiously idealistic ontology which repudiates material objects.   Such are the matters which it is the purpose of the present paper to set forth.

1. Analytic statements from the standpoint of non-modal logic.   All true statements which (like '$(x)\ (x = x)$') contain only logical signs are naturally to be classified as logically true.   But there are also other logically true statements (e. g. 'Socrates is mortal $\supset$ Socrates is mortal') which contain extra-logical signs.   Now every logical truth of the latter kind is (if for the present we disregard modal logic) either *provable within* the familiar logic of truth-functions and quantification alone, or else *deducible by* the logic of truth-functions and quantification *from* logical truths of the kind which contain only logical signs.   So *every* logical truth is either:

(a) a true statement containing only logical signs, or

(b) provable in the logic of truth-functions and quantification, or

(c) *deducible by the logic of truth-functions and quantification from true statements containing only logical signs.*

But (c) includes (b), since whatever is provable is also, vacuously, deducible from anything else.   Also (c) includes (a), since any statement is deducible from itself.   Thus (c) by itself might be adopted as an appropriate *definition of logical truth* (outside modal logic).   The "deducibility" spoken of in (c) can be expanded into purely syntactical terms by an enumeration of the familiar rules, which are known to be complete; and the reference to "logical signs" can likewise be expanded by enumeration of the familiar primitives.   The word 'true' in (c) cannot indeed be expanded; no enumeration of axioms or axiom-schemata would serve the purpose here, because of Gödel's proof that there can be no complete consistent system of higher logic.   We could desire otherwise, especially in view of the logical paradoxes which are known to be connected with the general concept of truth.[2]   Nevertheless (c) is not without explicative value, as marking out the special notion of logical truth within the general notion (such as it is) of truth.

Received July 17, 1946

[1] Ruth C. Barcan, *A functional calculus of first order based on strict implication*, this JOURNAL, vol. 11 (1946), pp. 1–16.

[2] See Alfred Tarski, *The semantic conception of truth and the foundation of semantics*, **Philosophy and phenomenological research,** vol. 4 (1944), pp. 341–376.

W. V. QUINE

The class of *analytic* statements is broader than that of logical truths, for it contains in addition such statements as 'No bachelor is married.' This example might be assimilated to the logical truths by considering it a definitional abbreviation of 'No man not married is married,' which is indeed a logical truth; but I should prefer not to rest analyticity thus on an unrealistic fiction of there being standard definitions of extra-logical expressions in terms of a standard set of extra-logical primitives. What is rather in point, I think, is a relation of *synonymy*, or sameness of meaning, which holds between expressions of real language though there be no standard hierarchy of definitions. In terms of synonymy and logical truth we could define analyticity: a statement is *analytic* if by putting synonyms for synonyms (e.g. 'man not married' for 'bachelor') it can be turned into a logical truth.

The particular synonymy relation wanted is one of several which have about equal right to the name "synonymy" and are all describable as "sameness of meaning"—in varying senses of "meaning." Synonymy of the kind which renders expressions interchangeable without violence to indirect quotation, for example, would be a narrower relation than the one here concerned; and the sense of synonymy proposed by Lewis[3] is yet a third relation, I believe, intermediate between the two.

The particular synonymy relation which I have in mind can easily be described in terms of analyticity, at least when the expressions related happen to be statements, names, or predicates. Statements are synonymous if the biconditional ('if and only if') which joins them is analytic; names are synonymous if the statement of identity which joins them is analytic; and predicates are synonymous if, when they are applied to like variables and then combined into a universally quantified biconditional, the result is analytic.

But of course we must seek some other definition of synonymy so as to avoid circularity, if synonymy is to be available for use in defining analyticity. Actually the synonymy relation sought is, insofar as applied to propositions, names, and predicates, precisely what Lewis (*loc. cit.*) calls *sameness of intension*; but expansion in turn of his definition of "intension" leaves us with phrases which I do not feel to be appreciably clearer than "synonymy" and "analyticity" themselves.

Synonymy, like other linguistic concepts, involves parameters of times and persons, suppressible in idealized treatment: the expression x is synonymous with the expression y for person z at time t. A satisfactory definition of this tetradic relation would no doubt be couched, like those of other general concepts of general linguistics, in behavioristic terms. I should like, as a service both to empirical semantics and to philosophy, to offer a satisfactory definition; but I have none. So long, however, as we persist in speaking of expressions as alike or unlike in meaning (and regardless of whether we countenance meanings themselves in any detached sense), we must suppose that there is an eventually formulable criterion of synonymy in some reasonable sense of the term—and probably, in particular, in the sense appropriate to present purposes. Given it,

---

[3] C. I. Lewis, *The modes of meaning*, ibid., vol. 4 (1943), p. 245.

and given the general notion of truth (in terms of which logical truth has been seen to be definable), we could define analyticity as previously indicated.

The notion of analyticity thus appears, at the present writing, to lack a satisfactory foundation. Even so, the notion is clearer to many of us, and obscurer surely to none, than the notions of modal logic; so we are still well advised to explain the latter notions in terms of it. This can be done, as sketched in the next section, so long as modal logic stops short of quantification theory.[4]

2. Interpretation of pre-quantificational modal logic. We need consider only the mode of logical *necessity*, symbolized by '$\square$'; for the other modal ideas (possibility, impossibility, and the strict conditional and biconditional) are expressible in terms of necessity in obvious fashion. Now '$\square$' is not quite interchangeable with 'is analytic,' for this reason: the former attaches to a *statement* (as '$\sim$' does) to form a statement *containing* the original statement, whereas 'is analytic' (like 'is true,' 'is false') attaches to the *name* of a statement to form a statement *about* the named statement. Grammatically '$\square$' is an adverb; 'is analytic' is a verb. The formal difference becomes immediately apparent in the case of iteration: '$\square$' can significantly be applied repeatedly (because the result of any application, being a statement, is the kind of expression to which '$\square$' can still significantly be prefixed) whereas 'is analytic' can be applied only once (because the result of the application is a statement, whereas 'is analytic' can be appended only to a name.)[5]

However, '$\square$' can be explained in terms of analyticity as follows:

(i) *The result of prefixing '$\square$' to any statement is true if and only if the statement is analytic.*

Let us speak of a statement as of *first intention* if it is non-modal; and let us speak of a statement as of $(n + 1)$st intention if '$\square$' occurs in it in application to statements of nth intention and no higher. The portion of modal logic which admits statements of nth intention at most (and includes also all non-modal logic) will be called the logic of nth intention; non-modal logic itself is the logic of first intention. Then (i) above may be taken as our explanation of all statements of second intention; and the word 'analytic' in it (explained in the preceding section) may be read 'analytic in first intention.' Relative to the logic of second intention, now, which has some new truths of its own in addition to those of the logic of first intention, we may adopt new definitions of logical truth

---

[4] Dr. Nelson Goodman has suggested (in conversation) the dismal possibility that what we think of as synonymy may be wholly a matter of degree, ranging from out-and-out orthographical sameness of expressions on the one hand to mere factual sameness of designatum (as in the case of 'nine' and 'the number of the planets') on the other. In this case analyticity in turn would become a matter of degree—a measure merely of our relative reluctance to give up one statement rather than another from among a set of statements whose conjunction has proved false. But if it does develop that the boundary between analytic and synthetic statements has thus to be rubbed out, no doubt it will be generally agreed that the logical modalities have to be abandoned as well. The explanation of modal logic in terms of analyticity remains of interest so long as there is interest in modal logic itself.

[5] Cf. my *Mathematical logic,* pp. 27–33.

46   W. V. QUINE

and analyticity paralleling those of the preceding section (but admitting un-
iterated use of '□' in addition to truth-functions in (c)).   There upon we may
repeat (i) above as an explanation now of all statements of third intention.
Supposing this process continued *ad infinitum*, we have an explanation of '□'
in application to any statements.

   I suppose that some such conception underlies the intuition where by axioms
are evaluated and adopted for modal logic.   The explanation of modal logic thus
afforded is adequate so long as modalities are not used inside the scopes of quantifiers; i. e., so long as '□' is applied only to statements and not to matrices.[6]   Of
course in actual presentations even of this part of modal logic the sign '□' commonly appears before non-statements such as 'p' or '$p \supset p$', but there is no harm
in this; such expressions are schemata, used diagrammatically and imagined
replaced in any given case by actual statements of the depicted forms.

   3. Quantification in modal logic.   It will be convenient now to think of our
basic modality not as '□' but as '◇' (possibility); the two are interdefinable,
amounting respectively to '$\sim\!\Diamond\!\sim$' and '$\sim\!\Box\!\sim$'.   And let us think of our
quantifiers as existential, since the universal quantifier '(x)' can be explained as
'$\sim\!(\exists x)\!\sim$'.

   When '◇' is applied to a matrix within a quantification, the whole context
admits, in certain cases, of reduction to the type of case dealt with in the preceding section.   For example, the combined prefix '$(\exists x)\Diamond$' is equated by Miss
Barcan[7] to '$\Diamond(\exists x)$', wherein '◇' applies no longer to the matrix but to the
statement formed by quantifying it (supposing there are no further free variables); and accordingly the explanation of the preceding section can thereupon
be brought to bear.   If every matrix containing '◇' were transformable into a
matrix containing '◇' only at the beginning, then repeated conversion of
$\ulcorner(\exists \alpha)\Diamond\urcorner$ to $\ulcorner\Diamond(\exists \alpha)\urcorner$ would be adequate to explaining the general case; but
unfortunately matrices are not generally thus transformable.

   Equating '$(\exists x)\Diamond$' with '$\Diamond(\exists x)$' gives us no clue to the interpretation of such
statements, for example, as:

$$(\exists x)\ (x \text{ is red } . \ \Diamond(x \text{ is round})).$$

No doubt a modal logician would regard this example as true, but only by virtue
of some supplementary intuitive criterion—perhaps this:

   (ii) *An existential quantification holds if there is a constant whose substitution for
the variable of quantification would render the matrix true.*

   This is at best a partial criterion (both in modal and non-modal logic), because
of unnameable objects; an unnameable object might satisfy the matrix though
there be no constant expression whose substitution for the variable would yield a

---

   [6] I use the word 'matrix' (as in *Mathematical logic*) for one of the meanings of the ambiguous phrase 'propositional function.'   A matrix is an expression which is like a statement except for containing, at grammatically permissible places, some free occurrences of
variables of the kind that are admissible in quantifiers.   Briefly, a matrix is a non-statement
which can be turned into a statement by applying quantifiers.

   [7] *Op. cit.*, theorem 38.

truth.   But let us adopt (ii) as a partial criterion (sufficient condition) and see how it fares.

What I shall show is that it has queer ontological consequences.   It leads us to hold that there are no concrete objects (men, planets, etc.), but rather that there are only, corresponding to each supposed concrete object, a multitude of distinguishable entities (perhaps "individual concepts," in Church's phrase). It leads us to hold, e. g., that there is no such ball of matter as the so-called planet Venus, but rather at least three distinct entities: Venus, Evening Star, and Morning Star.

To see this, let us use '**C**' (for 'congruence') to express the relation which Venus, the Evening Star, and the Morning Star, e. g., bear to themselves and, according to empirical evidence, to one another.   (It is the relation of *identity* according to materialistic astronomy, but let us not prejudge this.)   Then

$$\text{Morning Star } \mathbf{C} \text{ Evening Star . } \square \text{ (Morning Star } \mathbf{C} \text{ Morning Star).}$$

Therefore, according to (ii),

(1) $$(\exists x)\,(x \mathbf{C} \text{ Evening Star . } \square\,(x \mathbf{C} \text{ Morning Star})).$$

But also

$$\text{Evening Star } \mathbf{C} \text{ Evening Star . } \sim\square \text{ (Evening Star } \mathbf{C} \text{ Morning Star),}$$

so that, by (ii),

(2) $$(\exists x)\,(x \mathbf{C} \text{ Evening Star . } \sim\square\,(x \mathbf{C} \text{ Morning Star})).$$

Since the matrix quantified in (1) and the matrix quantified in (2) are mutual contraries, the x whose existence is affirmed in (1) and the x whose existence is affirmed in (2) are two objects; so there must be at least two objects x such that x **C** Evening Star.   If we were to introduce the term 'Venus' we could infer a third such object in similar fashion.

Thus it is that the contemplated version of quantified modal logic is committed to an ontology which repudiates material objects (such as the Evening Star properly so-called) and leaves only multiplicities of distinct objects (perhaps the Evening-Star-concept, the Morning-Star-concept, etc.) in their place. For, the ontology of a logic is nothing other than the range of admissible values of the variables of quantification.[8]

A quite parallel conclusion could be drawn in higher logical types, to show that the contemplated version of quantified modal logic is committed to an ontology which repudiates classes and admits only attributes.   But this consequence is likely to be regarded as less objectionable, from the point of view at least of modal logicians, than the consequence concerning individuals.

The modal logician who finds the repudiation of material objects (or, indeed, of classes) uncongenial may have recourse to either of the following alternatives.

(a) He may regard his quantified modal logic as only a fragment of the total logic to which he is prepared to subscribe, so that the undesirably limited ontology

---

[8] See my *Designation and existence,* **Journal of philosophy,** vol. 36 (1939), pp. 701–709.

48   W. V. QUINE

of the former comes to be only a fragment of a more inclusive ontology which embraces also material objects (and perhaps even classes). Those variables of the total logic which do admit material objects (or classes) as values would then be withheld from quantified modal contexts, or limited to harmless manners of occurrence in them,[9] by special grammatical rules. The total logic would not be one in which we could meaningfully apply a modal operator to any matrix at will and then meaningfully quantify the result at will with respect to any free variable.

(b) He may insist on the universality of his quantified modal logic, but disavow the criterion (ii) which underlies my argument. But then we have yet to see what might plausibly be put forward in its stead.

HARVARD UNIVERSITY

---

[9] Such is Church's procedure in *A formulation of the logic of sense and denotation* (abstract), this JOURNAL, vol. 11 (1946), p. 31. I am indebted to Professor Church for several helpful letters in this connection.—I am also indebted, along more general lines, to Professor Rudolf Carnap; correspondence with him on modal logic over recent years has been very instrumental in clarifying my general position.

6

Modalities and Intensional Languages

RUTH BARCAN MARCUS

Reprinted with the kind permission of the publisher (D. Reidel) from *Synthese*, XXVII (1962), 303-23.

MODALITIES AND INTENSIONAL
LANGUAGES*

RUTH BARCAN MARCUS is Professor of Philosophy at The University
of Illinois at Chicago Circle. She has written extensively
on logic and philosophy of science.

There is a normative sense in which it has been claimed that
modal logic is without foundation. Professor Quine, in *Word and Object*,
suggests that it was conceived in sin: the sin of confusing use and mention. The original transgressors were Russell and Whitehead. Lewis elaborated the error and constructed a logic in which an operator corresponding to "necessarily" operates on sentences whereas "is necessary" ought
to be viewed as a predicate of sentences. As Professor Quine reconstructs
the history of the enterprise,[1] the operational use of modalities promised
only one advantage: the possibility of quantifying into modal contexts.

---

* A revised version of a paper presented at the meeting of the Boston Colloquium for
the Philosophy of Science, February 7, 1962. Reprinted by kind permission of the author
and publisher from *Synthese*, Vol. 27, 1962, pp. 303–322.
[1] W. V. Quine, *Word and Object*, 1960, pp. 195–196.

Modalities and Intensional Languages   279

This several of us [2] were enticed into doing. But the evils of the sentential calculus were found out in the functional calculus, and with it—to quote again from *Word and Object*—"the varied sorrows of modality."

I do not claim that modal logic is wholly without sorrows, but only that they are not those which Professor Quine describes. I do claim that it is worthy of defense, for it is useful in connection with many interesting and important questions such as the analysis of causation, entailment, obligation and belief statements. My purpose in this paper is to allay some of the doubts concerning the systematic use of modalities.

INTENSIONAL LANGUAGES

I will begin with the notion of an intensional language. I will make a further distinction between languages which are explicitly and implicitly intensional. Our notion of intensionality does not divide languages into mutually exclusive classes but rather orders them loosely as strongly or weakly intensional. A language is *explicitly* intensional to the degree to which it does *not* equate the identity relation with some weaker form of equivalence. We will assume that we are here concerned with languages which have expressions for referring to objects (things), and expressions for describing a plurality of things. We will not go into the question as to how we come to regard some elements of experience as things, but one criterion for sorting out the elements of experience which we regard as things is that they may enter into the identity relation. In a formalized language, those symbols which name things will be those for which it is meaningful to assert that I holds between them, where "I" names the identity relation.

Ordinarily, and in the familiar constructions of formal systems, the identity relation must be held appropriate for individuals. If "x" and "y" are individual names then

(1)   xIy

is a sentence, and if they are individual variables, then (1) is a sentential function. Whether a language confers thinghood on attributes, classes, propositions, is not so much a matter of whether variables appropriate to them can be quantified upon (and we will return to this later), but rather whether (1) is meaningful where "x" and "y" may take as substitution instances names of attributes, classes, propositions. We note in passing

[2] (a) F. B. Fitch, *Symbolic Logic*, New York, 1952.

(b) R. Carnap, "Modalities and quantification," *Journal of Symbolic Logic*, Vol. XI (1946), pp. 33–64.

(c) R. C. Barcan (Marcus), "A functional calculus of first order based on strict implication," *Journal of Symbolic Logic*, Vol. XI (1946), pp. 1–16.

(d) R. C. Barcan (Marcus), "The identity of individuals in a strict functional calculus of first order," *Journal of Symbolic Logic*, Vol. XII (1947), pp. 12–15.

280   Contemporary Readings in Logical Theory

that the meaningfulness of (1) with respect to attributes and classes is more frequently allowed in formal systems than the meaningfulness of (1) in connection with propositions.

Returning now to the notion of explicit intensionality, if identity is appropriate to propositions, attributes, classes, as well as individuals, then any weakening of the identity relation with respect to any of these entities will be reflected in an extensionalizing of the language. By a weakening of the identity relation is meant equating it with some weaker equivalence relation.

On the level of individuals, one or perhaps two equivalence relations are customarily present: identity and indiscernibility. This does not preclude the introduction of others such as similarity or congruence, but the strongest of these is identity. Where identity is defined rather than taken as primitive, it is customary to define it in terms of indiscernibility. Indiscernibility may in turn be defined as

$$(2) \qquad\qquad x \operatorname{Ind} y = df (\phi) (\phi x \operatorname{eq} \phi y)$$

In a system of material implication (Sm) eq is taken as material equivalence ($\equiv$). In modal systems eq may be taken as strict equivalence ($\equiv$). In more strongly intensional systems eq may be taken as the strongest equivalence relation appropriate to such expressions as "ϕx." In separating (1) and (2) I should like to suggest the possibility that to equate (1) and (2) may already be an explicit weakening of the identity relation, and consequently an extensionalizing principle.[3]

Proceeding now to functional calculi with theory of types, an extensionality principle is of the kind

$$(3) \qquad\qquad x \operatorname{eq} y \rightarrow x I y.$$

The arrow may represent one of the implication relations named within the system or some metalinguistic conditional and eq one of the equivalence relations appropriate to x and y, but not identity. For example, within the system of material implication, "x" and "y" may be taken as symbols for classes, eq as class equality (in the sense of having the same members); or "x" and "y" may be taken as symbols for propositions and "eq" as the triple bar for material equivalence. In extended modal systems "eq" may be taken as the quadruple bar for strict equivalence where "x" and "y" are symbols for propositions. If the extended system is a modal system and has symbols for classes, eq may be interpreted as "having the same members," which with modalities can be expressed, within such a language. If we wish to distinguish classes from attributes in such a system

---

[3] F. P. Ramsey makes this point in *The Foundations of Mathematics*, London, 1931, pp. 30–32. Doubts about defining identity in terms of indiscernibility are plausible, since although it is obviously absurd to say of two things that they are the same thing, it seems less absurd to say of two things that they are indiscernible from one another. However, in my extensions of modal logic, identity is defined as indiscernibility.

"eq" may be taken as "necessarily applies to the same thing," which is similarly directly expressible within the system. In a language which permits epistemic contexts such as belief contexts, an even stronger equivalence relation than either material or strict equivalence would have to be present. Taking that stronger relation as eq, (3) would still be an extensionalizing principle (albeit weaker) in such a strongly intensional language. A system may therefore include a plurality of principles of extensionality, which vary with respect to strength as well as the object to which they apply.

I should now like to turn to the notion of *implicit* extensionality, which is bound up with the kinds of substitution theorems available in a language. Confining ourselves for the sake of simplicity of exposition to a sentential calculus, one form of the substitution theorem is

$$(4) \qquad\qquad x\ eq_1\ y \rightarrow z\ eq_2\ w$$

where x, y, z, w are well-formed, w is the result of replacing one or more occurrences of x by y in z, and "$\rightarrow$" symbolizes implication or a metalinguistic conditional. In the system of material implication (Sm), (4) is provable where eq_1 and eq_2 are both taken as material equivalence for appropriate values of x, y, z, w. That is

$$(5) \qquad\qquad (x \equiv y) \supset (z \equiv w).$$

Now (5) is clearly false if we are going to allow contexts involving belief, logical necessity, physical necessity and so on. We are familiar with the examples. If "x" is taken as "John is a featherless biped," and "y" as "John is a rational animal," then an unrestricted (5) fails. Our choice is to reject (5) as it stands, or to reject all contexts in which it fails. If the latter choice is made, the language is *implicitly* extensional since it cannot countenance *contexts* where (5) fails. Professor Quine's solution is the latter. All such contexts are consigned to a shelf labelled "referential opacity" or more precisely "contexts which confer referential opacity," and are disposed of. But the contents of that shelf are of interest and we would like to examine them in a systematic and formal manner. For this we need a language which is appropriately intensional.

In the modal calculi, since there are more than one kind of equivalence (4) represents several possible substitution theorems, some of which are provable. We will return to this below.

Similarly, if we are going to permit epistemic contexts, the modal analogue of (4), if unrestricted, fails in *those* contexts and a more appropriate one will have to supplement it.

IDENTITY AND SUBSTITUTION IN QUANTIFIED MODAL LOGIC

In the light of previous remarks I would like to turn specifically to the criticism raised against extended modal systems in connection with identity and substitution. In particular, I will refer to the [4] extension of Lewis' [5] S4 which consists of introducing quantification in the usual manner and the addition of the axiom [6]

$$(6) \qquad\qquad \Diamond \, (\exists x) \, (\phi x) \rightarrow (\exists x) \, \Diamond \, (\phi x)$$

I will call this system QS4. In QS4 (1) is defined in terms of (2). (2), and consequently (1), admit of alternatives for "eq" may be taken as material or strict equivalence: thus defining "I_m" and "I" respectively. But the following are theorems of QS4:

$$(7) \qquad\qquad (x I m y) \equiv (x I y)$$

$$(8) \qquad\qquad (x I y) \equiv \Box \, (x I y)$$

where "$\Box$" is the modal symbol for logical necessity. Given (7), "I_m" and "I" are strictly equivalent. Within such a modal language, they are therefore indistinguishable by virtue of a substitution theorem for strict equivalence. Contingent identities are disallowed by (8). Since

$$(9) \qquad\qquad (x I y) \cdot \Diamond \sim (x I y).$$

Professor Quine [7] finds these results offensive, for he sees (8) as "purifying the universe." Concrete entities are said to be banished and replaced by pallid concepts. The argument is familiar:

$$(10) \qquad\qquad \text{The evening star eq the morning star}$$

is said to express a "true identity," yet "evening star" and "morning star" are not validly intersubstitutable in

(11)   It is necessary that the evening star is the evening star.

But consider the claim that

$$(12) \qquad\qquad a I b$$

is a true identity. Now if (12) is such a true identity, then a and b are the same thing. It doesn't say that a and b are two things which happen,

---

[4] *Op. cit.* notes 2c, 2d.
[5] C. I. Lewis and C. H. Langford, *Symbolic Logic*, New York, 1932.
[6] See A. N. Prior, *Time and Modality*, Oxford, 1932, for an extended discussion of this axiom.
[7] W. V. Quine, *From a Logical Point of View*, Cambridge, 1953, pp. 152–154.

through some accident, to be one. True, we are using two different names for that same thing, but we must be careful about use and mention. If, then, (12) is true, it must have the same import as

(13)   aIa.

But if (13) is necessarily true (12) is necessarily true as well. This is precisely the import of theorem (8). We would therefore expect, indeed it would be a consequence of the truth of (12), that "a" is replaceable by "b" in any context except those which are about the names "a" and "b." Now suppose we come upon a statement like (10) or as in the other familiar example

(14)   Scott is the author of *Waverley*.

How are we to understand "eq" as it occurs in (10) or "is" as it occurs in (14)? It is possible to interpret the "eq" of (10) as an equivalence between propositions in accordance with the Russellian theory of descriptions or alternatively as class equivalence. It is possible to interpret the "is" of (14) as the "is" of attribution. To decide that "eq" in (10) and "is" in (14) stand for the identity relation is to decide that "the evening star" and "the morning star" are proper names for the same thing, and that "Scott" and "the author of *Waverley*" are proper names for the same things where the essential use of proper names is taken to be purely referential. As such they must be intersubstitutable in every context. In fact it often happens, in a growing changing language, that a descriptive phrase comes to be used as a proper name—an identifying tag—and the descriptive meaning is lost or ignored. Sometimes we use certain devices such as capitalization and dropping the definite article, to indicate the change in use. "The evening star" becomes "Evening Star," "the morning star" becomes "Morning Star," and they may come to be used as names for the same thing. Singular descriptions such as "the little corporal," "the Prince of Denmark," "the sage of Concord," or "the great dissenter," are as we know often used as alternative proper names of Napoleon, Hamlet, Thoreau and Oliver Wendell Holmes. One might even devise a criterion as to when a descriptive phrase is being used as a proper name. Suppose through some astronomical cataclysm, Venus was no longer the first star of the evening. If we continued to call it alternatively "Evening Star" or "the evening star" then this would be a measure of the conversion of the descriptive phrase into a proper name. If, however, we would, following such a cataclysm, then regard (10) as false, it would indicate that "the evening star" was not used as an alternative proper name of Venus. We might mention in passing that although the conversion of descriptions into proper names appears to be asymmetric; we do find proper names used in singular descriptions of something other than the thing named, as in the statement "Mao Tse-tung is the Stalin of China," where one intends to assert a similarity between the entities named.

That any language must countenance some entities as things would appear to be a precondition for language. But this is not to say that experience is given to us as a collection of things, for it would appear that there are cultural variations and accompanying linguistic variations as to what might be so singled out. It would also appear to be a precondition of language that the singling out of an entity as a thing is accompanied by many—and perhaps an indefinite number—of unique descriptions, for otherwise how would it be singled out? But to assign a thing a proper name is different from giving a unique description. The characterization of Venus as both the evening star and the morning star may be a contingent matter; it might have been otherwise. But the truth of

(16)   Venus I Venus

and if "a" is another proper name for Venus

(17)   Venus I a

cannot be contingent matters, for what could it possibly mean to say of a thing that it might not have been identical with itself? The import of (8) is simply that where an *identity* is true, it is necessarily true. Apparent counterexamples are generated by a confusion of identity with weaker equivalence relations.

Returning now to (10) and (14), if they express a true identity, then "Scott" ought to be anywhere intersubstitutable for "the author of *Waverly*" and similarly for "the morning star" and "the evening star." If they are not so universally intersubstitutable—that is, if our decision is that they are not simply proper names for the same thing; that they express an equivalence which is possibly false, e.g., someone else might have written *Waverley*, the star first seen in the evening might have been different from the star first seen in the morning—then they are not identities. One mode of analysis is Russell's which provides a translation of (10) and (14) such that the truth of (10) and (14) does not commit us to the logical truth of (10) and (14), and certainly not to taking the "eq" of (10) as identity, except on the *explicit* assumption of an extensionalizing axiom. Other and related analyses are in terms of membership in a non-empty unit class, or applicability of a unit attribute. But whatever the choice of explication; it will have to be one which permits intersubstitutability, or some analogue of intersubstitutability for the members of the pairs: "Scott" and "the author of *Waverley*," and "the evening star" and "the morning star," which is *short* of being universal. In a language which is implicitly strongly extensional that is, where all contexts in which such substitutions fail are simply eschewed, then of course there is no harm in equating identity with weaker forms of equivalence. But why restrict ourselves in this way when, in a more intensional language, we can still make all the substitutions permissible to this weaker form of equivalence, yet admit contexts in which

Modalities and Intensional Languages   285

such a substitutivity is not permitted. To show this, I would like to turn to the instances of (4) which are provable[8] in QS4. An unrestricted

(18) $$x \equiv y \rightarrow z \equiv w$$

is not provable whether "$\rightarrow$" is taken as material implication, strict implication or a metalinguistic conditional. It would involve us in a contradiction, if our interpreted system allowed statements such as

(19) $$(x \equiv y) \mathrel{.} \sim \square\, (x \equiv y)$$

as it must, if it is not to be reducible to the system of material implication. Indeed, the underlying assumption about equivalence which is implicit in the whole "evening star-morning star" controversy is that there are equivalences (misleadingly called "true identities") which are contingently true. Let x and y of (18) be taken as some p and q which satisfies (19). Let z be $\square(p \equiv p)$ and w be $\square(p \equiv q)$. Then (18) is

(20) $$(p \equiv q) \rightarrow (\square(p \equiv p) \equiv \square\,(p \equiv q))$$

From (19), simplification, modus ponens and $\square\,(p \equiv p)$, we can deduce $\square(p \equiv q)$. The latter, simplification of (19), and conjunction leads to the contradiction

(21) $$\square\,(p \equiv q) \mathrel{.} \sim \square\,(p \equiv q).$$

But a restricted form of (18) is provable. It is provable if z does not contain any modal operators. And this is exactly every context allowed in the system of material implications without at the same time banishing modal contexts. Indeed a slightly stronger (18) is provable. It is provable if x does not fall within the scope of a modal operator in z.

Where in (4), eq$_1$ and eq$_2$ are both taken as strict equivalence, the substitution theorem

(22) $$(x \equiv y) \rightarrow (z \equiv w)$$

is provable without restriction, and also where eq$_1$ is taken as strict equivalence and eq$_2$ is taken as material equivalence as in

(23) $$(x \equiv y) \rightarrow (z \equiv w).$$

But (22) is also an extensionalizing principle, since though it holds in modal context it fails in epistemic context such as those involving "knows that" or "believes that." For consider the statement.

(24) When Professor Quine reviewed the paper on identity in QS4, he knew that $\vdash a I_m b \equiv a I_m b$.

and

---

[8] *Op. cit.*, note 2c. Theorem XIX* corresponds to (23). The restricted (19), given the conditions of the restriction, although not actually proved, is clearly provable in the same manner as XIX*.

286   CONTEMPORARY READINGS IN LOGICAL THEORY

(25)   When Professor Quine reviewed the paper on identity in QS4 he knew that $\vdash aIb \equiv aI_mb$.

Given the truth of (7) and (24), it would follow from (22) that (25) is true; yet (25) is in fact false. But rather than repeat the old mistakes by abandoning epistemic contexts to the shelf labelled "referential opacity" after having rescued modal contexts, we need only conclude that (22) confines the limits of applicability of such modal systems. If it should turn out that statements involving "knows that" and "believes that" permit of formal analysis, then such an analysis would have to be embedded in a language with a still stronger equivalence relation than strict equivalence but short of identity. Carnap's intensional isomorphism, Lewis' analytical comparability, and perhaps Anderson and Belnap's mutual entailment are attempts in that direction. But even these stronger equivalence relations must be short of identity for there are surely contexts in which substitutions allowed by such stronger equivalences, would convert a truth into a falsehood. It seems plausible to argue [9] that the identity relation need not be introduced for anything other than the entities we clearly countenance as things, such as individuals. Increasingly strong substitution theorems give the force of universal substitutivity without explicit axioms of extensionality. We can talk of equivalence between propositions, classes, attributes, without thereby conferring on them thinghood by equating such equivalences with the identity relation.

Response to criticism of quantified modal logic would be incomplete without touching on another familiar example:

(26)   9 eq the number of planets

is said to be a true identity for which substitution fails in

(27) $\Box(9 > 7)$

for it leads to the falsehood

(28) $\Box$(the number of planets > 7).

Since the argument holds (26) to be contingent ($\sim \Box$(9 eq the number of planets)), "eq" of (26) is the appropriate analogue of material equivalence and consequently the step from (27) to (28) is not valid for the reason that the substitution would have to be made in the scope of the square. For it was shown above that (18) is not an unrestricted theorem in QS4. On the other hand, since in QS4

(29) $(5 + 4) =_s 9$

where "$=_s$" is the appropriate analogue for classes of *strict* equivalence,

[9] See R. Barcan Marcus, "Extensionality," *Mind*, Vol. LXIX, n.s., pp. 55–62 which overlaps to some extent the present paper.

Modalities and Intensional Languages 287

"5 + 4" may replace "9" in (27) in accordance with (22). If, however, the square were dropped from (27) as it validly can since

(30) $\Box p \dashv p$

is provable, then by the restricted (18), the same substitution permissible in systems of material implication is permissible here.

THE INTERPRETATION OF QUANTIFICATION

The previous sections have been directed toward those criticisms of modal systems which focus on problems of identity and substitution. The second prominent area of criticism of quantified modal logic involves interpretation of the operations of quantification when combined with modalities. It appears to me that at least some of the problems stem from an absence of an adequate, unequivocal, colloquial translation of the operations of quantification. It is often not quantification but our choice of reading and implicit interpretive consequences of such a reading which leads to difficulties. Such difficulties are not confined to modal systems. The most common reading of existential quantification is

(31)   There is (exists) at least one (some) thing (person) which (who) . . .

Strawson,[10] for example, does not even admit of significant alternatives, for he says of (31) ". . . we might think it strange that the whole of modern formal logic after it leaves the propositional logic and before it crosses the boundary into the analysis of mathematical concepts, should be confined to the elaboration of sets of rules giving the logical interrelations of formulae which, however complex, begin with these few rather strained and awkward phrases." What we would like to have and do not have, is a direct, unequivocal colloquial reading of

(32) $(\exists x)\phi x$

which gives us the *force* of either of the following:

(33)   Some substitution instance of "ϕx" is true

or

          There is at least one value of x for which ϕx is true.

I am not suggesting that (33) provides translations of (32), but only that what is wanted is a translation with the force of (32).

As seen from (33), quantification has primarily to do with truth and falsity, and open sentences. Reading in accordance with (31) may entangle us unnecessarily in ontological perplexities. For if quantification has to do

[10] P. F. Strawson, *Introduction to Logical Theory*, London, 1952, p. 216.

288   Contemporary Readings in Logical Theory

with things and if variables for attributes or classes can be quantified upon, then in accordance with (31) they are things. The solution is not to banish quantification on variables other than individual variables, but only not to be taken in by (31). We do in fact have some colloquial counterparts of (33). The non-temporal "sometimes" or "in some cases" or "in at least one case," which have greater ontological neutrality than (31). Such a relatively neutral interpretation of quantification is advantageous in a wide spectrum of contexts. We will focus on the way it may be employed to resolve doubts about the possibility of combining quantification with modalities.

· Consider first a quantified version of the "morning star-evening star" paradox. In QS4 the following definitions are introduced:[11]

(34) $(\phi =_m \psi) =_{df} (x)(\phi x \equiv \psi x)$

(35) $(\phi =_s \psi) =_{df} \Box (\phi =_m \psi)$

Individual descriptions may be taken as higher order terms between which weaker equivalence relations than identity may be defined. Two such relations (material and strict equality), are defined by (34) and (35). Since (10) is a contingency, it is the case that

(36)   (The evening star $=_m$ the morning star)

and

(37) $\Diamond \sim$ (the evening star $=_m$ the morning star);

but according to (11)

(38) $\Box$(the evening star $=_m$ the evening star).

By existential generalization on (38), it follows that

(39) $(\exists \phi) \Box (\phi =_m$ the evening star).

In the words of (31), (39) becomes

(40)   There is a thing such that it is necessary that it is equal to the evening star.

The stubborn unlaid ghost rises again. Which thing, the evening star which by (36) is equal to the morning star? But such a substitution would lead to the falsehood.

(41) $\Box$(the evening star $=_m$ the morning star).

---

[11] *Op. cit.*, note 2c. Abstracts are introduced and attributes (classes) may be equated with abstracts. Among the obvious features of such a calculus of attributes (classes), is the presence of equivalent, non-identical, empty attributes (classes). If the null attribute (class) is defined in terms of identity, then it will be intersubstitutible with any abstract on a contradictory function.

The argument may be repeated for (26) through (28). In QS4 the solution is clear. For since (37) holds, and since in (39) "ϕ" occurs within the scope of a square, then we cannot go from (39) to (41) by virtue of the substitution theorem. On the other hand the step from (38) to (39) (existential instantiation) is entirely valid. For surely (avoiding the ontological language of (31) and (40)) there is a case where

$$\square(\phi = \text{the evening star})$$

is true. In particular, the case where "ϕ" is replaced by "the evening star."

There is also the specific problem of interpreting quantification in $\lozenge(\exists x)\phi x \dashv (\exists x)\lozenge \phi x$ (6), which is a postulate of QS4. Read in accordance with (31) as

(42)   If it is logically possible that there is something which ϕ's, then there is something such that it is logically possible that it ϕ's.

It is admittedly odd. The antecedent seems to be about what is logically possible and the consequent about what there is. How can one go from possibility to existence? Read in accordance with (33) we have the clumsy but not so paradoxical

(43)   If it is logically possible that ϕx for some value of x, then there is some value of x such that it is logically possible that ϕx.

Although the emphasis has now been shifted from things and the ontological consequences of (42) are absent, it is still indirect and awkward. It would appear that questions such as the acceptability or non-acceptability of (6) are best solved in terms of some semantical construction. This will be returned to in conclusion, but first some minor matters.

MODALITIES MISUNDERSTOOD

In what preceded, the focus has been on problems connected with identity, substitution and quantification in interpreted modal systems. A defense of modal logic would be incomplete without touching on criticisms of modalities which stem from simple misunderstanding of what is or isn't provable in modal systems. Two examples will be cited, not because they are exhaustive but because they point up the need for more systematic study.

One example is from Rosenbloom [12] who seized on the fact that a strong deduction theorem is not available in QS4 as a reason for discarding strict implication as in any way relevant to the deducibility relation. He failed to

[12] P. Rosenbloom, *The Elements of Mathematical Logic*, New York, 1950, p. 60.

290   Contemporary Readings in Logical Theory

note [13] that a weaker and perhaps more appropriate deduction theorem is available. Indeed, Anderson and Belnap,[14] in their attempt to formalize entailment without modalities, reject the strong form of the deduction theorem as "counter-intuitive for entailment."

Another example occurs in *Word and Object* [15] which can be summarized as follows:

(44)   Modalities yield talk of a difference between necessary and contingent attributes.

(45)   Mathematicians may be said to be necessarily rational and not necessarily two-legged.

(46)   Cyclists are necessarily two-legged and not necessarily rational.

(47)   α is a mathematician and a cyclist

(48)   Is this concrete individual necessarily rational or contingently two-legged or vice versa?

(49)   "Talking referentially of the object with no special bias toward a background grouping of mathematicians as against cyclists . . . there is no semblance of sense in rating some of his attributes as necessary and others as contingent."

Professor Quine says that (44) through (47) are supposed to "evoke the appropriate sense of bewilderment" and they surely do. For I know of no interpreted modal system which treats of necessary attributes in the manner suggested. We may translate (45) by conjoining any one of the equivalent statements in (50) with any one of the equivalent statements in (51).

(50) $(x)(Mx \dashv Rx) \equiv (x)\square(Mx \supset Rx) \equiv (x) \sim \lozenge (Mx \cdot \sim Rx)$

(51) $(x) \sim \square (Mx \supset Tx) \equiv (x) \lozenge \sim (Mx \supset Tx) \equiv (x) \lozenge (Mx \cdot \sim Tx).$

Also we may translate (46) by conjoining any one of the equivalent statements in (52) with any one of the equivalent statements in (53).

(52) $(x)(Cx \dashv Tx) \equiv (x)\square(Cx \supset Tx) \equiv (x) \sim \lozenge (Cx \cdot \sim Tx)$

(53) $(x) \sim \square (Cx \supset Rx) \equiv (x) \lozenge \sim (Cx \supset Rx) \equiv (x) \lozenge (Cx \cdot \sim Rx).$

Let (48) be

(54) $Ma \cdot Ca$

---

[13] R. Barcan Marcus, "Strict implication, deducibility, and the deduction theorem," *Journal of Symbolic Logic*, Vol. XVIII (1953), pp. 234–236.
[14] A. R. Anderson and N. D. Belnap, *The Pure Calculus of Entailment* (preprint).
[15] *Op. cit.*, note 1, pp. 199–200.

Modalities and Intensional Languages   291

Among the non-bewildering conclusions we can draw from (50) through (54) are

$\Box(Ma \supset Ra)$, $\sim\Diamond(Ma \cdot \sim Ra)$, $\Diamond(Ma \cdot \sim Ta)$, $\sim\Box(Ma \supset Ta)$,
$\Box(Ca \supset Ta)$, $\sim\Diamond(Ca \cdot \sim Ta)$, $\Diamond(Ca \cdot \sim Ra)$, $\sim\Box(Ca \cdot \sim Ra)$,
Ta, Ra, $Ta \cdot Ra$

But nothing to answer question (48), or to make any sense of (49). It would appear that Professor Quine is assuming that

(55) $(p \dashv q) \dashv (p \dashv \Box q)$

is a theorem of modal logic, but it is not, except where $p \equiv \Box r$ for some r. Keeping in mind that we are dealing with logical modalities (or at best, analytic modalities), none of the attributes (M,R,T,C) in (50) through (54) taken separately, or conjoined, are necessary. It is not *that* sort of attribute which modal logic, even derivatively, countenances as being necessary. A word is appropriate here about the derivative sense in which we can speak of logically necessary and possible attributes.

In QS4, for example, abstracts are introduced such that to every function there corresponds an abstract

(56) $x \epsilon \hat{y} A =_{df} B$, where B is the result of substituting every free
         occurrence of y in A by x.

If r is some abstract then we can define

(57) $x \epsilon \boxed{\cdot}\, r =_{df} \Box(x \epsilon r)$, $\vdash \boxed{\cdot}\, r =_{df} (x)\, (x \epsilon \boxed{\cdot}\, r)$

and

(58) $x \epsilon \Diamond\, r =_{df} \Diamond(x \epsilon r)$, $\vdash \Diamond\, r =_{df} (x)\, (x \epsilon \Diamond\, r)$

It is clear that among the abstracts to which $\vdash \boxed{\cdot}$ may validly be affixed, will be those corresponding to tautological functions, e.g., $\hat{y}\,(y I y)$, $\hat{y}\,(\phi x \, v \sim \phi x)$, etc. It would be appropriate to call these necessary attributes, and the symbol "$\boxed{\cdot}$" provides a derivative way of applying modalities to attributes. There is a similar derivative sense for "possible attribute" (58), contingent attribute but these have little to do with the traditional problem of essentialism.

SEMANTIC CONSTRUCTIONS

I would like in conclusion to suggest that the polemics of modal logic are perhaps best carried out in terms of some explicit semantical construction. As we have seen in connection with (6) it is awkward at best and at worst has the character of a quibble, not to do so.

Let us reappraise (6) in terms of such a construction.[16] Consider for example a language (L), with truth functional connectives, a modal operator ($\Diamond$), a finite number of individual constants, an infinite number of individual variables, one two-place predicate (R), quantification and the usual criteria for being well-formed. A domain (D) of individuals is then considered which are named by the constants of L. A model of L is defined as a class of ordered couples (possibly empty) of D. The members of a model are exactly those pairs between which R holds. To say therefore that the atomic sentence R (a_1a_2) of L holds or is true in M, is to say that the ordered couple (b_1b_2) is a member of M, where a_1 and a_2 are the names in L of b_1 and b_2. If a sentence A of L is of the form $\sim$B, A is true in M if and only if B is not true in M. If A is of the form $B_1 \cdot B_2$ then A is true in M if and only if both B_1 and B_2 are true in M. If A is of the form $(\exists x)$B, then A is true in M if and only if at least one substitution instance of B is true (holds) in M. If A is $\Diamond$ B then A is true in M if and only if B is true in some model M_1.

We see that a true sentence of L is defined relative to a model and a domain of individuals. A logically true sentence is one which would be true in every model. We are now in a position to give a rough proof of (6). Suppose (6) is false in some M. Then

$$(59) \qquad \sim \Diamond \, (\, \Diamond \, (\exists x) \, \phi x \cdot \sim (\exists x) \, \Diamond \phi x)$$

is false in M. Therefore

$$(60) \qquad \Diamond \, (\, \Diamond \, (\exists x) \, \phi x \cdot \sim (\exists x) \, \Diamond \phi x)$$

is true in M. So

$$(61) \qquad \Diamond \, (\exists x) \, \phi x \cdot \sim (\exists x) \, \Diamond \phi x$$

is true in some M_1. Therefore

$$(62) \qquad \Diamond \, (\exists x) \, \phi x$$

and

$$(63) \qquad \sim (\exists x) \, \Diamond \phi x$$

are true in M_1. Consequently, from (62)

$$(64) \qquad (\exists x) \, \phi x$$

is true in some model M_2. Therefore there is a member of D (b) such that

---

[16] The construction here outlined corresponds to that of R. Carnap, *Meaning and Necessity*, Chicago, 1947. The statement of the construction is in accordance with the method of J. C. C. McKinsey. See also, J. C. C. McKinsey, "On the syntactical construction of systems of modal logic," *Journal of Symbolic Logic*, Vol. X (1946), pp. 88–94; "A new definition of truth," *Synthese*, Vol. VII (1948/49), pp. 428–433.

Reply to Professor Marcus   293

(65) ϕb

is true in M_2. But from (63)

$$(\exists x) \diamond \phi x$$

is not true in M_1. Consequently there is no member of D such that

(66) $\diamond \phi b$

is true in M_1. So there is no model M_2 such that ϕb is true in M_2. But this result contradicts (65). Consequently, in such a construction, (6) must be true in every model.

If this is the sort of construction one has in mind then we are persuaded of the plausibility of (6). Indeed, going back to (43), it can be seen that this was the sort of construction which was being assumed. If (6) is to be regarded as offensive, it must be in terms of some semantic construction which ought to be made explicit.[17]

We see, that though the rough outline above corresponds to the Leibnizian distinction between true in a possible world and true in all possible worlds, it is also to be noted that there are no specifically intensional objects. No new entity is spawned in a possible world that isn't already in the domain in terms of which the class of models is defined. In such a model, modal operators have to do with truth relative to the model, not with things. On this interpretation,[18] Professor Quine's "flight from intension" may have been exhilarating, but unnecessary.[19]